ATLANTIS COMPUTATIONAL INTELLIGENCE SYSTEMS
VOLUME 2

SERIES EDITOR: **DA RUAN**

Atlantis Computational Intelligence Systems

Series Editor:

Da Ruan, Belgian Nuclear Research Centre (SCK • CEN)
Mol & Ghent University, Gent, Belgium

(ISSN: 1875-7650)

Aims and scope of the series

The series 'Atlantis Computational Intelligence Systems' aims at covering state-of-the-art research and development in all fields where computational intelligence (CI) is investigated and applied. The series seeks to publish monographs and edited volumes on foundations and new developments in the field of computational intelligence, including fundamental and applied research as well as work describing new, emerging technologies originating from computational intelligence research. Applied CI research may range from CI applications in the industry to research projects in the life sciences, including research in biology, physics, chemistry and the neurosciences.

All books in this series are co-published with World Scientific.

For more information on this series and our other book series, please visit our website at:

www.atlantis-press.com/publications/books

ATLANTIS PRESS

AMSTERDAM – PARIS

World Scientific

Computational Intelligence in Complex Decision Systems

Da Ruan

Belgian Nuclear Research Centre (SCK • CEN)
Mol & Ghent University, Gent, Belgium

ATLANTIS PRESS

AMSTERDAM – PARIS

World Scientific

Atlantis Press

29, avenue Laumière
75019 Paris, France

For information on all Atlantis Press publications, visit our website at:

www.atlantis-press.com

Atlantis Computational Intelligence Systems

Volume 1: Linguistic Values Based Intelligent Information Processing: Theory, Methods, and Applications – Zheng Pei, Da Ruan, Jun Liu, Yang Xu

ISBN: 978-90-78677-27-7
ISSN: 1875-7650

Preface

In recent years there has been a growing interest in the need for designing computational intelligence to address complex decision systems. One of the most challenging issues for computational intelligence is to effectively handle real-world uncertainties that cannot be eliminated. These uncertainties include various type of information that is incomplete, imprecise, fragmentary, not fully reliable, vague, contradictory, deficient, and overloading. These uncertainties result in a lack of the full and precise knowledge of the decision system including the determining and selection of evaluation criteria, alternatives, weights, assignment scores, and the final integrated decision result. Computational intelligent techniques including fuzzy logic, neural networks, and genetic algorithms etc., as complimentary to the existing traditional techniques, have shown great potential to solve these demanding, real-world decision problems that exist in uncertain and unpredictable environments. These technologies have formed the foundation for computational intelligence.

To overview the role of computational intelligence in information–driven complex decision systems and illustrate the potential use and practical applications of computational intelligence related techniques in complex decision systems, this edited volume presents recent research results and provides a state-of-the-art on the future research directions. The book gathers a peer-reviewed collection of a number of representative applications of *Computational Intelligence in Complex Decision Systems*. It contains 13 chapters written by 25 authors from Australia, Belgium, Brazil, China, India, Japan, Portugal, Spain, Turkey, the UK, and the USA. These contributions and applications cover Complex Decision Systems ranging from Computational Intelligence (Chapter 1 by Kahraman *et al.*), Dynamically Changing Input Data (Chapter 2 by Pais *et al.*), Possibilistic Linear Programming (Chapter 3 by Guo), Virtual Reality (Chapter 4 by Machado and de Moraes), Many-Valued Temporal Logic and Reasoning (Chapter 5 by Lu *et al.*), Statistical Approach (Chapter 6 by Kunsch), Web based Assessment Tool (Chapter 7 by Xu), Intelligent Policy Simulator (Chapter 8 by Rao), Computing with Words (Chapter 9 by Mendel and Wu), Policy Realization (Chapter 10 by Kahraman and Kaya), Load Dispatch (Chapter 11 by Zhang *et al.*), Smart Home (Chapter 12 by Muñoz *et al.*), to Agile Supply Chain Strategies (Chapter 13 by Büyüközkan).

Each chapter of the book is self-contained. Academic and applied researchers and research students working on complex decision systems can also benefit from this book.

March 2010

Da Ruan
Belgian Nuclear Research Centre (SCK•CEN)
Mol & Ghent University, Gent, Belgium

Contents

Chapter 1

Computational Intelligence: Past, Today, and Future

Cengiz Kahraman, İhsan Kaya, and Didem Çınar

İstanbul Technical University, Department of Industrial Engineering, 34367- Maçka, İstanbul, Turkey

E-mails: {kahramanc, kayai, cinard}@itu.edu.tr

Computational intelligence is defined as the study of the design of intelligent agents. Since its relation to other branches of computer science is not well-defined, computational intelligence means different things to different people. In this chapter the history of computational intelligence with a wide literature review will be first given. Then, a detailed classification of the existing methodologies will be made. Later, the international computational intelligence journals will be handled and the characteristics of these journals will be examined. As an example, a special literature review on computational intelligence in complex decision systems will be also given. The direction of computational intelligence in the future will be evaluated.

1.1 Introduction

A definition of intelligence which is needed to be defined to research in a field termed artificial intelligence and computational intelligence has only rarely been provided, and the definitions in the literature have often been of little operational value. The intelligence was defined as the ability of solving the hard problems. However there are basic questions in this definition, such as how hard the problem is or who decides which problem is hard [11]. Intelligence comprises decision making. For any intelligent system, it must consistently make a decision to select of one from a number of alternative ways of allocating the available resources for a given purpose. Biological organisms satisfy the condition of intelligence as the derivation from their competition for the available resources. The primary goal of all living systems is survival and selection eliminates the weakest solutions variants while evolution as a process is purposeless. The weakest solution is the one which does not demonstrate adequately suitable behavior and it is eliminated stochastically. This basic idea has been recurred through the transitions of generations. But intelligence involves more than being restricted to biological organisms. So intelligence is the basic property of decision maker. Chellapilla and Fogel [11] defined the intelligence as "the capability of a system to adapt its behavior to meet its goals in a range of environments and the life process itself provides the most common form of intelligence".

The birth of Computational Intelligence (CI) is attributed to the IEEE World Congress on Computational Intelligence in 1994 Orlando, Florida. This term combines elements of learning, adaptation, evolution and fuzzy logic (rough sets) to create systems that is, in some sense, intelligent has been investigated by researchers until now. It is a necessity to answer the question what the "computational intelligence" is. CI can be broadly defined as the ability of a machine to react to an environment in new ways, making useful decisions in light of current and previous information. CI is generally accepted to include evolutionary computation, fuzzy systems, neural networks, and combinations thereof. CI, which consists of neural networks, fuzzy logic and evolutionary computing, and so on, is a novel technology to bring intelligence into computation. Compared with the traditional artificial intelligence, a significant characteristic of CI is that the precise model needs not to be established when dealing with imprecise, uncertain, and incomplete information.

IEEE Computational Intelligence Society defines its subjects of interest as neural networks, fuzzy systems and evolutionary computation, including swarm intelligence. The approach taken by the journals and by the book authors is to treat CI as an umbrella under which more and more methods will be added. A good definition of the field is therefore impossible, because different people include or exclude different methods under the same CI heading.

Despite the relatively widespread use of the term CI, there is no commonly accepted definition of the term. Since that time not only a great number of papers and scientific events have been dedicated to CI, but numerous explanations of the term have been published. In order to have a brief outline of history of the term the founding and most interesting definitions will be summarized now:

The term CI was first introduced by Bezdek in 1994. Bezdek says "... A system is computationally intelligent when it: deals with only numerical (low-level) data, has a pattern recognition component, does not use knowledge in the AI sense; and additionally when it (begins to) exhibit: (i) computational adaptivity; (ii) computational fault tolerance; (iii) speed approaching human-like turnaround, and (iv) error rates that approximate human performance".

Eberhart *et al.* [29] defined CI as follows: "Computational intelligence is defined as a methodology involving computing (whether with a computer, wetware, etc.) that exhibits an ability to learn and/or deal with new situations such that the system is perceived to possess one or more attributes of reason, such as generalisation, discovery, association, and abstraction."

"Computational intelligence is the study of the design of intelligent agents. [...] The central scientific goal of computational intelligence is to understand the principles that make intelligent behavior possible, in natural or artificial systems" [102].

"Computational intelligence is the field of studying how to build intelligent agents" [14].

"Computational intelligence is the study of adaptive mechanisms to enable or facilitate intelligent behavior in complex and changing environments. As such, computational intelligence combines artificial neural networks, evolutionary computing, swarm intelligence and fuzzy systems" [31].

"Computational Intelligence is a new paradigm of knowledge-based processing that dwells on three main pillars of granular computing, neural and fuzzy-neural networks, and evolutionary computing" [107].

In the face of these difficulties fuzzy logic (FL), neural networks (NN) and evolutionary computation (EC) were integrated under the name of CI as a hybrid system [122]. While some techniques within CI are often counted as artificial intelligence techniques (e.g., genetic algorithms, or neural networks) there is a clear difference between these techniques and traditional logic based artificial intelligence techniques. In general, typical artificial intelligence techniques are top-to-bottom, where the structure of models, solutions, etc. is imposed. CI techniques are generally bottom-up, where order and structure emerges from an unstructured beginning. An artificial neural network is a branch of CI that is closely related to machine learning. CI is further closely associated with soft computing, connectionist systems and cybernetics.

According to Bezdek [6], intelligence can be subdivided into CI, artificial intelligence, and biological intelligence according to the level of complexity as shown in Figure 1.1.

Computational processes deal with numeric data from sensors. Artificial intelligence is based on symbol processing techniques and augments computational processes with rules and other nonnumerical knowledge tidbits. Neural networks, self-organization map, genetic algorithms are examples of CI. Rule-based reasoning and case-based reasoning are in the style of artificial intelligence. Fuzzy logic is the most representative example of integrating numeric and semantic information.

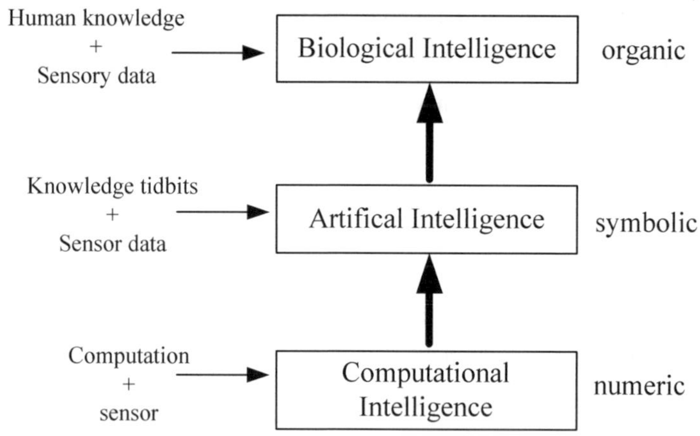

Figure 1.1 Structure of Intelligent Systems

The IEEE Computational Intelligence Society categorizes CI into three broad subjects:

- Neural Networks
- Fuzzy Systems
- Evolutionary computation, which includes
  - Evolutionary Algorithms
  - Swarm Intelligence

On the other hand, Fogel [35] summarized CI as "... These technologies of neural, fuzzy and evolutionary systems were brought together under the rubric of Computational Intelligence, a relatively new term offered to generally describe methods of computation that can be used to adapt solutions to new problems and do not rely on explicit human knowledge." According to Marks [70], CI consists of neural nets, genetic algorithms, fuzzy systems, evolutionary programming, and artificial life.

Irrespective of the way CI is defined above, its components should have the following characteristics: considerable potential in solving real world problems, ability to learn from experience, capability of self-organizing, and ability of adapting in response to dynamically changing conditions and constraints.

Because of the cloudy definition of intelligence, different statements of both artificial intelligence and CI have been developed [25]. Artificial intelligence is defined generally as the study of intelligent behavior. Another definition is making computer programs for doing intelligent things. For both statements the questions difficult to response are occurred: what are the intelligent behavior and intelligent things? [11] Artificial Intelligence (AI) which was the first large scientific community, established already in the mid 1950s. They are worked on comprehensive toolbox, issues of architecture and integration emerge as central.

CI is used on problems that are difficult to solve using artificial systems. Humans are capable of solving these problems so they are requiring intelligence [25]. According to the books and journals in literature, CI involves many methods and there is no consensus about methods under the same CI heading. Neural networks, fuzzy systems and evolutionary computation, including swarm intelligence are the subjects which are subjects of interest of IEEE Computational Intelligence Society. CI includes tools such as fuzzy logic, artificial neural networks, evolutionary computing, intelligent agents and probabilistic reasoning models. According to Marks [70] neural nets, genetic algorithms, fuzzy systems, evolutionary programming, and artificial life are the basic terms of CI.

This chapter aims to analyze the past and present of CI and make some evaluations for its future. For this aim, neural networks, fuzzy logic and evolutionary computing are explained in Sections 1.2, 1.3, and 1.4, respectively. Also hybrid systems, combination of these techniques, are defined in Section 1.5. The literature review and trends of CI in recent years are analyzed in Section 1.6. The international CI journals and the characteristics of these journals are examined in Section 1.7. CI's future and conclusions are discussed in Section 1.8.

1.2 Neural Networks

Artificial neural networks (ANN) are optimization algorithms which are recently being used in variety of applications with great success. ANN models take inspiration from the basic framework of the brain. Brain is formed by neurons and Figure 1.2 contains a schematic diagram of real neuron. The main parts of a neuron are cell body, axon and dendrites. A signal transport from axon to dendrites and passing through other neurons by synapses [37]. Figure 1.3 shows a representation of artificial neuron called perceptron. A perceptron consists of node as cell body and connections as synaptic links [15].

ANN consist of many nodes and connecting synapses. Nodes operate in parallel and communicate with each other through connecting synapses. ANN is used effectively for pattern recognition and regression. In recent years, experts prefer ANN over classical statistical methods as a forecasting model. This increasing interest can be explained by some basic properties of ANN. Extrapolating from historical data to generate forecasts, solving the

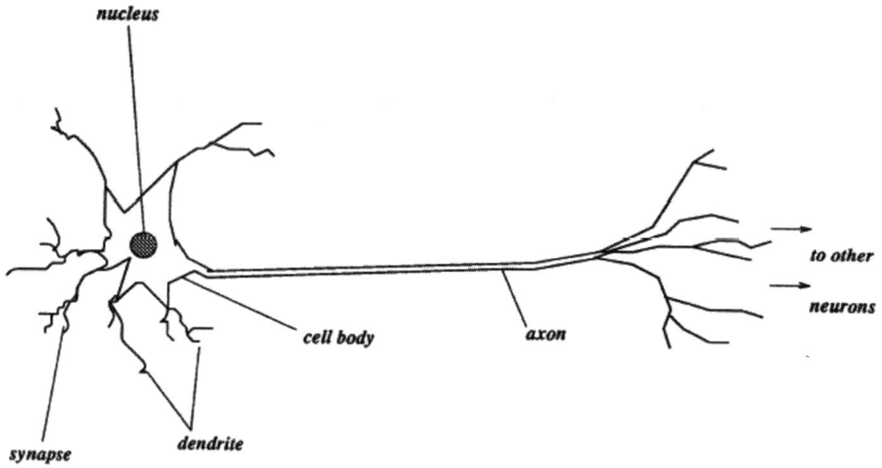

Figure 1.2 A schematic diagram of real neuron [15]

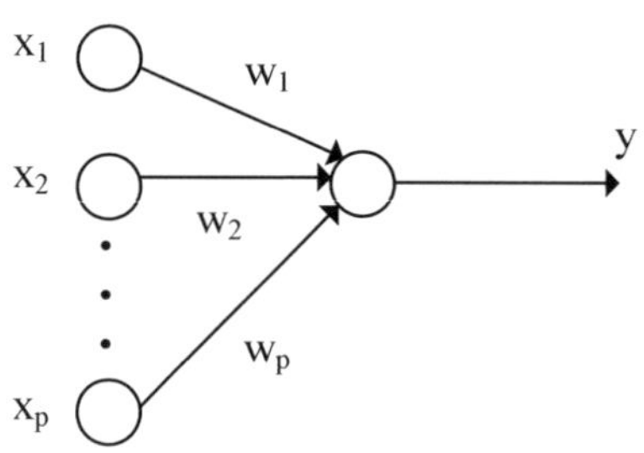

Figure 1.3 A simple perceptron

complex nonlinear problems successively and high computation rate are features that are the reasons for many experts to prefer ANN. Moreover, there is no requirement for any assumptions in ANN [88].

1.2.1 *Network Architectures*

Neural networks can be classified according to their architectures as single layer feed-forward networks, multilayer feed-forward networks and recurrent neural network. In feed-forward neural networks signals flow from the input layer to the output layer. Each layer has a certain number of neurons which are the basic processing elements of ANN. Neurons are connected with the other neurons in further layers and each connection has an associated weight. The neurons connect from one layer to the next layer, not to the previous layer

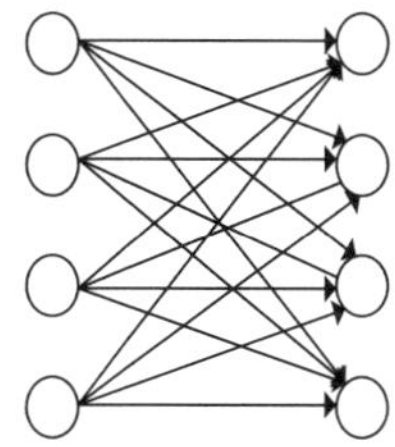

Figure 1.4 A sample single layer feed-forward neural network

or within the same layer. In Figure 1.4, there is a sample illustration of single layer feed-forward neural network architecture with four input and four output nodes. Only the output layer consists of computation nodes, so input layer is not counted when the architecture is defined [140].

A sample multilayer feed-forward neural network is shown in Figure 1.5. The network is composed of an input layer, some hidden layers and an output layer. Each neuron, except the neurons in input layer, is an operation unit in ANN. The process starts with summation of weighted activation of other neurons through its incoming connections. Then the weighted sum is passed through a function which is called activation function and this activated value is the output of the neuron. Activation function defines the output of a neuron. There are three basic activation function types [52]:

(i) *Threshold Function*: This type of function is shown in Figure 1.6(a). Generally if the signal coming through the previous layer is bigger than the threshold value, the output value of threshold function is 1, otherwise 0. In Figure 1.6-A the threshold value is 0 and this is the most widely used one.

$$f(x) = \begin{cases} 1, & x \geqslant 0 \\ 0, & x < 0 \end{cases} \tag{1}$$

Some threshold functions can take the value of -1 or 1, so if the output exceed the threshold value the value of the function will be 1, if the output is 0 the value of the function will be 0 and if the output is lower than the threshold value the value of the function will be -1 [140].

(ii) *Piecewise-Linear Function*: Piecewise-linear function is shown in Figure 1.6-B and defined as

$$f(x) = \begin{cases} 1, & x \geqslant -\dfrac{1}{2} \\ x + \dfrac{1}{2}, & -\dfrac{1}{2} \leqslant x \leqslant +\dfrac{1}{2} \\ 0, & x \leqslant -\dfrac{1}{2} \end{cases} \tag{2}$$

This function can be explained as an approximation of a nonlinear function [52].

(iii) *Sigmoid Function:* Because of the learning process in neural networks, nonlinear and differentiable activation functions are used as activation functions. Sigmoid functions are widely used activation functions since it is easy to derivative (Figure 1.6-C). An example of sigmoid functions called logistic function is defined as

$$f(x) = \frac{1}{1 + \mathrm{e}^{-\alpha x}} \tag{3}$$

where α is the slope parameter of sigmoid function. As the slope parameter approaches infinity the function becomes threshold function.

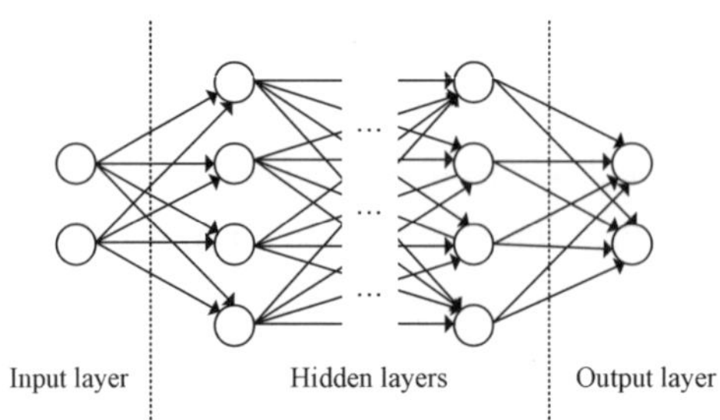

Figure 1.5 A sample multilayer feed-forward neural network [52]

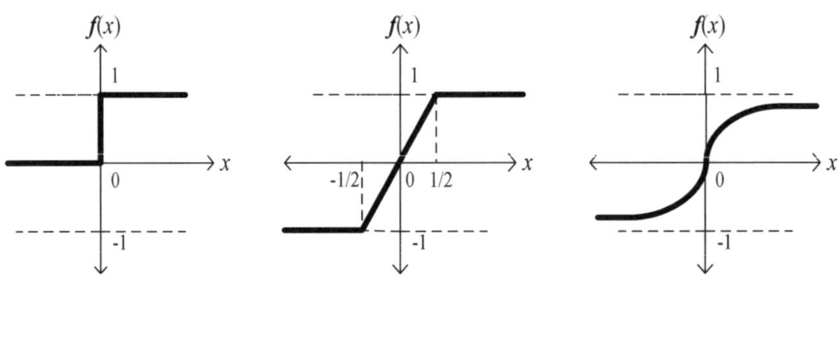

Figure 1.6 Basic activation function types

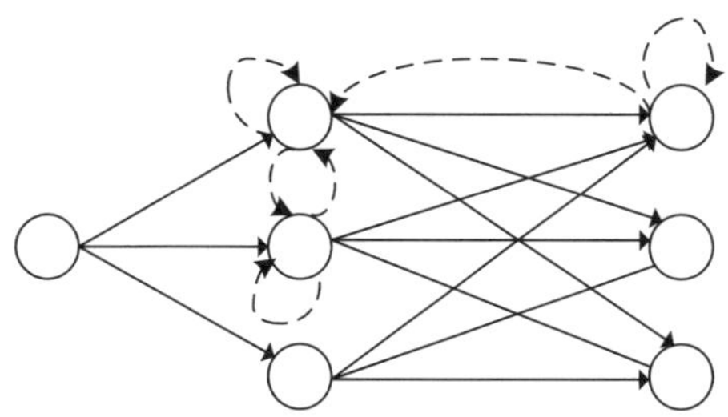

Figure 1.7 Recurrent network

The net input of neuron j is

$$net_j = \sum_i w_{ij} x_i + \theta_j \tag{4}$$

where x_i is the output of the neuron i in the previous layer, w_{ij} is the synaptic weight of neuron i to neuron j, and θ_j is the bias which is the constant value of the activation function. The last type of network architecture is recurrent networks shown in Figure 1.7. Recurrent neural networks can be commented as subsume of single layer and multilayer networks [103]. In recurrent networks, neurons have self connections and/or connections to nodes in the previous layers besides the forward connections between layers. This structure provides a short time memory and is used for remembering the past [1].

1.2.2 *Learning processes*

The most important section of ANN is training. Training is another name of seeking the correct weight values. While classical statistical techniques only estimate the coefficient of independent variables, ANN selects proper weights during training and keeps them for further use to predict the output [15]. Three types of learning processes are supervised, unsupervised and reinforcement learning.

1.2.2.1 *Supervised learning*

Supervised learning is used for regression and classification problems which concerns with the relationships between inputs and output values. Applications in literature have shown that neural networks with one hidden layer adequately learn the continuous functions. Second hidden layer can be used for continuous functions which have some break points that inhibit the continuity [140]. Among the several supervised learning algorithms, back-propagation algorithm is the most suitable method for training multilayer feed-forward networks [145]. While training the ANN, the weights are differentiated among neurons. In the learning phase, an input is presented to the network along with the desired output (y_p) and the weights are adjusted to produce the desired output. The most popular learning algorithm is the back-propagation (BP) algorithm. BP is a gradient descent algorithm which improves the resulting performance of the ANN by reducing the total error by adjusting the weights along its gradient.

Root Mean Square Error (RMSE) is the most widely used error value, which is calculated as

$$E = \frac{1}{2}\sum_{k}(y_k - o_k)^2 \tag{5}$$

where o_k is the output vector and k is the index for output units [52]. During back-propagation learning, weights are modified according to their contribution to the error function. For two layer feed-forward neural networks (one hidden layer and one output layer), the change of weights which are between neurons in hidden layer and ones in output layer can be found by least squares method and formulated as following:

$$\Delta v_h = -\eta \frac{\partial E}{\partial v_h} = \eta \sum_{t} \left(r^t - y^t\right) z_h^t \tag{6}$$

where t is the index of sample, v_h is the value of weight between output and the hth hidden neuron, y^t is the output value found by neural network, r^t is desired output value, z_h^t is the input value of hth hidden neuron and η is the learning rate which determines the magnitude of changes to be made in the parameter [52]. $(r^t - y^t)$ is the error between desired and output value and it is multiplied by z_h^t since the change of weight depends on the magnitude of input. So, for an input with small value an unnecessary training process will not be applied [1].

While the weights between input and hidden neurons are updated, least squares method is not applied. Because the error term resulted by hidden neuron cannot be found. The change of these weights can be found by chain rule as follows:

$$\begin{aligned}
\Delta w_{hj} &= -\eta \frac{\partial E}{\partial w_{hj}} \\
&= -\eta \sum_{t} \frac{\partial E^t}{\partial y^t} \frac{\partial y^t}{\partial z_h^t} \frac{\partial z_h^t}{\partial w_{hj}} \\
&= -\eta \sum_{t} - \left(r^t - y^t\right) v_h\, z_h^t \left(1 - z_h^t\right) x_j^t \\
&= \eta \sum_{t} \left(r^t - y^t\right) v_h\, z_h^t \left(1 - z_h^t\right) x_j^t
\end{aligned} \tag{7}$$

where $(r^t - y^t)\, v_h$ can be thought as error term of hth hidden neurons and it is backpropagated to the hidden neurons. $(r^t - y^t)$ is the error term of output and is weighted with the weight of hidden neuron v_h. $z_h^t\left(1-z_h^t\right)$ is derivative of sigmoid function and x_j^t is the derivative of weighted sum [1].

The performance can be analyzed with RMSE, however RMSE can be quite high or low depending on the unit of variables. In order to calculate the performance of different forecasting models, relative error (RE) can be used:

$$RE = \frac{\sum_k (y_k - o_k)^2}{\sum_k y_k^2} \tag{8}$$

Although BP is a simple and popular algorithm, there are several disadvantages. It is slow and needs much iteration to solve a simple problem [109]. An important disadvantage of BP is local convergence [126]. Solutions found by BP are dependent on the initially random weights [41]. So in order to find global optimum, BP is run with different random initial weights. Another drawback of BP is determining the parameters (number of hidden layers, number of hidden neurons, learning rate etc.) for finding the global optimum [145]. Many different combinations of the parameters are tried to generate a confidence that a global solution has been found. In the literature, most of the ANN applications use trial-and-error method to find appropriate parameters [126, 145].

1.2.2.2 *Unsupervised learning*

Another learning type is unsupervised learning. In supervised learning the values of inputs and outputs are known and the aim is seeking the structure of between inputs and outputs. In unsupervised learning only the input values are known and the aim is finding the pattern of inputs. Input space has a pattern and regular structures can be investigated [1]. After the pattern of input is defined, training procedure is completed and the classes of new input values can be determined.

Clustering problems are the examples of unsupervised learning. The aim of cluster analysis is determining the groups in data set or grouping the data. Such as, a firm sustaining demographic features and arrival frequencies of its customers can cluster the customers within different groups and define customer profiles [1].

1.2.2.3 *Reinforcement learning*

In the last type of learning process, reinforcement learning, signals, which are produced through a sequence of decisions and provide some measure of performance, are the sources of learning. Although the reinforcement learning provides developing profitable decision policies with minimal domain information, it generally requires a large number of training episodes and extensive CPU time [73]. Games are the examples of reinforcement learning. A single movement has not a meaning for a player. The sequence of movement is desired to give the best result. Chess is a popular game for reinforcement learning [1].

1.3 Fuzzy Set Theory

Zadeh published the first paper, called "fuzzy sets", on the theory of fuzzy logic (1965). He characterized non-probabilistic uncertainties and provided a methodology, fuzzy set theory, for representing and computing data and information that are uncertain and imprecise. Zadeh [149] defined the main contribution of fuzzy logic as "a methodology for computing with words" and pointed out two major necessities for computing with words: "First, computing with words is a necessity when the available information is too imprecise to justify the use of numbers, and second, when there is a tolerance for imprecision which can be exploited to achieve tractability, robustness, low solution cost, and better rapport with reality." While the complexity arise and the precision is receded, linguistic variables has been used to modeling. Linguistic variables are variables which are defined by words or sentences instead of numbers [148].

Many problems in real world deal with uncertain and imprecise data so conventional approaches cannot be effective to find the best solution. To cope with this uncertainty, fuzzy set theory has been developed as an effective mathematical algebra under vague environment. Although humans have comparatively efficient in qualitative forecasting, they are unsuccessful in making quantitative predictions. Since fuzzy linguistic models permit the translation of verbal expressions into numerical ones, thereby dealing quantitatively with imprecision in the expression of the importance of each criterion, some methods based on fuzzy relations are used. When the system involves human subjectivity, fuzzy algebra provides a mathematical framework for integrating imprecision and vagueness into the models [57].

Uncertainties can be reflected in mathematical background by fuzzy sets. Fuzzy sets have reasonable differences with crisp (classical) sets. Crisp set A in a universe U can be defined by listing all of its elements denoted x. Alternatively, zero-one membership function, $\mu_A(x)$, which is given below can be used to define x.

$$\mu_A(x) = \begin{cases} 1, & x \in A \\ 0, & x \notin A \end{cases} \tag{9}$$

Unlike crisp sets, a fuzzy set $\widetilde{A}$ in the universe of U is defined by a membership function

$\mu_{\widetilde{A}}(x)$ which takes on values in the interval $[0,1]$. The definition of a fuzzy set is the extended version of a crisp set. While the membership function can take the value of 0 or 1 in crisp sets, it takes a value in interval $[0,1]$ in fuzzy sets. A fuzzy set, $\widetilde{A}$, is completely characterized by the set of ordered pairs [152]:

$$\widetilde{A} = \left\{ (x, \mu_{\widetilde{A}}(x)) \mid x \in X \right\} \tag{10}$$

A fuzzy set $\widetilde{A}$ in X is convex if and only if for every pair of point x^1 and x^2 in X, the membership function of $\widetilde{A}$ satisfies the inequality

$$\mu_{\widetilde{A}}\left(\delta x^1 + (1-\delta)x^2\right) \geqslant \min\left(\mu_{\widetilde{A}}\left(x^1\right), \mu_{\widetilde{A}}\left(x^2\right)\right) \tag{11}$$

where $\delta \in [0,1]$ [49].

In fuzzy logic, basic sets operations, union, intersection and complement, are defined in terms of their membership functions. Let $\mu_{\widetilde{A}}(x)$ and $\mu_{\widetilde{B}}(x)$ be the membership functions of fuzzy sets $\widetilde{A}$ and $\widetilde{B}$. Fuzzy union has the membership function of

$$\mu_{\widetilde{A} \cup \widetilde{B}}(x) = \max\left\lfloor \mu_{\widetilde{A}}(x), \mu_{\widetilde{B}}(x) \right\rfloor \tag{12}$$

and fuzzy intersection has the membership function of

$$\mu_{\widetilde{A} \cap \widetilde{B}}(x) = \min\left\lfloor \mu_{\widetilde{A}}(x), \mu_{\widetilde{B}}(x) \right\rfloor \tag{13}$$

and fuzzy complement has the membership function of

$$\mu_{\overline{\widetilde{A}}}(x) = 1 - \mu_{\widetilde{A}}(x) \tag{14}$$

Most real world applications, especially in engineering, consist of real and nonnegative elements such as the Richter magnitudes of an earthquake [110]. However there are some applications that some strict numbers cannot be defined for given situation on account of uncertainty and ambiguity. Fuzzy set theory provides a representing of uncertainties. Zadeh [147] mentioned about fuzzy sets as: "The Notion of a fuzzy set provides a convenient point of departure for the construction of a conceptual framework which parallels in many respects the framework used in the case of ordinary sets, but is more general than the latter and, potentially, may prove to have a much wider scope of applicability, particularly in the fields of pattern classification and information processing."

There is a huge amount of literature on fuzzy logic and fuzzy set theory. In recent studies, fuzzy set theory has been concerned with engineering applications. Certain types of uncertainties are encountered in a variety of areas and fuzzy set theory has pointed out to be very efficient to consider these [57]. Automatic control, consumer electronics, signal processing, time-series prediction, information retrieval, database management, computer vision, data classification, and decision-making are some areas in which fuzzy logic and fuzzy set theory are applied [50].

1.4 Evolutionary Computation

Evolutionary computation concept based on Darwin's evolution theory by applying the biological principle of natural evolution to artificial systems for the solution of optimization problems has received significant attention during the last two decade, although the origins were introduced the late 1950's with works of Bremermann in 1962, Friedberg in 1958 and 1959, and Box in 1957, and others [3]. The domain of evolutionary computation involves the study of the foundations and the applications of computational techniques based on the principles of natural evolution. Evolutionary algorithms employ this powerful design philosophy to find solutions to hard problems from different domains, including optimization, automatic programming, circuit design, machine learning, economics, ecology, and population genetics, to mention but a few.

Evolutionary computation for solving optimization and other problems has considerable advantages. The first and important advantage is adaptability for fluxional situations. Unlike many traditional optimization procedures where the calculation must be restarted from the beginning if any variable in the problem changes, evolutionary computation does not need to restart from beginning since the current population serves as a memoir of stored knowledge that can be applied on the fly to a dynamic environment. Therefore, traditional optimization methods are more computationally expensive than the evolutionary computation. Another advantage of an evolutionary computation to problem solving comes in being able to generate good enough solutions quickly enough for them to be of use.

There are several techniques of evolutionary computations, among which the best known ones are genetic algorithms, genetic programming, evolution strategies, classifier systems and evolutionary programming; though different in the specifics they are all based on the same general principles [3, 20, 100].

An evolutionary computation (algorithm) begins by initializing a population of candidate solutions to a problem. New solutions are then created by randomly varying those of the initial population. This population is then selected in a guided random search using parallel processing to achieve the desired end.

1.4.1 *Genetic algorithms*

Genetic algorithms (GAs) which was first developed by Holland in 1975 are based on mechanics of natural selection and genetics to search through decision space for optimal solutions. The metaphor underlying GAs is natural selection. Genetic algorithm is a search technique used in computing to find exact or approximate solutions to optimization and search problems. GAs can be categorized as global search heuristics. GAs are a particular class of evolutionary algorithms (also known as evolutionary computation) that use techniques inspired by evolutionary biology such as inheritance, mutation, selection, and crossover (also called recombination). GAs are stochastic search methods based on the genetic process of biological organisms. Unlike conventional optimization methods, GAs maintain a set of potential solutions (populations) in each generation. A GA is encoding the factors of a problem by chromosomes, where each gene represents a feature of problem. In evolution, the problem that each species faces is to search for beneficial adaptations to the complicated and changing environment. In other words, each species has to change its chromosome combination to survive in the living world. In GA, a string represents a set of decisions (chromosome combination), that is a potential solution to a problem. Each string is evaluated on its performance with respect to the fitness function (objective function). The ones with better performance (fitness value) are more likely to survive than the ones with worse performance. Then the genetic information is exchanged between strings by crossover and perturbed by mutation. The result is a new generation with (usually) better survival abilities. This process is repeated until the strings in the new generation are identical, or certain termination conditions are met. A generic flow of GA is given in Figure 1.8. This algorithm is continued until the stopping criterion is reached. GAs are different from other search procedures in the following ways: (1) GAs consider many points in the search space simultaneously, rather than a single point; (2) GAs work directly with strings of characters representing the parameter set, not the parameters themselves; (3) GAs use probabilistic rules to guide their search, not deterministic rules. Because GAs consider many points in the search space simultaneously there is a reduced chance of converging to local optima. In a conventional search, based on a decision rule, a single point is considered and that is unreliable in multimodal space. GAs consist of four main sections that are explained in the following subsections: Encoding, Selection, Reproduction, and Termination [58, 32, 55, 56].

1.4.1.1 *Encoding*

While using GAs, encoding a solution of a problem into a chromosome is very important. Various encoding methods have been created for particular problems to provide effective implementation of GAs for the last 10 years. According to what kind of symbol is used as the alleles of a gene, the encoding methods can be classified as follows:

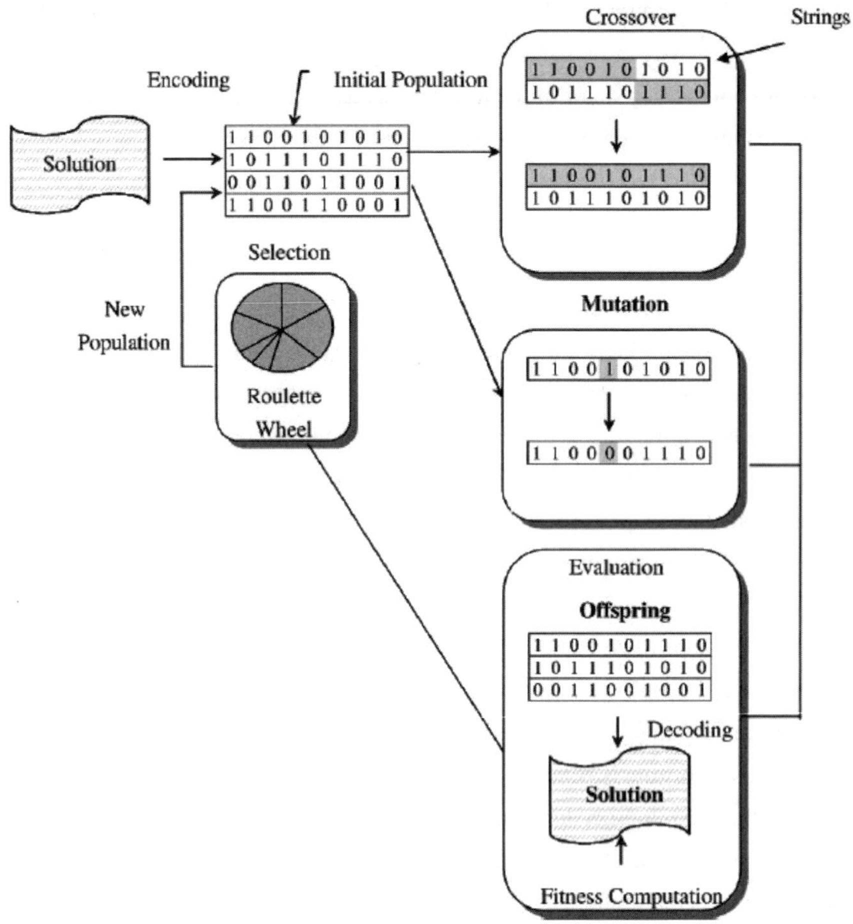

Figure 1.8 The fundamental cycle and operations of basic GAs [38]

- Binary encoding,
- Real number encoding,
- Integer or literal permutation encoding,
- General data structure encoding.

1.4.1.2 *Selection*

During each successive generation, a proportion of the existing population is selected to breed a new generation. Individual solutions are selected through a fitness-based process, where fitter solutions (as measured by a fitness function) are typically more likely to be selected. Certain selection methods rate the fitness of each solution and preferentially select the best solutions. Other methods rate only a random sample of the population, as this process may be very time-consuming. Most functions are stochastic and designed so that a small proportion of less fit solutions are selected. This helps keep the diversity of the population large, preventing premature convergence on poor solutions. Popular and well-studied selection methods include roulette wheel selection and tournament selection. The fitness function is the important section of selection. It is defined over the genetic representation and measures the quality of the represented solution. It is always problem dependent.

1.4.1.3 *Reproduction*

The next step of GAs is to generate a second generation population of solutions from those selected through genetic operators: crossover (also called recombination), and/or mutation. For each new solution to be produced, a pair of "parent" solutions is selected for breeding from the pool selected previously. By producing a "child" solution using the crossover and mutation, a new solution is created which typically shares many of the characteristics of its "parents". New parents are selected for each child, and the process continues until a new population of solutions of appropriate size is generated. These processes ultimately result in the next generation population of chromosomes that is different from the initial generation. Generally, the average fitness will have increased by this procedure for the population, since only the best organisms from the first generation are selected for breeding, along with a small proportion of less fit solutions, for reasons already mentioned above.

1.4.1.4 *Crossover*

In GAs, crossover is a genetic operator used to vary the programming of a chromosome or chromosomes from one generation to the next. It is an analogy to reproduction and biological crossover, upon which genetic algorithms are based.

1.4.1.5 *Mutation Operator*

The premature convergence of a new generation can be prevented by using the mutation operator. The purpose of the mutation in GAs is to allow the algorithm to avoid local minima by preventing the population of chromosomes from becoming too similar to each other, thus slowing or even stopping evolution.

1.4.1.6 *Termination*

This generational process is repeated until a termination condition has been reached. Common terminating conditions are as follows:

- A solution that satisfies minimum criteria is found,
- Fixed number of generations reached,
- Allocated budget (computation time/money) reached,
- The highest ranking solution's fitness such that successive iterations no longer produce better results,
- Combinations of the above.

1.4.2 *Genetic programming*

Genetic programming (GP) developed by Koza [61, 62] is an evolutionary algorithm-based methodology inspired by biological evolution to find computer programs that perform a user-defined task. It is defined by Koza [61] as "... genetic programming paradigm, populations of computer programs are genetically bred using the Darwinian principle of survival of the fittest and using a genetic crossover (recombination) operator appropriate for genetically mating computer programs." In GP, instead of encoding possible solutions to a problem as a fixed-length character string, they are encoded as computer programs. The individuals in the population are programs that — when executed — are the candidate solutions to the problem. It is a specialization of genetic algorithms where each individual is a computer program. Therefore, it is a machine learning technique used to optimize a population of computer programs according to a fitness landscape determined by a program's ability to perform a given computational task.
The basic steps in constructing a genetic program are as follows [80]:

1. Create an initial randomly generated population of trees.
2. Calculate the fitness of each tree in the initial population according to a suitable criterion.
3. Create a new population by applying the following operations:

    i) Copy existing individuals to the new population.
    ii) Randomly select a pair of existing trees and recombine subtrees from them to produce a new tree.

The operations of reproduction and recombination are carried out with the probability of selection for the operations skewed toward selecting individuals with higher levels of fitness.

4. Calculate the fitness of each individual in the new population.
5. Repeat these operations, keeping a record of the overall fittest individual.

1.4.3 *Evolution strategies*

Evolution strategies use natural problem-dependent representations, and primarily mutation and selection as search operators were introduced by Ingo Rechenberg and Hans Paul Schweffel in the 1960s [100] as a method for solving parameter-optimization problems. Mutation is the major genetic operator in evolution strategies. It also plays the role of a reproduction operator given that the mutated individual is viewed as an offspring for the selection operator to work on.

One of the commonly proposed advantages of evolution strategies (ESs) is that they can be easily parallelized. ESs with λ offspring per generation (population size λ) are usually parallelized by distributing the function evaluation for each of the offspring on a different processor. However, when the number of offspring is smaller than the number of available processors, the advantage of using evolution strategies in parallel cannot be fully exploited. Consequently, when large numbers of processors are available, it is desirable to develop an algorithm that can handle a large population efficiently [43].

1.4.4 *Evolutionary programming*

Evolutionary programming (EP) was first used by Fogel in 1960s in order to use simulated evolution as a learning process aiming to generate artificial intelligence. Fogel used finite state machines as predictors and evolved them. It has been applied with success to many numerical and combinatorial optimization problems in recent years. Like with evolution strategies, evolutionary programming first generates offspring and then selects the next generation. It is becoming harder to distinguish it from evolutionary strategies. Some of its original variants are quite similar to the later genetic programming, except that the program structure is fixed and its numerical parameters are allowed to evolve. The schematic diagram of the EP algorithm is depicted in Figure 1.9.

Optimization by EP can be summarized into two major steps as (i) mutate the solutions in the current population, and (ii) select the next generation from the mutated and the current solutions. These two steps can be regarded as a population-based version of the classical generate-and-test method, where mutation is used to generate new solutions (offspring)

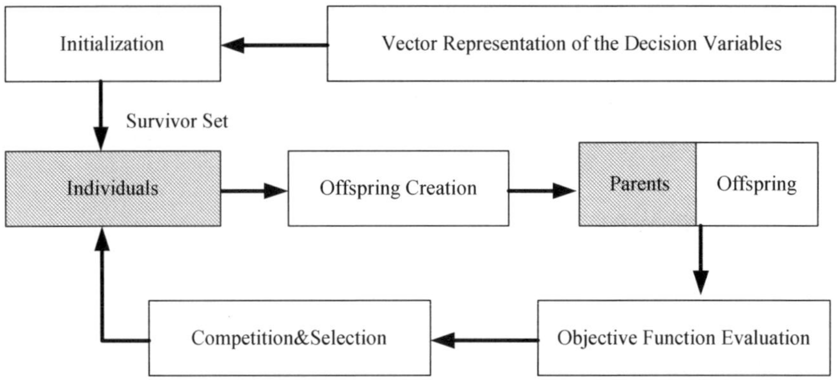

Figure 1.9 Schematic diagram of the evolutionary programming algorithm [144]

and selection is used to test which of the newly generated solutions should survive to the next generation. Formulating EP as a special case of the generate-and-test method establishes a bridge between EP and other search algorithms, such as evolution strategies, GAs, simulated annealing, tabu search, and others, and thus facilitates cross-fertilization among different research areas [146].

1.4.5 *Classifier systems*

Classifier systems (CSs), presented by Holland in 1970's, are evolution-based learning systems, rather than a 'pure' evolutionary algorithm. They can be thought of as restricted versions of classical rule-based systems, with the addition of input and output interfaces. A classifier system consists of three main components: (1) the rule and message system, which performs the inference and defines the behavior of the whole system, (2) the apportionment of credit system, which adapts the behavior by credit assignment, and (3) the GAs, which adapt the system's knowledge by rule discovery [100]. CSs exploit evolutionary computation and reinforcement learning to develop a set of condition-action rules (i.e., the classifiers) which represent a target task that the system has learned from on-line experience. There are many models of CSs and therefore also many ways of defining what a learning classifier system is. Nevertheless, all CS models, more or less, comprise four main components: (i) a finite population of condition action rules, called classifiers, that represents the current knowledge of the system; (ii) the performance component, which governs the interaction with the environment; (iii) the reinforcement component, which distributes the reward received from the environment to the classifiers accountable for the rewards obtained; (iv) the discovery component, which is responsible for discovering better rules and improving existing ones through a GA [45].

1.4.6 *Ant colony optimization*

In the early 1990s, ant colony optimization (ACO) which is a class of optimization algorithms modeled on the actions of a real ant colony was introduced by Dorigo and colleagues as a novel nature-inspired metaheuristic for the solution of hard combinatorial optimization problems.

The inspiring source of ACO is the foraging behavior of real ants. The working principles of ACO based on a real ant colony can be explained as follows [22]:

Real ants are capable of finding the shortest path from a food source to the nest without using visual cues. Also, they are capable of adapting to changes in the environment, e.g. finding a new shortest path once the old one is no longer feasible due to a new obstacle. Consider Figure 1.10-A: ants are moving on a straight line that connects a food source to their nest. It is well known that the primary means for ants to form and maintain the line is a pheromone trail. Ants deposit a certain amount of pheromone while walking, and each ant probabilistically prefers to follow a direction rich in pheromone. This elementary behaviour of real ants can be used to explain how they can find the shortest path that reconnects a broken line after the sudden appearance of an unexpected obstacle has interrupted the initial path (Figure 1.10-B). In fact, once the obstacle has appeared, those ants which are just in front of the obstacle cannot continue to follow the pheromone trail and therefore they have to choose between turning right or left. In this situation we can expect half the ants to choose to turn right and the other half to turn left. A very similar situation can be found on the other side of the obstacle (Figure 1.10-C). It is interesting to note that those ants which choose, by chance, the shorter path around the obstacle will more rapidly reconstitute the interrupted pheromone trail compared to those who choose the longer path. Thus, the shorter path will receive a greater amount of pheromone per time unit and in turn a larger number of ants will choose the shorter path. Due to this positive feedback (autocatalytic) process, all the ants will rapidly choose the shorter path (Figure 1.10-D). The most interesting aspect of this autocatalytic process is that finding the shortest path around the obstacle seems to be an emergent property of the interaction between the obstacle shape and ants distributed behaviour: although all ants move at approximately the same speed and deposit a pheromone trail at approximately the same rate, it is a fact that it takes longer to contour obstacles on their longer side than on their shorter side which makes the pheromone trail accumulate quicker on the shorter side. It is the ants' preference for higher pheromone trail levels which makes this accumulation still quicker on the shortest path.

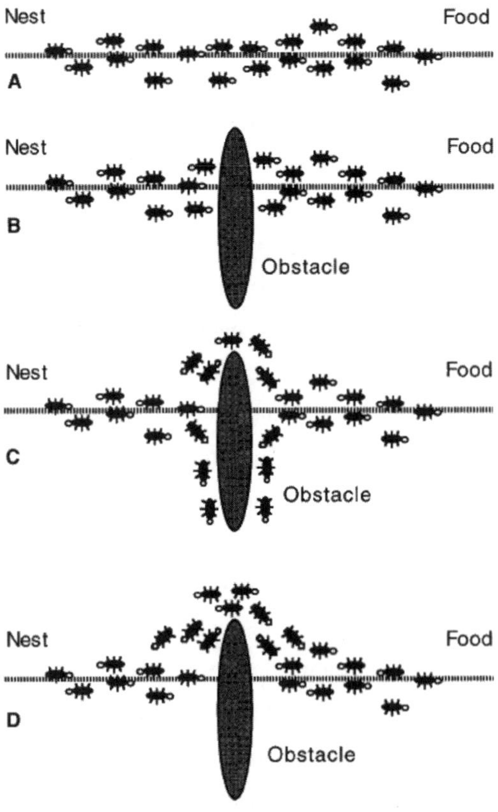

Figure 1.10 Real Ant Colony Movements from Nest to Food [22].

In general, the ACO approach attempts to solve an optimization problem by repeating the following two steps [21]:

- candidate solutions are constructed using a pheromone model, that is, a parameterized probability distribution over the solution space;
- the candidate solutions are used to modify the pheromone values in a way that is deemed to bias future sampling toward high quality solutions.

Dorigo and Gambardella [22] applied this philosophy to solve travelling salesman problem. After the initial proof-of-concept application to the traveling salesman problem (TSP),

ACO has been applied to many other optimization problems such as assignment problems, scheduling problems, and vehicle routing problems. Recently, researchers have been dealing with the relation of ACO algorithms to other methods for learning and optimization.

1.4.7 *Particle swarm optimization*

Particle swarm optimization (PSO) which is population based stochastic optimization technique developed by Kennedy and Eberhart [59], inspired by social behavior of bird flocking or fish schooling is a global optimization algorithm for dealing with problems in which a best solution can be represented as a point or surface in an n-dimensional space. PSO shares many similarities with evolutionary computation techniques such as Genetic Algorithms (GA). The system is initialized with a population of random solutions and searches for optima by updating generations. However, unlike GA, PSO has no evolution operators such as crossover and mutation. In PSO, the potential solutions, called particles, fly through the problem space by following the current optimum particles.

Each individual of the population, called a 'particle', flies around in a multidimensional search space looking for the optimal solution. Particles, then, may adjust their position according to their own and their neighboring-particles experience, moving toward their best position or their neighbor's best position. In order to achieve this, a particle keeps previously reached 'best' positions in a cognitive memory. PSO performance is measured according to a predefined fitness function. Balancing between global and local exploration abilities of the flying particles could be achieved through user-defined parameters. PSO has many advantages over other heuristic techniques such that it can be implemented in a few lines of computer code, it requires only primitive mathematical operators, and it has great capability of escaping local optima. In a PSO system, multiple candidate solutions coexist and collaborate simultaneously. Each solution candidate, called a 'particle', flies in the problem search space (similar to the search process for food of a bird swarm) looking for the optimal position to land. A particle, as time passes through his quest, adjusts its position according to its own 'experience', as well as according to the experience of neighboring particles. Tracking and memorizing the best position encountered build particle's experience. For that reason, the PSO algorithm possesses a memory (i.e. every particle remembers the best position it reached during the past). PSO system combines local search methods (through self experience) with global search methods (through neighboring experience), attempting to balance exploration and exploitation. Two factors characterize a particle status on the search space: its position and velocity [123].

Particle swarm optimization has been successfully applied in many research and application areas in recent years. It is demonstrated that PSO gets better results in a faster, cheaper way compared with other methods. Another reason that PSO is attractive is that there are few parameters to adjust.

1.5 Hybrid Systems

Solving complex problems, such as financial investment planning, foreign exchange trading, and knowledge discovery from large/multiple databases, involves many different components or sub-tasks, each of which requires different types of processing. To solve such complex problems, a great diversity of intelligent techniques, including traditional hard computing techniques (e.g., expert systems) and CI techniques (e.g., fuzzy logic, NN, and GAs), are required. For example, in financial investment planning, NN can be used as a pattern watcher for the stock market; GAs can be used to predict interest rates; and approximate reasoning based on fuzzy logic can be used to evaluate financial risk tolerance ability of clients. These techniques are complementary rather than competitive, and thus must be used in combination and not exclusively. These systems are called hybrid intelligent systems [150]. Although the sufficient results found by CI techniques, more effective solutions can be obtained when used combination of these techniques. Each combination has an aim to decrease the limitation of one method. For example, genetic algorithm has been used to improve the performance of ANN in literature. Usage of genetic algorithms in ANN for training or finding the appropriate architecture can keep from getting trapped at local minima. Another example is using fuzzy inference with other CI techniques. A fuzzy inference system can take linguistic information (linguistic rules) from human experts and also adapt itself using numerical data to achieve better performance. Generally, using hybrid systems provides synergy to the resulting system in the advantages of the constituent techniques and avoids their shortcomings [50]. The reader can find more details about intelligent hybrid systems, fuzzy logic and neural networks in Martin and Ralescu [71], Ruan [118], Song *et al.* [127], Zhang and Zhang [150], Kahraman [51], and Munakata [75].

1.6 Literature Review

In this section a literature review on CI has been realized. In Table 1.1, the results of this review are given. Here, the papers whose title including "computational intelligence" is listed for the years 1992 to 2008. In the first column, these papers are classified as roughly based on their CI technique(s) which is (are) used in the paper.

Table 1.1 CI Papers

CI Techniques	Authors	Main Topics
Fuzzy logic	Xue and Dong [143]	Conceptual Design
	Wang and Zou [137]	
	Zimmermann [153]	Environmental Planning
	Nucci *et al.* [82], Papageorgioua *et al.* [89]	Health
Fuzzy logic, Genetic algorithms	Gu *et al.* [39]	Conceptual Design
	Karray *et al.* [54]	Facility layout Planning
	Sebastian and Schleiffer [125]	Engineering Design
	Naso and Turchiano [78]	Manufacturing (AGVs)
	Naso and Turchiano [78]	Automated guided vehicles dispatching control
	Pedrycz and Reformat [99]	Decision Trees
Fuzzy logic, Genetic algorithms, Neural networks	Corne *et al.* [17], Park *et al.* [90], Park and Oh [92]	Modeling
	Liang and Chunguang [67]	Product packaging
	Tzafestas and Tzafestas [132]	Forecasting
	Pal and Pal [87]	Pattern Recognition
	Douligeris *et al.* [24]	Telecommunication Networks
	Alvarado *et al.* [2]	Petroleum Industry
	Oh *et al.* [84]	Design
	Huang *et al.* [46]	Conceptual Design
	Oh *et al.* [83], Pedrycz and Reformat [99], Pedrycz [97], Park *et al.* [91],	Optimization
	Wilson *et al.* [141]	Manufacturing
	Karr [53], Castellano *et al.* [8]	Computer systems
	Riziotis and Vasilakos [108]	Photonics technology
	Ruan [114]	Sensory Evaluation
	Stathakis and Athanassios [129]	Image Classification
Fuzzy logic, Neural networks	Sun and Kalenchuk [130]	Conceptual Design
	Dasey and Tzanakou	Medicine
	Duch and Hayashi [27]	Classification and prediction
	Vasilakos *et al.* [134]	Network
	Innocent *et al.* [47]	Research projects
	Duch *et al.* [26]	Data analysis
	Lau *et al.* [65]	Supply Chain
	Chen *et al.* [12]	Construction performance
Genetic algorithms	Ng and Leng [81]	Conceptual Design
	Lai *et al.* [64]	Power systems
	Li [66]	Optimization
	Wang *et al.* [136]	Modeling
Genetic algorithm, Neural networks	Ling *et al.* [69]	Forecasting
	Nakayama *et al.* [76]	Optimization
	Kubota [63]	Control of robots
Genetic programming, Neural networks	Narendra [77]	Cement stabilization

Table 1.1 continued.

CI Techniques	Authors	Main Topics
Neural networks	Venugopal and Naredran [135], Chang and Tsai [10], Park *et al.* [93]	Conceptual Design
	Cass and DePietro [7]	Process discovery (data analysis)
	Guimarães *et al.* [40]	Optimization
	Warne *et al.* [138]	Inferential model development
	Uhrig and Hines [133]	Nuclear Engineering
	Plikynas *et al.* [101]	Foreign investment
	Pavlidis *et al.* [95]	Forecasting
	Cherkassky *et al.* [16]	Earth sciences and Environment
	Quah and Sriganesh [104]	Online banking
Neural networks, Fuzzy logic	Edwards *et al.* [30]	Export behavior
	Santos *et al.* [124]	Forecasting
	Matics and Krost [72]	Energy management
Evolutionary algorithms, Neural networks;	Xu *et al.* [142]	Sound transmission
Evolutionary computation, Genetic algorithms, Neural networks	Reformat *et al.* [107]	Software quality analysis
Evolutionary computation, Particle swarm optimization,	Pavlidis *et al.* [94]	Game Theory
Neural networks, granular Computing, Rule-based computing	Pedrycz [96]	Software engineering
Neurocomputing, Evolutionary computing, Granular computing	Pedrycz and Peters [98]	Software engineering
Neuro-fuzzy modelling	Kothamasu *et al.* [60]	Hard turning
General overview	Feigenbaum [33]	CI
CI techniques are reviewed	Chen [13], Isasi *et al.* [48]	Finance and Economic
	Pal and Mudi [86]	Decision making
	Ovaska *et al.* [85]	The fusion of hard computing and soft computing techniques
	Dote and Ovaska [23]	Industrial applications

According to Table 1.1, the papers which include CI techniques have gained more attention in recent years. It should be noticed that two or more techniques (hybrid systems) are

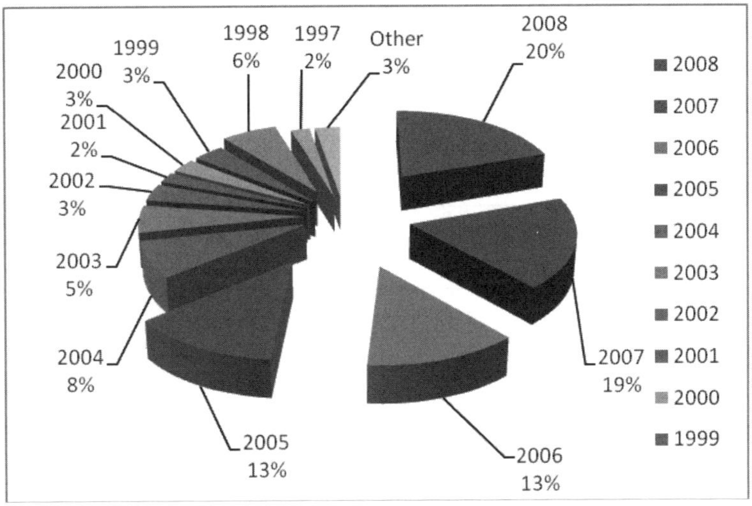

Figure 1.11 Distribution of articles whose title including CI.

integrated rather than using only one CI technique.

In Table 1.2, the literature review results for the number of papers whose titles including "computational intelligence" are given for the years from 1994 to 2008. When a search was made with respect to paper's title including "computational intelligence", totally 146 articles were viewed. At the same time, these papers were classified based on their keywords. As it is seen that 44 of these papers include the keyword *fuzzy set theory* (FST), 69 of them include the keyword *neural networks* (NNs), 39 of them include the keyword *genetic algorithms* (GAs).

In the other half of Table 1.2, the literature review has been extended to the papers whose keywords including "computational intelligence" for the years from 1994 to 2008. When a search was made for the papers whose keywords including "computational intelligence", totally 185 articles were viewed. At the same time, these papers were classified based on their keywords. In this case, total number of papers whose keywords including FST, GAs, and NNs were determined as 69, 57, and 90, respectively.

In Figure 1.11, a pie chart which summarizes the first half of Table 1.2 is given. According to Figure 1.11, CI has gained more attention year by year. 65 % of these papers have been published in the last 4 years.

The papers related to CI are also classified based on their subject areas and the obtained results are summarized in Table 1.4. The frequency distribution of these papers is illustrated

Table 1.2 Search Result Based on the Publication Years

Year	T: CI	T: CI + K: FST	T: CI + K: GAs	T: CI + K: NNs	T: CI + K: EC	T: CI + K: PSO	T: CI + K: ACO
2008	29	3	5	8	1	0	0
2007	27	7	4	12	2	0	0
2006	19	6	9	14	1	1	1
2005	19	9	8	11	2	1	0
2004	11	2	3	3	1	0	0
2003	8	2	1	3	0	0	0
2002	5	0	0	1	1	0	0
2001	3	3	1	3	1	0	0
2000	4	3	2	2	1	0	0
1999	5	4	3	4	1	0	0
1998	9	1	2	3	1	0	0
1997	3	1	0	2	0	0	1
1996	1	1	1	1	0	0	0
1995	1	1	0	1	1	0	0
1994	2	1	0	1	1	0	0
Total	**146**	**44**	**39**	**69**	**14**	**2**	**2**

Year	K: CI	K: CI + FST	K: CI + GAs	K: CI + NNs	K: CI + EC	K: CI + PSO	K: CI + ACO
2009	3	1	0	1	0	0	0
2008	37	13	7	12	5	3	0
2007	28	3	4	12	4	2	0
2006	19	8	8	8	2	1	1
2005	26	9	10	14	2	3	0
2004	13	7	6	7	1	1	0
2003	10	5	5	8	1	0	0
2002	8	4	3	5	1	0	0
2001	11	7	2	6	3	0	0
2000	5	3	0	1	1	0	0
1999	4	3	2	3	1	0	0
1998	7	2	3	5	1	0	0
1997	7	1	2	2	1	0	1
1996	3	1	2	2	1	0	0
1995	2	1	0	2	2	0	0
1994	2	1	0	2	1	0	0
Total	**185**	**69**	**57**	**90**	**27**	**10**	**2**

in Figure 1.12 as a bar chart. It is clearly understood that the most of CI papers are related to "computer science" while "engineering" and "mathematics" have consecutive importance. The pie chart for the papers, whose title including "computational intelligence" is given in Figure 1.13. According to this figure, NNs are the most used CI technique with 41 % of the papers. The second and third preferences are FST and GAs with percentages 26 and 23, respectively.

Table 1.3 Classification Results Based on Subject Areas

Subject Area	Count
Computer Science	76
Engineering	71
Mathematics	26
Decision Sciences	9
Physics and Astronomy	8
Biochemistry, Genetics and Molecular Biology	7
Materials Science	7
Earth and Planetary Sciences	5
Business, Management and Accounting	4
Energy	4
Environmental Science	4
Social Sciences	3
Multidisciplinary	3
Medicine	3
Chemistry	2
Neuroscience	2
Chemical Engineering	2
Agricultural and Biological Sciences	2
Health Professions	1
Economics, Econometrics and Finance	1

NNs and FST are the most used two CI techniques in the papers. These papers are also analyzed based on their publication years. Two pie charts illustrate the distribution of the papers with respect to the used technique in Figs. 1.14 and 1.15. According to Figure 1.14, the papers using NNs have the highest percentage in 2005 with 16 %. In addition, the largest increase in percentage is observed from 2004 (8 %) to 2005 (16 %) while the largest decrease in percentage is viewed from 2005 (16 %) to 2006 (9 %).

According to Figure 1.15, the papers using FST have the highest percentage in 2005 with 20 %. Also the largest increase in percentage is observed from 2004 (5 %) to 2005 (20 %) while the largest decrease in percentage is viewed from 2005 (20 %) to 2006 (14 %).

1.6.1 *Computational intelligence in complex decision systems*

CI techniques are required to solve complex problems, such as financial investment planning, foreign exchange trading, and knowledge discovery from large/multiple databases. They involve many different components or sub-tasks, each of which requires different

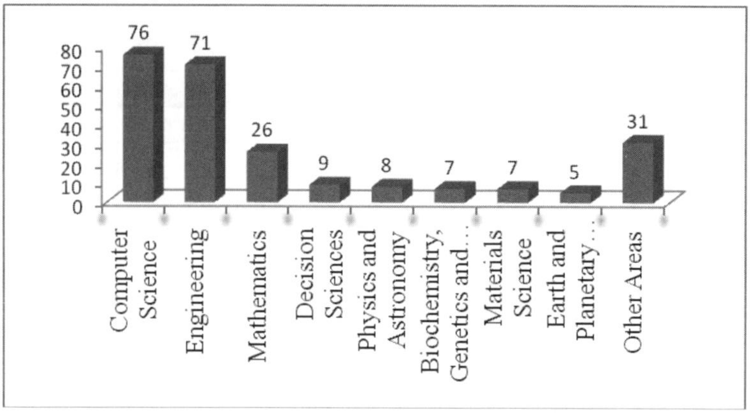

Figure 1.12 Frequency distribution of subject area classification.

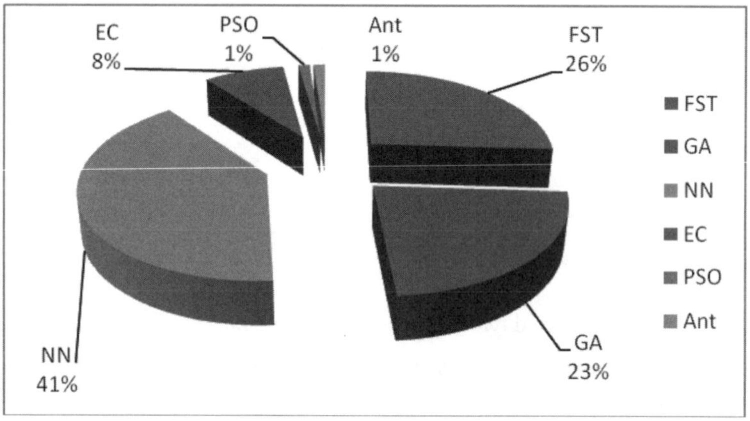

Figure 1.13 The distribution of CI techniques based on titles.

types of processing. For example, in financial investment planning, ANN can be used as a pattern watcher for the stock market; GAs can be used to predict interest rates; and approximate reasoning based on fuzzy logic can be used to evaluate financial risk tolerance ability of clients. Many techniques have been developed for complex problem solving and decision making. These techniques can be divided into two categories [150]:

- traditional hard computing techniques, including operations research, system science/engineering, expert systems, and
- CI techniques.

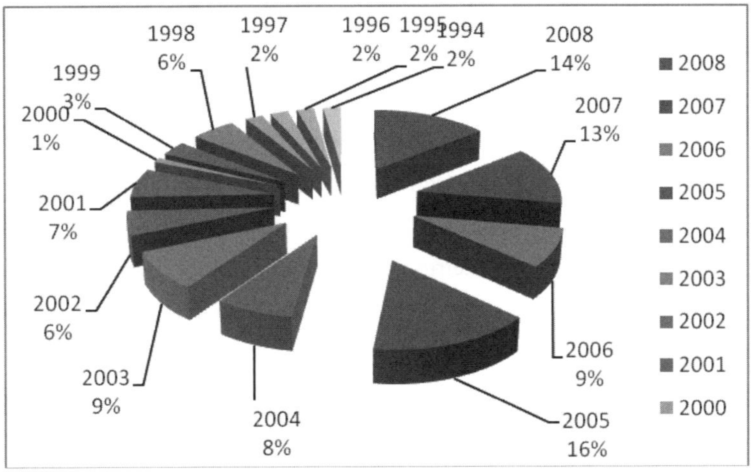

Figure 1.14 Distribution of the papers using NNs based on their publication years.

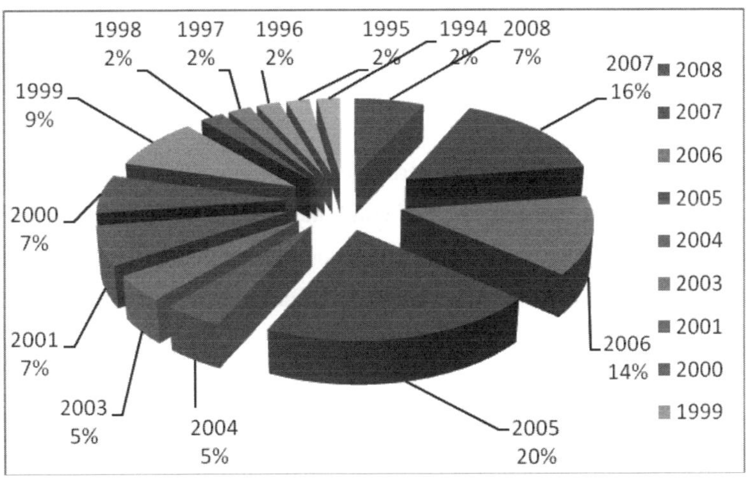

Figure 1.15 Distribution of the papers using FST based on their publication years.

In this subsection a literature review on computational intelligence in complex decision systems is given briefly. Many international conferences are organized to gather the latest development on CI and they publish those works in their proceedings. In the following, some papers published in these proceedings are summarized:

Benitez-Read and Rojas-Ramirez [4] presented the design, construction and real time performance of a mobile monitoring system based on a Khepera robot. They implemented a cascade fuzzy control algorithm for the robot navigation. Fuzzy sensor fusion related to the perception of the environment was used to reduce the complexity of the navigation function. The identification of test points was carried out by means of a Kohonen neural network. They also used one-dimensional image processing for the recognition of landmarks located at each test point. Han *et al.* [42] presented a new tissue classification system which combined both the classical fuzzy c-means classification algorithm and the human medical knowledge on geometric properties of different tissues and organs. They designed a user friendly interface so that medical knowledge could be easily transformed into these data structure in an interactive way. This system had been successfully applied to MRI images for classification of tissues of thigh. Rao [106] suggested a new computationally intelligent approach based on the Discerning Nuclear Intentions Model to support policy decision-making in a complex, non-linear manner. Muhsin *et al.* [74] presented an effective development process for a distributed workflow management system which was utilized to automate the management processes related to computer and peripheral repair requests in the Faculty of Engineering and Technology (FET) at the University of Jordan. They also investigated the distributed network layout and system security measures. Reduction of manual human intervention in the decision process was achieved through the implementation of a neuro-fuzzy computational intelligence processor to automate the major decision making process of tasks distribution. Ssali and Marwala [128] introduced a novel paradigm to impute missing data that combined a decision tree with an auto associative neural network based model and a principal component analysis-neural network based model. Ferreira and Ruano [34] presented RBF neural networks in order to implement a model-based predictive control methodology for a research greenhouse. Castillo and Melin [9] presented the development and design of two software tools which include a graphical user interface for construction, edition and observation of the intelligent systems for computational Intelligence. Betechuoh *et al.* [5] compared computational intelligence methods to analyze HIV in order to investigate which network was best suited for HIV classification. The methods analyzed were autoencoder multi-layer perception, autoencoder radial basis functions, support vector machines and neuro-fuzzy models. Quah and Ng [105] presented methodologies for equities selection based on soft-computing models which focused on applying fundamental analysis for equities screening. It compared the performance of three soft-computing models, namely Multi-layer Perceptrons, Adaptive Neuro-Fuzzy Inference Systems and General Growing and Pruning Radial Basis Function, and studied their computational time complexity. Rubin *et al.* [121] explored the interdependent roles of CI, data mining, and machine learning. Liau and Schmitt-Landsiedel [68] described a diagnosis method that worked with industrial semiconductor ATE (Automatic Test Equipment) for analyzing the robustness of the circuit (e.g. memory test chip) and used CI techniques. Teeuwsen *et al.* [131] introduced newly developed methods for on-line oscillatory stability assessment in large interconnected power systems. Instead of eigenvalue computation using the complete power system model, the new proposed OSA methods were based on computational intelligence such as neural networks, neuro fuzzy methods, and decision trees. Hirota *et al.* [44] analyzed Vehicle Dispatching Problem for Cooperative Deliveries from Multiple Depots (VDP/CD/MD) problem in the transport industries. They proposed a hierarchical multiplex structure (HIMS^{++}) calculation model to solve the VDP/CD/MD, problem. The HIMS^{++} model took advantage of object-oriented modeling, heuristic method, and fuzzy inference in (Atomic, Molecular, Individual) 3 layers, so it could find a utility decision (vehicles plan) close to expert dispatcher. Weber and Wu [139] described architecture for designing CI that included a knowledge management framework, allowing the system to learn from its own experiences, and those learned in external contexts. Zhang and Zhang [150] discussed the importance of hybrid intelligent systems for complex problem solving and decision-making, and explained why agent perspectives were suitable for modeling, designing and constructing hybrid intelligent systems. They presented some basic concepts and existing knowledge on hybrid intelligent systems. The advantages and disadvantages of different intelligent techniques were summarized. They also presented application system–agent-based hybrid intelligent system for data mining. Duch *et al.* [26] focused on the extraction and use of logical rules for data understanding. All aspects of rule generation, optimization, and application were described, including the problem of finding good symbolic descriptors for continuous data, tradeoffs between accuracy and simplicity at the rule-extraction stage, and tradeoffs between rejection and error level at the rule optimization stage. Zhang and Lin [151] proposed a new research area called Computational Web Intelligence based on both CI and Web Technology to increase the Quality of Intelligence of e-Business. Ndousse and Okuda [79] proposed a computationally based expert system for managing fault propagation in internetworks using the concept of fuzzy cognitive maps.

The reader can find full conference papers on CI applications in complex decision systems in Ruan *et al.* [111]–[120].

1.7 Computational Intelligence Journals

This section includes the brief descriptions of the CI journals. The journal, **Computational Intelligence: An International Journal**, has been published as quarterly since 1985 by Wiley-Blackwell Publishing. It focuses on topics about machine learning, which is including in particular symbolic multistrategy, and cognitive learning, web intelligence and semantic web, discovery science and knowledge mining, agents and multiagent systems, modern knowledge-based systems, Key application areas of AI. In the description of the journal it is clearly stated that: "This leading international journal promotes and stimulates research in the field of artificial intelligence (AI). Covering a wide range of issues – from the tools and languages of AI to its philosophical implications – the journal provides a vigorous forum for the publication of both experimental and theoretical research, as well as surveys and impact studies. The journal is designed to meet the needs of a wide range of AI workers in academic and industrial research."

The **International Journal of Computational Intelligence** that is a scholarly open access, peer-reviewed, interdisciplinary, quarterly and fully refereed journal has been published by WASET (World Academy Science, Engineering and Technology) since 2005. The journal is focusing on theories, methods and applications in CI.

The **International Journal of Computational Intelligence and Applications**, IJCIA, has been published since 2001 by World Scientific. The journal dedicated to the theory and applications of CI (ANN, fuzzy systems, evolutionary computation, and hybrid systems). The main goal of the journal is to provide the scientific community and industry with a vehicle whereby ideas using two or more conventional and CI based techniques could be discussed. The IJCIA welcomes works in areas such as neural networks, fuzzy logic, evolutionary computation, pattern recognition, hybrid intelligent systems, symbolic machine learning, statistical models, image/audio/video compression and retrieval. Areas include neural, fuzzy and evolutionary computation, pattern recognition, hybrid intelligent systems, symbolic machine learning, statistical models, image/audio/video compression and retrieval, encouraging "new ideas, combining two or more areas, such as neurofuzzy, neuro-symbolic, neuro-evolutionary, neuro-symbolic, neuro-pattern recognition, fuzzy-evolutionary, evolutionary-symbolic, fuzzy-evolutionary, evolutionary-symbolic, fuzzy-symbolic, etc."

The **International Journal of Computational Intelligence Research** that has been published by Research India Publications since 2005 is a free online journal. The aim and scope of the journal is defined by "Computational intelligence is a well-established paradigm, where new theories with a sound biological understanding have been evolving. The current experimental systems have many of the characteristics of biological computers and are beginning to be built to perform a variety of tasks that are difficult or impossible to do with conventional computers. In a nutshell, which becomes quite apparent in light of the current research pursuits, the area is heterogeneous as being dwelled on such technologies as neurocomputing, fuzzy systems, probabilistic reasoning, artificial life, evolutionary algorithms, multi-agent systems etc."

The **Journal of Computational Intelligence in Bioinformatics** which publishes articles describing recent fundamental contributions in the field of artificial intelligence and CI theory and their applications in Bioinformatics has been published by Research India Publications since 2008 with three issues in a year. This journal tries to cover all "advances in computational molecular/structural biology, encompassing areas such as computing in biomedicine and genomics, computational proteomics and systems biology, and metabolic pathway engineering. The topics covered include many CI methods.

The **International Journal of Computational Intelligence Systems** that aims at covering state-of-the-art research and development in all fields where CI is applied has been published by Atlantis Press since 2008. The journal publishes original papers on foundations and new developments of CI with an emphasis on applications, including current and potential applications of CI methods and techniques.

The **Computational Intelligence and Neuroscience** has been published by Hindawi Publishing since 2007. The journal is an open access journal interested in neural computing, neural engineering and artificial intelligence, where neuroscientists, cognitive scientists, engineers, psychologists, physicists, computer scientists, and artificial intelligence investigators among others can publish their work in one periodical that bridges the gap between neuroscience, artificial intelligence and engineering.

An other journal, **Applied Computational Intelligence and Soft Computing**, published by Hindawi Publishing in 2009, focuses on the disciplines of computer science, engineering, and mathematics. The scope of the journal includes developing applications related to all aspects of natural and social sciences by employing the technologies of CI and soft computing.

The **Journal of Advanced Computational Intelligence and Intelligent Informatics** has been published bimonthly by Fuji Technology Press since 1997. The journal focuses on the synergetic integration of neural networks, fuzzy logic and evolutionary computation, and building intelligent systems for industrial applications.

The **International Journal of Computational Intelligence: Theory and Practice** aims at publishing papers addressing theories, methods and applications in ANN, fuzzy systems, evolutionary computation, intelligent agents, hybrid systems and other areas of artificial intelligence. The journal has been published by Serials Publications since 2006.

The **International Journal of Computational Intelligence and Organizations** is a quarterly journal focusing on theories, methods and applications of CI in organizations. The journal that publishes original, high-quality articles dealing with the design, development, implementation and management of neural networks, genetic algorithms, fuzzy logic, uncertain reasoning techniques, and related machine learning methods has been published by Lawrence Erlbaum Associates since 1996.

The **IEEE Computational Intelligence Magazine** has been published by the IEEE Computational Intelligence Society since 2006. The journal is related to all areas of CI design and applications: applications oriented developments, successful industrial implementations, design tools, technology reviews, CI education, and applied research.

The **Journal of Computational Intelligence in Finance** has been published by Finance & Technology Publishing since 1993. The journal was focused on the financial applications of CI predictive methods.

Table 1.4 shows web page addresses of CI Journals introduced above.

1.8 Computational Intelligence's Future and Conclusions

In the future, one of the most important topics is the answer of the question how we will use CI. Duch [25] says "... Computational intelligence should protect us starting from birth, not only monitoring the health hazards, but also observing and guiding personal development, gently challenging children at every step to reach their full physical as well as mental potential. It should be a technology with access to extensive knowledge, but it also should help humans to make wise decisions presenting choices and their possible consequences. Although it may seem like a dangerous utopia perhaps deeper understanding of developmental processes, cognitive and emotional brain functions, real human needs, coupled with a technology that can recognize behavioral patterns, make sense of observations, understand natural language, plan and reason with extensive background knowledge, will lead to a better world in which no human life is wasted..."

CI techniques will probably be more used in robotics. In the future, pet robots, partner

Table 1.4 Web pages of CI Journals

Journal Name	Web Page
Computational Intelligence: An International Journal	http://www.wiley.com/bw/journal.asp?ref=0824-7935
International Journal of Computational Intelligence	http://www.waset.org/ijci/
International Journal of Computational Intelligence and Applications	http://www.worldscinet.com/ijcia/
International Journal of Computational Intelligence Research	http://www.softcomputing.net/ijcir/
Journal of Computational Intelligence in Bioinformatics	http://www.ripublication.com/jcib.htm
International Journal of Computational Intelligence Systems	http://www.atlantis-press.com/publications/ijcis/
Computational Intelligence and Neuroscience	http://www.hindawi.com/journals/cin/
Applied Computational Intelligence and Soft Computing	http://www.hindawi.com/journals/acisc/
Journal of Advanced Computational Intelligence and Intelligent Informatics	http://www.fujipress.jp/JACIII/
International Journal of Computational Intelligence: Theory and Practice	http://sofia.ocean.cs.siu.edu/index.php/ijcitp/ \newlineindex
International Journal of Computational Intelligence and Organizations	http://elib.cs.sfu.ca/Collections/CMPT/ cs-journals/P-Erlbaum/J-Erlbaum-IJCIO.html
IEEE Computational Intelligence Magazine	http://ieeexplore.ieee.org/xpl/RecentIssue.jsp? \newlinepunumber=10207
Journal of Computational Intelligence in Finance	http://ourworld.compuserve.com/homepages/ftpub/ \newlinejcif.htm

robots, and entertainment robots will be more developed than now as the next generation of human-friendly robots. CI techniques can be used to construct the interrelation between the human and robot through their actual interaction. The communication of a robot with a human requires the continuous interaction with the human, because the human tries to find out the causal relationship between human contact and its corresponding robotic action. Furthermore, the human can construct complicated relationship by expanding or integrating the found or constructed relationships. Therefore, the robot needs to accumulate the mapping structure between its perceptual system and action system through interaction with the human step by step. As a result, CI techniques will be used to realize this aim successfully. From this perspective, although inspirations drawn from cognitive and brain sciences, or biology in general, will continue to be very important, CI will become a solid branch of computer science more than now in the future.

CI's future is related to using of the hybrid systems. The future development of hybrid systems should incorporate various disciplinary knowledge of reservoir geo-science and maximize the amount of useful information extracted between data types so that reliable extrapolation away from the wellbores could be obtained.

In spite of the conflict on scope of the CI, there are many numbers of applications in industrial and academic researches. This is because the accurate results and different aspects of CI techniques for several problems. CI is coming into view that includes a highly interdisciplinary framework useful for supporting the design and development of intelligent systems. CI involves innovative models that often come with machine learning, but the researchers do not have any consensus on these models. Neural Networks, genetic algorithms, and fuzzy systems are common methods encountered in CI literature. Clusterization, classification, and approximation capabilities of CI systems are improving day by day and so many methods have been already developed that it is always possible to find alternative solutions with these CI techniques. While the problems getting more complex, the importance of CI is increasing. The trend of development of CI techniques will continue until systems as intelligent as human are created.

Bibliography

[1] Alpaydın, E., 2004, Introduction to machine learning, Chap. 11, The MIT Press, Cambridge, London, England.

[2] Alvarado, M., Sheremetov, L., Cantu, F., 2004, Autonomous agents and computational intelligence: the future of AI application for petroleum industry, Expert Systems with Applications, 26, 3–8.

[3] Back, T., Hammel, U., Schwefel, H.P, 1997, Evolutionary computation: comments on the history and current state, IEEE Transactions on Evolutionary Computation, 1 (1), 3–17.

[4] Benitez-Read, J.S., Rojas-Ramírez, E., 2008, A mobile monitoring system controlled by computational intelligence techniques, World Scientific Proceedings Series on Computer Engineering and Information Science 1; Computational Intelligence in Decision and Control - Proceedings of the 8th International FLINS Conference, Ruan, D., Montero, J., Lu, J., Martinez, L., D'hondt, P., and Kerre, E.E. (Eds.), pp. 981–986.

[5] Betechuoh, B.L., Marwala, T., Manana, J.V., 2008, Computational intelligence for HIV modeling, 12th International Conference on Intelligent Engineering Systems – Proceedings, INES 2008, pp. 127–132.

[6] Bezdek, J. C., 1994, What is computational intelligence?, In: Zurada, J.M., Marks, R.J., Robinson, C.J., (Eds.), Computational Intelligence, Imitating Life, IEEE Computer Society Press, 1–12.

[7] Cass, R., DePietro, J., 1998, Computational intelligence methods for process discovery, Engineering Applications of Artificial Intelligence, 11, 675–681.

[8] Castellano, G., Fanelli, A.M., Torsello, M.A., 2008, Computational Intelligence techniques for Web personalization, Web Intelligence and Agent Systems, 6 (3), 253–272.

[9] Castillo, O., Melin, P., 2008, Computational intelligence software: Type-2 fuzzy logic and modular neural networks, Proceedings of the International Joint Conference on Neural Networks, pp. 1820–1827.

[10] Chang, C.A., Tsai, C.Y., 1997, Using ART1 neural networks with destructive solid geometry for design retrieving systems, Computers in Industry, 34, 27–41.

[11] Chellapilla, K. and Fogel, D. B., 1999, Evolution, Neural Networks, Games, and Intelligence, Proceedings of the IEEE, 87 (9), 1471–1496.

[12] Chen, L., Pedrycz, W. and Chen P., 2006, Computational Intelligence Techniques for Building Transparent Construction Performance Models, IEEE International Conference on Systems, Man, and Cybernetics, 2, 1166–1171.

[13] Chen, S. H., 2005, Computational intelligence in economics and finance: Carrying on the legacy of Herbert Simon, Information Sciences, 170, 121–131.

[14] Chen, Z., 2000, Computational Intelligence for Decision Support, CRC Press, Boca Raton.

[15] Cheng, B. and Titterington, D.M., 1994, Neural Networks: A Review from a Statistical Perspective, Statistical Science, 9 (1), 2–54.

[16] Cherkassky, V., Krasnopolsky, V., Solomatine, D.P. and Valdes, J., 2006, Computational intelligence in earth sciences and environmental applications: Issues and challenges, Neural Networks, 19, 113–121.

[17] Corne, S., Murray, T., Openshaw, S., See, L., Turton, I., 1999, Using computational intelligence techniques to model subglacial water systems, Journal of Geographical Systems, 1, 37–60.

[18] Craenen, B.G.W., Eiben; A.E., 2008, Computational Intelligence; Encyclopedia of Life Support Sciences, EOLSS; EOLSS Co. Ltd., http://www.cs.vu.nl/ci/papers/Comp-Intell-Craenen-Eiben.pdf

[19] Dasey, T.J., Tzanakou, E.M., 2000, Detection of Multiple Sclerosis with Visual Evoked Potentials—An Unsupervised Computational Intelligence System, IEEE Transactions On Information Technology In Biomedicine, 4 (3), 216–224.

[20] Dimopoulos, C., Zalzala, A.M.S., 2000, Recent developments in evolutionary computation for manufacturing optimization: problems, solutions, and comparisons, IEEE Transactions on Evolutionary Computation, 4 (2), 93–113.

[21] Dorigo, M., Blum, C., 2005, Ant colony optimization theory: A survey, Theoretical Computer Science, 344, 243 – 278.

[22] Dorigo, M., Gambardella, L.M., 1997, Ant colonies for the travelling salesman problem, BioSystems, 43, 73–81.

[23] Dote, Y., Ovaska, S.J., 2001, Industrial applications of soft computing: A review, Proceedings of the IEEE 89 (9), 1243–1264.

[24] Douligeris, C., Pitsillides, A., Panno, D., 2002, Computational Intelligence in Telecommunications Networks, Computer Communications, 25, 1413–1414.

[25] Duch, W., 2007, What is Computational Intelligence and what could it become?, Duch, W., Mandziuk, J. (eds.) Challenges for Computational Intelligence. Studies in Computational Intelligence (J. Kacprzyk Series Editor), vol. 63. Springer, Heidelberg

[26] Duch, W., Setiono, R., Zurada, J.M., 2004, Computational intelligence methods for rule-based data understanding, Proceedings of the IEEE, 92 (5), pp. 771–805.

[27] Duch, W., Hayashi, Y., 2000, Computational intelligence methods and data understanding, Springer Studies in Fuzziness and Soft Computing, 54, 256–269.

[28] Duch, W., Setiono, R., Zurada, J.M., 2004, Computational Intelligence Methods for Rule-Based Data Understanding, Proceedings Of The IEEE, 92 (5), 771–805

[29] Eberhart, R., Simpson, P., Dobbins, R., 1996, Computational Intelligence PC Tools, Academic

Press, Boston.
[30] Edwards, R., Abraham, A. and Petrovic-Lazarevic, S., 2005, Computational Intelligence to Model the Export Behavior of Multinational Corporation Subsidiaries in Malaysia, Journal of the American Society for Information Science and Technology, 56 (11), 1177–1186.
[31] Engelbrecht, A.P., 2003, Computational Intelligence: An Introduction, Wiley.
[32] Engin, O., Çelik, A., Kaya, İ., 2008, A fuzzy approach to define sample size for attributes control chart in multistage processes: An application in engine valve manufacturing process, Applied Soft Computing, 8 (4), 1654–1663.
[33] Feigenbaum, E.A., 2003, Some Challenges and Grand Challenges for Computational Intelligence, Journal of the ACM, 50 (1), 32–40.
[34] Ferreira, P.M., Ruano, A.E., 2008, Application of computational intelligence methods to greenhouse environmental modeling, Proceedings of the International Joint Conference on Neural Networks, pp. 3582–3589.
[35] Fogel, D., 1995, Review of Computational intelligence: imitating life, IEEE Trans. Neural Networks, 6, 1562–1565.
[36] Fogel, G. B., Corne, D. W., 2003, Computational intelligence in bioinformatics, BioSystems, 72, 1–4.
[37] Fu, L., 1994. Neural Networks In Computer Intelligence, McGraw-Hill, United States of America.
[38] Gen, M., Cheng, R., 2000, Genetic Algorithms and Engineering Optimization. New York: John Wiley and Sons.
[39] Gu, P., Hashemian, M., Sosale, S., 1997, An integrated design methodology for life cycle engineering, Ann CIRP, 46 (1), 71–74.
[40] Guimarães, F.G., Barros, P.H.L., Ramírez, J.A., 2003, An Object-Oriented Library Based on Computational Intelligence Techniques for Optimization in Electromagnetics, IEEE Transactions On Magnetics, 39 (4), 2121–2124.
[41] Gupta, J.N.D. and Sexton, R.S., 1999, Comparing backpropagation with a genetic algorithm for neural network training, Omega, 27, 679–684.
[42] Han, K., Xianyi, Z., Taleb-Ahmed, A., Pinti, A., 2008, Integration of human knowledge for automatic tissue classification on medical images, World Scientific Proceedings Series on Computer Engineering and Information Science 1; Computational Intelligence in Decision and Control - Proceedings of the 8th International FLINS Conference, Ruan, D., Montero, J., Lu, J., Martinez, L., D'hondt, P., and Kerre, E.E. (Eds.), pp. 447–452.
[43] Hansen, N., Müller, S.D., Koumoutsakos, P., 2003, Reducing the Time Complexity of the Derandomized Evolution Strategy with Covariance Matrix Adaptation (CMA-ES), Evolutionary Computation, 11 (1), 1–18.
[44] Hirota, K., Chen, K., Dong, F., 2004, Computational intelligence approach to real-world cooperative vehicle dispatching problem, 2004 2nd International IEEE Conference 'Intelligent Systems' - Proceedings 1, pp. 7–12.
[45] Holmes, J.H., Lanzi, P.L., Stolzmann, W., Wilson, S.W., 2002, Learning classifier systems: New models, successful applications, Information Processing Letters, 82, 23–30.
[46] Huang, H.Z., Bo, R., Chen, W., 2006, An integrated computational intelligence approach to product concept generation and evaluation, Mechanism and Machine Theory 41, 567–583.
[47] Innocent, P.R., John, R.I., Garibaldi, J.M., 2001, The fuzzy medical group in the centre for computational Intelligence, Artificial Intelligence in Medicine, 21, 163–170.
[48] Isasi, P., Quintana, D., Saez, Y., Mochon, A., 2007, Applied Computational Intelligence for Finance and Economics, Computational Intelligence, 23 (2), 111–116.
[49] Jahanshahloo, G.R., Lotfi, F.H., Izadikhah, M., 2006, Extension of the TOPSIS method for

decision-making problems with fuzzy data, Applied Mathematics and Computation, 181, 1544–1551

[50] Jang, J.S.R. and Sun, C.T., 1995, Neuro-Fuzzy modeling and control, Proceedings of the IEEE, 83 (3), 378–406.

[51] Kahraman, C., (Ed.), 2008, Fuzzy multi-criteria decision making theory and applications with recent developments, Springer.

[52] Kalogirou, S.A., 2001, Artificial neural networks in renewable energy systems applications: a review, Renewable and Sustainable Energy Reviews, 5, 373–401.

[53] Karr, C.L., 2003, Control of a phosphate processing plant via a synergistic architecture for adaptive, intelligent control, Engineering Applications of Artificial Intelligence, 16 (1), 21–30.

[54] Karray, F., Zaneldin, E., Hegazy, T., Shabeeb, A., Elbeltagi, E., 2000, Computational Intelligence Tools for Solving the Facilities Layout Planning Problem, Proceedings of the American Control Conference, 3954–3958.

[55] Kaya, İ., 2009a, A genetic algorithm approach to determine the sample size for attribute control charts, Information Sciences, 179 (10), 1552–1566.

[56] Kaya, İ., 2009b, A genetic algorithm approach to determine the sample size for control charts with variables and attributes, Expert Systems with Applications, 36 (5), 8719–8734.

[57] Kaya, İ., Çınar, D., 2008, Facility Location Selection Using A Fuzzy Outranking Method, Journal of Multiple-Valued Logic and Soft Computing, 14, 251–263.

[58] Kaya, İ., Engin, O., 2007, A new approach to define sample size at attributes control chart in multistage processes: An application in engine piston manufacturing process, Journal of Materials Processing Technology, 183 (1), 38–48.

[59] Kennedy, J., Eberhart, R.C., 1995, Particle swarm optimization, Proceedings of the IEEE International Conference on Neural Networks, December, 1942–1948.

[60] Kothamasu, R., Huang, S. H. and Verduin, W. H., 2005, Comparison of computational intelligence and statistical methods in condition monitoring for hard turning, International Journal of Production Research, 43 (3), 597–610.

[61] Koza, J.R., 1990, Genetic programming: a paradigm for genetically breeding populations of computer programs to solve problems, Technical Report STANCS-90–1314, Department of Computer Science, Stanford University.

[62] Koza, J.R., 1992, Genetic Programming, Cambridge, MA: MIT Press.

[63] Kubota, N., 2005, Computational intelligence for structured learning of a partner robot based on imitation, Information Sciences, 171, 403–429.

[64] Lai, L.L., Sichanie, A.G., Gwyn, B.J., 1998, Comparison between evolutionary programming and a genetic algorithm for fault-section estimation, IEE Proceedings: Generation, Transmission and Distribution, 145 (5), 616–620.

[65] Lau, H.C.W., Hui, I.K., Chan, F.T.S., Wong, C.W.Y., 2002, Monitoring the supply of products in a supply chain environment: A fuzzy neural approach, Expert Systems, 19 (4), 235–243.

[66] Li, Y., 2007, An automatic parameter extraction technique for advanced CMOS device modeling using genetic algorithm, Microelectronic Engineering, 84 (2), 260–272.

[67] Liang, Y., Chunguang, Z., 2000, Advances in Identification of Nonlinear Characteristics of Packaging Based on Computational Intelligence, Mechanics Research Communications, 27 (1), 15–20.

[68] Liau, E., Schmitt-Landsiedel, D., 2005, Computational intelligence semiconductor ATE - Ultrashort worst case test, Proceedings of the 2005 IEEE International Conference on Computational Intelligence for Measurement Systems and Applications, CIMSA 2005, pp. 273–278.

[69] Ling, S. H., Leung, F. H. F., Wong, L. K., Lam, H. K., 2005, Computational Intelligence Techniques for Home Electric Load Forecasting And Balancing, International Journal

of Computational Intelligence and Applications, 3, 371–391.
[70] Marks, R., 1993, Computational versus artificial, IEEE Transactions on Neural Networks, 4, 737–739.
[71] Martin, T.; Ralescu, A. L. (Eds.), 1995, Fuzzy Logic in Artificial Intelligence, IJCAI '95 Workshop, Montreal, Canada, August 19–21, 1995, Selected Papers, Springer.
[72] Matics, J. and Krost, G., 2008, Micro combined heat and power home supply: Prospective and adaptive management achieved by computational intelligence techniques, Applied Thermal Engineering, 28, 2055–2061.
[73] Moriarty, D.E. and Miikkulainen, R., 1996, Efficient Reinforcement Learning through Symbiotic Evolution, Machine Learning, 22, 11–32.
[74] Muhsin, Z.J., El-Mousa, A.H., Al-Taee, M.A., 2008, A distributed workflow management system utilizing computational intelligence for decision support, 5th International Multi-Conference on Systems, Signals and Devices, SSD'08, pp. 1–6.
[75] Munakata, T., 2008, Fundamentals of the New Artificial Intelligence Neural, Evolutionary, Fuzzy and More, Springer.
[76] Nakayama, H., Arakawa, M., Sasaki, R., 2002, Simulation-Based Optimization Using Computational Intelligence, Optimization and Engineering, 3, 201–214.
[77] Narendra, B.S., Sivapullaiah, P.V., Suresh, S., Omkar, S.N., 2006, Prediction of uncon.ned compressive strength of soft grounds using computational intelligence techniques: A comparative study, Computers and Geotechnics, 33, 196–208.
[78] Naso, D. and Turchiano, B., 2005, Multicriteria Meta-Heuristics for AGV Dispatching Control Based on Computational Intelligence, IEEE Transactions on Systems, Man, and Cybernetics—Part b: Cybernetics, 35 (2), 208–226.
[79] Ndousse, T.D., Okuda, T., 1996, Computational intelligence for distributed fault management in networks using fuzzy cognitive maps, IEEE International Conference on Communications, 3, pp. 1558–1562.
[80] Neely, C., Weller, P., Dittmar, R., 1997, Is technical analysis in the foreign exchange market profitable? A genetic programming approach, The Journal of Financial and Quantitative Analysis, 32 (4), 405–426.
[81] Ng, T.T.H., Leng, G.S.B., 2002, Application of genetic algorithms to conceptual design of a micro-air vehicle, Engineering Applications of Artificial Intelligence, 15, 439–445.
[82] Nucci, E. R., Silva, R. G., Gomes, T. C., Giordano R. C., Cruz, A.J.G., 2005, A Fuzzy Logic Algorithm For Identification of The Harvesting Threshold During PGA production by Bacillus megaterium, Brazilian Journal of Chemical Engineering, 22 (4), 521–527,
[83] Oh, S.-K., Pedrycz, W., Park, H.-S., 2002, Implicit rule-based fuzzy-neural networks using the identification algorithm of GA hybrid scheme based on information granulation, Advanced Engineering Informatics, 16 (4), 247–263.
[84] Oh, S.K., Pedrycz, W., Park, H.S., 2005, Multi-layer hybrid fuzzy polynomial neural networks: a design in the framework of computational intelligence, Neurocomputing, 64, 397–431.
[85] Ovaska, S.J., VanLandingham, H.F., Kamiya, A., 2002, Fusion of soft computing and hard computing in industrial applications: An overview, IEEE Transactions on Systems, Man and Cybernetics Part C: Applications and Reviews, 32 (2), 72–79.
[86] Pal, N.R. and Mudi, R.K., 2003, Computational Intelligence for Decision-Making Systems, International Journal of Intelligent Systems, 18, 483–486.
[87] Pal, N.R., Pal, S., 2002, Computational Intelligence for Pattern Recognition, International Journal of Pattern Recognition and Artificial Intelligence, 16 (7), 773–779.
[88] Pal, S.K. and Mitra, S., 1992, Multilayer Perceptron, Fuzzy Sets, and Classification, IEEE Transactıons on Neural Networks, 3 (5), 683–697.
[89] Papageorgioua, E.I., Spyridonosc, P.P., Glotsosc, D. Th., Styliosb, C.D., Ravazoulad, P., Nikiforidisc, G.N., Groumposa, P.P., 2008, Brain tumor characterization using the soft com-

puting technique of fuzzy cognitive maps, Applied Soft Computing, 8 (1), 820–828.
[90] Park, B.J., Lee, D.Y., Oh, S.-K., 2003, Rule-based fuzzy polynomial neural networks in modeling software process data, International Journal of Control, Automation and Systems, 1 (3), 321–331.
[91] Park, B.J., Pedrycz, W., Oh, S.K., 2002, Fuzzy polynomial neural networks: Hybrid architectures of fuzzy modeling, IEEE Transactions on Fuzzy Systems, 10 (5), 607–621.
[92] Park, H.S., Oh, S.K., 2003, Rule-based fuzzy-neural networks using the identification algorithm of the GA hybrid scheme, International Journal of Control, Automation and Systems, 1 (1), 101–110.
[93] Park, J.-H., Seo, K.-K., Wallace, D., 2001, Approximate life cycle assessment of classified products using artificial neural network and statistical analysis in conceptual product design, in: Proceedings of Second International Symposium on Environmentally Conscious Design and Inverse Manufacturing, 321–326.
[94] Pavlidis, N.G., Parsopoulos, K.E., Vrahatis, M.N., 2005, Computing Nash equilibria through computational intelligence methods, Journal of Computational and Applied Mathematics, 175, 113–136.
[95] Pavlidis, N.G., Tasoulis, D.K., Plagianakos, V.P., Vrahatis, M.N., 2006, Computational Intelligence Methods for Financial Time Series Modeling, International Journal of Bifurcation and Chaos, 16 (7), 2053–2062.
[96] Pedrycz, W, 2002, Computational intelligence and visual computing: an emerging technology for software engineering, Soft Computing, 7, 33–44.
[97] Pedrycz, W., 2007, Genetic tolerance fuzzy neural networks: From data to fuzzy hyperboxes, Neurocomputing, 70 (7–9), 1403–1413.
[98] Pedrycz, W., Peters, J.F., (Eds.), 1998, Computational Intelligence in Software Engineering, Advances In Fuzzy Systems—Applications and Theory, vol. 16, World Scientific, Singapore.
[99] Pedrycz, W., Reformat, M., 2005, Genetically optimized logic models, Fuzzy Sets and Systems, 150 (2), 351–371.
[100] Pena-Reyes, C.A., Siper, M., 2000, Evolutionary computation in medicine: an overview, Artificial Intelligence in Medicine, 19, 1–23.
[101] Plikynas, D., Sakalauskas, L. and Poliakova, A., 2005, Analysis of foreign investment impact on the dynamics of national capitalization structure: A computational intelligence approach, Research in International Business and Finance, 19, 304–332.
[102] Poole, D., Mackworth, A., Goebel, R., 1998, Computational Intelligence – A Logical Approach, Oxford University Press, New York.
[103] Puskorius, G.V. and Feldkamp, L.A., 1994, Neurocontrol of Nonlinear Dynamical Systems with Kalman Filter Trained Recurrent Networks, IEEE Transactions on Neural Networks, 5 (2), 279–297.
[104] Quah, J. T.S., Sriganesh, M., 2008, Real-time credit card fraud detection using computational intelligence, Expert Systems with Applications, 35, 1721–1732.
[105] Quah, J.T.S., Ng, W.D., 2007, Utilizing computational intelligence for DJIA stock selection, IEEE International Conference on Neural Networks – Conference Proceedings, pp. 956–961.
[106] Rao, S., 2008, A nature-inspired computational approach to discern unhealthy nuclear intentions of nation states, World Scientific Proceedings Series on Computer Engineering and Information Science 1; Computational Intelligence in Decision and Control - Proceedings of the 8th International FLINS Conference, Ruan, D., Montero, J., Lu, J., Martinez, L., D'hondt, P., and Kerre, E.E. (Eds.), pp. 823–828.
[107] Reformat, M., Pedrycz, W., Pizzi, N.J., 2003, Software quality analysis with the use of computational intelligence, Information and Software Technology, 45, 405–417.

[108] Riziotis, C. and Vasilakos, A.V., 2007, Computational intelligence in photonics technology and optical networks: A survey and future perspectives, Information Sciences, 177, 5292–5315.

[109] Rooij, A.J.F., Jain, L.C. and Johnson, R.P., 1996, Neural network training using genetic algorithms, World Scientific Publishing Co. Pte. Ltd., Singapore.

[110] Ross, T., 1995, Fuzzy Logic with Engineering Applications, McGraw-Hill, USA.

[111] Ruan, D., Montero, J., Lu, J., Martinez, L., D'hondt, P., and Kerre, E.E., (Eds.), 2008, Computational intelligence in decision and control, Proceedings of the FLINS2008, World Scientific, Singapore.

[112] Ruan, D., D'hondt, P., Fantoni, P.F., De Cock, M., Nachtegael, M., and Kerre, E.E., (Eds.), 2006, Applied artificial intelligence, Proceedings of the FLINS 2006, World Scientific, Singapore.

[113] Ruan, D., D'hondt, P., De Cock, M., Nachtegael, M., and Kerre, E.E., (Eds.), 2004, Applied computational intelligence, Proceedings of the FLINS 2004, World Scientific, Singapore.

[114] Ruan, D., 2004, Role of computational intelligence in sensory evaluation, Journal of Dong Hua University (English Edition), 21 (3), 21–25.

[115] Ruan, D., D'hondt, P., and Kerre, E.E., (Eds.), 2002, Computational intelligent systems for applied research, Proceedings of FLINS the 2002, World Scientific, Singapore.

[116] Ruan, D., Aït Abderrahim, H., D'hondt, P., and Kerre, E.E., (Eds.), 2000, Intelligent technologies and soft computing in nuclear science and engineering, Proceedings of the FLINS 2000, World Scientific, Singapore.

[117] Ruan, D., Aït Abderrahim, H., D'hondt, P., and Kerre, E.E., (Eds.), 1998, Fuzzy logic and intelligent technologies for nuclear science and industry, Proceedings of the FLINS'98, World Scientific, Singapore.

[118] Ruan, D., (Ed.), 1997, Intelligent hybrid systems: fuzzy logic, neural networks, and genetic algorithms, Springer.

[119] Ruan, D., D'hondt, P., Govaerts, P., and Kerre, E.E., (Eds.), 1996, Intelligent systems and soft computing for nuclear science and industry, Proceedings of the FLINS'96, World Scientific, Singapore.

[120] Ruan, D., D'hondt, P., Govaerts, P., and Kerre, E.E., (Eds.), 1994, Fuzzy logic and intelligent technologies in nuclear science, Proceedings of the FLINS'94, World Scientific, Singapore.

[121] Rubin, S.H., Ceruti, M.G., Dai, W., 2005, The role of computational intelligence in data mining, Proceedings of the 2005 IEEE International Conference on Information Reuse and Integration, pp. 192–198.

[122] Rudas, I. J., Fodor, J., 2008, Intelligent Systems, International Journal of Computers, Communications & Control, III, 132–138

[123] Salman, A., Ahmad, I., Al-Madani, S., 2002, Particle swarm optimization for task assignment problem, Microprocessors and Microsystems, 26, 363–371.

[124] Santos, A.A.P., Costa Jr., N.C.A., Coelho, L.S., 2007, Computational intelligence approaches and linear models in case studies of forecasting exchange rates, Expert Systems with Applications, 33, 816–823.

[125] Sebastian, H.J., Schleiffer, R., 2000, Using Computational Intelligence in Fuzzy Engineering Design, Cybernetics and Systems: An International Journal, 31, 547–589.

[126] Sexton, R.S. and Gupta, J.N.D., 2000, Comparative evaluation of genetic algorithm and backpropagation for training neural networks, Information Sciences, 129, 45–59.

[127] Song, Y.H., Allan, J. Raj, A., 1997, Computational Intelligence Applications to Power Systems, Springer.

[128] Ssali, G., Marwala, T., 2008, Computational intelligence and decision trees for missing data estimation, Proceedings of the International Joint Conference on Neural Networks,

pp. 201–207.

[129] Stathakis, D., Athanassios, V., 2006, Comparison of Computational Intelligence Based Classification Techniques for Remotely Sensed Optical Image Classification, IEEE Transactions on Geoscience and Remote Sensing, 44 (8), 2305–2318.

[130] Sun, J., Kalenchuk, D.K., 2000, Design candidate identification using neural network-based fuzzy reasoning, Robotics and Computer-Integrated Manufacturing, 16 (5), 382–396.

[131] Teeuwsen, S.P., Erlich, I., El-Sharkawi, M.A., 2005, Small-signal stability assessment for large power systems using computational intelligence, 2005 IEEE Power Engineering Society General Meeting 3, pp. 2661–2668.

[132] Tzafestas, S., Tzafestas, E., 2001, Computational Intelligence Techniques for Short-Term Electric Load Forecasting, Journal of Intelligent and Robotic Systems, 31, 7–68.

[133] Uhrig, R.E. and Hines, J.W., 2005, Computational Intelligence in Nuclear Engineering, Nuclear Engineering and Technology, 37 (2), 127–138.

[134] Vasilakos, A.V., Anagnostakis, K.G., Pedrycz, W., 2001, Application of computational intelligence techniques in active networks, Soft Computing, 264–271.

[135] Venugopal, V., Naredran, T.T., 1992, Neural network model for design retrieval in manufacturing systems, Computers in Industry, 20 (1), 11–23.

[136] Wang, D.D., Tieu, A.K., D'Alessio, G., 2005, Computational Intelligence-Based Process Optimization for Tandem Cold Rolling, Materials and Manufacturing Processes, 20 (3), 479–496.

[137] Wang, L., Zou, H., 1998, Three-grade fuzzy synthetical decision for mechanism concept, Machine Design and Research, 14 (1), 9–11.

[138] Warne, K., Prasad, G., Rezvani, S. and Maguire, L., 2004, Statistical and computational intelligence techniques for inferential model development: a comparative evaluation and a novel proposition for fusion, Engineering Applications of Artificial Intelligence, 17, 871–885.

[139] Weber, R., Wu, D., 2004, Knowledge management for computational intelligence systems, Proceedings of IEEE International Symposium on High Assurance Systems Engineering 8, pp. 116–125.

[140] Welstead, S.T., 1994, Neural Networks and Fuzzy Logic Applications in C/C++, John Wiley & Sons, Canada.

[141] Wilson, E.L., Karr, C.L., Bennett, J.P., 2004, An Adaptive, Intelligent Control System for Slag Foaming, Applied Intelligence, 20 (2), 165–177.

[142] Xu, J., Nannariello, J. and Fricke, F.R., 2004, Predicting and optimising the airborne sound transmission of floor–ceiling constructions using computational intelligence, Applied Acoustics, 65, 693–704.

[143] Xue, D., Dong, Z., 1997, Coding and clustering of design and manufacturing features for concurrent design, Computers in Industry, 34, 139–153.

[144] Yang, H.T., Yang, P.C., Huang, C.L., 1996, Evolutionary programming based economic dispatch for units with non-smooth fuel cost functions, IEEE Transactions on Power Systems, 11 (1), 112–118.

[145] Yao, X. and Liu, Y., 1997, A New Evolutionary System for Evolving Artificial Neural Networks, IEEE Transactions on Neural Networks, 8 (3), 694–713.

[146] Yao, X., 1999, Evolutionary programming made faster, IEEE Transactions on Evolutionary Computation, 3 (2), 82–102.

[147] Zadeh, L.A., 1965, Fuzzy Sets, Information and Control, 8, 338–353.

[148] Zadeh, L.A., 1975, The concept of a linguistic variable and its application to approximate reasoning", Inf Sciences, 8, 199–249.

[149] Zadeh, L.A., 1996, Fuzzy Logic Equals Computing with Words, IEEE Transactions on Fuzzy Systems, 4 (2), 103–111.

[150] Zhang, Z.; Zhang, C. (Eds.), 2004, Agent-Based Hybrid Intelligent Systems An Agent-Based Framework for Complex Problem Solving, Springer.
[151] Zhang, Y.-Q., Lin, T.Y., 2002, Computational Web Intelligence (CWI): Synergy of computational intelligence and web technology, IEEE International Conference on Plasma Science 2, pp. 1104–1107.
[152] Zimmermann, H.-J. 1987, Fuzzy sets, decision making, and expert systems, Boston, Dordrecht, Lancaster.
[153] Zimmermann, H.-J., 2004, Computational Intelligence and Environmental Planning, Cybernetics and Systems: An International Journal, 35, 431–454.

Chapter 2

Uncertainty in Dynamically Changing Input Data

Tiago C. Pais, Rita A. Ribeiro, and Luís F. Simões

UNINOVA-CA3, Campus FCT/UNL, 2829-516 Caparica, Portugal

Email: rar@uninova.pt[1]

The main objective of multiple criteria decision making models is to select an alternative, from a finite number, regarding a set of pre-defined criteria. Usually, this type of problems includes two main tasks, rating the alternatives regarding each criterion and then ranking them. Once a decision is made (alternative selected) the problem is solved. However, for situations involving reaching consensus or requiring several steps before reaching a final decision, we must consider a dynamic and adaptable decision model, which considers previous solutions.

In this work we introduce multiple criteria dynamic decision making models (MCDDM) and discuss contributions to deal with the difficult problem of imprecision in dynamically changing input data. To illustrate the approach, a simplified example of autonomous spacecraft landing is presented.

2.1 Problem Statement

In general, the aim of Multiple Criteria or Multiple Attribute Decision Making problems [1] (henceforth called multiple criteria) is to find the best compromise solution from all feasible alternatives assessed by pre-defined criteria (or attributes). This type of problems is widespread in real life situations [1, 2]. A Multiple Criteria Decision Making (MCDM) problem is usually modeled as a decision matrix, as depicted in Eq. (1). Basically, a MCDM model includes two phases [3]:

(a) classify the alternatives regarding each criterion and then aggregate the respective classifications to obtain ratings per alternative;

[1] corresponding author

(b) order the alternatives (ranking), where the highest rate usually corresponds to the "best" alternative to be selected.

$$\begin{array}{c} \\ A_1 \\ A_2 \\ \vdots \\ A_n \end{array} \begin{array}{c} C_1 \; C_2 \; \cdots \; C_m \\ \begin{bmatrix} x_{11} & x_{12} & \cdots & x_{1m} \\ x_{21} & x_{22} & \cdots & x_{2m} \\ \vdots & \vdots & \ddots & \vdots \\ x_{n1} & x_{n2} & \cdots & x_{nm} \end{bmatrix} \end{array} \tag{1}$$

where A_i is the alternative i $(= 1,\ldots,n)$, C_j is the attribute j $(= 1,\ldots,m)$ and x_{ij} is the evaluation (or the satisfaction) of alternative A_i regarding attribute C_j.

In this work the context is Multiple Criteria Dynamic Decision Making (MCDDM) models, specifically decision paradigms with several iterations, which need to take into account past/historic information (feedback) to reach a decision (or decision consensus). In general, dynamic systems usually have spatial-temporal limitations such as, the search space varies for each step (iteration) and there are several steps (iterations) to reach a final decision [4]. According to Richardson and Pugh [5] system dynamics problems have two main features: "they involve quantities which change over time"; and "involves the notion of feedback". Moreover, when we are dealing with dynamic processes, the evaluation/selection process is more sophisticated because it must include information from previous iterations (historic data). Henceforth, this process is called "dynamic evaluation process" because it involves aggregation of past and current ratings, as well as selection of a sub-set of possible "good" candidates for the next iteration (historical feedback).

One important requirement that both static MCDM methods [1] and MCDDM methods face is that data must be both numerical and principally comparable. When in presence of both qualitative and quantitative variables, we need to transform and normalize the data to compare them.

In MCDDM a big challenge is how to represent dynamic input changing data. Here we also address another important aspect of many multicriteria decision problems: uncertainty in input data. Sometimes, there is a lack of confidence and accuracy on the available input data and we must devise ways of incorporating this uncertainty on the transformed input data. All these aspects fall under a general umbrella of data preparation [6] and they constitute the basis for dynamic spatial-temporal decision models.

Our main objective is to present contributions for handling the data preparation process in MCDDM models with imprecise input data. We will address four main aspects of any dynamic spatial-temporal decision problem:

(I) How to represent and normalize the input parameters within a dynamically changing input data;
(II) How to deal with uncertainty in dynamically changing input data;
(III) How to consider different criteria importance, depending on criteria satisfaction and decision process phase (iteration);
(IV) How to use feedback past information from the dynamic model to evaluate the alternatives at each decision point.

The first three questions belong to known literature processes about data preparation and multicriteria processes [7, 1, 6], respectively, and they will be discussed in detail. The fourth aspect is mostly concerned with suitable operators to aggregate current and past information that should be considered at each iteration of the decision process. The latter will only be addressed here briefly because the authors already proposed some contributions for this process [8].
Summarizing, the aim of single or dynamic Multiple Criteria Decision Making problems is to find the best compromise solution from all feasible alternatives, assessed by pre-defined criteria (or attributes) [7, 3]. There are many methods and techniques to deal with static MCDM [7, 1, 3]. However, when facing dynamic multiple criteria decisions, where several iterations are at stake and feedback from step to step is required, there are few contributions in the literature (see for example [9, 4, 10, 11]).
To better explain our proposed contributions to deal with uncertainty in dynamically changing input data during the temporal decision process, we use a simplified example of a site selection problem for spacecraft landing on planets [12]. This case study requires a dynamic and adaptable decision model to ensure robust and smooth site selection along the final descent.

2.2 Description of Methodology

In this chapter we present an architecture for a multiple criteria dynamic decision model. This architecture involves two important aspects: how to perform a correct data preparation when we are dealing with dynamically changing input data and how to deal with a complex evaluation process, which includes historic information to ensure a truly dynamic and adaptable decision algorithm. In Figure 2.1 we depict the conceptual design for the dynamic decision model.
The two main phases, shown in Figure 2.1, are:

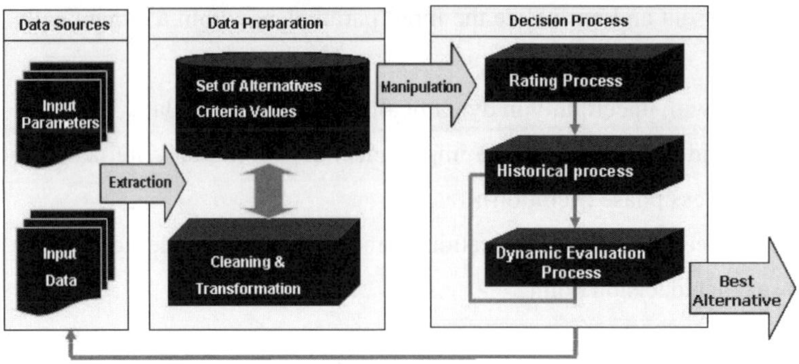

Figure 2.1 Conceptual design of the dynamic decision model.

(A) Phase A. Data preparation in dynamic environments – This process deals with transformation of inputs for the decision model. Its main tasks are to identify the criteria and the alternatives of the problem and then to clean and transform the input data to obtain parameters/variables that can be manipulated to achieve a decision. For this phase we propose six steps that are detailed in Sec. 2.2.1.

(B) Phase B. Decision Evaluation Process with Feedback – This process starts with rating the current alternatives (assessed by criteria) and then performs evaluation of alternatives, considering rating value plus the historic information available. Finally, the historic sub-set is created and is provided as feedback for the next iteration. This process goes on until a stoping criterion is reached.

As mentioned, in this work we focus on the first step, hence more emphasis is put on Phase A in the remaining sections.

2.2.1 *Phase A. Data Preparation in Dynamic Environments*

Here we discuss our proposed data preparation steps for handling dynamically changing input data, in presence of uncertainty. As mentioned, one important requirement of MCDM methods [1], both static and dynamic, is that data must be both numerical and principally comparable. When in presence of both qualitative and quantitative variables, we need to transform and normalize the data to compare them. This work also addresses an important aspect of many multiple criteria decision problems: uncertainty in input data. When dealing with MCDDM problems there are three important questions to answer: how to define and represent the variables? Is the raw input data extracted accurate and do we have confidence in it? Do we know if the search space includes all possible alternatives to be evaluated at each step? Our proposed data preparation steps for MCDDM with uncertainty are:

- Step 1. Parameters identification – This process is characterized by identifying the input variables (problem understanding). In a multiple criteria decision making environment these correspond to determine criteria for assessing candidate alternatives, as well as identifying the set of candidate alternatives [3].
- Step 2. Transformation – Data is transformed from a raw state into data suited for decision support, by normalizing and representing the input variables with fuzzy membership functions. This process is usually called fuzzification [2] and involves choosing the topology for the fuzzy sets representing the input variables. With a fuzzy logic approach we can guarantee normalized and comparable data definitions, besides allowing us to deal, in a simple fashion, with imprecision in data.
- Step 3. Cleaning – After defining the fuzzy set functions, for each criterion (i.e., representation and normalization) all candidate alternatives with membership values of zero, in any criterion, are discarded. Moreover, any other constraints that alternatives are required to obey will be used to further clean the data, thus further reducing the set of candidate alternatives. Another aspect of cleaning is how to handle missing input data (e.g., missing records, gaps in collect data etc.). A possible solution could be to use the previous value when there is missing data [13].
- Step 4. Fusion – transformed and cleaned data from each criterion is integrated using a conjunctive method [7] to define the general search space, i.e., number of alternatives to be evaluated with the defined criteria, per iteration. The Conjunctive method is an outranking method [7] so it does not give a score for each alternative like most common scoring methods, such as MaxiMin, WSM, WPM and TOPSIS. This method simply discards an alternative if it has a criterion value below a threshold. To obtain the final score a Pareto optimal strategy can be used (i.e., selects dominating alternatives – better or equal in each criteria – and from this set trade-off analysis can be performed).
- Step 5. Filtering uncertainty – Data should be filtered to consider both lack of accuracy and/or lack of confidence on the collected input data. A filtering function is presented that can handle this type of intrinsic uncertainty in input data. This process corresponds to including some degree of uncertainty (either given from experts or from statistical processes) when there are doubts about the correctness of collected data.
- Step 6. Weighting criteria – we should also consider the assignment of relative importance to criteria (weights). This process should elicit criterias importance, either per iteration or for a set of iterations. For this step we suggest using weighting func-

tions [14, 15], because they can penalize or reward satisfaction levels per criterion.

In Figure 2.2, we depict the proposed data preparation process with the six steps and their inter-relations.

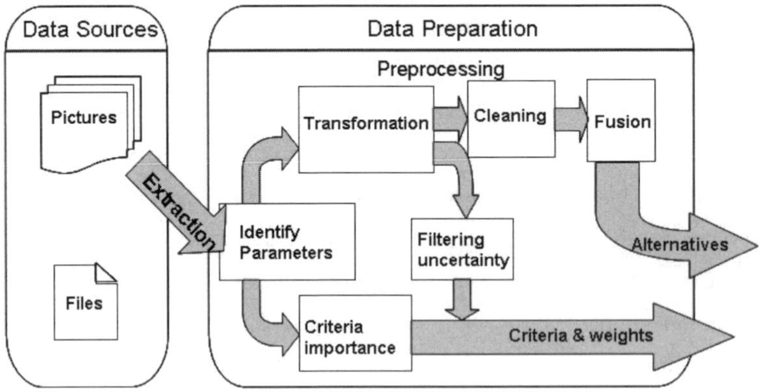

Figure 2.2 Data preparation process.

More details about each step and proposed formulations are discussed using the illustrative example to improve clarity of contributions.

2.2.2 *Phase B. Decision Evaluation Process with Feedback*

In a simple MCDM model this process would be a simple ordering of alternatives regarding the respective rating value, usually denoted ranking of alternatives [3]. However, in a dynamic model, besides using rating values to rank alternatives we also need to include historic information, about preliminary decisions taken along the decision process (iterations). The historical set is refreshed at each iteration, thus ensuring that best classified alternatives, during a certain number of previous iterations, have a better classification in the next iterations. The notion of feedback is introduced to express that at each step (iteration) we build a sub-set of good potential alternatives (historic set) that is re-fed into the system, as input for the next iteration. This feedback continues until a final decision is reached (consensus) or there are no more iterations. In summary, a dynamic decision process with feedback includes three processes for its evaluation of candidate alternatives, as shown in Figure 2.1:

(1) Rating process. During iteration t each alternative is classified, regarding all criteria, using an aggregation method such as the weighted average and weighted with crite-

ria relative importance. There are many aggregation methods that can be used for this purpose [7, 1]. The rating process deals with aggregation of all contributions per alternative regarding each criterion. During the decision process, we should compute these values for each alternative (per iteration). The proposed formulation for the rating process in our MCDDM is:

$$r_i = \bigoplus \left(W(ac_{i1}) \otimes ac_{i1}, \ldots, W(ac_{in}) \otimes ac_{in} \right) \qquad (2)$$

where $\bigoplus$ is the aggregation operator (in our case Weighted Sum Method); $\otimes$ is the product operator; $W(ac_{ij})$ represents the weighting function for accuracy and confidence (topics detailed in (see Sec. 2.3.2). As mentioned we propose to compute the weights to express the relative importance of each criterion, using weight generating functions [14, 15]:

(2) Evaluation Process. During iteration t, the previous historic set is combined with the rated sites at iteration t (obviously there is only combination if the same site exists in iterations t and $t-1$). This combination process, henceforth called evaluation process, ensures a continuous refreshment of the historic set for the next iteration (feedback). The dynamic evaluation algorithm for combining historical information ($H(t-1)$) and current rating values ($R(t)$), is based on the uninorm operator [16]. We chose the uninorm operator because it presents full reinforcement behavior [17] and this is what we are looking for in our adaptable and dynamic decision process based on historical data. We refined the uninorm, defining a hybrid operator [8] because we needed an operator with a compensatory nature outside the T-norms and S-norms [18] interval.

(3) Historic process. The Historic process defines the set k of rated alternatives that are worthwhile considering in the next decision iteration. The set k will record the most relevant information at the end of each iteration. The size of k is context dependent. For instance, if we had 262 144 alternatives it would be quite inefficient to pass all data sets from one iteration to another. Hence, for a specific MCDDM we should define an appropriate size for k (best classified alternatives) and then record their respective rating to act as feedback for the next iteration. Noteworthy that we will only mention one historic set because $T = 2$ and the last historic set is $H(T-1)$ $(= H(1))$.

There are a wide variety of operators and techniques [18, 16, 7, 1, 11] that could be considered to deal with this evaluation process, but, as pointed in previous works [8, 12], we propose to use specialized full-reinforcement operators [16, 17] because it provides flexibility within the search space. We will not discuss more details about this phase, because our focus is on data preparation in environments where input data changes dynamically, from iteration to iteration (i.e., decision step), and contains some intrinsic imprecision (i.e., we have lack confidence on available data and also have doubts about their accuracy).

2.3 Example in Practice

The example used in this section is a simplification of a real case study [12]. The objective of this multicriteria dynamic decision making case study was to decide which was the best target site, for spacecraft landing on planets. Of particular relevance to an autonomous hazard avoidance system is the ability to select landing sites in real-time as the spacecraft approaches the planet's surface, and to dynamically adjust that choice as better information becomes available along the descent (by performing one or more re-targetings). After several iterations, during the spacecraft final descent, a final decision about the best place to land is achieved [19, 12].

In previous works, we have shown good results of using a Fuzzy Multiple Criteria Decision Making approach to solve this problem [8, 20, 12]. However, we never discussed important aspects related with dynamically changing input data and how the data preparation process ought to be done. This example illustrates interesting contributions for an efficient data preparation process, and also summarizes the decision evaluation process with feedback [8, 12] to wrap-up the complete MCDDM approach.

2.3.1 *Background about Landing Site Selection*

Hazard avoidance includes three separate critical functions [12]:

- Hazard mapping that estimates ground features based on imaging sensor data (camera or Lidar), and creates hazard maps;
- Site selection that chooses a suitable landing site based on available hazard maps, mission, propulsion and guidance constraints - The context of this case study;
- A robust guidance to reach the selected target.

The goal of the site selection process is to provide an adequate target-landing site, evaluated with respect to a set of requirements (i.e., criteria):

- The site should be safe in terms of maximum local slope, light level and terrain roughness;
- The site should be reachable with the available fuel;
- The site should be visible from the camera along the descent phase.

In the final phase of descent, starting at around 2.7 km above the surface, the spacecraft is continuously mapping and evaluating the terrain below it, according to a set of criteria (e.g., Figure 2.3 depicts the shadow criterion). It then feeds that information to the site selection component, which will in turn provide the navigation system with the landing coordinates. At all times there is a degree of uncertainty with the evaluations of each site, that decreases (non-monotonically) as the spacecraft approaches the surface.

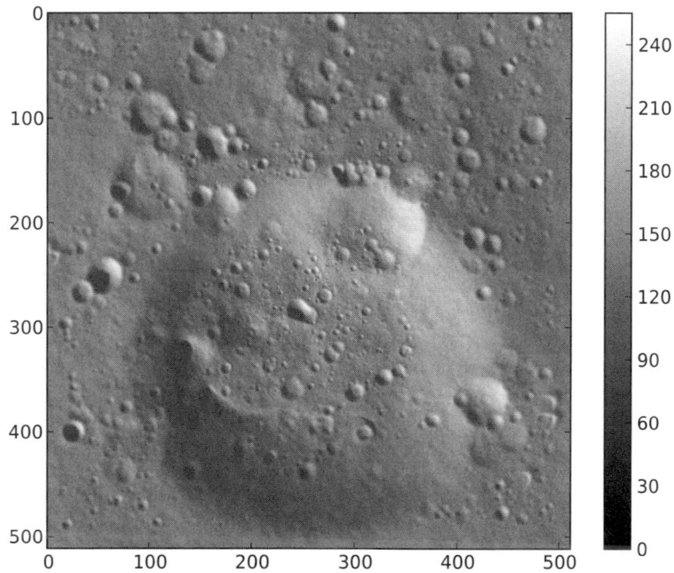

Figure 2.3 Representation of the Shadow criterion for all sites, in the 8th iteration of the CRATERS dataset

2.3.2 *Phase A. Data Preparation in Dynamic Environments*

2.3.2.1 *Step 1. Identification of parameters*

To illustrate the approach let us start by identifying the criteria (step 1 of data preparation Sec. 2.2.2). We identified six inputs (hazard maps), each with a matrix structure (512×512).

(1) Slope Map – provides the minimum angle to be feared by each pixel, in degrees;
(2) Texture Map – provides the variance value for each pixel;
(3) Shadow Map – provides the values of light in a grey scale (0-255);
(4) Fuel Map – provides the values, in kg, that are necessary to reach the spot corresponding to each pixel;

(5) Reachability Map – provides values between 0 and 1, meaning: 0 if the site is not reachable and 1 if the site is reachable;

(6) Distance Map – provides the distance (in meters) between each pixel to the current target;

An example of a Shadow map can be observed in Figure 2.3 and a texture map is shown in Figure 2.4. All other maps are provided in the same fashion except Distance, which is calculated.

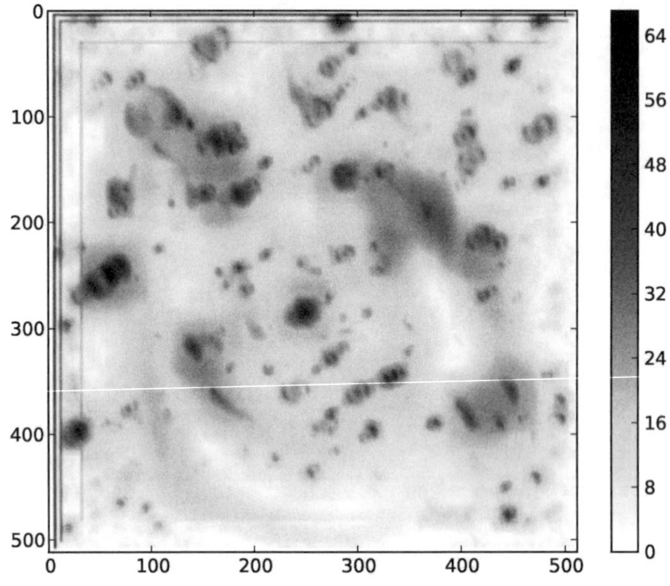

Figure 2.4 Representation of the Texture criterion for all sites, in the 8th iteration of the CRATERS dataset

2.3.2.2 *Step 2. Transformation*

Now let us deal with Step 2, data transformation. As mentioned, this process tries to answer the question on how to transform input data to be appropriately usable in the decision process. This transformation is two-folded: how to represent the variables and how to normalize the data. An important problem on how to fuzzify variables [2] is to choose the best topology for membership functions because we have to take into account our objective in the decision model. In our case we are trying to choose the best site for landing, i.e., the site, which best fulfils all criteria. Hence, our membership values have to be monotonically increasing towards the best criterion value, i.e., if criterion value is low our membership value is high and vice-versa. Another important aspect to deal with in this step, is to ensure that data is both numerical and comparable. As mentioned, when in presence of both qualitative and quantitative variables, we need to transform and normalize the data to compare them.

For our example we used fuzzy sets [2] to represent and normalize our input variables. To select which was the best topology for membership functions we used available test data to build three well-known functions (from the input data): triangle, trapezoid and gaussian. After, we compare them and select the most representative for usage with our spatio-temporal changing input data.

For example, the membership functions for texture represent "Low Texture Values" because it is what we want to maximize. The variable domain is $[0, 255^2]$ but we consider the upper bound to be the maximum value of texture map (see Figure 2.4) for all iterations until the current one. Figure 2.5 shows the membership functions for iteration 23 of a sampling scenario.

Moreover, to define the best morphology for criteria representation, we compared three types of membership functions more commonly used: trapezoidal, triangular and Gaussian. The trapezoidal, triangular and gaussian membership functions were build using the Equations 3, 4 and 5, respectively. Further, consider that x belongs to the interval $[0, \text{upperBound}]$.

$$\text{Trapzoidal}(x) = \begin{cases} 1 & \text{if } x \leqslant c \\ \dfrac{\text{upperBound} - x}{\text{upperBound} - c} & \text{if } x > c \end{cases} \tag{3}$$

where $c = \alpha \times \text{upperBound}$, and α defines the range for the function plateau.

$$\text{Triangular}(x) = \frac{\text{upperBound} - x}{\text{upperBound}} \tag{4}$$

$$\text{Gaussian}(x) = \exp\left(\frac{-x^2}{2\sigma^2}\right) \tag{5}$$

where

$$\sigma^2 = \frac{\text{upperBound}^2}{2\log(\beta)}, \tag{6}$$

and β is a parameter that satisfies the following condition: $\text{Gaussian}(\text{upperBound}) = \beta$. Concluding, for representing the Texture map criterion the Gaussian membership function seems the most adequate function because some values, for instance 40, have a too high membership value for triangular and trapezoidal functions when compared with the Gaussian and this can create "bias" in the decision results. Further, Gaussian penalizes high variable values and this is desirable because texture is a problem when values are high.

2.3.2.3 *Step 3. Cleaning*

In this illustrative case we start by setting to Zero all pixels in the 512×512 input matrix, which have membership value of zero. After, we proceed with other types of "cleaning", for instance, in the texture example all alternatives that have texture value higher than 68 are discarded. Since for our case study we do not have missing records there is no need to define a strategy to fill the gaps, as other dynamic decision problems might face. Hence, this aspect is not further discussed here.

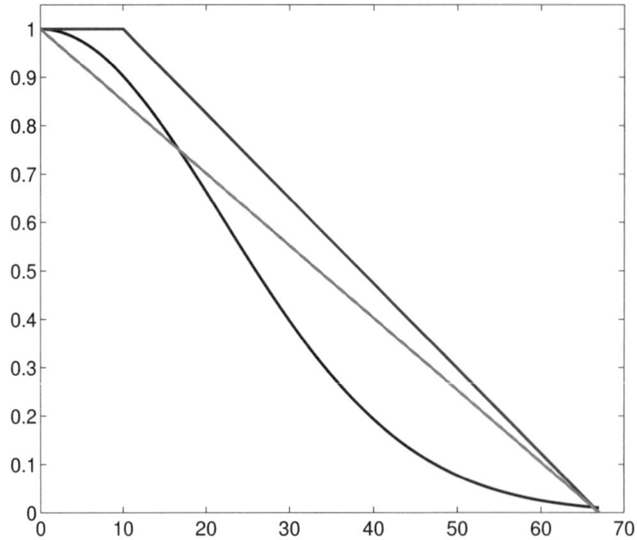

Figure 2.5 Membership functions for "Low Texture".

2.3.2.4 *Step 4. Fusion*

For fusing the different input parameters to obtain the common set of candidate alternatives for target landing, we used the the conjuntive method [7] with the min operator. With this method we can easily integrate all transformed and cleaned criteria (hazard maps), and obtain the set of 3-D coordinates of possible candidate alternatives. Moreover, this process allows reducing the number of alternatives (search space), which is quite important since there are around 262.000 original alternatives (image pixels corresponding to sites), corresponding to the 512×512 matrices. Conjunctive methods are normally used for discarding unacceptable alternatives [21, 7], hence our choice for the proposed approach.

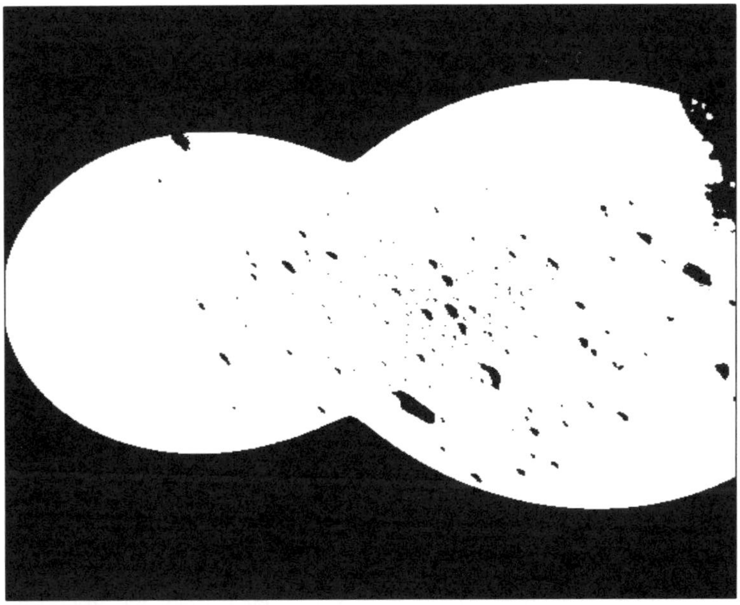

Figure 2.6 Image of all alternatives, whereas the black areas are those alternatives that have been discarded on the fusion process.

The procedure for this method is as follows:

(a) Decision maker specifies a minimal acceptable level for each criterion;
(b) For each alternative determine if all criterion values exceed the respective minimal acceptable threshold specified by the decision maker;
(c) If there is one value lower than the minimal acceptable level, the respective alternative is rejected.

Formally:

A_i is acceptable $\Leftrightarrow \forall j : x_{ij} > l_j$ where l_j is the minimal value for the criterion C_j

In Figure 2.6 we depict the final set of alternative pixels that remained after the cleaning and fusion processes took place. It can be observed with these two steps we clearly reduced the number of alternatives to be evaluated.

2.3.2.5 *Step 5. Filtering Uncertainty*

Step 5 deals with filtering uncertainty from data. The objective of this task is to deal with intrinsic imprecision/uncertainty found, at each iteration, in the input values. In this case we propose a filtering function that combines metrics to deal with both lack of accuracy and lack of confidence in the collected input values. Formally, the accuracy and confidence parameters (a_{ij} and wc_j, respectively) will be taken into account in the decision model using the following expression:

$$\text{Filter}(x_{ij}) = wc_j \times \left(1 - \max_{x\in[a,b]}\{|\mu(x) - \mu(x_{ij})|\}\right) \times \mu(x_{ij}) \tag{7}$$

where wc_j is the confidence associated to criterion j; x_{ij} is the value of jth criterion for site i; μ is a membership degree in a fuzzy set; and $[a,b]$ is defined as follows:

$$\begin{aligned} a &= \begin{cases} \min(D) & \text{if } x_{ij} - a_{ij} \leqslant \min(D) \\ x_{ij} - a_{ij} & \text{if } x_{ij} - a_{ij} > \min(D) \end{cases} \\ b &= \begin{cases} x_{ij} + a_{ij} & \text{if } x_{ij} + a_{ij} \leqslant \max(D) \\ \max(D) & \text{if } x_{ij} + a_{ij} > \max(D) \end{cases} \end{aligned} \tag{8}$$

where a_{ij} is the accuracy associated to criterion j for site i; and D is the variable domain. The accuracy is given as percentage of criterion value and confidence belongs to the unit interval. For example, an accuracy of 90 % for slope means that each slope value belongs to the interval $[a,b]$ where $a_{ij} = 0.9 \times x_{ij}$. On the other hand, a 0.9 confidence value means that we have a confidence on the $[a,b]$ interval of 0.9.

We can observe the result of using the *Filter* function in Figure 2.7. The membership function representing the fuzzy set "Low Slope" is shown with the circle shaped markers, and shown with the triangle shaped markers is the resulting function after using the *Filter*. For each x_{ij} we therefore obtain a filtered value that we call accuracy&confidence membership value, and represent by $ac_{ij} = \text{Filter}(x_{ij})$. For instance, in Figure 2.7 we can observe that for a texture value of 20 we have a membership value for "Low slope" of 0.52 and a filtered (with accuracy&confidence) membership value of 0.34. In the example, an accuracy value of $a_{ij} = 5$ is used, for all sites i. That means that a value read as 20 may actually come from anywhere in the interval $[20-5, 20+5]$. The confidence value $wc_j = 0.80$ indicates in general how confident one is with the quality of the process that generates the input values. In this case, the decision maker is indicating there will be room for a 20 % improvement in the determination of x_{ij}. Though the criterion may always have a degree of inaccuracy associated with values read, the process whereby they are obtained may be made more reliable.

As it can be observed, this formulation enables dealing with imprecision in the collected input hazard maps. Moreover, it allows dealing with two types of imprecision: lack of accuracy in the data and lack of confidence in the data. We believe this is a simple and easy way to tackle the problematic of how to handle imprecision in data in dynamic decision

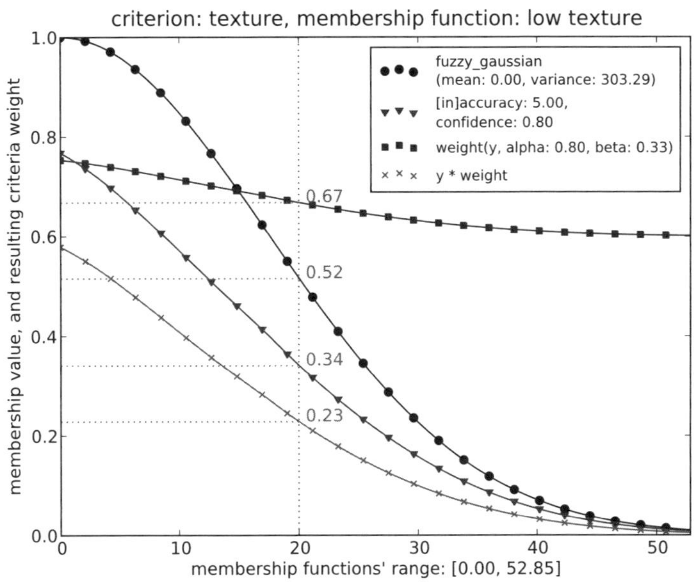

Figure 2.7 Membership function representing the set of values with *low texture*, before and after applying the accuracy and confidence factors. Given the final membership value, the linear weight generating function of Equation (10) is applied, and the criterion's final contribution to quality calculated. The different stages through which an alternative with an initial evaluation of 20 on the criterion passes is also shown.

models. However, in our approach to deal with accuracy we assumed that our decision maker has a pessimistic attitude towards the problem. Hence, Equation (7) can be seen as a particular case of a more general approach described by Eq. (9).

$$\text{Filter}_\alpha(x_{ij}) = wc_j \times \left(1 - \alpha \max_{x\in[a,b]} \left\{ \left|\mu(x) - \mu(x_{ij})\right| \right\}\right) \times \mu(x_{ij}) \tag{9}$$

where $\alpha \in [0,1]$ is a parameter that reflects the attitude of the decision maker (α value close to one represent a pessimistic attitude, close to zero an optimistic attitude). All other variables and parameters have the same meaning as in Eq. (7).

2.3.2.6 *Step 6. Weighting Criteria*

This step is the final one for completing the data preparation in MCDDM. It deals with defining the relative importance for each criterion. In dynamic processes it is rather important to consider the satisfaction level, of each alternative for each criterion, to ensure that a poorly satisfied criterion is not "emphasized" by a pre-determined high importance. Hence, we propose to compute the weights to express the relative importance of each criterion, using the following linear weight generating function [14, 15] :

$$L_j(ac_{ij}) = \alpha_j \frac{1+\beta_j ac_{ij}}{1+\beta_j} \tag{10}$$

where α_j, $\beta_j \in [0,1]$ and ac_{ij} is the accuracy and confidence membership value of jth criterion for site i. Note that ac_{ij} corresponds to the filtered value of x_{ij} from Eq. (7).

In Figure 2.7, the line with the square shaped markers depicts the behavior of the weight generating function for the texture criterion.

The logic of these weighting functions (see Eq. (11)) is that the satisfaction value of a criterion should influence its assigned relative importance. For example, if we are buying a car and the price is a "very important" criterion, if the car is quite expensive the final decision result should be less than the simple multiplication of weight and satisfaction value.

$$W(\mathbf{ac}) = \frac{L_j(ac_{ij})}{\sum_{k=1}^{m} L_k(ac_{ik})} \tag{11}$$

where $\mathbf{ac} = (ac_{i1}, \ldots, ac_{im})$; and L_j is a linear weight generating function presented in Eq. (10).

For our case study we considered that the relative importance of criteria has different morphologies for each criterion, depending on the altitude of the spacecraft in relation to the surface. The definition of these weighting functions morphologies is given by the parameters α and β. The α parameter provides the semantics for the weighting functions as follows:

(a) Very Important (VI= 1);
(b) Important (I= 0.8);
(c) Average importance (A= 0.6);
(d) Low importance (L= 0.4);
(e) Very Low importance (VL= 0.2).

The β parameter provides the slope for the weighting functions, which will depend on the criterion at hand, with the logic that higher values of β means higher slope. In this work this parameter has the following values:

(a) High (H= 1);
(b) Medium (M= 0.6667);
(c) Low (L= 0.3333);
(d) Null (N= 0);

For example, for high altitudes (> 1000 m; < 2000 m; 250 historic set size), we depict the proposed values for α and β parameters for this phase, and their respective plots (Figure 2.8).

Table 2.1 α and β parameters.

	Fuel	Reach	Slope	Dist	Shad	Text	ScIn
α	1	1	1	0.6	0.4	0.8	0.2
β	0.25	0.667	0.111	0.333	0	0.333	0

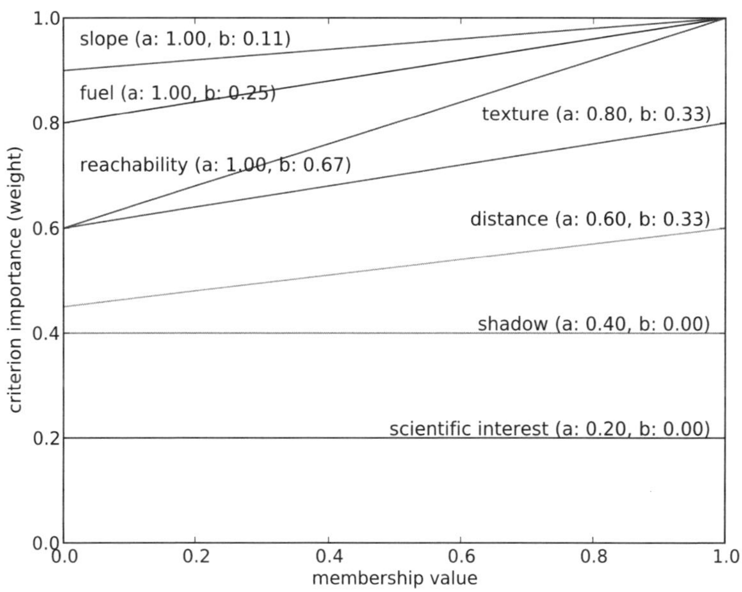

Figure 2.8 Weighting functions.

The rational above is expressed by the α parameter, while the β parameter provides more or less penalties for lower satisfaction values in the criteria, as depicted in the figures for each phase. For example, the rationale for "very important" is that although fuel, reachability and slope are all "very important" in this phase, a lower satisfaction for criteria should be much more penalized in the case of reachability, a little more for fuel and less for slope. In Figure 2.7 we see the weight generating function for the texture criterion. This is an Important criterion ($\alpha = 0.8$) with Low penalty ($\beta = 0.33$) for lower satisfaction values. In the example shown, when $x_{ij} = 20$, we have a somewhat low membership value of

$ac_{ij} = 0.34$ to which a weight of $L_j(ac_{ij}) = 0.67$ is attached, down from the criterion's base importance of 0.8. A simplification of the weighting functions could be to define "a priori" a slope for each importance, i.e., avoids having to define different β parameters for each weighting functions. This option simplifies the weight assignment process but it is less accurate. An important point to highlight is that the parameter values proposed for the phases (or iterations) can be tuned for any other dynamic decision applications. More details about this weighting process in the case study can be seen in Ref. [22].

2.3.3 *Phase B. Decision Evaluation Process with Feedback*

Since our scope is dynamically changing input data, in this section we just present a summary of required activities to solve the illustrative example, having in mind the evaluation alternatives when feedback is involved (phase B in Sec. 2.2.2). Details about contributions for this topic can be seen in our previous works [8, 20, 12].
The three steps for the evaluation process in our example are:

(i) Rating process – This process refers to the classification of each alternative regarding all criteria, weighted with their relative importance. There are many methods that can be used for this aggregation but a simple and sound method is the Weighted Sum rating method [1] and this is the one we used in our example.

(ii) Dynamic evaluation process – This process refers to the aggregation of historical information with the alternatives rating and then their respective ordering to obtain a set of ranked alternatives. This process is performed at each iteration of the decision process, by combining $R(T)$ with $H(T-1)$ with a hybrid uninorm operator [8]. When there are no more iterations the decision process stops and the best alternative is the one with the highest value.

(iii) Historical process – This process determines a subset of good alternatives, from the evaluated alternatives, to be considered as feedback information from iteration to iteration. Since this process takes place after evaluation, it means the historical information for a specific site "remembers" its past behavior plus the actual rating. We considered different sizes for (K) depending on different phases of the decision process. The K size changed 3 times in our example because it depended on the spacecraft altitude (distance from surface). This set K constitutes the feedback information that is made available for the next iteration.

2.4 Future Research Directions

We presented a general architecture for dynamic multiple criteria decision problems, divided into two main phases: data preparation and dynamic evaluation with feedback. Our scope was spatial-temporal multiple criteria decision problems, requiring feedback from iteration to iteration.

The focus of the work was on the first phase, data preparation, for which we proposed six steps, each with several contributions on how to perform them. We specifically proposed new contributions for dealing with uncertainty in dynamically changing input data and also for dealing with dynamic changes in criteria importance. We believe, these are interesting contributions to improve decision support approaches for MCDDM problems.

Finally, dealing with uncertainty in dynamically changing input data was a challenge and future contributions to improve the evaluation process, both at the level of better operators or new search methodologies to reduce the decision process are foreseeable. In addition, comparison studies between different methods and technologies may also prove to result in improved performance and accuracy for the selection of alternatives in presence of multiple criteria in dynamic decision processes.

Potential applications of this work could be on medical diagnose decision support and/ or fault, detection and isolation (FDI) problems, since both fields require several decision steps and feedback information.

Bibliography

[1] E. Triantaphyllou, *Multi criteria Decision Making Method: a Comparative Study*, vol. 44, *Applied Optimization Series*, Kluwer Academic Publishers, (2002).

[2] T. Ross, *Fuzzy Logic with Engineering Applications*, John Wiley & Sons, (2004).

[3] R. Ribeiro, Fuzzy multiple attribute decision making: a review and new preference elicitation techniques, *Fuzzy Sets and Systems*, **78**(2), 155–181, (1996).

[4] J. Busemeyer and J. Townsend, Decision field theory: a dynamic-cognitive approach to decision making in an uncertain environment, *Psychological Review*, **100**, 432–432, (1993).

[5] G. P. Richardson and A. L. Pugh III, *Introduction to System Dynamics Modeling with DYNAMO*, Productivity Press, Portland, Oregon, (1981).

[6] K. Cios, W. Pedrycz, and R. W. Swiniarski, *Data Mining Methods for Knowledge Discovery*, Kluwer Academic Publishers, (1998).

[7] S.-J. Chen and C.-L. Hwang, *Fuzzy Multiple Attribute Decision Making, Methods and Applications*, Number 375 in Lectures Notes in Economics and Mathematical Systems, Springer-Verlag, (1992).

[8] T. C. Pais, R. A. Ribeiro, Y. Devouassoux, and S. Reynaud, Dynamic ranking algorithm for landing site selection, In eds. L. Magdalena, M. Ojeda-Aciego, and J. L. Verdegay, *Proceedings of the 12th International Conference on Information Processing and Manage-*

ment of Uncertainty in Knowledge-Base Systems (IPMU), pp. 608–613, (2008). ISBN 978-84-612-3061-7.
URL: http://www.gimac.uma.es/ipmu08/proceedings/papers/080-PaisEtAl.pdf.

[9] R. Roe, J. Busemeyer, and J. Townsend, Multialternative decision field theory: a dynamic connectionist model of decision making, *Psychol Rev.*, **108**(2), 370–92, (2001).

[10] A. Diederich, Mdft account of decision making under time pressure, *Psychonomic Bulletin & Review*, **10**(1), 157–166, (2003).

[11] A. Diederich, Dynamic stochastic models for decision making under time constraints, *Journal of Mathematical Psychology*, **41**(3), 260–274, (1997).

[12] Y. Devouassoux, S. Reynaud, G. Jonniaux, R. A. Ribeiro, and T. C. Pais, Hazard avoidance developments for planetary exploration, In *GNC 2008: 7th International ESA Conference on Guidance, Navigation & Control Systems*, (2008).

[13] N. Viana, A. Pereira, R. A. Ribeiro, and A. Donati, Handling missing values in solar array performance degradation forecasting, In *Proceedings of the 15th Mini-EURO conference on Managing Uncertainty in Decision Support Models (MUDSM 2004)*, Coimbra, Portugal (September, 2004).

[14] R. Ribeiro and R. Marques Pereira, Generalized mixture operators using weighting functions: A comparative study with wa and owa, *European Journal of Operational Research*, **145** (2), 329–342, (2003).

[15] R. Pereira and R. Ribeiro, Aggregation with generalized mixture operators using weighting functions, *Fuzzy Sets and Systems*, **137**(1), 43–58, (2003).

[16] R. R. Yager and A. Rybalov, Uninorm aggregation operators, *Fuzzy Sets Systems*, **80**(1), 111–120, (1996).
ISSN 0165-0114.
http://dx.doi.org/10.1016/0165-0114(95)00133-6.

[17] R. Yager and A. Rybalov, Full reinforcement operators in aggregation techniques, *IEEE Transactions on Systems, Man and Cybernetics, Part B*, **28** (6), 757–769, (1998).

[18] H. Zimmermann, *Fuzzy Set Theory–and Its Applications*, Kluwer Academic Publishers, (2001).

[19] T. Jean-Marius and S. Strandmoe, Integrated vision and navigation for a planetary lander, In *49th International Astronautical Congress, Melbourne, Australia, Sept-Oct*, (1998).

[20] T. C. Pais, R. A. Ribeiro, Y. Devouassoux, and S. Reynaud, Regions rating for selecting spacecraft landing sites, In eds. D. Ruan, J. Montero, J. Lu, L. Martínez, P. D'hondt, and E. E. Kerre, *Computational Intelligence in Decision and Control – Proceedings of the 8th International FLINS Conference*, vol. 1, *World Scientific Proceedings Series on Computer Engineering and Information Science*, pp. 1039–1044, Singapore (Aug, 2008), World Scientific.
ISBN 978-981-279-946-3.

[21] R. M. Dawes, Social selection based on multidimensional criteria, *Journal of Abnormal and Social Psychology*, **68**(1), 104–109, (1964).

[22] T. Pais and R. A. Ribeiro, Contributions for dynamic multicriteria decision making models, In *International Fuzzy Systems Association World Congress – IFSA*, Lisbon, Portugal, (2009).

Chapter 3

Decision Making under Uncertainty by Possibilistic Linear Programming Problems

Peijun Guo

Faculty of Business Administration, Yokohama National University, Tokiwadai 79-4, Hodogaya-Ku, Yokohama, 240-8501 Japan

E-mail: guo@ynu.ac.jp

A decision making problem in an upper decision level is described in this chapter by a set of fuzzy satisfaction levels given by decision makers. Fuzzy solutions are used to approximate the feasible region of decision variables left by the given fuzzy satisfaction levels. Two different possibility distributions, i.e., symmetrical triangular possibility distributions and exponential possibility distributions are considered and their upper and lower possibility distributions are obtained. It can be said that a fuzzy solution associated with an upper possibility distribution leaves more rooms than the one associated with a lower possibility distribution.

3.1 Introduction

For some considerable time, linear programming (LP) has been one of the operation research techniques, which has been widely used and got many achievements in both applications and theories. But the strict requirement of LP is that data must be well defined and precise, which is often impossible in real decision problems. The traditional way to evaluate any imprecision in the parameters of an LP model is through post-optimization analysis, with the help of sensitivity analysis and parametric programming. However, none of these methods is suitable for an overall analysis of the effects of imprecision in parameters. Another way to handle imprecision is to model it in stochastic programming problems according to probability theory. A third way to cope with imprecision is to resort to fuzzy set theory, which gives the conceptual and theoretical framework for dealing with complexity, imprecision and vagueness R.E. Bellman and L.A. Zadeh [1], H. Tanaka and P. Guo [10, 11], L.A. Zadeh [15].

Generally speaking, in fuzzy linear programming models, the coefficients of decision variables are fuzzy numbers while decision variables are crisp ones. This means that in an uncertain environment, a crisp decision is made to meet some benefit criteria. On the other hand, Tanaka *et al.* H. Tanaka and K. Asai [13] initially proposed a possibilistic linear programming formulation where the coefficients of decision variables are crisp while decision variables are fuzzy numbers, and LP technique is used to obtain the largest possibility distribution of decision variables. As an extension of that idea, Guo *et al.* P. Guo *et al.* [4, 5], H. Tanaka *et al.* [9] proposed several approaches to obtain various fuzzy solutions to enable a decision maker select one preferable fuzzy decision among the obtained ones. In this chapter, a kind of decision problem in an upper decision level is described by a set of fuzzy satisfaction levels given by decision makers. Fuzzy solutions are used to approximate the feasible region of decision variables left by the given fuzzy satisfaction levels. Assuming fuzzy decision variables are governed by two different possibility distributions, i.e., symmetrical triangular possibility distributions and exponential possibility distributions, their upper and lower possibility distributions are obtained with different fuzzy degrees. It can be said that a fuzzy solution associated with an upper possibility distribution leaves more rooms than the one associated with a lower possibility distribution.

3.2 Fuzzy Decisions in Possibility Linear Programming Problems

Decision problems are often described in term of a multilevel functional hierarchy. From the bottom to the top, the objectives of decisions become large and complex because of the inherent fuzziness of decision problems. For the lower level decision problems, decision makers need to make a crisp decision under a fuzzy environment as widely researched by conventional fuzzy programming problems M. Inuiguchi *et al.* [2, 3], H. Rommelfange [7], M. Sakawa [8], H.-J. Zimmermann [14]. By contrast, fuzzy decisions are often required in the upper level because giving some rooms for lower level is necessary in real decision problems. The fuzzy decisions obtained in the upper level will be sent to the lower level where crisp decisions will be made within these fuzzy decisions. This chapter aims to obtain possibility distributions of fuzzy decision variables to reflect the fuzziness of decision problems. Mathematically, a kind of upper level decision problems can be described as follows:

$$\begin{aligned} &b_{i1}x_1 + \cdots + b_{in}x_n \approx^- C_i, \quad i = 1, \ldots, m_1, \\ &\quad \cdots\cdots \\ &b_{i1}x_1 + \cdots + b_{in}x_n \approx^+ C_i, \quad i = m_1 + 1, \ldots, m, \end{aligned} \tag{1}$$

where the symbols $\approx^-$ and $\approx^+$, defined later, represent two kinds of "approximately satisfy", C_i is a fuzzy number ($i = 1,\ldots,m$) representing a fuzzy satisfaction level offered by decision makers, and x_j is a decision variable ($j = 1,\ldots,n$) and b_{ij} is an associated crisp coefficient. In other words, the right-hand sides of the model (1) describe the desires of decision makers and the left-hand sides are some technical conditions to achieve them. Each fuzzy number C_i in (1), for example, can be regarded as a fuzzy goal from each department of a corporation given by its manager with only considering the benefit of his own department where the center of fuzzy number is an ideal point and the spread of fuzzy number represents some tolerance. As a result, a reasonable plan should be feasible for constraints from all of such departments.

Let us rewrite the fuzzy constraints (1) as follows.

$$b_{i1}x_1 + \cdots + b_{in}x_n \approx^- C_i, \quad i = 1,\ldots,m_1, \tag{2}$$

$$b_{j1}x_1 + \cdots + b_{jn}x_n \approx^+ C_j, \quad j = m_1+1,\ldots,m, \tag{3}$$

where the subscripts i and j correspond to symbols "$\approx^-$" and "$\approx^+$", respectively. Obviously, if "$Y_i \approx^- C_i$" and "$\approx^+$" (soft equal) become "=" (hard equal) and correspondingly C_i becomes a crisp value in (1), we can rarely obtain the feasible solutions for the case of $m > n$. However, each possibilistic constraint leaves some feasible region for decision variables. Because the feasible regions left from possibilistic constraints are conflicting and partially inconsistent in nature, the problem considered now is to obtain an integrated feasible region of decision vector, which satisfies all of possibilistic constraints. In what follows, let us consider how to obtain the feasible region from possibilistic constraints described in (1).

3.2.1 *Triangular Possibility Distributions of Fuzzy Decision Variables*

Assume that C_i is a symmetrical triangular fuzzy number denoted as $(c_i, d_i)_T$ where c_i and d_i are its center and spread with the condition $c_i - d_i \geqslant 0$. The feasible region of $\mathbf{x} = [x_1,\ldots,x_n]^t$ left from the ith fuzzy constraint is characterized by a symmetrical triangular fuzzy decision vector $\mathbf{A} = [A_1,\ldots,A_2]^t$. The possibility distribution of $\mathbf{A}$ is defined as follows:

$$\Pi_{\mathbf{A}}(\mathbf{x}) = \Pi_{A_1}(x_1) \wedge \Pi_{A_2}(x_2) \wedge \cdots \wedge \Pi_{A_n}(x_n) \tag{4}$$

where

$$\Pi_{A_i}(x_i) = \begin{cases} 1 - \dfrac{|x_i - a_i|}{r_i}, & a_i - r_i \leqslant x_i \leqslant a_i + r_i,\ r_i > 0 \\ 0, & \text{otherwise} \end{cases} \tag{5}$$

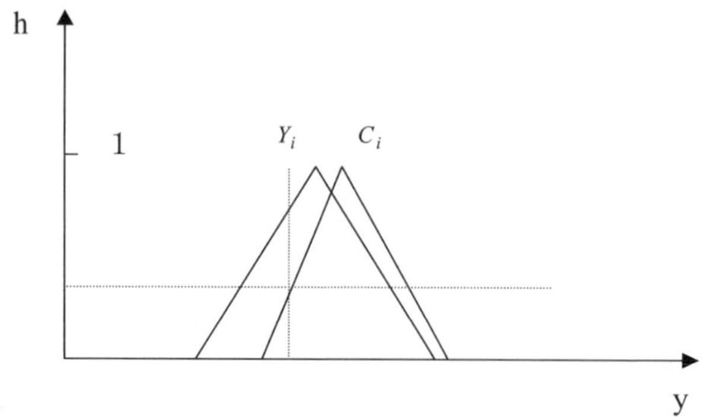

Figure 3.1 Explanation of $Y_i \approx^- C_i$ with degree h.

a_i and r_i are the center and spread of fuzzy number A_i. $\mathbf{A}$ is simply denoted as $(\mathbf{a},\mathbf{r})_T$, with $\mathbf{a} = [a_1,\ldots,a_n]^t$ ($a_i \geqslant 0$, $i = 1,\ldots,n$) and $\mathbf{r} = [r_1,\ldots,r_n]^t$ ($r_i \geqslant 0$, $i = 1,\ldots,n$).
The left-hand side of the fuzzy constraint (2) or (3) is written as

$$Y_i = b_{i1}x_1 + \cdots + b_{in}x_n. \tag{6}$$

Since $\mathbf{x} = [x_1,x_2,\ldots,x_n]^t$ becomes a possibilistic vector $\mathbf{A} = [A_1,\ldots,A_2]^t$, the possibility distribution of fuzzy set Y_i can be obtained by the extension principle as

$$\Pi_{Y_i}(y) = (y_i,s_i)_T = (\mathbf{b}_i^t\mathbf{a},\mathbf{b}_i^t\mathbf{r})_T, \tag{7}$$

where center y_i and spread s_i are $\mathbf{b}_i^t\mathbf{a}$ and $\mathbf{b}_i^t\mathbf{r}$, respectively, and $\mathbf{b}_i = [b_{i1},\ldots,b_{in}]^t \geqslant \mathbf{0}$.
Constraint $Y_i \approx^- C_i$ is explained as "Y_i is a little bit smaller than C_i", defined by the following inequalities.

$$y_i - (1-h)s_i \leqslant c_i - (1-h)d_i,\ i = 1,\ldots,m_1, \tag{8}$$

$$y_i + (1-h)s_i \leqslant c_i + (1-h)d_i,\ i = 1,\ldots,m_1, \tag{9}$$

$$y_i \geqslant c_i - (1-h)d_i, \qquad i = 1,\ldots,m_1, \tag{10}$$

where h is a predetermined possibility level by decision makers. It can be understood that the higher h is, the stricter constraints are. A graphical explanation of $Y_i \approx^- C_i$ is given by Figure 3.1 which shows that "Y_i is a little bit smaller than C_i", denoted as $Y_i \approx^- C_i$, means that the left and right endpoints of the h-level set of Y_i are smaller than the left and right ones of C_i, respectively described in (8) and (9), respectively, but the center of Y_i is confined to be larger than the left endpoint of C_i shown by the dotted line described in (10).
Similarly, the constraint $Y_j \approx^+ C_j$ is explained as "Y_j is a little bit larger than C_j", defined

by the following inequalities:

$$y_i - (1-h)s_i \geqslant c_i - (1-h)d_i, \;\; i = 1,\dots,m_1, \tag{11}$$

$$y_i + (1-h)s_i \geqslant c_i + (1-h)d_i, \;\; i = 1,\dots,m_1, \tag{12}$$

$$y_i \leqslant c_i + (1-h)d_i, \qquad i = 1,\dots,m_1. \tag{13}$$

It follows from the above definitions that fuzzy constraint conditions leave some feasible region for decision variables described by inequalities (8)-(13). Considering (7), fuzzy constraint (2) can be rewritten as:

$$\mathbf{b}_i^t\mathbf{a} - (1-h)\mathbf{b}_i^t\mathbf{r} \leqslant c_i - (1-h)d_i, \;\; i = 1,\dots,m_1, \tag{14}$$

$$\mathbf{b}_i^t\mathbf{a} + (1-h)\mathbf{b}_i^t\mathbf{r} \leqslant c_i + (1-h)d_i, \;\; i = 1,\dots,m_1, \tag{15}$$

$$\mathbf{b}_i^t\mathbf{a} \geqslant c_i - (1-h)d_i, \qquad i = 1,\dots,m_1, \tag{16}$$

and fuzzy constraint (3) can be rewritten as:

$$\mathbf{b}_j^t\mathbf{a} - (1-h)\mathbf{b}_j^t\mathbf{r} \geqslant c_j - (1-h)d_j, \;\; j = m_1+1,\dots,m, \tag{17}$$

$$\mathbf{b}_j^t\mathbf{a} + (1-h)\mathbf{b}_j^t\mathbf{r} \geqslant c_j + (1-h)d_j, \;\; j = m_1+1,\dots,m, \tag{18}$$

$$\mathbf{b}_j^t\mathbf{a} \leqslant c_j + (1-h)d_j, \qquad j = m_1+1,\dots,m. \tag{19}$$

From constraints (14)-(19), it is easy to understand that the center vector **a** should comply with the following constraints,

$$c_i - (1-h)d_i \leqslant \mathbf{b}_i^t\mathbf{a} \leqslant c_i, \; i = 1,\dots,m_1, \tag{20}$$

$$c_j \leqslant \mathbf{b}_j^t\mathbf{a} \leqslant c_j + (1-h)d_i, \; j = m_1+1,\dots,m. \tag{21}$$

It implies that the center vector must exist in the region formed by (20) and (21). The following LP problem is used to find out a candidate of the center vector.

$$\begin{aligned} \max_{\mathbf{a}} \;\; & g(\mathbf{a}) \\ \text{s. t.} \;\; & \mathbf{b}_i^t\mathbf{a} \geqslant (c_i - (1-h)d_i)(1+\beta), \;\; i = 1,\dots,m_1, \\ & \mathbf{b}_i^t\mathbf{a} \leqslant c_i(1-\beta), \;\; i = 1,\dots,m_1, \\ & \mathbf{b}_j^t\mathbf{a} \leqslant (c_j + (1-h)d_j)(1-\beta), \;\; j = m_1+1,\dots,m, \\ & \mathbf{b}_j^t\mathbf{a} \geqslant c_j(1+\beta), \;\; j = m_1+1,\dots,m, \\ & \beta \geqslant 0, \\ & \mathbf{a} \geqslant \mathbf{0}, \end{aligned} \tag{22}$$

where the objective function $g(\mathbf{a})$ is given by decision makers to characterize their preference for selecting the center vector, which is regarded as a reference point in the feasible region of decision variables. Parameter $\beta \geqslant 0$ is used to reduce the original feasible region to guarantee the obtained center vector inside the region formed by (20) and (21).

After determining one center vector, denoted as $\mathbf{a}_0$, we investigate two kinds of possibility distributions of fuzzy vector $\boldsymbol{A}$, i.e., upper and lower possibility distributions denoted as $\Pi_u(\mathbf{x})$ and $\Pi_l(\mathbf{x})$, respectively, with the condition $\Pi_u \geqslant \Pi_l$, which have some similarities with the concept of rough sets Z. Pawlak [6]. The upper possibility distribution of $\boldsymbol{A}$ corresponds to the upper possibility distribution of Y and the lower possibility distribution of $\boldsymbol{A}$ corresponds to the lower possibility distribution of Y. Figure 3.2 gives a graphic explanation of upper and lower possibility distributions of Y restricted by the possibility constraint $Y \approx^- C$. It shows that the region covered by the lower possibility distribution of Y is completely included by the h-level set of the given possibility information C while the region covered by the upper possibility distribution of Y completely includes the h-level set of the given possibility information C under the definition of $Y \approx^- C$. The upper and lower possibility distributions of Y are the upper and lower bounds of Y restricted by $Y \approx^- C$ for a fixed center of Y.

With considering a center vector $\mathbf{a}_0$, the problem for finding out the lower spread vector of $\boldsymbol{A}$ is formalized as the following LP problem.

$$\begin{aligned}
&\min_{\mathbf{r}_l} \ \mathbf{w}^t\mathbf{r}_l \\
&\text{s. t.} \quad -(1-h)\mathbf{b}_i^t\mathbf{r}_l \leqslant c_i-(1-h)d_i-\mathbf{b}_i^t\mathbf{a}_0, \ i=1,\ldots,m_1, \\
&\qquad (1-h)\mathbf{b}_i^t\mathbf{r}_l \leqslant c_i+(1-h)d_i-\mathbf{b}_i^t\mathbf{a}_0, \ i=1,\ldots,m_1, \\
&\qquad -(1-h)\mathbf{b}_j^t\mathbf{r}_l \geqslant c_j-(1-h)d_j-\mathbf{b}_j^t\mathbf{a}_0, \ j=m_1+1,\ldots,m, \\
&\qquad (1-h)\mathbf{b}_j^t\mathbf{r}_l \geqslant c_j+(1-h)d_j-\mathbf{b}_j^t\mathbf{a}_0, \ j=m_1+1,\ldots,m, \\
&\qquad \mathbf{r}_l \geqslant \mathbf{0},
\end{aligned} \tag{23}$$

where $\mathbf{w}$ is the weight vector of the lower spread vector $\mathbf{r}_l$.

Similarly, the problem for finding out the upper spread vector of $\boldsymbol{A}$ is formalized as the following LP problem.

$$\begin{aligned}
&\max_{\mathbf{r}_u} \ \mathbf{w}^t\mathbf{r}_u \\
&\text{s. t.} \quad -(1-h)\mathbf{b}_i^t\mathbf{r}_u \leqslant c_i-(1-h)d_i-\mathbf{b}_i^t\mathbf{a}_0, \ i=1,\ldots,m_1, \\
&\qquad (1-h)\mathbf{b}_i^t\mathbf{r}_u \leqslant c_i+(1-h)d_i-\mathbf{b}_i^t\mathbf{a}_0, \ i=1,\ldots,m_1, \\
&\qquad -(1-h)\mathbf{b}_j^t\mathbf{r}_u \geqslant c_j-(1-h)d_j-\mathbf{b}_j^t\mathbf{a}_0, \ j=m_1+1,\ldots,m, \\
&\qquad (1-h)\mathbf{b}_j^t\mathbf{r}_u \geqslant c_j+(1-h)d_j-\mathbf{b}_j^t\mathbf{a}_0, \ j=m_1+1,\ldots,m, \\
&\qquad \mathbf{r}_u \geqslant \mathbf{0}.
\end{aligned} \tag{24}$$

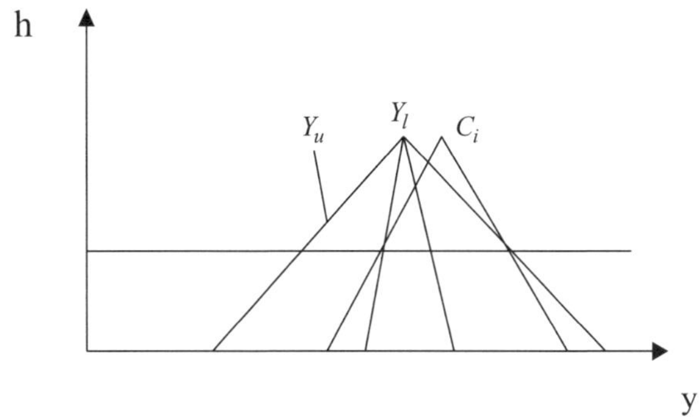

Figure 3.2 Illustration of upper and lower possibility distributions in $Y \approx^- C$.

With considering the inclusion relation between the upper and lower possibility distributions, the problem for obtaining the upper and lower spreads of $\boldsymbol{A}$ simultaneously is introduced as follows P. Guo *et al.* [5]:

$$
\begin{aligned}
\max_{\mathbf{r}_u,\mathbf{r}_l} \quad & \mathbf{w}^t(\mathbf{r}_u-\mathbf{r}_l) \\
\text{s. t.} \quad & -(1-h)\mathbf{b}_i^t\mathbf{r}_l \leqslant c_i-(1-h)d_i-\mathbf{b}_i^t\mathbf{a}_0,\ i=1,\ldots,m_1, \\
& (1-h)\mathbf{b}_i^t\mathbf{r}_l \leqslant c_i+(1-h)d_i-\mathbf{b}_i^t\mathbf{a}_0,\ i=1,\ldots,m_1, \\
& -(1-h)\mathbf{b}_j^t\mathbf{r}_l \geqslant c_j-(1-h)d_j-\mathbf{b}_j^t\mathbf{a}_0,\ j=m_1+1,\ldots,m, \\
& (1-h)\mathbf{b}_j^t\mathbf{r}_l \geqslant c_j+(1-h)d_j-\mathbf{b}_j^t\mathbf{a}_0,\ j=m_1+1,\ldots,m, \\
& -(1-h)\mathbf{b}_i^t\mathbf{r}_u \leqslant c_i-(1-h)d_i-\mathbf{b}_i^t\mathbf{a}_0,\ i=1,\ldots,m_1, \\
& (1-h)\mathbf{b}_i^t\mathbf{r}_u \leqslant c_i+(1-h)d_i-\mathbf{b}_i^t\mathbf{a}_0,\ i=1,\ldots,m_1, \\
& -(1-h)\mathbf{b}_j^t\mathbf{r}_u \geqslant c_j-(1-h)d_j-\mathbf{b}_j^t\mathbf{a}_0,\ j=m_1+1,\ldots,m, \\
& (1-h)\mathbf{b}_j^t\mathbf{r}_u \geqslant c_j+(1-h)d_j-\mathbf{b}_j^t\mathbf{a}_0,\ j=m_1+1,\ldots,m, \\
& \mathbf{r}_u-\mathbf{r}_l \geqslant \mathbf{0}, \\
& \mathbf{r}_l \geqslant \mathbf{0}.
\end{aligned} \tag{25}
$$

3.2.2 *Exponential Possibility Distributions of Fuzzy Decision Variables*

Assume that C_i is characterized by the following exponential possibility distribution

$$
\Pi_{C_i}(x) = \exp(-(x-c_i)^2/r_i), \tag{26}
$$

simply denoted as $(c_i, r_i)_e$, where $c_i \geqslant 0$ and $r_i > 0$ are the center value and the spread of C_i, respectively. Likewise, assume that $\mathbf{x} = [x_1,\ldots,x_n]^t$ is characterized by an exponential possibility distribution as

$$\Pi_{\mathbf{A}}(\mathbf{x}) = \exp\{-(\mathbf{x}-\mathbf{a})^t\mathbf{D}_{\mathbf{A}}^{-1}(\mathbf{x}-\mathbf{a})\}, \tag{27}$$

simply denoted as $\Pi_{\mathbf{A}}(\mathbf{x}) = (\mathbf{a}, \mathbf{D}_{\mathbf{A}})_e$, where $\mathbf{a} = [a_1, \ldots, a_n]^t$ $(a_i \geqslant 0)$ is an n-dimensional center vector, and $\mathbf{D}_{\mathbf{A}}$ is a symmetrical positive definite matrix, denoted as $\mathbf{D}_{\mathbf{A}} > 0$. The matrix $\mathbf{D}_{\mathbf{A}}$ is called a possibility distribution matrix.

Considering (6) and (27), the possibility distribution of the fuzzy set Y_i can be obtained by the extension principle as follows H. Tanaka and H. Ishibuchi [12]:

$$\Pi_{Y_i}(y) = (y_i, w_i)_e = (\mathbf{b}_i^t\mathbf{a}, \mathbf{b}_i^t\mathbf{D}_{\mathbf{A}}\mathbf{b}_i)_e, \tag{28}$$

where $\mathbf{b}_i = [b_{i1}, \ldots, b_{in}]^t$.

The constraint $Y_i \approx^- C_i$ is defined by the following inequalities:

$$y_i - \sqrt{(-\ln h)\cdot w_i} \leqslant c_i - \sqrt{(-\ln h)\cdot r_i}, \tag{29}$$

$$y_i + \sqrt{(-\ln h)\cdot w_i} \leqslant c_i + \sqrt{(-\ln h)\cdot r_i}, \tag{30}$$

$$y_i \geqslant c_i - \sqrt{(-\ln h)\cdot r_i}, \tag{31}$$

where h is a predetermined possibility level by decision makers. $Y_i \approx^- C_i$ means that the left and right endpoints of the h-level set of Y_i are smaller than the left and right ones of C_i, respectively described in (29) and(30), but the center of Y_i is confined to be larger than the left endpoint of C_i described in (31).

Similarly, The constraint $Y_j \approx^+ C_j$ is explained as "Y_j is a little bit larger than C_j", defined by the following inequalities:

$$y_j - \sqrt{(-\ln h)\cdot w_j} \geqslant c_j - \sqrt{(-\ln h)\cdot r_j}, \tag{32}$$

$$y_j + \sqrt{(-\ln h)\cdot w_j} \geqslant c_j + \sqrt{(-\ln h)\cdot r_j}, \tag{33}$$

$$y_j \leqslant c_j + \sqrt{(-\ln h)\cdot r_j}. \tag{34}$$

As a result, the fuzzy constraint conditions (2) and (3) can be rewritten as follows:

$$\mathbf{b}_i^t\mathbf{a} - \sqrt{(-\ln h)\mathbf{b}_i^t\mathbf{D}_{\mathbf{A}}\mathbf{b}_i} \leqslant c_i - \sqrt{(-\ln h)r_i}, \tag{35}$$

$$\mathbf{b}_i^t\mathbf{a} + \sqrt{(-\ln h)\mathbf{b}_i^t\mathbf{D}_{\mathbf{A}}\mathbf{b}_i} \leqslant c_i + \sqrt{(-\ln h)r_i}, \tag{36}$$

$$\mathbf{b}_i^t\mathbf{a} \geqslant c_i - \sqrt{(-\ln h)r_i}, \tag{37}$$

$$\mathbf{b}_j^t\mathbf{a} - \sqrt{(-\ln h)\mathbf{b}_j^t\mathbf{D}_{\mathbf{A}}\mathbf{b}_j} \geqslant c_j - \sqrt{(-\ln h)r_j}, \tag{38}$$

$$\mathbf{b}_j^t\mathbf{a}+\sqrt{(-\ln h)\mathbf{b}_j^t\mathbf{D}_{\mathbf{A}}\mathbf{b}_j}\geqslant c_j+\sqrt{(-\ln h)r_j}, \tag{39}$$

$$\mathbf{b}_j^t\mathbf{a}\leqslant c_j+\sqrt{(-\ln h)r_j}, \tag{40}$$

where $\mathbf{D}_{\mathbf{A}} > 0$.

Here, we investigate two kinds of possibility distributions of the fuzzy vector $\boldsymbol{X}$, i.e., upper and lower possibility distributions denoted as $\Pi_u(\mathbf{x})$ and $\Pi_l(\mathbf{x})$, respectively, with the condition that $\Pi_u \geqslant \Pi_l$ holds. $\Pi_u(\mathbf{x})$ and $\Pi_l(\mathbf{x})$ are represented as

$$\Pi_u(\mathbf{x})=\exp\{-(\mathbf{x}-\mathbf{a})^t\mathbf{D}_u^{-1}(\mathbf{x}-\mathbf{a})\}, \tag{41}$$

$$\Pi_l(\mathbf{x})=\exp\{-(\mathbf{x}-\mathbf{a})^t\mathbf{D}_l^{-1}(\mathbf{x}-\mathbf{a})\}. \tag{42}$$

Since $\Pi_u \geqslant \Pi_l$ is required, $\mathbf{D}_u \geqslant \mathbf{D}_l > 0$ should be satisfied.

The upper possibility distribution of $\boldsymbol{X}$ corresponds to the upper possibility distribution of Y and the lower possibility distribution of $\boldsymbol{X}$ corresponds to the lower possibility distribution of Y. Because $\mathbf{b}_i^t\mathbf{D}_{\mathbf{A}}\mathbf{b}_i$ is the spread of fuzzy number Y_i, the objective function for obtaining the upper possibility distribution of $\boldsymbol{X}$ is introduced as

$$\max_{\mathbf{D}_u}\sum_{i=1,\ldots,m}\delta_i(\mathbf{b}_i^t\mathbf{D}_u\mathbf{b}_i). \tag{43}$$

where m is the number of fuzzy constraint conditions of (1) and $\delta_i \geqslant 0$ is a weight of the spread of Y_i. Similarly, the objective function for obtaining the lower possibility distribution of $\boldsymbol{X}$ is introduced as

$$\min_{\mathbf{D}_l}\sum_{i=1,\ldots,m}\delta_i(\mathbf{b}_i^t\mathbf{D}_l\mathbf{b}_i), \tag{44}$$

From the constraints (35)-(40), we know that the center vector $\mathbf{a}$ should comply with the following constraint conditions:

$$c_i-\sqrt{(-\ln h)r_i}\leqslant\mathbf{b}_i^t\mathbf{a}\leqslant c_i \tag{45}$$

$$c_j\leqslant\mathbf{b}_j^t\mathbf{a}\leqslant c_j+\sqrt{(-\ln h)r_j}, \tag{46}$$

which imply the center vector must exist in the region formed by (45) and (46). Since (45) and (46) are necessity conditions for $\mathbf{a}$ being a center vector but not sufficiency conditions, the vector satisfying (45) and (46) is probably qualified as a center vector. The following LP problem is used to find out a candidate of the center vector of $\Pi_u(\mathbf{x})$ and $\Pi_l(\mathbf{x})$ in the middle of the feasible region formed by (45) and (46).

$$
\begin{aligned}
&\max_{\mathbf{a}} \;\; g(\mathbf{a}) \\
&\text{s. t.} \qquad \cdots\cdots \\
&\qquad \mathbf{b}_i^t\mathbf{a} \geqslant \left(c_i - \sqrt{(-\ln h)r_i}\right)(1+\beta), \\
&\qquad \mathbf{b}_i^t\mathbf{a} \leqslant c_i(1-\beta), \\
&\qquad \cdots\cdots \\
&\qquad \mathbf{b}_j^t\mathbf{a} \leqslant \left(c_j + \sqrt{(-\ln h)r_j}\right)(1-\beta), \\
&\qquad \mathbf{b}_j^t\mathbf{a} \geqslant c_j(1+\beta), \\
&\qquad \beta \geqslant 0,\ \mathbf{a} \geqslant \mathbf{0},
\end{aligned}
\tag{47}
$$

where the objective function $g(\mathbf{a})$ is used to characterize the preference of decision makers for selecting some center vector regarded as a reference point in the feasible region of decision variables. The parameter β is used to guarantee the obtained center vector inside the region formed by (45) and (46). The obtained optimal solution of (47) is denoted as $\mathbf{a}_0$. As mentioned before, constraints (45) and (46) are just necessity conditions for $\mathbf{a}_0$ being a center vector. Thus, $\mathbf{a}_0$ should be checked whether there is an admissible set in the following constraint conditions.

$$
\begin{aligned}
&\cdots\cdots \\
&\mathbf{b}_i^t\mathbf{a}_0 - \sqrt{(-\ln h)\mathbf{b}_i^t\mathbf{D_A}\mathbf{b}_i} \leqslant c_i - \sqrt{(-\ln h)r_i}, \\
&\mathbf{b}_i^t\mathbf{a}_0 + \sqrt{(-\ln h)\mathbf{b}_i^t\mathbf{D_A}\mathbf{b}_i} \leqslant c_i + \sqrt{(-\ln h)r_i}, \\
&\cdots\cdots \\
&\mathbf{b}_j^t\mathbf{a}_0 - \sqrt{(-\ln h)\mathbf{b}_j^t\mathbf{D_A}\mathbf{b}_j} \geqslant c_j - \sqrt{(-\ln h)r_j}, \\
&\mathbf{b}_j^t\mathbf{a}_0 + \sqrt{(-\ln h)\mathbf{b}_j^t\mathbf{D_A}\mathbf{b}_j} \geqslant c_j + \sqrt{(-\ln h)r_j}, \\
&\mathbf{D_A} > 0.
\end{aligned}
\tag{48}
$$

If there is an admissible set in (48), $\mathbf{a}_0$ is qualified for a center vector. Otherwise, The parameters β and h should be changed to obtain a suitable center vector. After finding out the center vector $\mathbf{a}_0$, other feasible solutions around it are investigated assuming that they are governed by a possibility distribution $(\mathbf{a}_0, \mathbf{D_A})_e$. Assume that $\mathbf{a}_0$ is a valid center vector. Then, the possibilistic programming problems for finding out the upper and the lower possibility distributions can be formalized as the following two crisp optimization problems P. Guo *et al.* [4].

$$
\begin{array}{ll}
\max\limits_{\mathbf{D}_u} & \sum\limits_{i=1,\dots,m} \delta_i(\mathbf{b}_i^t\mathbf{D}_u\mathbf{b}_i) \\
\text{s. t.} & \qquad\qquad \dots\dots \\
& \mathbf{b}_i^t\mathbf{a}_0 - \sqrt{(-\ln h)\mathbf{b}_i^t\mathbf{D}_u\mathbf{b}_i} \leqslant c_i - \sqrt{(-\ln h)r_i}, \\
& \mathbf{b}_i^t\mathbf{a}_0 + \sqrt{(-\ln h)\mathbf{b}_i^t\mathbf{D}_u\mathbf{b}_i} \leqslant c_i + \sqrt{(-\ln h)r_i}, \\
& \qquad\qquad \dots\dots \\
& \mathbf{b}_j^t\mathbf{a}_0 - \sqrt{(-\ln h)\mathbf{b}_j^t\mathbf{D}_u\mathbf{b}_j} \geqslant c_j - \sqrt{(-\ln h)r_j}, \\
& \mathbf{b}_j^t\mathbf{a}_0 + \sqrt{(-\ln h)\mathbf{b}_j^t\mathbf{D}_u\mathbf{b}_j} \geqslant c_j + \sqrt{(-\ln h)r_j}, \\
& \qquad\qquad \dots\dots \\
& \mathbf{D}_u > 0.
\end{array}
\tag{49}
$$

$$
\begin{array}{ll}
\min\limits_{\mathbf{D}_l} & \sum\limits_{i=1,\dots,m} \delta_i(\mathbf{b}_i^t\mathbf{D}_l\mathbf{b}_i) \\
\text{s. t.} & \qquad\qquad \dots\dots \\
& \mathbf{b}_i^t\mathbf{a}_0 - \sqrt{(-\ln h)\mathbf{b}_i^t\mathbf{D}_l\mathbf{b}_i} \leqslant c_i - \sqrt{(-\ln h)r_i}, \\
& \mathbf{b}_i^t\mathbf{a}_0 + \sqrt{(-\ln h)\mathbf{b}_i^t\mathbf{D}_l\mathbf{b}_i} \leqslant c_i + \sqrt{(-\ln h)r_i}, \\
& \qquad\qquad \dots\dots \\
& \mathbf{b}_j^t\mathbf{a}_0 - \sqrt{(-\ln h)\mathbf{b}_j^t\mathbf{D}_l\mathbf{b}_j} \geqslant c_j - \sqrt{(-\ln h)r_j}, \\
& \mathbf{b}_j^t\mathbf{a}_0 + \sqrt{(-\ln h)\mathbf{b}_j^t\mathbf{D}_l\mathbf{b}_j} \geqslant c_j + \sqrt{(-\ln h)r_j}, \\
& \qquad\qquad \dots\dots \\
& \mathbf{D}_l > 0.
\end{array}
\tag{50}
$$

In order to ensure the inclusion condition $\Pi_u \geqslant \Pi_l$, the matrices $\mathbf{D}_u$ and $\mathbf{D}_l$ will be solved by a primary problem and an auxiliary problem as follows P. Guo *et al.* [4].

Primary problem:

$$
\begin{aligned}
\max_{\mathbf{D}_u} \quad & \sum_{i=1,\ldots,m} \delta_i(\mathbf{b}_i^t \mathbf{D}_u \mathbf{b}_i) \\
\text{s. t.} \quad & \qquad \ldots\ldots \\
& \mathbf{b}_i^t \mathbf{D}_u \mathbf{b}_i \geqslant (\mathbf{b}_i^t \mathbf{a}_0 + \sqrt{(-\ln h)\cdot \mathrm{r}_i} - \mathrm{c}_i)^2/(-\ln h), \\
& \mathbf{b}_i^t \mathbf{D}_u \mathbf{b}_i \leqslant (\sqrt{(-\ln h)\cdot r_i} + c_i - \mathbf{b}_i^t \mathbf{a}_0)^2/(-\ln h), \\
& \qquad \ldots\ldots \\
& \mathbf{b}_j^t \mathbf{D}_u \mathbf{b}_j \leqslant (\mathbf{b}_j^t \mathbf{a}_0 + \sqrt{(-\ln h)\cdot r_j} - c_j)^2/(-\ln h), \\
& \mathbf{b}_j^t \mathbf{D}_u \mathbf{b}_j \geqslant (\sqrt{(-\ln h)\cdot r_j} + c_j - \mathbf{b}_j^t \mathbf{a}_0)^2/(-\ln h), \\
& \qquad \ldots\ldots \\
& \mathbf{D}_u > 0.
\end{aligned}
\tag{51}
$$

The optimization problem (51) is nonlinear because of the constraint condition $\mathbf{D}_u > 0$. In order to obtain $\mathbf{D}_u$ easily, we firstly solve the problem (51) without the constraint condition $\mathbf{D}_u > 0$. If the obtained matrix satisfies $\mathbf{D}_u > 0$ then it is a possibility distribution matrix. Otherwise a sufficient condition for $\mathbf{D}_u > 0$ shown in Theorem 3.1 is added to (51) by which (51) becomes an LP problem. If a positive matrix $\mathbf{D}_u$ can be obtained with the obtained vector $\mathbf{a}_0$, it also means that $\mathbf{a}_0$ is qualified for a center vector. Thus, solving (51) is also a procedure for checking $\mathbf{a}_0$ by (48).

Theorem 3.1 (P. Guo *et al.* [4]). *Given a real symmetric matrix $[d_{ij}] \in R^{n\times n}$, a sufficient condition for this matrix being positive definite is*

$$
d_{ii} > \sum_{j=1,\, j\neq i}^{n} (d_{ij}^{+} + d_{ij}^{-}), \quad (i = 1,\ldots,n) \tag{52}
$$

where $|d_{ij}| = |d_{ij}{}^{+} - d_{ij}{}^{-}|$ with $d_{ij}{}^{+} \geqslant 0$ and $d_{ij}{}^{-} \geqslant 0$.

After finding out the positive matrix $\mathbf{D}_u$, we set the spectral decomposition of $\mathbf{D}_u$ as follows:

$$
\mathbf{D}_u = \mathbf{P}\Lambda\mathbf{P}^t, \tag{53}
$$

where normalized eigenvectors are the columns of the matrix $\mathbf{P}$ and Λ is the diagonal matrix formed by the corresponding eigenvalues as follows:

$$
\begin{bmatrix}
\lambda_1 & 0 & \cdots & 0 \\
0 & \lambda_2 & \cdots & 0 \\
\vdots & \vdots & \ddots & \vdots \\
0 & 0 & \cdots & \lambda_n
\end{bmatrix}. \tag{54}
$$

Assume that upper and lower possibility distribution matrices have the same eigenvectors. Thus $\mathbf{D}_l$ can be expressed as $\mathbf{D}_l = \mathbf{P}\Phi\mathbf{P}^t$ where Φ is a positive diagonal matrix as follows:

$$\begin{bmatrix} \phi_1 & 0 & \cdots & 0 \\ 0 & \phi_2 & \cdots & 0 \\ \vdots & \vdots & \ddots & \vdots \\ 0 & 0 & \cdots & \phi_n \end{bmatrix}. \tag{55}$$

The matrix Φ is obtained by the following auxiliary problem P. Guo *et al.* [4].

Auxiliary problem:

$$\begin{aligned}
\min_{\Phi} \quad & \sum_{i=1,\ldots,m} \delta_i (\mathbf{b}_i^t\mathbf{P})\Phi(\mathbf{b}_i^t\mathbf{P})^t \\
\text{s. t.} \quad & \qquad \ldots\ldots \\
& (\mathbf{b}_i^t\mathbf{P})\Phi(\mathbf{b}_i^t\mathbf{P})^t \geqslant \left(\mathbf{b}_i^t\mathbf{a}_0 + \sqrt{(-\ln h)\cdot \mathrm{r}_i} - \mathrm{c}_i\right)^2/(-\ln h), \\
& (\mathbf{b}_i^t\mathbf{P})\Phi(\mathbf{b}_i^t\mathbf{P})^t \leqslant \left(\sqrt{(-\ln h)\cdot r_i} + c_i - \mathbf{b}_i^t\mathbf{a}_0\right)^2/(-\ln h), \\
& \qquad \ldots\ldots \\
& (\mathbf{b}_j^t\mathbf{P})\Phi(\mathbf{b}_j^t\mathbf{P})^t \leqslant \left(\mathbf{b}_j^t\mathbf{a}_0 + \sqrt{(-\ln h)\cdot r_j} - c_j\right)^2/(-\ln h), \\
& (\mathbf{b}_j^t\mathbf{P})\Phi(\mathbf{b}_j^t\mathbf{P})^t \geqslant \left(\sqrt{(-\ln h)\cdot r_j} + c_j - \mathbf{b}_j^t\mathbf{a}_0\right)^2/(-\ln h), \\
& \qquad \ldots\ldots. \\
& \varepsilon \leqslant \phi_k \leqslant \lambda_k, (k = 1, \ldots, n).
\end{aligned} \tag{56}$$

Here $\varepsilon \leqslant \phi_k \leqslant \lambda_k$ $(k = 1, \ldots, n)$ ensure that $\mathbf{D}_u \geqslant \mathbf{D}_l > 0$ holds such that $\Pi_u \geqslant \Pi_l$ is satisfied where ε is a given small positive value. After obtaining Φ, we have

$$\mathbf{D}_l = \mathbf{P}\Phi\mathbf{P}^t \tag{57}$$

Definition 3.1. Let us denote the feasible sets of decision variables obtained from upper and lower possibility distributions with a possibility level h as S_u^h and S_l^h, respectively. The sets S_u^h and S_l^h are defined as follows:

$$S_u^h = \{\mathbf{x} \in R^n | \Pi_u(\mathbf{x}) \geqslant h\}, \tag{58}$$

$$S_l^h = \{\mathbf{x} \in R^n | \Pi_l(\mathbf{x}) \geqslant h\}. \tag{59}$$

Theorem 3.2 (P. Guo *et al.* [4]). *For a possibility level h,* $S_l^h \subseteq S_u^h$.

3.3 Numerical Examples

In this section, two numerical examples are given to show how to obtain lower and upper possibility distributions of fuzzy decision variables.

Example 3.1 (P. Guo *et al.* [5]). *Let us consider the following possibilistic constraints,*

$$\begin{aligned} 2x_1 + x_2 &\approx^- \widetilde{15}, \\ x_2 &\approx^- \widetilde{4.5}, \\ 3x_1 + 4x_2 &\approx^- \widetilde{34}, \\ x_1 &\approx^- \widetilde{5.5}, \\ x_1 + 2x_2 &\approx^+ \widetilde{13}, \end{aligned} \tag{60}$$

where

$$\widetilde{15} = (15.,2.)_T,\ \widetilde{4.5} = (4.5,1.)_T,\ \widetilde{34} = (34.,4.)_T,\ \widetilde{5.5} = (5.5,0.9)_T,\ \widetilde{13} = (13.,2.)_T. \tag{61}$$

Assume that the possibility distribution of decision variables x_1 and x_2 is $X = (\mathbf{a},\mathbf{r})_T$ with $\mathbf{a} = [a_1,a_2]^t$, $\mathbf{r} = [r_1,r_2]^t$. Setting $h = 0.5$, a center vector was obtained by (22) with $\beta = 0.01$ and $g(\mathbf{a}) = 2x_1 + 3x_2$ as follows:

$$\mathbf{a} = [5.28,4.29]^t.$$

Upper and lower spread vectors were obtained by (25) with $\mathbf{w} = [1,1]^t$ as follows:

$$\begin{aligned} \mathbf{r}_u &= [0.64,1.02]^t, \\ \mathbf{r}_l &= [0.56,0.58]^t. \end{aligned}$$

The region of decision variables left by the possibilistic constraints of (60) is characterized by the possibility distribution of decision variables. The upper and the lower possibility distributions of fuzzy decision variables with $h = 0.5$ are shown in Figure 3.3. In Figure 3.3 the regions inside the two contours are feasible sets $S_u^{0.5}$ and $S_l^{0.5}$, respectively. It is obvious that the solution obtained from the upper possibility distribution leaves more room than the one from the lower possibility distribution.

Example 3.2. P. Guo *et al.* [4]. Let us consider the following fuzzy decision problem,

$$\begin{aligned} x_1 + 2x_2 &\approx^+ \widetilde{17}, \\ x_1 + x_2 &\approx^+ \widetilde{9}, \\ 2x_1 + x_2 &\approx^- \widetilde{15}, \\ x_1 &\approx^- \widetilde{3}, \end{aligned} \tag{62}$$

where x_1 and x_2 are decision variables. The fuzzy numbers are all governed by exponential possibility distributions as follows:

$$\widetilde{17} = (17.,10.)_e,\ \widetilde{9} = (9.,7.)_e,\ \widetilde{15} = (15.,10.)_e,\ \widetilde{3} = (3.,1.1)_e. \tag{63}$$

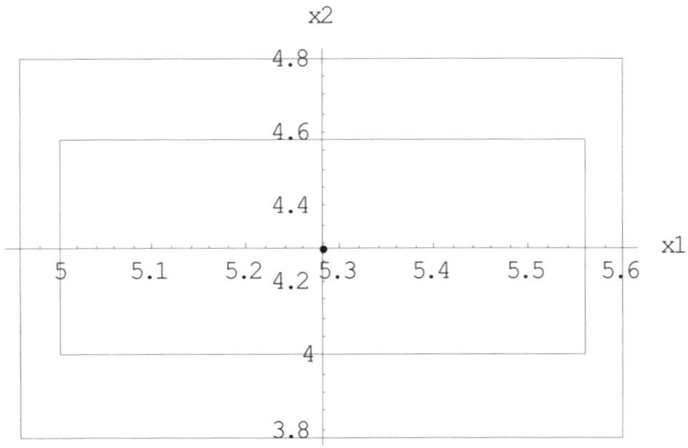

Figure 3.3 $S_u^{0.5}$ and $S_l^{0.5}$ (the outer is from the upper possibility distribution and the inner is from the lower possibility distribution).

Decision variables x_1 and x_2 are governed by an exponential possibility distribution $X = (\mathbf{a}, \mathbf{D_A})_e$, where

$$\mathbf{a} = [x_1, x_2]^t, \ \mathbf{D_A} = \begin{bmatrix} d_{11} & d_{12} \\ d_{12} & d_{22} \end{bmatrix}. \tag{64}$$

These four fuzzy constraints leave a feasible fuzzy region for decision variables. Setting $\beta = 0.05$ and $g(\mathbf{a}) = x_1 + 2x_2$ in the LP problem (47), a center vector was obtained with $h = 0.3$ as follows:

$$\mathbf{a} = [2.850, 8.298]^t, \tag{65}$$

and upper and lower possibility distribution matrices were obtained by (51), (56) and (57) with $\delta_i = 1$ as follows:

$$\begin{aligned} \mathbf{D}_u &= \begin{bmatrix} 1.405 & 1.357 \\ 1.357 & 5.560 \end{bmatrix}, \\ \mathbf{D}_l &= \begin{bmatrix} 1.003 & 0.006 \\ 0.006 & 1.022 \end{bmatrix}. \end{aligned} \tag{66}$$

The feasible region of decision variables left by the four fuzzy constraints (62) is characterized by the possibility distribution of decision variables. The upper and the lower possibility distributions of fuzzy decision variables with $h = 0.3$ are shown in Fig. 3.4 of which the regions inside the two contours are feasible sets $S_u^{0.3}$ and $S_l^{0.3}$, respectively. The fuzzy solution obtained from the upper possibility distribution leaves more room than the one from the lower possibility distribution. The feasible sets will be sent to lower decision levels where one specific solution will be chosen with considering the additional conditions.

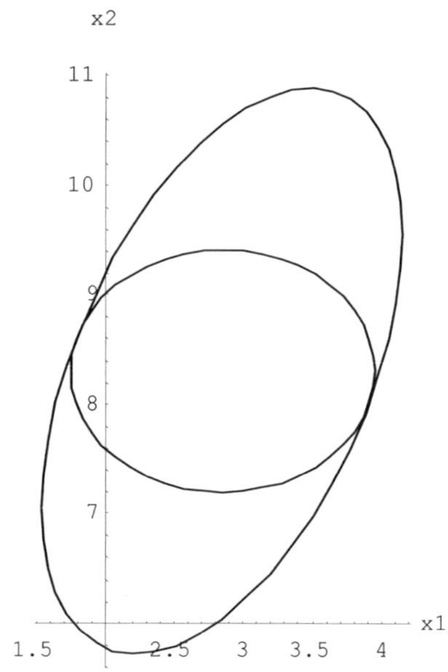

Figure 3.4 Possibility distributions of fuzzy decision variables (the outer is from the upper possibility distribution and the inner is from the lower possibility distribution).

3.4 Conclusions

For upper levels of decision-making systems, decision makers can always set some fuzzy satisfaction levels based on their experience. These fuzzy satisfaction levels can be represented by two kinds of soft equal, i.e., "$\approx^+$" and "$\approx^-$", which leave some feasible region for decision variables. In this chapter, the possibility distributions of fuzzy variables with symmetrical triangular and exponential distribution functions are studied to reflect the inherent fuzziness in this kind of decision-making problem. Upper and lower possibility distributions are obtained to represent solutions with different fuzzy degrees in decision-making procedure. An upper possibility distribution reflects the largest distribution and a lower possibility distribution reflects the smallest distribution of fuzzy decision variables for some given center vector. The fuzzy decision based on an upper possibility distribution leaves more room than the one based on a lower possibility distribution. The obtained fuzzy decision will be sent to lower levels of a decision-making system. Decision makers in lower levels can make some more detailed decisions within the region of decision variables obtained by the proposed methods with considering some practical situation.

Bibliography

[1] R. E. Bellman and L. A. Zadeh, Decision making in a fuzzy environment, Management Science, 17 (1970) 141–164.

[2] M. Inuiguchi, H. Ichihashi, and H. Tanaka, Fuzzy Programming: A survey of recent developments, in: R. Slowinski and J. Teghem, Eds., Stochastic Versus Fuzzy Approaches to Multiobjective Mathematical Programming under Uncertainty, Kluwer Academic Publishers, Dordrecht, (1990) 45–68.

[3] M. Inuiguchi, T. Tanino, and M. Sakawa: Membership Function Elicitation in Possibilistic Programming Problems, Fuzzy Sets and Systems, Vol. 111, No. 1, pp.29–45 (2000).

[4] P. Guo, H. Tanaka and H.-J. Zimmermann, Upper and lower possibility distributions of fuzzy decision variables in upper level decision problems, Fuzzy Sets and Systems, 111 (2000) 71–79.

[5] P. Guo, T. Entani, and H. Tanaka, Fusion of multi-dimensional possibilistic information via possibilistic linear programming, Journal of the Operations Research Society of Japan, 44 (2001) 220–229.

[6] Z. Pawlak, Rough set, International Journal of Computer and Information Science, 11 (1982) 341–356.

[7] H. Rommelfange, Fuzzy linear programming and applications, European Journal of Operational Research, 92 (1996) 512–527.

[8] M. Sakawa, Fuzzy Sets and Interactive Multiobjective Optimization (Plenum Press, New York, 1993).

[9] H. Tanaka, P. Guo, and H.-J. Zimmermann, Possibility distributions of fuzzy decision variables obtained from possibilistic linear programming problems, Fuzzy Sets and Systems, 113 (2000) 323–332.

[10] H. Tanaka and P. Guo, Possibilistic Data Analysis for Operations Research, (Physica-Verlag, Heidelberg, 1999).

[11] H. Tanaka and P. Guo, Portfolio selection based on upper and lower exponential possibility distributions, European Journal of Operational Research 114 (1998) 131–142.

[12] H. Tanaka and H. Ishibuchi, Evidence theory of exponential possibility distributions, International Journal of Approximate Reasoning, 8 (1993) 123–140.

[13] H. Tanaka and K. Asai, Fuzzy solution in fuzzy linear programming problems, IEEE Transactions on Systems, Man, and Cybernetics, 14 (1984) 325–328.

[14] H.-J. Zimmermann, Fuzzy programming and linear programming with several objective functions, Fuzzy Sets and Systems, 1 (1978) 45–56.

[15] L.A. Zadeh, The concept of a linguistic variable and its application to approximate reasoning – I, Information Science, 8 (1975) 199–249.

Chapter 4

Intelligent Decision Making in Training Based on Virtual Reality

Liliane dos Santos Machado [1] and Ronei Marcos de Moraes [2]

Laboratory of Technologies for Virtual Teaching and Statistics, Federal University of Paraiba – Brazil

http://www.de.ufpb.br/~labteve

[1] *liliane@di.ufpb.br,* [2] *ronei@de.ufpb.br*

Virtual reality (VR) is an evolving area for simulation and training applications. The area is related to realistic and interactive experiments in real time computational systems. Those systems generate data and information that can be used to intelligent decision making, as skills evaluation related to dexterity and reasoning power in critical procedures. This chapter includes the computational decision making based on statistical and fuzzy methodologies to perform user skills evaluation. An evaluation system must monitor the user's interactions with the VR application and be able to verify in real time the correctness degree of those interactions. From correctness degree the user will be qualified to perform the real task. Recently, publications in the literature show the use of continuous evaluation methods to measure the evolution of the user's performance. In the near future, methodologies for evaluation will be used to verify performance of multiple users in collaborative VR environments.

4.1 Training Aspects

The acquisition of knowledge can happen in several ways. The transmission of knowledge includes oral, visual and experimental approaches. In spite of the oral approach be the more traditional, the acquisition of knowledge can depend on the comprehension of physical phenomena. This aspect makes the experimentation an important stage in the learning process.

Technological advances provide new resources for learning to increase or facilitate the assimilation of contents. These new resources have as goal to enlarge the information access and allow that it could be obtained outside educational environments and in moments considered convenient by the apprentice. Additionally, the communication between apprentices and a tutor can be synchronous or asynchronous. The synchronous communication occurs when apprentices and the tutor share the same environment, real or virtual, and exchange information in real-time. In an opposite way, in the asynchronous communication the apprentices read, listen or watch a lesson and submit their doubts to the tutor. Thus, the answer will only be obtained after some time. In the context of the new resources, became possible to explore senses of reality and presence through the networks access and the availability of faster processors. It results in applications endowed of three-dimensional content, interactivity and/or real-time communication. These applications can be described as applications based on virtual reality or Web applications.

Generally, the training methods can be decomposed in four main categories: physical, assisted, computational and Web training. In the physical training the apprentice has direct contact with the subject contents and can handle and modify properties. Thus, the results of actions can be observed instantly. In a similar way, the apprentice also has physical contact in the assisted training, but a tutor aids them during the tasks execution. A computer program to simulate the tasks is used in the computational training. When the simulation occurs through the Internet, the training is known as Web training. It is important to observe that all these training methods have as goal provide to apprentice the opportunity of development of psychomotor capabilities. Particularly, the computational and Web training can use virtual reality to simulate real tasks.

Virtual reality is a recent research area that unites concepts of several other areas in order to digitally provide realistic environments. Its challenge is to explore the five human senses, through the use of devices and algorithms, to simulate environments or events. For training purposes, one of its main advantages is the possibility of simulation of micro and macroscopic realities, as well as those than could present risks in the real world. This feature allows the training in safe conditions. Additionally, it decreases or eliminates the consumption of materials, offers reuse and can be continuously available.

This chapter presents the main concepts necessary to the comprehension of virtual reality and systems that use it. Those will be necessary to understand how information from virtual reality applications can be used to intelligent decision making and which methods have been and could be used for this end.

4.2 Virtual Reality

In 1991, Rheingold published a book about a new and revolutionary technology called Virtual Reality (VR) [48]. This new technology referred to artificial worlds, created by computers, and electronic devices and promised to transform the society. Through the following decade, VR acquired fame from fiction movies, but keep its application restricted to games and military researches with flight simulators. Technological advances allowed it to be used in several other areas and to receive prominence as an important resource for training purposes.

Virtual Reality can be defined as a science that unites knowledge of several areas, as computer science, electronics, physics and cognition, beside others, in order to offer computational systems that integrate characteristics of immersion and interactivity to simulate real environments (Figure 4.1). In those environments, users have stimulated their several senses by the use of special devices and have the sensation of immersion in a virtual environment. VR systems react in real-time their users' actions and demand fast processing.

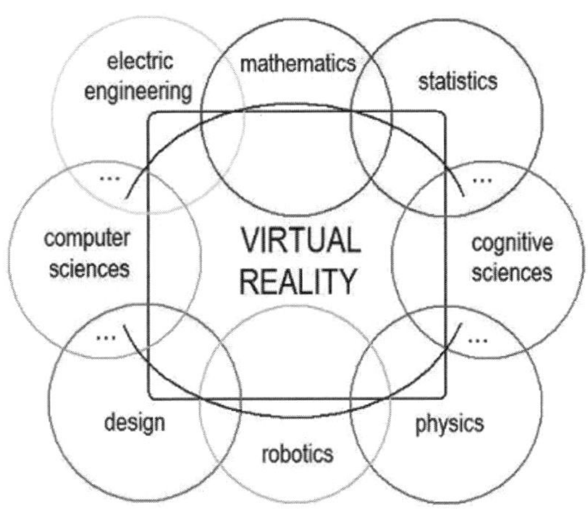

Figure 4.1 Virtual reality: the union of knowledge of several areas to provide immersion, interactivity and involvement.

The use of interaction devices and immersion is directly associated to cognitive aspects of human being and can explore visual, auditory, tactile, motor and smell stimuli. Those devices can be separated in two main categories: input and output. Input devices send to system information related to user movements and interactions. The information is used to the processing of new graphic scenes, sounds, vibrations and reaction forces. Examples of input devices are the tracking sensors, responsible by detect the position of an object or part of the body in which is attached; the interaction devices, as the traditional mouse, keyboard and joystick, and the data gloves; and the biological sensors that use voice recognition and muscular electrical signals. Figure 4.2 shows a tracking device attached to glasses to move an object in the virtual world according to users' head movements.

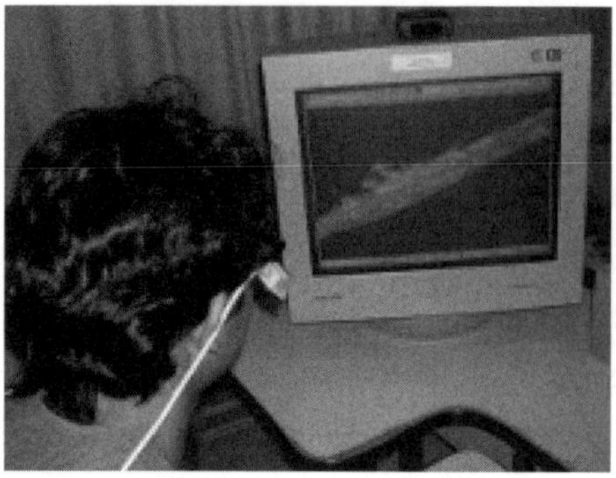

Figure 4.2 Tracking device send users' head movements and allows changing the point of view.

Output devices aim to stimulate users' senses, sending for them the answers of the system. In this category are the visual, aural, and haptic devices. Due to their function, the output devices are important to provide the sensation of presence and immersion in the VR environment. Visual devices are commonly the most used and can provide mono or stereoscopic visualization. When stereoscopic devices are used, users can observe floating in the space the objects of the virtual environment, inside or outside the projection plane (monitor or screen). The effect is obtained through the use of projection algorithms and glasses or head-based displays able to present different images to each observer's eye. Other output devices are: aural displays, three-dimensional systems that present sound according to user position, and haptic displays, devices that explore the sense of touch and proprioperception, as equilibrium, temperature and force resistance.

4.2.1 *Interaction Devices*

Interaction devices allow the user-application communication and can capture user actions in real-time to be used as source for the processing of application reactions. The reactions can occur as a change in the point-of-view of the graphical scene, objects deformation, presentation of sounds and vibration of devices. In spite of the restricted interaction possibilities, mouse and keyboard are the most economically accessible devices and can be used in

Table 4.1 Examples of interaction devices.

Device	Active	Reactive
Touch screen monitor	X	X
Mouse	X	
Data glove	X	
Data glove with exoesqueletum	X	X
Haptic devices	X	X
Tracking device	X	

conjunction with others in the interaction process. However, in order to achieve high levels of realism, VR applications use to integrate interaction devices whose shape or manipulation mode is similar to tools used in real procedures. Table 4.1 presents some examples of interaction devices that can be used in VR systems. The devices can provide bi-directional communication between user systems when they support the transfer of actions and reactions. As example, datagloves allow computers to identify users' fingers movements and can be used to tell the system that users are touching or grasping an object. In general, a tracking system is attached to datagloves to capture hand position also. In fact, tracking devices can be attached to any real object that, when handled by users, could inform the movement to the VR application.

A category of interaction devices allows both input and output of data and the computer can use them to receive and send information from/to users. Touch screen displays are an example of this category of device since they can present information (output) to users and also send users actions for computer. Other example is the set head-based displays with tracking devices attached. They can capture users' head movements and provide images according new points of view of the virtual environment. Haptic devices also can capture actions and provide reactions. From the examples presented, is important to mention that sight, hearing and tactile are the human senses most explored by VR. Technological limitations and high costs still prevent the use of devices that explore the other senses.

4.2.2 *Haptic Devices*

Haptic devices incorporate sensors and actuators to monitor user actions and provide touch and/or force feedback. The perception of touch is related to the nature of the contact with an object, as texture or temperature. In a complemental way, the perception of forces is related to the sense of position and movement associated to interaction with objects. In the last case, actuators are necessary to send reactions to users.

Haptic devices that provide force feedback can be separated in two main categories: ground-based or body-based. Ground-based haptic devices, as some joysticks, need to be physically attached to a platform or stable surface to provide force feedback. On the other hand, the body-based haptic devices use a connection point of the own device to provide force feedback. This feature makes them portable, most of the time, exoskeleton of data-gloves. In general, haptic devices allow movements with several degrees of freedom, support and react with different amplitudes, offer manipulation in a restricted space and use different technologies. Most of haptic devices for legs or arms provide force feedback. The reason they do not usually provide touch sensation is that hands are more suitable and sensitive to this perception. Those devices used to have their cost related to the amount of force supported and returned.

A group of ground-based devices uses a type of mechanical arm to provide touch and force feedback. They support six-degree-of-freedom movements (translations and rotations) are suitable for applications with stereoscopic visualization. The Phantom^{TM} – *Personal Haptic Interface Mechanism* – is one of those devices. A base in which the mechanical arm is attached and whose extremity is similar to a pen composes it. Available in different versions (Figure 4.3), the device uses potentiometers to offer force feedback with different intensities in three (translations) or six (translations + rotations) degrees. Its popularity is due to its shape and manipulation way that allows the intuitive simulation of hand tools, as scalpels, hammers and needles, as example.

Figure 4.3 Hapic device used to simulate a needle.

4.3 Training in Virtual Reality Systems

Training is one of the most promising areas in the context of VR applications. It includes simulators whose goal is allowing practice in environments that imitate the reality of a procedure. Users can practice in those environments and be technically and psychologically prepared to perform real tasks. In a similar way, simulators can also offer training of new techniques through the presentation of different and/or generic situations (detached from particularities of real cases). In those virtual environments users feel visually as well as physically involved in scenes with features similar of the real world, can interact with their objects and observe the consequences of their actions. As advantages: no one can be injured, there aren't risks involved, there isn't degradation of materials and the procedure can be repeated several times, so much it was necessary. During a training execution in a VR system, information from the simulation (user actions) can be collected and processed to evaluate users and assist decision making related to their abilities. Other possibility is the use of information to change in real-time the simulation, increasing or decreasing the complexity as well as modifying their parameters according to user evolution.

In order to teach motoric operating of machines for timber harvesting, Sweden groups developed a simulator to allow new workers to acquire skill and get used to the machines [16]. Since the harvest is an action that cannot be repeated without loss, the system can teach the best method to harvest and allows repetition of the method. The system is composed by a replica of the machine cockpit with specific software that reproduces forests with trees of several diameters and heights. This kind of simulator has been used in two steps of training: in the beginning for training motoric skills, when automating basic functions and training cognitive skills (e.g., bucking simulator), and in later stages of training, including the update of experienced operators. Such simulators use log files for evaluation in order to provide feedback for operator (trainee) and to allow the improvement of productivity and economy in operation.

Since the 90's, flight simulators have been used in the training of new pilots in military and civil aviation. Those simulators are constructed from a replica of a real cockpit of specific planes. Generally, the cockpit is set up in motion-platforms that can answer to user actions according to interaction movements. The VR system is composed by intelligent methods that present new levels of difficulty and can use past training data to provide continuity in the learning process. Nowadays, flight simulators are so precise and affordable that new pilots need to perform several hours of training in those systems before pilot a real aeroplane.

Also for military purposes, VR have used the games approach to prepare soldiers for the battlefield. The games are composed by intelligent modules that present virtual enemies and challenge situations. The experience in those virtual battlefields can minimize psychological impact of soldiers in real battles and training them to deal with surprise events and with fast decision making.

Another training possibility in VR simulators is related to microscopic or macroscopic situations. Nanotubes manipulation is an example of this kind of situation. It is applied to several procedures and requires the operations of characterizing, placing, deforming and connecting nanotubes. Gao and Lécuyer [15] developed a simulator for training and prototyping the telemanipulation of nanotubes to help students or new operators to understand the phenomenon. In order to provide a valid simulator, the system includes haptic manipulation and interactive deformation of the tubes. Additionally, new manipulation tasks can be simulated in order to find optimal solutions.

Health is probably one of the most benefited areas of training systems based on VR. Due to the fact that bad performed procedures can result in physical and/or psychological injuries, the simulation of them in virtual environments can help to reduce such situations. Additionally, the repetition of training in VR simulators is helpful when specific materials or procedures cannot be performed several times with plastic models or guinea pigs. In general, VR systems for medical training include three-dimensional visualization, realistic images obtained by tomography or magnetic ressonance imaging (MRI), models with deformation properties and haptic devices for touch and/or force feedback. Some categories with VR-based simulators are: suture practice, laparoscopy, bone marrow harvest, gynaecology exam and rehabilitation, among others. Those systems use haptic devices to simulate medical tools and propose to help apprentices to acquire dexterity to execute real tasks. In this context, minimally invasive procedures are particularly explored because of its feature of be performed with small cuts in patient body. In those procedures, dexterity is a key factor. In some cases, there isn't visual information available for the physician. The bone marrow harvest for transplant in children is an example of that. The simulator of this procedure [25] provides stereoscopic visualization only of the external body and the apprentice must identify physico-elastic properties of tissues when use a virtual needle to harvest bone marrow. Since the task must be quickly performed, the physician dexterity will result in lesser discomfort for patient and a faster recovery.

Laparoscopic procedures in virtual environments have been also developed due to the complexity of the tasks and the difficulty to understand how to manipulate the tools inside human body. In laparoscopic VR-based simulators the user visualizes a representation of the tweezers, manipulates haptic devices and observes and feels the results of his actions. Other possibility for medical simulators is the training of stages of pathologies, including rare cases. The SITEG system is dedicated to training the identification of cervix pathologies in women [23]. Its goal is to offer a virtual environment with different stages of cervix inflammation. The system presents two modules with phases for observation and palpation, both supervised by an evaluation system that informs user performance.

Physiotherapy and rehabilitation have used VR to teach users the right form to perform movements. The systems can evaluate users and rehabilitate cognitive and meta-cognitive processes as visual perception, attention and memory [50]. In this context, they depend on devices to monitor user movements. Important features in those systems are graphics realism and intuitive interaction: both must provide immersion to user and make him stay concentrated in the movements performed [61].

4.4 Collecting and Using Data from VR Simulators

The collect of data during interaction in a VR-based simulation can provide, in real-time, several data for decision making. Particularly, it can be done in real-time to modify simulation aspects, as variables and functions responsible for feedback. However, this information can also be utilized to verify the degree of accuracy of users when performing the simulation. Then, the system must supervise user interactions to evaluate the training performed in simulators based on VR. Theoretically, the system can collect information related to position, forces, torque, resistance, velocity, acceleration, temperature, angle of visualization, sound, smells, temperature, velocity and shape (Figure 4.4). Practically, devices must execute this task and some types of data cannot be collected nowadays due to technological restrictions.

Spacial position can be captured by tracking devices attached to some part of users' body or to an object manipulated by them. Those devices can collect movements in three or more degrees of freedom in constant intervals of time. Such information allows VR system to calculate object position in the virtual scene, the velocity of the movement and its acceleration. In a similar way, haptic devices also can do the same, but in a limited physical space. In both examples, sampling rates vary according to the device chosen. The positioning of objects manipulated by users can allow the identification of collision with other objects of the virtual scene, besides the direction of contact and its intensity. In order to achieve this, position vectors with last and present position are used to determine the collision velocity

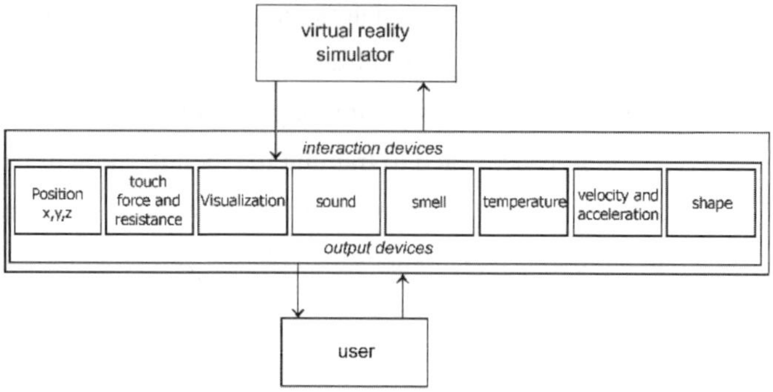

Figure 4.4 Interaction devices allow the collection of information from simulation.

and intensity. As example, it will be fundamental to decision making for evaluation purposes in simulators in which cuts and objects deformation is possible. Figure 4.5 show how data collected from VR simulators can be used to evaluate users.

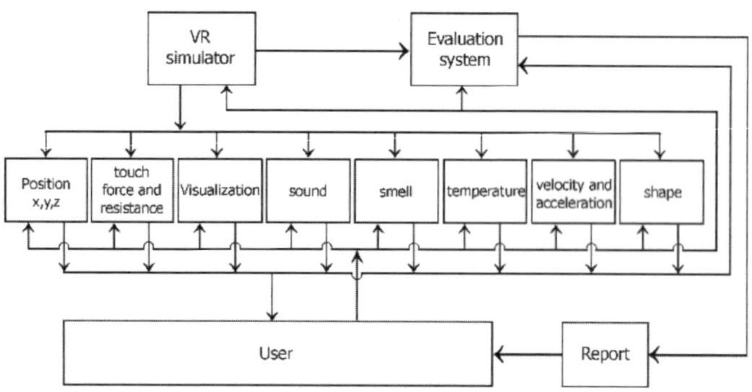

Figure 4.5 Evaluation systems collect data from VR-based simulations to evaluate user performance.

Reactions from data processing collected from interaction can be send to users as force feedback, a new point of view of the scene, deformation of objects, sound, increase or decrease of temperature, change of objects (as cuts or divisions) and smells. The intensity of feedback will depend on device capabilities. However, the continuity of reaction is an important factor in the levels of immersion.

4.4.1 *Online and Offline Evaluation*

Training procedures can be saved (video) for posterior analysis and used to inform users about their performance. Because users can have forgotten some decisions and actions done during the training, the main problem in this kind of evaluation is the interval between training and evaluation. Additionally, some performances cannot be classified as good or bad due to procedure complexity. Thus, the existence of an evaluation system coupled to a simulation allows fast feedback that can be used improve user performance.

Several methods have been proposed to offline and online evaluation. Offline methods evaluate users in a system independent of the VR system and data must be collected and stored for posterior use. In opposite, online methods are linked to VR system and can offer results of performance immediately after the execution of the simulation. Because they are coupled to the training system, online methods must present low computational complexity in order to not compromise the simulation performance. However, they must also have high accuracy that doesn't compromise the quality of evaluation. Figure 4.5 showed the independence between simulator and evaluation systems in spite of their simultaneous action. The choice of the variables to be monitored depends on the relevance of each one to the training subject.

It is possible to find several kinds of simulators based on virtual reality and also several evaluation systems. Gande and Devarajan [14] used an Instructor/Operator station to monitor users movements to increase or decrease the difficulty degree of a simulation. The station Instructor was prepared to evaluate the performance of a medical trainee based on predefined specifications and provided an effectivity report. The GeRTiSS System [1] was capable to create a report, with information about time of intervention, number of cuts, cauterisations, and others. The surgeon could use that information to improve his performance by himself. Other example is the WebSET System [18] that can simulate scenarios in which the users are trained. In that system, users are evaluated according to the speed of answers, number of mouse movements, answer accuracy, correct/wrong decisions and learning.

Other methods for training evaluation can be found and the next sessions will present some of them. Basically, they were separated in four sections: evaluation based on expert systems, evaluation based on mixture models, evaluation based hidden Markov models, and evaluation based on Bayesian models.

4.5 Evaluation Based on Expert Systems

4.5.1 *Using Classical Logic*

An intelligent evaluation using classical logic refers to a computational system that made an evaluation task in a similar way of one or more than one expert. In those systems, the knowledge from one or more experts is stored in a knowledge database using a logical representation, as for example rules. The control of rules utilization is done by an inference system, using facts that are obtained from beginning or after deduction process [8]. Using rules and facts, new facts can be obtained using one or more reasoning ways. The architecture formed by knowledge base and inference system is named "expert system" [49]. In expert systems, knowledge about a procedure is modelled by rules as:

IF <condition > THEN <conclusion>.

A rule can be composed by conjunctions and disjunctions and can take more than one conclusion simultaneously. For example:

IF (<condition 1> OR < condition 2>) AND (<condition 3>)
THEN (<conclusion 1> AND < conclusion 2>).

The rule above is equivalent to a set of rules with only one conclusion, as the following:

IF (<condition 1> OR <condition 2>) AND (<condition 3>)
THEN <conclusion 1>
IF (<condition 1> OR <condition 2>) AND (<condition 3>)
THEN <conclusion 2>.

Each rule is related to a variable of interest and experts can have their own opinion about a specific fact. However, it is important the prevention of conflicts among those opinions in order to keep the knowledge consistency. That means the system should never conclude "yes" and "no" from the same information. When variable values are measured by an external subsystem and sending to the expert system, the inference system must activate rules in a knowledge base, which is able to evaluate the data received and to generate conclusions.

4.5.2 *Using Fuzzy Logic*

As mentioned before, in intelligent evaluation systems the expert knowledge is stored in a knowledge database using a logical representation as, for example, rules. Then, the architecture formed by knowledge base and inference system is named "expert system". However, there are cases in which features cannot be measured with the precision requested or the expert recognizes that the knowledge is not valid in specific situations. In those situations, some coefficients of certainty can be introduced to measure that uncertainty in the conclusion of rule, which can be treated by probabilities [49], belief and plausibility [53], and possibilities [12], among others.

In (classical) set theory, each subset A of a universe X can be expressed by means of a membership function $\mu_A\colon X \rightarrow \{0,1\}$, where, for a given $a \in X$, $\mu_A\ (a) = 1$ and $\mu_A\ (a) = 0$ respectively, express the presence and absence of a in relation to A. A fuzzy set [63] is used to model an ill-known quantity. A fuzzy set A on X is characterized by its membership function $\mu_A\colon X \rightarrow [0,1]$, where [0,1] can be any bounded scale. We say that a fuzzy set A of X is "precise" when $\exists\ c^* \in X$ such that $\mu_A(c^*)=1$ and $\forall c \neq c^*$, $\mu_A(c)=0$. A fuzzy set A will be said to be "crisp" when $\forall c \in X$, $\mu_A(c) \in \{0,1\}$.

When there is subjectivity in the knowledge base, its representation can be done by fuzzy models [65], using fuzzy sets. In fuzzy expert systems, fuzzy rules model the knowledge about a procedure. For example, using a fuzzy expert system coupled to a surgical simulator based on virtual reality, experts can define, in an imprecise way, regions of tissue and bones in where is possible to find bone marrow harvest. To evaluate a user, values of variables are collected by a haptic device and sent to expert system for evaluation. The system must analyse each step performed by users and classify users, at the end of training, according to predefined performance classes. Machado *et al.* [24] used five performance classes, described by the following fuzzy sets: *you need much more training, you need more training, you need training, your training is good* or *your training is excellent*, to identify if more training of bone marrow harvest procedure is or not necessary. The fuzzy rules of expert system are modeled by membership functions according to specifications of experts. Several types of membership functions can be used as trapezoidal, triangular and pi-functions and the fuzzy inference system used is Mamdani-type [28]. An example of rule for this expert system is:

IF Position_x is left_center AND Position_y is up_center

AND Position_needle is acceptable AND Marrow_harvest is yes

THEN Trainee_class is you_need_training

where: Position_x, Position_y are coordinates which the needle touch the patient body; Position_needle is the angle of needle input to body of patient; Marrow_harvest shows the success or failure of trainee to harvest bone marrow and Trainee_class is the classification of trainee.

In case of bone marrow harvest, this procedure is blind made. Therefore, human experts can only evaluate the procedure through their external impressions of the patient's body, because it is only what they can see. The evaluation system proposed by Machado *et al.* [24] has privileged information because it can obtain external and internal data about patient's body.

Table 4.2 Visual and haptic properties description

	Color	Texture	Viscosity	Cervix elasticity
Normal	rosy	similar to buccal mucous membrane	smooth	Similar to an orthopedic rubber
Herpes / HPV	white with warts	spongy and irregular	with bubbles	very soft
Inflamed	red	similar to buccal mucous membrane	smooth	hard/tense

4.5.3 *Combining Expert Systems*

In some cases, knowledge modelling of a complex procedure can demand a particular approach. Some medical exams require sequential steps and different knowledge for each one. For example, gynaecological exam is one of the most important exams to female health and allows detecting pathologies that can evolve to cervix cancer. The gynaecological examination is performed in two steps. In the first stage is used an instrument named speculum to allow the visualization of the vagina walls and of the cervix to check colour and surface of these structures. In the second stage there isn't visual information. The doctor uses a lubricated glove to touch vagina walls and cervix to identify any wounds or lumps. When touch the cervix, the doctor will also feel its elasticity. In general, this kind of exam presents some difficulties. One example can be the patient's discomfort when this exam is performed in the presence of a medicine student (apprentice). This occurs because the only way of training is by the observation and experimentation. Other difficulty is related to the students' absence of opportunity to practice all possible cases, what result in an incomplete training. The Simulator for Gynaecological Exam (SITEG) [26] allows the training of gynaecological exam and simulates different phases of pathologies. The simulator presents randomly normal, HPV or Herpes and inflamed cases to the user. The two stages of a real exam were divided to compose a visual and a touch exam. In the visual exam, the user must observe the vagina walls and cervix and notice their colouring, as it is showed at Table 4.2. After the visual exam, the user will have only the external view of the vagina and must perform a touch examination perceive the texture and detect if there is wounds or lumps. A haptic device is used to allow touch and force feedback in the touch examination (Figure 4.6).

The evaluation system for SITEG is based on two fuzzy rule-based expert systems, each one according to the knowledge obtained from an expert, as presented in Figure 4.7. The first corresponds to the visual stage of the exam and the second corresponds to the touch stage. In the visual stage, the user must identify the cervix colouring according to a diagno-

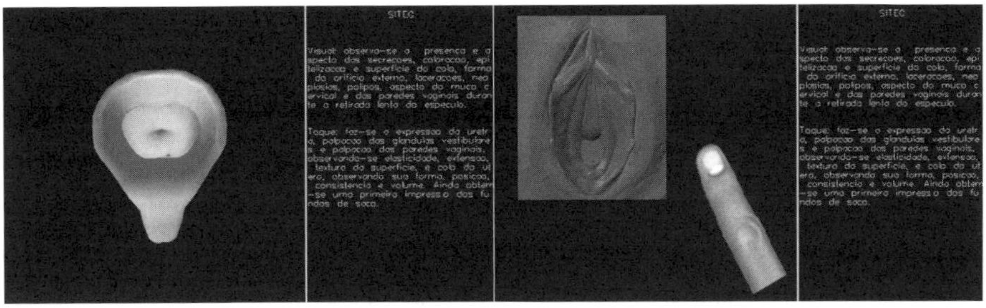

Figure 4.6 Gynaecological examination performed in a VR-based simulator: (left) visual exam with a speculum (grey object) and (right) external view of the unidigital exam.

sis of normality, Herpes/HPV or inflamed. Each colouring has its own fuzzy membership function: normal (rosy), Herpes or HPV (white) and inflamed (red). At the end of the first stage the user must provide to the system his opinion about the colouring and his diagnosis. The evaluation system compares it to the information related to the case presented and stores it in a database that will be used by the second fuzzy rule-based expert system in the second stage. In the second stage, the users perform the touch exam and emit again an opinion according to the possible diagnosis: normal, Herpes/HPV or inflamed. This information will be used and stored by the second fuzzy rule-based expert system. At the end of both stages, the evaluation system will request from the user a final diagnosis that should be chosen among:

$$D = \{\text{normal, inflamed, herpes or HPV, doubt}\}.$$

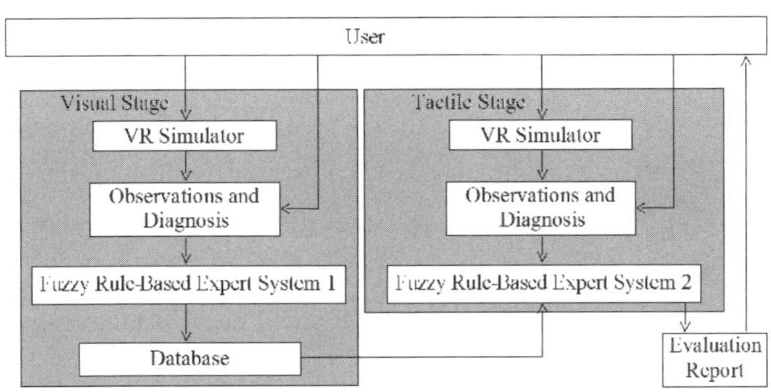

Figure 4.7 Diagram of the evaluation system.

In this case, the "doubt" option is pertinent due to the combination of information during a real exam that allows doctors to define a final diagnosis. It happens because contradictions about what the doctor decides on the patient's conditions between the first and second stage of the exam can occur.

Internally, the evaluation system executes in real-time the rules of each stage according to the case presented to users. The evaluation system is also capable to decide if the training was successful by the combination of the two stages and the final diagnosis with the case presented by the simulator. This way, the evaluation system can classify the user into classes of performance. This system uses five classes of performance:

(a) user is qualified to execute a real procedure;
(b) user is almost qualified to execute a real procedure, performance is good, but it can be better;
(c) user needs training to be qualified, performance is regular;
(d) user needs more training to be qualified, performance is bad;
(e) user is a beginner, performance is very poor.

It is important to mention that in cases of wrong diagnosis, the evaluation system is able to detect where the user made a mistake by the analysis of the degrees of pertinence of his information. All these information, including the users' class of performance, is provided to user in the evaluation report (Figure 4.7). Due to all those features, that assessment methodology can be used in continuous evaluation of training.

4.6 Evaluation Based on Mixture Models

4.6.1 *Gaussian Mixture Models*

There are cases in which statistical distributions of data cannot be assumed as Gaussian distributions (univariate or multivariate). Thus, a possible solution is modeling them using mixture models [29]. Moraes and Machado [32] presented a solution using Gaussian Mixture Models (GMM) as the kernel of an evaluation system. This section presents the GMM method for training evaluation. Parameter estimation equations for training expert models are presented first. After, the GMM method for training classification is then described as a maximum likelihood classifier. We follow the Tran *et al.* [59] explanation about GMM algorithm and classification.

Let $X = \{x_1, x_2, \ldots, x_T\}$ be a set of T vectors, where each one is a d-dimensional feature vector extracted by T different information at virtual space, obtained by the simulator. This information can be applied forces, angles, position and torque extracted at d different interval of time. Since the distribution of these vectors is unknown, it is approximately modeled by a mixture of Gaussian densities as the weighted sum of c component densities, given by (1).

$$p(x_t \mid \lambda_k) = \sum_{i=1}^{c} w_i N(x_t, \mu_i, \Sigma_i), \quad t = 1, \ldots, T, \tag{1}$$

where λ denotes a prototype consisting of a set of model parameters $\lambda = \{w_i,\ \mu_i,\ \Sigma_i\}$, w_i, $i = 1, \ldots, c$, are the mixture weights and $N(x_t, \mu_i, \Sigma_i)$ are the d-variate Gaussian component densities with mean vectors μ_i and covariance matrices Σ_i:

$$N(x_t,\ \mu_i,\ \Sigma_i) = \exp\{-1/2\}(x_t - \mu_i)' \Sigma_i^{-1} (x_t - \mu_i)\}/(2\pi)^{d/2} |\Sigma_i|^{1/2}. \tag{2}$$

To train the GMM, those parameters are estimated such that they best match the distribution of the training vectors. The maximum likelihood estimation is widely used as a training method. For a sequence of training vectors X for a λ, the likelihood of the GMM is done by:

$$p(X \mid \lambda) = \prod_{t=1}^{T} p(x_t \mid \lambda). \tag{3}$$

The aim of maximum likelihood estimation is to find a new parameter model $\overline{\lambda}$ such that $p(X \mid \overline{\lambda}) \geqslant p(X \mid \lambda)$. Since the expression in (3) is a nonlinear function of parameters in λ, its direct maximization is not possible. However, these parameters can be obtained iteratively using the Expectation-Maximization algorithm [10]. In this algorithm, an auxiliary function Q is used as follows:

$$Q(\lambda, \overline{\lambda}) = \sum_{t=1}^{T} \sum_{i=1}^{c} p(i \mid x_t, \lambda) \log \left[w_i N(x_t, \overline{\mu_i}, \overline{\Sigma_i}) \right] \tag{4}$$

where $p(i \mid x_t, \lambda)$ is the *a posteriori* probability for performance class i, $i = 1, \ldots, c$ and satisfies

$$p(i \mid x_t, \lambda) = \left[w_i N(x_t, \mu_i, \Sigma_i) \right] / \left\{ \sum_{k=1}^{c} w_k N(x_t, \mu_k, \Sigma_k) \right\} \tag{5}$$

The Expectation-Maximization algorithm is such that if $Q(\lambda, \overline{\lambda}) \geqslant Q(\lambda, \lambda)$ then $p(x \mid \overline{\lambda}) \geqslant p(x \mid \lambda)$ [46]. The setting of derivatives of Q function with respect to λ to zero, found the following reestimation formulas:

$$\overline{w_i} = \frac{1}{t} \sum_{t=1}^{t} p(i \mid x_t, \lambda) \tag{6}$$

$$\overline{\mu_i} = \sum_{t=1}^{t} [p(i \mid x_t, \lambda) x_t] / [\sum_{t=1}^{t} [p(i \mid x_t, \lambda)] \tag{7}$$

$$\overline{\Sigma_i} = \left\{ \sum_{t=1}^{T} p(i \mid x_t, \lambda)(x_t - \overline{\mu_i})(x_t - \overline{\mu_i})' \right\} / \left[\sum_{t=1}^{T} p(i \mid x_t, \lambda) \right] \tag{8}$$

The algorithm for training the GMM is described as follows:

1. Generate the *a posteriori* probability $p(i \mid x_t, \lambda)$ at random satisfying (5);
2. Compute the mixture weight, the mean vector, and the covariance matrix following (6), (7) and (8);
3. Update the *a posteriori* probability $p(i \mid x_t, \lambda)$ according to (5) and compute the Q function using (4);
4. Stop if the increase in the value of the Q function at the current iteration, relative to the value of the Q function at the previous iteration, is below a chosen threshold; otherwise go to step 2.

To provide GMM classification, several classes of performance λ are needed. So, let λ_k, $k = 1, \ldots, N$, denote models of N possible classes of performance. Given a feature vector sequence X, a classifier is designed to classify X into N classes of performance by using N discriminant functions $g_k(X)$, computing the similarities between the unknown X and each class of performance λ_k and selecting the class of performance λ_{k^*} if [59]:

$$k^* = \arg\max_{1 \leqslant k \leqslant N} \quad g_k(X) \tag{9}$$

In the minimum-error-rate classifier, the discriminant function is the *a posteriori* probability:

$$g_k(X) = p(\lambda_k \mid X) \tag{10}$$

It can be used the Bayes' rule

$$p(\lambda_k \mid x) = [p(\lambda_k)\, p(x \mid \lambda_k)]/p(x) \tag{11}$$

and assume equal likelihood of all performances, *i.e.*, $p(\lambda_k) = 1/N$. Since $p(X)$ is the same for all performance models, the discriminant function in (10) is equivalent to the following [19]:

$$g_k(X) = p(X \mid \lambda_k) \tag{12}$$

Finally, using the log-likelihood, the decision rule used for class of performance identification is:

$$\text{Select performance model } k^* \text{ if } k^* = \arg\max_{1 \leqslant k \leqslant N} \quad \sum_{t=1}^{t} p(x_t \mid \lambda_k) \tag{13}$$

where $p(x_t \mid \lambda_k)$ is given by (1) for each k, $k = 1, \ldots, N$.

4.6.2 *Fuzzy Gaussian Mixture Models*

In cases in which there is imprecision in variables measures or multiple ways of correct execution of a procedure, evaluation can use a fuzzy approach. In those cases a fuzzy approach for GMM can be used. Tran *et al.* [59] proposed an approach named FGMM that was followed by Moraes and Machado [33], as a kernel of another evaluation system. They used a modification of Fuzzy C-Means algorithm to estimate the GMM parameters. The main advantage of their approach is the ability of recognition of different geometric shape distributions in X using covariance matrices and mixture weights Tran and Wagner [56]. From within-groups sum of squared error function, Bezdek [4] defined as objective function:

$$J_m(U,\lambda) = \sum_{t=1}^{t} \sum_{i=1}^{c} u_{it}^m d_{it}^2 \tag{14}$$

where $U = \{u_{it}\}$ is a fuzzy c-partition of X, each u_{it} represents the degree of vector x_t belonging to the ith class. For $1 \leqslant i \leqslant c$ and $1 \leqslant t \leqslant T$, we have:

$$0 \leqslant u_{it} \leqslant 1, \quad \sum_{i=1}^{c} u_{it}^m = 1 \quad \text{and} \quad 0 < \sum_{t=1}^{t} u_{it} < T \tag{15}$$

$m \geqslant 1$ is a weighting exponent on each fuzzy membership u_{it} and it is called the degree of fuzziness; and a measure of dissimilarity, denoted by $d_{it}^2 > 0$, which is the distance in (14), given by:

$$\begin{aligned} d_{it}^2 &= -\log p(x_t, i \mid \overline{\lambda}) = -\log[\overline{w}_i N(x_t, \overline{\mu}_i, \overline{\Sigma}_i)] \\ &= -\log \overline{w}_i + \frac{1}{2}\log(2\pi)^d \mid \overline{\Sigma}_i \mid + \frac{1}{2}(x_t - \overline{\mu}_i)' \overline{\Sigma}_i^{-1} (x_t - \overline{\mu}_i). \end{aligned} \tag{16}$$

Substituting (16) in (14), it gives

$$\begin{aligned} J_m(U,\lambda) = -\sum_{t=1}^{t}\sum_{i=1}^{c} u_{it}^m \log \overline{w}_i - \sum_{t=1}^{t}\sum_{i=1}^{c} u_{it}^m \left[\frac{1}{2}\log(2\pi)^d \mid \overline{\Sigma}_i \mid\right] \\ - \sum_{t=1}^{t}\sum_{i=1}^{c} u_{it}^m \left[\frac{1}{2}(x_t - \overline{\mu_i})' \overline{\Sigma}_i^{-1} (x_t - \overline{\mu_i})\right] \end{aligned} \tag{17}$$

Minimizing J_m is performed using Lagrange multiplier Method and it gives [58]:

$$\overline{w_i} = \sum_{t=1}^{t} u_{it}^m \Big/ \sum_{i=1}^{c}\sum_{t=1}^{t} u_{it}^m \tag{18}$$

$$\overline{\mu_i} = \sum_{t=1}^{t} u_{it}^m x_t \Big/ \sum_{t=1}^{t} u_{it}^m \tag{19}$$

$$\overline{\Sigma_i} = \left\{ \sum_{t=1}^{t} u_{it}^m (x_t - \mu_i)'(x_t - \mu_i) \right\} \Big/ \sum_{t=1}^{t} u_{it}^m \tag{20}$$

The algorithm for training a FGMM is the following [55]:

1. Choose c and m, $2 < c < T$, $m > 1$. Generate matrix U at random satisfying (15);
2. For $i = 1, \ldots, c$, compute the fuzzy mixture weights, the fuzzy mean vectors, and the fuzzy covariance matrices following (18), (19) and (20).
3. Compute the d_{it}, $1 \leqslant i \leqslant c$ and $1 \leqslant t \leqslant T$, following (16). Update matrix U using:
$$u_{it} = \left[\sum_{k=1}^{c} \left(\frac{d_{it}}{d_{kt}} \right)^{(2/(m-1))} \right]^{-1}, \qquad (21)$$
if $d_{it} = 0$ for some t, set $u_{it} = 1$, $u_{is} = 0$, for all $s \neq t$.
4. Stop if the decrease in the value of the fuzzy objective function $J_m(U, \overline{\lambda})$ at the current iteration relative to the value of the $J_m(U, \overline{\lambda})$ function at the previous iteration is below a chosen threshold, otherwise go to step 2.

In the GMM algorithm, given the training sequence X, the model parameters $\overline{\lambda}$ are determined such that the function $Q(\lambda, \overline{\lambda})$ in (4) is maximized and thus the likelihood function $p(X \mid \overline{\lambda})$ is maximized too. Then, by use of log-likelihood in discriminant function done by (12), is obtained the decision rule for class of performance identification done by (13). In FGMM method, there are two cases [55] to select the discriminant function: m is closed to one (inclusive) or $m > 1$ and m is not close to one. In the first case, to minimize J_m is equivalent to maximize $Q(\lambda, \overline{\lambda})$ done by (4) in GMM. Thus, the decision rule used for identification in FGMM is the same that applied in GMM done by (13). In the second case, to minimize J_m is not equivalent to maximize $Q(\lambda, \overline{\lambda})$. Then, an alternative discriminant function must be chosen

$$Q_m(U, \lambda) = -J_m(U, \lambda) = \sum_{i=1}^{c} \sum_{t=1}^{t} u_{it}^{m} \log \left[\overline{w}_i N(x_t, \overline{\mu}_i, \overline{\Sigma}_i) \right] \qquad (22)$$

According to Tran and Wagner [55], the U matrix in $Q_m(U, \lambda)$ is replaced by (21) and (16) in order to reduce computations

$$Q_m(U, \lambda) = Q_m(\lambda) = \sum_{t=1}^{t} \left\{ \sum_{i=1}^{c} \left[-\log p(x_t, i \mid \overline{\lambda}) \right]^{(1/(m-1))} \right\}^{1-m} \qquad (23)$$

Let λ_k, $k = 1, \ldots, N$, denote models of N possible classes of performance. Given a feature vector sequence X, a classifier is designed to classify X into N classes of performance by using N discriminant functions $g_k(X)$, such as

$$g_k(X) = Q_m(\lambda_k). \qquad (24)$$

Finally, the decision rule used for class of performance identification is:

Select performance model k^* if

$$k^* = \arg\max_{1 \leqslant k \leqslant N} \sum_{t=1}^{t} \left\{ \sum_{i=1}^{c} \left[-\log p(x_t, i \mid \overline{\lambda}) \right]^{(1/(m-1))} \right\}^{1-m} \qquad (25)$$

It is important to note that the decision rule in (24) can also be applied to the first case when m is close to one.

4.6.3 *Sequential Methods*

There are ways of improve the results of a classifier using another classifier after that. In training evaluation based on virtual reality some methods based on 1) Gaussian Mixture Models and Relaxation Labeling and 2) Fuzzy Gaussian Mixture Models and Fuzzy Relaxation Labeling can be found in literature. Those methods are explained as follows.

4.6.3.1 *Gaussian Mixture Models and Relaxation Labeling*

The GMMs and FGMMs methods were presented in previous sections as a good option for training evaluation based on virtual reality. However, according to Tran *et al.* [59], the use of Relaxation Labeling (RL) after Gaussian Mixture Models can provide better results. Moraes and Machado [34] proposed the composition GMM-RL as a kernel of a training evaluation system in virtual reality based environments.

Rosenfeld *et al.* [51] introduced the Relaxation Labeling (RL): an interactive approach to update probabilities of a previous classification. It has been successfully employed in image classification [13]. For VR evaluation purposes, RL will be used after a GMM classification. Then, denote a set of objects $A = \{a_1, a_2, \ldots, a_N\}$ and a set of labels $\Lambda = \{\lambda_1, \lambda_2, \ldots, \lambda_N\}$. An initial probability is given to each object a_t having each label λ_k, which is denoted by $p_t(\lambda_k)$. These probabilities satisfy the following condition:

$$\sum_{k=1}^{N} p_t(\lambda_k) = 1, \text{ for all } a_t \in A \tag{26}$$

The RL updates the probabilities $p_t(\lambda_k)$ using a set of compatibility coefficients $r_{tt'}(\lambda_k, \lambda_l)$, where $r_{tt'}(\lambda_k, \lambda_l) : \Lambda \times \Lambda \to [-1, 1]$, whose magnitude denotes the strength of compatibility. The meaning of these compatibility coefficients can be interpreted as [59]:

a) If $r_{tt'}(\lambda_k, \lambda_l) < 0$, then λ_k, λ_l are incompatible for a_t and $a_{t'}$;
b) If $r_{tt'}(\lambda_k, \lambda_l) = 0$, then λ_k, λ_l are independent for a_t and $a_{t'}$;
c) If $r_{tt'}(\lambda_k, \lambda_l) > 0$, then λ_k, λ_l are compatible for a_t and $a_{t'}$;

Two possible methods employ the concepts of statistical correlation and mutual information for computing coefficients. The two methods are based on those developed by Peleg and Rosenfeld [45]. The correlation-based estimation of the compatibility coefficients is defined as

$$r_{tt'}(\lambda_k)(\lambda_l) = \frac{\sum_{t=1}^{t} [p_t(\lambda_k) - p(\lambda_k)][p_{t'}(\lambda_l) - p(\lambda_l)]}{\sigma(\lambda_k)\sigma(\lambda_l)} \tag{27}$$

where $p_{t'}(\lambda_l)$ is the probability of $a_{t'}$ having label λ_l and $a_{t'}$ are the neighbors of a_t, $p(\lambda_l)$ is the mean of $p_{t'}(\lambda_l)$ for all $a_{t'}$, and $\sigma(\lambda_l)$ is standard deviation of $p_{t'}(\lambda_l)$. In order to minimize the effect of dominance among labels, the modified coefficients are [59]:

$$r^*_{tt'}(\lambda_k)(\lambda_l) = [1 - p(\lambda_k)][1 - p(\lambda_l)]r_{tt'}(\lambda_k)(\lambda_l) \tag{28}$$

and the mutual-information based estimate of compatibility coefficient is

$$r_{tt'}(\lambda_k)(\lambda_l) = \log \frac{t \sum_{t=1}^{t} p_t(\lambda_k)p_{t'}(\lambda_l)}{\sum_{t=1}^{t} p_t(\lambda_k)\, p_{t'}(\lambda_l)} \tag{29}$$

The compatibility coefficients in (29) must be scaled in the range $[-1,1]$. The updating factor for the estimation $p_t(\lambda_k)$ at the mth interaction is:

$$q_t^{(m)}(\lambda_k) = \sum_{t'=1}^{t} d_{tt'} \left[\sum_{l=1}^{N} r_{tt'}(\lambda_k)(\lambda_l) p_{t'}^{(m)}(\lambda_l) \right] \tag{30}$$

where $d_{tt'}$ are the parameters that weight the contributions to a_t coming from its neighbors $a_{t'}$ and subject to

$$\sum_{t'=1}^{t} d_{tt'} = 1 \tag{31}$$

The updated probability $p_t^{(m+1)}(\lambda_k)$ for object a_t is given by:

$$p_t^{(m+1)}(\lambda_k) = \frac{p_t^{(m)}(\lambda_k)\left[1 + q_t^{(m)}(\lambda_k)\right]}{\sum_{k=1}^{N} p_t^{(m)}(\lambda_k)\left[1 + q_t^{(m)}(\lambda_k)\right]} \tag{32}$$

The RL algorithm can be outlined as follows:

1. estimate the initial probabilities for each object satisfying (26);
2. compute the compatibility coefficients using (28) or (29);
3. calculate the updating factor defined in (30);
4. update the probabilities for each object using the updating rule in (32);
5. repeat steps 3 and 4 until the change in the probability is less than a chosen threshold or equal to a chosen number of interactions.

Clearly, for a successful performance in a relaxation method processing, the initial label probabilities and the compatibility coefficients need to be well determined. Wrong estimations of these parameters will lead to algorithmic instabilities. In the GMM-based classification, the initial probabilities in the RL are defined as the *a posteriori* probabilities. Objects are now feature vectors considered in the GMM and labels are classes of performance identification. Unlike the relaxation labeling for image recognition where the m-connected neighbouring pixels may belong to different regions, in performance identification, all unknown feature vectors in the sequence $X = \{x_1, x_2, \dots, x_T\}$ are known to belong to a certain class of performance λ. Therefore, there isn't necessity to consider the compatibility between an input vector and its adjacent vectors [59]. This leads to:

$$p_{t'}(\lambda_l) = p_t(\lambda_l) \tag{33}$$

which means that compatibility between different labels is only considered for a same object. Thus, the updating rule in (32) should be now rewritten [59] as follows:

$$p_t^{(m+1)}(\lambda_k) = \frac{p_t^{(m)}(\lambda_k)\left[1 - q_t^{(m)}(\lambda_k)\right]}{\sum\limits_{k=1}^{N} p_t^{(m)}(\lambda_k)\left[1 - q_t^{(m)}(\lambda_k)\right]} \tag{34}$$

The GMM-RL algorithm for class of performance identification is stated as follows.

1. Estimate the initial probabilities for each class of performance using the *a posteriori* probabilities in (3):

$$p_t(\lambda_k) = p(\lambda_k \mid x_t) = \frac{[p(x_t \mid \lambda_k)p(\lambda_k)]}{\left[\sum\limits_{k=1}^{N} p(x_t \mid \lambda_k)\, p(\lambda_k)\right]} \tag{35}$$

   where $p(\lambda_k) = 1/N$ and $p(x_t \mid \lambda_k)$ is computed as in (1);
2. Compute the compatibility coefficients using (28) or (29), where $t' = t$ (no neighbours considered);
3. Calculate the updating factor defined in (30), where $t' = t$ and $d_{tt'} = 1/T$ for simplicity;
4. Update the probabilities for each class of performance using the updating rule in (32);
5. Repeat steps 3 and 4 until the change in the probability is less than chosen threshold or equal to a chosen number of interactions;
6. The probability of each class of performance $p(\lambda_k)$ after RL algorithm is computed by:

$$p(\lambda_k) = \prod_{t=1}^{T} p_t(\lambda_k) \tag{36}$$

where $p_t(\lambda_k)$ is the *a posteriori* probability used in (10). Therefore, the decision rule for class of performance identification is as follow [59]:

$$\text{Select class of performance } k^* \text{ if}$$
$$k^* = \underset{1 \leqslant k \leqslant N}{\arg\max}\, p(\lambda_k) \tag{37}$$

4.6.3.2 *Fuzzy Gaussian Mixture Models and Fuzzy Relaxation Labeling*

The RL model proposed by Rosenfeld *et al.* [51] has been widely used for several applications with good performance [45]. However, several non-normalized models were also proposed [17]. According to Borotschnig *et al.* [7] non-normalized models are widely used as Fuzzy Relaxation Labeling (FRL). The main advantage is that non-normalized models allow multiple labels for one object.

Machado and Moraes [22] proposed the use of a two-stage evaluator where: FGMM is the first stage and FRL is the second stage. It is possible to consider previous results obtained from the FGMM method as initial degrees of membership to each object a_t having each label λ_k which is denoted by $\phi_t(\lambda_k)$ [5]. The FRL method updates the membership degrees $\phi_t(\lambda_k)$ and $\phi_t^{(n+1)}(\lambda_k)$ is obtained. Among existing FRL methods in literature, it was chosen that proposed by Borotschnig *et al.* [7]:

$$\phi_t^{(m+1)}(\lambda_k) = \frac{1}{N} \sum_{j=1}^{N} \max_{T} \left[r_{tj} \wedge \phi_t(\lambda_k) \right] \tag{38}$$

where $\wedge$ means the logical operator "AND" which can be translated by a t-norm (as for example *min*).

The FRL method stops when the changes in the pertinence degrees are smaller than a chosen threshold or when ends the number of interactions previously defined.

4.7 Evaluation Methods Based on Hidden Markov Models

4.7.1 *Discrete Hidden Markov Models (DHMM)*

Baum and his colleagues published in the late 1960s and early 1970s the basic theory of Hidden Markov Models (HMM) [2, 3]. In the classical HMM five elements are necessary to specify a discrete HMM [46]. Denote a HMM by $\lambda = (A, B, \pi)$, when is needed:

(i) the number N of states in the model;
(ii) the number M of distinct observation symbols per state, *i.e.*, the discrete output of system;

(iii) the state transition probability distribution matrix, denoted by $A = \{a_{ij}\}$;
(iv) the observation symbol probability distribution in state j, denoted by $B = \{b_j(k)\}$; and
(v) the initial state distribution $\pi = \{\pi_i\}$, where $1 \leqslant i, j \leqslant N$ and $1 \leqslant k \leqslant M$.

Given the HMM form, there are three basic problems of interest that must be solved for the model to be useful in real applications. These problems are:

1. Evaluation problem: Given the observation sequence in time $O = o_1, o_2, \ldots, o_T$ and a model λ, how to efficiently compute $P(O \mid \lambda)$, the probability of the observation sequence, given a model?
2. Uncover the hidden part of the model: Given the observation sequence $O = o_1, o_2, \ldots, o_T$ and a model λ, how to choose a corresponding state sequence $S = s_1, s_2, \ldots, s_T$ which is optimal in some meaningful sense (*i.e.*, best "explains" the observations)?
3. Optimise the model parameters: How to adjust the model parameters $\lambda = (A, B, \pi)$ to maximise $P(O \mid \lambda)$?

To solve the first problem, we can use the *Forward-Backward Procedure* [46]. The second problem is an optimisation problem and it can be solved by using the *Viterbi Algorithm* [52]. The last problem can be solved by an iterative procedure such as the Baum-Welch Method (or equivalently the EM - expectation-maximisation-method) [46]. In next section, the notation used by Rabiner [46] will be followed.

4.7.2 *Continuous Hidden Markov Models*

For most applications, the observations are continuous vectors. It can be used Vector Quantization (VQ) to generate codebooks and use DHMM. However, to do this it is necessary training data for all classes. When a new class is added, the system must be trained from the beginning again. In CHMM, is only needed to train the newly added class. The densities are considered as a mixture of Gaussians.

$$b_j(o_t) = P(o_t \mid \lambda) = \sum_{k=1}^{M} w_{jk}\, N(o_t, \mu_{jk}, \Sigma_{jk}) \tag{39}$$

where o_t, $t = 1, \ldots, T$, are observation vectors being modelled, w_{jk}, $j = 1, \ldots, N$, $k = 1, \ldots, M$, are mixture coefficients and $N(o_t, \mu_{jk}, \Sigma_{jk})$ is a Gaussian with a mean vector μ_{jk} and covariance matrix Σ_{jk} for the kth mixture component in the state j, done by:

$$N(o_t, \mu_{jk}, \Sigma_{jk}) = \frac{1}{(2\pi)^{N/2} \mid \Sigma_{jk} \mid^{1/2}} \times \exp\left\{ -\frac{1}{2}(o_t - \mu_{jk})'(\Sigma_{jk})^{-1}(o_t - \mu_{jk}) \right\} \tag{40}$$

and the following constrains are satisfied:

$$w_{jk} > 0; \quad \sum_{k=1}^{M} w_{jk} = 1; \quad \int_{-\infty}^{+\infty} b_j(o_t)do_t = 1 \tag{41}$$

An iterative reestimation process is used to found the coefficients. Rabiner [46] described a procedure for providing good initial estimates of the model parameters called the segmental K-means [20]. It is a variant of the classical K-means algorithm [19] for clustering data.

4.7.3 *Comparison of Hidden Markov Models*

In a training evaluation is important to compare two HMMs. Let be $\lambda_1 = (A_1, B_1, \pi_1)$ and $\lambda_2 = (A_2, B_2, \pi_2)$, two different HMMs. It is wanted to measure the similarity of two models, which is done by a distance measure between two HMMs, denoted by $D(\lambda_1, \lambda_2)$:

$$D(\lambda_1, \lambda_2) = \frac{1}{T}\left[\log P(O^{(2)} \mid \lambda_1) - \log P(O^{(2)} \mid \lambda_2)\right] \tag{42}$$

where $O^{(2)} = O_1, O_2, \ldots, O_T$ is a sequence of observations generated by model λ_2. Thus, (42) is a measure of how well model λ_1 matches observations generated by λ_2, relative to how well model λ_2 matches observations generated by itself [46]. Unfortunately, this measure is nonsymmetrical. Hence, a natural expression for this measure is the symmetrised version:

$$D_S(\lambda_1, \lambda_2) = \frac{D(\lambda_1, \lambda_2) + D(\lambda_2, \lambda_1)}{2} \tag{43}$$

4.7.4 *Fuzzy Hidden Markov Models*

There are several fuzzy approaches for HMM and the continuous versions of Fuzzy HMMs are particularly interesting for training evaluation [35]. Among those approaches, it can be cited those proposed by Tran and his colleagues [57, 60] and by Mohamed and Gader [30]. In this section, the first one is followed and denoted by FHMM.

Let $u_{ijt} = u_{ijt}(O)$ be the membership function, denoting the degree, to which the observation sequence O belongs to state i at time t and to state j at time $t+1$, satisfying:

$$0 \leqslant u_{ijt} \leqslant 1; \quad \sum_{i=1}^{N}\sum_{j=1}^{N} u_{ijt} = 1; \quad 0 < \sum_{t=1}^{T} u_{ijt} < T \tag{44}$$

Using the fuzzy EM Algorithm [57], it can be shown that the reestimation equations for coefficients of the mixture of densities done by (39) are:

$$\overline{w}_{jk} = \left\{ \sum_{t=1}^{T} \overline{u}_{jkt}^{m} \right\} \Big/ \left\{ \sum_{t=1}^{T} \sum_{k=1}^{M} \overline{u}_{jkt}^{m} \right\}$$

$$\overline{\mu}_{jk} = \left\{ \sum_{t=1}^{T} \overline{u}_{jkt}^{m} o_t \right\} \Big/ \left\{ \sum_{t=1}^{T} \overline{u}_{jkt}^{m} \right\} \tag{45}$$

$$\overline{\Sigma}_{jk} = \left\{ \sum_{t=1}^{T} \overline{u}_{ikt}^{m} (o_t - \overline{\mu}_{jk})(o_t - \overline{\mu}_{jk})' \right\} \Big/ \left\{ \sum_{t=1}^{T} \overline{u}_{jkt}^{m} \right\}$$

where the prime denotes vector transposition, $m \geqslant 1$ is a weighting exponent on each fuzzy membership $u_y(x)$ (and is called a degree of fuzziness) and

$$\overline{u}_{jkt} = \left[\sum_{i=1}^{N} \sum_{l=1}^{M} \left(\frac{d_{jkt}}{d_{ilt}} \right)^{(2/(m-1))} \right]^{-1}; \quad m > 1$$
$$\overline{u}_{jkt} = \eta_t(j,k); \quad m = 1 \tag{46}$$

where

$$d_{jkt}^2 = d_{jkt}^2(O) = -\log P(O, s_t = j, k_t = k \mid \lambda)$$
$$= -\log \left\{ \sum_{i=1}^{N} \alpha_t(i) a_{ij} \, w_{jk} \, N\left(o_t, \mu_{jk}, \sum_{jk} \right) \beta_{t+1}(j) \right\} \tag{47}$$

and

$$\eta_t(j,k) = P(s_t = j; k_t = k \mid O, \lambda)$$
$$= \{\alpha_t(j)\beta_t(j)\} / \left\{ \sum_{j=1}^{N} \alpha_t(j)\beta_t(j) \right\} \tag{48}$$
$$\times \left\{ w_{jk} N\left(o_t, \mu_{jk}, \sum_{jk} \right) \right\} \Big/ \left\{ \sum_{k=1}^{M} w_{jk} \, N\left(o_t, \mu_{jk}, \sum_{jk} \right) \right\}$$

where $\alpha_t(j)$ and $\beta_t(j)$ are the forward and backward respectively [47].

Let λ_z, $z = 1, \ldots, Z$, denote models of Z FHMMs modeled. Given a new feature vector sequence O', it is possible to classify O' in two different ways:

1) To verify the distances between each pair λ_z and $\lambda_{O'}$ and find the smaller [46], or
2) To use a discriminant criteria, to classify O' into one of Z models [60].

4.8 Evaluation Methods Based on Bayesian Models

4.8.1 *Maximum Likelihood*

Maximum Likelihood decision rule is the most common statistical technique used in data classification. Its application for training evaluation based on VR was presented by Moraes and Machado [36]. Formally, the classes of performance for an user are done by: w_i, $i = 1,\dots,M$, where M is the total number of classes of performance. It is possible to determine the most probable class of a vector of training data X, by conditional probabilities [19]:

$$P(w_i \mid X), \text{ where } i = 1,\dots,M. \tag{49}$$

The probability done by (49) gives the likelihood that for a data vector X, the correct class is w_i. Classification rule is performed according to

$$X \in w_i \text{ if } P(w_i \mid X) > P(w_j \mid X) \text{ for all } i \neq j. \tag{50}$$

However, all the probabilities done by (59) are unknown. So, probabilities denoted by $P(X \mid w_i)$ can be estimated if there is sufficient information available for each class of performance. Using the Bayes Theorem:

$$P(w_i \mid X) = \frac{P(X \mid w_i)P(w_i)}{P(X)}, \tag{51}$$

where $P(X) = \sum_{i=1}^{M} P(X \mid w_i)P(w_i)]$.
As $P(X)$ is the same for all classes w_i, then it is not relevant for data classification. In Bayesian theory, $P(w_i)$ is called *a priori* probability for w_i and $P(w_i \mid X)$ is *a posteriori* probability for w_i where X is known. Then, the classification rule done by (50) is modified:

$$X \in w_i \text{ if } P(w_i \mid X)P(w_i) > P(w_j \mid X)P(w_i) \text{ for all } i \neq j. \tag{52}$$

Equation (52) is known as the maximum likelihood decision rule or maximum likelihood classification. However, it can be convenient to use [19]:

$$g(X) = \ln[P(X \mid w_i)P(w_i)] = \ln[P(X \mid w_i)] + \ln[P(w_i)] \tag{53}$$

where $g(X)$ is known as the log-likelihood function and it is known as discriminant function. Equation (53) can be used to modify the formulation done by (52):

$$X \in w_i \text{ if } g_i(X) > g_j(X) \text{ for all } i \neq j. \tag{54}$$

It is important to note that if statistical distribution of training data can assume multivariate Gaussian distribution, the use of (54) has interesting computational properties [19]. If training data cannot assume that distribution, (54) can provide a significant reduction of computational cost of implementation. Thus, the user's interactions with the system are monitored and the information is sent to the evaluation system, where Maximim Likelihood is in its kernel.

4.8.2 *Fuzzy Bayes Rule*

Moraes and Machado [38] proposed an evaluation system based on Fuzzy Bayes Rule [54] that has similarities to the method presented in previous section and based on conditional probabilities.

The probability of a fuzzy event is defined by [64]: let $(\mathbb{R}^n, \phi, P)$ a space of probability where ϕ is an σ-algebra in $\mathbb{R}^n$ and P is a probability measure over $\mathbb{R}^n$. Then a fuzzy event in $\mathbb{R}^n$ is a set A in $\mathbb{R}^n$, with a membership function $\mu_A(x)$, where μ_A: $\mathbb{R}^n \rightarrow \{0,1\}$ is Borel-mensurable. The probability of a fuzzy event A is defined by Lebesgue-Stieltjes integral:

$$P(A) = \int_{\mathbb{R}^n} \mu_A(x) dP = E(\mu_A) \tag{55}$$

In others words, the probability of a fuzzy event A with the membership function μ_A is the expected value of the membership function μ_A.

Again, let the classes of performance for an user be done by w_i, $i = 1, \ldots, M$, where M is the total number of classes of performance. However, now is assumed that w_i are fuzzy sets over space of decision Ω. Let $\mu_{wi}(X)$ be the fuzzy membership function for each class w_i given by a fuzzy information font (for example, a rule composition system of the expert system, or a histogram of the sample data), according a vector of data X. In this case, we assume that the fuzzy information font is a histogram of the sample data.

By the use of fuzzy probabilities and fuzzy Bayes rule [54] in the classical Bayes rule, the fuzzy probability of the w_i class is given by the vector of data X:

$$P(w_i \mid X) = \frac{\mu_{wi}(X) P(X \mid w_i) P(w_i)}{P(X)} \tag{56}$$

where $P(X) = \sum_i \mu_{wi}(X) = 1$.

However, as the denominator is independent, then the Fuzzy Bayes classification rule is to assign the vector of training data X from the user to w_i class of performance if:

$$X \in w_i \text{ se } \mu_{wi}(X) P(w_i \mid X) P(w_i) > \mu_{wj}(X) P(w_j \mid X) P(w_i) \text{ for all } i \neq j \tag{57}$$

As in evaluation system based on Maximim Likelihood, the evaluation system based on Fuzzy Bayes Rule analyses data from user's interaction and emits a report about the user's performance at the end of the training.

4.8.3 *Naive Bayes*

The Naive Bayes (NB) method, also called discrete or multinomial NB, is a robust method for data classification. Formally, let performance classes w_i, be in space of decision $\Omega = \{1, \ldots, M\}$, where M is the total number of performance classes available. Based on that space of decision, a Naive Bayes classifier computes conditional class probabilities to predict the most probable class of a vector of training data X, where X is a vector with n features obtained when a training is performed, *i.e.* $X = \{X_1, X_2, \ldots, X_n\}$. From (51):

$$P(w_i \mid X) = \frac{P(X \mid w_i)P(w_i)}{P(X)} \Leftrightarrow$$

$$\Leftrightarrow P(w_i \mid X_1, X_2, \ldots, X_n) = \frac{P(X_1, X_2, \ldots, X_n \backslash w_i)P(w_i)}{P(X)} \tag{58}$$

However, as $P(X)$ is the same for all classes w_i, it is not relevant for data classification and can be rewritten as:

$$P(X \mid w_i)P(w_i) = P(X_1, X_2, \ldots, X_n \backslash w_i)P(w_i) \tag{59}$$

Equation (59) is equivalent to the joint probability model:

$$P(X_1, X_2, \ldots, X_n \backslash w_i)P(w_i) = P(X_1, X_2, \ldots, X_n, w_i) \tag{60}$$

From successive applications of the conditional probability definition over (60), can be obtained:

$$\begin{aligned} P(X_1, X_2, \ldots, X_n, w_i) &= P(w_i)P(X_1, X_2, \ldots, X_n \backslash w_i) \\ &= P(w_i)P(X_1 \backslash w_i)P(X_2, \ldots, X_n \backslash w_i, X_1) \\ &= P(w_i)P(X_1 \backslash w_i)P(X_2 \backslash w_i, X_1)P(X_3, \ldots, X_n \backslash w_i, X_1, X_2) \\ &\ldots \\ &= P(w_i)P(X_1 \backslash w_i)P(X_2 \backslash w_i, X_1) \ldots P(X_n \backslash w_i, X_1, X_2, \ldots, X_{n-1}) \end{aligned} \tag{61}$$

The Naive Bayes classifier receives this name because its naive assumption of each feature X_k is conditionally independent of every other feature X_l, for all $k \neq l \leqslant n$. It means that knowing the class is enough to determine the probability of a value X_k. This assumption simplifies the equation above, due to:

$$P(X_k \backslash w_i, X_l) = P(X_k \backslash w_i) \tag{62}$$

for each X_k and (60) can be rewritten as:

$$P(X_1, X_2, \ldots, X_n, w_i) = P(w_i)P(X_1 \backslash w_i)P(X_2 \backslash w_i) \cdots P(X_n \backslash w_i) \tag{63}$$

unless a scale factor S, which depends on $X_1, X_2, \ldots, X_n$. Finally, (58) can be expressed by:

$$P(w_i \mid X_1, X_2, \ldots, X_n) = \frac{1}{S} P(w_i) \prod_{k=1}^{n} P(X_k \backslash w_i) \tag{64}$$

Then, the classification rule for Naive Bayes is similar those done by (52):

$$\begin{gathered} X \in w_i \text{ if } P(w_i \mid X_1, X_2, \ldots, X_n) > P(w_j \mid X_1, X_2, \ldots, X_n) \\ \text{for all } \; i \neq j \text{ and } i, j \in \Omega, \end{gathered} \tag{65}$$

and $P(w_* \mid X_1, X_2, \ldots, X_n)$ with $^* = \{i, j \mid i, j \in \Omega\}$, is done by (64).
To estimate parameters for $P(X_k \backslash w_i)$ for each class i, it was used a maximum likelihood estimator, named P_e:

$$P_e(X_k \backslash w_i) = \#(X_k, w_i)/\#(w_i) \tag{66}$$

where $\#(X_k, w_i)$ is the number of sample cases belonging to class w_i and having the value X_k, $\#(w_i)$ as the number of sample cases that belong to the class w_i.
Previously, an expert performs several times the procedure labeling them into M classes of performance. The information of variability about these procedures is acquired using probability models, from the vector of the training data. When users perform the training in virtual reality simulator, the Assessment Tool based on Naive Bayes collects the data from their manipulation. All probabilities of that data for each class of performance are calculated by (66) and, at the end, the user is assigned to a w_i class of performance by (65) [39].

4.8.4 *Quantitative and Qualitative Evaluation Based on Naive Bayes*

The evaluation system based on Naive Bayes can be adapted to analyze simultaneously qualitative and quantitative information and improve decision quality for special cases. For example, in the bone marrow harvest procedure, some special cases can occur and it can require specific skills of physician. In the traditional transplant technique, multiple penetrations are required (up to 20 per patient) in order to obtain enough bone marrow for that transplant. This procedure requires specific applied force to trespass the bone and to reach the marrow, but to do not bypass it. For this reason, the repetitive procedures can cause loss of control or fatigue of physician. Another problem is the proximity between a first penetration and the next (generally about millimetres), which require sufficient dexterity of the operator. In the paediatric oncology, it is easy to find children with soft bone structures or bones with deterioration caused by disease. In these cases, mistaken procedures can cause serious injuries to the patient, as a fracture of the pelvic bone.
Machado and Moraes [27] proposed a modified Naive Bayes to lead simultaneously with qualitative and quantitative variables and assist other requirements of an evaluation system for training based on VR [41]. Based on equation (64), it is possible to apply Naive Bayes classifier in data with quantitative and qualitative variables using a discretisation method in the first stage to allow the use of the Naive Bayes method after. However, this approach can affect classification bias and variance of the NB method [62]. Other approach is to use quantitative and qualitative variables simultaneously [11] and to compute its parameters from D.

Formally, let $X_{\text{cat}} = \{X_1, X_2, \ldots, X_c\}$, c $(0 \leqslant c \leqslant n)$ be categorical or discrete variables obtained from training data, as in classical Naive Bayes and $X_{\text{cont}} = \{X_{c+1}, X_{c+2}, \ldots, X_n\}$, n-c continuous variables, obtained from training data too. Thus, X is a vector with n features, with $X = X_{\text{cat}} \cup X_{\text{cont}}$. According [6], it can be written as:

$$P(w_i \mid X_1, X_2, \ldots, X_n) = \frac{1}{S} P(w_i) \prod_{k=1}^{c} P(X_k \backslash w_i) \prod_{k=c+1}^{n} P(X_k \backslash w_i) \tag{67}$$

and the classification rule is done by (65).

Equation (67) defines a modification of Naive Bayes method. Categorical variables can be modeled by multinomial distributions. Discrete variables can be modeled by count of events in sample data D or by discrete statistical probability distributions. The continuous variables can be modeled by probability density functions. All these distributions models can be adjusted and verified by statistical tests over the data [31].

Based on the same space of decision with M classes, the modified Naive Bayes method computes conditional class probabilities and then predicts the most probable class of a vector of training data X, according to sample data D. The parameters of the method are learning from data. The final decision about vector of training data X is done by (65), where $P(w_* \mid X_1, X_2, \ldots, X_n)$ with $^* = \{i, j \mid i, j \in \Omega\}$, is done by (67).

4.8.5 *Bayesian Networks*

A Bayesian network is a probabilistic model that can represent a set of probabilities distributions from all variables in a complex process and also establish their relationships [44]. Formally, a Bayesian network is defined as directed acyclic graphs, denoted by G and a probabilistic distribution denoted by P. The graph G is a set of nodes and oriented arcs, where nodes represent variables in process and oriented arcs encode conditional dependencies between variables [44]. The dependencies are modeled by specific conditional probabilistic distributions [21].

Cheng and Greiner [9] proposed a classification for Bayesian networks, according to their graph structure, in five classes: Naive-Bayes, Tree Augmented Naive-Bayes, Augmented Naive-Bayes, Bayesian Multi-net nets e General Bayesian Networks (GBNs). The choice of a specific structure to knowledge representation depends on dependencies relationship between variables which describe that process. That choice is critical, because it changes the final results. The GBN is a generalized form of Bayesian networks, which allows nodes to form an arbitrary graph, rather than just a tree. Another important characteristic is that each child node cannot be connected to the final classes of evaluation.

The General Bayesian Network is convenient to serve as base for a training evaluation due to its generality. In that network, the dependencies between nodes can adjust itself to real dependencies. Thus, it is possible to verify dependencies between variables during network modeling and put them in structure nodes of GBN, which did not occur in other structures. Formally, let the classes of performance be in space of decision Ω with M classes of performance. Let be w_j, $j \in \Omega$, the class of performance for a user and X_i, $1 \leqslant i \leqslant n$, represents a node in GBN with n as the number of nodes in a graph. The joint probability distribution in GBN for an event is done by:

$$P(X_1, X_2, \ldots, X_n) = \prod_{i=1}^{n} P(X_n \mid X_{n-1}, X_{n-2}, \ldots, X_1) \tag{68}$$

where $P(X_1, X_2, \ldots, X_n)$ is the joint probability distribution and $P(X_n \mid X_{n-1}, X_{n-2}, \ldots, X_1)$ is the conditional probability of X_n conditioned by its predecessor nodes $X_{n-1}, X_{n-2}, \ldots, X_1$. If the conditional independence between variables is verified, this permits simplifications in (68). Then,

$$P(X_1, X_2, \ldots, X_n) = P(X_1 \mid w_j)\, P(X_2 \mid w_j)\, P(X_3 \mid w_j) \tag{69}$$

The node probabilities are associated to probability distribution. For example, a node A can have a Gaussian distribution and a node B, which depends on A, can have a bivariate Gaussian distribution, with a mean vector and a covariance matrix [19].

The structure of GBN is learned from data, as well as the parameters of conditional probabilities. By the use of probabilities calculus is possible to find dependencies among nodes in a Bayesian network. If those dependencies are founding and, if is possible to assume Gaussian distribution for nodes, dependencies can be estimated using multivariate linear regression [44]. Scores are used to help the estimation of the final structure of GBN for each class of assessment. In a first moment, a network is created with all independent nodes and an initial score is calculated. Following, all combinations are searched and an arc is designed between two nodes to obtain an increment of initial score. Then, the parameters for that nodes set are re-estimated using linear regression. This cycle is repeated until the total network score could be less than a predetermined value or a fixed number of cycles.

Previously, an expert calibrates the system, according M classes of performance. The information of variability about these procedures is acquired using GBN based method [43]. The users perform their training in the VR simulator and the Assessment Tool based on GBN collects the data from that manipulation. All probabilities of data for each class of performance are calculated by GBN and a wj class of performance is assigned to the user at the end of simulation, according (68). At the end of the training, the assessment system reports the classification to the trainee.

4.9 Considerations About Evaluation Methods

Evaluation methods present in literature could be characterized in four main groups based on: descriptive measures (in general, statistical measures), logical methods, machine learning methods and mixed methods (combining two or more of them for intelligent decision making). The effectiveness of each methodology depends on the context of the training simulated by VR and its adaptation to such context. In some cases, could be enough to inform users about their condition. However, complex simulations could demand a detailed report about errors and successes in the procedure execution.

Other way to characterize evaluation methods for training could be related to the number of users evaluated simultaneously. In this case, there are two types of evaluation: that analyse one user and that analyse more than one user and also their interactions during the training simulation. In the second mode, the evaluation is performed for each user and also for all users in order to generate a report about individual performance and its relation to the other users performance.

A third perspective for the characterization of methods could take into account the training of each user or all performed trainings for a continuous evaluation. In the first case, users perform training and receive evaluation reports about the training. But, in the second case, each time the training is performed, the evaluation reports about the present training and also about the previous training. This report includes a profile to allow users to identify recurrence of mistakes and strong points in the performance.

The most important point related to evaluation methods for training based on virtual reality is the observation of the particularities of each training. These particularities define a set of evaluation methods that can be used. As example can be mentioned the training of bone marrow harvest in which a specific region of the body must be selected to insert the needle. In this case, the target is the internal region of the iliac bone for extraction of bone marrow. Thus, the path of needle is the main attribute to be measured. However, there are other measures important to define the success of the procedure, as applied forces and angles of needle path. It means that the evaluation method to be used must evaluate the geometric design and also the variation related to the bone marrow harvest process. Other example can be the simulator for training gynaecological exam. In this training the user must palpate softly the vagina and cervix region with an angle that don't hurt patient. Then, evaluation method must verify variations in forces and angles of touch. Additionally, it should identify if user touched all region necessary to complete the patient examination. Therefore, it is possible to affirm that the evaluation methods adequate to the first type of training could not be able to deal with the features of the second type of training.

It is important to observe that evaluation methods are more robust than a simple application of a pattern recognition method. In fact, it is the kernel of a larger system, whose architecture is shown in Figure 4.5, and collects data from several devices and user's interactions to perform evaluation. For those reasons, and because VR simulators are real time systems, a training simulator and its correspondent evaluation system are limited by the computational power available. It explains why is difficult to cut functionalities of VR simulators: the sense of presence in the virtual environment cannot be compromised. For example, haptic loops need to work at 1 000 Hz to allow user to feel tactile sensations and realistic 3D environments demand the processing and exhibition of two images with 30 frames per second rates. Those technical limitations must be taken into account to construct a realistic simulator based on VR.

As the research area of evaluation methods for training based on virtual reality is recent, the several methodologies proposed cannot lead with all training situations because each training can use specific devices and/or specific interaction modes. Additionally, computers limitation can demand specific architectures as flight simulators used for training pilots. In this case, the evaluation method should fit to the architecture to take advantage of its functionalities.

4.10 Future Trends and Conclusions

Intelligent decision making for VR systems, particularly for training evaluation, allows the development of safe, realistic, affordable and reliable tools for the training of new professionals. Socially, it results in better-qualified professionals and, consequently, in better quality services.

Future trends point to systems in which multiple users can be immersed in a same virtual environment, locally or through networks (collaborative activities) [40]. The technologies for immersion in virtual environments still require the use of special glasses and other wearable devices. Researches about autostereoscopic displays are in progress, but their results will be improved in next years. Nowadays, most haptic devices are little intuitive and need improvements to allow comfortable use for training purposes. Besides, computational power and new algorithms are necessary to process multiple points of contact for haptic devices in order to provide realistic haptic reactions. Mostly, technologies for high immersion still are very expensive for social applications and this is a huge limitation for its use in large scale.

Computational performance is the most significant limitation for the use of evaluation methods in training based on VR. As VR systems must be real time systems by definition, the use of more complex and sophisticated evaluation methods is only limited by computational power. Some solutions were recently proposed and use embedded systems coupled to computer systems to execute evaluation methods [42]. However, it is a temporary solution while computers with larger processing power are not available at lower costs.

Recently, another trend arose: continuous evaluation methods [37]. Continuous evaluation is a good tool used in present and distance learning to help the construction of the knowledge and the cognitive training. In training based on VR environments, the goal is to construct a diagnostic to help trainees to understand their difficulties along their several trainings.

Bibliography

[1] Alcañiz, M. *et al.* (2003), GeRTiSS: Generic Real Time Surgery Simulation, *Studies in Health Technology and Informatics*, **94**, pp. 16–18, IOSPress.

[2] Baum, L.E. (1972), An inequality and associated maximization technique in statistical estimation for probabilistic functions of Markov processes, *Inequalities*, (3), pp. 1–8.

[3] Baum, L.E. and Petrie, T. (1996), Statistical inference for probabilistic functions of finite state Markov chains, *Ann. Math. Stat.*, (37), pp. 1554–1563.

[4] Bezdek, J.C. (1993), A review of probabilistic, fuzzy and neural models for pattern recognition, *Journal of Intelligent and Fuzzy Systems*, **1** (1), pp. 1–26.

[5] Bonnet, N. and Cutrona, J. (2001), Improvement of unsupervised multi-component image segmentation through fuzzy relaxation, *Proc of IASTED Int. Conf. on Visualization, Imaging and Image Processing*, pp. 477–482, Spain.

[6] Borgelt, C. and Kruse, R. (2002), Graphical Models: Methods for Data Analysis and Mining, Wiley.

[7] Borotschnig, H, *et al.* (1998), Fuzzy relaxation labeling reconsidered, *Proc. IEEE World Congress On Computational Intelligence*, FUZZ-IEEE, pp. 1417–1423.

[8] Buchanan, B.G. and Shortlife, E.H. (1985), Rule-Based Expert Systems: The MYCIN experiments of the Stanford Heuristic Programming Project, Addison-Wesley.

[9] Cheng, J. and Greiner, R. (2001), Learning Bayesian Belief Network Classifiers: Algorithms and System, *Proc. Fourteenth Canadian Conference on Artificial Intelligence.*

[10] Dempster, A.P., Laird, N.M. and Rubin, D.B. (1977), Maximum Likelihood from Incomplete Data via EM Algorithm, *Journal of Royal Statistical Society*, Ser. B. 39, pp. 1–38.

[11] Doring, C., Borgelt, C. and Kruse, R. (2004), Fuzzy clustering of quantitative and qualitative data, *Proc. of the 2004 NAFIPS*, pp. 84–89.

[12] Dubois, D. and Prade, H. (1996), What are fuzzy rules and how to use them. *Fuzzy Sets and Systems*, **84** (1), pp. 169–185.

[13] Fu, K.S. and Yu, T.S. (1980), Statistical Pattern Classification Using Contextual Information, Research Studies Press.

[14] Gande, A. and Devarajan, V. (2003), Instructor station for virtual laparoscopic surgery: requirements and design, *Proc. of Computer Graphics and Imaging*, USA, pp. 85–90.

[15] Gao, Z. and Lécuyer, A. (2008), A VR Simulator for Training and Prototyping of Telemanip-

ulation of Nanotubes, *Proc. ACM Simp. on Virtual Reality Software and Technology*, Bordeaux/France, pp. 101–104.

[16] Harstela, P. (1999), The Future of Timber Harvesting in Finland, *Int. Journal of Forest Engineering*, **10** (2), pp. 33–36.

[17] Hummel, R.A. and Zucker, S.W. (1983), On the foundations of relaxation labeling processes, *IEEE Transactions on Pattern Analysis and Machine Intelligence*, **5** (3), pp. 267–287.

[18] John, N.W. *et al.* (2001), Web-based surgical educational tools, *Studies in Health Technology and Informatics*, **81**, pp. 212–217. IOSPress.

[19] Johnson, R.A. and Wichern, D.W. (2001), Applied Multivariate Statistical Analysis, 5th edition, Prentice Hall.

[20] Juang, B.-H. and Rabiner, L.R. (1990), The segmental K-means algorithm for estimating parameters of hidden Markov models, *IEEE Trans. Acoustics, Speech and Signal Processing*, **38** (9), pp. 1639–1641.

[21] Krause, P.J. (1998), Learning Probabilistic Networks, *Knowledge Engineering Review*, **13**, pp. 321–351.

[22] Machado, L.S. and Moraes, R.M. (2003), An Online Evaluation Of Training in Virtual Reality Simulators Using Fuzzy Gaussian Mixture Models and Fuzzy Relaxation Labeling, *Proc. IASTED International Conference on Computers and Advanced Technology in Education* (CATE'2003), pp. 192–196, Greece.

[23] Machado, L.S. and Moraes, R.M. (2006), VR-Based Simulation for the Learning of Gynaecological Examination. Lecture Notes in Computer Science, 4282, pp. 97–104.

[24] Machado, L.S., Moraes, R.M. and Zuffo, M.K. (2000), A Fuzzy Rule-Based Evaluation for a Haptic and Stereo Simulator for Bone Marrow Harvest for Transplant, *Proc. Phantom Users Group Workshop*, USA.

[25] Machado, L.S., Mello, A.N., Lopes, R.D., Odone Fo., V. and Zuffo, M.K. (2001), A Virtual Reality Simulator for Bone Marrow Harvest for Transplant, *Studies in Health Technology and Informatics*, Amsterdam/The Netherlands, **81**, pp. 293–297.

[26] Machado, L.S. *et al.* (2006), Assessement of Gynecological Procedures in a Simulator Based on Virtual Reality, *Proc. 7th International FLINS Conference on Applied Artificial Intelligence*, pp. 799–804, Italy.

[27] Machado, L.S. and Moraes, R.M. (2009), Qualitative and Quantitative Assessment for a VR-Based Simulator, *Studies in Health Technology and Informatics*, **142**, pp. 168–173, IOS Press.

[28] Mamdani, E.H. and Assilian, S. (1975), An Experiment in Linguistic Synthesis with a Fuzzy Logic Controller, *International Journal of Man-Machine Studies*, **7**, pp. 1–13.

[29] McLachlan, G. and Peel, D. (2000), Finite Mixture Models, New York: Wiley-Interscience.

[30] Mohamed, M.A. and Gader, P. (2000), Generalized hidden Markov models - Part I: theoretical frameworks, *IEEE Trans. On Fuzzy Systems*, **8** (1), pp. 67–81.

[31] Mood, A.M., Graybill, F. and Boes, D.C. (1974), Introduction to the Theory of Statistics, 3rd ed., McGraw-Hill.

[32] Moraes, R.M. and Machado, L.S. (2003), Online Training Evaluation in Virtual Reality Simulators Using Gaussian Mixture Models, *Studies in Health Technology and Informatics*, **94**, pp. 42–44, IOSPress.

[33] Moraes, R.M. and Machado, L.S. (2003), Fuzzy Gaussian Mixture Models for On-line Training Evaluation in Virtual Reality Simulators. *Annals of the International Conference on Fuzzy Information Processing (FIP'2003)*, **2**, pp. 733–740, China.

[34] Moraes, R.M. and Machado, L.S. (2003), Gaussian Mixture Models and Relaxation Labeling for Online Evaluation of Training in Virtual Reality Simulators, *Proc. Int. Conf. on Engineering and Computer Education (ICECE'2003)*, Brasil.

[35] Moraes, R.M. and Machado, L.S. (2004), Using Fuzzy Hidden Markov Models for Online

Training Evaluation and Classification in Virtual Reality Simulators, *International Journal of General Systems*, **33** (2-3), pp. 281–288.

[36] Moraes, R.M. and Machado, L.S. (2005), Maximum Likelihood for On-line Evaluation of Training Based on Virtual Reality, *Proc. Global Congress on Engineering and Technology Education (GCETE'2005)*, pp. 299–302, Brazil.

[37] Moraes, R.M. and Machado, L.S. (2005), Continuous Evaluation in Training Systems Based on Virtual Reality, Proc. Global Congress on Engineering and Technology Education (GCETE'2005), pp. 1048–1051, Brazil.

[38] Moraes, R.M. and Machado, L.S. (2006), On-line Training Evaluation in Virtual Reality Simulators using Fuzzy Bayes Rule, *Proc. 7th International FLINS Conference on Applied Artificial Intelligence (FLINS'2006)*, pp. 791–798, Italy.

[39] Moraes, R.M. and Machado, L.S. (2007), Assessment Based on Naive Bayes for Training Based on Virtual Reality, *Proc. Int. Conference on Engineering and Computer Education (ICECE'2007)*, pp. 269–273, Brazil.

[40] Moraes, R.M. and Machado, L.S. (2007), Multiple Assessment for Multiple Users in Virtual Reality Training Environments, *Lecture Notes in Computer Science*, **4756**, pp. 950–956, Berlin.

[41] Moraes, R.M. and Machado, L.S. (2008), A Modified Naive Bayes to Online Training Assessment in Virtual Reality Simulators, *Proc. 3th Int. Conf. on Intelligent System and Knowledge Engineering (ISKE'2008)*, China.

[42] Moraes, R.M. and Machado, L S. (2008), Using Embedded Systems to Improve Performance of Assessment in Virtual Reality Training Environments, *Proc. Int. Conference on Engineering and Technology Education (Intertech'2008)*, pp. 140–144, Brazil.

[43] Moraes, R.M., Machado, L.S. and Souza, L.C. (2009), Online Assessment of Training in Virtual Reality Simulators Based on General Bayesian Networks, *Proc. VI International Conference on Engineering and Computer Education (ICECE'2009)*, Argentina, In Press.

[44] Neapolitan, R.E. (2003), Learning Bayesian Networks, Prentice Hall Series in Artificial Intelligence, Prentice Hall.

[45] Peleg, S. and Rosenfeld, A. (1978), Determining Compatibility Coefficients for Curve Enhancement Relaxation-Process, *IEEE Trans. on Systems, Man and Cybernetics*, **8** (7), pp. 548–555.

[46] Rabiner, L.R. (1989), A Tutorial on Hidden Markov Models and Selected Application in Speech Recognition, *Proc. of the IEEE*, **77** (2).

[47] Rabiner, L.R and Juang, B.-H. (1993), *Fundamentals of Speech Recognition*, Prentice Hall PTR, New Jersey.

[48] Rheingold, H. (1991), Virtual Reality, Touchstone, New York.

[49] Rich, E. and Knight, K. (1993), Artificial Intelligence. New York: McGrawHill.

[50] Rose, F., Brooks, B. and Rizzo, A. (2005), Virtual Reality in Brain Damage Rehabilitation: Review, *CyberPsychology and Behavior*, **8** (3), pp. 241–262.

[51] Rosenfeld, A., Hummel, R.A. and Zucker, S.W. (1976), Scene labelling by relaxation operations, *IEEE Transactions on Systems, Man and Cybernetics*, **6** (6), pp. 420–433.

[52] Ryan, M.S. and Nudd, G.R. (1993), The Viterbi algorithm, *Research Report CS-RR-238*, Department of Computer Science, University of Warwick, UK.

[53] Shafer, G. (1976), A Mathematical Theory of Evidence, Princeton University Press.

[54] Terano, T., Asai, K. and Sugeno, M. (1987), Fuzzy systems theory and it's applications, Academic Press Inc., San Diego.

[55] Tran, D. and Wagner, M. (1998), Fuzzy Gaussian Mixture Models for Speaker Recognition, *Proc. Int. Conf. Spoken Language Processing (ICSLP98) special issue of the Australian Journal of Intelligent Information Processing Systems (AJIIPS)*, **5** (4), pp. 293–300.

[56] Tran, D. and Wagner, M. (1999), Fuzzy approach to Gaussian mixture models and generalised

Gaussian mixture models, *Proc. Computation Intelligence Methods and Applications, (CIMA'99)*, 154–158, USA.

[57] Tran, D. and Wagner, M. (1999), Fuzzy hidden Markov models for speech and speaker recognition, *Proc. 18th Int. Conf. North American Fuzzy Information Society (NAFIPS'99)*, pp. 426–430, USA.

[58] Tran, D., VanLe, T. and Wagner, M. (1998), Fuzzy Gaussian Mixture Models for Speaker Recognition, *Proc. Int. Conf. on Spoken Language Processing (ICSLP98)*, **2**, pp. 759–762, Australia.

[59] Tran, D., Pham, T. and Wagner, M. (1999), Speaker recognition using Gaussian mixture models and relaxation labeling, *Proc. 3rd World Multiconf. on Systemetics, Cybernetics and Informatics/ 5th Int. Conf. Information Systems Analysis and Synthesis (SCI/ISAS99)*, **6**, pp. 383–389.

[60] Tran, D., Wagner, M. and Zheng, T. (1999), A fuzzy approach to statistical models in speech and speaker recognition, *Proc. FUZZ-IEEE'99 Conference 3*, pp. 1275–1280, Korea.

[61] Weiss, P., Rand, D., Katz, N. and Kizony, R. (2004), Video capture virtual reality as a flexible and effective rehabilitation tool. *Journal of NeuroEngineering and Rehabilitation*, **1** (12), online (http://www.jneuroengrehab.com/content/1/1/12), BioMed Central.

[62] Yang, Y and Webb, F.I. (2003), On Why Discretization Works for Naive-Bayes Classifiers, *Lecture Notes on Artificial Intelligence*, **2903**, pp. 440–452.

[63] Zadeh, L.A. (1965), Fuzzy Sets, *Information and Control*, **8**, pp. 338–353.

[64] Zadeh, L.A. (1968), Probability Measures of Fuzzy Events, *Journal of Mathematical Analisys and Applications*, **10**, pp. 421–427.

[65] Zadeh, L.A. (1988), Fuzzy Logic, *Computer*, **1**, pp. 83–93.

Chapter 5

A Many-Valued Temporal Logic and Reasoning Framework for Decision Making

Zhirui Lu, Jun Liu, Juan C. Augusto, and Hui Wang

School of Mathematic and Computing, University of Ulster at Jordanstown, Newtownabbey, BT37 0QB, Northern Ireland, UK

E-mail: Lu-Z1@email.ulster.ac.uk, {j.liu, jc.augusto, h.wang}@ulster.ac.uk

Temporality and uncertainty are important features of real world systems where the state of a system evolves over time and the transition through states depends on uncertain conditions. Examples of such application areas where these concepts matter are smart home systems, disaster management, and robot control etc. Solving problems in such areas usually requires the use of formal mechanisms such as logic systems, statistical methods and other reasoning and decision-making methods. In this chapter, we extend a previously proposed temporal reasoning framework to enable the management of uncertainty based on a many-valued logic. We prove that this new many-valued temporal propositional logic system is sound and complete. We also provide extended reasoning algorithms that can now handle both temporality and uncertainty in an integrated way. We illustrate the framework through a simple but realistic scenario in a smart home application.

5.1 Introduction

Decision making is a process of leading to a selection of a course of action among many alternatives and happening all over the world all the time. People try to collect as much information as they can to help them to perform the most appropriate decision for further steps. In nowadays society, large amount of information can be provided by media or other sources and loads of it may affect to people's problems, however, it is rather difficult and even impossible for human being to manually deal with such amount of information. In such case, scientists have developed computer systems which help people to analyze that information according to some specific methodologies and return feedbacks which may guide people what and how to make the most suitable decision under certain situation.

These systems are usually called Decision Support Systems (DSS), which couple the intellectual resources of individuals with the capabilities of computers to improve the quality of decisions [29].

Decision support system is an essential component in many real world systems, e.g., smart homes, disaster management, and robot control. These real world systems are characterized by *uncertainty*, where the states and transition between states are not deterministic due to various reasons, and *temporality*, where the transition between states is dependent not just on the current state but also on the time when the transition happens. Solving problems in such systems depends on the formal mechanisms used, e.g., logic systems, statistical methods, reasoning, and decision making methods. Logic is the study of principle of inference and demonstration [30]. In a formal system, logic should be able to investigate and classify the statements and arguments, through the study of inference and argument in natural languages. Logic-based formalisms play an important role in artificial intelligence realm and have made significant contributions both to the theory and practice of artificial intelligence. A completed logic should have its own axioms and inference rules to help it analyze the arguments or information from certain sources, and release the most reliable and reasonable result, which is what we require in the new DSS. Hence, a logic-based Decision Support System should be more rational, especially DSS based on the formal logic tools being able to represent and handle dynamic, inconsistent and uncertain information. There are logic reasoning systems that can be used to solve problems under temporal conditions, or under uncertain conditions. It is not hard to see that such a logic reasoning system would be quite complicated. The problem of decision making under uncertainty in a dynamic domain is computationally demanding and has recently been investigated by many researchers.

Figure 5.1 shows the objective for our research framework to build up a many-valued temporal logic system for decision support, which is used to solve the decision-making problem containing uncertain information within dynamic environment, and expected to target many applications such as medical diagnosis problem, risk analysis, or some other similar problems which contain complex preference, uncertainty and dynamic environment. The present work only covers the preliminary results regarding the combination of two typical propositional logic systems with its theoretical properties, and the corresponding reasoning algorithms, illustrated by a simple but realistic scenario in smart homes.

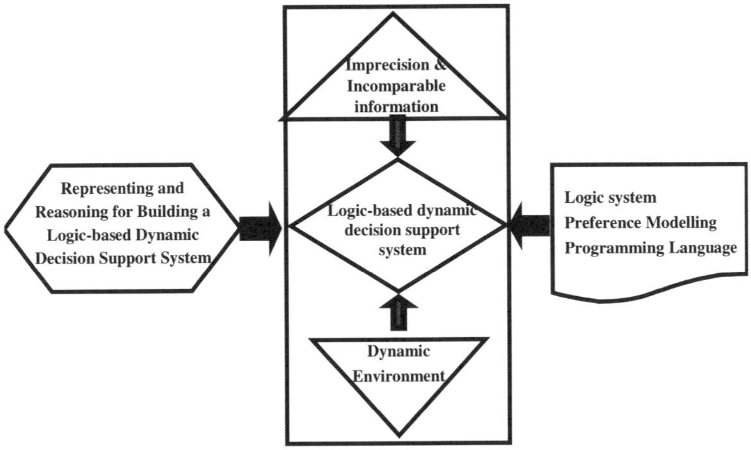

Figure 5.1 Our Research Framework Illustration.

5.1.1 *Problem Description: a Realistic Scenario*

The ability to reason about both time and uncertainty is very important and desirable in a knowledge-based system. There are numerous applications with the need of reasoning about both time and uncertainty. For example, Smart Home systems (A Smart Home can be described as a house that is supplemented with technology, for example sensors and devices, in order to increase the range of services provided to its occupants by reacting in an intelligent way [5]), which rely on data gathered by sensors, have to deal with the storage, retrieval, and processing of uncertain and time constrained data. Consider a scenario where the task is to model a kitchen monitored by sensors in a Smart Home system. Let us assume the cooker is on (*cookerOn,* a sensor detecting cooker being activated), but the motion sensor is not activated (*-atKitchen, atKitchen* is a sensor detecting location of the patient in the kitchen). If no motion is detected after more than three units of time (*umt3u*), then we consider the cooker is unattended (*cu*). In this case, at the next unit of time, the alarm will be on (*alarmOn*) to notify the occupant. In this scenario, the cooker and the occupant are both monitored by sensors, but there may be a problem with these sensors which can not return accurate information about the status of cooker or position of the occupant, and some causal relationships may not be always certain. For example, due to the likely malfunction of sensor "*atKitchen*", we can only assume that the patient is in the kitchen with e.g., 80 % certainty, or with 'high' confidence. What we want to know is if the alarm would be on or off under such uncertain and dynamic situation can be automatically inferred in order to decide for further steps. The proposed reasoning framework aims to help deal with such uncertain and time constrained situations to make rational decisions.

5.1.2 *Relevant Works*

From the scenario giving above, it shows that the smart home systems provided two kinds of information at least, uncertain and temporal information. To handle uncertainty through logic approaches, many works have been done by researchers, which, among others, can be referred to [26, 24, 25, 19, 18, 8, 10, 31]. For the temporal property in logic can be referred to [16, 12, 14, 32, 6, 7, 20], among others. Allen suggested to separate the time issue into interval, provided 13 relations between different time intervals [1, 2]. However, in this scenario, the uncertainty and temporality may exist at the same time, such that, how to solve this case is the main issue for developing the combined logic system.

One of the common approaches used to solve such decision-making problems with these characteristics is by combining many-valued and temporal logics. For example, Escalada-Imaz [13] provided a many-valued temporal reasoning method which extends the truth value of a state to indicate the uncertainty of an element for real-time control systems. In this system, it implemented a valid area (only the interaction area of condition states) of conclusion part of rule, which is one of interval temporal logic applications. Cardenas Viedma *et al.* [9] extended temporal constraint logic (TCL) into fuzzy temporal constraint logic (FTCL) which allows FTCL to handle uncertainty of time representation such as 'approximately 90 minutes', such that, within the implementation of fuzzy set into time representation, it improves the ability of system for handling the decision-making problem which contains uncertain time issue, however, they did not consider the uncertain information of state. Mucientes *et al.* [23] suggested a fuzzy temporal reasoning method for robot control; and Schockaert and Cock [28] extended classic time interval as used in temporal reasoning into fuzzy-time interval to make the reasoning system more flexible, the proposed system is similar to the one in [9], but it provided more mathematical definitions, lemmas and theorems which built up a theoretical foundation.

From the above brief literature review, it shows that some of decision-making systems combining with fuzzy logic and temporal logic still have some weakness. Some of them only considered the uncertainty of state and extend the truth value of state and gave the valid time interval for conclusion part, some of them just focused on the uncertainty of time issue. However, from the real world experience, we know that the rule may not always be true in some special case, such that, the uncertainty may not only exist in states; it still possibly exists in rule. How to handle such a problem is the main objective in this chapter. In this chapter, we present a novel reasoning framework for decision making under uncertainty and temporality, which integrates many-valued logic (mainly focus on Łukasiewicz logic) and temporal logic [15]. As a difference with other proposals, our many-valued approach allows the consideration of uncertainty not only on states but also on rules. We adopted a many-valued logic with truth values in the interval $[0,1]$ by using the Łukasiewicz implication operator, i.e., Łukasiewicz logic $L[0,1]$ [26, 31, 21], where 0 means 'false' and 1 means 'true'. The temporal logic element is simpler than in the approaches cited above, we follow the work from [15], which provided a simple stratified causal rule for the time issue (only same-time rule and next-time rule) to allow a way to reason about the dynamic aspects of a system with less computational cost. With it, we can provide a simple program to identify if the system is suitable or not. After this step, the temporality of this reasoning can be extended into time interval way for further research.

This chapter aims to build up a framework of many-valued temporal reasoning in theory and provide an applicable algorithm for decision-making system to solve the real-world decision making problem. Within this system, it should be able to solve the dynamic decision making problem which contains uncertainty of state and rule. We would like to build up a generic algorithm, which allows users insert their owned problem and situation and return a reliable result which may lead the most acceptable choice.

In the rest of this chapter, we provide the basic definitions for syntax, semantic and inference rules, and prove the soundness and completeness theorems over the defined logical system. We also present algorithms for forward and backward reasoning based on this logic framework. We illustrate this framework through a simple but realistic scenario extracted from current research on the use of artificial intelligence applied to the design and implementation of Smart Home [3].

5.2 Many-valued Temporal Propositional Logic Systems

In this section, we outline a formal framework, which extends a temporal reasoning framework presented in [15] so that the representation and reasoning with uncertainty is allowed within the system. Uncertainty is introduced in the form of a many-valued logic and reasoning framework, by means of the Łukasiewicz logic [26, 31, 21].

Łukasiewicz logic $L[0,1]$ with truth-values in $[0,1]$ is a well known many-valued logic, where the implication operator "$\rightarrow$" is the Łukasiewicz implication given by $x \rightarrow y = \min\{1, 1-x+y\}$ $(x, y \in [0,1])$ and $-x = 1-x$ is the ordinary negation operation.

Łukasiewicz logic has been studied in numerous papers on fuzzy and many-valued logic. More importantly, Pavelka showed in [26] that the only natural way of formalizing fuzzy logic for truth values in the unit interval $[0,1]$ is by using the Łukasiewicz implication operator or some isomorphic forms of it. In extending the classical logical approach, most important proposals and results used the Kleene implication ($x \to y = \max(-x, y)$). It implies that the formulae of their logics are syntactically equivalent to the formulae in classical logic. One can easily check that the truth-value degrees of the formulae derivable in the Kleene's system and in the Łukasiewicz system do not, in general, coincide. So the development of a relatively efficient calculus based on the Łukasiewicz system seems desirable. Formally, we have:

Definition 5.1. Let $L = <[0,1], \wedge, \vee, -, \to, \otimes>$; $x, y \in [0,1]$. If the operations are defined as follows:

$$x \wedge y = \mathrm{Min}(x, y),$$
$$x \vee y = \mathrm{Max}(x, y),$$
$$-x = 1 - x,$$
$$x \otimes y = \mathrm{Max}(0, x + y - 1),$$

Then L is called the Łukasiewicz implication algebra on $[0,1]$, where $\otimes$ is called the Łukasiewicz product and $\to$ is called Łukasiewicz implication. Note that, $-x = 1 - x = x \to 0$, $x \otimes y = \mathrm{Max}(0, x + y - 1) = -(x \to (-y))$. From now on, L will represent Łukasiewicz implication algebra.

5.2.1 *Syntax and Semantics*

Following the notations given in [15], we assume a set of *atomic states*, denoted as S, and $s_1, s_2, \ldots, s_n \in S$. We also assume a set of rules, denoted as R, characterizing relationships amongst states of the system. $Q = S \cup R$ refers to as the set of all atomic states and rules. Each *atomic state* comes in pairs, each positive atomic state s being paired with its negation $-s$. $s_1 \wedge s_2$ denotes the (non-atomic) state that holds when s_1 and s_2 both hold. S_I denotes the set of the *independent* atomic states which does not depend on other states holding at the same time, whereas a dependent state can do so, S_D denotes the set of the *dependent atomic states*. An independent state can only be initiated by the occurrence of initiating *events*. We also propose a set of time slot, denoted as T, and $t_1, t_2, \ldots, t_n \in T$, and every time slot is independent to each other. In this system, it only considers two kinds of rules:

Same-time rules: $s_1 \wedge s_2 \wedge \cdots \wedge s_n \rightarrow s$;

Next-time rules: $s_1 \wedge s_2 \wedge \cdots \wedge s_n \rightarrow Os$,

where each s_i is an atomic state and $s \in S_D$. $s_1 \wedge s_2 \wedge \cdots \wedge s_n \rightarrow s$ represents the influence of $s_1 \wedge s_2 \wedge \cdots \wedge s_n$ over s, and $s_1 \wedge s_2 \wedge \cdots \wedge s_n \rightarrow$ Os represents delayed (next time) influence of $s_1 \wedge s_2 \wedge \cdots \wedge s_n$ over s. Same-time rules are required to be *stratified*, i.e., they are ordered in such a way that the states in a rule are either independent or dependent on states which are heads of rules in previous levels of the stratification, see more details on this in [15]. Time is represented as a discrete series of atomic instances, labelled by natural numbers.
In order to manage uncertainty, we express that a state is not just true or false, but certain to some degree, which is taken from [0, 1]. The certainty degree dictates to which extent a state is true. The semantic extension is also applied to rules, which may occur when an expert is unable to establish/predict a precise correlation between premise and conclusion but only with degrees of certainty. Let $A \in F_L(Q)$, $F_L(Q)$ represents the set of all the fuzzy sets on Q, called a fuzzy premise set. If $p \in Q, A(p) = \alpha \in [0,1]$ expresses that a state holds or a correlation holds with a certainty degree α. A is called a non-logical fuzzy axiom set or fuzzy premise set. Every $p \in Q$ is associated with a value $A(p) \in [0,1]$. In a real-world application one may suppose that $A(p)$ is the minimal truth-value degree (or possibility degree, or credibility degree) of a proposition p (based on the application context). Hence, the knowledge in the proposed formal system can be represented as a triplet: (p, t, θ) which means p holds with the truth-value level θ at time t, and denoted as *HoldsAt*(p, t, θ). We assume that *HoldsAt*$(-p,t,\theta)$ is equivalent to *HoldsAt*$(p,t,1-\theta)$, $s \in S$, $\theta \in [0,1]$. If p is a state, it may be that both p and $-p$ are dependent, independent, or one of each. We also provide events to model impingements from outside of the system. These events represent ingressions to a state, represented as *Ingr(s)*, where $s \in S$. *Ingr(s)* is the event of s being initiated.
The semantic definition follows a universal algebraic point of view, as in [26, 31, 21].

Definition 5.2. Let X be a set of propositional variables, $TY = L \cup \{-, \rightarrow\}$ be a type with $ar(-) = 1$, $ar(\rightarrow) = 2$ and $ar(a) = 0$ for every $a \in L$. The propositional algebra of the many-valued propositional calculus on the set of propositional variables is the free T algebra on X and is denoted by $LP(X)$.
Note that L and $LP(X)$ are the algebras with the same type *TY*, where $TY = L \cup \{-, \rightarrow\}$. Moreover, note that $\vee$, $\wedge$, $\otimes$ can all be expressed by – and $\rightarrow$, so $p \vee q, p \wedge q, p \otimes q \in LP(X)$ if $p, q \in LP(X)$. In addition, notice that $Q = S \cup R \subseteq LP(X)$.

Definition 5.3. Let T be the time set. If a mapping γ: $LP(X) \times T \rightarrow L$ satisfies the following properties:

(1) For any $\alpha \in [0,1], t \in T, \gamma(\alpha,t) = \alpha$;
(2) γ is a propositional algebra homomorphism with respect to the first argument;
(3) For any $t_1, t_2 \in T$, if $t_1 \neq t_2$, then $\gamma(^*,t_1) \not\equiv \gamma(^*,t_2)$, where * means any state belong to S.

Then γ is called a temporal valuation of $LP(X)$.

Definition 5.4. Let $p \in LP(X)$, $\alpha \in [0,1]$. If there exists a temporal valuation γ such that $\gamma(p) \geqslant \alpha$ at time t, then p is said to be α-satisfiable at time t. If $\gamma(p) \geqslant \alpha$ for every temporal valuation γ of $LP(X)$ at time t, then p is said to be valid with the truth-value level α at time t. If $\alpha = 1$ at time t, then p is valid in time t.

5.2.2 *Inference Rules*

This section explains how reasoning with uncertainty in a dynamic system is performed in our system. The definitions below cover all the possible ways the system can use to compute the value of a state based on other states and incoming events (which can also alter the truth value of states).

Definition 5.5. Same-time β-Rule:

$$(s_1 \wedge s_2 \wedge \cdots \wedge s_n \rightarrow s, \beta),$$

which means that if s_1 and s_2 and ... and s_n holds, then the truth-value level stating that s holds at the same time slot immediately is β, where s_1 and s_2 and ... and $s_n \in S$, $\beta \in [0,1]$.

Definition 5.6 (Same Time Many-valued Temporal Modus Ponens Rule). The same time MTMP rule (s-MTMP) is defined as:

$$\frac{\{(s_1,t,\alpha_1),\ldots,(s_n,t,\alpha_n)\},(s_1 \wedge \cdots \wedge s_n \rightarrow s,t,\beta)}{(s,t,\alpha \otimes \beta)},$$

where $\alpha = Min(\alpha_1, \alpha_2, \ldots, \alpha_n)$, $\alpha_i \in [0,1]$ $(i = 1,\ldots,n)$, $\beta \in [0,1]$.
According to the above definition, the same-time rule calculus is built up for application. The same-time rule is used to solve the truth value of the dependent state which is affected by independent state and/or another dependent state instantly.

Definition 5.7. Next-time β-Rule:

$$(s_1 \wedge s_2 \wedge \cdots \wedge s_n \rightarrow \text{O}s, \beta),$$

which means that: if s_1 and s_2 and ... and s_n holds, then the truth-value level stating that s holds in the next time slot is β.
The symbol 'O' indicates that change on the truth value of state s will be delayed and take effect in the next time unit.

Definition 5.8 (Next Time Many-valued Temporal Modus Ponens Rule). The next time MTMP rule (n-MTMP) is defined as:

$$\frac{\{(s_1,t,\alpha_1),\ldots,(s_n,t,\alpha_n)\},(s_1 \wedge s_2 \wedge \cdots \wedge s_n \rightarrow \mathrm{O}s,t,\beta)}{(s,t+1,\alpha \otimes \beta)},$$

where $\alpha = Min(\alpha_1,\alpha_2,\ldots,\alpha_n)$, $\alpha_i \in [0,1]$ $(i = 1,\ldots,n)$, $\beta \in [0,1]$. In addition, if $s_1 \wedge \cdots \wedge s_n \rightarrow$ O(-s), then the consequence would be $(-s,t+1,\alpha \otimes \beta)$, i.e., $(s,t+1,1-(\alpha \otimes \beta))$.
According to the above definitions, the next-time rule calculus is built up for application. The next-time rule is used to solve the truth value of the dependent state which is affected by independent states and/or another dependent state in next time slot. However, this rule does not affect to the truth value of the related states instantly.
Different from the dependent state, the independent states can only be initiated by the occurrence of the initiating events. We write $(Ingr(s),t,\sigma)$ to denote an ingression to s, at t, with the truth-value $\sigma \in [0,1]$.

Definition 5.9. Assume events occur instantly and an instant between t and $t+1$ is denoted as t^*. *Occurs*(*Ingr*(s), t^*, v) is used to express the event occurs and the rule for the occurrence of an event is defined as:

$$\text{Occurs(Ingr}(s),t^*,v) \leftrightarrow \text{HoldsAt}(s,t,v^*) \wedge \text{HoldsAt}(s,t+1,v),$$

where $s \in S_I$ and v^*, $v \in [0,1]$.

Definition 5.10. Event Modus Ponens Rule (E-MP) The Event Modus Ponens Rule is defined as:

$$\frac{(s,t-1,\alpha),Occurs(s,(t-1)*,\beta)}{(s,t,\beta)}.$$

Definitions 5.9 and 5.10 provide a calculus for event, such that, while an event occurs, then the truth value of state should be changed by E-MP.

Definition 5.11 (Persistence rule). An atomic state is said to follow the persistence rule if there is no event or rule that can be applied to affect the truth value of state s at time t. Then at time $t+1$, it inherits the same truth value as that one at time t, i.e., $(s,t,v) \rightarrow (s,t+1,v)$, where $s \in S_I$ and $v \in [0,1]$.

Definition 5.12 (Persistence Modus Ponens Rule (P-MP)). The Persistence Modus Ponens Rule is defined as:

$$\frac{(s,t-1,\alpha), Persistence(s,t-1,\alpha)}{(s,t,\alpha)}$$

The P-MP is used to handle the state which is not affected by any event or rule in specific time slot, such that, from the inference rule, we can see that it just inherits the truth value from the previous time slot.

From the above definitions, there are four different Modus Ponens types of inference rules in our logical system. At a meta-logical level the following priority applies in their applications:

E-MP>>s-MTMP>>n-MTMP>>Persistence,

which means they are considered from left to right until one can be applied.

5.2.3 *Logical Calculus*

Definition 5.13 (Logical Consequence). Let M be an inference rule and p, p_1 and $p_2 \in LP(X)$. Then $p = M(p_1, p_2)$ is called a logical consequence of p_1 and p_2, if:

$$\gamma(p) = \gamma(M(p_1, p_2)) \geqslant \gamma(p_1) \otimes \gamma(p_2)$$

holds for any temporal valuation γ in $LP(X)$.

Lemma 5.1. *Let MTMP denote both same-time and next time MTMP rules and p, p_1 and $p_2 \in LP(X)$. Then $p =$ MTMP(p_1, p_2) is a logical consequence of p_1 and p_2.*

Proof. for any a, b, $c \in L$, it follows from the property of Lukasiewicz implication that: $a \to (b \to c) = b \to (a \to c)$, $a \to b = (-b) \to (-a)$, and $a \leqslant b$ iff $a \to b = 1$.

Consider the s-MTMP rule, suppose $p_1 = s_1 \wedge s_2 \wedge \cdots \wedge s_n \to s$ and $p_2 = s_1 \wedge s_2 \wedge \cdots \wedge s_n$, so $p =$ s-MTMP$(p_1, p_2) = s$, and γ is any temporal valuation in $LP(X)$ (so γ is a propositional algebra homomorphism with respect to any formulae in $LP(X)$). Hence

$$\begin{aligned}
[\gamma(p_1) \otimes \gamma(p_2)] \to \gamma(p) &= [\gamma(p_2 \to p) \otimes \gamma(p_2)] \to \gamma(p) \\
&= [[\gamma(p_2) \to \gamma(p)] \otimes \gamma(p_2)] \to \gamma(p) \\
&= -\gamma(p) \to [[\gamma(p_2) \to \gamma(p)] \to -\gamma(p_2)] \\
&= [\gamma(p_2) \to \gamma(p)] \to [-\gamma(p) \to -\gamma(p_2)] \\
&= 1.
\end{aligned}$$

That is, $\gamma(p) = \gamma(M(p_1, p_2)) \geqslant \gamma(p_1) \otimes \gamma(p_2)$. It follows from Definition 5.13 that $p =$ MTMP(p_1, p_2) is a logical consequence of p_1 and p_2. The result for n-MTMP rule can be proved in the similar way. □

Definition 5.14. Let $A \in F_L(LP(X))$ be a fuzzy premise set. A temporal valuation γ in $LP(X)$ is called satisfying A at time t if $\gamma(p) \geqslant A(p)$ at time t for each $p \in LP(X)$.

Definition 5.15 (α-Logical Consequence). Let $A \in F_L(LP(X))$ and $p \in LP(X)$. C is called an α-logical consequence of A at time t, denoted by $A| =_{(t,\alpha)} C$, if for any temporal valuation γ in $LP(X)$, γ satisfies A at time t implies that $\gamma(C) \geqslant \alpha$ at time t. Set $Con(A)(C) = \wedge\{\gamma(C);\, \gamma$ is a temporal valuation γ in $LP(X)$ satisfying $A\}$.

Definition 5.16 (Many-valued Temporal Deduction). Let $A \in F_L(LP(X))$ be a fuzzy premise set, and $C \in LP(X)$. An α-temporal deduction of C from A is defined as follows:

I) At a specific time t, an α-deduction of C from A at time t, denoted as (ω, t), is a finite sequence in the following form:

$$(\omega,t) : (C_1,t,\alpha_1),(C_2,t,\alpha_2),\ldots,(C_n,t,\alpha_n),$$

where $C_n = C$, $\alpha_n = \alpha$. For each i, $1 \leqslant i \leqslant n$, $C_i \in LP(X)$, $\alpha_i \in L$, and

(1) If $C_i \in LP(X)$ and $\alpha_i = A(C_i)$ at time t; or
(2) If there exist j, $k < i$, such that $C_i =$ s-MTMP(C_j, C_k) and $\alpha_i = \alpha_j \otimes \alpha_k$ at time t.
(3) If there exists an α-deduction of C from A at t, then denoted it as $A +_{(t,\alpha)} C$.

II) If there exists a finite sequence in the following form:

$$(\omega,t) : (C_1,t,\alpha_1),(C_2,t,\alpha_2),\ldots,(C_n,t,\alpha_n),$$

where $C_n = OC$, $\alpha_n = \alpha$. For each i, $1 \leqslant i \leqslant n$, $C_i \in LP(X)$, and $\alpha_i \in [0,1]$. If $i \neq n$, (C_i,t,α_i) is the same as the above same time process, and for $i = n$,

(1) if $C \in LP(X)$ and $\alpha = A(C)$ at time $t+1$, or,
(2) if there exist j, $k < n$, such that $C_n = n$-MTMP(C_j, C_k) and $\alpha_n = \alpha_j \otimes \alpha_k$ at time $t+1$.

Then it is called an α-deduction of C from A at time $t+1$, denoted it as $A \vdash_{(t,\alpha)} OC$.

III) In case there is no event or rule changing the truth value of a state at time t.

(1) If there is an event *Occurs*(C, $(t-1)^*, \alpha$), where $C \in LP(X)$ and $\alpha = A(C)$, occurs between time $t-1$ and time t, then $C \in LP(X)$ and $\alpha = A(C)$ at time t.
(2) If $C \in LP(X)$ and C is not effected by the same-time rule, next-time rule, or event occurring, and $\alpha = A(C)$ at time $t-1$, then it should follow the Persistence rule, such that, we will have $C \in LP(X)$ and $\alpha = A(C)$ at time t.

Here we set $Ded(A)(C) = \vee\{\alpha; A \vdash_{(t,\alpha)} C\} = \vee\{B(C);\, B$ can be deduced from A at time $t\}$.

5.2.4 *Soundness and Completeness Theorems*

Theorem 5.1 (Soundness). *Let $A \in F_L(LP(X))$, $\alpha \in [0,1]$, and $C \in LP(X)$. If there exists an α-temporal deduction of C from A in the following form:*

$$(C_1, t_1, \alpha_1), (C_2, t_2, \alpha_2), \ldots, (C_n, t_n, \alpha_n),$$

where $C_n = C$ or OC, $\alpha_n = \alpha$. For each i, $1 \leqslant i \leqslant n$, $C_i \in LP(X)$, $\alpha_i \in L$, then for any temporal valuation γ in $LP(X)$, γ satisfies A at time t_n implies that $\gamma(C) \geqslant \alpha$ at time t_n.

Proof. The proof is given as follows considering the different cases: □

Case 1. If $t_1 = t_2 = \ldots = t_n = t$ and $C_n = C$, we shall prove by deduction on the length of ω (denoted as $l(\omega)$) that if γ satisfies A at time t, then $\gamma(C) \geqslant \alpha$ at time t.
If $l(\omega) = 1$, then $A(C_n) = \alpha_n$, since γ satisfies A at time t, then $\gamma(C) = \gamma(C_n) \geqslant A(C_n) = \alpha_n = \alpha$ at time;
If $1 < l(\omega) < n$, the conclusion holds for each deduction, then we have to prove that it holds for $l(\omega) = n$. Suppose we have $i, j < n$, and $C_n = s$-MTMP(C_i, C_j) and $\alpha_n = \alpha_i \otimes \alpha_j$ at time t, then by induction hypothesis, $\gamma(C_i) \geqslant \alpha_i$ and $\gamma(C_j) \geqslant \alpha_j$ at time t. Without lose of generality, assume that $C_i = s_{i1} \wedge s_{i2} \wedge \cdots \wedge s_{in}$ and $C_j = s_{i1} \wedge s_{i2} \wedge \cdots \wedge s_{in} \rightarrow C_n$, at time t. Then it follows from Lemma 5.1 that

$$\gamma(C_n) \geqslant \gamma(C_i) \otimes \gamma(C_j) \geqslant \alpha_n = \alpha_i \otimes \alpha_j.$$

Case 2. If $t_1 = t_2 = \cdots = t_{n-1} = t$, $t_n = t+1$ and $C_n = \mathrm{O}C$, $\alpha_n = \alpha$, we shall prove by deduction on $l(\omega)$ that γA-satisfies S at time $t+1$, then $\gamma(C) \geqslant \alpha$ at time $t+1$.

(1) If $l(\omega) = 1$, then $A(C_n) = \alpha_n$, since γ satisfies A at time $t+1$, then, $\gamma(C) = \gamma(C_n) \geqslant A(C_n) = \alpha_n = \alpha$ at time $t+1$;
(2) If $1 < l(\omega) < n$, the conclusion holds for each deduction, then we have to prove that it holds for $l(\omega) = n$. Suppose we have $i, j < n$, and $C_n = n$-MTMP(C_i, C_j) and $\alpha_n = \alpha_i \otimes \alpha_j$ at time $t+1$, then by induction hypothesis, $\gamma(C_i) \geqslant \alpha_i$ and $\gamma(C_j) \geqslant \alpha_j$ at time $t+1$. Without lose of generality, assume that $C_i = s_{i1} \wedge s_{i2} \wedge \cdots \wedge s_{in}$ and $C_j = s_{i1} \wedge s_{i2} \wedge \cdots \wedge s_{in} \rightarrow C_n$, at time t. Then it follows from Lemma 5.1 that

$$\gamma(C_n) \geqslant \gamma(C_i) \otimes \gamma(C_j) \geqslant \alpha_n = \alpha_i \otimes \alpha_j$$

holds at time $t+1$.

Case 3. If $t_1 = t_2 = \cdots = t_{n-1} = t-1$, $t_n = t$, and $C_n = C$, $\alpha_n = \alpha$. If $1 < l(\omega) < n$, the conclusion holds for each deduction, then we have to prove that it holds for $l(\omega) = n$.

Suppose we have $i < n$, and C_n =E-MP((C, $t-1$,β), *Occurs*(C, $(t-1)^*$, α)). It is easy to see that the conclusion holds as well.

Case 4. If $t_1 = t_2 = \ldots = t_n = t$, $C_n = C$, $\alpha_n = \alpha$, Suppose that C is not taken effect by any same-time rule, next-time rule or event occurring rule at time t, then according to P-MP rule, we have:

$$\text{P-MP}((C,t-1,\alpha),\text{Persistence}(C,(t-1),\alpha)) = (C,t,\alpha)$$

It is easy to see the conclusion holds. Equivalently, Theorem 5.1 can be stated as $Ded(A) \leqslant Con(A)$.

Theorem 5.2 (Completeness). *Let $A \in F_L(LP(X))$, $\alpha \in L$, and $C \in LP(X)$. If C is an α-logical consequence of A at time t, then there exists an α-temporal deduction of C from A in the following form:*

$$(C_1,t_1,\alpha_1),(C_2,t_2,\alpha_2),\ldots,(C_n,t_n,\alpha_n),$$

where $C_n = C$ or OC, $t_n = t$, and $\alpha_n = \alpha$. For each i, $1 \leqslant i \leqslant n$, $C_i \in LP(X)$, $\alpha_i \in L$.

Proof. If $\alpha = 1$, $A \in F_{\{0,l\}}$ (*LP*(X)). For any temporal valuation γ of *LP*(X), if γ satisfies A, i.e., for any $p \in LP(X)$, $\gamma(p) \geqslant A(p) \in \{0,1\}$, then $\gamma(p) = 1$. Obviously, γ is now a binary valuation. This is just the classical Boolean logic case, so according to the definitions of syntax and semantic in *LP*(X), it is easy to see that $A| =_{(t,1)} C$ implies that $A \vdash_{(t,1)} C$. Hence, there exists a deduction of C from A in the following form:

$$(C_1,t_1),(C_1,t_1),\ldots,(C_n,t_n).$$

So we need to prove the consistency of *Ded*(A) and *Con*(A). From the above soundness theorem, the completeness theorem can be equivalent to the statement that $Con(A) \leqslant Ded(A)$. According to the definition of *Con*(A), it only needs to prove that the temporal valuation γ_{Ded} of *LP*(X) induced by the *Ded*(A) satisfies A.

Because the system we focused on only considers a set of atomic states (denoted as S), and a set of rules (denoted as R), so we assume that $C_i = s \in S$ which is an atomic state. Then it follows from the definition of *Ded*(A) that $\gamma_{Ded}(s) \geqslant A(s)$. Without lose of generality, assume that $C_j = s_1 \to s_2 \in R$. Suppose that $\gamma_{Ded}(s_1 \to s_2) < A(s_1 \to s_2)$. Then it follows from the definition of *Ded*(A) that $\gamma_{Ded}(s_1 \to s_2) < A(s_1 \to s_2) < B(s_1 \to s_2) < 1$, where $B \in F_L$ (*LP*(X)) is the fuzzy set which is deduced from A. In addition, it follows from the properties of $\to$ and $\otimes$ that $\gamma_{Ded}(s_1) \otimes B(s_1 \to s_2) > \gamma_{Ded}(s_2)$. Based on the definition of *Ded* (A), there exists a $B' \in F_L(LP(X))$ (also deduced from A) such that

$$B'(s_1) \otimes B(s_1 \to s_2) > \gamma_{Ded}(s_2).$$

Set $B^* = B \vee B'$, it is obvious that B^* is also deduced from A. So we have $B^*(s_1) \otimes B^*(s_1 \rightarrow s_2) > \gamma_{Ded}(s_2)$. Therefore, there exists a $\widetilde{B} \in F_L(LP(X))$ which is deduced from B^* (based on MTMP rule in Definition 5.16) such that

$$\widetilde{B}(s_2) = B'(s_1) \otimes B(s_1 \rightarrow s_2) > \gamma_{Ded}(s_2).$$

This leads to a contradiction, i.e.,

$$\gamma_{Ded}(s_2) = Ded(A)(s_2) \geqslant \widetilde{B}(s_2) > \gamma_{Ded}(s_2).$$

This means that $\gamma_{Ded}(s_1 \rightarrow s_2) \geqslant A(s_1 \rightarrow s_2)$, completes the proof. □

According to Theorems 5.1 and 5.2, it shows that although the system is simple, it is sound and complete, such that, both of them provide a theoretical foundation for us to implement such a system into a program (e.g. Prolog). So, in the future, we can provide a program (e.g., Prolog) to identify how this system works and whether the result is reliable.

5.3 Practical Many-valued Temporal Reasoning

There are two algorithms to implement reasoning within our system. One follows a forward reasoning style and the other works by backward reasoning. They complement each other and are useful at different stages of the design of a system. The forward reasoning algorithm is mainly used for simulations that can show how the system changes (all state truth values) as time evolves. The main drawback of this algorithm is that to find out if *HoldsAt(p, t, α)* the algorithm will compute the value of all states time after time, from 0 until t. The backward reasoning based algorithm instead is more efficient. It is a goal based mechanism and to find out if *HoldsAt(p, t, α)*, then it will only considers those states and times the rule base indicate are strictly needed to answer the query, very much as a query is answered in Prolog.

5.3.1 *Forward Reasoning Algorithm*

The forward reasoning algorithm is used to simulate the given decision-making problems containing their owned initial assumptions and list all the running results from $t = 1$ to n. The classical forward reasoning algorithm for stratified causal theory is introduced [15], which means that there are only two statuses in state, true or false, and it also assumes that all the rules in knowledge base are always true. In this section, it extends the classical forward reasoning algorithm into many-valued one which allows users to do the simulation with uncertain information, included both states and rules under uncertainty.

Input: a stratified set (see Section 2.2) of same-time rules, a set of next-time rules, initial conditions, which are specified by determining $\alpha \in [0,1]$ in $(s,0,\alpha)$ for $s \in S_I$ and $\beta \in [0,1]$ in $(r,0,\beta)$ for $r \in R$, and an event occurrence list, which is a set of formula in the form *Occurs(Ingr*(s)*,*$t^*, \alpha)$.

Output: a history of the values of all states up to a time t.

We say a rule is *live* if it can be applied. A threshold λ is assumed and used to determine if a state has supportive evidence of holding (when its degree of truth is in $[\lambda,1]$) or not (when its degree of truth is in $[0,\lambda)$). We compute the resulting history as follows:

(1) At $t = 0$, notice that unless otherwise known $(s,0,\alpha)$ is assumed for all $s \in S_I$, apply any live same-time rules under the order of increasing stratification level. Once all possible same-time rules were applied, then apply any next-time rule.

(2) For $t = 1, 2, 3, \ldots,$

 (a) for each *Occurs(Ingr(s)*, $(t-1)*, \alpha)$ that arrives, if $(s,t-1,1-\alpha)$ holds then assert (s,t,α).

 (b) for each co-independent state s, if $(s,t-1,\alpha)$ holds and $(s,t,1-\alpha)$ was not asserted, then assert (s,t,α).
 This is called 'applying persistence' to the state s.

  (i) For $k = 1, 2, 3, \ldots$, apply any live same-time rule of Stage k.

  (ii) Apply persistence: for any co-k-dependent state s, if $(s,t,1-\alpha)$ has not been asserted, and $(s,t-1,\alpha)$, then assert (s,t,α).

 (c) Apply any live next-time rule.

5.3.2 *Backward Reasoning Algorithm*

The classical backward reasoning algorithm for this system has already been provided in [15, 4]. In the paper [4], it applied such an algorithm to solve a healthcare scenario which is used to check if some specific case is true or false in a specific time slot under the initial assumption. In this section, we extend such a backward reasoning algorithm under classical level into many-valued level. This extension allows users to enquiry some uncertain temporal decision-making problem in specific way under their assumption.

Input: a stratified set of same-time rules (R_s), a set of next-time rules (R_n), where R_s, $R_n \in R$, and $\beta \in [0,1]$ in $(r, 0, \beta)$ for $r \in R$, an event occurrence list (E), which is a set of formula in the form *Occurs(Ingr(s)*, t^*, α), an initial condition list (I_c), and a query of type

holds(q, t, α) by which we ask the system to prove that the truth value of state q is equal or greater than α at time t.
Output: the answer to the query *holds*(q,t,α) (this could easily be extended to also provide a justification).
We then apply the following steps (where α_i represents the truth-value of p_i at time t):

(1) IF $t > 0$ THEN REPEAT

a) IF *HoldsAt*$(q,t,\theta) \in I_c$ OR *Occurs*(*Ingr*$(q),(t-1)*,\theta) \in E$ and $\theta \geqslant \alpha$, THEN the query is true.

b) ELSE IF *HoldsAt*$(q,t,\theta) \in I_c$ OR *Occurs*(*Ingr*$(q),(t-1)*,\theta) \in E$ and $\theta < \alpha$, THEN the query is false.

c) ELSE IF there is a same-time rule $(p_1 \wedge p_2 \wedge \cdots \wedge p_n \rightarrow q,t,\beta)$
THEN IF $\alpha_i \geqslant 1+\alpha-\beta$, for $i = 1, 2, \ldots, n$, at time t
(i.e., applies this algorithm recursively for each member of the antecedent of the rule)
THEN the query is true.

d) ELSE IF there is a next-time rule $(p_1 \wedge p_2 \wedge \cdots \wedge p_n \rightarrow \text{O}q,t,\beta)$
THEN IF $\alpha_i \geqslant 1+\alpha-\beta$, for $i = 1, 2, \ldots, n$, at time $t-1$
(i.e., applies this algorithm recursively for each member of the antecedent of the rule)
THEN the query is true.

e) ELSE $t = t$-1 (i.e., try to find if there is a proof that is true at an earlier time and the value persists)
UNTIL (the proof of q or $-q$ is found) OR ($t = 0$)

(2) IF $t = 0$
THEN IF *HoldsAt*$(q,0,\theta) \in I_c$ and $\theta \geqslant \alpha$,
THEN answer the query is true
ELSE the query is false.

5.4 Scenarios

Consider a simplified scenario where the task is to model a kitchen monitored by sensors in a smart home system as mentioned in Section 5.1.1. Let us assume the cooker is on (*cookerOn*, i.e., a sensor detecting cooker being activated), but the motion sensor is not activated (*-atKitchen, atKitchen* is a sensor detecting location of the house occupant is in the kitchen). If no motion is detected after more than three units of time (*umt3u*), then we consider the cooker is unattended (*cu*). In this case, at the next unit of time, the alarm will be on (*alarmOn*) to notify the occupant that the cooker has been left unattended. In this scenario, the cooker and the occupant are both monitored by sensors. Sensors are, for various reasons, unreliable and some relationships, e.g., status of cooker or position of the occupant, may not be always certain. For example, due to the likely malfunction of sensor "*atKitchen*", we can only assume that the house occupant is in the kitchen with, e.g., 80% certainty. We need to decide if the alarm should be activated under such uncertain situation. The proposed reasoning framework aims to help to represent and reasoning with such situations and to help in the design and development of systems with such characteristics. Let us assume the following representation of the scenario discussed above:

Independent atomic states: *cookerOn*, $\pm$*atKitchen, umt3u.*

Dependent atomic states: $\pm$*cu*, $\pm$*hazzard*, $\pm$*alarmOn*, $-$*umt3u*, $-$*cookerOn.*

Same-time rules:

Stage 1: $R1$. *–atKitchen*$\wedge$*cookerOn*$\wedge$*umt3u*$\rightarrow$ *cu*

R2. $-$cookerOn$\rightarrow$ $-$*alarmOn*

R3. $-$cookerOn$\rightarrow$ $-$*hazzard*

R4. $-$cookerOn$\rightarrow$ $-$*umt3u*

R5. $-$cookerOn$\rightarrow$ $-$*cu*

Stage 2: $R6$. *cu* $\rightarrow$ *alarmOn*.$R7$.*cu* $\rightarrow$ *hazzard*

Next-time rule: $R8$. *alarmOn* $\rightarrow$ O($-$*cookerOn*)

Lets assume the rules above have different degrees of confidence attached: ($R1$ being the less reliable given the sensors involved: $R1(0.9)$, $R2(0.95)$, $R3(0.95)$, $R4(0.95)$, $R5(0.95)$, $R6(1)$, $R7(1)$, $R8(1)$.

Besides, we define the trigger level of all rules to be 0.5 and provide the events as follows:

Occurs(ingr(atKitchen), 0^*, 0.9),

Occurs(ingr(cookerOn), 0^*, 0.9),

Occurs(ingr($-$atKitchen), 1^*, 0.9),

Occurs(ingr(umt3u), 4^*, 0.9)

Questions:

1) The occupant wants to know what will happen from time= 1 to time= 6.

2) The occupant wants to check if the alarm will turn on automatically by the system at time= 5.

Answer for question 1)

Let us follow the evolution of some key states in this scenario (Forward Reasoning algorithm):

$t = 1$: Because of *Occurs*(*ingr*(*atKitchen*, 0^*, 0.9)) and *Occurs*(*ingr*(*cookerOn*,0^*,0.9)), the value of *atKitchen* is set to be 0.9 and *cookerOn* to be 0.9;

$t = 2$: *Occurs*(*ingr*($-$*atKitchen*,1^*, 0.9)) changes the value of *atKitchen* to be 0.1 by E-MP;

$t = 3$ and 4, the values of the states we follow do not vary;

$t = 5$: *Occurs*(*ingr*(*umt3u*, 4^*, 0.9)) then the value of *umt3u* changes to be 0.9 by E-MP. This makes *R1 live*, thus, the value of *cu* becomes 0.8 by s-MTMP. According to *R*6, the value of *alarmOn* becomes 0.8 by s-MTMP. By *R*7, the truth value of hazzard becomes 0.8 by s-MTMP. Besides, the change of *alarmOn* causes the value of *cookerOn* changes to be 0.2 at next time unit by *R*8 and by *n*-MTMP;

$t = 6$: The triggering of *R*8 makes *R*2 live, the value of *alarmOn* becomes 0.25 by s-MTMP. It also triggers *R*3, then the value of *hazzard* becomes 0.25 by s-MTMP. By *R*4, the value of *umt3u* changes to be 0.25 by s-MTMP. According to *R*5, the value of *cu* is changed into 0.25 by s-MTMP.

The result of applying the forward reasoning algorithm up to time unit 6 to the scenario described above is summarized in Table 5.1 above.

From the forward reasoning algorithm, we can see that it provides a simulation of the scenario according the initial assumptions. Through it, we can see what happened during the time passed, and what the result is at each time slot. From Table 5.1, when $t = 5$, the alarm is activated because of the unattended cooker is on for more than 3 time units, but it is uncertain and only contain 0.8 not 100 percent true. However, 0.8 is in a high level of trust, such that, the system believes that it may lead to dangerous situation and turn on the alarm to notify the occupant that the cooker is on and unattended at the moment. Such that, the system turns off the cooker automatically at time 6 and provides a low truth value of *cookerOn*. By this change, other related states are also changed their truth values into a low level.

Answer for question 2):

Assume we want to know with a confidence level of at least 75 % whether the alarm will be triggered $t = 5$, then we can use the following query (via Backward Reasoning algorithm): *holds*(*alarmOn*,5,0.75) and apply backward reasoning.

Table 5.1 Exhaustive simulation by forward reasoning

Time State	1	2	3	4	5	6
cookerOn	0.9	0.9	0.9	0.9	0.9	0.2
atKitchen	0.9	0.1	0.1	0.1	0.1	0.1
umt3u	0	0	0	0	0.9	0.25
cu	0	0	0	0	0.8	0.25
hazzard	0	0	0	0	0.8	0.25
alarmOn	0	0	0	0	0.8	0.25
Time implication	**1**	**2**	**3**	**4**	**5**	**6**
R1	0.9	0.9	0.9	0.9	0.9	0.9
R2	0.95	0.95	0.95	0.95	0.95	0.95
R3	0.95	0.95	0.95	0.95	0.95	0.95
R4	0.95	0.95	0.95	0.95	0.95	0.95
R5	0.95	0.95	0.95	0.95	0.95	0.95
R6	1	1	1	1	1	1
R7	1	1	1	1	1	1
R8	1	1	1	1	1	1

Because *alarmOn* is a dependent state, then the system will start by finding a related rule, in this case $R6$. From $R6$, the system will calculate that *cu* must be greater than 0.75 to change the truth value of *alarmOn* greater than 0.75. Because *cu* is a dependent state the system will identify the states it depends on: *–atKitchen*, *cookerOn* and *umt3u*. Because at $t = 5$ *atKitchen* is under the 0.5 threshold and *cookerOn* and *umt3u* are above the 0.5 threshold they can trigger rule 6. The system can trace back in time the knowledge to the points where specific events triggered those values: *Occurs*(*ingr*(*cookerOn*),$0^*, 0.9$), *Occurs*(*ingr*($-$*atKitchen*), $1^*, 0.9$), and *Occurs*(*ingr*(*umt3u*), $4^*, 0.9$), so the system has a way to prove that each state involved in the query is supported at the right level (under or above the threshold 0.5 as requested by the rules).

The results show that according to the initial setting of the scenario and the inference performed by our system, the intuitive outcome is obtained, i.e., the alarm will be triggered to notify the occupant when the cooker has been left on without attention for a specified length of time.

Compared to the forward reasoning algorithm, the backward reasoning algorithm provides a more sufficient way to identify the specific query than only forward reasoning algorithm in the decision-making system. From the above example, we can see that the backward reasoning algorithm always traces the related state of the query, such that, it would ignore some unrelated components and avoid the unnecessary paths, so it decreases the time of searching and calculating process to improve the sufficient of the query process.

5.5 Discussions

According to the simple scenario, the uncertainty is not only implemented into states, but also applied into rules. So, the uncertain information collection from Smart Home systems, such as sensors can be reflected into our reasoning system. Moreover, the truth values of rules show that rules may not be always true in smart home systems and they may contain uncertain information in some specific cases. For example, there is only a 80 % truth degree of $R1$, which means that $R1$ is available for most of cases, but not all of them, and if the system wants to trigger $R1$, it needs to provide a high truth degree of each state in condition part, such that, it requires more accurate information for trigger. The results from the reasoning system may be more reliable by handling uncertainty both on states and rules. So far, all the truth values are in the $[0,1]$ interval, but in the real world application, it is not sufficient to represent all the uncertain information. If the information can not be represented in a numerical form, this system can not be applicable, such that, from the uncertainty issue, the further research should be implementing the lattice values which can handle the non-numerical uncertain information based on [31].

However, by the definitions, the system can only predict or handle some situations in the same time slot (same-time rule effect) or next time slot (next-time rule effect), but if there are some effects which may last several time slots (time interval case), it may need to create more states or events to handle it. For example, if the occupant sets up the cooker that should be open for 30 minutes (time controller), so the system may need to have an event *Occurs*(-cookerOn,30, 1), but if we can extend the same-time rule and next-time rule into time interval form based on [17], this added event may be avoided. So, the further research we may do is how to extend the time issue into a time interval situation.

5.6 Conclusions

In this chapter, we have provided basic definitions of syntax, semantic, and inference rules for a many-valued temporal propositional logic system that allows us reason under both temporality and uncertainty. We have proved the soundness and completeness of this logic system, and we have also presented practical algorithms for forward and backward reasoning. In future work we will implement our reasoning framework in Prolog and explore problems in other domains. We will also consider extending the reasoning framework to a more general lattice valued logic framework and to consider different types of time durations whilst retaining simplicity.

Acknowledgment

This work is partially supported by the research project TIN2009-08286 and P08-TIC-3548.

Bibliography

[1] J. Allen, Time and time again: the many ways to represent time, *Intl J. of Intelligent Systems*, 6 (4): 1–14, 1991.

[2] J. Allen and G. Ferguson, Actions and events in interval temporal logic, *Journal of Logic and Computation, Special Issue on Actions and Processes*, 4: 531–579, 1994.

[3] J.C. Augusto and D. Cook, Ambient intelligence: applications in society and opportunities for AI, *Tutorial Lecture Notes, 20th Int. Joint Conf. on Artificial Intelligence* (IJCAI-07), Hyderabad, India, 2007.

[4] J.C. Augusto, P.J. McCullagh, V. Croft and J.-A. Walkden, Enhanced healthcare provision through assisted decision-making in a smart home environment, *Proceedings of 2nd Workshop on Artificial Intelligence Techniques for Ambient Intelligence (AITAmI07)*, pp. 27–32. Co-located event of IJCAI 2007. 6th-7th of January 2007. Hyderabad, India.

[5] J. Augusto, J. Liu, P. McCullagh, H. Wang, and J. Yang, Management of uncertainty and spatio-temporal aspects for monitoring and diagnosis in a Smart Home, *International Journal of Computational Intelligence System*, 1(4): 361–378, December, 2008.

[6] J.C. Augusto, *A General framework for Reasoning about Change*, *New Generation Computing*, 21 (3) 209–247, Ohmsha, Ltd and Springer-Verlag, 2003.

[7] J.C. Augusto, *Temporal reasoning for decision support in medicine*, *Artificial Intelligence in Medicine*, Vol. 33/1 pp. 1–24, Elsevier, 2005.

[8] L. Bolc and P. Borowik, *Many-Valued Logics, 1. Theoretical Foundations*. Springer, Berlin, 1992.

[9] M.A. Cardenas Viedma, R. Marin Morales, and I. Navarrete Sanchez, Fuzzy temporal constraint logic: a valid resolution principle, *Fuzzy Sets and Systems*, 117: 231–250, 2001.

[10] R. Cignoli, I. D'Ottaviano, and D. Mundici, *Algebraic foundations of many-valued reasoning*, Dordrecht: Kluwer, 2000.

[11] D. Dubois, A. HadjAli, and H. Prade, Fuzziness and uncertainty in temporal reasoning, *JUCS*, 9 (9): 1168–1195, 2003.

[12] E.A. Emerson, Temporal and modal logic, *Handbook of Theoretical Computer Science*, Chapter 16, the MIT Press, 1990.

[13] G. Escalada-Imaz, A temporal many-valued logic for real time control systems, In *Proceedings of the 9th Int. Conf. on Art. Int.: Methodology, Systems, and Applications*, pp. 91–100. 2000, Bulgaria.

[14] D.M. Gabbay, I. Hodkinson, and M. Reynolds, *Temporal Logic (Volume 1): Mathematical Foundations and Computational Aspects*, Oxford University Press, 1994.

[15] A. Galton and J. C. Augusto, Stratified causal theories for reasoning about deterministic devices and protocols, In *Proc. of 9th Int. Symposium on Temporal Representation and Reasoning*, pp. 52–54, U.K.

[16] A.P. Galton, *Temporal Logics and Their Applications*, London: Academic Press, 1987.

[17] A. Galton, Causal Reasoning for Alert Generation in Smart Homes, J. C. Augusto and C. D. Nugent (eds.), *Designing Smart Homes*, Springer, pp. 57–70, 2006.

[18] S. Gottwald, *A Treatise on Many-Valued Logics*, Studies in Logic and Computation, vol. 9, Research Studies Press Ltd., Baldock, 2001.

[19] P. Hajek, *Metamathematics of Fuzzy Logic*, Dordrecht: Kluwer, 1998.

[20] F. Kröger and S. Merz, *Temporal Logic and State Systems*, The Springer, 2008.

[21] J. Liu, D. Ruan, Y. Xu, and Z. Song, A resolution-like strategy based on a lattice-valued logic, *IEEE Trans. on Fuzzy Systems*, 11(4): 560–567, 2003.

[22] Z. Lu, J. Liu, J. C. Augusto and H. Wang, Multi-valued temporal reasoning framework for decision-making, In *Proc. of the* 8th *Int. FLINS Conference on Computational Intelligence in Decision and Control*, pp. 301–306, September 21–24, 2008, Spain.

[23] M. Mucientes, R. Iglesias, C.V. Regueiro, A. Bugarin, and S. Barro. A fuzzy temporal rule-based velocity controller for mobile robotics, *Fuzzy Sets and System*, 134:83–99, 2003.

[24] V. Novak, *Fuzzy Sets and Their Applications*. Bristol: Adam Hilger, 1989.

[25] V. Novak, I. Perfilieva, and J. Mockor, *Mathematical Principles of Fuzzy Logic*, Dordrecht: Kluwer, 2000.

[26] J. Pavelka, On fuzzy logic I: multiple-valued rules of inference, II: enriched residuated lattices and semantics of propositional calculi, III: semantical completeness of some multiple-valued propositional calculi, *Zeitschr. F. Math. Logik und Grundlagend. Math.*, 25: 45–52, 119–134, 447–464, 1979.

[27] N. Rescher, *Many-Valued Logic*, McGraw Hill, New York, 1969.

[28] S. Schockaert and M. De Cock, Temporal reasoning about fuzzy intervals, *Artificial Intelligence*, 172: 1158–1193, 11, Dec. 2008.

[29] E. Turban, and J.E. Aronson, *Decision Support Systems and Intelligent Systems*, Fifth Edition, Prentice Hall, 1997.

[30] P. Suppes, *Introduction to Logic*, New York: Litton Educational Publishing, Inc., 1957.

[31] Y. Xu, D. Ruan, K. Qin, and J. Liu, *Lattice-valued Logic: An Alternative Approach to Treat Fuzziness and Incomparability*, Springer-Verlag, 2003.

[32] Y. Venema, Temporal Logic, in Goble, Lou, ed., *The Blackwell Guide to Philosophical Logic*. Blackwell, 2001.

Chapter 6

A Statistical Approach to Complex Multi-Criteria Decisions

Pierre L. Kunsch
MOSI department, Vrije Universiteit Brussel, Pleinlaan 2, BE-1050 Brussels, Belgium
E-mail: pkunsch@vub.ac.be

Complex decision problems have most of the time multi-criteria dimensions. Many existing multi-criteria decision tools are however plagued with difficulties due to uncertainties on data and preference weights, multiple decision-makers, correlations between criteria, etc., and last but not least, undesirable properties, like rank reversal. This chapter investigates an original approach using the correlations between criteria, as a measure of distance between ranking solutions. Geometrical interpretations are given for two and three-dimensional problems. It is shown how the proposed framework, which is valid for any dimension, addresses uncertainties, and how it enhances the rank-reversal immunity. This methodology serves two objectives: firstly, it provides a statistical tool for interpreting decision-making processes for large samples of customers, or clients on markets; secondly, it provides a support for multiple-criteria ranking of alternatives in the presence of uncertainties. The on-going development of the approach, and several future research directions are also indicated.

6.1 Background

Multi-criteria decision-making (MCDM) has become a very important instrument of Operations Research. It has been moving in recent decades towards Multi-criteria-decision aid (MCDA) (see Roy [1, 2], Vincke [3], Belton and Stewart [4]; Figueira *et al.* [5] for overviews of existing techniques). The proposed methodologies are therefore basically normative: the intention is to assist the decision-making process, rather than to provide a final decision. Such normative approaches necessitate a rather tedious process of preference elicitation, and there are therefore practical limitations on the number of participating decision-makers. As a consequence, such methods are not directly adapted to descriptive models, like in many marketing-research applications, see e.g., Malhotra [6]; system-dynamics simulation models like the choice of a departure time of car commuters by Springael *et al.* [7,8], De Smet *et al.* [9, 10], moving decisions in urban areas by Kunsch *et al.* [11]; agent-based modelling (ABM), see e.g., Ferber [12], etc.

These MCDM problems are characterized by a large number of decision-makers, and therefore statistical treatments are required. The main objective is here to apprehend in a credible way the behaviours of usually many agents with different preferences, for analysis, and/or mimicking. A simple example is extrapolating the market-share evolution of different product brands, based on initial consumers' enquiries, and giving some improvement capabilities of the brands. Outranking methods are based on pair-wise comparisons, like ELECTRE developed by Roy [1, 2, 13], see also Maystre *et al.* [14]; PROMETHEE, see Brans and Vincke [15], Brans *et al.* [16], Brans and Mareschal [17, 18, 19, 20]. All require assumptions on scales, indifference and preference thresholds, weights, etc. For large sets of decision-makers, e.g., consumers in some market, it is therefore difficult, or impossible, to gather all relevant technical parameters, and to validate them against the observations. This constitutes an important obstacle for meaningful modelling.

Another very important drawback for the correct and robust use of MCDA methodologies in a statistical framework is the important anomaly of rank reversal: there is no independence of the ranking of two alternatives with respect to a third, irrelevant one. In many situations it is impossible to find a justification for this disturbing phenomenon. Belton and Stewart [4] first identified the mechanism of rank reversal in the Analytical Hierarchy Process of Saaty [21]. The latter is not an outranking method, but it is also based on pair-wise comparisons of alternatives. De Keyser and Peeters [22], Macharis *et al.* [23], Kunsch [24], have shown that rank reversals appear quite frequently with the PROMETHEE method. It is only recently that rank reversal has been shown to appear many times in the ELECTRE methodology, see Awang and Triantaphyllou [25], and an answer note by Figuera and Roy [26]. Ref. [25] makes reference to important test criteria concerning the invariance properties regarding rank reversals that must be claimed for robust MCDM methodologies. For the coming discussion I draw from my own contribution [24] to this problem, more specifically when using the PROMETHEE methodology.

Furthermore, in outranking methodologies, it is difficult to include dependencies between criteria, and to establish how they affect the comparisons. Finally, because MCDA approaches are normative, by definition of decision aiding, they leave no space to the way real people are coming to a final ranking. These difficulties are an obstacle for using these well-known techniques in many practical problems, e.g., in Marketing Research [6], for which there are strong needs to adjust parameters to observed data. In this chapter, it is shown that basic concepts of Multivariate statistics, see e.g., Härdle and Hlávka [27], can provide an extremely simple, and robust MCDM technique with a dual use: this technique can be as well used for interpreting statistical data from observations, as serving as a normative MCDA instrument. It is easily shown that the technique is immune against the denounced non-rational rank reversals [24].

In Section 6.2, the author presents the basics of the proposed MCDM procedure. The latter is first developed in the case when only ordinal rankings of alternatives are available from the decision-makers for multiple criteria. In Section 6.3, illustrative examples are presented with 2-D and 3-D geometrical representations. Section 6.4 presents the more general methodology, and how it can be extended to the case of mixed ordinal and cardinal data. Section 6.5 presents conclusions, and an outlook is given on future research on this approach.

6.2 Basic Elements of the MCDM Methodology

6.2.1 *An ordinal procedure for finding the Rank Matrix*

In the following it is assumed that there are many decision-makers representing multiple possible preferences between n alternatives, given K criteria. To make statistical evaluations, it will be assumed that weights representing the priorities between criteria are fully stochastic in the ranges $[0,1]^K$. It is also assumed that all decision-makers share the same knowledge about the criteria, which is provided in a $n \times K$ evaluation table, containing real ordinal or cardinal data, independent of preferences. Note that these assumptions are made without loss of generality, and they may be easily removed when needed.

Let me first introduce some useful definitions, bringing important properties described with more details in Appendix A.1.

n-vector: any real vector in $\mathbb{R}^n$;

Unit n-vector: vector obtained by centring the n-vector to its mean value and normalising it to one;

V^n: *the set of all unit n-vectors;*

Criteria: $C_1, C_2, \ldots, C_k, \ldots; k = 1, 2, \ldots, K$ criteria, unambiguously defined by their rank vectors;

Alternatives: $A_1, A_2, \ldots, A_i, \ldots;\ i = 1, 2, \ldots, n$; n alternatives measured by their evaluation vectors;

Evaluation vector: n-vector providing ordinal or cardinal evaluations of the n alternatives for some criterion;

Preference ranking: $A_i > A_j > A_k = A_l > \ldots$; indicates the preferences between alternatives: $A_i > A_j$ *indicates that* A_i *is better ranked than* A_j;

$A_k = A_l$ *indicates that* A_k *and* A_l *have the same rank.*

Rank vector: n-vector of ranks r_{ik} of n alternatives A_i, $i = 1,2,\ldots,n$, for criteria $k = 1,2,\ldots,K$. The traditional way of indicating a rank, in case of a tie, say p alternatives at position l in the rank vector, is to use the average tie rank:

$$r_{ik}^{\text{trad}} = l + \frac{1}{2}(p-1) \tag{1}$$

In this chapter, for reasons that will become clear later on, the integer value of the rank is used, thus simply:

$$r_{ik} = l \tag{2}$$

For example, a preference ranking $A_1 > A_5 = A_4 > A_3 > A_2$ gives in this notation the rank vector $(1,5,4,2,2)$, rather than $(1,5,4,2.5,2.5)$, as traditionally used.

Associated rank vector (to an evaluation vector): Rank vector, which is obtained by ranking the alternatives on the basis of an evaluation vector, and using an adequately defined indifference threshold for identifying ties of alternatives;

Criteria rank vector: Rank vector containing the ranking obtained for some criterion;

Unit criteria rank vector: unit n-vector of the criteria rank vector;

Overall rank vector: n-vector indicating the ranks of the n alternatives in the overall ranking, obtained by aggregating all criteria rank vectors by means of MCDM procedures for vector optimisation to be defined later in this chapter;

Overall ranking: Ranking provided by the overall rank vector;

$P(n)$: Number of ordinal rankings with ties for n alternatives. $P(n)$ is given by the recursive formula:

$$P(n) = \sum_{i=1}^{n-1} P(i)C_n^i + 1;\ \ n \geqslant 2;\ \ P(1) = 1 \tag{3}$$

$P(2) = 2+1; P(3) = 12+1; P(4) = 74+1; P(5) = 540+1; P(6) = 4,682+1; P(7) = 47,292+1$; etc.

$P(n)$ is always an odd number because it contains the trivial ranking $(1,1,\ldots,1)$ in which all alternatives belong to the same indifference tie.

Rank Matrix: the $n \times n$ matrix indicating the probability of any of the n alternatives to occupy any rank, with the possibility of ties, given fully stochastic weights with rectangular probability distributions in ranges $[0,1]^K$.

On the basis of these definitions, I now introduce a seemingly harmless, but very powerful Basic Property A.1.1, and its Corollary A.1.2. Proofs are provided in Appendix A.1:

Basic Property A.1.1. *Any matrix, with column vectors from V^n, has a rank at most equal to $(n-1)$, which is the dimension of the space of all unit n-vectors. Every vector in V^n may be obtained as a linear combination of a basis made of $(n-1)$ independent vectors in V^n, in short basis vectors.*

Corollary 6.1. *Consider a set $\{K\}$ of $K \leqslant n-1$ independent unit vectors in V^n. Call $V^n_{\{K\}}$ the subset of V^n, which is generated by all possible linear combinations of these vectors serving as basis vectors. The set $V^n_{\{K\}} \subset V^n$ has dimension K, i.e., that any matrix consisting of column vectors from $V^n_{\{K\}}$ has at most rank K.*

These results have very important consequences for ordinal MCDM ranking problems. Assuming K independent unit criteria rank vectors, they constitute a basis in $V^n_{\{K\}}$. Consider now all possible unit n-vectors obtained by combining those K basis vectors with random non-negative coefficients, distributed according to rectangular distributions in $[0,1]^K$, and normalising them to unit vectors – note that the n-vectors are automatically centred through the property of unit basis vectors. Herewith a combination unit n-vector is obtained for each instance of the weight set. Let us further consider the *associated rank vectors to the combination unit n-vector* (see definitions, above in this section), obtained from these unit n-vectors, ignoring for the time how to identify ties by means of indifference thresholds. The following Theorem 6.1 applies:

Theorem 6.1. *Using K independent unit criteria rank vectors, and combining them linearly with K non-negative weights from $[0,1]^K$ generate a set of n-vectors; the set of associated rank vectors to these n-vectors certainly contains all ordinal overall rank vectors which are Pareto-optimal, i.e., solutions of the vector-optimisation MCDM problem with stochastic weights.*

Proof. If a possible Pareto-optimal overall ranking would not appear in the set of associated rank vectors, it could not be associated with any linear combination of the unit criteria rank vectors showing non-negative coefficients. But all Pareto-optimal linear combinations must necessarily lie within the solid angle spanned by the unit criteria rank vectors, and all have non-negative coefficients; otherwise some negative preferences would be introduced. □

Theorem 6.1 does not imply that the positive coefficients in the linear combination of basis vectors are identical to the actual preference weights used by decision-makers to mark their priorities between the criteria. Indeed, this is not always the case. Due to the use of unit n-vectors, the normalisation process is a mathematical operation, which has nothing to do with actual preferences. To see that, let us consider the criteria rank vectors and the normalisation process in the following simple example with two criteria (C_1; C_2; $K = 2$) and three alternatives (A_1, A_2, A_3). Call R_1 and R_2 the criteria rank vectors:

$$\begin{aligned} &C_1 : A_1 > A_2 > A_3;\ \mathrm{R}_1 = (1,2,3);\ w_1 = 0.5 \\ &C_2 : A_2 > A_1 = A_3;\ \mathrm{R}_2 = (2,1,2);\ w_2 = 0.5 \\ &\text{OR (overall ranking)} : A_1 = A_2 > A_3 \end{aligned} \tag{4}$$

w_1, w_2 are the preference weights associated to C_1, C_2, respectively. Because the weights are equal, A_1 and A_2 have symmetrical positions, so that there are in a tie regarding the overall ranking (OR); A_3 is dominated by both.

The centring and normalising process to unit rank vectors UR_1, and UR_2 gives:

$$\begin{aligned} &\mathrm{UR}_1 = \frac{R_1 - (2,2,2)}{\sigma_1\sqrt{2}};\ \mathrm{UR}_2 = \frac{R_2 - (5/3,5/3,5/3)}{\sigma_2\sqrt{2}} \\ &\sigma_1 = 1;\ \sigma_2 = \frac{1}{\sqrt{3}} \end{aligned} \tag{5}$$

where σ_1, σ_2 are the standard deviations of the rank vectors. Because there is a tie in C_2, the standard deviations used in the normalising process are not the same. Combine now linearly these basis vectors with positive coefficients c_1, c_2. The mean values of R_1, R_2 are different, because of the use of (2), rather than the traditional notation of (1), but this difference is the same for all three alternatives, so that it will not affect the overall ranking associated to the linear combination. The overall ranking will however be affected by the fact that $\sigma_2 < \sigma_1$, given less dispersion in the case of C_2, because of the tie presence. This is just a mathematical trick: it is not meaningful from the point of view of preferences represented by the weights. In order to preserve the ranks with respect to the normalisation constants, the following transformation must be applied:

$$c_1 = w_1\,;\ c_2 = w_2 \frac{\sigma_2}{\sigma_1} \leqslant w_2 \tag{6}$$

In general, σ_0 being the standard deviation of the natural rank $(1,2,\ldots,n)$, the positive coefficients to be used in the linear combination of the basis vectors are linked to the preference weights by the following relationship:

$$c_j^k = w_k \frac{\sigma_k}{\sigma_0};\ i = 1,2,\ldots,n;\ k = 1,2,\ldots,K \tag{7}$$

In the case that there is no tie in the criteria rank vector, the positive coefficient is thus equal to the preference weight.

The rank-reversal phenomenon could also occur when the linear combination depends on the normalising process. Using the weighed sum of criteria unit vectors without the adaptation of (7) could produce a rank-reversal situation. In the example of (4), using the unit criteria rank vectors with equal weights produces the following overall ranking, as easily verified:

$$\text{OR}: \quad (A_2 > A_1 > A_3) \tag{8}$$

This ranking is different from $A1 = A2 > A3$, indicated in (4), which is obtained by a simple equivalence consideration; the latter result is the same as obtained by simply adding the weighed un-normalised rank vectors, and finding the associated rank vector.
Consider now in addition that $C_2 : (2,1,2)$ in (2.14) changes to $C_2' : (2,1,3)$, i.e., a third alternative A_3 gets worse in the second criteria. It is expected that the overall ranking would not be affected, because A_3 is dominated in all cases. But the corresponding overall ranking is now certainly as indicated in (4), whatever the used approach, because there is no tie any more in the second basis vector:

$$\text{OR}': \quad (A_2 = A_1 > A_3) \tag{9}$$

The only way for avoiding such influence of a third irrelevant alternative A_3 on a pair (A_1,A_2), when ties are present in some criteria, is indeed using (7). This looks like a complication, but in fact it is not: a strikingly simple procedure indeed results for obtaining the overall ranking, given the individual rank vectors per criterion, as follows:
Combination rule of rank vectors: The linear combination of the unit criteria rank vectors with the positive coefficients c_j's defined in (7) gives the same final ranking as the direct combination of the un-normalised criteria rank vectors with the preference weights w_j's.
The proof is trivial, because after the transformation in (7) the denominators of the linear combination terms of the unit criteria rank vectors are now the same; the same associated rank vector is obtained than simply adding the weighed un-normalised rank vectors. This immediately defines the procedure for aggregating rankings vectors corresponding to different independent criteria:

Ordinal MCDM procedure: In a MCDM problem with only ordinal data for n alternatives, and $K \leqslant n-1$ independent unit rank vectors representing the criteria, given some set of K preference non-negative weights, any Pareto-optimal overall rank vector is the associated rank vector to the weighted sum of the K rank vectors. All Pareto-optimal overall rankings are obtained by considering non-negative fully random weights drawn from $[0,1]^K$.

The Pareto-optimal overall rank vectors obtained with this procedure satisfy the following invariance property:

Invariance property of the ordinal MCDM procedure: When the ordinal MCDM procedure is applied for obtaining the overall rank vectors, the ranks of alternatives in a pair are not affected when an alternative, which is dominated by the pair in all criteria, gets worse. The same property applies when alternatives dominated by the pair in all criteria are added to the alternative set.

The proof of this invariance property is trivial, as by the given procedure the overall rank vectors is the weighed sum of the criteria rank vectors, and the ranks of the alternatives in the pair are not affected, when a third alternative with no better ranks, becomes worse, or new dominated alternatives are introduced.

Note that this simple invariance property, which excludes not-explainable rank reversals, is not respected by outranking methods, as shown in Awang and Triantaphyllou [25], Kunsch [24]. Rank reversals appear because these approaches, in particular ELECTRE [25] and PROMETHEE [24], introduce interdependence between alternatives, so that the ranking within a pair is not immune against a third irrelevant alternative getting worse, or the addition of additional dominated alternatives. This rank-reversal phenomenon would also occur here if the linear combination would be dependent on the normalising process; it is why (7) has to be applied to remove this dependency, and the linear combination must be made directly on the ranks. The need for avoiding interdependency between alternatives also justifies clearly why the ranks must be defined according to (2), rather than to (1), to avoid the dependency of the rank on the number of alternatives p involved in a tie.

Note finally that some explainable rank reversals are unavoidable, with any procedure, in case of purely ordinal rank vectors. This is due to the missing cardinal data, providing information about the relative positions, and changes of positions of alternatives, see Kunsch [24]. This phenomenon may be interpreted as resulting from Arrow's impossibility theorem [26].

In order to identify ties in the overall ranking obtained in the weighed sum of criteria rank vectors, the following approach is best used: before calculating the weighed sum of ranks re-normalise the sum of weights to one. The components of the resulting combined n-vector are numbers belonging to the interval $[1,n]$. Consider an indifference thresholds Q, e.g., $Q = 0.1$, and while ranking give the same rank to two numbers differing by less than Q.

The proposed procedure is disappointingly simple, though it is convincing, and it has sufficient mathematical underpinning, as further developed in appendix A.1. But it may not be possible to demonstrate by mathematical means only that this approach is the only 'correct one' to the ill-defined vector-optimisation problem. Nevertheless this procedure is expected to be close to the way actual people reason while aggregating partial rankings of individual criteria. It is certainly not to be expected that people have a computer in their head, or that they use sophisticated graph-theoretical approaches, like in ELECTRE, or threshold-rich preference functions, like in PROMETHEE. Finally we are brought back to rather unsophisticated weighed sums of ranks. The point is here that all criteria are made commensurable by working with unit vectors.

6.2.2 *The maximum number of criteria*

The ordinal MCDM procedure in sub-section 6.2.1 imposes a restriction on the maximum number of criteria. This restriction has never been pointed out before, to my knowledge, but it is certainly well justified.

Note first that, when considering $(n-1)$ independent unit criteria vectors, it is always possible to add a dummy $(n+1)$ alternative, so that now up to $K = n$ independent criteria, and basis vectors, may be considered. The $(n+1)$ dummy alternative is chosen such that it is dominated by all n 'real' alternatives, in all n criteria. This addition brings the trivial n-vector ranking $(1,1,\ldots,1)$ into the game, which now becomes $(1,1,\ldots,1,n+1)$ in the space of higher dimension $(n+1)$. The corresponding $(n+1)$-vector is shown to be orthogonal to the set of n-vectors, and its projection is at the origin of the coordinate system using $(n-1)$ orthogonal basis vectors in V^n, see sub-sections 6.3.1 and 6.3.2 for additional explanations.

If for example $n = 2$, $K = 2$; C_1: $(1,2)$ and C_2: $(2,1)$, the two unit criteria rank vectors are obviously linearly dependent, as confirmed by $K > n-1$, because they are anti-correlated, pointing in opposite directions along the 1-D axis. To solve the MCDM problem a third dummy dominated alternative is introduced, so that now the unit vectors corresponding to $(1,2,3)$; $(2,1,3)$ are used as a basis, see sub-section 6.3.1. The projection of these basis vectors on the 1-D axis perpendicular to the vector corresponding to $(1,1,3)$ gives the 1-D situation; the trivial 1-D ranking $(1,1)$ is the point projection at the axis origin of $(1,1,3)$ on the 1-D axis, see below the 2-D visualisation in Fig. 6.1.

A dummy $(n+1)$ alternative stays for all alternatives, why are not considered in detail by the decision-makers, because they are quite bad in all respects: they are placed in a dominated indifference tie at the very end of the ranking, for all criteria. An interesting

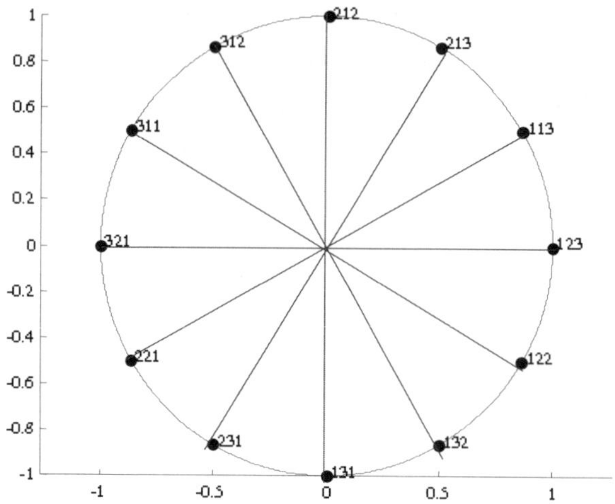

Figure 6.1 Shows the 12 non-trivial rank vectors for $n = 3$ alternatives.

question is to know how many such dummy alternatives may be added to the dominated unique indifference tie? In other words, with $(n-1)+x=K$, what is the largest possible positive integer x, and thus the largest acceptable K, the number of independent criteria, given n alternatives?

When the criteria vector does not exhibit ties between the significant alternatives, $x = 1$ at most, because for $x > 1$, i.e., with two or more dummy variables in the dominated tie, the x last rows would be identical in the matrix built by the basis vectors as columns. This leads us to the following upper bound on the number of criteria:

Upper bound on the number of criteria, given n alternatives: The actual maximum number of acceptable criteria in any MCD problem is given by the maximum rank of the basis matrix built with the criteria unit rank vectors as columns, placing dummy alternatives in a tie, in position $(n+1)$, in each criteria rank vector. This number is, in any case, smaller than, or equal to n, the number of alternatives, plus the number of criteria, which show ties in the n alternatives.

Some more theoretical investigation may precise the value of this upper bound on the maximum number of criteria in the general case.

Other dependency situations between criteria may happen in practice, like:

(1) Two or more criteria rank vectors are identical. In this case they may be combined into

one criterion, and their weights may be added;

(2) In case K is above the limit, say L, and some unit criteria rank vectors are linear combinations with non-negative coefficients of a basis of L independent unit criteria rank vectors, their weights are shared according to this combination between these basis vectors;

(3) It may happen that K does not exceed the limit, but some basis vectors are linearly dependent, such that the maximum rank of the basis matrix is $r < K$. In this case, the dependent basis vectors have to be eliminated from the set, such as to maximise the sum of criteria weights;

(4) In case the number of criteria exceeds the upper acceptable limit, and (2) is not applicable, the more important criteria with respect to the weights have to be selected, up to this acceptable limit;

(5) When several important criteria have equal weights, so that more criteria than the limit, say L, have to be considered, say N, it may be appropriate to decompose the problem by selecting random weights in $[0.45, 0.55]^N$, and to consider for each instance of the weight set, used for calculating the Rank Matrix, the L most important criteria; etc.

The proposed procedure presented in sub-section 6.2.1 is thus only valid in practice for a number of independent criteria, generally not much larger than n, the number of alternatives. According to our knowledge this restriction has never been reported before in MCDM problems. Space is lacking for discussing in detail this important aspect, and its full implications, but such limitation looks quite reasonable: when no limit is placed on the number of criteria, the latter may grow forever, as it suits the decision-makers: it is clear from intuition, and confirmed by the Basic Property A.1.1, and Corollary A.1.2, see section 6.2.1, that the more criteria beyond n, the more correlations between criteria appear, that may artificially ‘push’ some alternatives in an unmerited way towards the top of the ranking. Consider, for example, the purchase of a car: when more and more small design features are added as criteria in the MCDM analysis, there may be a point when they start outweighing by their very number more essential criteria like the technical performances, the price, etc.

In such cases it is better to adopt a hierarchical structure, like in AHP of Saaty [21], before starting the analysis. In this way separate MCDM analyses are performed at different levels, by first combining commensurate criteria of the same nature, pursuing the analysis at higher level on the obtained more global criteria, etc., see Macharis *et al.* [23] for similar suggestions. Simulation tests [25] also indirectly confirm these conclusions for ELECTRE

II and ELECTRE III. In these tests, the rates of rank reversals in some sample examples from the literature are plotted against the number of criteria K for different numbers of alternatives n. The curves are bell-shaped, and their maximum values are observed to be around $K = n$. The authors [25] observe that the decrease with larger numbers of criteria is due to the fact that 'if the number of criteria is beyond some value, the pair-wise outranking relations and the subsequent ranking of the alternatives is more likely to become stable than before'. This is in my opinion coherent with the above remark that the increased correlations between criteria may consolidate ranks in an artificial way.

6.2.3 *The inverse procedure for finding preference weights*

In sub-section 6.2.1, a normative procedure has been discussed for aggregating the criteria rank vectors to an overall ordinal ranking. The inverse question is also useful, when analysing data from multiple decision-makers, e.g., for market surveys: given statistical results on overall rankings, how to reconstruct the preference rankings of criteria, and how to perform a statistical analysis of the different preference groups in the decision-makers sample?

Assume for applying the reverse procedure the example presented in Kunsch [29] from Ruan *et al.* [28]: $n = 3$ car types, are offered on the market; $K = 2 = n - 1$ evaluation criteria, C_1, C_2 are considered. A pay-off table is available from which ordinal rankings are deduced for each criterion, independently of individual preferences:

$$C_1 : (1,2,3); \quad C_2 : (3,1,2) \tag{10}$$

An enquiry is performed on a sufficiently large sample of individuals ('interviewees') to collect their opinions on car rank vectors, on the basis of an evaluation table with two criteria. According to (3) there are for each criterion $P(3) = 12 + 1$ possibilities for the alternative rankings, corresponding to the permutations with ties of $(1,2,3)$; this includes the trivial ranking $(1,1,1)$ to be ignored. The rank vectors provided by several groups of interviewees are given in the upper part of Table 6.1, with their percentages with respect to the full sample (100 %). For validation purposes a preference ranking of the criteria is asked as well. The objective is here to deduce the preferences between criteria for each group, and to validate these results against the collected interviewees' data. The analysis in this first step is expected to provide enough information on preferences. These results are used in a second step, and in later steps, when the car characteristics change, or new brands enter the car market. In this way the changing market shares may be re-computed, without performing anew an expensive market enquiry.

Table 6.1 The rankings with their percentages for five group of interviewees from the observed sample in the Market survey enquiry from Kunsch [29] in Ruan *et al.* [28].

Label R % sample	$R_1 = C_1$ (15 %)	$R_2 = C_2$ (8 %)	R_3 (36 %)	R_4 (25 %)	R_5 (16 %)
Ranking	(1, 2, 3)	(3, 1, 2)	(1, 1, 3)	(2, 1, 3)	(2, 1, 2)
Weight C_1	1	0	1.155	1	0.577
Weight C_2	0	1	0.577	1	1.155
Preference	C_1 alone	C_2 alone	$C_1 > C_2$	$C_1 = C_2$	$C_1 < C_2$

The two criteria in Table 6.1 correspond to the direction of the unit criteria rank vectors representing $C_1 : (1,2,3)$, and $C_2 : (3,1,2)$ (see Fig. 6.1). Any other ranking is obtained by combining linearly the criteria rank vectors used as basis vectors, according to the Basic Property A.1.1 and its corollary A.1.2, see sub-section 6.2.1.

Because the two basis vectors contain no tie, the positive coefficients in the linear combination of the basis vectors for obtaining the rank vectors are equal to the preference weights, indicated in the lower part of Table 6.1, according to (7). They are easily calculated from (A.5) in appendix A.1, by inverting the correlation matrix of the two basis vectors.

The preferences are indicated in the lowest row of Table 6.1: $C_1 > C_2$ indicates that C_1 is more important that C_2; $C_1 = C_2$ indicates that both criteria have the same importance; C_1 (C_2) alone indicates that C_2 (C_1) has a vanishing weight in the linear combination. These results are then compared to the interviewees' declarations about their criteria preferences; appropriate corrections to non-rational rankings are made; there is no need for such corrections in this example, as all five groups have chosen Pareto-optimal rankings, all weights being positive, or zero. The market-shares vector (MS_1) for the three cars is computed as being:

$$\mathrm{MS}_1 : \; (33\,\%,\ 67\,\%,\ 0\,\%) \tag{11}$$

In this evaluation, equal shares of ranks are assumed for the cars involved in a tie. In a second step assume that the criteria rank vectors change, due to some evolution of the brands, as follows:

$$C_1' : \; (2,1,3); \quad C_2' : \; (2,2,1) \tag{12}$$

Assuming that preferences of the interviewees' groups have remained the same, it is easy to recalculate the new markets shares. This is done for each group by using the sets of two weights, compatible with the preferences indicated in Table 6.1 for each preference group. Because now, C_2' has a tie, the c_2 coefficient positive coefficient is related to the weight w_2

as indicated in (7), and it becomes:

$$c_2' = \frac{\sigma_2}{\sigma_0} w_2 = \frac{1}{\sqrt{3}} w_2 \tag{13}$$

For the three groups R_1, R_2, R_4, the two weights are immediately obtained, as either one is vanishing, or both are equal, and so is the associated rank vector. For group $R_3 :\ C_1 > C_2$; $R_5 :\ C_2 > C_1$, Monte Carlo calculations are performed using the weight ranking of the group, according to the MCDM ordinal procedure in sub-section 6.2.1. A Rank Matrix is obtained for each interviewees group. Multiplying the probabilities of each car brand of being ranked first by the group percentages in the whole interviewees sample gives the modified market-shares vector (MS2):

$$\text{MS}_2 :\ (0\,\%, 84\,\%, 16\,\%) \tag{14}$$

The inverse procedure to the MCDM ordinal procedure in sub-section 6.2.1 is easy to perform, assuming that the aggregation procedure is indeed a weighed sum of ranks. Note also that because the basis criteria are independent, each overall rank vector is determined in a unique way by a fixed set of combination coefficients of the basis vectors.

6.3 2-D and 3-D Visualisation in the Ordinal Case

In order to illustrate the ordinal procedure, and to visualise the results in the 2-D and 3-D space the two cases of $n = 3$; $K = 2$, and $n = 4$; $K = 3$ are discussed in detail in this section.

6.3.1 *The 2-D case*

For $n = 3$, $K = (n-1) = 2$, there are $P(3) = 12$ rank vectors according to (3), not including the trivial rank vector $(1,1,1)$, which we first ignore. According to the Basic Property A.1.1 and Corollary A.1.2, the matrix, which has all unit rank vectors as columns, has rank= $n-1 = 2$, making a 2-D representation possible.

The 12 non-trivial rank vectors are shown in Fig. 6.1. The trivial rank vector $(1,1,1)$ is perpendicular at the origin to the plane of this figure. The orthogonal unit rank vectors corresponding to the rankings $(1,2,3)$, and $(2,1,2)$ have zero correlations: they may be chosen as orthogonal positive X-axis, and Y-axis, respectively. The Pearson's correlation between two unit rank vectors is equal to $\cos(\theta)$, $0 \leqslant \theta \leqslant \pi$ is the angle between these vectors [27]. This angle is equal to 30° between any two adjacent rank vectors.

Assuming two maximum criteria, the sequence of rankings in Fig. 6.1 is a logical one: starting from any ranking in any direction: e.g., starting from $(1,2,3)$ counter clockwise, one finds successively: an increase of (2) towards (1) first leading to $(1,1,3)$; then a further increase of (2) beyond (1), leading further to $(2,1,3)$; then an increase in (3) leading to $(2,1,2)$, etc. Consider the rank vectors correspond to $K=2$ criteria given as $C_1:(1,2,3)$; $C_2:(2,1,3)$; the corresponding unit rank vectors are:

$$\begin{aligned} C_1 &: \left(-\frac{1}{\sqrt{2}}, 0, +\frac{1}{\sqrt{2}}\right) \\ C_2 &: \left(0, -\frac{1}{\sqrt{2}}, +\frac{1}{\sqrt{2}}\right) \end{aligned} \tag{15}$$

Using these vectors as basis vectors, combining them linearly by means of two non-negative random coefficients in $[0,1]$ [2], identical to the preference weights in this basis without ties, see (7), and re-normalising, produces a unit vectors lying in the circle sector between C_1 and C_2. It is clear that all Pareto-optimal solutions of the (C_1,C_2) MCDM problem must necessarily be one of the overall rankings associated with such combination vectors, i.e., they must be overall rank vectors lying in the circle sector between C_1, and C_2. In this example, only $(1,2,3)$; $(1,1,3)$; or $(2,1,3)$ are possible Pareto-optimal overall rank vectors, because of the logical evolution sequence starting counter-clockwise from $(1,2,3)$; or clockwise from $(2,1,3)$. Choosing e.g., $(1,2,2)$ would not be logical: starting from $C_1:(1,2,3)$ it would move clockwise towards non-increasing A_2 values, and increasing A_3 values, away from $C_2:(2,1,3)$. Thus the possible compromise rank vectors, and their positive coefficients, c_1, c_2 in the combinations, are the following ones, where both the ordinary and unit rank vector are indicated:

$$\begin{aligned} C_1 &:(1,2,3): c_1 = w_1 = 1; c_2 = w_2 = 0; \text{ see (15) for the unit vector} \\ &(1,1,3): c_1 = w_1 = c_2 = w_2 = 1; \left(-\frac{1}{\sqrt{6}}, \frac{-1}{\sqrt{6}}, \frac{+2}{\sqrt{6}}\right) \\ C_2 &:(2,1,3): c_1 = w_1 = 0; c_2 = w_1 = 1; \text{ see (15) for the unit vector} \end{aligned} \tag{16}$$

The positive combination coefficients are calculated by means of (A.5) in appendix A.1. Note again that the positive coefficients are equal to the preference weights, in the absence of ties in the basis vectors. The MCDM compromise obtained with equal preference weights being given to both criteria is thus $(1,1,3)$. The sum of the linear-combination coefficients is not necessarily equal to one, as the combination result must be a unit vector, and a quadratic normalisation rule applies.

The ranks frequencies of alternatives, as given by the Rank Matrix, are obtained by performing Monte Carlo calculations on the weights. These frequencies are visualized, in this simple case, as corresponding to the relative surfaces of the sectors lying between the basis vectors. For arbitrary weights from $[0,1]^2$, and the (C_1,C_2) basis vectors, one obtains immediately equal ranks frequencies for both A_1, A_2, while A_3 is dominated:

$$\begin{aligned} &A_1 : (50\%;50\%;0\%) \\ &A_2 : (50\%;50\%;0\%) \\ &A_3 : (0\%;0\%;100\%) \end{aligned} \tag{17}$$

It is also clear from the 2-D representation why the preference weights are not the same as the positive coefficients in the linear combinations of basis vectors, when the latter show ties. Using $C_2' : (2,1,2)$ instead of $C_2 : (2,1,3)$ must not change the ranks frequencies; but an additional 30° sector is now added, see Fig. 6.1, that seem to favour A_2 for being ranked first. But by application of (7) the frequency invariance is re-established, and any rank reversal is avoided.

Note that for $n = 3$, the 2-D overall rank vectors must always lie within the solid angle defined by the basis vector. This is not necessarily true for cases with $n > 3$, and higher dimensional spaces. In these cases the Pareto-optimal overall rank vectors will either lie within, or close-by the edges of the solid angle spanned by the basis vectors, i.e., the criteria rank vectors. This is elaborated in the following sub-section, when discussing the 3-D case with $n = 4$.

6.3.2 *The 3-D Case*

For $n = 4$, $K = (n-1) = 3$, there are $P(4) = 74$ rank vectors according to (3), not including the trivial rank vector $(1,1,1,1)$, which may be first ignored. According to the Basic Property A.1.1 and Corollary A.1.2., see sub-section 6.2.1, the matrix, which has all unit rank vectors as columns, has rank$= n-1 = 3$, so that their representation in the 3-D space is easy. They appear on the unit sphere in Fig. 6.2. The six permutations in the rank vector $(1,1,3,3)$ provide here the six directions of orthogonal XYZ axes. Projections in the plane from above and below perpendicular to the (X,Y) plane are shown in two Figs. A.1, A.2 in Appendix A.2.

This visualisation shows that the rank vectors are organised in a symmetrical way around the unit sphere: they build a symmetry group, which is certainly interesting to analyse, but this is beyond the scope of the present chapter. Two types of octants are observed for each $Z \geqslant 0$, $Z \leqslant 0$ with respectively 16 and 13 unit rank vectors, so that there is no C_4 symmetry around the orthogonal XYZ axes. This symmetry lowering is due to the use of integer ranks in (2). It is interesting to note that the traditional representation in (1) would produce the higher C_4 symmetry, and four identical octants for each $Z \geqslant 0$; $Z \leqslant 0$: but, as discussed earlier, this representation would not be suitable, because it introduces

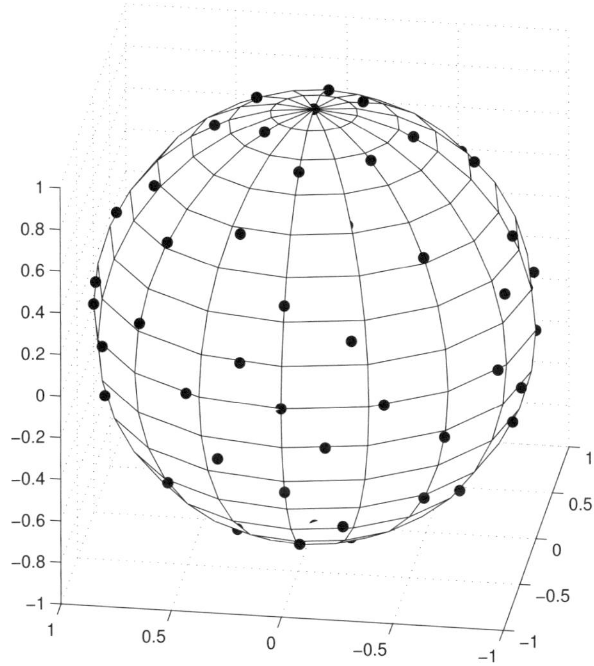

Figure 6.2 The unit sphere shows for $n = 4$ the $p(4) = 74$ non-trivial ranking vectors indicated by dark points.

dependencies between alternatives, which may lead to rank reversal situations, impossible to explain on a rational basis.

To further illustrate the proposed approach, let us consider the 16-vector octant shown in Fig. 6.3. Assume the following three independent basis vectors, being the criteria rank vectors:

$$C_1 : (1,3,4,1);\; C_2 : (1,2,4,3);\; C_3 : (3,1,4,1) \quad (18)$$

A Monte-Carlo analysis is performed by using random weights in $[0,1]$ [3], and using (7) for taking into account the tie effect on the weights in C_1 and C_3. The computed Rank Matrix is obtained:

$$\begin{aligned} A_1 &: (45\%, 30\%, 25\%, 0\%) \\ A_2 &: (13\%, 30\%, 57\%, 0\%) \\ A_3 &: (0\%, 0\%, 0\%, 100\%) \\ A_4 &: (42\%, 41\%, 17\%, 0\%) \end{aligned} \quad (19)$$

An equal-sharing rule of ranks probabilities is applied to alternatives involved in a tie. This explains why A_1 has a somewhat larger probability of occupying the first rank than A_4, though both alternatives are equivalent regarding their criteria ranks. Nevertheless A_4 has to share one time the first rank with A_2, this explains the observed difference in the first-rank frequency.

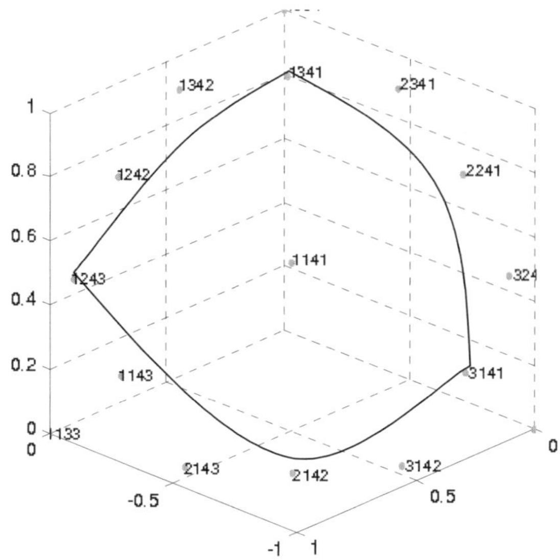

Figure 6.3 An upper octant with 16 vectors. The sketched solid angle spanned by the unit basis vectors described in the text is evidenced. The rank vectors within this solid angle, or close to its edges, are the $P(3) = 12$ rank vectors of Fig. 6.1, considering that the dominated A_3 has the fixed 4th rank.

It can be remarked that alternative A_3 is always dominated, so that this MCDM problem is equivalent to three 2-D problems, obtained by combining pair-wise the three criteria. This is a case where a dummy dominated variable (here A_3) is added in order to be able to address the larger $K = 3$ MCDM problem. This has been discussed in sub-section 6.2.2. All 13 permutations of $(1,2,(4),3)$ are present, including the trivial $(n-1=3)$ rank vector $(1,1,(4),1)$, the diagonal of the octant shown in Fig. 6.3, A_3 being fixed in the 4th position. When projected on a plane perpendicular to the $(1,1,4,1)$ diagonal these $12+1$ solutions reconstitute all unit $(n-1)$-vectors in the 2-D example (see Fig. 6.1). This may be immediately verified from Fig. 6.3, by looking at all permutations rankings of $(1,2,(4),3)$ with the fixed third position (4). The trivial $(1,1,1)$ ranking for $(n-1) = 3$ is located at the origin as discussed for the case $n = 2$ in section 6.3.1.

For example the Pareto-optimal rank vectors located about the edge $(1,2,(4),3)$ to $(1,3,(4),1)$ are in the sequence $(1,2,(4),3)$; $(1,2,(4),2)$, $(1,3,(4),2)$; $(1,3,(4),1)$, compare Fig. 6.1 and Fig. 6.3.

This graphical analysis confirms that the introduction of a dummy dominated alternative will not cause any rank reversal among the dominating solutions. It also shows that Pareto-optimal rank vectors are not all located within the solid angle spanned by the basis vectors, but some are located outside, but close to its edges, on which some combination coefficients are vanishing. Because they come somewhat outside the edges of the solid angle, these rank vectors have one of several negative linear-combination coefficients with respect to some basis vectors: it means that they are each solutions of a reduced MCDM problem, in which some criteria rank vectors have vanishing preference weights, being less important for the decision-makers. The cases in which all criteria have comparable importance will bring the solution $(1,1,4,1)$, located in the octant diagonal, corresponding to the trivial $(1,1,1)$ solution in the projected 2-D case for $n-1=3$, see Fig. 6.3.

6.4 An Extension of the Approach to Cardinal Scales

6.4.1 *A MCDM procedure*

The nice thing about the Basic Property A.1.1 and Corollary A.1.2, used in subsection 6.2.1 for designing the ordinal MCDM procedure, is that it is not only applicable to unit basis vectors corresponding to ordinal rankings but to any unit n-vector in the K-dimensional subspace $V^n_{\{K\}} \subset V^n$, $K \leqslant n-1$, given n alternatives, and K criteria. It would mean, at least in principle, that unit n-vectors obtained from the cardinal evaluations of alternatives may be used as basis vectors, in the same way as basis vectors with integer components are used in the case of purely ordinal scales. But this is not so easy in practice, as additional difficulties arise here. First, the correct use of (7) is not fully clear, concerning the relationship between the positive combination coefficients to be affected to the basis vectors, given a set of preference weights. While the number of discrete ordinal rank vectors is finite, the set of evaluation vectors is infinite; which reference vector should be used to calculate σ_0 in (7)? A second difficulty arises because some alternative evaluations are uncertain, and any modification in some values affects the re-normalising process of unit vectors serving as a basis; the same happens when dominated alternatives are added to the set; some could be given arbitrarily bad values, but they must not change the final overall rankings: the required invariance properties of the ranks of dominating alternatives would not be granted if unit evaluation vectors are used without care as basis vectors.

For cardinal scales things are thus far less clear than for ordinal scales, but a procedure satisfying the property of invariance to rank reversals must be worked out, though it may not be unique. In addition it must be inspired by the wish of keeping things simple, and close to the way the rather limited human brain is able to combine criteria evaluations by means of preference weights, using simple 'mental rules'.

To achieve that result first consider that all criteria scales are cardinal. To address the mentioned difficulties the evaluations of alternatives with any criterion should be transformed into well-defined and discrete scores. The following approach [24] is proposed:

Assume without loss of generality a minimum criterion, the adjustment for maximum criteria being trivial. Perform an affine transformation of cardinal evaluations to an m-point-scale $(1,m)$, so that for each criterion — one obtains an integer n-vector with five possible echelons in the interval $[0,m]$:

$$\begin{aligned} &\text{score (best)} = 1 \\ &\text{score (worst)} = m \\ &\text{score (value)} = \text{INT}\left[1 + \frac{\text{value-best}}{\text{worst-best}} \cdot (m-1)\right] \end{aligned} \tag{20}$$

where: 'best' corresponds to the best value expected for the criterion; 'worst' corresponds to the threshold value beyond which the score takes the worst value$= m$; 'INT' computes the closest integer value.

In this way integers scores in $[0,m]$ are obtained; they are in first approximation independent of the precise value of the alternatives; this is important considering that evaluations are many times imprecise or uncertain. Without loss of generality, the first-ranked alternatives in the criterion evaluation vector may be given a score$= 1$, so that the 'best' value is chosen close-by and fixed, independently of possible uncertainties on its evaluation. Of course should the best value change drastically – due for example to technology development, and the coming up of new, better alternatives, it should be acceptable to modify this value.

Let us elaborate on this approach by using the language of fuzzy logic, see e.g., Klir and Yuan [30].

Select the 'universe of discourse' for each criterion. Consider as an example a minimum criterion, e.g., some pertinent cost: the universe of discourse would be in the open interval:]Most preferred, Least preferred[, meaning that values left, or right of the boundaries keep the value 'Most Preferred', or 'Least Preferred', respectively. Consider five echelons covering the universes of discourse uniformly by means of five triangular membership functions MF_i, $i = 1,2,\ldots,5$, with flat ramps to the left and right of the universe-of-discourse boundaries. They thus produce a 5-point scale for the scoring. An example is shown in Fig. 6.4 for cost data in the universe of discourse $]20,120[$, $n \geqslant 5$.

In this case the fuzzy rules are different from the usual Mamdani rules used in control theory

[31]; for each criterion, and an alternative with a given criterion VALUE, an application is considered between the membership grade (MG_i) of the MF_i, $i = 1,2,\ldots,5$, and an integer, or half-integer score SC(VALUE), as follows:

$$\begin{aligned}&IF\ MG_i(VALUE) > 0.55\ THEN\ SC(VALUE) = i\\&IF\ MG_{i+1}(VALUE) \leqslant 0.55\ AND\ MG_i(VALUE) \geqslant 0.45\ THEN\ SC(VALUE) = i+0.5\\&i = 1,2,\ldots,5\end{aligned} \tag{21}$$

This rule system attributes the integer score $SC(VALUE) = i$ in case there is no hesitation between two echelons; and the half-score $SC(VALUE = (i+0.5)$ in case there is a hesitation between two echelons (i); $(i+1)$. Thanks to the rounding down, or up to the next integer, except for some hesitation in the middle range, the scores are robust against changes in the evaluations of the alternatives due to uncertainties.

In this procedure, three parameters must be fixed: (a) The 'most-preferred' left boundary, (b) The 'least-preferred' right boundary, and (c) '*m*' the number of preference echelons, i.e., the number of points in the scoring scale.

(a) The choice of the most-preferred left boundary in the universe of discourse is not an issue, assuming a constant range of values: an equal shift in the scores of all alternatives does not affect the final ranking. This value may be fixed such that the first ranked alternatives indeed gets score 1, corresponding to the most preferred alternatives in the provided set. Of course, if a new better alternative shows up later on, the choice of a value for score 1 may be revisited.
(b) The choice of the least preferred value in the universe of discourse is more delicate, because it influences all other scores, creating an unwanted dependency between alternatives, that may cause rank reversals [24]. A simple way is choosing this value such as to give the highest '*m*' score, i.e., 5, in the example of a 5-point scale to the least ranked solution. This value should however be fixed, such as not to be influenced by uncertainties, modifications of evaluations of least-preferred alternatives, or the introduction of new, still worse alternatives. It is better to choose a threshold value indicating a least preferred value for some criterion: all alternatives beyond this threshold will be given the same worst score, indicating that they are indifferent to the decision-makers, being equally unattractive regarding this criterion.
(c) The last important parameter is the number of echelons '*m*' in the scoring scale. Consider first the case when there are no purely ordinal criteria: a comparison has to be made between any alternative and the best available one, which receives score 1; five

echelons seem to give a sufficient precision to the judgments. If $n > 5$ decision-makers may not be able, or willing, to establish a fine distinction between least-preferred alternatives, and the same score$= m$ is given, in order to indicate indifference between 'least preferred alternatives'.

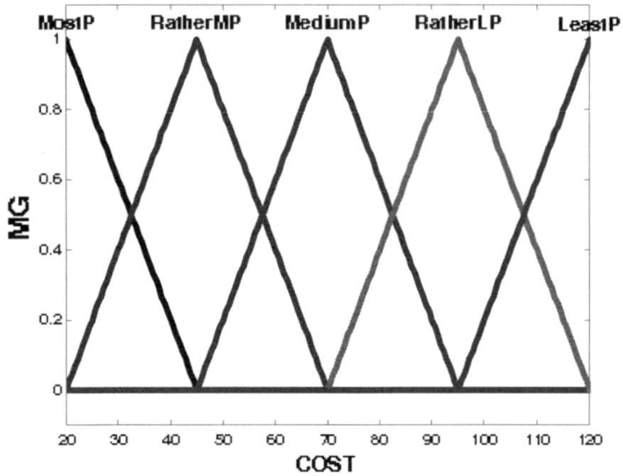

Figure 6.4 The five Memberships functions for the minimum criterion 'COST' using a 5-point scoring scale with Most Preferred (MostP); Rather Most Preferred (RatherMP); Medium Preferred (MediumP); Rather Least Preferred (RatherLP); Least Preferred (LeastP).

Five echelons in a 5-point scale give $(5^n - 4^n)$ possibilities for scoring n alternatives, the score 1 being always present at least once, and not including possible hesitations between half scores. For $n = 5$, $5^5 - 4^5 = 2101$ integer scores are possible to evaluate ($n = 5$) alternatives, to be compared with $P(5) = 540(+1)$ rank vectors available with ordinal scales, see (3).

Of course the number 'm' of echelons must be the same for all criteria. When there are ordinal scales, the number of echelons must not be larger than n: this is because a ranking like $(1,2,3)$ cannot be distinguished from $(1,3,5)$, which is meaningless in an ordinal setting. I therefore recommend the following formula for choosing an 'm' value:

$$\begin{aligned} m &= n & n &\leqslant 5 \\ m &= 5 & n &= 6 \\ m &= 5,7 & n &\geqslant 7 \end{aligned} \tag{22}$$

When there are seven, or more, alternatives I recommend to use 5 or 7-point scales. This is because again the human brain is probably not in a position to make refined distinctions between more than seven echelons indicating relative preferences. The MCDM procedure developed in subsection 6.2.1 for ordinal rank vectors is applicable to the scoring vectors obtained by means of the m-point scale. This is easy to verify, because the Basic Property A.1.1 and Corollary A.1.2 described in sub-section 6.2.1 are valid for any set of independent basic vectors in $V^n_{\{K\}}$. Regarding the presence of ties in some basis vectors the same line of reasoning, as in sub-section 6.2.1, leads again to (7), for transforming the preference weights into positive combination coefficients of the basis vectors. The score vector with the largest standard deviation σ_0 may be chosen as a reference for (7). For example with an odd $n = 5$ and $m = 5$, $(1,1,3,5,5)$ has the largest standard deviation of all evaluation vectors, and it may be used for the σ_0 reference; for an even $n = 6$, and $m = 5$, $(1,1,1,5,5,5)$ may take this part. The same conclusion is obtained, as before in sub-section 6.2.1 applicable to ordinal rankings, that the un-normalised basis vectors must be directly combined in order to obtain an overall score n-vector for the alternatives, from which the associated rank vector may be obtained. The following procedure would then be adapted to cardinal data, and mixed ordinal/cardinal data:

MCDM Procedure with cardinal or mixed data:

- For each criterion with cardinal evaluation data, choose the 'most preferred' value to be given the score '1'; choose the 'least preferred' value serving as a threshold for the least attractive alternatives receiving the same score m; choose the 'm' number of preference echelons as indicated in (22).
- Evaluate all alternatives on the m-point scale using the rule system described in (21); K n-vectors are obtained, containing the score evaluations, integer or half-integers values on the m-point scales: call them criterion evaluation vectors;
- Calculate K basis vectors obtained by centring and normalising the K criterion evaluation vectors. Verify that the K basis vectors are independent. Otherwise reduce the dimension of the basis, as explained in sub-section 6.2.2;
- Select weights in $[0,1]^K$; use each instance of the normalised weights to combine the independent basis vectors, and to obtain a combined evaluation vector with components in the interval $[1,m]$;
- Find for each weight instance the associated overall rank vectors to the combined evaluation vector by using an indifference threshold Q, e.g., $Q = 0.1$ for identifying ties;
- Calculate the Rank Matrix in case of stochastic weights.

Invariance Property of the cardinal/mixed-data MCDM procedure: When the MCDM

procedure is applied to cardinal, or mixed data for obtaining overall rank vectors, the ranks of alternatives in a pair are not affected when a third alternative gets worse, which was dominated by the pair in the overall rank vector. The same property applies when dominated alternatives are added to the set of alternatives.
The proof of this property is the same as for the ordinal MCDM procedure presented in sub-section 6.2.1. Note however that it is here sufficient that the third alternative be dominated in the overall rank vector: it is no longer required, as in the ordinal case, that it should be dominated in all criteria rank vectors, see sub-section 6.2.1. This is because the scores of the dominating alternatives in the pair are unaffected whatever happens to the third alternatives in any criterion, while this is not necessarily true in case of ordinal ranks. Of course this invariance is only granted if the worsening of dominated alternatives does not modify the m-point-scale range of values.

6.4.2 *An application of the cardinal procedure*

For comparing existing methodologies with the present one, a MCDM application is presented in this sub-section. It is the localisation of a composting plant in Ticino (Switzerland) developed in Maystre *et al.* [32] for illustrating the ELECTRE methodologies. There are $n = 7$ alternatives and $K = 5$ linearly independent criteria. The cardinal evaluation data, the nature and units of criteria, and ranges for the criteria weights are given in Table 6.2. The indifference and preference thresholds appear in the lower part of this table. They are used for the evaluation with ELECTRE III [32], and also for the comparison with PROMETHEE I, II, for which linear criteria with two P (preference), Q (indifference) thresholds are assumed [18, 19, 20].
Table 6.3 provides the rankings resulting from the application of the different methodologies on the MCDM problem described in Table 6.2. In the last column on the right the correlations are indicated between the obtained rankings from the different methodologies, and the 5-point scale (5-pts) approach introduced in section 6.4.1. Note that ELECTRE and PROMETHEE have two rankings, because of the possibility of incomparability between pairs of alternatives; these rankings are also shown in the comparison in Table 6.3.

- In ELECTRE II and III [14] (EII, EIII) there are ascending (asc) and descending (desc) distillation processes leading each to two complete rankings;
- In PROMETHEE I [18, 19, 20] there are two complete rankings corresponding to the positive (dominance) flows (PROM+), and the negative (dominating) flows (PROM−) respectively.

Table 6.2 The evaluation data for the MCDM localisation problem[32]. Minimum criteria appear with a negative sign (SF=Swiss Francs).

Criteria **Alternati-ves**	**Site Price** **SF/m²**	**Transport** **10³ km/y**	**Environmental status** **Qualitative**	**#Residents affected** **Qualitative**	**Availability of site** **Qualitative**
A1	-120	-284	5	3.5	18
A2	-150	-269	2	4.5	24
A3	-100	-413	4	5.5	17
A4	-60	-596	6	8	20
A5	-30	-1321	8	7.5	16
A6	-80	-734	5	4	21
A7	-45	-982	7	8.5	13
Weights min-average-max	20-25-30	35-45-55	8-10-12	10-12-14	6-8-10
Indifference thresholds	15	80	1	0.5	1
Preference thresholds	40	350	3	3.5	5

- The PROMETHEE II [18,19,20] complete ranking (PROM II) is obtained from the net flows, which are equal to the difference between the positive and the negative flows.
- The results of ordinal MCDM procedure, see section 6.2.1, are also indicated for comparison in Table 6.3. An interesting result [24] is that they are identical to the complete ranking provided by the negative flows in the ordinal version of PROMETHEE I, i.e., assuming that the preference thresholds $P = 0$ for all criteria. In general it can be shown that the complete ranking induced by negative flows in PROMETHEE I provides more robust results than the net flows used for the complete ranking in PROMETHEE II, though there are also not entirely immune against rank reversals with preference thresholds $P \neq 0$.

For the sake of keeping assumptions to a minimum, the range of the m-point-scale for each criterion is chosen to be the interval between the best value (score '1') and the worst value (score 'm'). Of course this assumption deserves to be further analysed by means of sensitivity studies depending on actual preferences of the decision-maker groups.
The comparison in Table 6.3 is very instructive as far as it confirms the following results:

2. ELECTRE II and III provide results, which are very different from those obtained by other methodologies, except for the ascending distillation in ELECTRE III [14], which

Table 6.3 A comparison between the rankings of ELECTRE II, III; PROMETHEE I; PROMETHEE II; the ordinal MCDM procedure in sec. (6.2.1); the 5-point (5 pts) and 7-point (7 pts) scales in the MCDM procedure in sec. (6.4.1). The abbreviations are further explained in the text.

	A1	A2	A3	A4	A5	A6	A7	Correlation 5-pt scale
EII asc	4	1	4	2	7	4	6	0.580
EII desc	4	1	4	2	7	4	6	0.580
EIII asc	2.5	2.5	4	1	6	7	5	0.873
EIII desc	5.5	5.5	2.5	1	5.5	5.5	2.5	0.663
PROM+	3.5	2	5.5	1	5.5	7	3.5	0.633
PROM-	3	4	2	1	7	5.5	5.5	0.973
PROMII	2.5	4	2.5	1	7	6	5	0.982
Ordinal	3	2	4.5	1	6	7	4.5	0.800
5-pts	3	4	2	1	6.5	6.5	5	1.000
7-pts	2	4.5	3	1	7	6	4.5	0.945

comes acceptably close to other results; the ascending distillation could be compared to the PROMETHEE I negative flow ranking [24], discussed below;

2. The negative flows in PROMETHEE I provide a ranking, which is closely related to both 5-point-scale, and 7-point-scale results. This indicates that, in this example, the evaluations of the criteria are sufficiently well apart: the interdependency between alternatives introduced by preference thresholds remains rather small [24]. Nevertheless, changes in threshold values, the addition of new dominated alternatives, etc. may introduce unwanted rank reversals to the PROMETHEE I results. For the same reason the very high correlation of PROMETHEE II with the 5-point-scale results should be considered with caution, as it gives no guarantee for robust results in case technical parameters or evaluation data would change.

Maystre *et al.* [32] assume crisp weights, indicated as average weights in Table 6.2. It is important in the present approach to make statistical analyses on these weights as well. Table 6.4 provides the Rank Matrix for the 5-point scale, when the weights are taken to be stochastic in the ranges $[\min, \max]$ indicated in Table 6.2. These results show that the crisp ranking is relatively stable in this range, i.e.,

$$A_4 > A_3 > A_1 > A_2 > A_7 > A_5 = A_6 \tag{23}$$

Table 6.4 The Rank Matrix obtained from stochastic weights varying according to a rectangular distribution in the range indicated in Table 6.2.

	Rank 1	Rank 2	Rank 3	Rank 4	Rank 5	Rank 6	Rank 7
A_1	0.0 %	15.8 %	74.8 %	8.8 %	0.7 %	0.0 %	0.0 %
A_2	0.0 %	0.0 %	1.4 %	69.0 %	21.6 %	8.0 %	0.1 %
A_3	0.0 %	84.0 %	16.1 %	0.0 %	0.0 %	0.0 %	0.0 %
A_4	100.0 %	0.0 %	0.0 %	0.0 %	0.0 %	0.0 %	0.0 %
A_5	0.0 %	0.0 %	0.0 %	0.7 %	7.5 %	42.8 %	49.2 %
A_6	0.0 %	0.0 %	0.0 %	0.0 %	2.2 %	47.1 %	50.8 %
A_7	0.0 %	0.3 %	7.8 %	21.6 %	68.2 %	2.2 %	0.0 %

6.5 Conclusions and Outlook

This chapter presents simple procedures for solving MCDM problems, though they have a strong mathematical underpinning detailed in appendix A.1. These procedures may be used either as interpretative instruments of statistical data in multi-criteria enquiries, or directly as normative, i.e., decision aiding tools for MCDA.

The simplicity of the approach enhances its credibility, by making it more realistic, and close to 'mind computing' in many every day's MCDM problems. Many applications are certainly thinkable, not only quite technical ones in Marketing Research, agent-based modelling, etc., but also in many cases of ordinary life. The key statistical concept is a measure of distance by means of the ordinary (Pearson) correlation between two rank vectors. Garcia and Pérez-Román [33] in Ruan *et al.* [28] have shown that the cosine is the most adequate measure of distance between rank vectors when trying to achieve a collective consensus for group decision-making. In particular this approach eliminates dependencies between alternatives, not explainable rank-reversals, or non-transitivity situations, quite common in popular outranking methods. Note, however that explainable rank reversals are always possible with ordinal rankings, due to the poor information available on the dynamic positioning of alternatives, as shown in [24].

Regarding the properties of different correlation measures, the Spearman's rank correlation [6] gives the same correlation values as Pearson's correlation in the absence of ties, but it is not applicable to tie situations, which are common in MCDM. Kendall-τ [6], though it has the capability of handling ties, has not the satisfactory property of Pearson's correlation providing the cosine as a measure of distance between unit vectors. It is thus not useable in the MCDM context, because it does not make possible the development in K-criteria basis vectors of any unit rank vector, like proposed in this chapter. Springael [34] has investigated more in detail the Kendall-τ as a measure of distance between unit vectors; its properties substantially differ from these of the Pearson's correlation explicated in appendix A.1. One result obtained numerically for $n \leqslant 7$ is that the Kendall's correlation matrix of the $P(n)$ rank vectors has rank $2(n-1)$, and two sets of $(n-1)$ degenerate eigenvalues, instead of one, see Property A.1.4. The first non-vanishing eigenvalue is close to the expected value $P(n)/(n-1)$, see Property A.1.4; the second degenerate eigenvalue has a much smaller value. A formal proof of this property for all n values is still outstanding.

The present chapter insists on the need to consider stochastic analyses of the preferences as manifested by groups of decision-makers. In most applications the only information available on the many preferences is ordinal, generally in the form of some criteria ranking, shared by more or less homogeneous decision-maker groups with similar priorities. In each such group a Rank Matrix is obtained by Monte-Carlo simulation, showing the ranks probabilities of the different alternatives. More complicated constraints on the weight sets may be handled as well, and make the results much more credible than crisp values of the weights, which are in general impossible to justify, and do not make superfluous detailed sensitivity analyses.

Of course some important concepts introduced in outranking methods [1, 2, 3, 5, 14] like the incomparability between actions, veto thresholds, compensatory or non-compensatory effects, etc. are partially, or totally lost in the approach proposed in this chapter. But perhaps in many cases prior pre-conditioning of data may bring an adequate substitute for these concepts. Such treatment avoids the purely mechanical processing by elaborated, but not always well-understood techniques. Some possibilities to be further explored in practice may be the following ones in addressing several incomparability and compensation issues:

- Eliminate beforehand alternatives, which are beyond any acceptable range for some criteria;
- Introduce IF rules for avoiding undue compensations between ranks, like the following: *IF alternative I has rank* $\geqslant 5$ *for one criterion at least, it may not be elected for the first rank in the overall ranking, etc.*

In the case of ordinal data, the set of Pareto-optimal rankings may be fully, and univoquely determined by means of fully stochastic weights in $[0,1]^K$ intervals, K being the number of independent criteria. An aspect to be discussed is the choice of indifference thresholds in both situations of establishing criteria rankings, and in aggregating them into an overall ranking with ties. Also an analysis from a group-theoretic point of view of the $P(n)$ permutations with ties of n alternatives is of great interest for characterising the Pareto-optimal set given arbitrary preference weights for the criteria.

In both cases of only cardinal data, or of a mix of ordinal and cardinal data, the situation is not so straightforward, as more information is needed from the side of the decision-makers to achieve the statistical analysis of the Pareto-optimal rankings. If the m-point-scale MCDM procedure is adopted, as introduced in sub-section 6.4.1, there is more space for discussions regarding some important choices to be made than in the ordinal case. This stresses the fact that MCDM problems are, and will always be ill-defined problems. Moreover, the human freedom in defining preferences makes it impossible to design completely mechanical MCDM algorithms, even if the assumption is made of fully stochastic weights for obtaining the Rank Matrix.

The approach proposed in this chapter is certainly not a final answer to all MCDM aspects. Key problems on which further research could elaborate, mainly regarding the MCDM procedure for cardinal and mixed data presented in sub-section 6.4.1, are the following ones:

- How to convert cardinal data into scores? Is the proposed linear transformation sufficient, should more complicated cases be considered, like logistic curves, or other non-linear functions, at the risk of being less close to the 'mind computing' way of ordinary people?
- How many preference echelons to choose? I have assumed that the human mind is not really in a position of evaluating more than five to seven echelons on a scale, but this is certainly open for discussion;
- How to take into account hesitations between two adjacent preference echelons? A half-score approach has been proposed in the procedure of sub-section 6.4.1: is it useful to have a finer score graining? How does the graining influence the final aggregation of the score vectors for individual criteria?
- How to choose the $[1, m]$ range of cardinal values corresponding to the scores? While the choice of an origin for the best score 1 is not really an issue, choosing the least preferred threshold corresponding to the 'm' score depends on variable decision-maker preferences; it is why additional sensitivity analyses may have to be performed to capture this uncertain dimension of the scoring process of alternatives;
- May different scales be used when both ordinal and cardinal data are present?
- How to choose an indifference threshold for finding the associated overall rank vectors to combined evaluation vectors? The same issue appears in both ordinal and cardinal cases, but in the cardinal case it only arises at the level of aggregating criteria through

the weighed sum of criteria scores, but not at the level of defining individual criteria rank vectors with possible ties in the ordinal case.

Another point for future research is elaborating the relationship between the number of alternatives, and the maximum number of admissible independent criteria in the basis set, see a discussion on this aspect for the ordinal case in sub-section 6.2.2. It may be expected that more freedom is given in case of cardinal data, and the use of m-point scales for cardinal data, but this needs to be verified and quantified.
To complete this discussion, note again that the present chapter primarily discusses the ranking of alternatives of MCDM problems in the presence of many decision-makers showing various preferences profiles. Therefore statistical aspects are in the foreground. MCDA is more concerned over decision-aid for individual decision-makers $[1,2,3,5]$. Therefore the impression should not be awakened that all sophistication introduced in current MCDA methodologies, and particularly outranking methods, is superfluous in all circumstances. Figueira and Roy [26], and Roy at many places $[1,2,13]$ insist on several objectives of outranking methods; the latter are not primarily, or not only interested in complete ranking of alternatives. Other aspects of pair-wise comparisons in outranking methods are classification, description, identification of incomparability, etc. A further field of investigation is to assess the possible theoretical input of the proposed vector-optimisation methodology to these MCDA aspects.

Appendix A

A.1 *Properties of the space of n-vectors*

In this theoretical appendix the mathematical properties of the space of normalised and centred real vectors with n components, in short unit n-vectors, are detailed, and demonstrated. This theory serves as a basis for the MCDM procedures developed in the main text of this chapter.

Definition A.1.1. Call $V^n \subset \mathbb{R}^n$ the set of all real centred and normalised n-component vectors, in short unit n-vectors v:

$$v = (v_1, v_2, \ldots, v_n) \in V^n \tag{A.1}$$

$$\sum_{i=1,2,\ldots,n} v_i = 0 \tag{A.2}$$

$$\sum_{i=1,2,\ldots,n} v_i^2 = 1 \tag{A.3}$$

Basic Property A.1.1. *Any matrix, with column vectors from V^n, has a rank at most equal to $(n-1)$, which is the dimension of the space of all unit n-vectors. Every vector in V^n may be obtained as a linear combination of a basis made of $(n-1)$ independent vectors in V^n, in short basis vectors.*

Proof. The rank of any such a matrix can obviously not be larger than n. Its rows are linearly dependent, as their sum is equal to zero, according to (A.2). Therefore the rank of such matrix is at most equal to $(n-1)$. The second part of the proposition is obvious because by definition any $n \times n$ matrix consisting of $(n-1)$ independent column vectors plus any other column vector $v \in V^n$ has a rank equal to $(n-1)$. Thus v is linearly dependent on the $(n-1)$ independent vectors, which constitute a basis by definition. □

Corollary A.1.2. *Consider a set $\{K\}$ of $K \leqslant n-1$ independent unit vectors in V^n. Call $V^n_{\{K\}}$ the subset of V^n, which is generated by all possible linear combinations of these vectors serving as basis vectors. The sub-set $V^n_{\{K\}} \subset V^n$ has dimension K, i.e., that any matrix consisting of column vectors from $V^n_{\{K\}}$ has at most rank K.*

Proof. This corollary is trivial, because it is not possible to find more than K independent vectors in the sub-set $V^n_{\{K\}}$; the latter includes all possible linear combinations of the set $\{K\}$ of independent basis vectors. □

Definition A.1.2. Call $C_K^{(m)}$ the Pearson's correlation matrix of $m \geqslant K$ vectors in $V^n_{\{K\}}$; $K \leqslant n-1$.

Property A.1.2. *The rank of $C_K^{(m)}$ is at most equal to K.*

Proof. Consider that the top left K sub-matrix of $C_K^{(m)}$ is the correlation matrix of the K basis vectors. If there would be any linear relationship between the rows and columns of this correlation sub-matrix, the same linear relationship would exist between the basis vectors; this is excluded because the basis vectors are independent. The rank of this sub-matrix is thus equal to K. On the contrary any additional vector $\in V^n_{\{K\}}$ in the matrix is a linear combination of the K basis vectors. Thus the corresponding row and column in the correlation matrix are linear combinations of the K first rows or columns respectively. □

Definition A.1.3. Call C_b^K the correlation matrix of $K \leqslant n-1$ basis vectors in $V^n_{\{K\}}$.
Call $\rho_v^{(b)}$ the column vector containing the correlation coefficients of v with the K basis vectors.

Further call $c_v^{(b)}$ the column vector containing the coefficients of the linear development of v in the basis vectors.

The next property gives us the means for calculating the coefficients of the linear combination of basis vectors for any vector $v \in V^n_{\{K\}}$, see sub-section 6.2.3 in the main text.
Property A.1.3. *Consider any vector $v \in V^n_{\{K\}}$ and the basis matrix $B = (b_1, b_2, \ldots, b_K)$ where b_i are the basis column vectors. The following relationships hold, given Definitions A.1.3:*

$$\rho_v^{(b)} = C_b^K c_v^{(b)} \tag{A.4}$$

$$c_v^{(b)} = \left[C_b^K\right]^{-1} \rho_v^{(b)} \tag{A.5}$$

Proof. (A.4) immediately results when using the relation $v = Bc_v^{(b)}$ for calculating the correlation coefficients in matrix $\rho_v^{(b)}$ of v with the K basis vectors. (A.5) results from (A.4) by considering that the correlation matrix of the K basis vectors is invertible, having the rank$= K$, according to Property A.1.2.
The following properties refers to the matrix built with the $P(n)$ rank vectors of n alternatives, not including the trivial rank vector $(1, 1, \ldots, 1)$, see (3) in the main text. □
Property A.1.4. *Consider the matrix X ($m = P(n), n$), the rows of which are the $P(n)$ normalised and centred rank vectors (unit rank vectors) in V^n:*

(1) *The rank of the matrix X is $q = n - 1$;*
(2) *The $m \times m$ correlation matrix $C^{(n)} = XX'$ and the $n \times n$ matrix $D^{(n)} = X'X$ have the same rank $q = (n-1)$, and q non-vanishing eigenvalues;*
(3) *All unit n-vectors in V^n are eigenvectors of $D^{(n)}$ with the same eigenvalue $\lambda = P(n)/q$, which is the q-denerate eigenvalue of $C^{(n)}$, $D^{(n)}$;*
(4) *All rows r_i and columns c_j of the correlation matrix $C^{(n)}$ are eigenvectors of the q non-vanishing eigenvalues $\lambda = P(n)/q$.*

Proof.

(1) is obvious from the definition of the matrix X. Its rank can be at most equal to n; but each row sums up to zero, so that its rank is equal to $(n-1)$.
(2) It is obvious that the correlation matrix is $C^{(n)} = XX'$ by definition of the data matrix X. Denote:

$$\begin{aligned} D^{(n)} u_\alpha &= \lambda_\alpha u_\alpha \\ C^{(n)} v_\alpha &= \mu_\alpha v_\alpha \end{aligned} \tag{A.6}$$

where $\lambda_1 \geqslant \lambda_2 \geqslant \cdots \geqslant \lambda_q$ are the q non-vanishing eigenvalues of $D^{(n)}$, and $\mu_1 \geqslant \mu_2 \geqslant \cdots \geqslant \mu_q$ are the non-vanishing eigenvalues of $C^{(n)}$.

Considering the first eigenvalue $\alpha = 1$ in (A.6), and multiplying the first equation on the left by X, one obtains:

$$XD^{(n)}u_1 = XX'Xu_1 = C^{(n)}Xu_1 = \lambda_1 Xu_1 \tag{A.7}$$

(A.7) shows that Xu_1 is an eigenvector, and λ_1 is an eigenvalue of $C^{(n)}$, and thus $\lambda_1 \leqslant \mu_1$, as μ_1 is the largest eigenvalue by definition.

Multiplying now the second equation on the left by X', one also sees that $X'v_1$ is an eigenvector of $D^{(n)}$ with respect to the eigenvalue μ_1 and thus $\lambda_1 \geqslant \mu_1$. Therefore $\lambda_1 = \mu_1$. Using the same approach the same result is obtained for other non-vanishing q eigenvalues. Because $D^{(n)}$ has the same eigenvalues as $C^{(n)}$, it is also of rank $q = n-1$. Note that this is a well-known result of factor analysis, see Härdle and Hlávka **?**.

(3) $D^{(n)}$ is by definition the variance-covariance matrix of the n alternative positions in the rankings with ties. Because all alternatives are equivalent regarding all possible positions, this matrix has n equal diagonal elements, say d, and $n(n-1)$ equal non diagonal element, say o.

The sum of eigenvalues is the trace of $C^{(n)}$, equal to $P(n)$, which it is thus equal to the trace of $D^{(n)}$ according to (2), therefore $d = P(n)/n$. Consider any unit vector $v \in V^n$. It is immediately seen that:

$$D^{(n)}v = (d-o)v \tag{A.8}$$

(A.8) indicates that any unit n-vector is an eigenvector. There is thus only one non-vanishing q-denerate, $q = (n-1)$, eigenvalue λ of $C^{(n)}$, $D^{(n)}$, such that:

$$\lambda = \frac{P(n)}{q} = d - o \tag{A.9}$$

$$o = \frac{P(n)}{n} - \frac{P(n)}{n-1} = -\frac{P(n)}{n(n-1)} \tag{A.10}$$

(4) results from the equivalence of $C^{(n)}$, and $D^{(n)}$ regarding eigenvalues. According to (A.7):

$$v_\alpha = Xu_\alpha \tag{A.11}$$

Take for the eigenvector u_α any of the $P(n)$ unit rank vector. According to (A.11) v_α has for components the correlation coefficient of itself with the $P(n)$ rank vectors, i.e., this vector is an eigenvector of the correlation matrix, and it is at the same time one of its row, or column. □

Property A.1.5. *The correlation matrix* $C^{(n)}$ *is such that*

$$\left[C^{(n)}\right]^k = \left(\frac{P(n)}{n-1}\right)^{k-1} C^{(n)} = \lambda^{k-1} C^{(n)} \quad \forall k = 1,2,3,\ldots \tag{A.12}$$

Proof. The formula results immediately for $k = 2$ from Property A.1.4, as $C^{(n)}$ has $q = (n-1)$ degenerate non-vanishing eigenvalues, and all its rows and columns are eigenvectors. The formula for any k power results by successive application of this formula. □

A.2 *Projection in the XY-plane of the 74 ranking vectors (n = 4) on the unit sphere in* $\mathbb{R}^3$

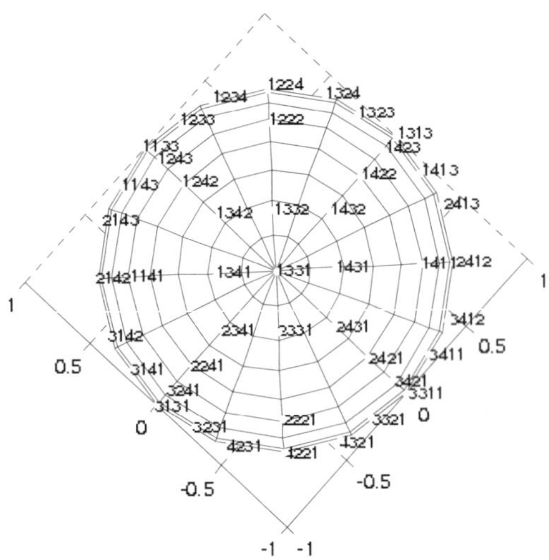

Figure A.1 The unit sphere with the $p(4) = 74$ non-trivial ranking vectors, as seen from above. The ending point of the unit rank vector comes approximately at the position of the first label component.

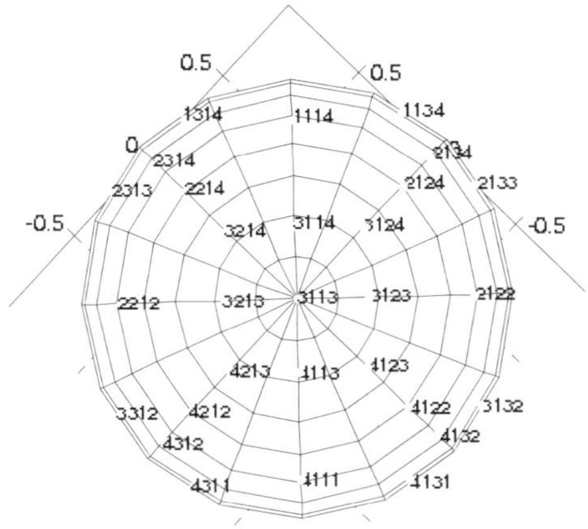

Figure A.2 The unit sphere with the $p(4) = 74$ non-trivial ranking vectors, as seen from below. The ending point of the unit rank vector comes approximately at the position of the first label component.

Bibliography

[1] B. Roy, *Méthodologie multicritère d'aide à la decision*, (Economica, Paris 1985).

[2] B. Roy, *Multicriteria Methodology for Decision Aiding*, (Kluwer, Dordrecht, 1996).

[3] Ph. Vincke, *Multi-criteria Decision Aid*, (John Wiley&Sons, Chichester, 1992).

[4] V. Belton and T. Stewart, *Multiple Criteria Decision Analysis: An Integrated Approach*, (Kluwer, Boston, MA, 2002).

[5] J. Figueira, S. Greco, M. Ehrgott Eds. *Multiple Criteria Decision Analysis, State of the Art Surveys*, (Springer Science+Business Media, Inc., NY, 2005).

[6] N. Malhotra, *Marketing Research: an Applied Orientation*, 5th edition, (Prentice Hall, Inc., Upper Saddle River, NJ, 2007).

[7] J. Springael , P.L. Kunsch and J.P. Brans (2000) Traffic crowding in cities - Control with urban tolls and flexible working hours A group multicriteria aid and system dynamics approach, JORBEL, **40** (1-2), 81–90 (2000), Corrigendum in **41** (3-4), 189–202 (2001).

[8] J. Springael, P.L. Kunsch and J.-P. Brans, A multicriteria-based system dynamics modelling of traffic congestion caused by urban commuters, Central European Journal of Operational Research, **10**, 81–97 (2002).

[9] Y. De Smet, J. Springael and P.L. Kunsch, Towards statistical multicriteria decision modelling: a model and its application, *Journal of Multicriteria Decision Aid*, **11/6**, 305–313 (2002).

[10] Y. De Smet, J. Springael and P.L. Kunsch, A new framework for describing the decision behaviour of large groups, *Research Paper*, **2004-011** (Universiteit Antwerpen, Antwerpen, 2004).

[11] P.L. Kunsch, E. Martens and M. Despontin "A socio-economic model of moving decisions in cities", *VUB/MOSI working document*, **17** (VUB, Brussels, 2005).

[12] J. Ferber, *Multiagents Systems: An Introduction to Distributed Artificial Intelligence*, (Addison-Wesley, London, 1999).

[13] B. Roy, The outranking approach and the foundations of the ELECTRE Methods, *Theory and Decision*, **31**, 49–73 (1991).

[14] L.Y. Maystre, J. Pictet, J. Simos, *Méthodes multicritères ELECTRE. Description, conseils pratiques et cas d'application à la gestion environnementale*, (Presses Polytechniques et Universitaires Romandes, Lausanne, 1994).

[15] J.P. Brans and Ph. Vincke A preference ranking organisation method: The PROMETHEE method for MCDM, *Management Science*, **31(6)**, 647–656 (1985).

[16] J.P. Brans, Ph. Vincke and B. Mareschal, How to select and to rank projects: The PROMETHEE method, *European Journal of Operational Research*, **24**, 228–238 (1986).

[17] J.P. Brans and B. Mareschal, The PROMETHEE Methods for MCDM; The PROMCALC, GAIA and BANKADVISER Software, in, *Readings in Multiple Criteria Decision Aid*, C.A. Bana Costa Ed. (Springer, Berlin, 1990) p. 216–242.

[18] J.P. Brans and B. Mareschal PROMETHEE-GAIA. *Une méthodologie d'aide à la décision en présence de critères multiples*, (Ellipses, France, 2002).

[19] J.P. Brans and B. Mareschal The PROMCALC and GAIA decision support system for MCDA, *Decision Support Systems*, **12**, 297–310 (2004).

[20] J.P. Brans and B. Mareschal, PROMETHEE methods, in J. Figueira, S. Greco, M. Ehrgott Eds., *Multiple Criteria Decision Analysis: state of the art surveys* (Springer, New York, 2005) p. 163–195.

[21] T.L. Saaty, *The Analytic Hierarchy Process* (McCraw-Hill Inc., New York, 1980).

[22] W. De Keyser and P. Peeters, A note on the use of PROMETHEE multicriteria methods, *European Journal of Operational Research*, **89**, 457–461 (1996).

[23] C. Macharis, J. Springael, J., K. De Brucker and A. Verbeke, PROMETHEE and AHP: The design of operational synergies in multicriteria analysis. Strengthening PROMETHEE with ideas of AHP, *European Journal of Operational Research*, **153**, 307–317 (2004).

[24] P.L. Kunsch, Remedies to rank reversal in multi-criteria decision methodologies, submitted for publication (2010).

[25] X. Awang and E. Triantaphyllou, Ranking irregularities when evaluating alternatives by using some ELECTRE methods, *Omega*, **36**, 45–63 (2008).

[26] J. Figueira and B. Roy A note on the paper, "Ranking irregularities when evaluating alternatives by using some ELECTRE methods", by Wang and Triantaphyllou, *Omega*, **37**, 731–733 (2009).

[27] W. Härdle and Z. Hlávka, *Multivariate Statistics*, (Springer, Berlin, 2007).

[28] D. Ruan, J. Montero, J. Lu, L. Martinez, P. D'hondt, E.E. Kerre Eds., *Computational Intelligence in Decision and Control, Proceedings of the* 8th *International FLINS Conference*, (World Scientific, New Jersey, 2008).

[29] P.L. Kunsch, A statistical Multicriteria Decision Aiding technique, in *Ref. 28*, p. 629.

[30] G.J. Klir and B. Yuan *Fuzzy sets and Fuzzy logic – Theory and Applications* (Prentice-Hall, London, 1995).

[31] D. Driankov, H. Hellendoorn, M. Reinfrank *An Introduction to Fuzzy Control*, 2nd ed. (Springer, Berlin, 1996).

[32] L.Y. Maystre, J. Pictet, J. Simos, Exemple didactique commun: localisation d'une usine de compostage au Tessin, in Ref. 14, Chap. 3.

[33] J.L. Garcia, D. Pérez-Román, Some consensus measures and their applications in group decision-making, in Ref. 28, p. 611.

[34] J. Springael, Comparison of the properties of different rank correlations formulas used as a distance measure, *private communication* (2008).

Chapter 7

A Web Based Assessment Tool via the Evidential Reasoning Approach

Dong-Ling Xu

Manchester Business School, The University of Manchester, Manchester, M15 6PB, UK

Ling.Xu@mbs.ac.uk

This chapter describes the interface design and the applications of a web based assessment tool on the basis of the Evidential Reasoning (ER) approach. The tool has been validated and used by a number of business users and examples of the application areas include business innovation assessment, supplier evaluation, and performance assessment. The ER approach is developed to handle multi-criteria decision analysis (MCDA) and assessment problems possibly with hybrid types of uncertainties. It uses belief decision matrices for problem modelling and data collection. Combined with thoughtfully designed interfaces, the tool offers a flexible and friendly environment for web users to express their assessment judgments consistently, objectively and accurately. By applying the ER algorithm for information aggregation, assessment outcomes generated from the tool can include average scores and ranking, sensitivity of the outcomes to uncertainties in different parameters, distributed assessments revealing variations in performances, and user specific reports highlighting key areas for attention. The interfaces of the tool allow users to enter data using a built-in assessment criteria hierarchy and to display aggregated outcomes in both text and graphic formats.

7.1 Introduction

With the advance of computer and Internet technologies, web based voting, discussion forum, opinion survey and assessment have become increasingly common, providing new ways for supporting decision making processes. Some web sites also allow users to construct their own decision models through the Internet [10].

This chapter describes the interface design of a web based assessment tool based on the Evidential Reasoning (ER) approach [29, 31]. The ER approach is a generic method that can be used for modelling and investigating MCDA problems under various types of uncertainties [31]. It offers unique features and flexibilities for supporting users to conduct comprehensive assessments and make informative decisions in a way that is consistent and reliable.

Many assessment schemes, such as impact assessment of policies, customer satisfaction survey and business performance assessment, are structured as typical multi-criteria decision making problems [30, 1]. Typical assessment schemes include the EFQM (European Foundation for Quality Management) model [7] for business excellence assessment and many pre-qualification questionnaires (PQQ) used to select suppliers by different organisations including the public sector in the UK. These schemes normally consist of a criteria hierarchy, criteria weights, the detailed explanation of each criterion, and a scoring standard for assessing each criterion. The construction of an assessment scheme requires domain specific knowledge and is normally completed by experts in the assessed areas possibly with the help of decision analysts.

The web based assessment tool discussed in this paper is developed by the requests of a number of industrial collaborators and business advisors. It has been applied to implement a number of assessment schemes used in supplier selection, business innovation assessment and policy impact assessment. The interfaces of the tool are supported by a relational database which is specifically designed to manage the assessment schemes and related knowledge. Assessment information entered by users through the interfaces is also stored in the database. To aggregate information on sub criteria in order to obtain overall performance assessments of an entity such as a business or a policy, the ER algorithm [31] is built into the tool. The tool has an automatic report generator and interfaces for displaying aggregated outcomes in both text and graphical formats.

In the ER approach, belief decision matrices are used to model multiple criteria assessment problems and record assessment information. Using belief decision matrices, users are able to select multiple answers and associate a belief degree with each answer. This is useful in situations where an assessment is felt to be somewhere between two adjacent grades, or where an assessment is provided by a group of people with different opinions. Belief decision matrices can also accommodate missing or unknown information in an assessment. This flexibility is one of the unique features of the tool.

The tool can be used in a wide range of assessment activities such as customer satisfaction surveys, product assessment and selection, and identification and ranking of consumer preferences. It can be used in both individual and group assessment situations. Most importantly, it can handle hybrid types of uncertainties including missing data, randomness and subjective judgments rationally and consistently.

The chapter is organised as follows. First the ER approach and its features are briefly described in Section 7.2. An illustrative example is given in Section 7.3 to demonstrate how the ER approach can be applied to model assessment problems and aggregate information with uncertainties. In Section 7.4, the interfaces and the specific considerations about how to accommodate the special features of the ER approach in the interfaces are illustrated using examples and screen snapshots from applications. Using the examples, the aggregated results and features are explained. Concluding remarks are made in the Section 7.5.

7.2 The ER Approach

The ER approach is developed to deal with MCDA problems having both quantitative and qualitative information with uncertainties [29, 30, 31]. Using the ER approach for MCDA includes two major steps. The first step is to use a distributed modelling framework in the format of a *belief decision matrix* to model a MCDA problem. The second step is to aggregate the assessment information of alternatives using the *ER algorithm*.

The belief decision matrix is an extension to a traditional *decision matrix* [22, 9, 11] for modelling a MCDA problem. In a decision matrix, each element is a single value, representing the "accurate" or average assessment of an alternative or option on a criterion. In the belief decision matrix, an assessment is represented by a paired vector, rather than a single value. A paired vector, referred to as a *belief structure* or a *distributed assessment* in the ER approach, consists of the permissible referential values of a criterion and their associated degrees of belief. For example, if people are asked to rate the impact if UK adopts the Euro, the answers could be positive and negative to certain degrees. In a belief decision matrix, such distributed judgements are allowed and various types of uncertainties are captured and explicitly modelled. The criterion referential values can be quantitative scores, qualitative assessment grades in different terms and numbers, or a mixture of both. Assessments made on different scales and terms can be converted to a common scale in terms of utility equivalence using the rule and utility based information transformation techniques [29].

The ER algorithm is developed on the basis of Dempster-Shafer theory of evidence [17, 4, 31]. The theory is related to the Bayesian probability theory in the sense that they both deal with subjective beliefs. However, according to Shafer [17], the evidence theory includes the Bayesian probability theory as a special case. Its subjective beliefs are also required to obey the probability rules. The biggest difference being in that the former is able to deal with ignorance, while the latter is not. The evidence theory has found wide applications in many areas such as expert systems [4, 2, 27], pattern recognition [8, 12], information fusion [18], database and knowledge discovery [5], multiple attribute decision analysis [3, 31], and audit risk assessment [21, 20]. The ER algorithm is used for aggregating distributed assessment information recorded in a belief decision matrix. The outcome of the aggregation is also a distribution, rather than a single score. If necessary, a score can be calculated from a distribution by first quantifying the assessment grades and then adding the grade values weighted by their associated belief degrees in the distribution [29, 31, 32]. Note that a score generated using the ER algorithm may be different from that generated using the weighted sum method because a distribution is generated through a nonlinear aggregation process.

There are two main reasons for not using the weighted sum method for information aggregation in the ER approach. Firstly, unlike the ER algorithm, the weighted sum method requires the stringent additive preferential independence condition to be met by assessment criteria [13], which is difficult to satisfy and hard to check if many criteria need to be taken into account. Secondly, the weighted sum method can only provide an average score for assessing an alternative with little capability to handle uncertainty, whilst the ER algorithm can generate a distribution and, when there is missing information, a lower and an upper bound of a belief degree to which an assessment statement is believed to be true. Such pragmatic yet rigorous outcomes provide scopes for global sensitivity analysis of alternative rankings under uncertainties [14, 15].

The above features of the ER approach bring the following three practical benefits. Firstly, assessment questions and choices of answers can be presented to users in a user friendly format. Secondly, the distributed assessment information generated by the ER algorithm reveals performance diversities and supports the identification of strengths and weaknesses. Thirdly, the number of criteria in the assessment model is much less of a concern to the ER approach than to other conventional approaches, because the former does not require the satisfaction of the additive preferential independence condition. The ER approach including the ER aggregation algorithm and some of its features is illustrated using a simple example in Section 7.3.

7.3 Illustration of the ER Approach

The following example is based on an excerpt from a real world application of the ER approach.

To assess and help to improve the innovation capability of small to medium sized enterprises in the UK and Europe, assessment criteria and grading standards were developed by Xu *et al.* [28]. One of the criteria is *Company Culture* which is assessed through several sub-criteria including the following two:

(1) How well does the company motivate talented people?
(2) Are employees empowered to test new ideas?

The directors, managers and some representatives of the employees of a company were asked to self-assess its performance on the sub-criteria using the three grades {Not Very Well, Fairly Well, Well} for sub-criterion (1) and the other three grades {No, Some Times, Yes} for sub-criterion 2.

Not every one agrees with each others assessments. On the first sub-criterion, 30 % of the answers are Not Very Well, 50 % Fairly Well, and 20 % Well. On the second one, the answers are 40 % No, 30 % Some Times, and 20 % Yes. It should be noted that the total percentage for the second one did not add up to 100 % because some of the employees did not provide an answer to the assessment question.

Instead of approximating the company performances on each sub-criterion using a single grade, which is normally the case if a decision matrix is used, the ER approach representing the two assessments using the following two belief structures:

$$P(S_1) = \{(\text{Not Very Well}, 0.3),\ (\text{Fairly Well}, 0.5),\ (\text{Well}, 0.2)\} \tag{1}$$

$$P(S_2) = \{(\text{No}, 0.4),\ (\text{Some Times}, 0.3), (\text{No}, 0.2)\} \tag{2}$$

The numbers associated with the assessment grades are called belief degrees. Because belief degrees are in essence probabilities, the sum of them in each assessment, $P(S_1)$ or $P(S_2)$, should be 1 or less. If the sum is less than 1, this means that there is some missing information. When the sum of the belief degrees in a belief structure is 1, it is said that the assessment is *complete*, otherwise *incomplete*. Accordingly, the assessment $P(S_1)$ in (1) is complete while $P(S_2)$ is incomplete.

Suppose the utilities [13] of the above two sets of assessment grades are evenly distributed in the utility space. Based on the assumption, if the three grades are denoted by $\{H_1, H_2, H_3\}$ and their utilities by $u(H_1)$, $u(H_2)$ and $u(H_3)$ respectively, then we have

$$\{H_1, H_2, H_3\} = \{\text{Not Very Well, Fairly Well, Well}\} = \{\text{No, Some Times, Yes}\} \tag{3}$$

and

$$u(H_1) = 0,\ u(H_2) = 0.5,\ \text{and}\ u(H_3) = 1 \tag{4}$$

If the utilities of the two sets of grades are distributed differently, then both sets of grades need to be converted to a common set using utility equivalent transformation techniques developed by Yang [29]. Using the notation in (3), (1) and (2) become

$$P(S_1) = \{(H_1, 0.3), (H_2, 0.5), (H_3, 0.2)\} \tag{5}$$

$$P(S_2) = \{(H_1, 0.4), (H_2, 0.3), (H_3, 0.2)\} \tag{6}$$

To know how well the company is doing on the *Company Culture* criterion, its performance on the sub-criteria needs to be aggregated. The ER aggregation algorithm is given as follows.

Suppose sub-criterion (1) is more important with a weight of 0.3, and the weight for sub-criterion (2) is 0.2. In the ER algorithm, the weights of sub-criteria need to be normalised to 1. Suppose there are L sub-criteria and ω_i is the weight of the ith sub-criterion ($i = 1, \ldots, L$), then the normalisation is defined so that

$$0 \leqslant \omega_i \leqslant 1 \tag{7}$$

and

$$\sum_{i=1}^{L} \omega_i = 1. \tag{8}$$

In the example, the normalised weights for sub-criteria (1) and (2) are

$$\omega_1 = 0.3/(0.3+0.2) = 0.6 \text{ and } \omega_2 = 0.2/(0.3+0.2) = 0.4$$

respectively.

The ER aggregation algorithm takes the two assessments $P(S_1)$ and $P(S_2)$ as its input and generates a combined assessment, denoted by $P(C) = \{(H_1, \beta_1), (H_2, \beta_2), (H_3, \beta_3)\}$, as its output. The belief degrees in the assessment, β_1, β_2, and β_3, are obtained through the following steps:

Step 1: Calculate basic probability masses p_n and q_n ($n = 1, 2, 3$):

$$p_n = \omega_1 \beta_{n,1} \quad (n = 1, 2, 3) \tag{9a}$$

$$\overline{p}_H = 1 - \omega_1 = 0.4 \tag{9b}$$

$$\widetilde{p}_H = \omega_1 \left(1 - \sum_{n=1}^{3} \beta_{n,1}\right) = 0 \tag{9c}$$

$$p_H = \overline{p}_H + \widetilde{p}_H = 1 - \omega_1 \sum_{n=1}^{3} \beta_{n,1} = 1 - \omega_1 = \quad 0.4 \tag{9d}$$

Table 7.1 Probability Masses

$P(S_1) \oplus P(S_2)$		$P(S_1)$				
		$p_1 = 0.18$ $\{H_1\}$	$p_2 = 0.3$ $\{H_2\}$	$p_3 = 0.12$ $\{H_3\}$	$\overline{p}_H = 0.4$ $\{H\}$	$\widetilde{p}_H = 0$ $\{H\}$
$P(S_2)$	$q_1 = 0.16$ $\{H_1\}$	$p_1q_1 = 0.0288$ $\{H_1\}$	$p_2q_1 = 0.048$ $\{\Phi\}$	$p_3q_1 = 0.0192$ $\{\Phi\}$	$\overline{p}_Hq_1 = 0.064$ $\{H_1\}$	$\widetilde{p}_Hq_1 = 0$ $\{H_1\}$
	$q_2 = 0.12$ $\{H_2\}$	$p_1q_2 = 0.0216$ $\{\Phi\}$	$p_2q_2 = 0.036$ $\{H_2\}$	$p_3q_2 = 0.0144$ $\{\Phi\}$	$\overline{p}_Hq_2 = 0.048$ $\{H_2\}$	$\widetilde{p}_Hq_2 = 0$ $\{H_2\}$
	$q_3 = 0.08$ $\{H_3\}$	$p_1q_3 = 0.0144$ $\{\Phi\}$	$p_2q_3 = 0.024$ $\{\Phi\}$	$p_3q_3 = 0.0096$ $\{H_3\}$	$\overline{p}_Hq_3 = 0.032$ $\{H_3\}$	$\widetilde{p}_Hq_3 = 0$ $\{H_3\}$
	$\overline{q}_H = 0.6$ $\{H\}$	$p_1\overline{q}_H = 0.108$ $\{H_1\}$	$p_2\overline{q}_H = 0.18$ $\{H_2\}$	$p_3\overline{q}_H = 0.072$ $\{H_3\}$	$\overline{p}_H\overline{q}_H = 0.24$ $\{H\}$	$\widetilde{p}_H\overline{q}_H = 0$ $\{H\}$
	$\widetilde{q}_H = 0.04$ $\{H\}$	$p_1\widetilde{q}_H =$ 0.0072 $\{H_1\}$	$p_2\widetilde{q}_H = 0.012$ $\{H_2\}$	$p_3\widetilde{q}_H =$ 0.0048 $\{H_3\}$	$\overline{p}_H\widetilde{q}_H = 0.016$ $\{H\}$	$\widetilde{p}_H\widetilde{q}_H = 0$ $\{H\}$

$$q_n = \omega_2 \beta_{n,2} \quad (n = 1, 2, 3) \tag{10a}$$

$$\overline{q}_H = 1 - \omega_2 = 0.6 \tag{10b}$$

$$\widetilde{q}_H = \omega_2 \left(1 - \sum_{n=1}^{3} \beta_{n,2}\right) = 0.4 \times 0.1 = 0.04 \tag{10c}$$

$$q_H = \overline{q}_H + \widetilde{q}_H = 1 - \omega_2 \sum_{n=1}^{3} \beta_{n,2} = 1 - \omega_2 \times 0.9 = 1 - 0.36 = 0.64 \tag{10d}$$

where $\beta_{n,1}$ and $\beta_{n,2}$ are the belief degrees associated with H_n $(n = 1, 2, 3)$ in (5) and (6) respectively. For example, $\beta_{1,1} = 0.3$ and $p_1 = \omega_1 \beta_{1,1} = 0.6 \times 0.3 = 0.18$. The calculated p_n and q_n are called probability masses assigned to grade H_n. The terms p_H and q_H in (9d) and (10d) are the remaining probability masses initially unassigned to any individual grades. The term p_H consists of two parts, $\overline{p}_H$ and $\widetilde{p}_H$, as shown in (9d). The first part $\overline{p}_H$ represents the degree to which other criteria can play a role in the assessment. It should eventually be assigned to individual grades in a way that is dependent upon how all criteria are weighted and assessed. The second part $\widetilde{p}_H = 0$ because $\sum_{n=1}^{3} \beta_{n,1} = 1$ as calculated using (9c). Similarly, q_H consists of two parts, $\overline{q}_H$ and $\widetilde{q}_H$. Note that $\widetilde{q}_H$ is not zero due to the incompleteness of the assessment $P(S_2)$, or $\sum_{n=1}^{3} \beta_{n,2} = 0.9$. In fact, $\widetilde{p}_H$ and $\widetilde{q}_H$ represent the remaining probability mass unassigned due to the incompleteness in their corresponding original assessments. They are proportional to their corresponding missing belief degrees and criterion weights, and will cause the subsequently aggregated assessments to be incomplete [31]. The values of those calculated probability masses are given in the 1st row and 1st column of Table 7.1.

Step 2: Calculate combined probability masses:

The ER algorithm aggregates the above probability masses to generate combined probability masses, denoted by r_n ($n = 1, 2, 3$), $\overline{r}_H$ and $\widetilde{r}_H$, using the following equations:

$$r_n = k(p_n q_n + p_H q_n + p_n q_H) \;\; (n = 1, 2, 3) \tag{11}$$

$$\overline{r}_H = k(\overline{p}_H \overline{q}_H) \tag{12}$$

$$\widetilde{r}_H = k(\widetilde{p}_H \widetilde{q}_H + \widetilde{p}_H \overline{q}_H + \overline{p}_H \widetilde{q}_H) \tag{13}$$

where

$$k = \left(1 - \sum_{t=1}^{3} \sum_{\substack{n=1 \\ n \neq t}}^{3} p_t q_n \right)^{-1} \tag{14}$$

From Table 7.1, we have

$$\begin{aligned}
k &= (1 - (0.0192 + 0.048 + 0.0144 + 0.0216 + 0.024 + 0.0144))^{-1} \\
&= 0.8584^{-1} = 1.1650 \\
r_1 &= k(p_1 q_1 + p_H q_1 + p_1 q_H) \\
&= 1.1650 \times (0.0288 + 0.064 + 0.108 + 0.0072) \\
&= 0.2423 \\
r_2 &= k \times (p_2 q_2 + p_H q_2 + p_2 q_H) \\
&= 1.1650 \times (0.036 + 0.048 + 0.18 + 0.012) \\
&= 0.3215 \\
r_3 &= k \times (p_3 q_3 + p_H q_3 + p_3 q_H) \\
&= 1.1650 \times (0.0096 + 0.032 + 0.072 + 0.0048) \\
&= 0.1379 \\
\overline{r}_H &= k(\overline{p}_H \overline{q}_H) = 1.1650 \times 0.24 = 0.2796 \\
\widetilde{r}_H &= k(\widetilde{p}_H \widetilde{q}_H + \widetilde{p}_H \overline{q}_H + \overline{p}_H \widetilde{q}_H) = 1.1650 \times 0.016 = 0.0186
\end{aligned}$$

If there are more than two sub-criteria, the combined probability masses can then be combined with the assessment on the third criterion in the same way. The process is repeated until the assessments on all sub-criteria are aggregated. The combined probability masses are independent of the order in which individual assessments are aggregated [17]. If there are several levels in a criteria hierarchy, the aggregation process is carried out from the bottom level until the top of the hierarchy is reached.

The belief degrees in the aggregated performance distribution are calculated from the combined probability masses. Suppose the final aggregated assessment is represented as follows:

$$P(C_1) = \{(H_1, \beta_1), (H_2, \beta_2), (H_3, \beta_3)\} \tag{15}$$

Then β_n $(n = 1, 2, 3)$ are generated by:

$$\beta_n = \frac{r_n}{1 - \bar{r}_H} \tag{16}$$

For the example, they are given by

$$\beta_1 = \frac{0.2423}{1-0.2796} = 0.3364,\ \beta_2 = \frac{0.3215}{1-0.2796} = 0.4463, \text{ and } \beta_3 = 0.1915.$$

Because of the incompleteness in one of the assessments, the aggregated assessment is also incomplete and it is shown by the sum of the three belief degrees which is 0.9741, indicating only 97.41 % of the belief degrees are assigned. The unassigned part is given by,

$$\beta_H = 1 - 0.9741 = 0.0259$$

It could be partially or completely assigned to any combination of the three grades depending on the message in the missing information. If it were assigned to grade H_1, the belief degree associated to the grade could be as high as $Pl(H_1) = \beta_1 + \beta_H = 0.3623$. The same applies to the belief degrees associated with grades H_2 and H_3. Therefore β_H represents the combined effects on aggregated outcomes of missing information in the assessments on any sub-criteria.

If necessary, a utility score [13] can be calculated from the aggregated assessment. Suppose the utilities for the 3 grades are given in (4). The expected utility score of the assessment given by (15), denoted by U, can be calculated as follows with the belief degrees as weights,

$$U = \sum_{i=1}^{3} u(H_i)\beta_i = 0.4147 \tag{17}$$

The score will normally be different from that calculated by using the weighted sum approach because the ER aggregation is a nonlinear process in which harmonic judgments will be reinforced more than proportionally and conflicting ones weakened accordingly. More details on the properties of the ER algorithm can be found in Yang and Xu [32] and Yang [29].

Applying the ER approach manually as discussed above is tedious but unnecessary. The algorithm can be easily programmed and incorporated into different applications. It has been applied to a wide range of real world problems, such as organisational self-assessment in quality management [30], new product design selection [16, 6], product evaluation [25], safety and risk assessment [24, 23] and supplier evaluation [19]. One of its latest applications is the prioritisation of customer voices for the General Motors Corporation [25].

7.4 Interfaces for Data Input

To take full advantages of the ER approach, a web based assessment tool is developed. The interfaces of the web assessment tool are designed using ASP.Net and supported by a MySQL database. The following are some of the features of the interfaces.

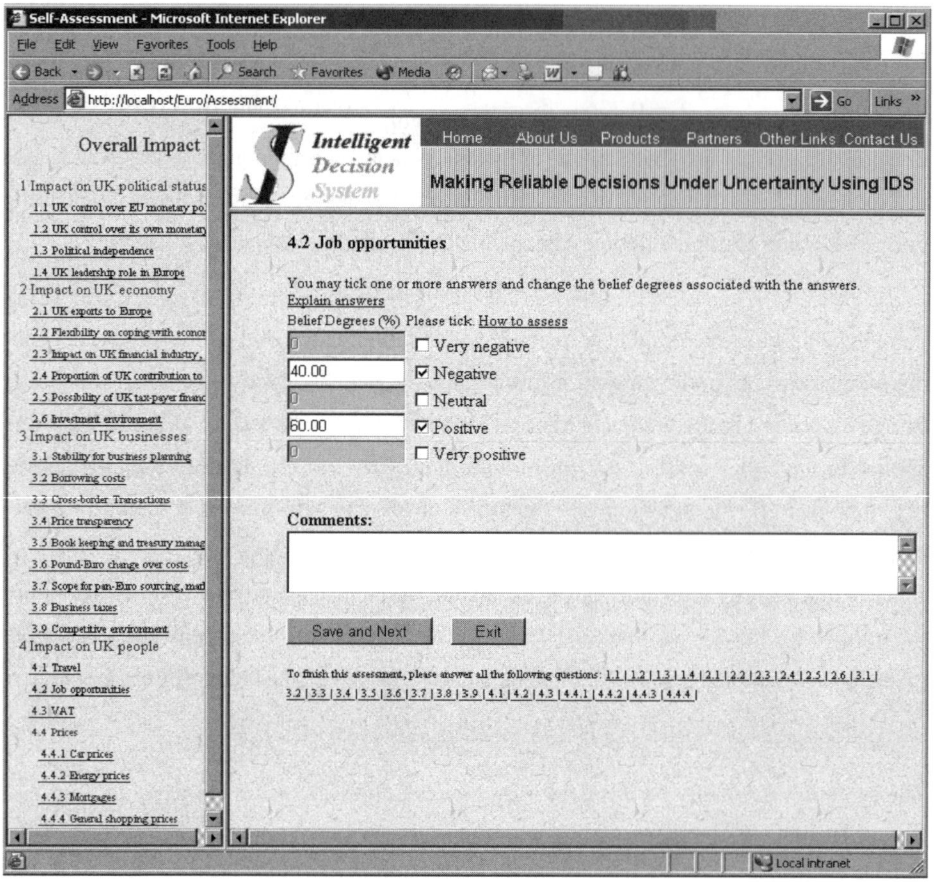

Figure 7.1 Criterion Hierarchy Displayed in Left Pane.

Display the overview of the assessment scheme: The assessment questions are displayed in the left frame of the interface (Figure 7.1), in a hierarchical (tree) format. The hierarchy provides users with a panoramic view of the assessment scheme – how many questions need to be answered and how they are related to each other in the hierarchy. There is a hyperlink to each question which directly leads users to the page (interface) where they can enter or review their answers and comments to this question.

Answer questions: Each question is given a dedicated page. The page is located in the lower right frame (Figure 7.1). It displays an assessment question and its multiple choice answers. To answer the question, users can tick one or more check boxes beside the appropriate assessment grades or answers, and assign a belief degree to each grade. It is different from and provides more flexibilities than most other assessment tools which normally allow only one assessment grade to be selected.

Considering that users may not be familiar with the flexibility provided, the interface is designed in such a way that as soon as an answer is selected, a belief degree in percentage is assigned and displayed automatically beside the ticked box. Initially, the belief degrees are assigned equally to the selected answers and add up to 100 %. Users may then edit the automatically assigned belief degrees to match a performance with grading standards which can be accessed from the interface if required, as described later.

If only one answer is selected, the automatically assigned belief degree will be 100 %. This is equivalent to conventional assessment schemes. Therefore for users who are unwilling to deal with belief degrees and prefer conventional single-answer assessment, they still have the flexibility. However for those who feel uncomfortable to categorise a mixed performance into a single grade, using belief structures to represent their assessments can boost their confidence in the aggregated assessment outcomes, as remarked by many industrial users and practitioners.

Model uncertainty: If uncertainty means not 100 % sure, then a belief structure can model almost all types of uncertainty, some obvious ones being subjective judgments, probability distribution and ignorance. Therefore belief structures allow different formats of uncertainty to be modelled and handled in a unified way.

The purposes of uncertainty modelling are to encourage users to understand, clarify and reduce it as much as possible, instead of just living with it. We believe that using belief structures to model it can fulfill such purposes.

Uncertainty is common in many decision making and assessment situations. If there is uncertainty in collected data and an approach based on decision matrices is used for data analysis and information aggregation, it will normally be required to eliminate the uncertainty first. For example, when there are missing answers to some assessment questions, a common practice is to either guess the missing answers or reject the whole data set. This results in not only information loss or distortion, but also a false sense of certainty in the outcomes.

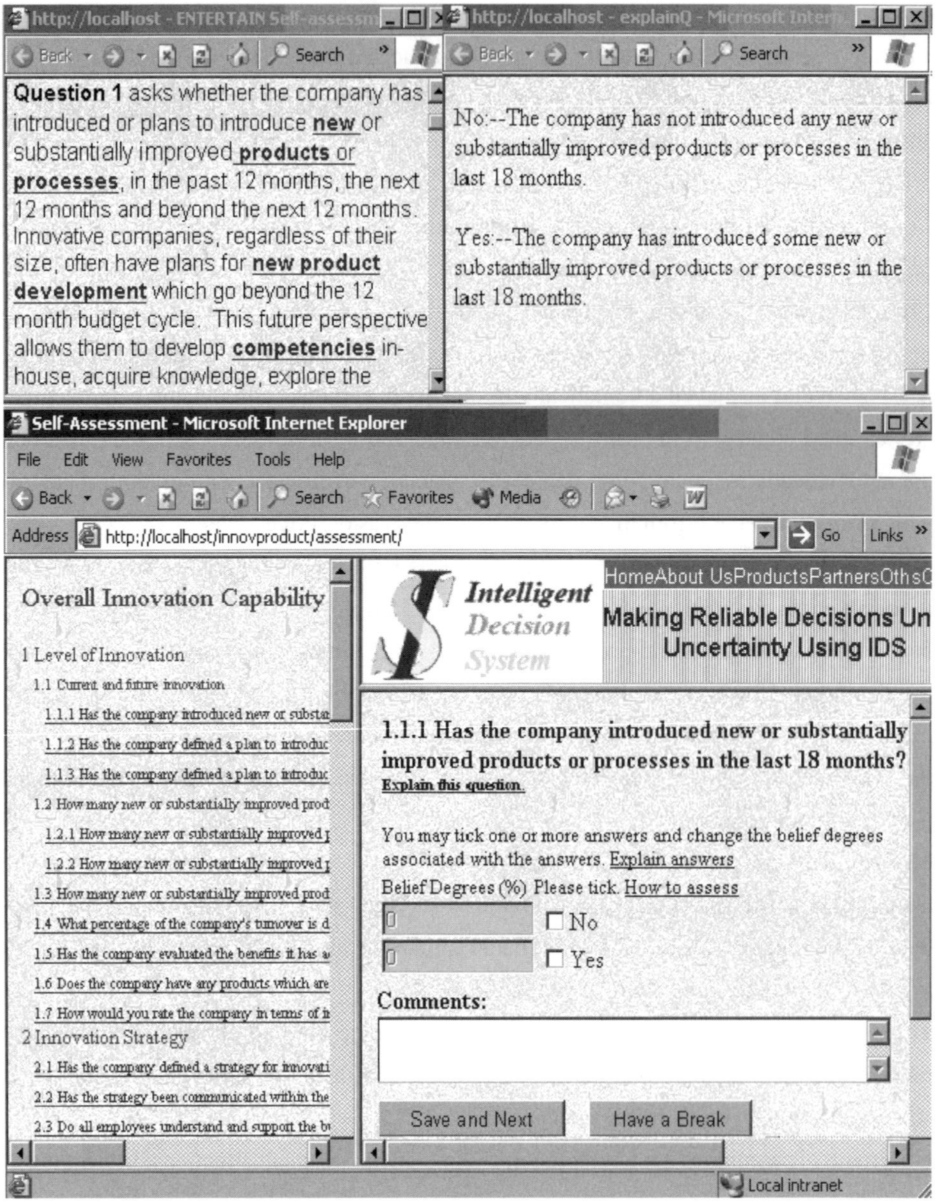

Figure 7.2 Side by Side Explanations of Question and Answers.

By modelling uncertainties using belief structures, the originality of data can be maintained, the information in all available data can be fully used in an assessment process, and meanwhile the effects of the uncertainties can be considered, analysed and revealed. Those are also some of the main purposes of modelling uncertainties in the ER approach.

In addition to accepting qualitative assessments through grades and belief degrees as discussed above, the interface can also be used to collect quantitative data with or without probability uncertainty. Data with missing information is accommodated by assigning less than 100 % belief degrees. The collected data are then recorded in the format of belief structures and stored in the supporting database.

The process of assigning belief degrees is also a process of prompting users to exam and clarify any uncertainty. Such a process can help to reduce uncertainty in a number of ways. For example, users neither have to approximately classify a mixed performance to a single grade, nor do they need to guess missing answers.

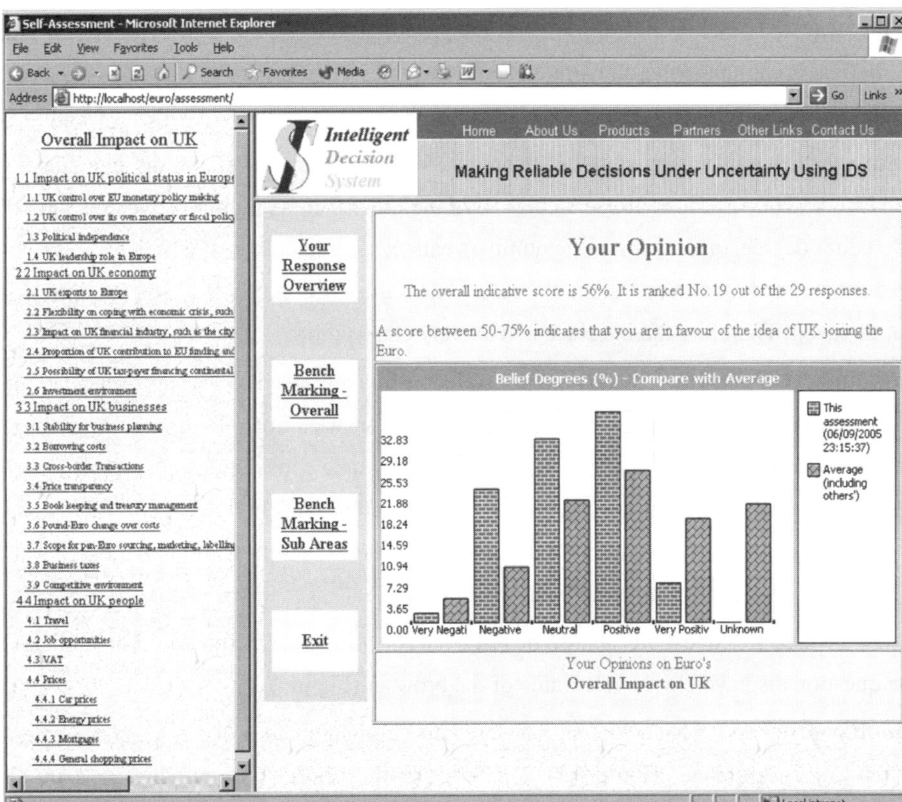

Figure 7.3 Aggregated Assessment Outcomes – Distributed Assessment Information.

Explain Question: It is often the case that a set of assessment criteria are developed by experts in the related area and words with special meanings may be used when assessment questions are asked. If a question needs to be explained in more detail, a link "Explain this question" is placed beside the question (Figure 7.2). The explanation can be displayed in a separate browser at the top left corner of the main browser (Figure 7.2).

Explain Answers: Answers to assessment questions are often given in forms of qualitative grades. The standards of those grades may need to be clearly defined in order to maintain consistency in assessments for different alternatives conducted by different web users in different locations at different times. The link "Explain answers" located at the top of the answers leads to a new web browser displaying the standards (Figure 7.2).

Note that the **Explain Question** and **Explain Answers** browsers are in much smaller sizes and are placed in positions that are least likely to interfere with the focal points of the users. In this way, the assessment question and the grading standards are displayed side by side so that users can map what they know about the assessed alternatives into the assessment grade or grades with appropriate belief degrees. We call this process "Evidence Mapping".

Data validation: The sum of belief degrees assigned to the answers of any one question needs to be 100 % or less. If users enter anything other than a number between 0 and 100 as a belief degree, or the sum of the numbers entered is greater than 100 %, a message will be displayed to remind them about the rule. Unless the correction is made the answers will not be saved. Therefore the interface is relatively error-proof.

Save and retrieve data: The answers to each question are saved as soon as users click the "Save and Next" button (Figure 7.1), given that the answers are valid. For some comprehensive assessment tasks, it is possible that they may take considerable amount of time to finish. If it is the case, users can "Have a Break" and come back to finish it later. To use this function, users have to give their email or user names as identities so that data associated to a specific user can be retrieved later.

Saved answers to a question can also be retrieved for editing at any time by simply clicking the question displayed in the left frame of the browser (Figure 7.1).

Monitor progress: A list of the un-answered question numbers is displayed at the bottom of the lower right pane (Figure 7.1). The list is getting shorter as more questions are answered, which serves as a progress bar. The hyper link behind each question number can also be clicked to display the unanswered question if a user wishes to answer the questions in a different order. After all questions are answered, the aggregated overall performance and the performance in each sub-area are computed in the background by the ER algorithm. When the calculation is complete, users are directed to the pages where results are displayed (Figures 7.3 and 7.4).

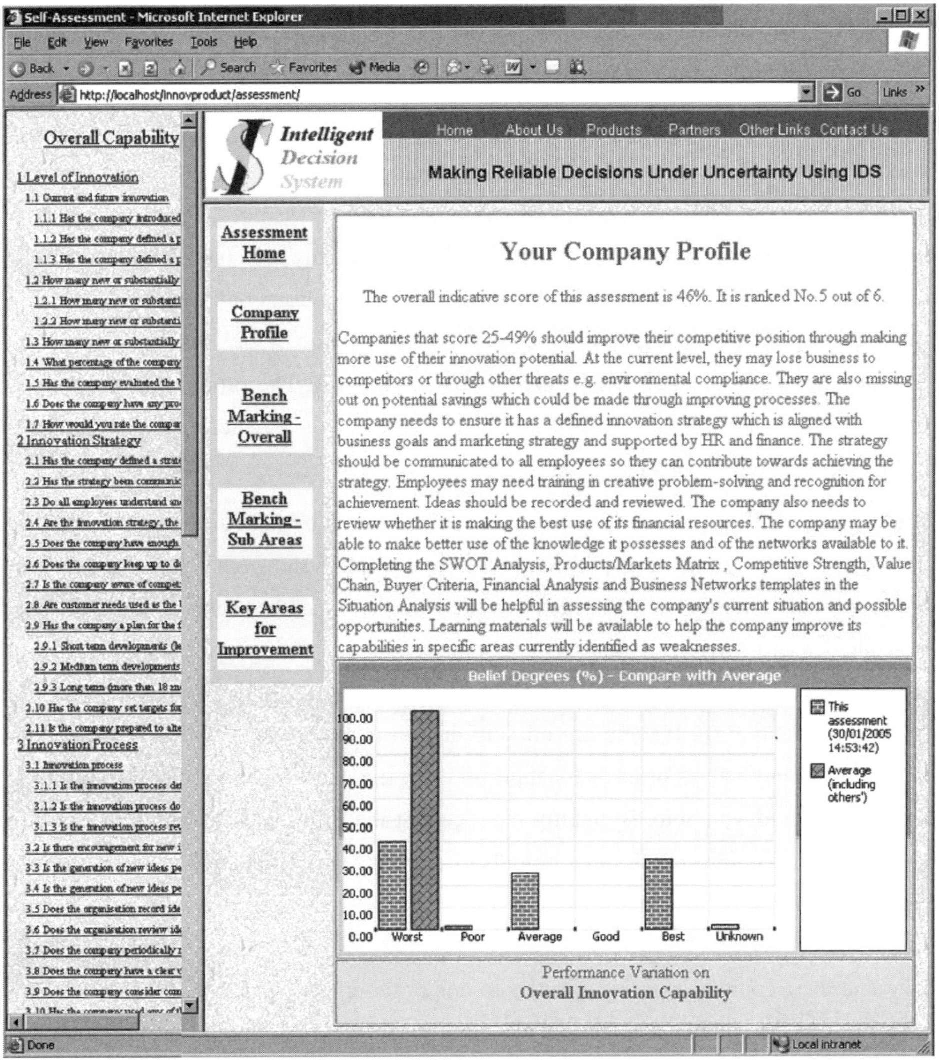

Figure 7.4 Aggregated Assessment Outcomes – Performance Assessment Overview with Tailored Text Report.

7.5 Interfaces for Outcome Display

The outcomes displayed in browsers are similar to those shown in Figures 7.3-7.6. The tool provides four types of aggregated assessment information – text summary, distributed performance assessments, scores and sensitivity of the scores when there are uncertainties.

Text summary explains what an assessment score means, the position of the user's opinion (Figures 7.3 and 7.4) and the key areas that the user needs to pay attention to regarding the performance of the assessed alternative (Figure 7.5).

The distributed performance graph displays the aggregated performance distributions based on the assessments conducted by the current user and all the previous users as a group, as shown in Figure 7.6. From the graph, the user knows not only the variations of the aggregated performance of the assessed alternative in any area (sub-criteria), but also how different their judgments are from those of all previous users on average.
The distributed assessment graph also displays the proportion of any missing information. It is labeled as unknown as shown in Figures 7.3 and 7.4. The proportion of unknown elements will be non-zero and shown in the graph if the sum of belief degrees assigned to the answers of a question is less than 100 %.

The expected utility scores of the assessments conducted by the current user and all the previous users as a group are displayed in a different graph as shown in Figure 7.6. For users who have made a number of assessments over a period of time, the scores are displayed in a chronological order to reflect trend of their opinions that may change over time (Figure 7.6).
Sensitivity of scores or rankings is displayed as grey areas in the graphs representing the scores (Figure 7.6). If there are missing data, it is assumed in the ER approach that they could be any values or answers appropriate to the question; they may turn out to be favourable or unfavourable. By taking into account the full ranges in which the missing data may vary, the lower and upper bounds of the scores are calculated using the built-in ER algorithm. The score ranges reveal whether alternative rankings could result from the missing data.
Note that there could be missing answers to one or more assessment questions. The score ranges reflect the combined effects of all missing data. From Saltelli *et al.* [15], analyses on the sensitivity of outcomes to simultaneous uncertain changes of different variables are normally referred to as global sensitivity analysis, in contrast to local sensitivity analysis found in most literature, in which uncertainty is considered for one factor at a time. From this point of view, the ER approach provides a means for global sensitivity analysis in MCDA.
Different formats of outcomes can be accessed from the same interface as follows. The text summary giving an overview of assessment outcomes can be accessed by clicking on the top criterion in the criteria hierarchy displayed in the left pane of the browser (Fig-

ures 7.3-7.6). The other types of information are available for any criterion in any level of the hierarchy and can be accessed by clicking the questions listed in the hierarchy. Note that the hierarchy serves different purposes in different stages. In the assessment stage when the focus of its users is on answering questions, the links hosted in the pane direct users to "answering the question" page. After all the questions are answered, the links direct the users to the "displaying outcomes" page.

7.6 Applications

The tool has been used in a number of areas including business innovation capability assessment, supplier assessment and impact assessment of UK adopting the Euro. Those assessment schemes are developed through a number of research projects conducted in the Manchester Business School and tested by business users from the UK and other European countries [28].

The users have provided valuable feedbacks on how to improve the interfaces so that the tool can be more user-friendly and be used by users with different levels of computer literacy. Some of the interface features described earlier are added by taking into account the feedback, such as the "explain questions" and "explain answers" features. Further improvement and development are still under way. The snapshots of the application of the tool to business innovation capability assessment are shown in Figures 7.4-7.6.

7.7 Concluding Remarks

Real world decisions are often based on assessments and comparisons of alternative courses of action. They are complex in the sense that they often involve many criteria and uncertain knowledge. To make a rational and reliable decision, it is crucial that information in all available data in different formats and from different sources is fully utilised and undistorted in an assessment process. It is also crucial that uncertainty in data and its effects are taken into account so that risks of a decision associated with the uncertainty is fully understood and prepared for. It is demonstrated in this chapter by examples that the ER approach meets such crucial requirements by using belief decision matrices for problem modelling and the ER algorithm for information aggregation.

A web based assessment tool is developed based on the ER approach. Considering the data structure used in belief decision matrices and the new features provided by the ER approach, it is described how interfaces of the tool are designed to support users to take advantages of the features. In the chapter the advantages offered by the tool are also illustrated using examples. The flexibility offered by its data input interfaces helps users to express their judgments more precisely and consistently. The assessment criteria hierarchy on the left pane provides users with a holistic view of the assessment problem. The outputs of the tool include performance distributions and effects of uncertainties which allow users to gain more insights into the assessment problem. By using different web design techniques, such as data validation and automatic assignment of belief degrees, the interfaces are made user friendly.

The web based assessment tool is also an effective and efficient knowledge management tool. Domain expert knowledge in the applied areas are structured and stored in the assessment framework. Knowledge can be retrieved at where and when it is most needed by users, such as through the "Explain Question" and "Explain Answers" links.

The tool can be used in a variety of applications such as contractor pre-qualification in supply chain and project management, impact assessment in supporting policy making, business performance self-diagnosis in business management, and opinion surveys.

Acknowledgement

The author would like to thank the support of the UK Engineering and Physical Science Research Council under grant No: EP/F024606/1, and Lin Yang of University College London for converting the pictures in the paper to the requested format by the publisher.

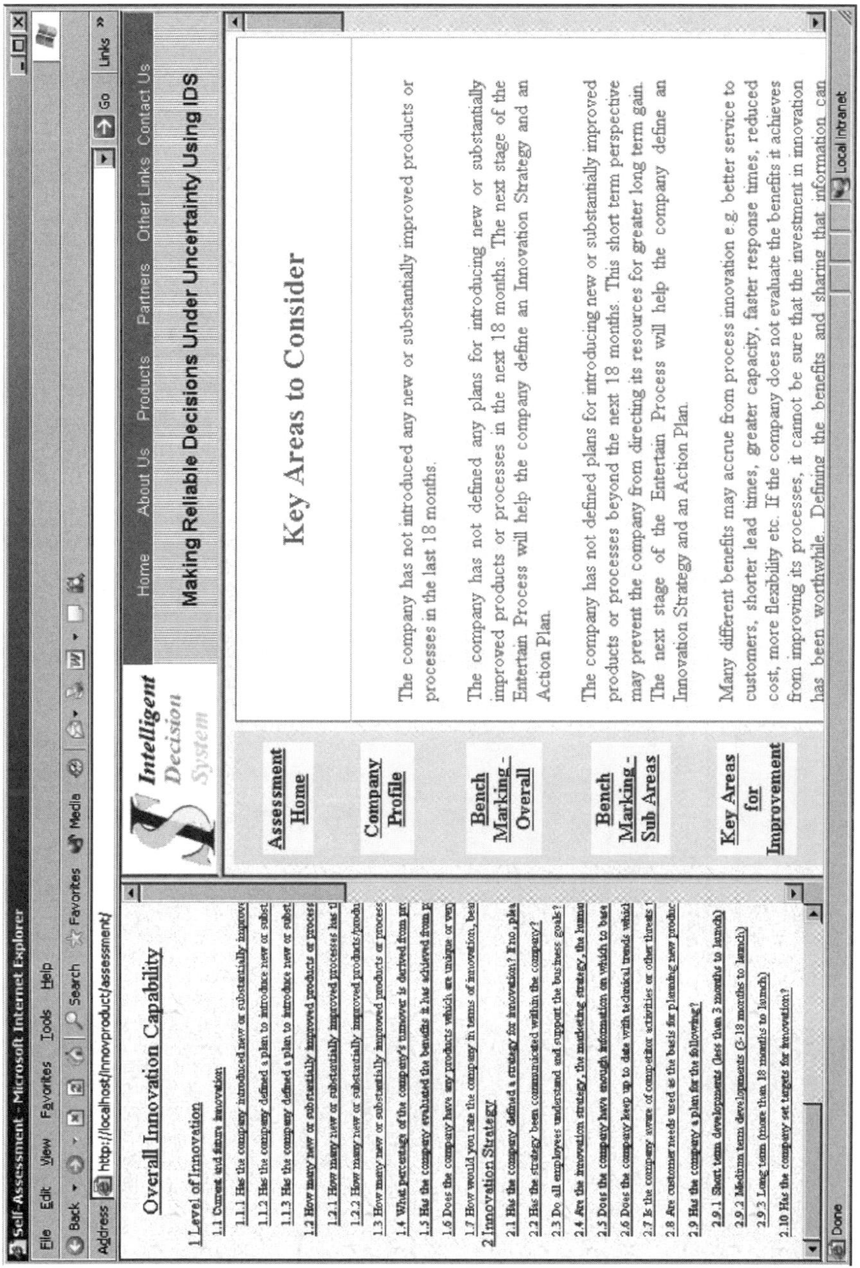

Figure 7.5 Aggregated Assessment Outcomes – Key Areas to Consider for Performance Improvement.

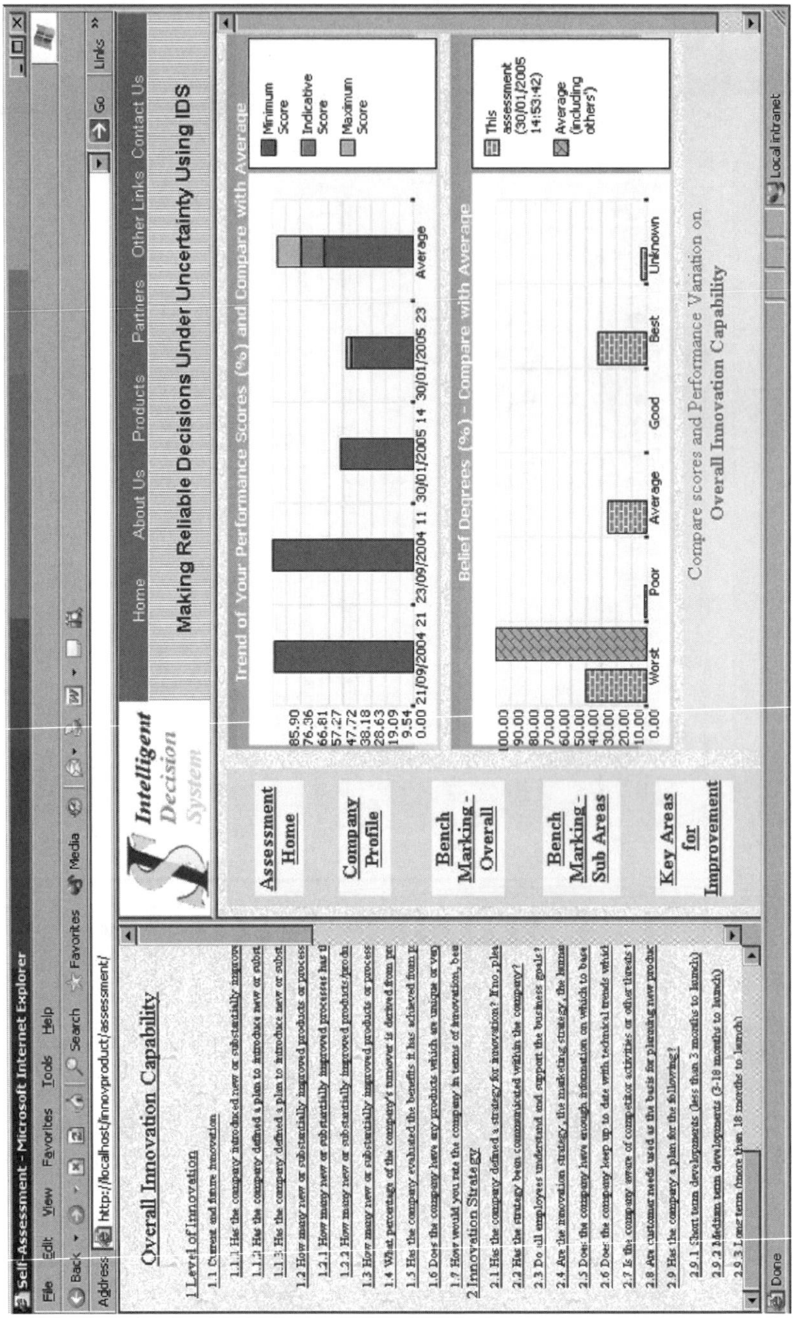

Figure 7.6 Aggregated Assessment Outcomes – Scores Ranges Showing Rank Sensitivity to Missing Data.

Bibliography

[1] V. Belton and T. J. Stewart (2002), *Multiple Criteria Decision Analysis — An Integrated Approach*, Kluwer Academic Publishers.

[2] M. Beynon, D. Cosker and D. Marshall (2001), "An expert system for multi-criteria decision making using Dempster Shafer theory", *Expert Systems with Applications*, **20**, 357–367.

[3] M. Beynon, B. Curry and P. Morgan (2000), "The Dempster-Shafer theory of evidence: an alternative approach to multicriteria decision modelling", *Omega*, **28**, 37–50.

[4] B. G. Buchanan and E. H. Shortliffe (1984), *Rule-Based Expert Systems*, Reading, MA: Addison-Wesley.

[5] D. Cai, M. F. McTear and S. I. McClean (2000), "Knowledge discovery in distributed databases using evidence theory", *International Journal of Intelligent Systems*, **15**, 745–761.

[6] K. S. Chin, J. B. Yang, J. Lam and M. Guo (2007), "An evidential reasoning-interval based method for new product design assessment", *IEEE transactions on Engineering Management*, in press.

[7] T. A. Conti (2007), "A history and review of the European Quality Award Model", *The TQM Magazine*, **19** (2), 112–128.

[8] T. Denoeux (1997), "Analysis of evidence-theoretic decision rules for pattern classification", *Pattern Recognition*, **30** (7), 1095–1107.

[9] S. French (1986), Decision theory - An introduction to the mathematics of rationality, Ellis Horwood, Chichester.

[10] R. P. Hämäläinen (2003), "Decisionarium-aiding decisions, negotiating and collecting opinions on the web", *Journal of Multi-Criteria Decision Analysis*, **12** (2-3), 101–110.

[11] C. L. Hwang and K. Yoon (1981), Multiple Attribute Decision Making Methods and Applications, Springer-Verlag.

[12] Q. Ji and M. M. Marefat (2003), "A Dempster–Shafer approach for recognizing machine features from CAD models", *Pattern Recognition*, **36** (6), 1355–1368.

[13] R. L. Keeney and H. Raiffa (1976), *Decisions with Multiple Objectives*, Cambridge University Press.

[14] A. A. Salo and R. P. Hämäläinen (1995), "Preference programming through approximate ratio comparisons", *European Journal of Operational Research*, **82**, 458–475.

[15] A. Saltelli, S. Tarantola and K. Chan (1999), "A quantitative, model independent method for global sensitivity analysis of model output", *Technometrics*, **41** (1), 39–56.

[16] P. Sen and J. B. Yang (1995), "Multiple criteria decision making in design selection and synthesis", *Journal of Engineering Design*, **6** (3), 207–230.

[17] G. A. Shafer (1976), *Mathematical Theory of Evidence*, Princeton, N.J.: Princeton University Press.

[18] S. Y. Sohn and S. H. Lee (2003), "Data fusion, ensemble and clustering to improve the classification accuracy for the severity of road traffic accidents in Korea", *Safety Science*, **41**, 1–14.

[19] M. Sonmez, J. B. Yang and G. D. Holt (2001), "Addressing the contractor selection problem using an evidential reasoning approach", *Engineering Construction and Architectural Management*, **8** (3), 198–210.

[20] R. P. Srivastava (1995), "The belief-function approach to aggregating audit evidence", *International Journal of Intelligent Systems*, **10** (3), 329–356.

[21] R. P. Srivastava and G. R. Shafer (1992), "Belief-function formulas for audit risk", *The Accounting Review*, **67** (2), 249–283.

[22] E. Triantaphyllou (2000), *Multi-criteria Decision Making Methods: a Comparative Study*, Kluwer Academic Publishers.

[23] J. Wang, H. S. Sii, A. Pillay, J. B. Yang, S. Kim and A. Saajedi (2004), "Use of advances in technology in marine risk assessment", *Risk Analysis*, **24** (4), 1011–1033.

[24] J. Wang, J. B. Yang and P. Sen (1996), "Multi-person and multi-attribute design evaluations using evidential reasoning based on subjective safety and cost analysis", R*eliability Engineering and System Safety*, **52**, 113–127.

[25] X. L. Xie, D. L. Xu, J. B. Yang, J. Wang, J. Ren and S. Yu (2007), "Ship selection using a multiple criteria synthesis approach", *Journal of Marine Science and Technology*, in press.

[26] X. Xie, J. B. Yang, D. L. Xu, and A. K. Maddulapalli (2007), "An investigation into multiple criteria evaluation of consumer preferences under uncertainty", Submitted to *19th International Conference on Multiple Criteria Decision Making*, Auckland, New Zealand.

[27] D. L. Xu, J. Liu, J. B. Yang, G. P. Liu, J. Wang, I. Jenkinson and J. Ren (2007), "Inference and learning methodology of belief-rule-based expert system for pipeline leak detection", *Expert Systems with Applications*, **32** (1), 103–113.

[28] D. L. Xu, G. McCarthy and J. B. Yang (2006), "Intelligent decision system and its application in business innovation self assessment", *Decision Support Systems*, **42**, 664–673.

[29] J. B. Yang (2001), "Rule and utility based evidential reasoning approach for multiple attribute decision analysis under uncertainty", *European Journal of Operational Research*, **131**, 31–61.

[30] J. B. Yang, B. G. Dale and C. H. R. Siow (2001), "Self-assessment of excellence: an application of the evidential reasoning approach", *International Journal of Production Research*, **39** (16), 3789–3812.

[31] J. B. Yang and D.L. Xu (2002a), "On the evidential reasoning algorithm for multiple attribute decision analysis under uncertainty", *IEEE Transactions on Systems, Man and Cybernetics Part A: Systems and Humans*, **32**, 289–304.

[32] J. B. Yang and D. L. Xu (2002b), "Nonlinear information aggregation via evidential reasoning in multiple attribute decision analysis under uncertainty", *IEEE Transactions on Systems, Man, and Cybernetics Part A: Systems and Humans*, **32**, 376–393.

Chapter 8

An Intelligent Policy Simulator for Supporting Strategic Nuclear Policy Decision Making

Suman Rao

Risk Analytics and Solutions, 401, "Valentina", Hiranandani Estate, Patlipada, Thane (W), 400 607 India

E-mail: sumanashokrao@yahoo.co.in

One of the biggest challenges for strategic nuclear policy decision-makers is to discern nuclear proliferation intentions of nation states despite information deficiencies. This chapter suggests a new computationally intelligent nuclear policy simulator called DiNI (**Di**scerning **N**uclear **I**ntentions) to objectively discern nuclear proliferation intentions of nation states in real time. DiNI is inspired from the well-validated theme of socio-biological evolution of altruistic behavior and works on a NetLogo platform. By using DiNI, policy makers can objectively assess the nuclear proliferation intentions of states based on the current policy situation and also assess the effectiveness of new policy instruments in influencing nuclear intentions through simulation. Simulation conducted on DiNI using strategic decisions made under the historic "Atoms for Peace" program demonstrates that DiNI can indeed be used to proactively inform strategic policy decision-makers on unhealthy proliferation intentions of nation states.

8.1 Introduction

"It is easier to denature Plutonium than to denature the evil spirits of man"

– Albert Einstein.

At the root of denaturing and predicting man's 'evil' lies the assessment of his intentions. While assessing individual human intentions is in itself a difficult task, assessing intentions of nation-states is even more difficult. The dilemma faced by strategic policy makers regarding nuclear intentions of Iran and North Korea is a case in point as to how ambivalent this assessment can be. Conventional intelligence methods to detect proliferation intentions have been found to be inadequate/controversial in such cases [1]. These methods are usually centered on capability versus intent considerations. While capability is a "tangible" characteristic and can be objectively assessed to some extent by various physical means, objective assessment of intent which is an "intangible" is a challenge. Consequently, the key elements of the international policy responses towards such states and the Decision Support Systems (DSS) for these policy responses rely on an unstructured combination of technical capability assessments and strategic intelligence information rather than on any objective modeling basis that integrates these elements. By itself, technical capability assessment, though belonging to a tangible domain, is often not conclusive, as there have been many instances in the past where such assessments (e.g., International Atomic Energy Agency (IAEA) safeguard investigations) have been unable to detect clandestine developments of military applications of nuclear technologies. In addition, the strategic/military intelligence information to strategic policy decision makers on capability and intention is (in many cases) sketchy, incomplete and vague.

An additional issue consists of time-lag of information feeding the policy decision-makers. For instance, by the time the U.S. National Intelligence Estimate report on Iran was released in late 2007 with a 'high-confidence' that Iran had halted its nuclear weapons program in 2003 itself, the Bush Administration in the U.S. was almost close to war with Iran based on Iran's suspected nuclear ambitions*[ibid]*.

Problem Statement:

Considering the above practical circumstances, how can strategic policy decision makers objectively assess the proliferation intentions of nation-states in real-time under given policy situations? In particular, can influence of strategic policy instruments e.g., deterrence/incentives on nuclear intentions of target states be objectively evaluated prior to their deployment?

As a response to the above question, this chapter proposes a nature-inspired real-time Policy Simulator called DiNI (**Di**scerning **N**uclear **I**ntentions). DiNI is a NetLOGO Agent Based Model (ABM) built using the socio-biological phenomenon of genetic evolution of altruistic behavior. First, the chapter gives a brief background of the existing methods, followed by a discussion of the socio-biological background of the policy simulator and then the simulator construction in NetLogo is explained. Subsequently, the simulation runs are performed using hypothetical parameter values and the insights that were obtained to proactively support decision makers are highlighted. In order to demonstrate the practical applicability of the policy simulator, the experience of the USA vis-à-vis India in the historic Atoms for Peace program is simulated and the results are discussed. Sections on validity and model verification, the ethical and security aspects of simulation modeling as well as further directions for research are also included in this chapter. The DiNI Policy Simulator is designed to serve DSS needs for national strategic policy decision makers as in the national defense, military and strategic intelligence agencies apart from multilateral safeguard agencies such as the IAEA.

8.2 Existing Intelligence Methods in Discerning Proliferation Intentions of Nation-states

Application of 'intelligent' methods for policy decision support is not new. Social simulations to support policy decision making are generally regarded as belonging to two categories:

(i) Simulation pertaining to a single observed system and
(ii) Simulation of a "typical system" – not of one particular instance.

Type (i) is a normal architecture for most Dynamic Data Driven Simulation systems. However, this type does not fit most social science scenarios and an architecture that is somewhere in the spectrum between (i) and (ii) is recommended [2].
Advanced models such as Real-Time Adversarial Intelligence and Decision-Making (RAID) of Defense Advanced Research Projects Agency (DARPA), use architectures based on game theoretic and cognitive approaches to discern the intention of opponents in war action. However, by design, these models rely on the world view of the analyst(s), e.g., as reflected by the choice of model variables. But are these methods sufficient to address complex problems such as discerning the nuclear proliferation intentions of nation-states? According to a senior defense expert [3] "What technologies must we develop to understand and influence nation states... WMD proliferators... the path to understand people, their cultures, motivations, intentions, opinions and perceptions lies in applying interdisciplinary quantitative and computational social science methods from mathematics, statistics, economics, political science, cultural anthropology, sociology, neuroscience, and modeling and simulation."
Are existing models geared to meet the complex and multi-disciplinary nature of the above requirements? A limited survey of existing methods of 'modeling' nuclear intentions was performed and reveals different insights. Two such models are briefly explained below:
Discourse Based Models [4]: E.g., Sagan's Security, Domestic Politics and Norms Model. As per the security model, States will seek to develop nuclear weapons when they face a military threat to their security that cannot be met through alternative means. If they do not

face such threats, they will willingly remain non-nuclear states. The domestic policy model focuses on the domestic actors who encourage or discourage governments from pursuing the bomb building. Important domestic actors within the state are: 1) State's nuclear energy establishment; 2) Units within the professional military; 3) Politicians or parties who favor nuclear weapons. This model focuses on norms concerning weapons acquisition and postulates that States behavior is not determined by leaders or parochial bureaucratic interests, but rather by deeper norms and shared beliefs about what actions are legitimate [5].

Computer Models [5]: These are typically Type (i) Models such as the ones being built by Prof. de Mesquita (USA) based on rational choice/game theoretic approaches. De Mesquita models are reported to be accurate 90 % of the time. E.g., in the case of Iran this model assumed game theoretic interactions between 80 players. These players were stand-ins for real-life people who influenced a negotiation or decision. Experts were asked narrow, carefully delineated questions about which outcome each player would prefer, how important the issue is to each player, and how much influence each player can exert. Based on these inputs the model was run and the outcomes concluded. The history of the conflict, the cultural norms of the area, or what the experts think will happen is not part of the model [7].

While existing methods have distinct advantages, they have a few limitations as outlined below:

(i) They lay an excessive emphasis on single disciplines –e.g., Sagan model on International theories and Mesquita models on game theory/rational choices.
(ii) Real-time capabilities of the models are limited.
(iii) Model construction depends on the world-view of the analysts and experts. This is especially reflected in the choice of model variables and specific pre-determined questions posed to experts for their opinion.
(iv) Capability to incorporate emergence properties of the problem is limited.

8.3 A Suggested Policy Simulator Based on the Genetic Evolution of Altruism

Overcoming the lacunae (as described in Section 8.2) of existing models for predicting nuclear intentions, this chapter proposes a nature-inspired real-time Agent Based Model (ABM) called 'Discerning Nuclear Intentions' (DiNI). DiNI is a policy simulator for strategic policy support which accepts real-time inputs from multiple sources/disciplines and helps objectively inform policy decision makers in assessing and influencing the nuclear intentions of target/suspect nation-states. DiNI takes inputs not only from experts but also from other sources/data bases in real-time. DiNI is inspired from a natural phenomenon: the socio-biological evolution of altruistic behavior and is therefore not dependent on the world-view of the analysts. A brief background of the phenomenon of socio-biological altruistic behavior is given below.

8.3.1 *Inspiration from Nature: The Genetic Evolution of Altruism*

In socio-biological parlance, an organism is said to behave 'altruistically' when its behavior benefits other organisms at a cost to itself. The costs and benefits are measured in terms of reproductive fitness. For example, Vervet monkeys warn fellow monkeys of predators, even though in doing so, they increase their own chance of being attacked. Under the conventional Darwinist intuition 'survival of the fittest', this altruism should have actually wiped itself out in subsequent generations, leading to the proliferation of the 'selfish' members of the species. However, this does not happen in reality. Evolutionary socio-biologists hold that altruism triumphs due to the phenomenon of 'inclusive fitness', wherein the altruistic gene, though it reduces the reproductive fitness of the bearer, survives due to an increase in the overall group fitness enabled due to altruistic behavior [7]. In a world comprising of both altruists and their selfish counterparts, the altruists are successful if $c < b^{*}r$ (called Hamilton's inequality) [8], where $c =$ cost of altruism, $b =$ altruistic benefit conferred and $r =$ Sewall's coefficient of relatedness.

8.3.2 *Peace as a State of Dynamic Equilibrium: Altruism in the Nuclear World*

In the nuclear world of dual-use technologies, the spread of nuclear cooperation is essential for constructive applications of nuclear energy. Parasiting on this spread of peaceful intentions are the unhealthy intentions of target/suspect nation-states that intend to take undue/illegal advantage of dual-use nuclear technologies and proliferate. Policing multilateral agencies and individual/groups of nation-states are involved in detecting proliferation intentions and keeping such intentions under control with a 'suitable' policy package of incentives and/or deterrents. These policy package incentives may range from restricted technology transfers, multibillion-dollar loans and economic reconstruction packages to national security guarantees. The deterrents may range from diplomatic admonition and United Nations (UN) sanctions to an outright attack on installations/war. The objective of the policymaking is to overcome proliferation intentions of the target state and achieve the end objective of peace. From a modeling perspective, this peace, which is a function of continuous interactions of peaceful and proliferation intentions, is a Dynamic Equilibrium

(DE) of a complex dynamic nuclear world system requiring Dynamic State Estimations (DSE). The DE of peace is achieved by overcoming the spread of unhealthy nuclear intentions (analogous to the selfish agents) by the peaceful intentions (analogous to the altruists) who offer the policy package at a cost to themselves. The analogy between the socio-biological evolution of altruism and the nuclear proliferation context are now fairly evident. The DE of peace exists in the system as long as the peace agents triumph over the proliferation agents. Information on the conditions/events/changes in motivations is then input in real time into this system. Assessing the effectiveness of various policy instruments is, therefore, analogous to the DSE of this system based on the policy-driven change in the parameter input values.

While the above seems to be a plausible model construction basis, can nature's altruism model abstraction be regarded as a valid inspiration for DiNI?

8.3.3 *DiNI Policy Simulator: Validity and Verification*

Policy simulations are used in a variety of situations ranging from agricultural/ land use planning to HIV policies. These are typically built on ABM platforms.

ABM-based simulations are widely regarded to offer tremendous advantages, especially pertaining to interdisciplinary collaboration. Simulation by itself has been described as a "third way of doing science" [9]. However, it has also been acknowledged (by the same author) that "While a mathematical proof can usually be checked for accuracy without great difficulty, the same cannot be said for an agent-based simulation program" [10]. Therefore, it becomes essential to validate and verify the model and its premise very carefully. The following discussion gives key aspects of DiNI model validity/verification and is not exhaustive due to space limitations.

Nature's altruism model is based on the socio-biological evolution of altruistic genes, whereas DiNI's analogy to nature has been drawn with (abstract) intention agents. Is there an inconsistency involved? Some experts argue that the biological models of animal altruism are based on reproductive fitness consequences where no 'intention' as such in 'helping' other animals exists and, therefore, caution attributing such behaviors to intentions. However, it needs to be clarified here that such claims also have their criticisms. Also, the DiNI model has been 'translated' from animal data/modeling to humans and this translation involves making adjustments to human contexts, particularly by way of drawing analogies between biological genes and human intentions. A more complete explanation of this analogy cuts across disciplines ranging from biology to social-psychology and is beyond the scope of this chapter.

DiNI is based on an abstraction of the altruism model as built on NetLogo. The NetLogo altruism model is freely available for download from the internet. Based on a paper of Mitteldorf and Wilson, this model has been verified and validated from a computational modeling perspective [11]. Further details on the modeling are provided in the next section.

8.4 Modeling Basis for DINI - Nature's Altruism Model in NetLogo [12]

In this model, Abstract agents called "patches" interact in a von Neumann Neighborhood (VNN) under conditions of harshness and disease (see Fig. 8.1). The model simulations provide insights into the circumstances under which the pink "altruistic" agents survive and the green "selfish" agents are contained in an environment that is made tough with Black "Void" agents.

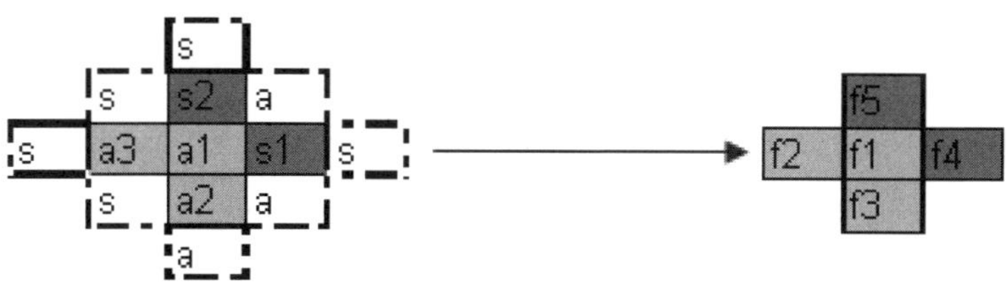

Figure 8.1 A single ASASA VNN in the model with fitness representation.

There are four input parameters:

- cost to altruist (c)
- benefit of altruism (b)
- harshness (h) and
- disease (d).

Agent rules are as follows:

- Each patch first calculates its "fitness" and then contributes to a genetic "lottery" for its space.
- Based on the outcome of this lottery, a patch "survives" or "fails". Fitness of an altruist patch $= 1 - c + b$ (No. of altruistic neighborhood agents)$/5$.
- Fitness of selfish patch$= 1 + b$ (No. of altruistic neighborhood agents).
- Fitness of void agents is a constant value$= h$.

In Fig. 8.1 above, $f_1 = 1 - c + b(3/5)$, $f_2 = 1 - c + b(2/5)$, $f_3 = 1 - c + b(4/5)$, $f_4 = 1 + b(3/5)$, $f_5 = 1 + b(2/5)$.

Steps in the genetic lottery: (Illustrations for the VNN depicted in Fig. 8.1)

- Calculate Fitness sum $F = f_1 + f_2 + f_3 + f_4 + f_5 + d$.
- Calculate Alt wt $= (f_1 + f_2 + f_3)/F$, Self wt $= (f4 + f5)/F$, Void wt $= (0 + d)/F$. (In this case Figure 8.1, there are no "void" agents in the neighborhood.)
- Conduct genetic lottery: Let Major seed $\mathrm{M_{alt}}$ = Max (Alt wt, Self wt) and Minor Seed m_{alt} = Min (Alt wt, Self wt). A random number $n_t \in [0,1]$ is generated for agent a_1's genetic lottery at time t. Suppose $\mathrm{M_{alt}}$ = Alt wt for patch a_1 at time t. If $0 < n_t < m_{\mathrm{alt}}$, patch turns green, for $m_{\mathrm{alt}} < n_t < m_{\mathrm{alt}} + \mathrm{M_{alt}}$, patch turns pink, for $m_{\mathrm{alt}} + \mathrm{M_{alt}} < n_t < 1$, patch turns black (void).

8.5 DiNI Model Construction

The DiNI Model construction involves suitably adapting NetLogo Altruism model parameters (see Table 8.1) to the nuclear world analogies (see Section 8.3) and computing input parameter values *c*, *b*, *h* and *d* (Section 8.4) based on the existing circumstances, policy and instruments.

All Parameter values are dynamic and will change real-time. If the model is maintained static with limited periodic updates to input values, then its utility will be greatly limited.

8.5.1 *Calculating Parameter Values* c, b, h *and* d *for DiNI*

The choice of parameters *c*, *b*, *h* and *d* has been made based on an inspiration from nature's altruism model and does not depend on analyst's world-view. These values are determined based on the following steps:

- Tabulate driving motivations (Motivational Indicators –MI) for the parameters based on assessment of economic, cultural, sociological, political motives of target Nation State.
- Use a suitable method to normalize the multi-disciplinary inputs and compute values for *c*, *b*, *h*, *d* (conforming to the altruism parameter ranges). The multi-disciplinary inputs are normalized based on a combination of PR (Perception Rating) and CI (Confidence Index).

Table 8.1 Adapting altruism model parameters to DiNI.

Altruism Model Elements	**DiNI Elements**	**Altruism Input Parameters**	**DiNI Parameters**
Agent patches represent genetic units of social behavior (either altruistic or selfish)	Agent patches represent **units of Nation State intention under particular situations of nuclear policy** (either peaceful or proliferating)	Cost of altruism (c)	Net costs of incentivisation/deterrence policy packages (for P agents)
Pink altruist agents	Peaceful intentions of policy making Nation state Represented by P agents	Benefit of altruism (b)	Net benefits of the policy package to the target state (for U agents)
Green "Selfish" Agents	Unhealthy intentions of suspect/target Nation State Represented by U agents	Harshness of environment (h)	Strength of policy package provisions
Black Void Agents	Policy intentions Represented by V agents	Disease (d)	Conditions under which both the P agents and U agents will die
Initial proportion of altruists and selfish agents ~Initial proportion of positive (p) and unhealthy (u) intentions.			

Tables 8.2-8.5 present an illustration of the base case value tables for parameter b, c, h and d. PR and CI are derived relative to the policy-making state. PR is an objective assessment of motive strength affecting the model parameter; CI denotes the confidence with which these perceptions are expressed. Both PR and CI are based on a synthesis of information pertaining to key motive indicators, expert opinions, intelligence agency estimates etc. The PR is in fact a number arrived at as an outcome of the perception stage assessment of Situation Awareness (e.g., Level 1 of the commonly known Endsley Model of Situation Awareness).

Note: Situation Awareness is described as the "perception of elements in the environment within a volume of time and space, the comprehension of their meaning and their projection in the near future" [13].

The CI is an index number with which the confidence of the PR of the MI needs to be weighed in the DSS. In strategic/military contexts, this confidence is an integral part of intelligence that is considered 'actionable'. Various advanced information synthesis methods are available with which to arrive at the PR and CI numbers as also their methods of weighting and normalization. The DiNI model illustration below takes hypothetical PR and CI numbers (on a scale of 1-5, 5 reflecting the highest strength) and weighs the MIs using a simple weighted average method of normalization. Each value of *c*, *b*, *h* and *d* is thus obtained after taking into account a complex assessment based on multi-disciplinary MIs e.g., economical, political, cultural, and sociological etc.

Table 8.2 Value table for b – estimated net policy package benefits to targeted nation state.

MIs that reduce the perceived benefits received from the policy packages (b)	PR	CI	PR	CI	MIs that increase the perceived benefits received from the policy packages (b)
National security and pride	4	3	4	5	Economic
Regional competition	3	3	5	4	Admission into the world order
Level of Mis-Trust in policy-making state	2	3	5	3	Energy Security
Wtd. Normalization of PR × CI	$\frac{12+9+6}{75} = 0.36$		$\frac{20+20+15}{75} = 0.73$		Net Benefit value $b = 0.73 - 0.36 = 0.37$

Table 8.3 Value table for c – estimated net policy costs to the policy-making nation state.

MIs that increase the cost to the policy-making Nation State (c)	PR	CI	PR	CI	MIs that reduce the perceived cost of the policy-making Nation State (c)
Financial Cost of putting together the incentive/deterrent policy package	4	5	4	4	Long term Economic gains
Costs of Policing	5	5	3	3	National/International popularity gain in as an upholder of peace
NPT status and adherence to the treaty obligations by the target state.	5	3	2	2	Reduced risks of nuclear terrorism in own country
Wtd. Normalization of PR × CI	$\frac{20+25+15}{75} = 0.80$		$\frac{16+9+4}{75} = 0.39$		Net Cost value $c = 0.80 - 0.39 = 0.41$

Where MI = Motivational Indicator, PR = Perceived Rating and CI = Confidence Index as explained above

All the factors/motivations in Tables 8.2-8.5 have been the outcome of learning from various world nuclear proliferation experiences in the past. They are clearly not exhaustive in their scope and have only been mentioned here by way of illustration.

Table 8.4 Value table for h– strength of (existing) policy package provisions.

Factors/Forces/Features that increase the strength of the policy package (h)	**PR**	**CI**	**PR**	**CI**	**Factors/Forces/Features that reduce the perceived strength of the policy package (h)**
Quality and Quantum of Deliverables (policy covenants) of the target state according to the policy package.	4	3	4	2	Reputation of the policy-making country in punishing package violations in the past
End use verification provisions	3	3	5	1	Lack of widespread support to the package in own country
			5	2	Lack of support for the package from other key international actors in the policy-making arena
Wtd. Normalization of PR × CI	$\frac{12+9}{50} = 0.42$		$\frac{8+5+10}{75} = 0.31$		Net strength of policy $h = 0.42 - 0.31 = 0.11$

Table 8.5 Value table for d – conditions under which both agents will die.

Factors/Forces/Features that can increase the disease (d)	**PR**	**CI**	**PR**	**CI**	**Factors/Forces/Features that reduce the disease (d)**
Natural calamities	4	5	4	3	Weak political governance/administration
Internal strife in target country	5	4	1	1	Global Economic depression
An overriding influence of a third player	5	3			
Wtd. Normalization of PR × CI	$\frac{20+20+15}{75} = 0.73$		$\frac{12+1}{50} = 0.26$		Net Disease value $d = 0.73 - 0.26 = 0.47$

8.6 DiNI Model Simulation and Results

The DiNI simulation results (time ticks > 200) are summarized in Table 8.6 and are interpreted in Table 8.7. The survival of pink P agents signifies effectiveness of the strategic policy package instruments and their extinction signifies policy failure. The values p, u, c, b, d and h in Table 8.7 are hypothetical.

The above hypothetical case illustrations of DiNI simulation results show how to discern

Table 8.6 DiNI simulation run cases.

Case 1 (Base case)*		Case 2		Case 3	
$p = 0.26$ $u = 0.26$ $c = 0.37$ $b = 0.33$ $d = 0.47$ $h = 0.11$	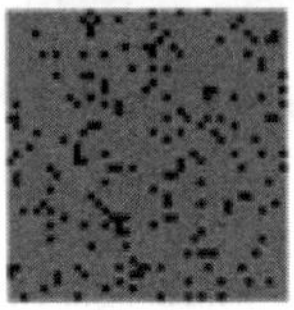	$p = 0.26$ $u = 0.26$ $c = 0.10$ $b = 0.70$ $d = 0.20$ $h = 0.53$	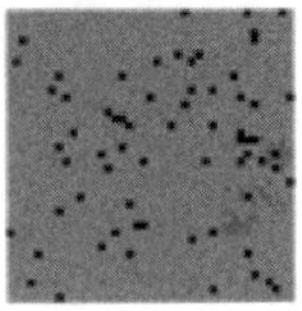	$p = 0.26$ $u = 0.26$ $c = 0.13$ $b = 0.48$ $d = 0.31$ $h = 0.88$	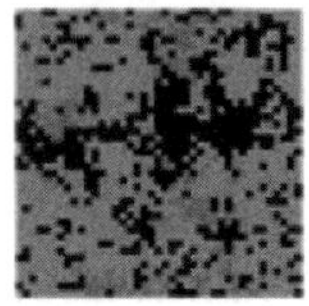

Table 8.7 Illustration of how a policy maker can use DiNI for strategic decision-making.

Case	Case Description	Simulation results and Interpretation
1	Base Case: Equal probabilities of unhealthy intentions of target states and positive intentions of policy-making states i.e., $p = 0.26$, $u = 0.26$ with assessed values of c, b, h and d based on existing policy. (based on Tables 8.2-8.5)	**Result: Green U Agents survive, Pink P agents extinct** The Unhealthy intentions dominate indicating that current state of the system of policy-making is ineffective in containing unhealthy intentions of the target Nation State.
2	The policy maker has now introduced new policy instruments (incentives) in such a way that $c < b^{*}0.2$ (Hamilton's inequality), with changes in d, h.	**Result: Pink P Agents survive, Green U agents extinct** Success for the positive intentions of the policy-making nation state with the revised policy package of incentives and deterrents keeping proliferation risks under control
3	The policy maker has increased strength of policy provisions h though c and b do not satisfy Hamilton's inequality	**Result: Pink P Agents survive, Green U agents extinct** Despite $c > b^{*}0.2$, and a reduction in disease conditions (as compared to base case) , the new policy package still succeeds by getting proliferation risks under control through suitably increasing policy provision fitness (h).

nuclear intentions of target nation states under various policy situations and evaluate the proliferation (intention) response to specific policy measures.

The DiNI Policy simulator is now illustrated with a real-life nuclear policy situation in order to demonstrate its validity and utility

8.7 Policy Simulation on DiNI: The Experience of USA vis-à-vis India under the Atoms for Peace program

8.7.1 *Nuclear Cooperation Between USA and India - A Brief Background*

As part of the 1950s-era Atoms for Peace (AfP) program, the United States actively promoted nuclear energy cooperation with India from the mid-1950s, building nuclear reactors

(Tarapur), providing heavy water for the CIRUS reactor, and allowing Indian scientists to study at U.S. nuclear laboratories. However, India did not join the NPT on the basis that it was discriminatory [14]. In 1974, India exploded a "peaceful" nuclear device, demonstrating that nuclear technology transferred for peaceful purposes could be used to produce nuclear weapons. As a result, the United States refused nuclear cooperation with India for more than three decades and influenced other states to do the same. This policy stand has now been dramatically reversed through the recent (2008) Indo-US nuclear deal under the GNEP program.

8.7.2 *Construction of the DiNI Atoms for Peace Policy Simulator*

Table 8.8 characterizes the DiNI AfP policy simulator constituents.

Problem definition: On the basis of available information at that time (1950s–1960s) could the policy makers have objectively predicted the outcome of the cooperation of US with India under the AfP program? What further potential insights could DiNI provide for policy making countries such as the USA?

As a solution construct to the above problem, Motivational Indicators (MIs) as elicited from historical published Strategic Intelligence information available during the era of AfP until the 1974 Indian explosion would be input into DiNI to objectively demonstrate how the policy simulation insights compare with reality as it unfolded.

Table 8.8 DiNI Atoms for Peace (AfP) policy simulator – characterization.

Altruism Model Elements	**DiNI Elements**	**Altruism Input Parameters**	**DiNI Parameters**
Agent patches represent genetic units of social behavior (either altruistic or selfish)	Agent patches represent **units of Nation State intention under particular situations of nuclear policy** (either peaceful or proliferating)	Cost of altruism (c)	Net costs of incentivisation/deterrence policy packages (for P agents)
Pink altruist agents	Peaceful intentions of USA Represented by P agents	Benefit of altruism (b)	Net benefits of the policy package to the target state (for U agents)
Green "Selfish" Agents	Unhealthy/Proliferation intentions of India Represented by U agents	Harshness of environment (h)	Strength of policy package provisions
Black Void Agents	AfP Policy intentions Represented by V agents	Disease (d)	Conditions under which both the P agents and U agents will die

Initial proportion of P and U agents ~Initial proportion of positive (p) and unhealthy (u) intentions.

Note 1: This illustration is for the sole purpose of demonstrating the utility and validity of DiNI and is not to be construed as throwing adverse light on either India or the USA.
Note 2: Information sources used for this illustration are cited under [15, 16, 17, 18], and [19]

- Declassified strategic intelligence documents of the government of USA (NIE) have been used for the purposes of this illustration. In order to avoid a "wisdom in hindsight" bias, and to test the ability of DiNI Policy Simulator to proactively inform decision-makers:

  (a) no information source post the 1974 'peaceful' explosion of India has been included,
  (b) no Indian interpretation of the events has been included since DiNI simulation in this example is run from the view point of USA. Rather the perceptions of USA on the motives of India is what is input into the policy simulator.

- The strategic intelligence documentation included in this simulation is illustrative and not exhaustive. The intelligence information is limited to the extent of declassification by the U.S. Government.
- There is scope for including information from civilian sources e.g., economic databases, to feed into the Motivation Indicators. However this has not been included for present illustration purposes due to constraints in space and time.

8.7.3 *Calculating Parameter Values for* c, b, h *and* d *for the DiNI Atoms for peace policy simulator*

First driving motivations (Motivational Indicators – MI) for the parameters based on assessment of economic, cultural, sociological, political motives of target Nation State are tabulated time-period wise (In this case year wise). Then a simple method is used to normalize the strategic intelligence inputs (as was discussed in section 8.5) and values for c, b, h, d (conforming to the simulator parameter ranges) computed. The multi-disciplinary inputs are normalized based on a combination of PR (Perception Rating) and CI (Confidence Index). PR and CI are derived relative to the viewpoint of USA.
Since the information is over 50 years old and it is now not possible to obtain a Perception Rating and Confidence Index without wisdom in hindsight bias, some necessary assumptions have been made:

(i) Default PR and CI is 4 on a scale of 1-5 (5 being the strongest)

(ii) Depending on the qualifying adjectives for the MI, CI rating is then varied.

a. E.g., the words 'strong', 'very clearly' are taken to indicate high confidence and get a CI of 5,
b. The words probably, likely etc. which are indicators of weak confidence get a CI of 3.

8.7.4 *The AfP Experience of USA vis-à-vis India - Base Case*

Tables 8.9 and 8.10 present an illustration of the base case value tables for parameter *c* and *b*. The 1957 joint progress reports submitted by the State Department and the AEC on implementation of NSC 5507/2 "Peaceful uses of atomic energy" have been used in framing the base case values [20].

Table 8.9 Value table for *c* – Estimated net policy costs to the USA.

MI Description	Parameter	+/−	Perception Rating	Confidence Index	PR*CI	Year	Source
Maintain US's Leadership Position in the development of peaceful uses of nuclear energy	*c*	−	5	5	−25	1957	Joint progress report
To promote peaceful uses of nuclear energy in free nations abroad as rapidly as possible	*c*	−	5	5	−25	1957	Joint progress report
to promote cohesion within the free world nations	*c*	−	5	5	−25	1957	Joint progress report
to forestall Soviet Union's similar objectives	*c*	−	5	5	−25	1957	Joint progress report
to assure continued access of nuclear materials to the US	*c*	−	5	5	−25	1957	Joint progress report
to prevent diversion of fissionable materials to non-peaceful uses	*c*	−	5	5	−25	1957	Joint progress report
Distribution of nuclear material	*c*	−	5	5	−25	1957	Joint progress report
Conferences, Missions and Info programs	*c*	−	5	5	−25	1957	Joint progress report

Continued on next page...

Table 8.9 – continued from previous page

MI Description	Parameter	+/−	Perception Rating	Confidence Index	PR*CI	Year	Source
Power reactor agreements and prospects of nuclear commerce	*c*	−	5	5	−25	1957	Joint progress report
Power reactors required for use abroad to be developed in US to maintain US technological leadership	*c*	−	5	5	−25	1957	Joint progress report
Aid for Research reactors to be provided for select countries	*c*	−	5	5	−25	1957	Joint progress report
Educate and train foreign students	*c*	−	5	5	−25	1957	Joint progress report

Overall value for c is -1.

Table 8.10 Value table for b – Estimated net policy package benefits to India.

MI Description	Parameter	+/−	Perception Rating	Confidence Index	PR*CI	Year	Source
Distribution of nuclear material	*b*	+	5	5	25	1957	Joint progress report
Conferences, Missions and Info programs	*b*	+	5	5	25	1957	Joint progress report
Power reactor agreements and prospects of nuclear commerce	*b*	+	5	5	25	1957	Joint progress report
Power reactors required for use abroad to be developed in US to maintain US technological leadership	*b*	+	5	5	25	1957	Joint progress report
Aid for Research reactors to be provided for select countries	*b*	+	5	5	25	1957	Joint progress report
Educate and train foreign students	*b*	+	5	5	25	1957	Joint progress report

Applying scale translation, $c = -1 + 1 = 0$

Overall value for b is 1.

Note: There is no specific mention on the benefits for recipient countries in the Joint progress report. Subsequently the author has assumed those relevant points from Table 8.9 above to be repeated as benefits in Table 8.10.

A conservative (subjective) value of 0.2 for h and 0.05 for d have been assumed based on literature study of the crucial AfP decade (1957–1967). There is scope to further validate these two values with more information pertaining to that decade.

8.7.5 *Evaluating the AfP Experience of USA vis-à-vis India - The 1960s*

For this evaluation, a total of 77 MIs were elicited from the strategic intelligence information (NIE Reports). The MIs were first classified as belonging to either of b, c, h or d category. If the same MI could have been classified under two categories, then the overwhelming categorization was considered, thereby restricting the complexity in calculations. (However DiNI provides flexibility to include multiple classifications as well.) Overall net values of b, c, h and d were calculated in year-wise value tables (Tables 8.11-8.16) similar to the methods demonstrated in Section 8.5 illustrations.

The individual year wise value tables are provided below for information (1962 data were unavailable to the author).

Table 8.11 Value tables for year 1961.

Year			1961
b			25
	–		–50
		Neighbor (China's) foreign policy	–25
		Security, Prestige and ability to be neutral (due to potential Chinese nuclear program)	–25
	+		75
		Cost and reluctance to divert resources from current economic programs	25
		Leadership decision on program not to go the weapons way	25
		Psychological and political factors opposing nuclear weapons	25
c			15
	–		–25
		Lack of technical capability (snags)	–25
	+		40
		Developing plutonium separation plant	20
		Developing indigenous uranium resources	20
h			–20
	–		–20
		Expressed desire to avoid safeguards	–20

Table 8.12 Value tables for year 1963.

Year			1963
b			20
	–		–25
		Chinese threat may affect the progress and direction of the Indian nuclear program	–25
	+		45
		political leadership unlikely to go ahead with the weaponisation	20
		Psychological and political factors opposing nuclear weapons	25
c			50
			50
		If dependency on US for heavy water is eliminated then can independently produce plutonium without safeguards	25
		India improving overall nuclear capabilities	25

Table 8.13 Value tables for year 1964.

Year			1964
b			**–40**
	–		**–40**
		Changes in Sino-soviet relations	–20
		scope and pace of the Chinese nuclear program	–20
c			**20**
	+		**20**
		Basic facilities existing including plutonium separation plant	20

Table 8.14 Value tables for year 1965.

Year			1965
b			**–270**
	–		**–375**
		As China's arsenal improves the views of the military leaders are likely to change	–15
		Chinese test in late 64	–20
		Development costs of nuclear weapons not a sufficient deterrent to India	–25
		Economic burden in developing few simple fissile weapons is not great and only small parts of these would involve foreign exchange	–15
		If India tested, it will claim it was for peaceful purposes thereby avoiding damage to prestige and not violated its agreement with Canada on the CIR	–25
		Inability to stand up to a nuclear-armed China	–25
			–15
		Indian prestige and acknowledgment as a great power is not possible without nuclear weapons	–25
		Political leadership will support technical efforts to shorten time between decision and detonation of a test device	–25
		Public sentiment for nuclear weapon building	–25
		Severe economic difficulties might deter the testing decision	–15
		Indo-Pakistani war has strengthened shift towards nuclear weapons	–25
		Threat of Chinese intervention in Indo-Pak fighting has given a boost to weapons proponents	–20
		No scientific spectacular achievement to counter Chinese achievements of nuclear tests	–25

Continued on next page...

Table 8.14 – continued from previous page

Year		**1965**
	Pace and scope of the Chinese nuclear program	−25
	A renewal of war with China supporting Pakistan might cause New Delhi to opt for the bomb	−15
	Declining legacy of Gandhi (Non-violence and Nehru)	−15
	Costs would be prohibitive (as per some Indian quarters)	−20
+		**105**
	Apprehensions of Setting up a nuclear weapons race with Pakistan	15
	Build up of conventional weapon strength is preferred by military leadership	15
	Conventional arms are what is required the most in view of the Indo-Pak war	20
	Indian military focussed on borders and not on strategic capabilities and hence not pressing for nuclear weapons	15
	Reversal of Nehru's position will lead to damage of international prestige	15
	Political leadership's position strengthened who has non-proliferation leanings	25
c		**35**
−		**−40**
	No evidence of advanced weapons design and test site identification	−25
	Limited work on missile technology so far and sourcing missile systems will be a challenge	−15
+		**75**
	India has capability to test a device within a year of the decision	15
	India has the capability to develop nuclear weapons	20
	Plutonium production facilities make it doubtful whether it is for only peaceful purposes	15
	New Delhi will probably detonate a nuclear device and proceed to produce nuclear weapons within next few years	25
d		**15**
+		**15**
	If China attacks India with nuclear weapons, the US and USSR may become inevitably involved.	15
h		−100
−		−180
	India regards that Moscow won't cut off aid to influence nuclear policy	−15
	Moscow's silence when China threatened to intervene in the Indo-Pak war	−20
	Moscow's support will ensure Western support as well	−15
	Not willing to insure security through a test ban treaty	−15
	Political leadership will avoid committing to international agreements that will curtail India's options	−25
	stiff stand on non-proliferation treaty	−20
	Suspension of US military aid to India and US's failure to prevent Pakistan's use of US weapons against India	−20
	New Delhi won't accede to NPT since China is not limited in weapons devpt as per NPT and China won't accept such restrictions	−25
	China has not suffered any set-backs on account of its nuclear capability and its status has been enhanced	−25
+		**80**
	Meaningful international progress in disarmament might deter the testing decision	15
	Political leadership will weigh assurances, inducements and pressures forthcoming from other nuclear powers	25
	Political leadership's immediate course of action is to keep diplomatic and technical options open	25
	Securing international gurantess	15

Table 8.15 Value tables for year 1966.

Year			1966
b			−85
	−		−110
		China's growing nuclear strength	−15
		National Security	−15
		Prestige	−15
		Spectre of Pakistani-Chinese collaboration	−25
		New Delhi won't accede to NPT since China is not limited in weapons devpt as per NPT and China won't accept such restrictions	−25
		Strengthening its bargaining position	−15
	+		25
		Political leadership believe that this is not reqd	25
c			−75
	−		−75
		Food situation critical	−25
		Present and prospective economic difficulties	−25
		India has capability to produce nuclear weapons and test a first device within one year of decision	−25

Table 8.16 Value tables for year 1967.

Year			1967
b			−95
	−		−95
		Fear of Sino-Pakistani collaboration	−20
		War with Pakistan (Self-reliance in Defence matters)	−20
		Chinese detonation of 1966	−25
		No sign of satisfactory security guarantee from USA/USSR	−15
		Cessation of US assistance during 1965 Indo-Pak war	−15
c			−10
	−		−10
		Huge demand for cost, foreign exchange and trained manpower a deterrent	−10

Every year c, b, h and d values were cumulated and DiNI was run again.

The cumulated c, b, h and d values are mentioned in Tables 8.17 and 8.18 below for all the years ranging from 1961 to 1967. There is a data availability gap on NIE sources the author faced for 1962-hence there is a break in the yearly time series).

Table 8.17 Cumulative value tables for years 1961, 1963 and 1964.

	Initial Values	1961			1963			1964		
		Revised b, c, h and d values tailored to model scale								
	Base case	**From Value Table**	**Cumu-lative**	**After scale trans-lation**	**From Value Table**	**Cumu-lative**	**After scale trans-lation**	**From Value Table**	**Cumu-lative**	**After scale trans-lation**
b	0.90	0.00	0.90	0.90	−0.10	0.80	0.80	−0.80	0.00	0.00
c	0.00	−0.20	−0.20	0.00	1.00	0.80	0.80	0.80	1.60	0.90
h	0.20	−0.80	−0.60	0.00	0.00	−0.60	0.00	0.00	−0.60	0.00
d	0.05	0.00	0.05	0.05	0.00	0.05	0.05	0.00	0.05	0.05

Table 8.18 Cumulative value tables for years 1965, 1966 and 1967.

	1965			1966			1967		
	From Value Table	**Cumu-lative**	**After scale trans-lation**	**From Value Table**	**Cumu-lative**	**After scale trans-lation**	**From Value Table**	**Cumu-lative**	**After scale transla-tion**
b	−0.13	−0.13	0.00	0.27	0.13	0.13	−0.76	−0.63	0.00
c	−0.05	1.55	0.90	−1.00	0.55	0.55	−0.40	0.15	0.15
h	0.00	−0.60	0.00	0.00	−0.60	0.00	0.00	−0.60	0.00
d	0.60	0.65	0.65	0.00	0.65	0.65	0.00	0.60	0.65

8.7.6 *DiNI Atoms for Peace Simulation and Results*

The DiNI simulation results (time ticks > 200) are summarized in Table 8.19 and insights are interpreted in Table 8.20. The survival of pink P agents signifies effectiveness of the strategic policy package instruments of USA and their extinction signifies policy failure. The values p, u, c, b, d and h in Table 8.7 are as derived from Section 8.7.2 above.

Table 8.19 DiNI AfP simulation results.

p = 0.26 **u** = 0.26 **c** = 0.00 **b** = 0.90 **d** = 0.05 **h** = 0.20	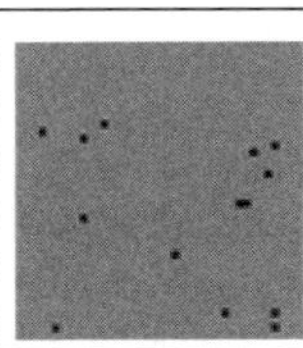	**p** = 0.26 **u** = 0.26 **c** = 0.00 **b** = 0.90 **d** = 0.05 **h** = 0.00	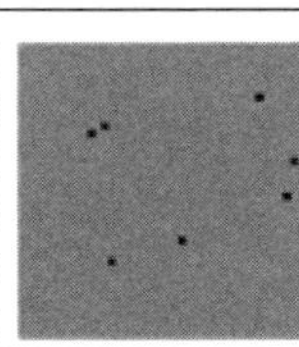	**p** = 0.26 **u** = 0.26 **c** = 0.80 **b** = 0.80 **d** = 0.05 **h** = 0.00	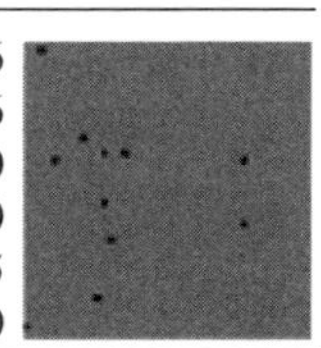

Continued on next page...

Table 8.19 – continued from previous page

1964		1965		1966	
p = 0.26 **u** = 0.26 **c** = 0.90 **b** = 0.00 **d** = 0.05 **h** = 0.00	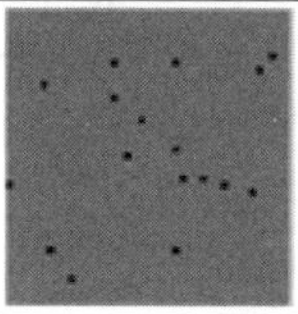	**p** = 0.26 **u** = 0.26 **c** = 0.90 **b** = 0.00 **d** = 0.65 **h** = 0.00	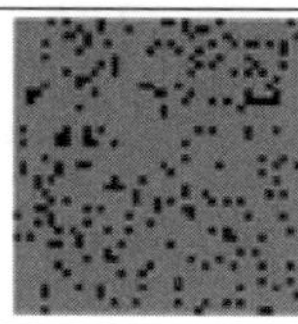	**p** = 0.26 **u** = 0.26 **c** = 0.55 **b** = 0.13 **d** = 0.65 **h** = 0.00	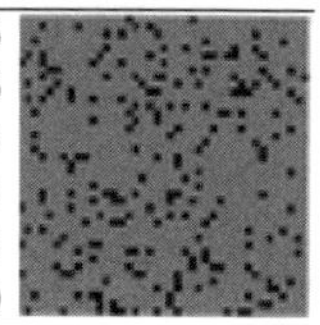

1967	
p = 0.26 **u** = 0.26 **c** = 0.15 **b** = 0.00 **d** = 0.65 **h** = 0.00	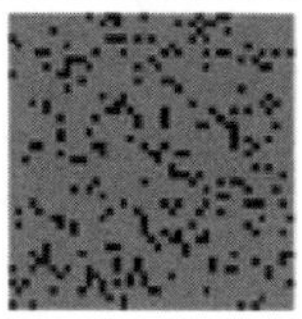

Table 8.20 Illustration of proactive DiNI insights on Atoms for Peace policies.

Case Year	Case Description	Simulation results and Interpretation
1957 Base Case	Equal probabilities of unhealthy intentions of target states and positive intentions of policy-making states, i.e. $p = 0.26$, $u = 0.26$ with assessed values of *c*, *b*, *h* and *d* based on existing policy. (based on Tables 8.2-8.5)	**Result: Green U Agents survive, Pink P agents extinct** The US intentions dominate indicating that current state of the system of policy-making is effective in containing unhealthy intentions of the target nation states.
1961	No change in Simulator parameter values despite cumulating parameter values and applying scale transitions (see Table above)	**Result: Green U Agents survive, Pink P agents extinct** The US intentions dominate indicating that current state of the system of policy-making is effective in containing unhealthy intentions of the target nation states
1963	There has been a disproportionate increase in costs with *d* and h not changing. This results in a violation of Hamilton's rule	**Result: Pink P Agents extinct, Green U agents survive** Signifies policy failure. Proliferation intentions of India are stronger than the peaceful intentions of the USA.
1964	Further increase in costs with *d* and *h* not changing. This results in a violation of Hamilton's rule	**Result: Pink P Agents extinct, Green U agents survive** Signifies policy failure. Proliferation intentions of India are stronger than the peaceful intentions of the USA.

Continued on next page...

Table 8.20 – continued from previous page

Case Year	Case Description	Simulation results and Interpretation
1965, 1966, 1967	Both cumulative costs and benefits are at their maximum, with Hamilton's inequality still not prevailing. h has now increased but the increase is not sufficient to offset the disproportions between b and c	**Result: Pink P Agents extinct, Green U agents survive** Signifies policy failure. Proliferation intentions of India are stronger than the peaceful intentions of the USA. **1974- India conducted its first 'peaceful' nuclear explosion signifying policy failure and triumph of green U agents**

As has been practically demonstrated in Table 8.20, DiNI has successfully simulated AfP policy situations and accurately predicted the proliferation intentions of India.

There would be a counter argument that whether or not DiNI was available, India's leanings towards proliferation were already well known to the intelligence community. Hence what is the value-add DiNI brings to the whole process of discerning nuclear intentions?

Apart from the fact that DiNI provides an objective basis to assess nuclear intentions (which was hitherto based on subjective opinions of state leaders, scientists, military leaders and the like), DiNI can help evaluate the effectiveness of policy decisions and options.

8.7.7 *Atoms for Peace: Some Policy Options for the USA*

During this period (1957–1967), there were various policy options available to the USA to influence nuclear intentions of India. Some of them were

(i) Security guarantees [21, 22];

a. Providing unilateral security guarantee to India in the event of nuclear attack by China,
b. Providing Joint-guarantee with USSR to India in the event of nuclear attack by China.

(ii) Intensifying peaceful cooperation with India; [23]

a. Indo-US cooperation on peaceful uses of nuclear energy to enhance scientific prestige,
b. Collaborative project on recycling Plutonium for India's nuclear reactors,
c. Cooperative "Plowshare" projects-nuclear explosions for civilian uses,
d. Collaborative reactor construction projects.

None of the above policy options were objectively analyzed for policy impacts. Rather the policy decision not to implement the above went more on the basis of opinion held by key influencers in the US e.g., Joint chiefs, Ambassador at Large etc.
Instead of the above policy options, the following policy decisions were taken which had little impact on influencing the Indian intentions (U agents). The US diplomatic channels were briefed to: [24]

(i) Abandon rhetoric suggesting special prestige of nuclear-weapon nations
(ii) Emphasize Wisdom of a national decision to forego development of nuclear weapons
(iii) Exhort the benefits of civilian nuclear energy use
(iv) As far as China's nuclear attack possibility is concerned, accentuate US's capacity for retaliation

Again the above were a result of discourse oriented strategic thinking and had no objective policy impact analysis basis.
DiNI facilitates an objective evaluation of such policy options using simulation. Such an evaluation can be performed by suitably reworking the c, b, h and d parameter values and running them through the simulator under various policy scenarios. However due to limitations of space individual proliferation impact assessment of the above policy options of Atoms for Peace have not been considered in this chapter.

8.8 Advantages of the DiNI Policy Simulator

As demonstrated both by a hypothetical example and the Atoms for Peace Program illustration, DiNI avoids the lacunae in existing policy simulation modeling (Section 8.3) and offers the following distinct advantages

(i) Provides a platform to combine multi-disciplinary inputs with a scope to include a wide range of objective/mathematical methods of aggregation,
(ii) Provides an objective, emergent view of proliferation to serve the DSS needs of strategic policy decision-makers in real-time,
(iii) DiNI Inputs are predominantly driven by analogies to nature's altruism model and thus reduces the chances of analyst world-view biases,
(iv) The results of DiNI are easily 'visible' and conducive to interpretation even to a predominantly non-technical audience such as politicians, strategic advisors to governments and nuclear strategic policy decision-makers.

8.9 Ethical and Security Aspects of DiNI Policy Simulator

According to the code of ethics for simulationists, an ethical simulationist is expected to "support studies which will not harm humans (current and future generations) as well as environment" [25]. Would harm to humans be possible if DiNI falls into the wrong hands? The design philosophy of DiNI is based firmly on Claude Shannon's maxim that "the enemy knows your system". Also supported by DiNI design is Kerchoff's design principle for military ciphers – "it must be able to fall into the hands of the enemy without inconvenience" [26]. In accordance with these maxims, the entire platform of DiNI is based on the open architectural model of altruism available on the net freely for anyone to download. From a model misuse point of view, assuming that the latest real – time DiNI model is available to a rogue user:

(i) The rogue user can take on the 'role' as the altruist and consider benevolent states as selfish (viz. evil, infidel etc.). However this goes against the very conceptualization of 'helping others at a cost to oneself' which is inherent in the model and hence will render the whole simulation exercise meaningless.

(ii) The rogue user can identify himself/herself with the selfish agent and look for events/circumstances when the altruists lose and selfish agents win in the model thereby objectively and systematically countering strategies of the Altruist strategic policy makers. However DiNI is a dynamic model by design and multi-disciplinary inputs feed into the system real-time based on changes in events and circumstances e.g., an orchestrated terror attack will trigger real-time change in DiNI simulator parameter values (e.g., d values will increase in the case of terrorism) and prompt strategic policy decision makers/politicians to act in a manner so as to bring back the dynamic equilibrium of peace.

8.10 Further Research Directions

Further research directions include extending the DiNI Policy Simulator into different cellular automata neighborhoods, different neighborhood values within VNN, additional parameters etc., building low-level 'intelligence' into the agent patches, dealing with groups of agent behavior rather than individual agents, constructing and analyzing second-order emergence and self-organizing approaches to containment of nuclear proliferation.

8.11 Conclusions

This chapter suggested a nature-inspired policy simulator called DiNI (**Di**scerning **N**uclear **I**ntentions) for objectively discerning unhealthy nuclear proliferation intentions of target nation states. DiNI is based on the socio-biological evolution phenomenon of altruism and works on a NetLOGO ABM platform. It serves DSS needs of strategic policy decision makers from intelligence agencies/governments /defense etc. who need to make key decisions on the basis of a reliable proliferation intention assessment of target nation states. By mimicking nature's model of altruism, DiNI enables simulation modeling which is fairly independent of the world-view of the analyst and also provides the flexibility to include inputs from multiple disciplines in a strategic decision-making environment. Simulation runs of DiNI with hypothetical parameter values demonstrated how DiNI can help discern current state of proliferation intentions as also evaluate how future policy changes will impact these intentions. The experience of USA vis-à-vis India in the historic Atoms for Peace program was simulated in DiNI and DiNI demonstrated the inevitability of India moving towards nuclear-weaponisation based on the contemporary strategic intelligence information. The ethical aspects of the DiNI Policy simulator and possible further research directions were also discussed in brief.

Acknowledgement

I am grateful to M. Ludo VEUCHELEN (SCK•CEN) and Prof (Dr.) Da RUAN (SCK•CEN) for their encouragement in making this chapter happen. I devote this chapter to the precious affection bestowed on me by my dear elder Brother and the pure sincerity of my dear younger Sister Mrs. Padma Prakash.

Bibliography

[1] National Intelligence Estimate, Iran: Nuclear Intentions and Capabilities, Intelligence Report of National Intelligence Council (USA), November 2007.

[2] Kennedy C. and Theodoropoulos G., Towards Intelligent Data-Driven Simulation for Policy Decision Support in the Social Sciences can be accessed at http://www.ncess.ac.uk/research/sgp/aimss/20051001_kennedy_PolicyDecisionSupport.pdf

[3] Popp R., Utilizing Social Science Technology to Understand and Counter the 21st Century Strategic Threat, Presentations of DARPA Tech 2005, Aug 2005.

[4] Schimdt O., Understanding & Analyzing Iran's Nuclear Intentions – Testing Scott Sagan's Argument of "Why do States build Nuclear Weapons" MA International relations Dissertation Lancaster University, 2008.

[5] Bergundthal M., Why do states build nuclear weapons? Scott Sagan – 1996/97 as accessed at http://home.etu.unige.ch/~grafale3/spo/spo-read/2b2_sagan_mathias.pdf

[6] Rehmeyer J., Mathematical Fortune-telling How well can game theory solve business and political disputes?, Web edition of ScienceNews can be accessed at http://www.sciencenews.org/view/generic/id/9041/title/Math_Trek__Mathematical_Fortune-Telling

[7] Okasha S., "Biological Altruism", The Stanford Encyclopedia of Philosophy (Summer 2005 Edition), Edward N. Zalta (ed.), http://plato.stanford.edu/archives/sum2005/entries/altruism-biological/

[8] Hamilton W.D., The genetical evolution of social behavior, I, J. Theor. Biol. 7:1-16, 1964.

[9] Axelrod R., Advancing the Art of Simulation in the Social Sciences Journal of the Japanese Society for Management Information Systems, Vol. 12, No. 3, Dec. 2003d.

[10] Axelrod R., "Agent-based Modeling as a Bridge Between Disciplines," in: Leigh Tesfatsion & Kenneth L. Judd (ed.), Handbook of Computational Economics, edition 1, volume 2, chapter 33, pp. 1565–1584, Elsevier, 2006.

[11] NetLogo Models Library download URL: http://ccl.northwestern.edu/netlogo/models/

[12] Wilensky U., (1998), NetLogo Altruism model, Center for Connected Learning and Computer-Based Modeling, Northwestern University, Evanston, IL http://ccl.northwestern.edu/netlogo/models/Altruism

[13] Endsley M.R., Garland D.J., Situation Awareness: Analysis and Measurement, Lawrence Erlbaum Associates, ISBN 0805821341, 9780805821345, 2000 Preview courtesy: Google book search.

[14] Squassoni S., U. S. Nuclear Cooperation With India: Issues for Congress, CRS Report for Congress, 2005.

[15] National Intelligence Estimate (NIE) 4-3-61 Nuclear Weapons and Delivery Capabilities of freeworld countries other than the US and the UK, 1961 Declassified

[16] National Intelligence Estimate, 4-63, Likelihood and Consequences of a proliferation of Nuclear Weapon Systems, 1963 Declassified.

[17] National Intelligence Estimate, 4-2-64, Prospects for a proliferation of Nuclear Weapons over the next decade, 1964 Declassified.

[18] National Intelligence Estimate, 4-66, The likelihood of further nuclear proliferation 1966 Declassified.

[19] National Intelligence Estimate, 4-67, Proliferation of Missile Delivery Systems for nuclear weapons, 1967 Declassified.

[20] Joint Progress Report (State Department and AEC) on implementation of NSC 5507/2 – "Peaceful uses of nuclear energy", 1957 Declassified

[21] Memorandum from the State Department, Ambassador at Large: "New Delhi's 1862 of December 31, 1964," December 31, 1964 Declassified can be accessed at http://www.gwu.edu/~nsarchiv/NSAEBB/NSAEBB6/index.html

[22] Memorandum from the State Department, Ambassador at Large: "Indian Nuclear Weapons Capability," January 30, 1965 Declassified can be accessed at http://www.gwu.edu/~nsarchiv/NSAEBB/NSAEBB6/index.html

[23] Memorandum from the State Department, Ambassador at Large: "Indian Nuclear Weapons Capability," January 30, 1965 Declassified can be accessed at http://www.gwu.edu/~nsarchiv/NSAEBB/NSAEBB6/index.html

[24] US State Department Cable Regarding a U.S. Public Stance Nuclear Proliferation, October 27, 1966, Declassified can be accessed at http://www.gwu.edu/~nsarchiv/NSAEBB/NSAEBB6/index.html

[25] Ören, TI, et.al, A Code of Professional Ethics for Simulationists, Proceedings of the 2002 Summer Computer Simulation Conference, 2002

http://www.scs.org/ethics/scsEthicsCode.pdf
[26] Encyclopedia entry Shannon's Maxim, download available at http://www.nationmaster.com/encyclopedia/Shannon's-Maxim

Chapter 9

Computing with Words for Hierarchical and Distributed Decision-Making

Jerry M. Mendel and Dongrui Wu

Signal and Image Processing Institute, Ming Hsieh Department of Electrical Engineering, University of Southern California, Los Angeles, CA 90089-2564, USA

Email: mendel@sipi.usc.edu, dongruiw@usc.edu

According to Zadeh, Computing with Words (CWW) is a methodology in which the objects of computation are words and propositions drawn from a natural language. A specific architecture for subjective decision-making using CWW, called Perceptual Computer — Per-C for short — is introduced in this chapter. Its three components — encoder, CWW engine and decoder — are briefly described. The main focus is on how the Per-C can be used to assist in hierarchical and distributed decision-making. A Journal Publication Judgment Advisor (JPJA) is designed as an example to show how the journal paper review process can be automated by the Per-C. The JPJA has the potential to relieve much of the burden of the reviewers and the associate editors, and moreover, it may be more accurate and less subjective.

9.1 Introduction

Zadeh coined the phrase "*computing with words*" (CWW) [1, 2]. According to him [2], CWW is "*a methodology in which the objects of computation are words and propositions drawn from a natural language.*" There are at least two types of uncertainties associated with a word [3]: intra-personal uncertainty and inter-personal uncertainty. The former is explicitly pointed out by Wallsten and Budescu [3] as "*except in very special cases, all representations are vague to some degree in the minds of the originators and in the minds of the receivers,*" and they suggest to model it by type-1 fuzzy sets (T1 FSs). The latter is pointed out by Mendel [4] as "*words mean different things to different people*" and Wallsten and Budescu [3] as "*different individuals use diverse expressions to describe identical situations and understand the same phrases differently when hearing or reading them.*"

Because an interval type-2 FS [4] (IT2 FS) (see Appendix A.1) can be viewed as a group of T1 FSs, it can model both types of uncertainty; hence, we suggest IT2 FSs be used in CWW [5,4,6].

A specific architecture [7] shown in Fig. 9.1 is proposed for making subjective judgments by CWW. It is called a *perceptual computer*—Per-C for short. In Fig. 9.1, the *encoder*[1] transforms linguistic perceptions into IT2 FSs that activate a *CWW engine*. The CWW engine performs operations on the IT2 FSs. The *decoder*[2] maps the output of the CWW engine into a recommendation, which can be a word, rank, or class.

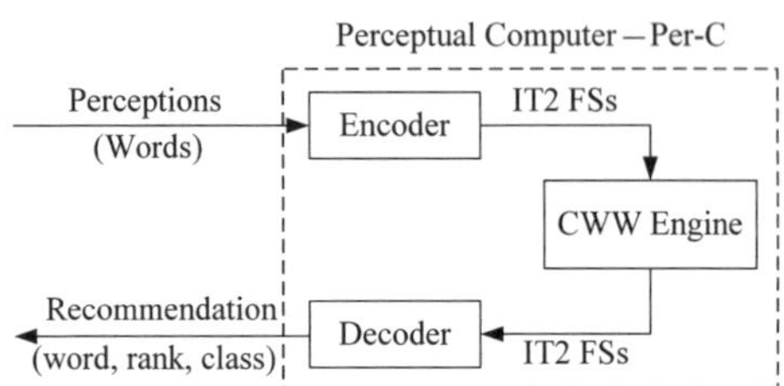

Figure 9.1 Conceptual structure of the Perceptual Computer (Mendel [7], © 2002, AMCS).

To operate the Per-C, one needs to solve the following problems:

(1) *How to transform words into IT2 FSs, i.e., the encoding problem.* This can be done with Liu and Mendel's *Interval Approach* [10] (IA). First, for each word in an application-dependent encoding vocabulary, a group of subjects are asked the following question:

> *On a scale of 0-10, what are the end-points of an interval that you associate with the word ____?*

After some pre-processing, during which some intervals (e.g., outliers) are eliminated, each of the remaining intervals is classified as either an interior, left-shoulder or right-shoulder IT2 FS. Then, each of the word's data intervals is individually mapped into its respective T1 interior, left-shoulder or right-shoulder MF, after which the union of all of these T1 MFs is taken. The result is a footprint of uncertainty (FOU) for an IT2 FS model of the word. The words and their FOUs constitute a *codebook*.

(2) *How to construct the CWW engine, which maps IT2 FSs into IT2 FSs.* There are different kinds of CWW engines, e.g.,

(a) The *linguistic weighted average* [11, 12] (LWA) (see Appendix A.2), which is

[1]Zadeh [1,2] calls this *constraint explicitation*. In [8,9] and some of his recent talks, he calls this *precisiation*.
[2]Zadeh [1,2] calls this *linguistic approximation*.

defined as

$$\widetilde{Y}_{\mathrm{LWA}} = \frac{\sum_{i=1}^{N} \widetilde{X}_i \widetilde{W}_i}{\sum_{i=1}^{N} \widetilde{W}_i} \tag{1}$$

where $\widetilde{X}_i$, the sub-criteria (e.g., data, features, decisions, recommendations, judgments, scores, etc), and $\widetilde{W}_i$, the weights, are usually words modeled by IT2 FSs; however, they can also be special cases of IT2 FSs, e.g., numbers, intervals, or T1 FSs. It has been shown [11, 12] that the upper membership function (UMF) of $\widetilde{Y}_{\mathrm{LWA}}$ is a fuzzy weighted average [13] of the UMFs of $\widetilde{X}_i$ and $\widetilde{W}_i$, and the lower membership function (LMF) of $\widetilde{Y}_{\mathrm{LWA}}$ is a fuzzy weighted average of the LMFs of $\widetilde{X}_i$ and $\widetilde{W}_i$.

(b) *Perceptual reasoning* [14, 15] (PR), which considers the following problem:

Given a rulebase with K rules, each of the form:

$$R^k : \textit{If } x_1 \textit{ is } \widetilde{F}_1^k \textit{ and } \ldots \textit{ and } x_p \textit{ is } \widetilde{F}_p^k, \textit{ Then } y \textit{ is } \widetilde{G}^k \tag{2}$$

where $\widetilde{F}_j^k$ and $\widetilde{G}^k$ are words modeled by IT2 FSs, and a new input $\widetilde{\mathbf{X}}' = (\widetilde{X}_1, \ldots, \widetilde{X}_p)$, where $\widetilde{X}_j$ $(j = 1, \ldots, p)$ are also words modeled by IT2 FSs, then what is the output IT2 FS $\widetilde{Y}_{PR}$?

In PR [14] one computes

$$\widetilde{Y}_{PR} = \frac{\sum_{k=1}^{K} f^k(\widetilde{\mathbf{X}}')\widetilde{G}^k}{\sum_{k=1}^{K} f^k(\widetilde{\mathbf{X}}')} \tag{3}$$

where $f^k(\widetilde{\mathbf{X}}')$ is the firing level of R^k, i.e.,

$$f^k(\widetilde{\mathbf{X}}') = \prod_{j=1}^{p} s_J(\widetilde{X}_j, \widetilde{F}_j^k) \tag{4}$$

in which $s_J(\widetilde{X}_j, \widetilde{F}_j^k)$ is the Jaccard similarity for IT2 FSs [16], i.e.,

$$s_J(\widetilde{X}_j, \widetilde{F}_j^k) = \frac{\sum_{i=1}^{N} \min(\overline{X}_j(x_i), \overline{F}_j^k(x_i)) + \sum_{i=1}^{N} \min(\underline{X}_j(x_i), \underline{F}_j^k(x_i))}{\sum_{i=1}^{N} \max(\overline{X}_j(x_i), \overline{F}_j^k(x_i)) + \sum_{i=1}^{N} \max(\underline{X}_j(x_i), \underline{F}_j^k(x_i))}. \tag{5}$$

where, e.g., $\overline{X}_j(x_i)$ and $\underline{X}_j(x_i)$ are upper and lower MFs of $\widetilde{X}_j$. Another approach that uses firing intervals instead of firing levels is described in [17].

(3) *How to map the output of the CWW engine into a recommendation, i.e., the decoding problem.* Thus far, there are three kinds of decoders according to three forms of recommendations:

(a) *Word:* To map an IT2 FS into a word, it must be possible to compare the *similarity* between two IT2 FSs. The Jaccard similarity measure [16] described by (5) can be used to compute the similarities between the CWW engine output and all words in the codebook. Then, the word with the maximum similarity is chosen as the Decoder's output.
(b) *Rank:* Ranking is needed when several alternatives are compared to find the best. Because the performance of each alternative is represented by an IT2 FS obtained from the CWW engine, a ranking method for IT2 FSs is needed. A centroid-based ranking method [16] for IT2 FSs has been proposed.
(c) *Class:* A classifier is necessary when the output of the CWW engine needs to be mapped into a decision category. Vlachos and Sergiadiss subsethood measure [18–20] is useful for this purpose. One first computes the subsethood of the CWW engine output for each of the possible classes. Then, the final decision class is the one corresponding to the maximum subsethood.

This chapter applies Per-C to a hierarchical and distributed decision-making process. By "hierarchical and distributed decision-making" is meant decision-making that is ultimately made by a single individual, group or organization, but is based on aggregating *independently* made recommendations about an *object* from other individuals, groups or organizations (i.e., *judges*). An *object* could be a person being considered for a job, an article being reviewed for publication in a journal, a military objective, etc. It is the independent nature of the recommendations that leads to this being called "distributed," and it is the aggregation of the distributed recommendations at a higher level that leads to this being called "hierarchical."

There can be multiple levels of hierarchy in this process, because each of the independent recommendations may also involve a hierarchical decision-making process. Additionally, the individuals, groups or organizations making their independent recommendations may not be of equal expertise, and so a weight has to be assigned to each of them when they are aggregated. The independent recommendations can involve aggregating numbers, intervals, T1 FSs, and words modeled by IT2 FSs. The final recommendation (or decision) is made by a decision maker who not only uses an aggregated recommendation that is made across all of the judges but may also use the aggregated recommendation from each of the judges. In this chapter our attention is directed at the hierarchical and distributed *journal publication judgment advisor* (JPJA) in which for the first time only words are used at every level. This application is representative of other distributed and hierarchical decision-making applications, so its results should be extendable to them.

The rest of this chapter is organized as follows: Section 9.2 introduces the traditional journal paper review process. Section 9.3 describes how Per-C is used to construct the JPJA. Section 9.4 illustrates the performance of the JPJA using several examples. Finally, Section 9.5 draws conclusions. Background materials on IT2 FSs and the LWA are given in the Appendices.

9.2 The Journal Publication Judgment Advisor (JPJA) [3]

When an author submits a paper to a journal [11], the Editor usually assigns its review to an Associate Editor (AE), who then sends it to at least three reviewers. The reviewers send their reviews back to the AE who then makes a publication-recommendation to the Editor based on these reviews. The Editor uses this publication-recommendation to assist in making a final decision about the paper.

In addition to the "comments for the author(s)," each reviewer usually has to complete a form similar to the one shown in Table 9.1 in which the reviewer has to evaluate the paper based on two major criteria, *Technical Merit* and *Presentation*. *Technical Merit* has three sub-criteria *Importance, Content* and *Depth*, and *Presentation* has four sub-criteria *Style, Organization, Clarity* and *References*. Observe that each of the sub-criteria has an assessment level that is characterized by a starting word and an ending word (e.g., *Valuable* is the starting word for *Importance* and *Useless* is its ending word) and there are five boxes between them. A reviewer chooses one assessment level by checking-off one of the five boxes. This is very subjective because no one knows what words are associated with the middle three boxes. Usually, the reviewer is also asked to give an overall evaluation of the paper and make a recommendation to the AE. The AE then makes a final decision based on the opinions of the three reviewers.

The distributed and hierarchical nature of the decision–making process is shown in Fig. 9.2. Observe that there are three levels in the hierarchy: (1) Aggregation of the sub-criteria for the two major criteria, (2) aggregation of the two major criteria, and (3) aggregation of the three reviewers' recommendations.

Sometimes a reviewer may feel it is difficult to give an overall evaluation of a paper because it gets high assessment levels on some of the sub-criteria but does poorly on the others. In that case, the reviewer may give an evaluation based on the reputation of the author(s) or randomly choose an evaluation from several comparable evaluations. A similar situation

[3] The material in Sections 9.2 and 9.3 will also appear in [19].

may occur at the AE level, e.g., if one reviewer suggests rejection of the paper, another suggests a revision of the paper, and a third reviewer suggests acceptance of the paper, what should the final decision be?

Table 9.1 Paper review form for a generic journal.

Technical Merit:							
Importance	Valuable	( )	( )	( )	( )	( )	Useless
Content	Original	( )	( )	( )	( )	( )	Derivative
Depth	Deep	( )	( )	( )	( )	( )	Shallow
Presentation:							
Style	Readable	( )	( )	( )	( )	( )	Incoherent
Organization	Precise	( )	( )	( )	( )	( )	Ambiguous
Clarity	Clear	( )	( )	( )	( )	( )	Confusing
Reference	Complete	( )	( )	( )	( )	( )	Incomplete
Overall:							
Overall Evaluation	Excellent	( )	( )	( )	( )	( )	Dreadful

Recommendation:	
( )	ACCEPT: as written (editorial corrections as noted are necessary)
( )	REWRITE: needs substantial changes and re-review
( )	REJECT: materials is unsuitable for publication in this journal
( )	TRANSFER: more suitable for publication in ____________

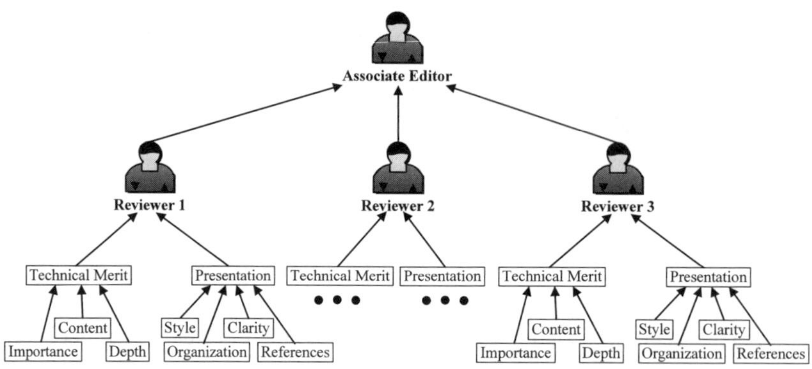

Figure 9.2 The paper review process (Wu and Mendel [11], © 2007, IEEE).

Because this evaluation process is often difficult and subjective, it may be better to leave it to a computer, i.e., each reviewer should only be asked to provide a subjective evaluation of a paper for each of the seven sub-criteria, after which LWAs would automatically compute the reviewer's overall judgment of the paper. Once the opinion of all the reviewers are obtained, another LWA would compute an overall aggregated opinion for the AE. This automatic process has the potential to relieve much of the burden of the reviewers and the AE, and, moreover, it may be more accurate and less subjective.

9.3 Perceptual Computing for the JPJA

This section explains how a Per-C can be used as a JPJA.

9.3.1 *Modified Paper Review Form*

To begin, a modified version of the Table 9.1 paper review form is needed, one that removes the uncertainty about the words that are associated with the three middle boxes for each sub-criterion, and that asks each reviewer to indicate their level of expertise for reviewing the paper. The modified paper review form (for a generic journal) is depicted in Table 9.2.

Table 9.2 Modified paper review form for a generic journal.

	Poor	Marginal	Adequate	Good	Excellent
Technical Merit:					
Importance	( )	( )	( )	( )	( )
Content	( )	( )	( )	( )	( )
Depth	( )	( )	( )	( )	( )
Presentation:					
Style	( )	( )	( )	( )	( )
Organization	( )	( )	( )	( )	( )
Clarity	( )	( )	( )	( )	( )
Reference	( )	( )	( )	( )	( )

Expertise:	Low	Moderate	High
Your Expertise	( )	( )	( )

Comparing the review forms in Tables 9.1 and 9.2, observe that:

(1) The same words are now used for all seven sub-criteria, namely: *Poor, Marginal, Adequate, Good* and *Excellent*. These five words are linguistically appropriate for each of the seven sub-criteria. Of course, fewer or more than five words could be used, and different words could be used for each sub-criterion.

(2) Three words are used for a reviewer's level of expertise: *Low, Moderate* and *High*. While it is doubtful that fewer than three words should be used, it is possible that more than three words could be used.

(3) A reviewer is no longer asked to provide a recommendation.

When perceptual computing is used for the JPJA each of the three components of a Per-C—encoder, CWW engine and decoder—must be considered.

9.3.2 *Encoder*

Two codebooks are needed, one for the words that will be used by a reviewer and the other for weights, and each of these codebooks has sub-codebooks, as explained next.

9.3.2.1 *Codebook words used by a reviewer*

The reviewer codebook has two sub-codebooks, each of which is described next.

- Sub-codebook R1: This codebook contains the five words (*Poor, Marginal, Adequate, Good* and *Excellent*) and their FOUs that are used to assess the seven sub-criteria. FOUs for these words are depicted in Fig. 9.3. They were not obtained by collecting data from a group of subjects[4], e.g., AEs and reviewers, but instead were generated by the authors. Consequently, all of the results that are in this chapter are synthetic. In order to get more accurate results, a pool of knowledgeable AEs and reviewers should be surveyed and then their data intervals should be mapped into word FOUs using the IA [10].

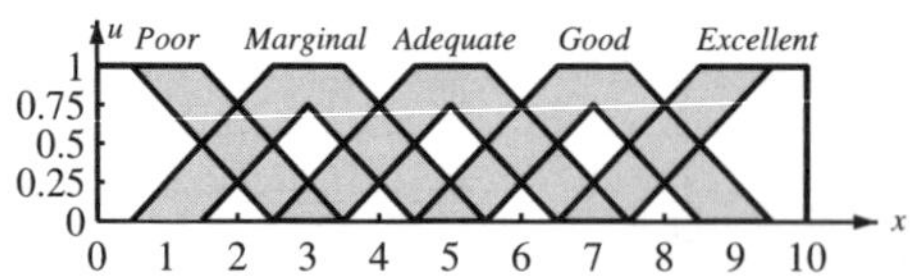

Figure 9.3 FOUs for the five-word Sub-codebook R1.

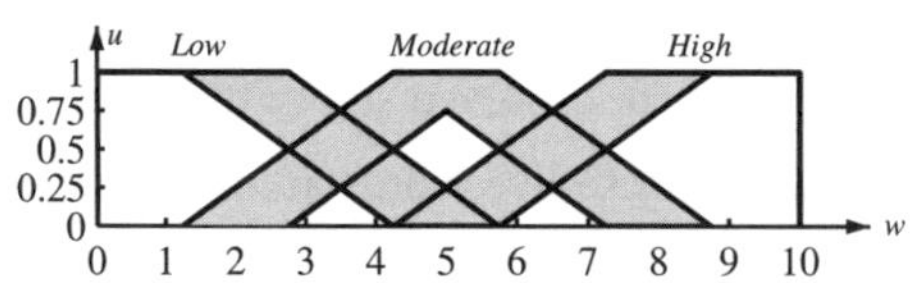

Figure 9.4 FOUs for the three-word Sub-codebook R2.

[4]Intervals could be collected from a group of subjects by stating:

You are to assign an interval or a "range" of numbers that falls somewhere between 0–10 to each of following three criteria that are associated with judging the Technical Merit of a journal article submission: Content, Importance and Depth. The interval corresponds to the importance weighting that you assign to each criterion. It is important to note that not all ranges have to be the same and ranges can overlap. Subjects are then asked a question like: *"Where on a scale of 0–10 would you locate the ends points of an interval that you assign to weight the importance to Technical Merit of* Content*?"*

- Sub-codebook R2: This codebook contains the three words (*Low, Moderate* and *High*) and their FOUs that describe a reviewer's level of expertise. FOUs for these words are depicted in Fig. 9.4. They also were not obtained by collecting data from a group of subjects, but instead were generated by the authors; so the admonition just given for the FOUs in Sub-codebook R1 applies here as well.

9.3.2.2 *Codebook for the weights*

This weights codebook has three sub-codebooks each of which is described next. A major difference between the weights sub-codebooks and the two reviewer sub-codebooks is that for the latter each FOU has a word associated with it, whereas for the weight sub-codebooks each FOU is associated with a weight that has no word associated with it. The weight FOUs are only used in LWAs and are not available to a reviewer, hence, they are assigned symbols rather than words.

- Sub-codebook W1: This codebook contains labels and FOUs for the relative weighting of the three sub-criteria that are associated with the criterion of *Technical Merit*. FOUs for these weights are depicted in Fig. 9.5. These FOUs were also generated by the authors, however, the relative orderings of the three sub-criteria were first established (in 2007) with the help of Dr. Nihil Pal (Editor-in-Chief of the *IEEE Trans. on Fuzzy Systems*). That ordering is: *Content (Co)* is more important than *Importance (I)* which in turn is more important that *Depth (D)*, hence, $\widetilde{W}_{Co} > \widetilde{W}_I > \widetilde{W}_D$.

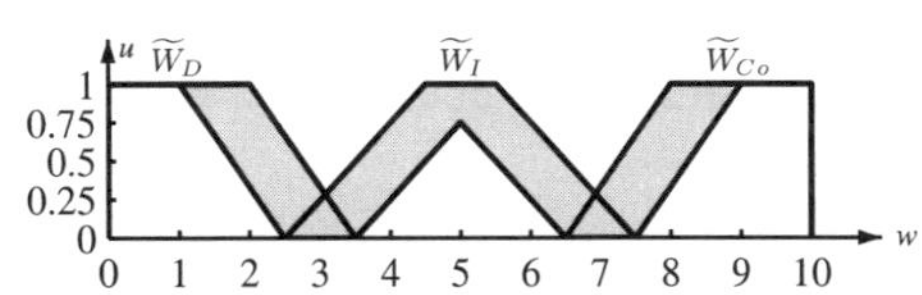

Figure 9.5 FOUs for the three-word Sub-codebook W1. Weights correspond to *Importance* ($\widetilde{W}_I$), *Content* ($\widetilde{W}_{Co}$) and *Depth* ($\widetilde{W}_D$).

- Sub-codebook W2: This codebook contains labels and FOUs for the relative weighting of the four sub-criteria that are associated with the criterion of *Presentation*. FOUs for these weights are depicted in Fig. 9.6. Again, with the help of Dr. Nihil Pal, it was decided that *Organization (O)* and *References (R)* were indistinguishable as were *Style (S)* and *Clarity (C)*, and that *Style* and *Clarity* are more important than *Organization and References*, hence, $\widetilde{W}_S = \widetilde{W}_{Cl} > \widetilde{W}_O = \widetilde{W}_R$.

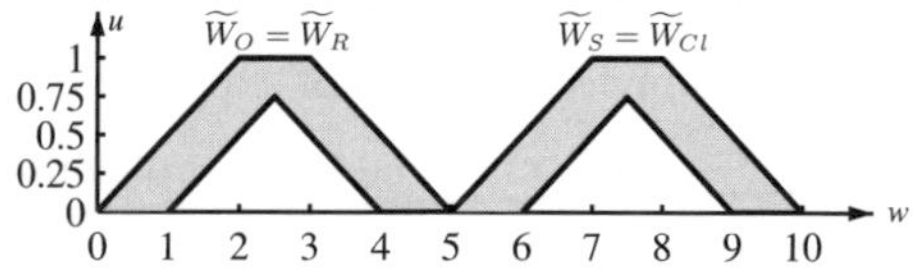

Figure 9.6 FOUs for the four-word Sub-codebook W2. Weights correspond to *Style* ($\widetilde{W}_S$), *Organization* ($\widetilde{W}_O$), *Clarity* ($\widetilde{W}_{Cl}$) and *Reference* ($\widetilde{W}_R$).

- Sub-codebook W3: This codebook contains labels and FOUs for the relative weighting of the two criteria *Technical Merit* and *Presentation*. Clearly *Technical Merit (T)* is more important than *Presentation (P)*, i.e., $\widetilde{W}_T > \widetilde{W}_P$. Again, with the help of Dr. Nihil Pal, it was decided that the FOUs for these weights should be located as depicted in Fig. 9.7.

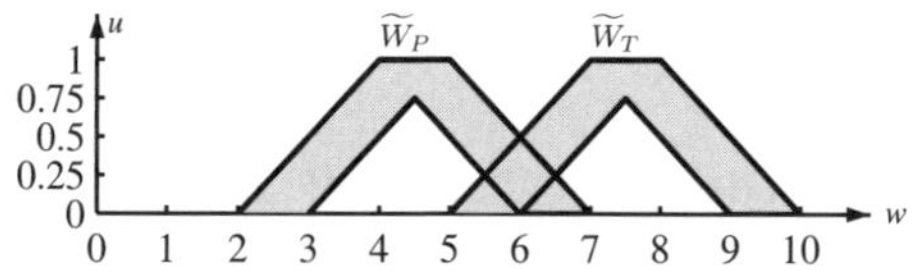

Figure 9.7 FOUs for the two-word Sub-codebook W3. Weights correspond to *Technical Merit* ($\widetilde{W}_T$) and *Presentation* ($\widetilde{W}_P$).

If interval data are collected from AEs and reviewers for sub-codebooks W1, W2 and W3, and the FOUs are determined using the IA, then the shapes of the FOUs as well as the amount that they overlap will be different from the ones in Figs. 9.5–9.7. Those details, while important for the application of the JPJA to a specific journal, do not change the methodology of the JPJA that is further explained below.

9.3.3 *CWW Engine*

For the CWW Engine of the JPJA, LWAs [11,12] (see Appendix A.2) are used because one of the unique features of this application is that all assessments and weights are words (or FOUs). To begin, each of the two major criteria (*Technical Merit* and *Presentation)* has an LWA computed for it, i.e., $(j = 1, 2, \ldots, n_R)$:

$$\widetilde{Y}_{jT} = \frac{\widetilde{X}_{jI}\widetilde{W}_I + \widetilde{X}_{jCo}\widetilde{W}_{Co} + \widetilde{X}_{jD}\widetilde{W}_D}{\widetilde{W}_I + \widetilde{W}_{Co} + \widetilde{W}_D} \tag{6}$$

$$\widetilde{Y}_{jP} = \frac{\widetilde{X}_{jS}\widetilde{W}_S + \widetilde{X}_{jO}\widetilde{W}_O + \widetilde{X}_{jCl}\widetilde{W}_{Cl} + \widetilde{X}_{jR}\widetilde{W}_R}{\widetilde{W}_S + \widetilde{W}_O + \widetilde{W}_{Cl} + \widetilde{W}_R} \tag{7}$$

where n_R is the number of reviewers[5], $\widetilde{Y}_{jT}$ is the LWA for *Technical Merit* in which $\widetilde{X}_{jI}, \widetilde{X}_{jCo}$ and $\widetilde{X}_{jD}$ are the linguistic assessments provided by Reviewer-j for *Importance, Content* and *Depth*, respectively, and $\widetilde{Y}_{jP}$ is the LWA for *Presentation* in which $\widetilde{X}_{jS}$, $\widetilde{X}_{jO}$, $\widetilde{X}_{jCl}$ and $\widetilde{X}_{jR}$ are the linguistic assessments provided by Reviewer-j for *Style, Organization, Clarity* and *References*, respectively.

Next, $\widetilde{Y}_{jT}$ and $\widetilde{Y}_{jP}$ are aggregated using the following Reviewer LWAs, $\widetilde{Y}_{Rj}$ $(j = 1, 2, \ldots, n_R)$:

$$\widetilde{Y}_{Rj} = \frac{\widetilde{Y}_{jT}\widetilde{W}_T + \widetilde{Y}_{jP}\widetilde{W}_P}{\widetilde{W}_T + \widetilde{W}_P} \tag{8}$$

Finally, the n_R Reviewer LWAs are aggregated using the following AE LWA:

$$\widetilde{Y}_{\text{AE}} = \frac{\sum_{j=1}^{n_R} \widetilde{Y}_{Rj}\widetilde{W}_{Rj}}{\sum_{j=1}^{n_R} \widetilde{W}_{Rj}} \tag{9}$$

in which $\widetilde{W}_{Rj} \in \{\text{Low, Moderate, High}\}$.

9.3.4 *Decoder*

The decoder for the JPJA is actually a classifier, i.e., it classifies the overall quality of a paper, $\widetilde{Y}_{\text{AE}}$, into one of three classes: *Accept*, *Rewrite*, or *Reject*. A *decoding codebook* is needed to store the FOUs for these three words. Two approaches for constructing such a codebook are described next.

9.3.4.1 *Construct the decoding codebook using a survey*

In this approach, AEs are surveyed using a statement and question like:

> *A reviewer of a journal submission must score the submission using a number between 0–10 where 0 is the lowest score and 10 is the highest score. The reviewer's score must then be mapped into one of three classes—*Accept, Rewrite *or* Reject. *Where on the scale of 0–10 would you locate the ends points of an interval that you assign to* Accept (Rewrite, Reject)*?*

The IA can then be used to map the crisp intervals into IT2 FS FOUs for *Accept, Rewrite* and *Reject*.

9.3.4.2 *Construct the decoding codebook using training examples*

A *training data set* is a collection of *training examples*, each of which consists of n_R reviewers' completed review forms, the AE's FOU for a specific journal submission, and the final

[5]Although Fig. 9.2 shows three reviewers, the number of reviewers is treated here as a variable.

recommendation made for the paper by the Editor-in-Chief (*Accept*, *Rewrite* or *Reject*), i.e., for the kth submission ($k = 1, \ldots, N_T$) in the training data set, a training example is

$$\left\{(\widetilde{X}^k_{jI}, \widetilde{X}^k_{jCo}, \widetilde{X}^k_{jD}, \widetilde{X}^k_{jS}, \widetilde{X}^k_{jO}, \widetilde{X}^k_{jCl}, \widetilde{X}^k_{jR}, \widetilde{W}^k_{Rj}),\ j = 1, \ldots, n_R;\ \widetilde{Y}^k_{\text{AE}},\ \textit{Final Recommendation}(k)\right\}$$

Instead of pre-specifying the FOUs for *Accept, Rewrite* and *Reject*, their shapes are chosen like the ones in Fig. 9.8 but their specific parameters that completely define each FOU are not fixed ahead of time. Instead, the FOU parameters are tuned using search algorithms to minimize the errors between the given *Final Recommendation* and an *Estimated Recommendation* for all N_T elements in the training data set. The *Estimated Recommendation* for each training example is obtained as follows: (1) FOU parameters for *Accept*, *Rewrite*, and *Reject* are specified (or updated using an optimization algorithm), (2) Vlachos and Sergiadiss subsethoods of $\widetilde{Y}^k_{\text{AE}}$ in *Accept*, *Rewrite*, and *Reject* are computed, and (3) the paper is assigned to the class with the maximum subsethood.

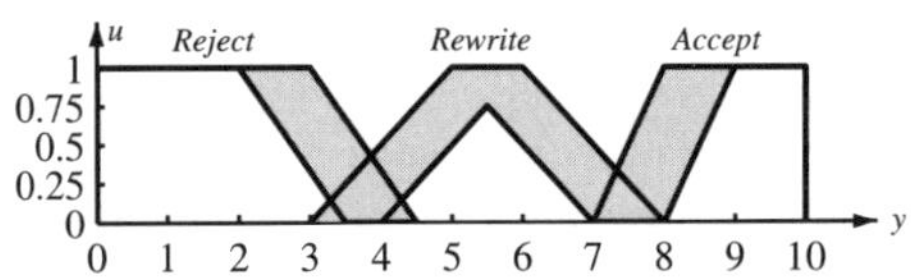

Figure 9.8 FOUs for the three-classes decoding codebook.

9.3.4.3 *Remarks*

In principle either approach could be used; however, because the generic review form in Table 9.2 has yet to be used, no training examples are available. So, for the present, only the approach described in Section 9.3.4.1 can be used for constructing the decoding codebook. Because we did not have access to a pool of AEs and reviewers, the decoding codebook used in this chapter is shown in Fig. 9.8. Its FOUs were synthesized with the help of Dr. Nihil Pal.

9.3.4.4 *Decoder*

Vlachos and Sergiadis's subsethoods [18–20] are computed between $\widetilde{Y}_{\text{AE}}$ and *Accept*, *Rewrite* and *Reject*, namely $ss(\widetilde{Y}_{\text{AE}}, Accept)$, $ss(\widetilde{Y}_{\text{AE}}, Rewrite)$ and $ss(\widetilde{Y}_{\text{AE}}, Reject)$, after which the decoder recommends to the AE the publication class of maximum subsethood. The decoder also provides $\widetilde{Y}_{\text{AE}}$ and the values of the three subsethoods to the AE, because the AE may want to make some subjective adjustments to the publication class when two subsethoods are very close.

9.4 Examples[6]

This section contains some examples that illustrate the automatic paper review process. First the different levels of aggregation are examined to demonstrate that reasonable results are obtained, and then three complete paper reviews are provided.

9.4.1 *Aggregation of Technical Merit Sub-criteria*

To consider all possible combinations of the inputs to the criterion of Technical Merit, one would need to examine a total of $5^3 = 125$ cases, because each of its three sub-criteria has five possible linguistic terms (Fig. 9.3) that can be chosen by a reviewer. This is impractical for us to do, so instead our focus is on whether or not *Content* dominates the other sub-criteria of *Importance* and *Depth* as it should, since in (6) and Sub-codebook W1 it has already been established that $\widetilde{W}_{Co} > \widetilde{W}_I > \widetilde{W}_D$. To do this 15 of the 125 possible cases are studied. In all cases, $\widetilde{Y}_T$ in (6) is computed for the three weight FOUs that are depicted in Fig. 9.5, and only $\widetilde{X}_I$, $\widetilde{X}_{Co}$ and $\widetilde{X}_D$ are varied. If *Content* dominates the other sub-criteria of *Importance* and *Depth*, then regardless of the words chosen for *Importance* and *Depth*, one expects to see $\widetilde{Y}_T$ move from left-to-right as $\widetilde{X}_{Co}$ moves from left-to-right.

9.4.1.1 *Importance is Excellent, Depth is Good, and Content varies from Poor to Excellent*

The FOUs of $\widetilde{Y}_T$ for these five cases are depicted in the right-hand figures of Fig. 9.9. Each of the left-hand figures in Fig. 9.9 depicts the respective FOUs for $\widetilde{X}_I$, $\widetilde{X}_{Co}$ and $\widetilde{X}_D$. Note that $\widetilde{X}_I = Excellent$ and $\widetilde{X}_D = Good$ are the ones in Fig. 9.3. Only $\widetilde{X}_{Co}$ changes in the left-hand figures, and its FOUs match the ones in Fig. 9.3 for all five words.

Observe that as the reviewer's response to *Content* varies from *Poor* to *Excellent*, $\widetilde{Y}_T$ does move from left-to-right towards the maximal score of 10 which supports our expectation that *Content* dominates.

9.4.1.2 *Importance is Poor, Depth is Good, and Content varies from Poor to Excellent*

Starting with the choices that were made for *Importance*, *Depth* and *Content* in Fig. 9.9, *Importance* is changed from *Excellent* to *Poor*, and everything else is kept the same. The FOUs of $\widetilde{Y}_T$ for the present five cases are depicted in the right-hand figures of Fig. 9.10. Each of the left-hand figures in Fig. 9.10 depicts the respective FOUs for $\widetilde{X}_I$, $\widetilde{X}_{Co}$ and $\widetilde{X}_D$.

[6] The examples in this section are similar to those in [19].

Note that $\widetilde{X}_I = Poor$ and $\widetilde{X}_D = Good$ are the ones in Fig. 9.3. As in Fig. 9.9, only $\widetilde{X}_{Co}$ changes in the left-hand figures, and its FOUs match the ones in Fig. 9.3 for all five words.

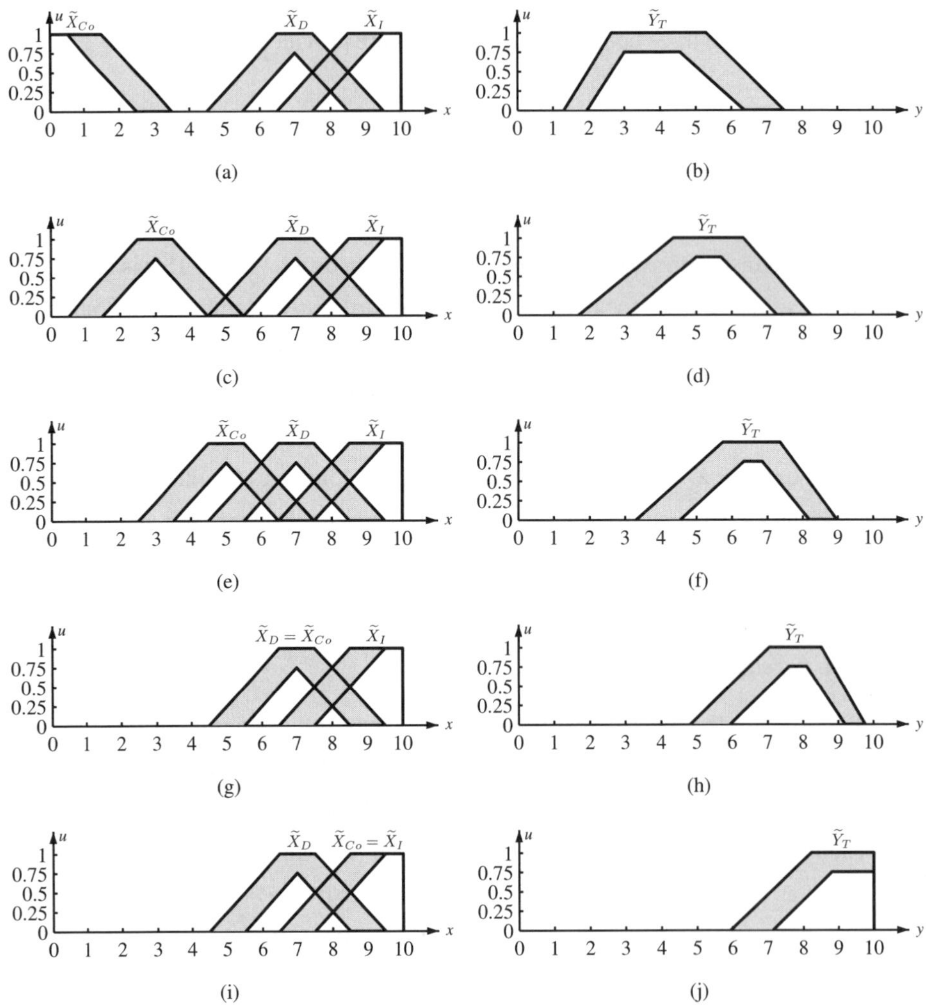

Figure 9.9 Technical Merit when *Importance* is *Excellent*, *Depth* is *Good* and *Content* varies. (a), (c), (e), (g), (i): Input FOUs when a reviewer's response to *Content* changes from *Poor* to *Excellent*; (b), (d), (f), (h), (j): Output $\widetilde{Y}_T$ when a reviewer's response to *Content* changes from *Poor* to *Excellent*. The corresponding weights for the three sub-criteria are shown in Fig. 9.5.

Observe that as the reviewer's response to the sub-criterion *Content* varies from *Poor* to *Excellent*, $\widetilde{Y}_T$ moves from left-to-right towards the maximal score of 10 (but never reaching it), which again supports our expectation that *Content* dominates.

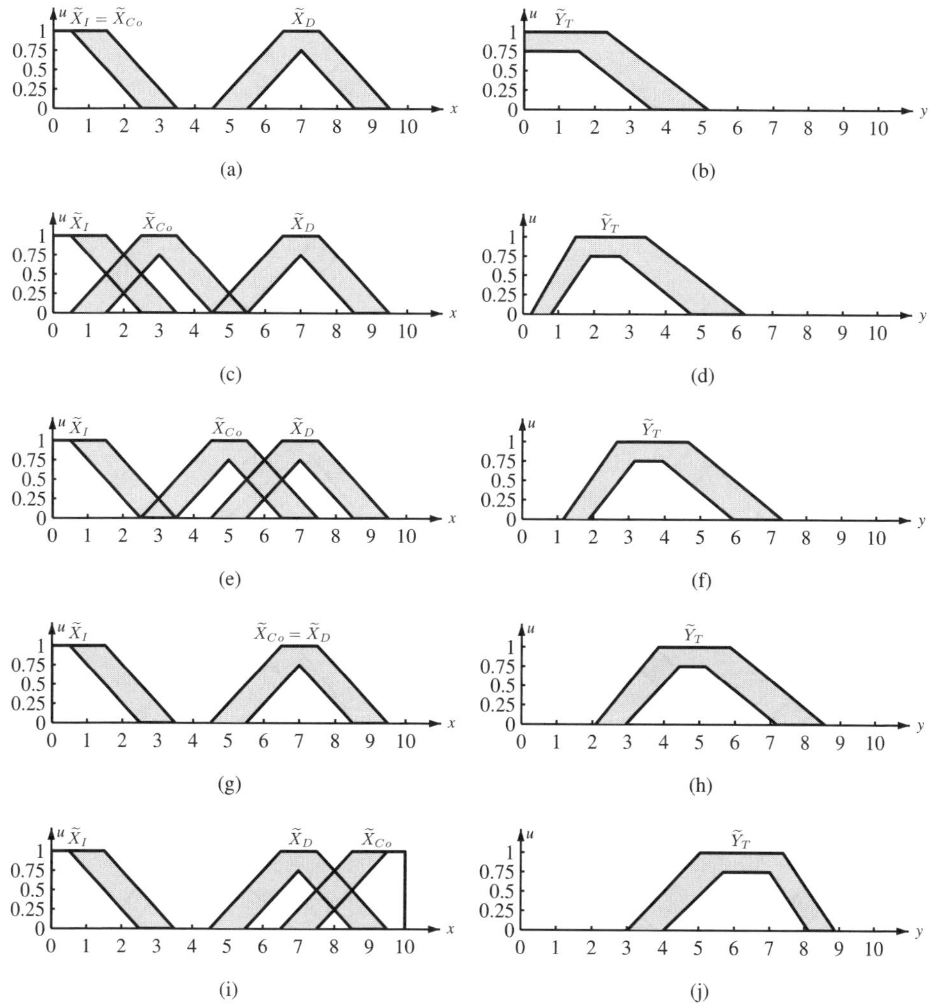

Figure 9.10 Technical Merit when *Importance* is *Poor*, *Depth* is *Good* and *Content* varies. (a), (c), (e), (g), (i): Input FOUs when a reviewer's response to *Content* changes from *Poor* to *Excellent*; (b), (d), (f), (h), (j): Output $\widetilde{Y}_T$ when a reviewer's response to *Content* changes from *Poor* to *Excellent*. The corresponding weights for the three sub-criteria are shown in Fig. 9.5.

By comparing each line of the two sets of right-hand figures in Figs. 9.9 and 9.10, observe that each of the FOUs of $\widetilde{Y}_T$ for when *Importance* is *Excellent* lies farther to the right of its respective FOU for when *Importance* is *Poor*. This also agrees with our expectation, because improving the assessment of *Importance* should improve $\widetilde{Y}_T$, i.e., move $\widetilde{Y}_T$ further to the right.

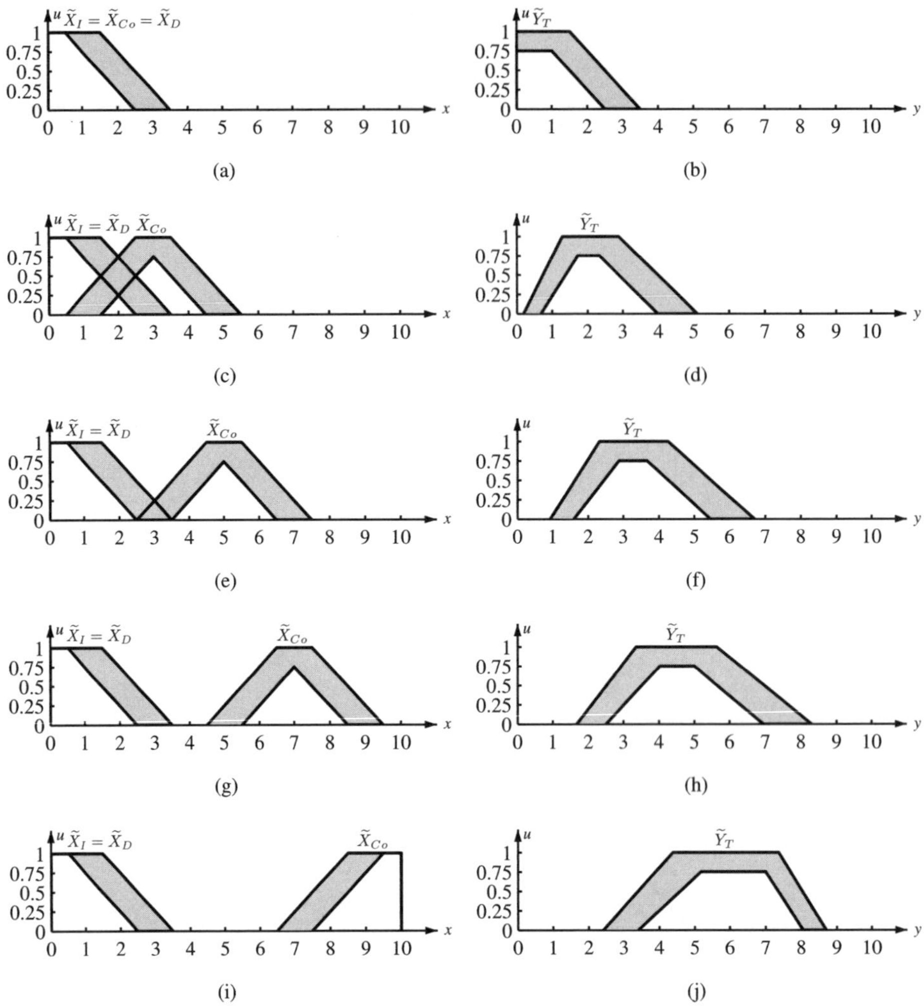

Figure 9.11 Technical Merit when both *Importance* and *Depth* are *Poor* and *Content* varies. (a), (c), (e), (g), (i): Input FOUs when a reviewer's response to *Content* changes from *Poor* to *Excellent*; (b), (d), (f), (h), (j): Output $\widetilde{Y}_T$ when a reviewer's response to *Content* changes from *Poor* to *Excellent*. The corresponding weights for the three sub-criteria are shown in Fig. 9.5.

9.4.1.3 *Importance is Poor, Depth is Poor, and Content varies from Poor to Excellent*

Starting with the choices that were made for *Importance*, *Depth* and *Content* in Fig. 9.10, *Depth* is changed from *Good* to *Poor*, and everything else is kept the same. The FOUs of $\widetilde{Y}_T$ for the present five cases are depicted in the right-hand figures of Fig. 9.11. Each of the left-hand figures in Fig. 9.11 depicts the respective FOUs for $\widetilde{X}_I$, $\widetilde{X}_{Co}$ and $\widetilde{X}_D$. Note that

$\widetilde{X}_I = \widetilde{X}_D = Poor$ is the one in Fig. 9.3. As in Figs. 9.9 and 9.10, only $\widetilde{X}_{Co}$ changes in the left-hand figures, and its FOUs again match the ones in Fig. 9.3 for all five words.

Observe again that as the reviewer's response to the sub-criterion *Content* varies from *Poor* to *Excellent*, $\widetilde{Y}_T$ moves from left-to-right towards the maximal score of 10 (which, again, it never reaches), which again supports our expectation that *Content* dominates.

By comparing each line of the two sets of right-hand figures in Figs. 9.10 and 9.11, observe that each of the FOUs of $\widetilde{Y}_T$ for when *Depth* is *Good* lies farther to the right of its respective FOU for when *Depth* is *Poor*. This also agrees with our expectation, because improving the assessment of *Depth* should improve $\widetilde{Y}_T$, i.e., move $\widetilde{Y}_T$ further to the right.

Finally, observe that the five cases in Fig. 9.10 represent a deterioration of the respective cases in Fig. 9.9, and the five cases in Fig. 9.11 represent an even greater deterioration of those cases. These deteriorations (which correspond to poorer reviews within the criterion of Technical Merit) are evident in all respective right-hand figure FOUs in Figs. 9.9–9.11 by their moving towards the left. For example, comparing Fig. (j) in these figures, one observes that in Fig. 9.9(j) the very left portion of $\widetilde{Y}_T$ reaches $y = 6$, but in Figs. 9.10(j) and 9.11(j) the very left portion of $\widetilde{Y}_T$ only reaches $y = 3$ and $y \approx 2.4$. This all seems quite sensible in that one would expect poorer assessments of any of the three sub-criteria to move $\widetilde{Y}_T$ to the left.

9.4.1.4 *Conclusions*

These 15 cases have demonstrated that *Content* does indeed dominate *Importance* and *Depth* and that a higher assessment for any of the three sub-criteria will move $\widetilde{Y}_T$ to the right.

9.4.2 *Aggregation of Presentation Sub-criteria*

To consider all possible combinations of the inputs to the criterion of Presentation, one would need to examine a total of $5^4 = 625$ cases, because each of its four sub-criteria has five possible linguistic terms (Fig. 9.3) that can be chosen by a reviewer. This is even more impractical to do than it was to examine all 125 possible cases for Technical Merit, so instead our focus is on observing the effect that sub-criterion *Clarity* has on $\widetilde{Y}_P$ when *Style* is fixed at *Excellent* and *Organization* and *References* are varied by the same amounts (recall that the weights for both *Organization* and *References* are the same – see Fig. 9.6). To do this 15 of the 625 possible cases are studied. In all cases, $\widetilde{Y}_P$ in (7) is computed for the four weight FOUs that are depicted in Fig. 9.6. Because $\widetilde{W}_S = \widetilde{W}_{Cl}$, one expects to see $\widetilde{Y}_P$ move from left-to-right as $\widetilde{X}_S$ moves from left-to-right and also as $\widetilde{X}_O$ and $\widetilde{X}_R$ simultaneously move from left-to-right.

9.4.2.1 *Style is Excellent, Organization and References are Poor, and Clarity varies from Poor to Excellent*

The FOUs of $\widetilde{Y}_T$ for these five cases are depicted in the right-hand figures of Fig. 9.12. Each of the left-hand figures in Fig. 9.12 depicts the respective FOUs for $\widetilde{X}_{Cl}$, $\widetilde{X}_O$, $\widetilde{X}_R$ and $\widetilde{X}_S$. Note that $\widetilde{X}_S = Excellent$ and $\widetilde{X}_O = \widetilde{X}_R = Poor$ are the ones in Fig. 9.3. Only $\widetilde{X}_{Cl}$ changes in the left-hand figures, and its FOUs match the ones in Fig. 9.3 for all five words.

Observe that as the reviewer's response to *Clarity* varies from *Poor* to *Excellent*, $\widetilde{Y}_P$ does move from left-to-right towards the maximal score of 10 which supports our expectation that $\widetilde{Y}_P$ moves from left-to-right as $\widetilde{X}_{Cl}$ moves from left-to-right.

9.4.2.2 *Style is Excellent, Organization and References are Adequate and Clarity varies from Poor to Excellent*

The FOUs of $\widetilde{Y}_T$ for these five cases are depicted in the right-hand figures of Fig. 9.13. Each of the left-hand figures in Fig. 9.13 depicts the respective FOUs for $\widetilde{X}_{Cl}$, $\widetilde{X}_O$, $\widetilde{X}_R$ and $\widetilde{X}_S$. Note that, as in Fig. 9.12, $\widetilde{X}_S = Excellent$ but now $\widetilde{X}_O = \widetilde{X}_R = Adequate$ and these FOUs are the ones in Fig. 9.3. Again, only $\widetilde{X}_{Cl}$ changes in the left-hand figures, and its FOUs match the ones in Fig. 9.3 for all five words.

Observe that as the reviewer's response to *Clarity* varies from *Poor* to *Excellent*, $\widetilde{Y}_P$ does move from left-to-right towards the maximal score of 10 which again supports our expectation that $\widetilde{Y}_P$ moves from left-to-right as $\widetilde{X}_{Cl}$ moves from left-to-right.

By comparing each line of the two sets of right-hand figures in Figs. 9.12 and 9.13, observe that each of the FOUs of $\widetilde{Y}_P$ for when *Organization* and *References* are *Adequate* are somewhat to the right of its respective FOU for when *Organization* and *References* are *Poor*. This also agrees with our expectation, because improving the assessments of *Organization* and *References* should improve $\widetilde{Y}_P$, i.e., move $\widetilde{Y}_P$ further to the right.

9.4.2.3 *Style, Organization and References are Excellent and Clarity varies from Poor to Excellent*

The FOUs of $\widetilde{Y}_T$ for these five cases are depicted in the right-hand figures of Fig. 9.14. Each of the left-hand figures in Fig. 9.14 depicts the respective FOUs for $\widetilde{X}_{Cl}$, $\widetilde{X}_O$, $\widetilde{X}_R$ and $\widetilde{X}_S$. Note that, as in Figs. 9.12 and 9.13, $\widetilde{X}_S = Excellent$ but now $\widetilde{X}_O = \widetilde{X}_R = Excellent$ where *Excellent* is depicted in Fig. 9.3. Again, only $\widetilde{X}_{Cl}$ changes in the left-hand figures, and its

FOUs match the ones in Fig. 9.3 for all five words.

Observe that as the reviewer's response to *Clarity* varies from *Poor* to *Excellent*, $\widetilde{Y}_P$ once again moves from left-to-right towards the maximal score of 10 which continues to support our expectation that $\widetilde{Y}_P$ moves from left-to-right as $\widetilde{X}_{Cl}$ moves from left-to-right.

By comparing each line of the two sets of right-hand figures in Figs. 9.13 and 9.14, observe that each of the FOUs of $\widetilde{Y}_P$ for when *Organization* and *References* are *Excellent* are somewhat to the right of its respective FOU for when *Organization* and *References* are *Adequate*. This also continues to agree with our expectation, because improving the assessments of *Organization* and *References* should improve $\widetilde{Y}_P$, i.e., move $\widetilde{Y}_P$ further to the right.

Observe that as the reviewer's response to *Clarity* varies from *Poor* to *Excellent*, $\widetilde{Y}_P$ once again moves from left-to-right towards the maximal score of 10 which continues to support our expectation that $\widetilde{Y}_P$ moves from left-to-right as $\widetilde{X}_{Cl}$ moves from left-to-right.

By comparing each line of the two sets of right-hand figures in Figs. 9.13 and 9.14, observe that each of the FOUs of $\widetilde{Y}_P$ for when *Organization* and *References* are *Excellent* are somewhat to the right of its respective FOU for when *Organization* and *References* are *Adequate*. This also continues to agree with our expectation, because improving the assessments of *Organization* and *References* should improve $\widetilde{Y}_P$, i.e., move $\widetilde{Y}_P$ further to the right.

Finally, observe that the five cases in Fig. 9.13 represent an improvement of the respective cases in Fig. 9.12, and the five cases in Fig. 9.14 represent an even greater improvement of those cases. These improvements (which correspond to better reviews within the criterion of Presentation) are evident in all respective right-hand figure FOUs in Figs. 9.12-9.14 by their moving towards the right. For example, comparing Fig. (j) in these figures, one observes that in Fig. 9.12(j) the left portion of $\widetilde{Y}_P$ begins at $y \approx 3.3$ and the very right portion of $\widetilde{Y}_P$ reaches $y = 10$, in Fig. 9.13(j) the left portion of $\widetilde{Y}_P$ begins at $y \approx 4.5$ and the very right portion of $\widetilde{Y}_P$ also reaches $y = 10$, and, in Fig. 9.14(j) the left portion of $\widetilde{Y}_P$ begins at $y \approx 6.5$ and not only does the very right portion of $\widetilde{Y}_P$ also reach $y = 10$, but $\widetilde{Y}_P$ has changed its shape from that of an interior FOU to that of a right-shoulder FOU.

This all seems quite sensible in that one would expect higher assessments of any of the three sub-criteria to move $\widetilde{Y}_P$ to the right.

9.4.2.4 *Conclusions*

These 15 cases have demonstrated that $\widetilde{Y}_P$ moves from left-to-right as $\widetilde{X}_{Cl}$ moves from left-to-right and also as $\widetilde{X}_O$ and $\widetilde{X}_R$ simultaneously move from left-to-right.

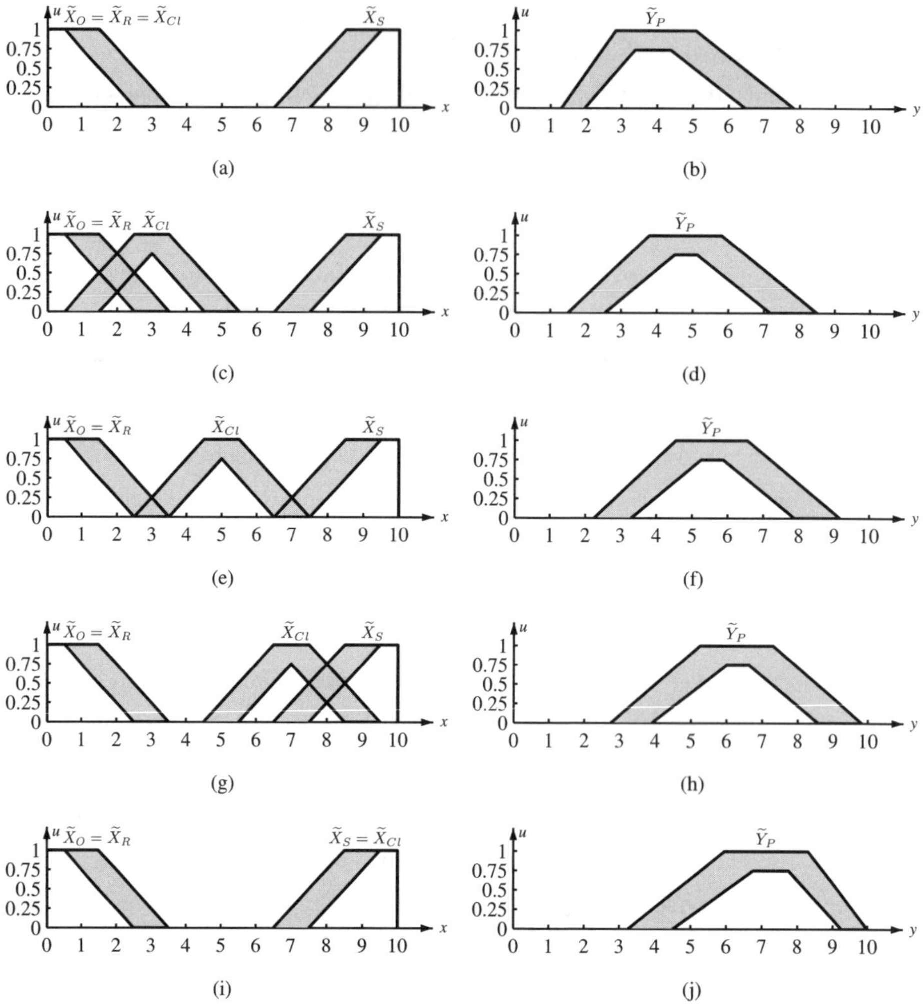

Figure 9.12 Presentation when *Style* is *Excellent*, *Organization* and *References* are *Poor*, and *Clarity* varies. (a), (c), (e), (g), (i): Input FOUs when a reviewer's response to *Clarity* changes from *Poor* to *Excellent*; (b), (d), (f), (h), (j): Output $\widetilde{Y}_P$ when a reviewer's response to *Clarity* changes from *Poor* to *Excellent*. The corresponding weights for the three sub-criteria are shown in Fig. 9.6.

9.4.3 *Aggregation at the Reviewer Level*

This section assumes that there are three reviewers for a paper submission, and that *Technical Merit* and *Presentation* have already had their sub-categories aggregated, leading to $\widetilde{Y}_{jT}$ and $\widetilde{Y}_{jP}$ $(j = 1,2,3)$. $\widetilde{Y}_{jT}$ and $\widetilde{Y}_{jP}$, whose shapes in this section are pre-specified by us[7], are then aggregated using the LWA in (8) in which $\widetilde{Y}_{jT}$ and $\widetilde{Y}_{jP}$ are weighted using their respec-

[7] In Section 9.4.5 they will be determined by beginning with three completed generic review forms.

tive weight FOUs that are depicted in Fig. 9.7, where, as previously agreed upon, heavier weight is given to Technical Merit than to Presentation. The results are $\widetilde{Y}_{R_j}$, $j = 1, 2, 3$.

9.4.3.1 *Presentation is Adequate and Technical Merit Varies*

In this case all of the reviewers agree that Presentation is *Adequate*, but they disagree about Technical Merit. Reviewer 1 rates Technical Merit as *Poor*, Reviewer 2 rates Technical Merit as *Adequate* and Reviewer 3 rates Technical Merit as *Excellent*, where *Poor*, *Adequate* and *Excellent* are in Fig. 9.3. $\widetilde{Y}_{jT}$ and $\widetilde{Y}_{jP}$ are depicted in Figs. 9.15(a)–(c) for Reviewers 1-3, respectively. In those figures $\widetilde{Y}_{jP}$ is fixed at *Good* and only $\widetilde{Y}_{jT}$ varies from one figure to the next. Fig. 9.15(d) depicts $\widetilde{Y}_{R_1}$, $\widetilde{Y}_{R_2}$ and $\widetilde{Y}_{R_3}$. Observe that these FOUs are spread out indicating substantial disagreement among the reviewers, and that as the rating for Technical Merit improves $\widetilde{Y}_{R_j}$ moves to the right; hence, $\widetilde{Y}_{R_3} > \widetilde{Y}_{R_2} > \widetilde{Y}_{R_1}$, where $>$ is used here to denote "further to the right of."

9.4.3.2 *Technical Merit is Adequate and Presentation Varies*

In this case all of the reviewers agree that Technical Merit is *Adequate*, but they disagree about Presentation; hence, this case is the opposite of the one in Section 9.4.3.1. Reviewer 1 now rates Presentation as *Poor*, Reviewer 2 rates Presentation as *Adequate*, and Reviewer 3 rates Presentation as *Excellent*. $\widetilde{Y}_{jT}$ and $\widetilde{Y}_{jP}$ are depicted in Figs. 9.16(a)–(c) for Reviewers 1-3, respectively. In those figures, $\widetilde{Y}_{jT}$ is fixed at *Good* and only $\widetilde{Y}_{jP}$ varies from one figure to the next. Fig. 9.16(d) depicts $\widetilde{Y}_{R_1}$, $\widetilde{Y}_{R_2}$ and $\widetilde{Y}_{R_3}$.

Observe that these FOUs are much more bunched together and have considerably more overlap than the ones in Fig. 9.15(d). So, even though there is considerable disagreement among the reviewers about Presentation, this does not make as much difference in $\widetilde{Y}_{R_j}$ as did the disagreement about Technical Merit in Fig. 9.15(d). While it is true that an improved rating for Presentation moves $\widetilde{Y}_{R_j}$ further to the right, this effect on $\widetilde{Y}_{R_j}$ is nowhere as dramatic as the effect of an improved rating for Technical Merit has on $\widetilde{Y}_{R_j}$.

9.4.3.3 *Conclusions*

As expected, a higher rating for Technical Merit has a much greater effect on $\widetilde{Y}_{R_j}$ than does a comparable rating for Presentation.

9.4.4 *Aggregation at the AE Level*

This section builds upon the results in Section 9.4.3, i.e., it assumes there are three reviewers of a submission and their reviews have been aggregated using (8). Here the focus is on what effects different levels of reviewer expertise have on $\widetilde{Y}_{\mathrm{AE}}$ as computed by (9). One expects that reviews from reviewers who have high expertise will have more effect on $\widetilde{Y}_{\mathrm{AE}}$ than those from reviewers who have moderate or low levels of expertise, because according to Fig. 9.4, $High > Moderate > Low$, where again $>$ is used to denote "further to the right of."

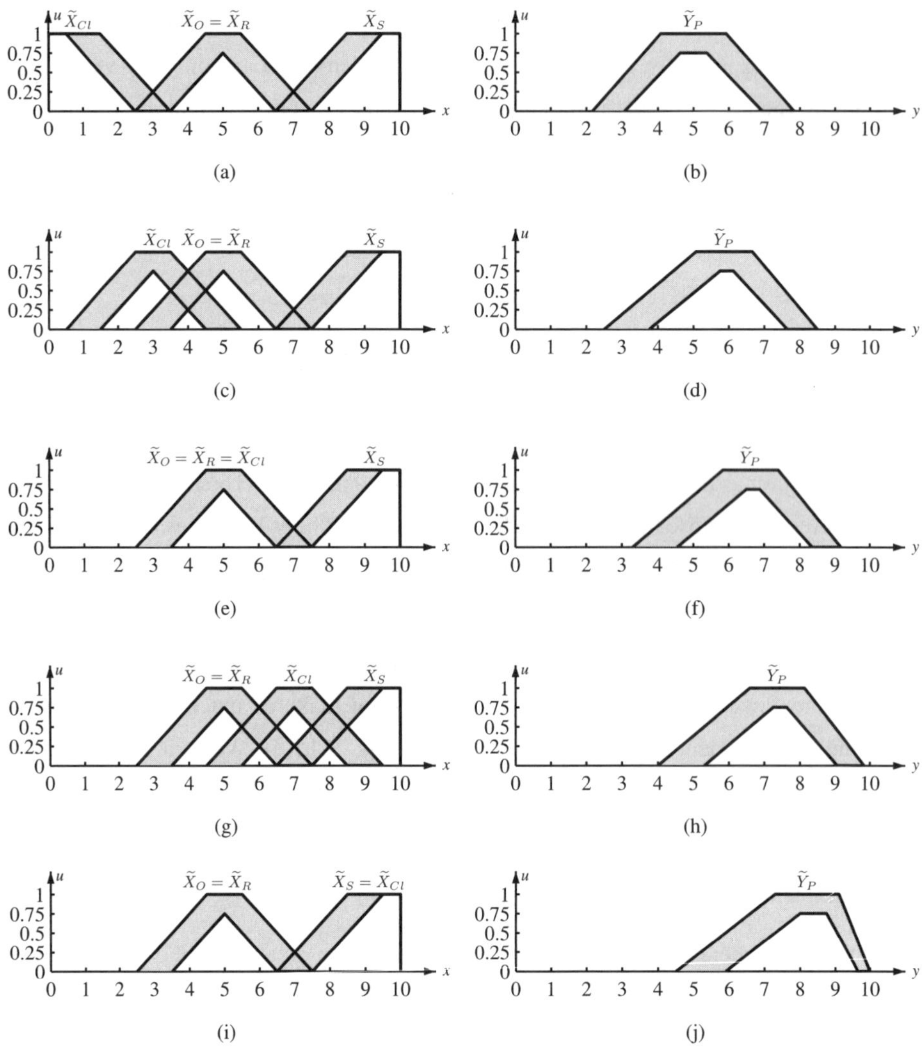

Figure 9.13 Presentation when *Style* is *Excellent*, *Organization* and *References* are *Adequate*, and *Clarity* varies. (a), (c), (e), (g), (i): Input FOUs when a reviewer's response to *Clarity* changes from *Poor* to *Excellent*; (b), (d), (f), (h), (j): Output $\widetilde{Y}_P$ when a reviewer's response to *Clarity* changes from *Poor* to *Excellent*. The corresponding weights for the three sub-criteria are shown in Fig. 9.6.

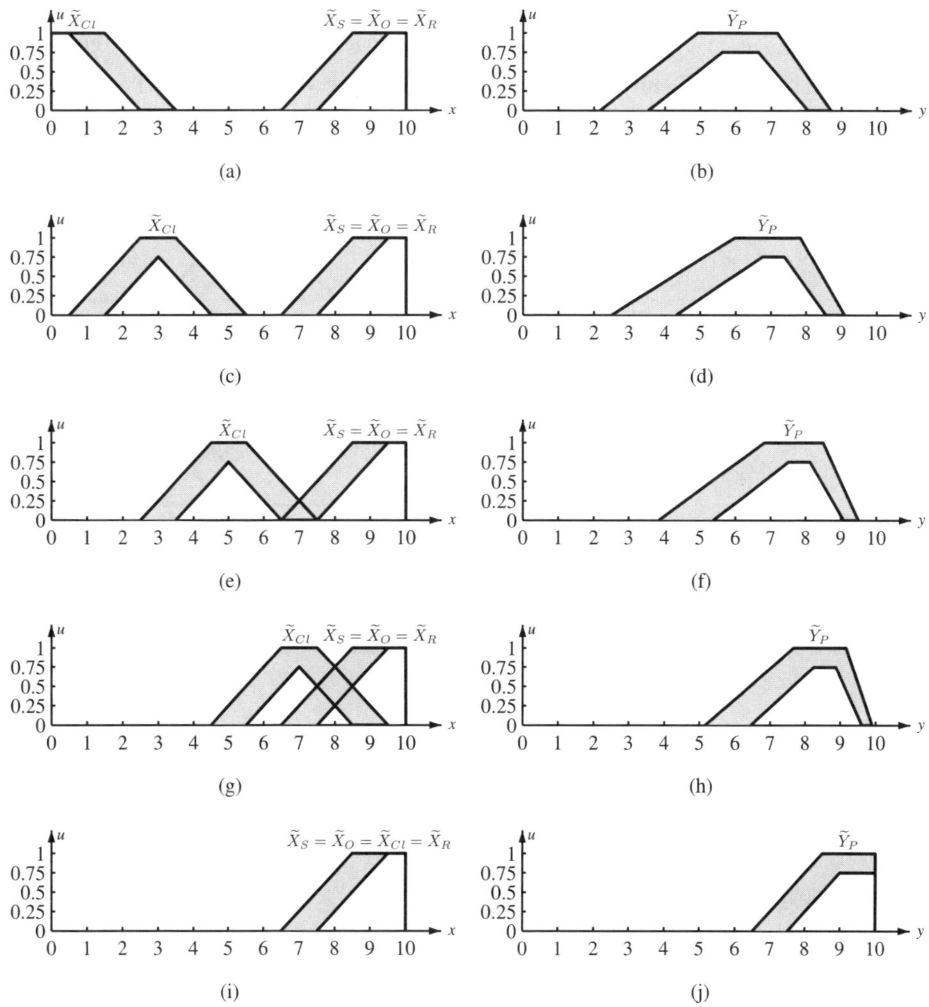

Figure 9.14 Presentation when *Style*, *Organization* and *References* are *Excellent*, and *Clarity* varies. (a), (c), (e), (g), (i): Input FOUs when a reviewer's response to *Clarity* changes from *Poor* to *Excellent*; (b), (d), (f), (h), (j): Output $\widetilde{Y}_P$ when a reviewer's response to *Clarity* changes from *Poor* to *Excellent*. The corresponding weights for the three sub-criteria are shown in Fig. 9.6.

9.4.4.1 *Presentation is Adequate, Technical Merit Varies, and Reviewer Expertise Varies*

This is a continuation of Section 9.4.3.1, and starts with $\widetilde{Y}_{R_1}$, $\widetilde{Y}_{R_2}$ and $\widetilde{Y}_{R_3}$ that are in Fig. 9.15(d) and that are quite spread out. When Reviewer 1 is of *high expertise*, Reviewer 2 is of *moderate expertise* and Reviewer 3 is of *low expertise*, their weights are depicted in Fig. 9.17(a), and (9) leads to $\widetilde{Y}_{\text{AE}}$ that is depicted in Fig. 9.17(b). On the other hand, when all three reviewers are of *moderate expertise*, their weights are depicted in Fig. 9.17(c), and the resulting $\widetilde{Y}_{\mathrm{AE}}$ is in Fig. 9.17(d). Finally, when Reviewers 1 and 3 are of *high expertise* and Reviewer 2 is of *low expertise*, their weights are depicted in Fig. 9.17(e), and the resulting $\widetilde{Y}_{\mathrm{AE}}$ is depicted in Fig. 9.17(f).

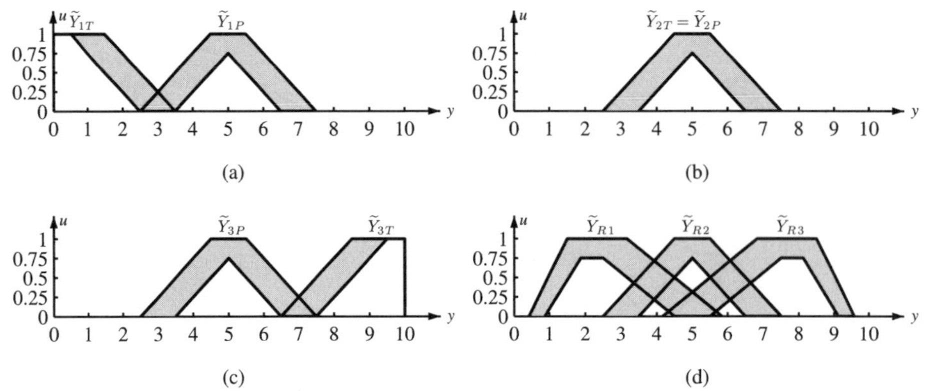

Figure 9.15 The three reviewers have the same opinion about Presentation (*Adequate*) and different opinions about Technical Merit. (a), (b) and (c): Reviewers 1, 2 and 3's aggregated FOUs on Technical Merit and Presentation, respectively. (d): Reviewers 1, 2 and 3's overall FOU. The corresponding weights for the two criteria are shown in Fig. 9.7.

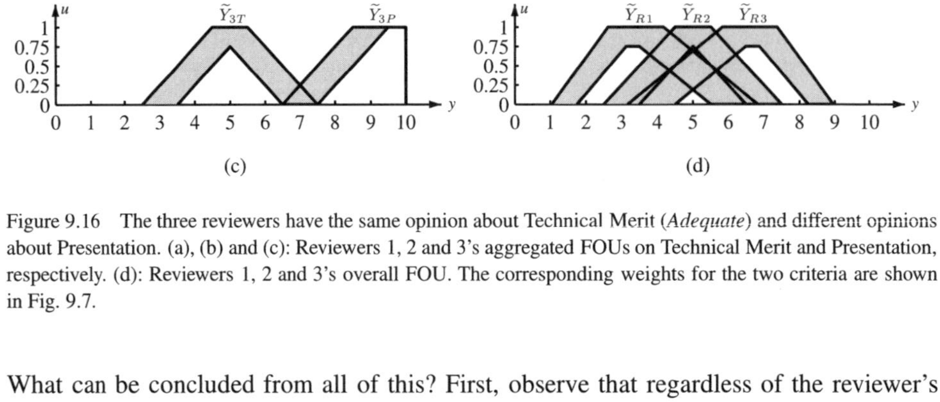

Figure 9.16 The three reviewers have the same opinion about Technical Merit (*Adequate*) and different opinions about Presentation. (a), (b) and (c): Reviewers 1, 2 and 3's aggregated FOUs on Technical Merit and Presentation, respectively. (d): Reviewers 1, 2 and 3's overall FOU. The corresponding weights for the two criteria are shown in Fig. 9.7.

What can be concluded from all of this? First, observe that regardless of the reviewer's expertise $\widetilde{Y}_{\mathrm{AE}}$ is very spread out, so that it is very likely that the AE will recommend that the paper be rewritten. Next, observe that a better $\widetilde{Y}_{\text{AE}}$ is obtained when a reviewer's $\widetilde{Y}_{R_j}$ in Fig. 9.15(d) is farther to the right (e.g., Reviewer 3) and the reviewer is of *high expertise*. So, the expertise of the reviewer is important, as can be seen by comparing $\widetilde{Y}_{\text{AE}}$ in Figs. 9.17(b), (d) and (f).

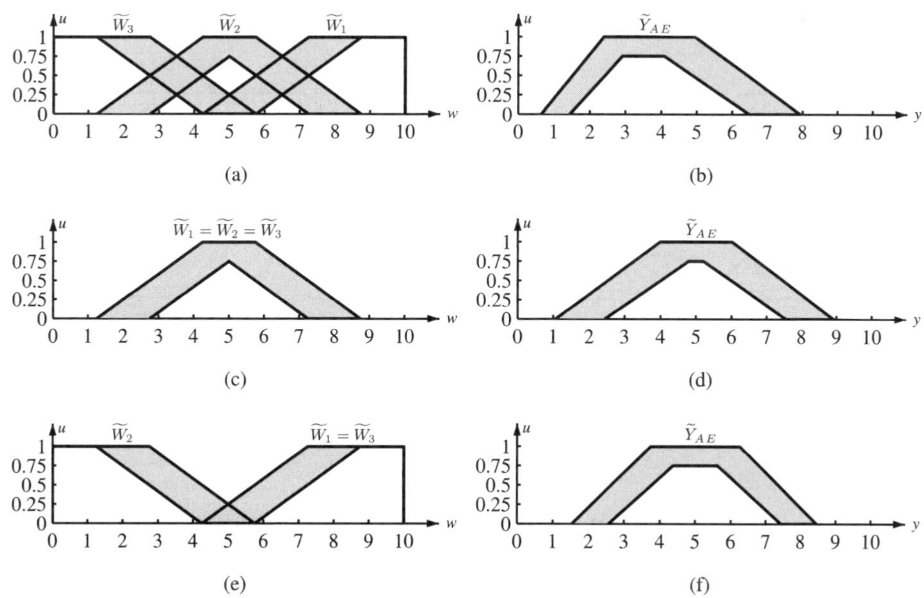

Figure 9.17 Aggregation at the AE level for the three reviewers' opinions shown in Fig. 9.15(d), when reviewer expertise varies. (a), (c), (e): weights for the three reviewers; (b), (d) and (f): the corresponding $\widetilde{Y}_{\text{AE}}$.

9.4.4.2 *Technical Merit is Adequate, Presentation Varies, and Reviewer Expertise Varies*

This is a continuation of Section 9.4.3.2, and starts with $\widetilde{Y}_{R_1}$, $\widetilde{Y}_{R_2}$ and $\widetilde{Y}_{R_3}$ that are in Fig. 9.16(d) and that are much more bunched together and have considerably more overlap than the ones in Fig. 9.15(d). When Reviewer 1 is of *high expertise*, Reviewer 2 is of *moderate expertise* and Reviewer 3 is of *low expertise*, their weights are depicted in Fig. 9.18(a), and (9) leads to $\widetilde{Y}_{\text{AE}}$ that is depicted in Fig. 9.18(b). On the other hand, when all three reviewers are of *moderate expertise*, their weights are depicted in Fig. 9.18(c), and the resulting $\widetilde{Y}_{\text{AE}}$ is in Fig. 9.18(d). Finally, when Reviewers 1 and 3 are of *high expertise* and Reviewer 2 is of *low expertise*, their weights are depicted in Fig. 9.18(e), and the resulting $\widetilde{Y}_{\text{AE}}$ is depicted in Fig. 9.18(f).

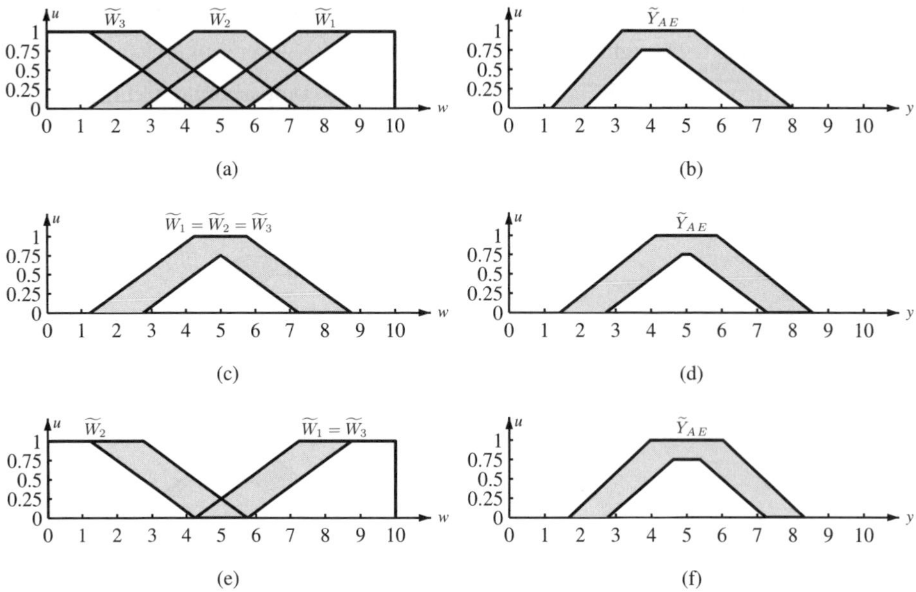

Figure 9.18 Aggregation at the AE level for the three reviewers' opinions shown in Fig. 9.16(d), when reviewer expertise varies. (a), (c), (e): weights for the three reviewers; (b), (d) and (f): the corresponding $\widetilde{Y}_{\text{AE}}$.

As in Fig. 9.17, one may ask: "What can be concluded from all of this?" Again, observe from Fig. 9.18 that, regardless of the reviewer's expertise, $\widetilde{Y}_{\text{AE}}$ is very spread out (although not quite as much as in Fig. 9.17), so that again it is very likely that the AE will recommend that the paper be rewritten. Observe again that a better $\widetilde{Y}_{\text{AE}}$ is obtained when a reviewer's $\widetilde{Y}_{R_j}$ in Fig. 9.16(d) is farther to the right (e.g., Reviewer 3) and the reviewer is of *high expertise*. So, again the expertise of the reviewer is important, as can be seen by comparing $\widetilde{Y}_{\text{AE}}$ in Figs. 9.18(b), (d) and (f).

9.4.4.3 *Conclusions*

In practice when an AE receives three widely different reviews the result is a recommendation that the paper be rewritten. The JPJA gives results that seem to be consistent with this.

9.4.5 ***Complete Reviews***

This section provides three examples of the complete JPJA for different kinds of reviews so that one can gain confidence that the JPJA will be a useful assistant to an AE. In all examples there are three reviewers.

9.4.5.1 *A Submission that would be Accepted*

The reviewer's three completed generic review forms are depicted in Figs. 9.19(a)–(c). Observe that all of the linguistic assessments are in the *Good* or *Excellent* columns suggesting that this paper probably will be accepted. Will the JPJA arrive at this recommendation?

The three reviewers' aggregated FOUs for Technical Merit and Presentation are depicted in Figs. 9.19(d)–(f). These FOUs were computed using (6) and (7). Observe that all of the FOUs are towards the right side of the scale 0–10, suggesting that things are looking good for this submission.

The reviewer's overall FOUs are shown in Fig. 9.19(g). These FOUs were computed using (8). The three overall FOUs look very similar because the three review forms are very similar. Observe that all of the overall FOUs are also towards the right side of the scale 0–10, suggesting that things are looking even better for this submission.

The weights for each of the reviewers are shown in Fig. 9.19(h). They are used together with the overall FOUs in Fig. 9.19(g) in (9) to obtain the aggregated FOU for the AE, $\widetilde{Y}_{\text{AE}}$, depicted in Fig. 9.19(i). Observe that $\widetilde{Y}_{\text{AE}}$ is also towards the right side of the scale 0–10, suggesting that things are looking very good for this submission; however, we are not going to leave things to a subjective "look" to make the final publication judgment. Instead, $\widetilde{Y}_{\text{AE}}$ is sent to the decoder.

The decoder computes Vlachos and Sergiadis's subsethood measure between $\widetilde{Y}_{\text{AE}}$ and the three words in the decoding codebook (Fig. 9.8), i.e.,

$$ss(\widetilde{Y}_{\text{AE}}, \text{Reject}) = 0$$

$$ss(\widetilde{Y}_{\text{AE}}, \text{Rewrite}) = 0.26$$

$$ss(\widetilde{Y}_{\text{AE}}, \text{Accept}) = 0.72$$

Because $ss(\widetilde{Y}_{\text{AE}}, \text{Accept})$ is much larger than the other two subsethoods and it is greater than 0.5, the AE can recommend "Accept" with high confidence, so the JPJA has made the recommendation that agrees with our earlier stated intuition.

9.4.5.2 *A Submission that would be Rejected*

The reviewer's three completed generic review forms are depicted in Figs. 9.20(a)–(c). Reviewer 1 has assessed all of the sub-categories as either *Adequate* or *Good*, but his expertise is *Low*. Reviewers 2 and 3 have assessed all of the sub-categories as *Poor*, *Marginal* or *Adequate*, and their levels of expertise are *High* and *Moderate*, respectively. An AE will tend to put more credence on the reviews from Reviewers 2 and 3 than on the review from Reviewer 1, suggesting that this paper will probably be rejected. Will the JPJA also arrive at this recommendation?

	Poor	Marginal	Adequate	Good	Excellent
Technical Merit:					
Importance	( )	( )	( )	(X)	( )
Content	( )	( )	( )	( )	(X)
Depth	( )	( )	( )	( )	(X)
Presentation:					
Style	( )	( )	( )	(X)	( )
Organization	( )	( )	( )	( )	(X)
Clarity	( )	( )	( )	( )	(X)
Reference	( )	( )	( )	(X)	( )
Expertise:	Low		Moderate		High
Your Expertise	( )		(X)		( )

(a)

	Poor	Marginal	Adequate	Good	Excellent
Technical Merit:					
Importance	( )	( )	( )	(X)	( )
Content	( )	( )	( )	( )	(X)
Depth	( )	( )	( )	(X)	( )
Presentation:					
Style	( )	( )	( )	( )	(X)
Organization	( )	( )	( )	( )	(X)
Clarity	( )	( )	( )	( )	(X)
Reference	( )	( )	( )	(X)	( )
Expertise:	Low		Moderate		High
Your Expertise	( )		( )		(X)

(b)

	Poor	Marginal	Adequate	Good	Excellent
Technical Merit:					
Importance	( )	( )	( )	( )	(X)
Content	( )	( )	( )	(X)	( )
Depth	( )	( )	( )	( )	(X)
Presentation:					
Style	( )	( )	( )	(X)	( )
Organization	( )	( )	( )	( )	(X)
Clarity	( )	( )	( )	(X)	( )
Reference	( )	( )	( )	(X)	( )
Expertise:	Low		Moderate		High
Your Expertise	(X)		( )		( )

(c)

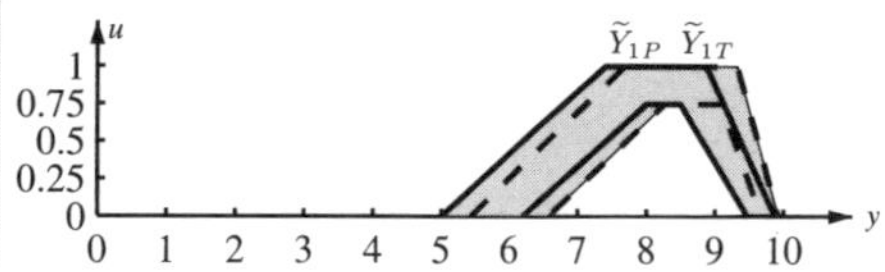

(d)

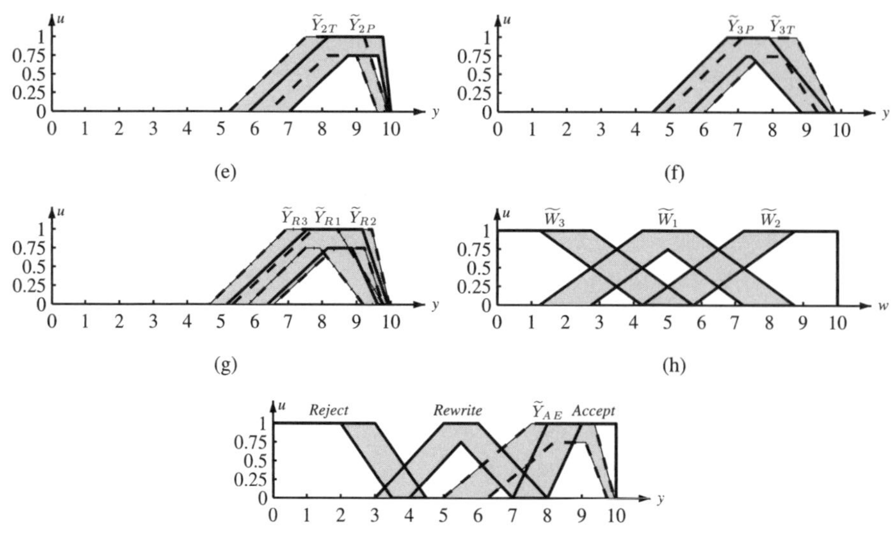

(e) (f) (g) (h) (i)

Figure 9.19 The first complete paper review example. (a), (b), (c): the completed review forms; (d), (e), (f): aggregated Technical Merit and Presentation FOUs for the three reviewers; (g): overall FOUs of the three reviewers; (h): the weights associated with the three reviewers; (i): the aggregated AE's FOU in relation to the three categories.

The three reviewers' aggregated FOUs for Technical Merit and Presentation are depicted in Figs. 9.20(d)–(f). Observe that the FOUs for all three reviewers are towards the left on the scale 0–10. This suggests that things are not looking good for this submission.

The reviewer's overall FOUs are shown in Fig. 9.20(g). The overall FOUs for all three reviewers are very clearly shifted to the left on the scale 0–10, suggesting that things are looking even worse for this submission.

The weights for each of the reviewers are shown in Fig. 9.20(h). They are used together with the overall FOUs in Fig. 9.20(g) in (9) to obtain the aggregated FOU for the AE, $\widetilde{Y}_{\mathrm{AE}}$, depicted in Fig. 9.20(i). Observe that $\widetilde{Y}_{\mathrm{AE}}$ is also towards the left side of the scale 0–10, suggesting that things are looking very bad for this submission.

Indeed, when $\widetilde{Y}_{\mathrm{AE}}$ is sent to the decoder the following results are obtained:

$$ss(\widetilde{Y}_{\mathrm{AE}},\mathrm{Reject}) = 0.74$$
$$ss(\widetilde{Y}_{\mathrm{AE}},\mathrm{Rewrite}) = 0.30$$
$$ss(\widetilde{Y}_{\mathrm{AE}},\mathrm{Accept}) = 0$$

Because $ss(\widetilde{Y}_{\mathrm{AE}},\mathrm{Reject})$ is much larger than the other two subsethoods and it is larger than 0.5, the AE can recommend *Reject* with high confidence. Once again the JPJA has provided a recommendation that agrees with our earlier stated intuition.

9.4.5.3 *A Submission that would be Rewritten*

The reviewer's three completed generic review forms are depicted in Figs. 9.21(a)–(c). The three reviewers have assessed all of the sub-categories as *Adequate*, *Good* or *Excellent*; however, it is not clear from the actual reviews whether the paper will be accepted or will have to be rewritten. How (or) will this ambiguity be seen by the JPJA?

The three reviewers' aggregated FOUs for Technical Merit and Presentation are depicted in Figs. 9.21(d)–(f). The reviewer's overall FOUs are shown in Fig. 9.21(g). Comparing this figure with Fig. 9.19(g), it is clear that the reviewer's overall FOUs for the accepted paper are all to the right of 5 on the scale of 0–10, whereas the reviewer's overall FOUs for the present case cover a larger range on that scale.

The weights for each of the reviewers are shown in Fig. 9.21(h). They are used together with the overall FOUs in Fig. 9.21(g) in (9) to obtain the aggregated FOU for the AE, $\widetilde{Y}_{\mathrm{AE}}$, depicted in Fig. 9.21(i). Observe that $\widetilde{Y}_{\mathrm{AE}}$ covers a large range on the scale of 0–10. It seems that the AE is getting mixed reviews for this submission.

Indeed, when $\widetilde{Y}_{\text{AE}}$ is sent to the decoder the following results are obtained:

$$ss(\widetilde{Y}_{\text{AE}}, \text{Reject}) = 0.06$$
$$ss(\widetilde{Y}_{\text{AE}}, \text{Rewrite}) = 0.76$$
$$ss(\widetilde{Y}_{\text{AE}}, \text{Accept}) = 0.20$$

Because $ss(\widetilde{Y}_{\text{AE}}, Rewrite)$ is much larger than the other two subsethoods and it is larger than 0.5, the AE can recommend *Rewrite* with high confidence.

9.4.5.4 *Conclusions*

From these three complete examples, the JPJA is providing recommendations that agree with anticipated recommendations. This suggests that the JPJA will be a very useful assistant to an AE.

9.5 Conclusions

The examples in this chapter have demonstrated that the Per-C is a very useful tool for hierarchical and distributed decision-making. In this chapter, all inputs to the JPJA have been words that were modeled as IT2 FSs; however, the Per-C can also easily aggregate mixed inputs of numbers, intervals and words; hence, the Per-C has great potential in complex decision-making problems.

Acknowledgment

Much of the material in this chapter will appear in the authors' book [19], and is being published in this chapter with the permission of IEEE Press and John Wiley. The authors would like to thank Dr. Nihil Pal, the Editor-in-Chief of the *IEEE Trans. on Fuzzy Systems*, for his helps in establishing the FOUs used in this chapter.

	Poor	Marginal	Adequate	Good	Excellent
Technical Merit:					
Importance	( )	( )	(X)	( )	( )
Content	( )	(X)	( )	( )	( )
Depth	( )	(X)	( )	( )	( )
Presentation:					
Style	( )	(X)	( )	( )	( )
Organization	( )	( )	(X)	( )	( )
Clarity	( )	(X)	( )	( )	( )
Reference	( )	(X)	( )	( )	( )
Expertise:	Low		Moderate		High
Your Expertise	(X)		( )		( )

(a)

	Poor	Marginal	Adequate	Good	Excellent
Technical Merit:					
Importance	(X)	( )	( )	( )	( )
Content	( )	(X)	( )	( )	( )
Depth	( )	(X)	( )	( )	( )
Presentation:					
Style	( )	( )	(X)	( )	( )
Organization	( )	(X)	( )	( )	( )
Clarity	( )	( )	(X)	( )	( )
Reference	(X)	( )	( )	( )	( )
Expertise:	Low		Moderate		High
Your Expertise	( )		( )		(X)

(b)

	Poor	Marginal	Adequate	Good	Excellent
Technical Merit:					
Importance	(X)	( )	( )	( )	( )
Content	( )	(X)	( )	( )	( )
Depth	(X)	( )	( )	( )	( )
Presentation:					
Style	( )	(X)	( )	( )	( )
Organization	( )	( )	(X)	( )	( )
Clarity	( )	(X)	( )	( )	( )
Reference	(X)	( )	( )	( )	( )
Expertise:	Low		Moderate		High
Your Expertise	( )		(X)		( )

(c)

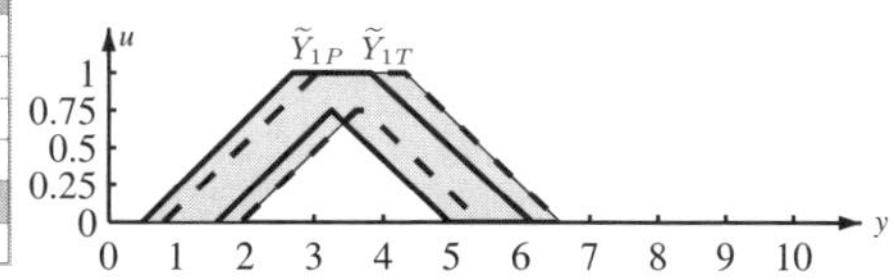

(d)

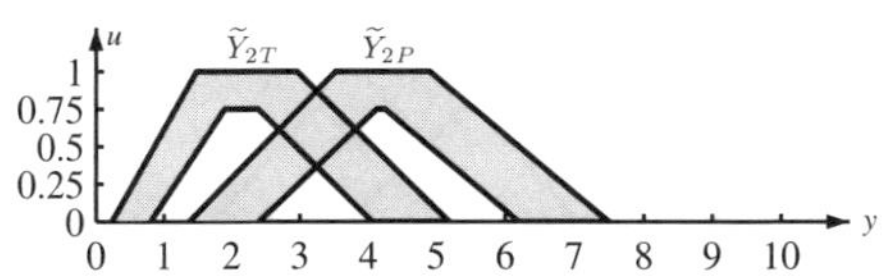

(e)

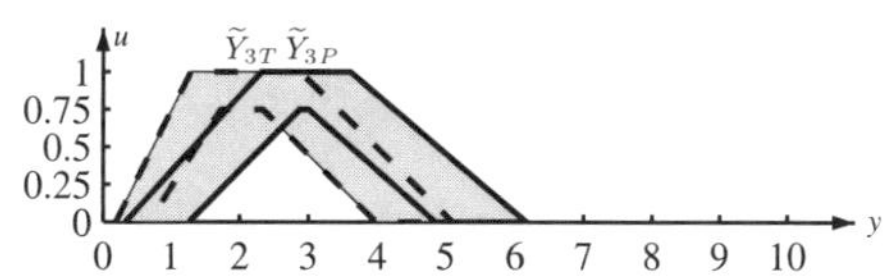

(f)

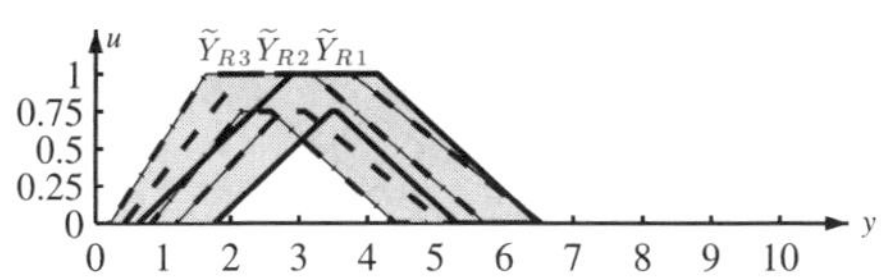

(g)

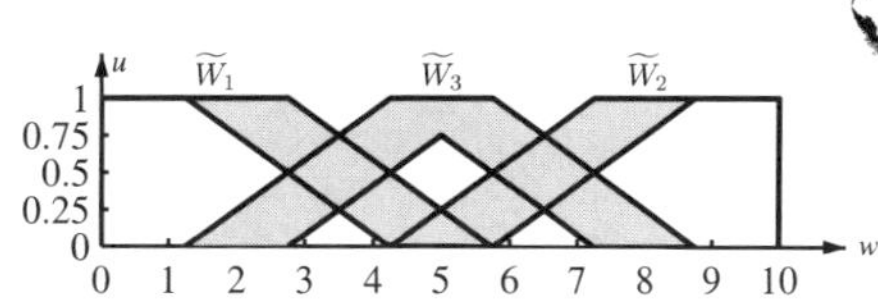

(h)

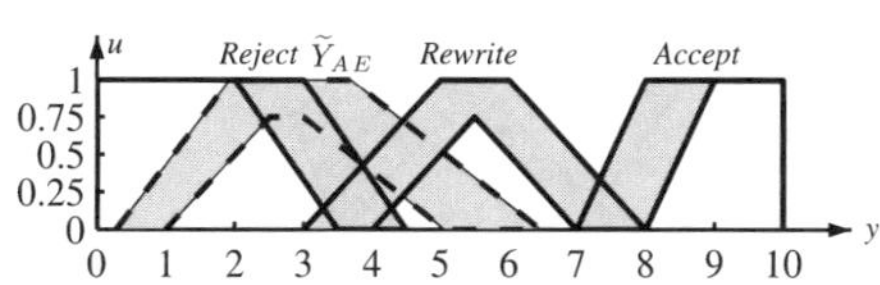

(i)

Figure 9.20 The second complete paper review example. (a), (b), (c): the completed review forms; (d), (e), (f): aggregated Technical Merit and Presentation FOUs for the three reviewers; (g): overall FOUs of the three reviewers; (h): the weights associated with the three reviewers; (i): the aggregated AE's FOU in relation to the three categories.

	Poor	Marginal	Adequate	Good	Excellent
Technical Merit:					
Importance	( )	( )	( )	(X)	( )
Content	( )	( )	(X)	( )	( )
Depth	( )	( )	( )	( )	(X)
Presentation:					
Style	( )	( )	( )	( )	(X)
Organization	( )	( )	( )	(X)	( )
Clarity	( )	( )	( )	( )	(X)
Reference	( )	( )	( )	(X)	( )
Expertise:	Low		Moderate		High
Your Expertise	( )		(X)		( )

(a)

	Poor	Marginal	Adequate	Good	Excellent
Technical Merit:					
Importance	( )	( )	(X)	( )	( )
Content	( )	( )	( )	(X)	( )
Depth	( )	( )	(X)	( )	( )
Presentation:					
Style	( )	( )	( )	(X)	( )
Organization	( )	( )	( )	(X)	( )
Clarity	( )	( )	(X)	( )	( )
Reference	( )	( )	( )	( )	(X)
Expertise:	Low		Moderate		High
Your Expertise	( )		(X)		( )

(b)

	Poor	Marginal	Adequate	Good	Excellent
Technical Merit:					
Importance	( )	( )	(X)	( )	( )
Content	( )	( )	(X)	( )	( )
Depth	( )	( )	( )	(X)	( )
Presentation:					
Style	( )	( )	( )	(X)	( )
Organization	( )	( )	( )	( )	(X)
Clarity	( )	( )	( )	(X)	( )
Reference	( )	( )	( )	(X)	( )
Expertise:	Low		Moderate		High
Your Expertise	( )		( )		(X)

(c)

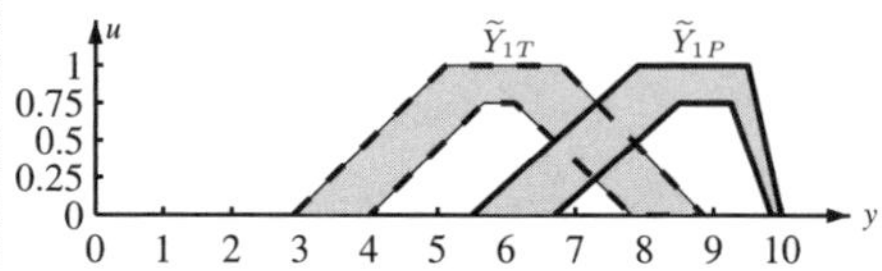

(d)

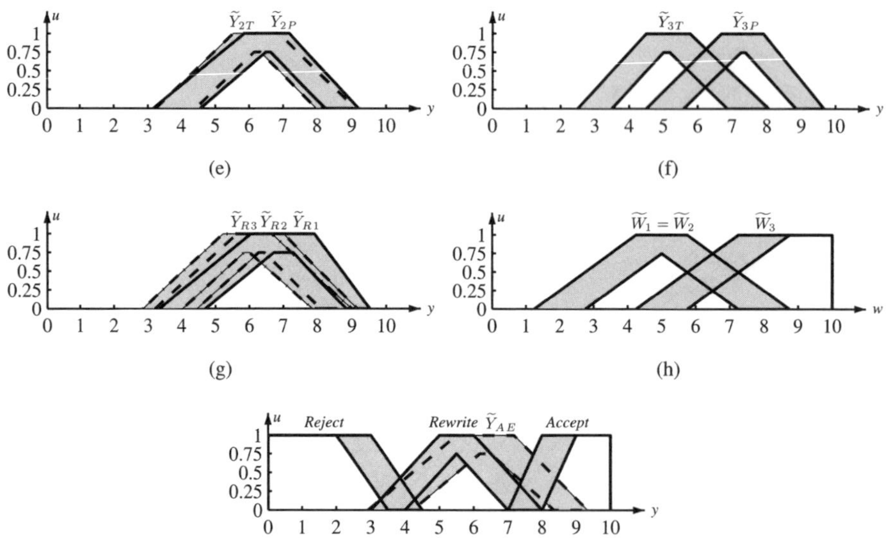

Figure 9.21 The third complete paper review example. (a), (b), (c): the completed review forms; (d), (e), (f): aggregated Technical Merit and Presentation FOUs for the three reviewers; (g): overall FOUs of the three reviewers; (h): the weights associated with the three reviewers; (i): the aggregated AE's FOU in relation to the three categories.

Appendix A

A.1 *Interval Type-2 Fuzzy Sets (IT2 FSs)*

An IT2 FS, $\widetilde{A}$, is to-date the most widely used kind of T2 FS, and is the only kind of T2 FS that is considered in this chapter. It is described as [4, 21]

$$\widetilde{A} = \int_{x\in X}\int_{u\in J_x} 1/(x,u) = \int_{x\in X}\left[\int_{u\in J_x} 1/u\right]\Big/ x, \tag{A.1}$$

where x is the *primary variable*; J_x, an interval in $[0,1]$, is the *primary membership* of x; u is the *secondary variable*; and $\int_{u\in J_x} 1/u$ is the *secondary membership function* (MF) at x. Note that (A.1) means: $\widetilde{A} : X \to \{[a,b] : 0 \leqslant a \leqslant b \leqslant 1\}$. Uncertainty about $\widetilde{A}$ is conveyed by the union of all of the primary memberships, called the *footprint of uncertainty* of $\widetilde{A}$ [$\widetilde{A}$], i.e.,

$$FOU(\widetilde{A}) = \bigcup_{x\in X} J_x \tag{A.2}$$

An IT2 FS is shown in Fig. 9.22. The FOU is shown as the shaded region. It is bounded by an *upper MF* (UMF) $\overline{A}$ and a *lower MF* (LMF) $\underline{A}$, both of which are T1 FSs; consequently, the membership grade of each element of an IT2 FS is an interval $[\mu_{\underline{A}}(x), \mu_{\overline{A}}(x)]$.

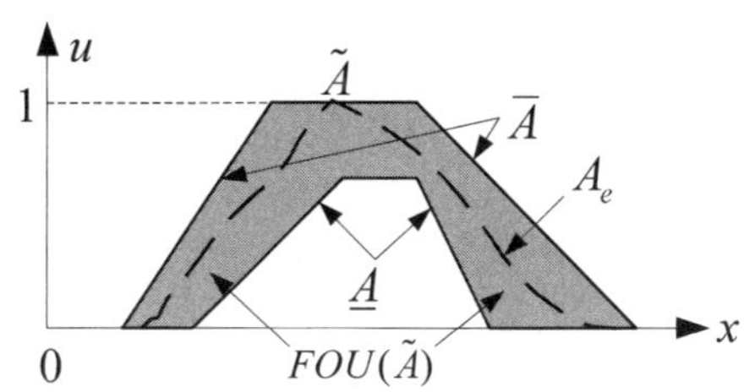

Figure 9.22 An IT2 FS. A_e is an embedded T1 FS (Wu and Mendel [11], © 2007, IEEE).

Note that an IT2 FS can also be represented as

$$\widetilde{A} = 1/FOU(\widetilde{A}) \tag{A.3}$$

with the understanding that this means putting a secondary grade of 1 at all points of $\widetilde{A}$. For discrete universes of discourse $X = \{x_1, x_2, \ldots, x_N\}$ and discrete J_x, an *embedded T1 FS* A_e has N elements, one each from $J_{x_1}, J_{x_2}, \ldots, J_{x_N}$, namely $u_1, u_2, \ldots, u_N$, i.e.,

$$A_e = \sum_{i=1}^{N} u_i/x_i, \qquad u_i \in J_{x_i} \subseteq [0,1].$$

Examples of A_e are $\mu_{\overline{A}}(x)$ and $\mu_{\underline{A}}(x)$; see, also Fig. 9.22. Note that if each J_{x_i} is discretized into M_i levels, there will be a total of n_A A_e, where

$$n_A = \prod_{i=1}^{N} M_i. \tag{A.4}$$

Mendel and John [22] have presented a Representation Theorem for a general T2 FS, which when specialized to an IT2 FS can be expressed as:

Theorem A.1.1 (Representation Theorem for an IT2 FS). *Assume that primary variable x of an IT2 FS $\widetilde{A}$ is sampled at N values, $x_1, x_2, \ldots, x_N$, and at each of these values its primary memberships u_i are sampled at M_i values, $u_{i1}, u_{i2}, \ldots, u_{iM_i}$. Let A_e^j denote the jth embedded T1 FS for $\widetilde{A}$. Then $\widetilde{A}$ is represented by (A.3), in which*[8]

$$FOU(\widetilde{A}) = \bigcup_{j=1}^{n_A} A_e^j = \bigcup_{x \in X} \{\mu_{\underline{A}}(x), \ldots, \mu_{\overline{A}}(x)\} \equiv \bigcup_{x \in X} [\mu_{\underline{A}}(x), \mu_{\overline{A}}(x)] \equiv [\underline{A}, \overline{A}]. \quad \blacksquare \tag{A.5}$$

This representation of an IT2 FS, in terms of simple T1 FSs, the embedded T1 FSs, is very useful for deriving theoretical results, such as the centroid, cardinality, fuzziness, variance and skewness of IT2 FSs [16], the Jaccard similarity measure [16], Rickard *et al.*'s subsethood measure [18].

A.2 *Linguistic Weighted Average (LWA)*

$\widetilde{Y}_{\text{LWA}}$, as expressed by (1), is itself an IT2 FS that is characterized by its $FOU(\widetilde{Y}_{\text{LWA}})$, i.e.,

$$FOU(\widetilde{Y}_{\text{LWA}}) = [\underline{Y}_{\text{LWA}}, \overline{Y}_{\text{LWA}}] \tag{A.6}$$

where $\underline{Y}_{\text{LWA}}$ and $\overline{Y}_{\text{LWA}}$ are the LMF and UMF of $\widetilde{Y}_{\text{LWA}}$, respectively. So, to compute $\widetilde{Y}_{\text{LWA}}$, one only needs to compute $\underline{Y}_{\text{LWA}}$ and $\overline{Y}_{\text{LWA}}$.

Recall from the Representation Theorem [(A.3) and (A.5)] that

$$\widetilde{X}_i = 1/FOU(\widetilde{X}_i) = 1/[\underline{X}_i, \overline{X}_i] \tag{A.7}$$

$$\widetilde{W}_i = 1/FOU(\widetilde{W}_i) = 1/[\underline{W}_i, \overline{W}_i] \tag{A.8}$$

as shown in Figs. 9.23 and 9.24. Because in (1) $\widetilde{X}_i$ only appears in the numerator of $\widetilde{Y}_{\text{LWA}}$, it follows that

$$\underline{Y}_{\text{LWA}} = \min_{\forall W_i \in [\underline{W}_i, \overline{W}_i]} \frac{\sum_{i=1}^{n} \underline{X}_i W_i}{\sum_{i=1}^{n} W_i} \tag{A.9}$$

$$\overline{Y}_{\text{LWA}} = \max_{\forall W_i \in [\underline{W}_i, \overline{W}_i]} \frac{\sum_{i=1}^{n} \overline{X}_i W_i}{\sum_{i=1}^{n} W_i} \tag{A.10}$$

[8] Although there are a finite number of embedded T1 FSs, it is customary to represent $\widetilde{A}$ as an interval set $[\mu_{\underline{A}}(x), \mu_{\overline{A}}(x)]$ at each x. Doing this is equivalent to discretizing with infinitesimally many small values and letting the discretizations approach zero.

An α-cut [24] based approach has been proposed [11, 12] to compute $\underline{Y}_{\text{LWA}}$ and $\overline{Y}_{\text{LWA}}$ efficiently, and it is briefly introduced next.

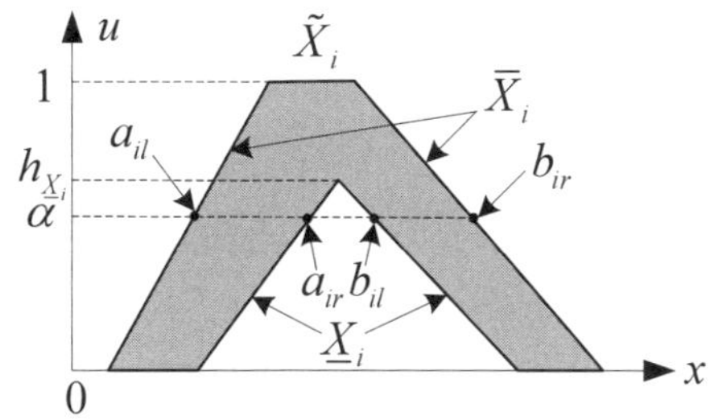

Figure 9.23 $\widetilde{X}_i$ and an α-cut (Wu and Mendel [11], © 2007, IEEE).

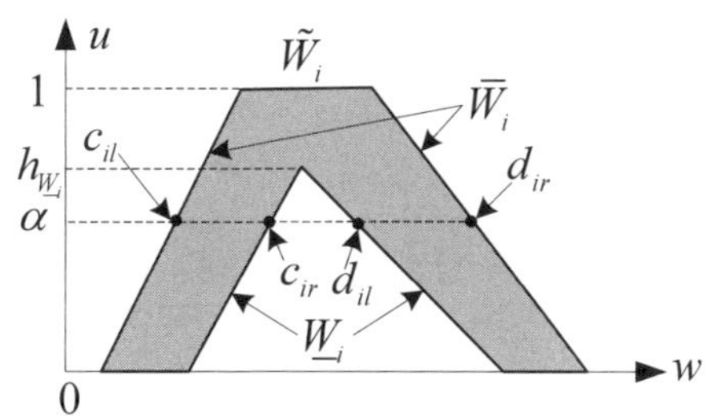

Figure 9.24 $\widetilde{W}_i$ and an α-cut (Wu and Mendel [11], © 2007, IEEE).

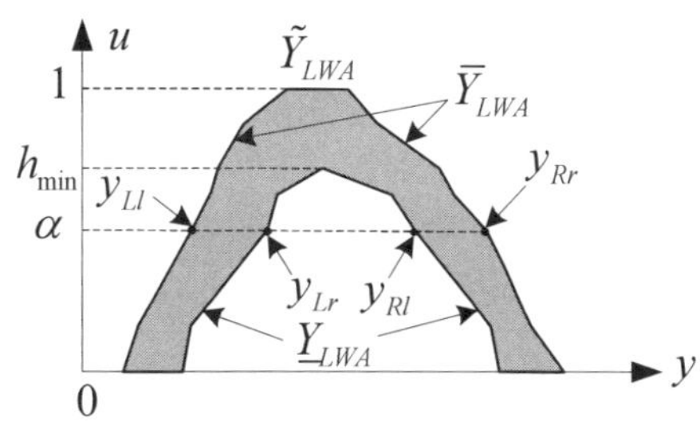

Figure 9.25 $\widetilde{Y}_{\text{LWA}}$ and associated quantities (Wu and Mendel [11], © 2007, IEEE).

First, the heights of $\underline{Y}_{\text{LWA}}$ and $\overline{Y}_{\text{LWA}}$ need to be determined. Because all UMFs are normal T1 FSs, $h_{\overline{Y}_{\text{LWA}}} = 1$. Denote the height of $\underline{X}_i$ as $h_{\underline{X}_i}$ and the height of $\underline{W}_i$ as $h_{\underline{W}_i}$. Let

$$h_{\min} = \min\{\min_{\forall i} h_{\underline{X}_i}, \min_{\forall i} h_{\underline{W}_i}\}. \tag{A.11}$$

Then [12], $h_{\underline{Y}_{\text{LWA}}} = h_{\min}$.

Let $[a_{il}(\alpha), b_{ir}(\alpha)]$ be an α-cut on $\overline{X}_i$, $[a_{ir}(\alpha), b_{il}(\alpha)]$ be an α-cut on $\underline{X}_i$ (see Fig. 9.23), $[c_{il}(\alpha), d_{ir}(\alpha)]$ be an α-cut on $\overline{W}_i$, $[c_{ir}(\alpha), d_{il}(\alpha)]$ be an α-cut on $\underline{W}_i$ (see Fig. 9.24), $[y_{Ll}(\alpha), y_{Rr}(\alpha)]$ be an α-cut on $\overline{Y}_{\text{LWA}}$, and $[y_{\text{Lr}}(\alpha), y_{\text{Rl}}(\alpha)]$ be an α-cut on $\underline{Y}_{\text{LWA}}$ (see Fig. 9.25), where the subscripts l and L mean *left* and r and R mean *right*. The end-points of the α-cuts on $\widetilde{Y}_{\text{LWA}}$ are computed as solutions to the following four optimization problems [11, 12]:

$$y_{Ll}(\alpha) = \min_{\forall w_i \in [c_{il}(\alpha), d_{ir}(\alpha)]} \frac{\sum_{i=1}^n a_{il}(\alpha) w_i}{\sum_{i=1}^n w_i}, \quad \alpha \in [0,1] \tag{A.12}$$

$$y_{Rr}(\alpha) = \max_{\forall w_i \in [c_{il}(\alpha), d_{ir}(\alpha)]} \frac{\sum_{i=1}^n b_{ir}(\alpha) w_i}{\sum_{i=1}^n w_i}, \quad \alpha \in [0,1] \tag{A.13}$$

$$y_{\text{Lr}}(\alpha) = \min_{\forall w_i \in [c_{ir}(\alpha), d_{il}(\alpha)]} \frac{\sum_{i=1}^n a_{ir}(\alpha) w_i}{\sum_{i=1}^n w_i}, \quad \alpha \in [0, h_{\min}] \tag{A.14}$$

$$y_{\text{Rl}}(\alpha) = \max_{\forall w_i \in [c_{ir}(\alpha), d_{il}(\alpha)]} \frac{\sum_{i=1}^n b_{il}(\alpha) w_i}{\sum_{i=1}^n w_i}, \quad \alpha \in [0, h_{\min}] \tag{A.15}$$

Furthermore [11, 12]:

Theorem A.2.2. *(a) $y_{Ll}(\alpha)$ in (A.12) is computed as*

$$y_{Ll}(\alpha) = \frac{\sum_{i=1}^{L_l^*} a_{il}(\alpha) d_{ir}(\alpha) + \sum_{i=L_l^*+1}^n a_{il}(\alpha) c_{il}(\alpha)}{\sum_{i=1}^{L_l^*} d_{ir}(\alpha) + \sum_{i=L_l^*+1}^n c_{il}(\alpha)}, \quad \alpha \in [0,1] \tag{A.16}$$

(b) $y_{Rr}(\alpha)$ in (A.13) is computed as

$$y_{Rr}(\alpha) = \frac{\sum_{i=1}^{R_r^*} b_{ir}(\alpha) c_{il}(\alpha) + \sum_{i=R_r^*+1}^n b_{ir}(\alpha) d_{ir}(\alpha)}{\sum_{i=1}^{R_r^*} c_{il}(\alpha) + \sum_{i=R_r^*+1}^n d_{ir}(\alpha)}, \quad \alpha \in [0,1] \tag{A.17}$$

(c) $y_{Lr}(\alpha)$ in (A.14) is computed as

$$y_{Lr}(\alpha) = \frac{\sum_{i=1}^{L_r^*} a_{ir}(\alpha) d_{il}(\alpha) + \sum_{i=L_r^*+1}^n a_{ir}(\alpha) c_{ir}(\alpha)}{\sum_{i=1}^{L_r^*} d_{il}(\alpha) + \sum_{i=L_r^*+1}^n c_{ir}(\alpha)}, \quad \alpha \in [0, h_{\min}] \tag{A.18}$$

(d) $y_{Rl}(\alpha)$ in (A.15) is computed as

$$y_{Rl}(\alpha) = \frac{\sum_{i=1}^{R_l^*} b_{il}(\alpha) c_{ir}(\alpha) + \sum_{i=R_l^*+1}^n b_{il}(\alpha) d_{il}(\alpha)}{\sum_{i=1}^{R_l^*} c_{ir}(\alpha) + \sum_{i=R_l^*+1}^n d_{il}(\alpha)}, \quad \alpha \in [0, h_{\min}] \tag{A.19}$$

In these equations L_l^*, R_r^*, L_r^* and R_l^* are switch points that are computed using KM or EKM Algorithms [4, 25]. ■

Observe from (A.16), (A.17), and Figs. 9.23 and 9.24 that $y_{Ll}(\alpha)$ and $y_{Rr}(\alpha)$ only depend on the UMFs of $\widetilde{X}_i$ and $\widetilde{W}_i$, i.e., they are only computed from the corresponding α-cuts on the UMFs of $\widetilde{X}_i$ and $\widetilde{W}_i$; so,

$$\overline{Y}_{\text{LWA}} = \frac{\sum_{i=1}^n \overline{X}_i \overline{W}_i}{\sum_{i=1}^n \overline{W}_i}. \tag{A.20}$$

Because all $\overline{X}_i$ and $\overline{W}_i$ are normal T1 FSs, $\overline{Y}_{\text{LWA}}$ is also normal. The algorithm for computing $\overline{Y}_{\text{LWA}}$ is:

(1) Calculate $y_{Ll}(\alpha_j)$ and $y_{Rr}(\alpha_j)$, $j = 1,\ldots,m$. To do this:

(a) Select appropriate m α-cuts for $\overline{Y}_{\text{LWA}}$ (e.g., divide $[0,1]$ into $m-1$ intervals and set $\alpha_j = (j-1)/(m-1)$, $j = 1,2,\ldots,m$).
(b) Find the corresponding α-cuts on $\overline{X}_i$ and $\overline{W}_i$ ($i = 1,\ldots,n$) for each α_j; denote the end-points of the α-cuts as $[a_{il}(\alpha_j), b_{ir}(\alpha_j)]$ and $[c_{il}(\alpha_j), d_{ir}(\alpha_j)]$, respectively.
(c) Use a KM or EKM algorithm to find $y_{Ll}(\alpha_j)$ in (A.16) and $y_{Rr}(\alpha_j)$ in (A.17).
(d) Repeat Steps (b) and (c) for every α_j ($j = 1,\ldots,m$), and then go to Step 2.

(2) Construct $\overline{Y}_{\text{LWA}}$ from the m α-cuts. To do this:

(a) Store the left-coordinates $(y_{Ll}(\alpha_j), \alpha_j)$, $j = 1,\ldots,m$.
(b) Store the right-coordinates $(y_{Rr}(\alpha_j), \alpha_j)$, $j = 1,\ldots,m$.
(c) (Optional) Fit a spline curve through the $2m$ coordinates just stored.

Similarly, observe from (A.18), (A.19), and Figs. 9.23 and 9.24 that $y_{\text{Lr}}(\alpha)$ and $y_{\text{Rl}}(\alpha)$ only depend on the LMFs of $\widetilde{X}_i$ and $\widetilde{W}_i$; hence,

$$\underline{Y}_{\text{LWA}} = \frac{\sum_{i=1}^{n} \underline{X}_i \underline{W}_i}{\sum_{i=1}^{n} \underline{W}_i}. \tag{A.21}$$

Unlike $\overline{Y}_{\text{LWA}}$, which is a normal T1 FS, the height of $\underline{Y}_{\text{LWA}}$ is $h_{\min}$, the minimum height of all $\underline{X}_i$ and $\underline{W}_i$. The algorithm for computing $\underline{Y}_{\text{LWA}}$ is:

(1) Calculate $y_{\text{Lr}}(\alpha_j)$ and $y_{\text{Rl}}(\alpha_j)$, $j = 1,\ldots,p$. To do this:

(a) Determine $h_{\underline{X}_i}$ and $h_{\underline{W}_i}$, $i = 1,\ldots,n$, and $h_{\min}$ in (A.11).
(b) Select appropriate p α-cuts for $\underline{Y}_{\text{LWA}}$ (e.g., divide $[0, h_{\min}]$ into $p-1$ intervals and set $\alpha_j = h_{\min}(j-1)/(p-1)$, $j = 1,2,\ldots,p$).
(c) Find the corresponding α-cuts $[a_{ir}(\alpha_j), b_{il}(\alpha_j)]$ and $[c_{ir}(\alpha_j), d_{il}(\alpha_j)]$ on $\underline{X}_i$ and $\underline{W}_i$.
(d) Use a KM or EKM algorithm to find $y_{\text{Lr}}(\alpha_j)$ in (A.18) and $y_{\text{Rl}}(\alpha_j)$ in (A.19).
(e) Repeat Steps (c) and (d) for every α_j, $j = 1,\ldots,p$, and then go to Step 2.

(2) Construct $\underline{Y}_{\text{LWA}}$ from the p α-cuts. To do this:

(a) Store the left-coordinates $(y_{\text{Lr}}(\alpha_j), \alpha_j)$, $j = 1,\ldots,p$.
(b) Store the right-coordinates $(y_{\text{Rl}}(\alpha_j), \alpha_j)$, $j = 1,\ldots,p$.

(c) (Optional) Fit a spline curve through the $2p$ coordinates just stored.

In summary, computing $\widetilde{Y}_{\text{LWA}}$ is equivalent to computing two FWAs, $\overline{Y}_{\text{LWA}}$ and $\underline{Y}_{\text{LWA}}$. A flowchart for computing $\underline{Y}_{\text{LWA}}$ and $\overline{Y}_{\text{LWA}}$ is given in Fig. 9.26. For triangular or trapezoidal IT2 FSs, it is possible to reduce the number of α-cuts for both $\underline{Y}_{\text{LWA}}$ and $\overline{Y}_{\text{LWA}}$ by choosing them only at *turning points*, i.e., points on the LMFs and UMFs of X_i and W_i $(i = 1,2,\ldots,n)$ at which the slope of these functions changes.

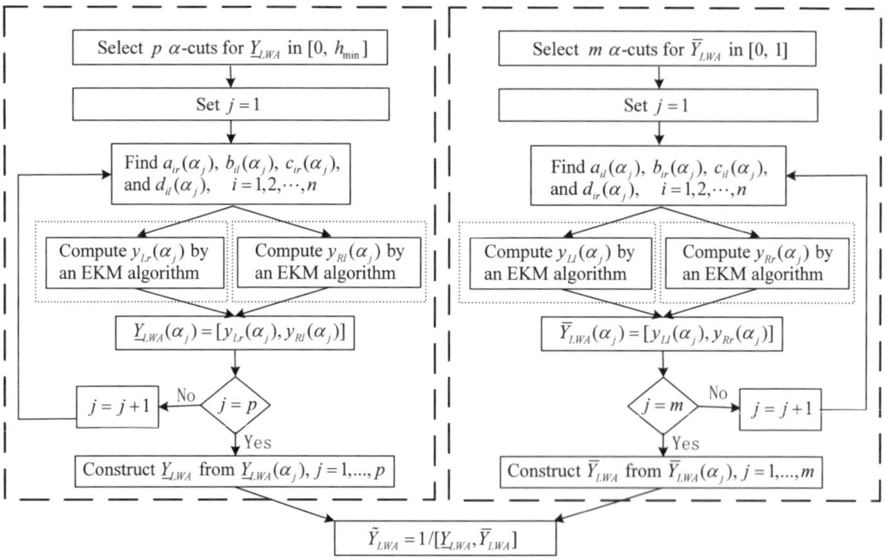

Figure 9.26 A flowchart for computing the LWA (Wu and Mendel [12], © 2008, IEEE).

Bibliography

[1] L. A. Zadeh, Fuzzy logic = Computing with words, *IEEE Trans. on Fuzzy Systems*, **4**, 103–111, (1996).

[2] L. A. Zadeh, From computing with numbers to computing with words – From manipulation of measurements to manipulation of perceptions, *IEEE Trans. on Circuits and Systems–I*, **46** (1), 105–119, (1999).

[3] T. S. Wallsten and D. V. Budescu, A review of human linguistic probability processing: General principles and empirical evidence, *The Knowledge Engineering Review*, **10**(1), 43–62, (1995).

[4] J. M. Mendel, *Uncertain Rule-Based Fuzzy Logic Systems: Introduction and New Directions*, (Prentice-Hall, Upper Saddle River, NJ, 2001).

[5] J. M. Mendel, Computing with words, when words can mean different things to different people, In *Proc. 3rd Int'l ICSC Symposium on Fuzzy Logic and Applications*, pp. 158–164, Rochester, NY (June, 1999).

[6] J. M. Mendel, Computing with words and its relationships with fuzzistics, *Information Sciences*, **177**, 988–1006, (2007).

[7] J. M. Mendel, An architecture for making judgments using computing with words, *Int'l Journal of Applied Mathematics and Computer Science*, **12**(3), 325–335, (2002).

[8] L. A. Zadeh, Toward a generalized theory of uncertainty (GTU)–an outline, *Information Sciences*, **172**, 1–40, (2005).

[9] L. A. Zadeh, Toward human level machine intelligence – Is it achievable? The need for a paradigm shift, *IEEE Computational Intelligence Magazine*, **3**(3), 11–22, (2008).

[10] F. Liu and J. M. Mendel, Encoding words into interval type-2 fuzzy sets using an interval approach, *IEEE Trans. on Fuzzy Systems*, **16**(6), 1503–1521, (2008).

[11] D. Wu and J. M. Mendel, Aggregation using the linguistic weighted average and interval type-2 fuzzy sets, *IEEE Trans. on Fuzzy Systems*, **15**(6), 1145–1161, (2007).

[12] D. Wu and J. M. Mendel, Corrections to "Aggregation using the linguistic weighted average and interval type-2 fuzzy sets", *IEEE Trans. on Fuzzy Systems*, **16**(6), 1664–1666, (2008).

[13] F. Liu and J. M. Mendel, Aggregation using the fuzzy weighted average, as computed using the Karnik-Mendel algorithms, *IEEE Trans. on Fuzzy Systems*, **12**(1), 1–12, (2008).

[14] D. Wu and J. M. Mendel, Perceptual reasoning for perceptual computing: A similarity-based approach, submitted for publication in *IEEE Trans. on Fuzzy Systems*, **17** (6), 1397–1411, (2009).

[15] D. Wu and J. M. Mendel, Similarity-based perceptual reasoning for perceptual computing, *Proc. IEEE Int'l Conf. on Fuzzy Systems*, pp. 700–705, Jeju Island, South Korea (August, 2009).

[16] D. Wu and J. M. Mendel, A comparative study of ranking methods, similarity measures and uncertainty measures for interval type-2 fuzzy sets, *Information Sciences*, **179**(8), 1169–1192, (2009).

[17] J. M. Mendel and D. Wu, Perceptual reasoning for perceptual computing, *IEEE Trans. on Fuzzy Systems*, **16**(6), 1550–1564, (2008).

[18] D. Wu and J. M. Mendel, Interval type-2 fuzzy set subsethood measures as a decoder for perceptual reasoning, USC-SIPI Report 398, Signal and Image Processing Institute, University of Southern California, Los Angeles, CA, (2010).

[19] J. M. Mendel and D. Wu, *Perceptual Computing: Aiding People in Making Subjective Judgments*, (Wiley-IEEE Press, to appear in 2010).

[20] I. Vlachos and G. Sergiadis, Subsethood, entropy, and cardinality for interval-valued fuzzy sets – an algebraic derivation, *Fuzzy Sets and Systems*, **158**, 1384–1396, (2007).

[21] J. M. Mendel, H. Hagras, and R. I. John, Standard background material about interval type-2 fuzzy logic systems that can be used by all authors, http://ieee-cis.org/_files/standards.t2.win.pdf.

[22] J. M. Mendel and R. I. John, Type-2 fuzzy sets made simple, *IEEE Trans. on Fuzzy Systems*, **10** (2), 117–127 (2002).

[23] J. T. Rickard, J. Aisbett, and G. Gibbon, Fuzzy subsethood for fuzzy sets of type-2 and generalized type-*n*, *IEEE Trans. on Fuzzy Systems*, **17**(1), 50–60, (2009).

[24] G. J. Klir and B. Yuan, *Fuzzy Sets and Fuzzy Logic: Theory and Applications*, (Prentice-Hall, Upper Saddle River, NJ, 1995).

[25] D. Wu and J. M. Mendel, Enhanced Karnik-Mendel Algorithms, *IEEE Trans. on Fuzzy Systems*, **17**(4), 923–934, (2009).

Chapter 10

Realizing Policies by Projects Using Fuzzy Multiple Criteria Decision Making

Cengiz Kahraman and İhsan Kaya

İstanbul Technical University, Department of Industrial Engineering, 34367 Maçka, İstanbul, Turkey

E-mail: {kahramanc, kayai}@itu.edu.tr

The policy-making process is flexible and innovative, questioning established ways of dealing with things, encouraging new and creative ideas; and where appropriate, making established ways work better. The advice and decisions of policy makers are based upon the best available evidence from a wide range of sources; all key stakeholders are involved at an early stage and throughout the policy's development. The policy-making process takes into account of the impact on and/or meets the needs of all people directly or indirectly affected by the policy; and involves key stakeholders directly. Determining the best policy can be taken into consideration as a decision making problem which is the process of finding the best option from all of the feasible alternatives. In real-case problems, because of incomplete or non-obtainable information, the data (attributes) are usually vague. Consequently fuzziness is a necessity that must be taken into account in policy making since it is based on human beings' judgments. An expression like "This policy has more importance with respect to a considered criterion than the other policy with respect to the same criterion" should be evaluated using fuzzy sets which are one of the main computational techniques. In this chapter, a fuzzy analytic hierarchy process technique is used to evaluate the proposed alternative policies to decrease traffic congestion in Istanbul.

10.1 Introduction

A policy is a course or principle of action adopted or proposed by a government, party, business or individual. Policy making is the process by which governments translate their political vision into programmes and actions to deliver 'outcomes' - desired changes in the real world. Effective policy making is one of the most important services that the public service provides to government. For policy making to be fully effective, civil servants involved in policy development not only need all the 'traditional' attributes (knowledge of relevant law and practice, understanding of key stakeholders' views, ability to design implementation systems), but they must also understand the context within which they (and the policy) have to work. Figure 10.1 sets out the analyses and process which policy-makers need to apply (`http://www.ofmdfmni.gov.uk`). There are tools and techniques that can help in making a policy more effectively.

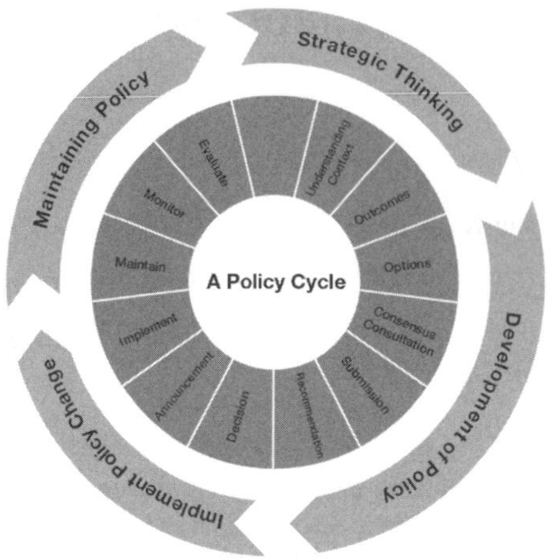

Figure 10.1 A policy cycle.

The birth of computational intelligence (CI) is attributed to the IEEE World Congress on Computational Intelligence in 1994 at Orlando, Florida [22]. Since that time not only a great number of papers and scientific events have been dedicated to CI, but also numerous explanations of the term have been published. In order to have a brief outline of history of the term the founding and most interesting definitions will be summarized below:

The first one was proposed by Bezdek [2] as follows: "A system is called computationally intelligent if it deals only with numerical (low-level) data, has a pattern recognition component, and does not use knowledge in the artificial intelligence (AI) sense; and additionally, when it (begins to) exhibit (i) computational adaptivity; (ii) computational fault tolerance; (iii) speed approaching human-like turnaround, and (iv) error rates that approximate human performance." Marks [18] defined CI by listing the building blocks being neural nets, genetic algorithms, fuzzy systems, evolutionary programming, and artificial life. Eberhart *et al.* [8] defined CI as follows: "Computational intelligence is defined as a methodology involving computing (whether with a computer, wetware, etc.) that exhibits an ability to learn and/or deal with new situations such that the system is perceived to possess one or more attributes of reason, such as generalisation, discovery, association, and abstraction." Computational intelligence, which consists of neural network, fuzzy logic and evolutionary computing, and so on, is a novel technology to bring intelligence into computation. CI techniques have been used to solve different problems successfully. The readers can find more details about CI techniques in Chapter 1.

In this chapter, a multiple criteria decision making technique based on analytic hierarchy process (AHP), introduced by Saaty [23], is proposed under fuzzy environments to evaluate alternative projects which aim at decreasing traffic congestion in Istanbul.

The rest of this chapter is organized as follows: The decision making process and some multiple criteria decision making approaches are summarized in Section 10.2. The proposed fuzzy multiple criteria decision making (FMCDM) methodology is explained in Section 10.3. The details of application that the proposed methodology is applied to decrease traffic congestion in Istanbul are illustrated in Section 10.4. Conclusions and future research directions are explained in Section 10.5.

10.2 Multiple Criteria Decision Making

Decision-making problem, such as making decision on order of the projects, is the process of finding the best option among all of the feasible alternatives. It has been one of the fastest growing areas during the last decades depending on the changing in the business sector. In almost all such problems there may be so many criteria and the process of evaluating the efficiency of alternatives is a complicated problem. That is, for many such problems, decision makers put multiple criteria decision making (MCDM) techniques into account. Especially in the last years, where computer usage has increased significantly, the application of MCDM methods has considerably become easier for the users and the decision makers as the application of most of the methods are corresponded with complex mathematics. Generally the primary concern of MCDM problems is to choose the most preferred alternative, or ranking alternatives in order of importance for selection problems, or screening alternatives for the final decision.

There are many MCDM approaches which differ in how they combine and utilize the data. MCDM approaches can be classified on the basis of the major components of multiple criteria decision analysis. Three different classifications can be made as follows: multi-objective decision-making (MODM) versus multi-attribute decision-making (MADM); individual versus group decision-making problems; and decisions under certainty versus decisions under uncertainty. The distinction between MADM and MODM is based on the evaluation criteria which are the standards of judgments or rules on which the alternatives are ranked according to their desirability. *Criterion* is a general term and includes both the concepts of attributes and objectives. An attribute is a measurable quantity whose value reflects the degree to which a particular objective is achieved. An objective is a statement about the desired state of the system under consideration. It indicates the directions of improvement of attributes. Objectives are functionality-related to, or derived from, a set of attributes [10].

The main steps of multiple criteria decision making are as follows [12]:

(a) Establishing system evaluation criteria that relate system capabilities to goals;
(b) Developing alternative systems for attaining the goals (generating alternatives);
(c) Evaluating alternatives in terms of criteria (the values of the criterion functions);
(d) Applying a normative multiple criteria analysis method;
(e) Accepting one alternative as "optimal" (preferred);
(f) If the final solution is not accepted, gather new information and go into the next iteration of multiple criteria optimization.

In the literature some multiple criteria approaches are available to help decision making process as briefly explained below:

Analytic Hierarchy Process

Analytic Hierarchy Process is a structured approach to decision making developed by Saaty [23]. It is a weighted factor-scoring model and has the ability to detect and incorporate inconsistencies inherent in the decision making process. Therefore, it has been applied to a wide variety of decision making problems, including the evaluation of alternatives.

Outranking Methods

The outranking methods are based on the construction and the exploitation of an outranking relation. The underlying idea consists of accepting a result less rich than the one yielded by Multiattribute Utility Theory (MAUT) by avoiding the introduction of mathematical hypotheses which are too strong and asking the decision maker (DM) some questions which are too intricate. The concept of an outranking relation is introduced by Bernard Roy who is the founder of outranking methods. According to Roy [21] an outranking relation is a binary relation S defined on the set of alternatives A such that for any pair of alternatives $(a,b) \in A \times A$: aSb if, given what is known about the preferences of the DM, the quality of the evaluations of the alternatives and the nature of the problem under consideration, there are sufficient arguments to state that the alternative a is at least as good as the alternative b, while at the same time there does not exist any strong reason to refuse this statement [3].

The Preference Ranking Organization Method for Enrichment Evaluations (PROMETHEE) is a multiple criteria decision-making method developed by Brans *et al.* [5]. It is a quite simple ranking method in conception and application compared to other methods for multiple criteria analysis. It is well adapted to problems where a finite number of alternative actions are to be ranked considering several, sometimes conflicting, criteria [29].

Technique for Order Performance by Similarity to Ideal Solution

Technique for Order Performance by Similarity to Ideal Solution (TOPSIS) is one of the well known classical Multi-Attribute Decision Making (MADM) methods. TOPSIS views a MADM problem with m alternatives as a geometric system with m points in an n-dimensional space. It was developed by Hwang and Yoon [11]. The method is based on the concept in which the chosen alternative should have the shortest distance from the positive-ideal solution and the longest distance from the negative-ideal solution. TOPSIS defines an index called similarity (or relative closeness) to the positive-ideal solution and the remoteness from the negative-ideal solution. Then the method chooses an alternative with the maximum similarity to the positive-ideal solution.

Multiattribute Utility Theory

Multiattribute Utility Theory (MAUT) allows the decision-maker to quantify and aggregate multiple objectives even when these objectives are composed of conflicting attributes. The decision-maker's preferences are modeled in order to obtain a multiattribute utility function, for instance $U(c_i,t_i,d_i)$. This function aggregates utility functions for all criteria or attributes. That is, an analytical function is obtained which combines all criteria through a synthesis function. Each particular analytical form for this function has preferential independence conditions to be evaluated, in order to guarantee that the decision maker's preferences are associated to the basic axioms of the theory [1, 15].

Simple Additive Weighting Method

The Simple Additive Weighting Method, which is also known as Weighted Sum Method [11] is probably the most commonly used MADM approach, particularly in dealing with a single dimensional problem. This approach is based on the hypothesis that in any decision problem, there exists a real utility function defined by the set of feasible actions, which the DM wishes to evaluate. The method is characterized by the additive utility assumption, referring to the total value of each alternative being equal to the sum of the products of the criteria ratings and their weight from the respective alternatives.

Weighted Product Method

For a multi-dimensional MADM problem involving different units of measurement, the Weighted Product Method is supposed to be more appropriate for application when the attributes are connected by a multiplication operation. Accordingly, the weights become exponents with respect to each attribute value, which takes a positive value in the case of maximization and a negative value for minimization problems.

VIKOR

The VIKOR method was developed for multiple criteria optimization of complex systems. It determines the compromise ranking-list, the compromise solution, and the weight stability intervals for preference stability of the compromise solution obtained with the initial (given) weights. This method focuses on ranking and selecting from a set of alternatives in the presence of conflicting criteria. It introduces the multiple criteria ranking index based on the particular measure of "closeness" to the "ideal" solution. Assuming that each alternative is evaluated according to each criterion function, the compromise ranking could be performed by comparing the measure of closeness to the ideal alternative [20].

Multiobjective Methods

In multiple objective decision-making (MODM), application functions are established to measure the degree of fulfillment of the DM's requirements (achievement of goals, closeness to an ideal point, satisfaction, etc.) on the objective functions and are extensively used in the process of finding "good compromise" solutions. MODM methodologies can be categorized in a variety of ways, such as form of model (e.g., linear, nonlinear, stochastic), characteristic of decision space (e.g., finite or infinite), or solution process (e.g., prior specification of preferences or interactive). Among MODM methods, we can list multi-objective linear programming (MOLP) and its variants such as multi-objective stochastic integer linear programming, interactive MOLP and mixed 0-1 MOLP; multi-objective goal programming (MOGoP); multi-objective geometric programming (MOGeP); multi-objective non-linear fractional programming; multi-objective dynamic programming and multi-objective genetic programming.

Analytic hierarchy process is one of the most used group decision making techniques. The traditional AHP needs exact judgments. In addition, due to the complexity and uncertainty involved in real world decision problems, it is sometimes unrealistic or even impossible to perform exact comparisons. It is therefore more natural or realistic that a decision-maker is allowed to provide fuzzy judgments instead of precise comparisons. In this chapter, AHP based on the fuzzy set theory is applied on decision making process.

10.3 The Proposed Methodology

Sometimes a decision maker's judgments are not crisp, and it is relatively difficult for the decision maker to provide exact numerical values. Therefore most of the evaluation parameters cannot be given as precisely and the evaluation data of the alternative project's suitability for various subjective criteria and the weights of the criteria are usually expressed in linguistic terms by the DMs. In this case, fuzzy logic that provides a mathematical strength to capture the uncertainties associated with human cognitive process can be used. In this chapter, a fuzzy multiple criteria decision making methodology is proposed to select the best project alternative to avoid traffic congestion.

The fuzzy set theory was specifically designed to mathematically represent uncertainty and vagueness and provide formalized tools for dealing with the imprecision intrinsic to many problems. The roots of fuzzy set theory go back to 1965 when Zadeh initiated the concept of Fuzzy Logic Zadeh [30]. It uses approximate information and uncertainty to generate decisions. This is why it looks somewhat similar to human reasoning. Since knowledge can be expressed in a more natural way by using fuzzy sets, many engineering and decision problems can be greatly simplified. Fuzzy set theory implements groupings of data with loosely defined boundaries. Keeping this in mind, any methodology or theory implementing "crisp" definitions may be "fuzzified", if needed, by generalizing the concept of a crisp set to a fuzzy set with blurred boundaries. The main benefit of extending crisp analysis methods to fuzzy techniques is the strength in solving real-world problems, which has imprecision in the variables and parameters measured and processed for the application. To achieve this benefit, linguistic variables are used as a critical aspect of some fuzzy logic applications. If a variable can take words in natural languages as its value, it is called a linguistic variable, where the words such as "good", "mediocre", and "bad" are characterized by fuzzy sets defined in the universe of discourse in which the variable is defined. Several geometric mapping functions have been widely adopted, such as triangular, trapezoidal and S-shaped membership functions (MF) where the triangular MF is a special case of trapezoidal one. Within this chapter, standardized trapezoidal fuzzy numbers (STFNs) are used.

A trapezoidal fuzzy number, $\widetilde{A}(a,b,c,d)$, is a normal, convex fuzzy set, on the real line, with a piecewise continuous membership function, as illustrated in Fig. 10.2, such that there are four points $a \leqslant b \leqslant c \leqslant d$ with the following properties and membership function shown in (1):

(1) $\mu(x) = 0$ for every $x \in (-\infty, a) \cup (d, \infty)$
(2) μ is increasing on $[a,b]$ and decreasing on $[c,d]$
(3) $\mu(a) = \mu(d) = 0$ and $\mu(x) = 1$, for every $x \in [b,c]$

$$\mu_{\widetilde{A}}(x) = \begin{cases} \dfrac{x-a}{b-a}, & \text{for} \quad a \leqslant x \leqslant b \\ 1 & \text{for} \quad b \leqslant x \leqslant c \\ \dfrac{d-x}{d-c}, & \text{for} \quad c \leqslant x \leqslant d \\ 0 & \text{for} \quad \text{Otherwise} \end{cases} \tag{1}$$

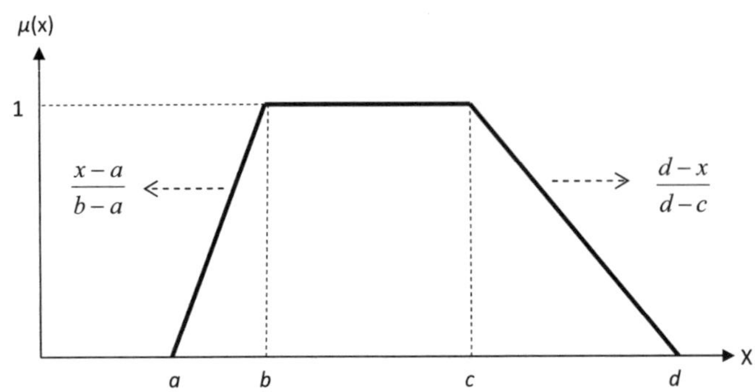

Figure 10.2 Membership function of an STFN.

The cases $a = -\infty$ and $d = \infty$ are admitted and, then, the fuzzy number will be, by the left or by the right, asymptotically zero, so its support will not be bounded.

As mentioned in the preceding sections, both the benefits and the costs embedded in a very important strategic investment projects are mostly intangible. This is the main reason making the investment decision evaluation extremely hard. If sufficient objective data were available, the probability theory would be preferred in such a decision analysis. Unfortunately, decision makers do not have enough information to perform such a decision analysis, since probabilities can never be known with certainty and the decisions about strategic level information technology investments are attributable to many uncertain derivations. In this situation, decision makers should rely on decision makers' knowledge in modeling projects which are investments to decrease traffic congestion. To deal quantitatively with such an imprecision or uncertainty, the fuzzy set theory is used.

According to Zeng *et al.* [31], influential factors can be decomposed by brainstorming or checklist techniques, scored by fuzzy membership functions and weighed by AHP. However, one drawback of the current AHP method is that it can only deal with definite scales in reality. To deal with this drawback, fuzzy AHP is proposed. A fuzzy AHP is an important extension of the typical AHP method which was first introduced by Laarhoven and Pedrycz [16]. Later, some other fuzzy AHP approaches were developed and applied to some industrial problems [6, 7, 13].

In this chapter, a modified AHP method proposed by Zeng *et al.* [31] combined with a different fuzzy ranking method is used for selecting the traffic congestion project best fitting the municipality's policies. In this method, fuzzy aggregation is used to create group decisions, then defuzzication is employed to transform the fuzzy scales into crisp scales for the computation of priority weights. The group preference of each factor is then calculated by applying fuzzy aggregation operators, i.e., fuzzy multiplication and addition operators. Here are the steps of the methodology [31]:

Step 1: Measure the factors in the hierarchy. The decision makers are required to provide their judgments on the basis of their knowledge and expertise for each factor at the bottom level in the hierarchy. As different decision makers having different perspectives could have different influence on the final decision, a fuzzy eigenvector based weighting is used in the model to calculate the decision makers' competence. The decision makers can provide a precise numerical value, a range of numerical values, a linguistic term or a fuzzy number. For m decision makers in the evaluation group, the ith decision maker is assigned a weight, c_i where $c_i \in [0,1]$, and $c_1 + c_2 + \cdots + c_m = 1$.

Step 2: Compare the factors using pair-wise comparisons. The attributes having impacts on the selection of a project are listed and classified in a hierarchical structure as can be seen in Figure 10.3. The pair-wise comparison matrixes for the main and sub-criteria are built by a simple Microsoft Excel based evaluation form. A modified fuzzy AHP method is applied to work out the priority weights of selected attributes. In a typical AHP method, decision makers would have to give a definite number from Table 10.1 to the pair-wise comparison so that the priority vector can be computed.

However, attribute comparisons often involve certain amount of uncertainty and subjectiv-

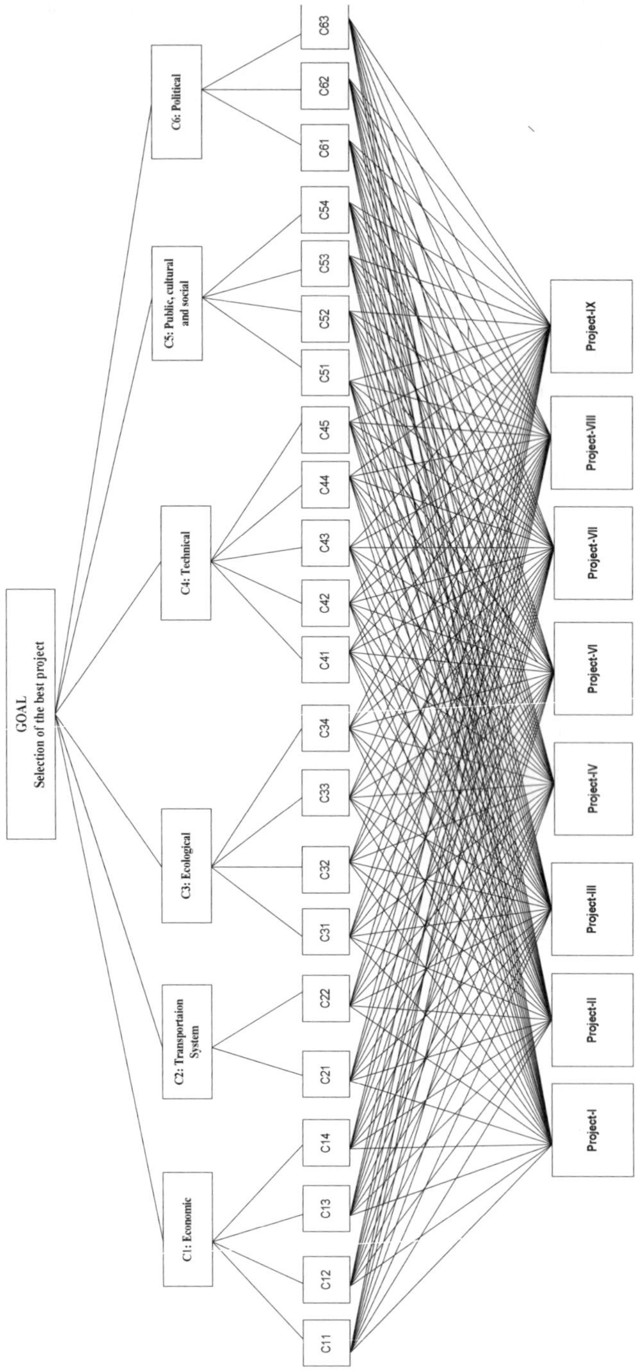

Figure 10.3 Hierarchical structure of the alternative projects.

Table 10.1 Scale of relative importances [23]

Intensity of importance	Definition	Explanation
1	Equal importance	Two activities contribute equally to the objective
3	Weak importance of one over another	Experience and judgment slightly favor one activity over another
5	Essential or strong importance	Experience and judgment strongly favor one activity over another
7	Demonstrated importance	An activity is strongly favored and its dominance demonstrated in practice
9	Absolute importance	The evidence favoring one activity over another is of the highest possible order of affirmation
2, 4, 6, 8	Intermediate values between the two adjacent judgments	When compromise is needed
Reciprocals of above non-zero	If activity i has one of the above non-zero numbers assigned to it when compared with activity j, then j has the reciprocal value when compared with i.	

ity. Here are two very important special examples to illustrate this situation: (*i*) Assume that, a decision maker is sure that attribute 1 is more important than attribute 2, but he/she cannot give a definite score to the comparison because of being not sure about the degree of importance for attribute 1 over attribute 2. In this case, the decision maker may prefer to provide a range of 3–5 to describe the comparison as, "attribute 1 is between weakly more important to strongly more important than attribute 2". (*ii*) Assume that, the decision maker cannot compare two attributes due to the lack of adequate information. In this case, a typical AHP method has to be discarded due to the existence of fuzzy or incomplete comparisons.

A modified fuzzy AHP is used in this study to overcome these shortcomings. The decision makers are required to compare every attribute pair-wise in their corresponding group structured in the hierarchy attached in Figure 10.3, and define scores of the project alternatives against these attributes.

Step 3: Convert preferences into STFNs. As described in Steps 1 and 2, because the values of factors provided by experts are crisps, e.g., a numerical value, a range of numerical value, a linguistic term or a fuzzy number, the STFN is employed to convert these experts' judgments into a universal format for the composition of group preferences. A crisp numerical value, a range of crisp numerical values and a triangular fuzzy number can be converted to an STFN as follows:

(1) A crisp number "n" is converted to the STFN as $\widetilde{A} = (n,n,n,n)$ (*i.e.*, $a = b = c = d = n$);
(2) A linguistic term, "*about n*", is converted to the STFN as $\widetilde{A} = (n-1,n,n,n+1)$ (*i.e.*, $a = n-1$, $b = c = n$, $d = n+1$);
(3) A range, the scale is likely between (n,m), is converted to the STFN as $\widetilde{A} = (n,n,m,m)$ (*i.e.*, $a = b = n$, $c = d = m$);
(4) A triangular fuzzy number, $\widetilde{T} = (x,y,z)$, is converted to the STFN as $\widetilde{A} = (x,y,y,z)$ (*i.e.*, $a = x$, $b = c = y$, $d = z$);
(5) If a decision maker cannot compare any two factors at all, then it is represented with $\widetilde{A} = (0,0,0,0)$ (*i.e.*, $a = b = c = d = 0$).

The decision makers are encouraged to give fuzzy scales if they are not sure about the exact numerical values or leave some comparisons absent as they cannot compare two attributes at all. In each case, as can be understood from the conversion information in the brackets above, a single STFN is employed to convert these decision makers' judgments into a generic format for the composition of group preferences.

Step 4: Aggregate individual STFNs into group STFNs. This step aims to apply an appropriate operator to aggregate individual preferences made by individual expert into a group preference of each factor. The aggregation of STFN scores is performed by applying the fuzzy weighted trapezoidal averaging operator, which is defined by

$$\widetilde{S}_i = \widetilde{S}_{i1} \otimes c_1 \oplus \widetilde{S}_{i2} \otimes c_2 \oplus \cdots \oplus \widetilde{S}_{im} \otimes c_m \tag{2}$$

where $\widetilde{S}_i$ is the fuzzy aggregated score of the factor F_i, $\widetilde{S}_{i1}, \widetilde{S}_{i2}, \ldots, \widetilde{S}_{im}$ are the STFN scores of the factor F_i measured by m decision makers $DM_1, DM_2, \ldots, DM_m$, respectively, $\otimes$ and $\oplus$ denote the fuzzy multiplication operator and the fuzzy addition operator, respectively, and $c_1, c_2, \ldots, c_m$ are contribution factors (CFs) allocated to decision maker, $DM_1, DM_2, \ldots, DM_m$ and $c_1 + c_2 + \cdots + c_m = 1$.

Similarly, the aggregation of STFN scales is defined as

$$\widetilde{a}_{ij} = \widetilde{a}_{ij1} \otimes c_1 \oplus \widetilde{a}_{ij2} \otimes c_2 \oplus \cdots \oplus \widetilde{a}_{ijm} \otimes c_m \tag{3}$$

where $\widetilde{a}_{ij}$ is the aggregated fuzzy scale of attribute i comparing to attribute j for $i, j = 1, 2, \ldots, n$; $\widetilde{a}_{ij1}, \widetilde{a}_{ij2}, \ldots, \widetilde{a}_{ijm}$ are the corresponding STFN scales of attribute i comparing to attribute j measured by decision makers $DM_1, DM_2, \ldots, DM_m$, respectively.

It should be noted that the aggregation should discard the absent scale while it comes with non zero scales provided by other decision makers under the same comparison. This process can be defined as follows.

$$\widetilde{a}_{ij} = \frac{\widetilde{a}_{ij1} \otimes c_1 + \widetilde{a}_{ij2} \otimes c_2 + \cdots + \widetilde{a}_{ijm} \otimes c_m}{1 - \sum c_r} \tag{4}$$

where $\sum c_r$ is the total weight of decision makers who provide zero scales. If none of the decision makers can evaluate a particular comparison, this comparison should be left absent.

Step 5: After having all the required aggregated STFNs, it is now time for defuzzification to find the representative crisp numbers. Assume an aggregated STFN, $\widetilde{a}_{ij} = \left(a^a_{ij}, a^b_{ij}, a^c_{ij}, a^d_{ij}\right)$, the representative crisp value a_{ij} can be obtained as follows:

$$a_{ij} = \frac{a^a_{ij} + 2\left(a^b_{ij} + a^c_{ij}\right) + a^d_{ij}}{6} \tag{5}$$

where $a_{ii} = 1$, and $a_{ji} = 1/a_{ij}$.

Consequently, all the aggregated fuzzy scales $\widetilde{a}_{ij}$ $(i, j = 1, 2, \ldots, n)$ are transferred into crisp scales a_{ij} within the range of $[0, 9]$.

Step 6: Calculate the priority weights of factors. Let $F_1, F_2, \ldots, F_n$ be a set of factors in one section, a_{ij} be the defuzzified scale representing the quantified judgment on F_i comparing to F_j. Assuming $A_1, A_2, \ldots, A_n$ represent a set of attributes in one group, pair-wise comparisons between A_i and A_j in the same group yield an n-by-n matrix defined as follows:

$$A = a_{ij} = \begin{array}{c|cccc} & F_1 & F_2 & \ldots & F_4 \\ F_1 & 1 & a_{12} & \ldots & a_{1n} \\ F_2 & {}^1/_{a_{12}} & 1 & \ldots & a_{2n} \\ F_3 & \ldots & \ldots & \ldots & \ldots \\ F_4 & {}^1/_{a_{1n}} & {}^1/_{a_{2n}} & \ldots & 1 \end{array} \quad , \quad i, j = 1, 2, \ldots, n \tag{6}$$

where $a_{ii} = 1$, $a_{ji} = 1/a_{ij}$.

The priority weights of factors in the matrix A can be calculated by using the arithmetic averaging method

$$w_i = \frac{1}{n}\sum_{j=1}^{n} \frac{a_{ij}}{\sum_{k=1}^{n} a_{kj}} \quad i, j = 1, 2, \ldots, n. \tag{7}$$

where w_i is the section weight of F_i. Assume F_i has t upper sections at different level in the hierarchy, and $w^{(i)}_{\text{section}}$ is the section weight of the ith upper section which contains F_i in the hierarchy, the final weight w'_i of F_i can be derived by

$$w'_i = w_i \times \prod_{i=1}^{t} w^{(i)}_{\text{group}} \tag{8}$$

All individual upper section weights of $w^{(i)}_{\text{group}}$ can also be derived by (7) to prioritize sections within the corresponding cluster in the hierarchy.

Step 7: Calculate final fuzzy scores. When the scores and the priority weights of factors are obtained, the final fuzzy scores $\left(\widetilde{FS}\right)$ can be calculated by

$$\left(\widetilde{FS}\right) = \sum_{i=1}^{n} \widetilde{S}_i w_i' \qquad i = 1, 2, \ldots, n \tag{9}$$

Step 8: Compare the $\left(\widetilde{FS}\right)$ values using an outranking method.
In this chapter a method proposed by Tran and Duckstein [26] is used to ranking final fuzzy scores. The method is based on the comparison of distances from fuzzy numbers (FNs) to some predetermined targets: the crisp maximum (Max) and the crisp minimum (Min). The idea is that a FN is ranked first if its distance to the crisp maximum ($D_{\max}$) is the smallest but its distance to the crisp minimum ($D_{\min}$) is the greatest. If only one of these conditions is satisfied, the FN might be outranked by the others depending upon context of the problem (for example, the attitude of the decision maker in a decision situation).
The Max and Min are chosen as follows:

$$\begin{aligned} \mathrm{Max}(I) &\geqslant \sup\left(\bigcup_{i=1}^{I} s\left(\widetilde{A}_i\right)\right) \\ \mathrm{Min}(I) &\leqslant \inf\left(\bigcup_{i=1}^{I} s\left(\widetilde{A}_i\right)\right) \end{aligned} \tag{10}$$

where $s(A_i)$ is the support of FNs A_i, $i = 1, \ldots, n$. Then $D_{\max}$ and $D_{\min}$ of fuzzy number A can be computed as follows:

$$D^2\left(\widetilde{A}, M\right) = \begin{cases} \left[\begin{array}{l} \left(\frac{a_2+a_3}{2} - M\right)^2 + \frac{1}{2}\left(\frac{a_2+a_3}{2} - M\right) \times [(a_4-a_3)-(a_2-a_1)] \\ +\frac{1}{3}\left(\frac{a_3-a_2}{2}\right)^2 + \frac{1}{6}\left(\frac{a_3-a_2}{2}\right) \times [(a_4-a_3)+(a_2-a_1)] \\ +\frac{1}{9}\left[(a_4-a_3)^2 + (a_2-a_1)^2\right] - \frac{1}{9}[(a_2-a_1)\times(a_4-a_3)] \end{array}\right] \\ \qquad \text{if } \widetilde{A} \text{ is a trapezoidal fuzzy number} \\ \left[\begin{array}{l} (a_2-M)^2 + \frac{1}{2}(a_2-M)[(a_3+a_1)-2M] \\ +\frac{1}{9}\left[(a_3-a_2)^2 + (a_2-a_1)^2\right] - \frac{1}{9}[(a_2-a_1)(a_3-a_2)] \end{array}\right] \\ \qquad \text{if } \widetilde{A} \text{ is a triangular fuzzy number} \end{cases} \tag{11}$$

where M is either *Max* or *Min*. Hence,

$$D_{\max} = \sqrt{D^2\left(\widetilde{A}, \mathrm{Max}\right)} \text{ and } D_{\min} = \sqrt{D^2\left(\widetilde{A}, \mathrm{Min}\right)} \tag{12}$$

Table 10.2 The Population of Istanbul [27]

Year	Population	Change (%)
1990	7,195,773	–
2000	10,018,735	39.23
2007	12, 573, 836	25.50

10.4 An Application

Istanbul is Europe's most populous city and Turkey's cultural and financial center. Istanbul has a population of 12, 573, 836 residents according to the latest count as of 2007. Istanbul is located in the north-west Marmara Region of Turkey. The city covers 27 districts of the Istanbul province. It extends both on the European (Thrace) and on the Asian (Anatolia) side of the Bosphorus, and is thereby the only metropolis in the world which is situated on two continents. In its long history, Istanbul served as the capital city of the Roman Empire (330-395), the Byzantine Empire (395-1204 and 1261-1453), the Latin Empire (1204-1261), and the Ottoman Empire (1453-1922). The city was chosen as joint European Capital of Culture for 2010. The historic areas of Istanbul were added to the UNESCO World Heritage List in 1985. The population of Istanbul has begun to rapidly increase as people from Anatolia migrated to the city since it is the most-industrialized city in Turkey, having the 40 % of industry of Turkey. In Table 10.2, the population of Istanbul and changes with respect to the years 1990-2007 are presented. Since the population's excessive increase, the city has been face to face by many problems [14].

Istanbul has been suffering from traffic for over 20 years since it is the vital part of the industry and being overpopulated. As a result of the lack in public transportation vehicles, excessive number of private cars, lacks of expert staff, employees, private cars carrying only 1-2 passengers, geographical features, unplanned expansion, infeasibilities in the existing structure, problems in parking, and coordination problems with authority the traffic problem of Istanbul arises more and more.

The present number of vehicles in Istanbul is 2.5 million that is 20 % of Turkey. The total number of cars is 1.8 million that is 29 % of Turkey and the daily number of vehicles in traffic is 1.7 million that 1.6 million of them are private cars and daily number of vehicles joining Istanbul traffic is 400. Also, the total length of highway is nearly 12,000 kilometers and approximately 15 million journeys are made every day in the metropolitan area. Istanbul has two bridges in which the first called Boğaziçi Bridge and the second called

Table 10.3 The Distribution of Highway Transportation

Type of Vehicle	Number of Vehicles	Daily Passenger
Private cars	1,600,000	2,100,000
IETT Buses	2,500	1,700,000
Public Buses	1,300	1,100,000
Minibuses	7,000	2,000,000
Dolmuş	590	80,000
Taxis	18,000	1,100,000
Company Services	35,500	2,150,000
TOTAL	1,664,890	10,230,000

Fatih Sultan Mehmet Bridge to links Asia and Europe. The daily number of travels between Asia and Europe is 1.3 million that 34 % of which are made by private cars, 49 % of which are made by public transportation vehicles, and 17 % of which is made by waterborne [4]. 90 % of Istanbul transportation is made by land-based transportation which includes private cars, public buses, minibuses, metro buses, taxis, and vehicles for company services; 3.5 % is made by waterborne which includes ships, fast ferries and private motorboats and 6.5 % is made by rail transportation which includes trains, subways, tramcars, IETT nostalgic tramcars and tunnel, light metro. Istanbul's traffic is managed by three local organizations administrated by Istanbul Metropolitan Municipality (IMM) and two central governmental organizations. The largest and first local organization which controls highway and railway public transportation mostly is Istanbul Establishment of Electricity, Trams and Tunnel (IETT). The other two local organizations are Istanbul Fast Ferries Co. (IDO) which is in charge of sea transportation which was established in 1988. The governmental organizations are Turkish Republic Railways Organization (TCDD) and Turkish Sea Transportation Organization (TDI). Besides, transportation is also met by the private sector in Istanbul. Taxis, minibuses, private motorboats, and public buses carry a high percentage of passengers.

Tables 10.3-10.5 show distributions of highway transportation, sea transportation and railway transportation, respectively [4].

According to Table 10.3, the most important part belongs to company services, private cars, minibuses and IETT Buses while the TDI ships are the most important vehicles among sea based transportation as can be seen from Table 10.4.

According to Table 10.5, all vehicle types except tunnel and nostalgic tramcar are almost equally important among railway transportation vehicles.

Table 10.4 The Distribution of Sea Transportation

Type of Vehicle	Number of Vehicles	Daily Passenger
TDI Ships	74	250,000
IDO Ferries	26	30,000
Motorboats	236	160,000
TOTAL	336	440,000

Table 10.5 The Distribution of Railway Transportation

Type of Vehicle	Number of Vehicles	Daily Passenger
TCDD Trains	72	125,000
Light Metro	19	190,000
Tramcars	11	160,000
Subway	9	130,000
IETT Tunnel & Nostalgic Tramcar	5	11,000
TOTAL	116	616,000

Republic of Turkey Ministry of Transportation and Communication has managed two important projects which are Marmaray and Third Bosphorus Bridge in Istanbul.

Istanbul Strait Rail Tube Crossing and Commuter Railway Upgrading (MARMARAY) Project comprises of three phases as following; (i) Constructing an immersed tube tunnel under the Istanbul Strait with approaching tunnels, three underground and one surface stations, (ii) upgrading the existing commuter rail system including a new third track on ground and completely new electrical and mechanical systems, (iii) procurement of the rolling stock [19].

The Marmaray project which can be shown in Figure 10.4 is the upgrading of approximately 76 km of commuter rail from Halkali, European end, to Gebze, Asian end. It includes the new railway system that will be constructed in tunnels under the Bosphorus and it is called bosphorus crossing (BC Project), which is currently in the early stage of design and construction. The total length of the project is 13.6 km, mainly consisting of 1.4 km of immersed tube, 10.1 km of bored tunnels, 1.3 km of cut and cover tunnels and four numbers of stations [24].

Marmaray Project is finished in 2012. Rail travelers (and rail cargo) currently have to transfered to a ferry for a three-hour journey across the city. Then that will drop to less than two hours. Ideally, the tunnel will also relieve some of the pressure on those bridges. And when

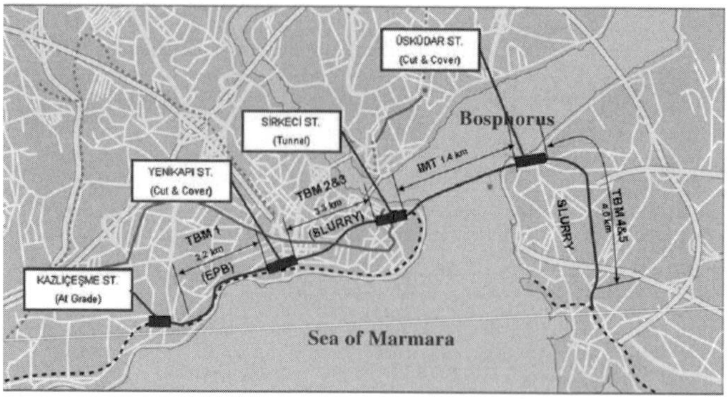

Figure 10.4 Marmaray Project Location [24].

the Marmaray Project is integrated into a planned railway through Azerbaijan, Georgia, and Turkey, you'll be able to hop on a train in London, wave at the Hagia Sofia, and step off days later in Beijing [25].

The Bosphorus, a strait that physically divides Istanbul into two parts, is currently spanned by two bridges. The first bridge was constructed in 1973 and the second bridge, called as Fatih Sultan Mehmet Bridge, was subsequently constructed in 1989 when the first bridge became inadequate after a short period of time. Currently they are both inadequate in providing the required capacity. For this reason, the construction of a third bridge is considered at the northern end of the Bosphorus, north of the other two bridges, in Istanbul.

These two projects and under construction-projects such as the subway line from "Fourth Levent" to "ITU" and the tramcar line from "ehitlik" to "Topkapı" are reckoned without when the alternative projects are discussed in this chapter. The municipality's policy is that more investment should be made in railway systems. As a result the following nine projects which are located in Figure 10.5 are evaluated with the proposed fuzzy decision making methodology to decrease traffic congestion in Istanbul:

- Project-I: Subway Line from Bağcılar to İkitelli,
- Project-II: Subway Line from Beşiktaş to Otogar,
- Project-III: Ferryboat line from Ortaköy to Beylerbeyi,
- Project-IV: Light Rail System from Üsküdar to Tepeüstü,
- Project-V: Light Rail System from Tepeüstü to Samandıra,
- Project-VI: Tramcar line from Kabataş to Beşiktaş,
- Project-VII: Subway Line from Yenikapı to Bağcılar,

Table 10.6 Main Characteristics of Proposed Projects

Project	Length (km)	Capacity (passenger/day)	Cost ($/million)
I	14.2	70,000	700
II	14	140,000	600
III	2	6,000	30
IV	11.5	70,000	800
V	9.5	70,000	800
VI	1.5	30,000	5
VII	11.8	140,000	600
VIII	10	70,000	800
IX	14.6	70,000	800

- Project-VIII: Light Rail System from Bakırköy to E-5 Bridge,
- Project-IX: Light Rail System from Küçükçekmece to Beylikdüzü.

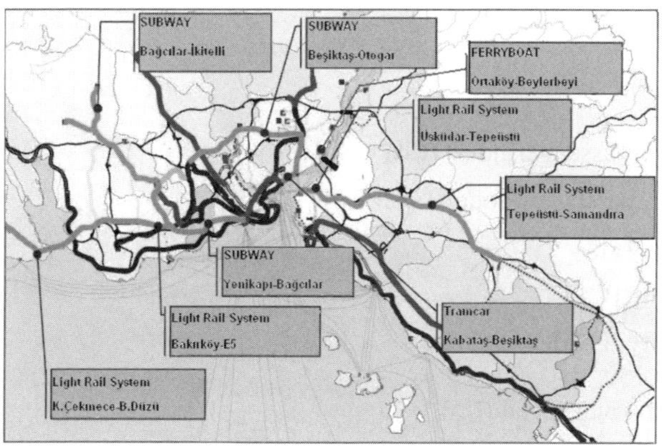

Figure 10.5 The Suggested Projects to Decrease Traffic congestion in Istanbul.

The estimated main characteristics of these projects are shown in Table 10.6.

The following criteria whose hierarchical structure is shown in Figure 10.3 are taken into consideration when the proposed AHP approach is used to evaluate the alternative projects for decreasing traffic congestion in Istanbul. The four level hierarchy composed of 6 main criteria and 22 sub-criteria and nine alternatives is given in Figure 10.3. These criteria have been derivated from the related literature [17, 32, 9, 28] and the interviews with four experts from the municipality and one professor from Istanbul Technical University (ITU), Management Faculty, Department of Industrial Engineering.

- Economic (C1),

(a) Set up cost (C11),
(b) Operation cost (C12),
(c) Economic Value (PW, IRR, B/C) (C13),
(d) Maintenance cost (C14).

- Transportation system (C2),

(a) Contribution to the general transportation system (C21),
(b) Compatibility with the municipality's master plan (C22).

- Ecological (C3),

(a) Negative impacts on the ecosystems during the construction phase (C31),
(b) Negative impacts on the ecosystems during the operation phase (C32),
(c) Contribution/harm to green(C33),
(d) Aesthetic appeal (C34).

- Technical (C4),

(a) Capacity (passenger/hour) (C41),
(b) Demand (passenger/hour) (C42),
(c) Safety (C43),
(d) Feasibility (C44),
(e) Reliability (C45).

- Public, cultural and social (C5),

(a) Negative impacts on the historical environment during the construction phase (C51),
(b) Compatibility with the development of the city, region, and country (C52),
(c) Contribution/harm to social development (C53)
(d) Labour impact (C54).

- Political (C6),

(a) Compatibility with the transportation policy of the government (C61),
(b) Financial possibilities of the government (C62),
(c) Dependency on foreign countries for construction (C63).

In this chapter, the most appropriate project alternative is selected by a FMCDM technique. Five experts evaluate the considered criteria to determine the most appropriate project alternative. Each criterion of the hierarchy is evaluated by experts under the defined criteria. A score system is shown in Figure 10.6. Experts may provide a decision about their judgment as a precise numerical value, a possible range of numerical value, a linguistic term, or a fuzzy number. Then these evaluations are converted into STFNs as defined in Table 10.7.

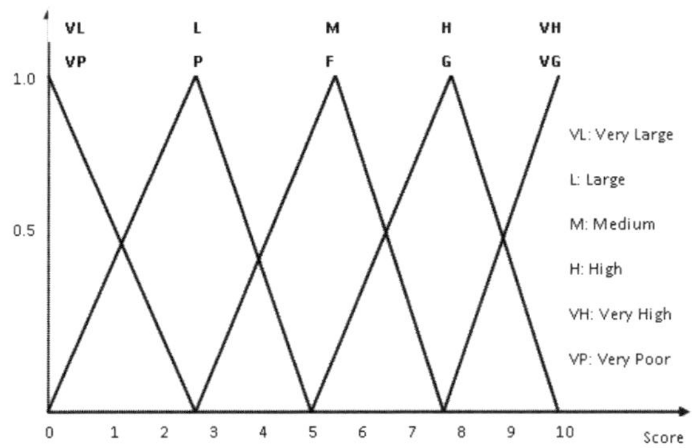

Figure 10.6 Membership Functions for Evaluation.

Table 10.7 provides the fuzzy weights of the criteria for Project VI. The aggregations of the obtained scores are calculated by Eq. (2). For instance, the aggregation of "Set up Cost" under "Economic" section is calculated as follows:

$$
\begin{aligned}
\widetilde{S}_{\text{setup}} &= (5.0,7.5,7.5,10.0)\otimes 0.20 \oplus (5.0,7.5,7.5,10.0)\otimes 0.20 \\
&\oplus (3.0,3.0,5.0,5.0)\otimes 0.20 \oplus (7.0,8.0,8.0,9.0)\otimes 0.20 \\
&\oplus (8.0,9.0,9.0,10.0)\otimes 0.20 \\
\widetilde{S}_{\text{setup}} &= (5.60,7.00,7.40,8.80)
\end{aligned}
$$

The other values for aggregation are shown in Table 10.7. The pair-wise comparisons of "Economic Criteria" and the corresponding STFNs are shown in Table 10.8. The aggregation of STFN scales are calculated by Eq. (3). For example, the STFN scale of comparing

Table 10.7 Scores and Converted STFN for Project VI

		E1		E2		E3		E4		E5		Aggregated
		Score	STFN	Score	STFN	Score	STFN	Score	STFN	Score	STFN	
Technological	C1	VH	(7.5, 10, 10, 10)	10	(10, 10, 10, 10)	9	(9, 9, 9, 9)	A7	(6, 7, 7, 8)	A10	(8, 9, 9, 10)	(8.1, 9, 9, 9.4)
	C2	VH	(7.5, 10, 10, 10)	10	(10, 10, 10, 10)	8	(8, 8, 8, 8)	7	(7, 7, 7, 7)	8	(8, 8, 8, 8)	(8.1, 8.6, 8.6, 8.6)
	C3	H	(5, 7.5, 7.5, 10)	9	(9, 9, 9, 9)	9	(9, 9, 9, 9)	6	(6, 6, 6, 6)	8	(8, 8, 8, 8)	(7.4, 7.9, 7.9, 8.4)
	C4	9	(9, 9, 9, 9)	9	(9, 9, 9, 9)	8,9	(8, 8, 9, 9)	7	(7, 7, 7, 7)	9,10	(9, 9, 10, 10)	(8.4, 8.4, 8.8, 8.8)
	C5	VH	(7.5, 10, 10, 10)	9	(9, 9, 9, 9)	8,9	(8, 8, 9, 9)	G	(5, 7.5, 7.5, 10)	VH	(7.5, 10, 10, 10)	(7.4, 8.9, 9.1, 9.6)
Economic	C1	L	(5, 7.5, 7.5, 10)	L	(5, 7.5, 7.5, 10)	3,5	(3, 3, 5, 5)	A8	(7, 8, 8, 9)	A10	(8, 9, 9, 10)	(5.6, 7, 7.4, 8.8)
	C2	H	(0, 2.5, 2.5, 5)	5	(5, 5, 5, 5)	5,6	(5, 5, 6, 6)	A6	(5, 6, 6, 7)	7	(7, 7, 7, 7)	(4.4, 5.1, 5.3, 6)
	C3	VG	(7.5, 10, 10, 10)	7	(7, 7, 7, 7)	G	(5, 7.5, 7.5, 10)	A9	(8, 9, 9, 10)	9,10	(9, 9, 10, 10)	(7.3, 8.5, 8.7, 9.4)
	C4	L	(5, 7.5, 7.5, 10)	8	(8, 8, 8, 8)	L	(5, 7.5, 7.5, 10)	A9	(8, 9, 9, 10)	7,9	(7, 7, 9, 9)	(6.6, 7.8, 8.2, 9.4)
Ecological	C1	L	(5, 7.5, 7.5, 10)	A4	(3, 4, 4, 5)	8	(8, 8, 8, 8)	A3	(2, 3, 3, 4)	A7	(5, 6, 6, 7)	(4.6, 5.7, 5.7, 6.8)
	C2	L	(5, 7.5, 7.5, 10)	7	(7, 7, 7, 7)	7,8	(7, 7, 8, 8)	A3	(2, 3, 3, 4)	7,8	(7, 7, 8, 8)	(5.6, 6.3, 6.7, 7.4)
	C3	9	(9, 9, 9, 9)	7	(5, 5, 6, 6)	6,8	(6, 6, 8, 8)	A7	(6, 7, 7, 8)	7,9	(7, 7, 9, 9)	(6.6, 6.8, 7.8, 8)
	C4	9,10	(9, 9, 10, 10)	A7	(6, 7, 7, 8)	7,8	(7, 7, 8, 8)	A6	(5, 6, 6, 7)	7,9	(7, 7, 9, 9)	(6.8, 7.2, 8, 8.4)
Transportation System	C1	VH	(7.5, 10, 10, 10)	8,10	(8, 8, 10, 10)	9,10	(9, 9, 10, 10)	A9	(8, 9, 9, 10)	8,9	(8, 8, 9, 9)	(8.1, 8.8, 9.6, 9.8)
	C2	VH	(7.5, 10, 10, 10)	10	(10, 10, 10, 10)	8,8	(8, 8, 8, 8)	H	(5, 7.5, 7.5, 10)	10	(5, 7.5, 7.5, 10)	(7.1, 8.6, 8.6, 9.6)
Public, Cultural and Social	C1	VL	(7.5, 10, 10, 10)	9,10	(9, 9, 10, 10)	9,10	(9, 9, 10, 10)	A7	(6, 7, 7, 8)	8	(8, 8, 8, 8)	(7.9, 8.6, 9, 9.2)
	C2	H	(5, 7.5, 7.5, 10)	8	(8, 8, 5, 8)	8,9	(8, 8, 9, 9)	A5	(4, 5, 5, 6)	7,8	(7, 7, 8, 8)	(6.4, 7.1, 6.9, 8.2)
	C3	H	(5, 7.5, 7.5, 10)	5,6	(5, 5, 6, 6)	8	(8, 8, 8, 8)	A4	(3, 4, 4, 5)	7	(7, 7, 7, 7)	(5.6, 6.3, 6.5, 7.2)
	C4	G	(5, 7.5, 7.5, 10)	A7	(6, 7, 7, 8)	G	(5, 7.5, 7.5, 10)	6,7	(6, 6, 7, 7)	6	(6, 6, 6, 6)	(5.6, 6.8, 7, 8.2)
Political	C1	8	(7, 8, 8, 9)	A7	(6, 7, 7, 8)	9,10	(9, 9, 10, 10)	A9	(8, 9, 9, 10)	7	(7, 7, 7, 7)	(7.4, 8, 8.2, 8.8)
	C2	VG	(7.5, 10, 10, 10)	9	(9, 9, 9, 9)	8	(8, 8, 8, 8)	G	(5, 7.5, 7.5, 10)	G	(5, 7.5, 7.5, 10)	(6.9, 8.4, 8.4, 9.4)
	C3	VL	(7.5, 10, 10, 10)	A8	(7, 8, 8, 9)	7,9	(7, 7, 9, 9)	A7	(6, 7, 7, 8)	8	(8, 8, 8, 8)	(7.1, 8, 8.4, 8.8)

"Operation Cost" with "Maintenance Cost" is aggregated as follows:

$$\begin{aligned}\tilde{a}_{24} = \; & (5.0, 5.0, 6.0, 6.0) \otimes 0.20 \oplus (5.0, 5.0, 5.0, 5.0) \otimes 0.20 \\ & \oplus (5.0, 5.0, 5.0, 5.0) \otimes 0.20 \oplus (4.0, 4.0, 5.0, 5.0) \otimes 0.20 \\ & \oplus (3.0, 3.0, 5.0, 5.0) \otimes 0.20 \\ \tilde{a}_{24} = \; & (4.4, 4.4, 5.2, 5.2)\end{aligned}$$

Then STFN scale of comparisons should be defuzzified. By using Eq. (5), the STFN scale of comparing "Operation Cost" with "Maintenance Cost" is defuzzified as

$$a_{24} = \frac{4.4 + 2(4.4 + 5.2) + 5.2}{6} = 4.80$$

Using Eqs. (6)-(7) the pair-wise comparisons matrix of "Economic Criteria" is obtained as follows:

$$A_{\text{Economic}} = \begin{bmatrix} 1.000 & 0.475 & 2.400 & 8.700 \\ 2.105 & 1.000 & 1.100 & 4.800 \\ 0.417 & 0.909 & 1.000 & 5.200 \\ 0.114 & 0.208 & 0.192 & 1.000 \end{bmatrix}$$

By taking into account this matrix and using Eq. (8) the weights of the sub-criteria of "Economic Criteria" are calculated as follows:

$$w = \{0.3528, 0.3607, 0.2356, 0.0509\}$$

The final weights of the criteria are calculated by using Eq. (8). Then the $\widetilde{FS}$ of Project VI is calculated by using Eq. (9) as follows:

$$\widetilde{FS}_{\text{Pr}-VI} = (6.68, 7.55, 7.83, 8.89)$$

$\widetilde{FS}$ values of project alternatives are also calculated. The results are shown in Table 10.9. The membership functions of these fuzzy scores are shown in Figure 10.7.

In the last step of the proposed methodology, the fuzzy scores need to be ranked. To rank the fuzzy scores the method explained in Section 10.3 is used. The ranking results are summarized in Table 10.10.

According to Table 10.10, Project VI whose D_{max} and D_{min} values are minimum, and maximum, respectively is determined as the best project alternative to decrease traffic congestion in Istanbul. The ranking of project alternative is determined as follows: {VI – II - IV - V - VII - I - IX – VIII-III}.

Table 10.8 Fuzzy Aggregation of Economic Criteria for Project-VI

	C11			C12			C13			C14		
	Experts	Scale	STFN	Scale		STFN	Scale		STFN	Scale		STFN
C11	E1			0.50	0.75	(0.5, 0.5, 0.75,0.75)	3.00	3.00	(3,3,3,3)	9.00	10.00	(9,9,10,10)
	E2			0.25	0.50	(0.25, 0.25, 0.5, 0.5)	2.00	2.00	(2, 2, 2,2)	9.00	9.00	(9, 9, 9, 9)
	E3			0.50	0.50	(0.5, 0.5, 0.5, 0.5)	2.00	3.00	(2, 2, 3,3)	8.00	8.00	(8, 8, 8, 8)
	E4			0.50	0.50	(0.5, 0.5, 0.5, 0.5)	2.00	3.00	(2, 2, 3,3)	9.00	9.00	(9, 9, 9, 9)
	E5			0.25	0.50	(0.25, 0.25, 0.5, 0.5)	2.00	2.00	(2, 2, 2,2)	7.00	9.00	(7, 7, 9, 9)
	Aggregation		1.00			(0.4, 0.4, 0.55, 0.55)			(2.2, 2.2,2.6, 2.6)			(8.4, 8.4, 9, 9)
C12	E1						1.00	1.00	(1, 1, 1, 1)	5.00	6.00	(5, 5, 6, 6)
	E2						1.00	2.00	(1, 1, 2, 2)	5.00	5.00	(5, 5, 5, 5)
	E3						1.00	1.00	(1, 1, 1, 1)	5.00	5.00	(5, 5, 5, 5)
	E4						1.00	1.00	(1, 1, 1, 1)	4.00	5.00	(4, 4, 5, 5)
	E5						1.00	1.00	(1, 1, 1, 1)	3.00	5.00	(3, 3, 5, 5)
	Aggregation					1.00			(1, 1, 1.2, 1.2)			(4.4, 4.4, 5.2, 5.2)
C13	E1									5.00	7.00	(5, 5, 7, 7)
	E2									5.00	5.00	(5, 5, 5, 5)
	E3									4.00	6.00	(4, 4, 6, 6)
	E4									3.00	5.00	(3, 3, 5, 5)
	E5									5.00	7.00	(5, 5, 7, 7)
	Aggregation								1.00			(4.4, 4.4, 6, 6)
C14	E1											
	E2											
	E3											
	E4											
	E5											
	Aggregation											1.00

Table 10.9 Fuzzy Scores of Alternative Projects

Alternatives	Fuzzy Scores
Project-I	(4.43, 5.26, 5.47, 6.59)
Project-II	(5.11, 5.94, 6.13, 7.22)
Project-III	(3.71, 4.58, 4.76, 5.91)
Project-IV	(5.05, 5.84, 6.03, 7.1)
Project-V	(4.98, 5.77, 5.93, 7.02)
Project-VI	(6.68, 7.55, 7.83, 8.89)
Project-VII	(4.91, 5.71, 5.89, 7.01)
Project-VIII	(3.93, 4.8, 4.95, 6.1)
Project-IX	(3.99, 4.83, 5, 6.11)

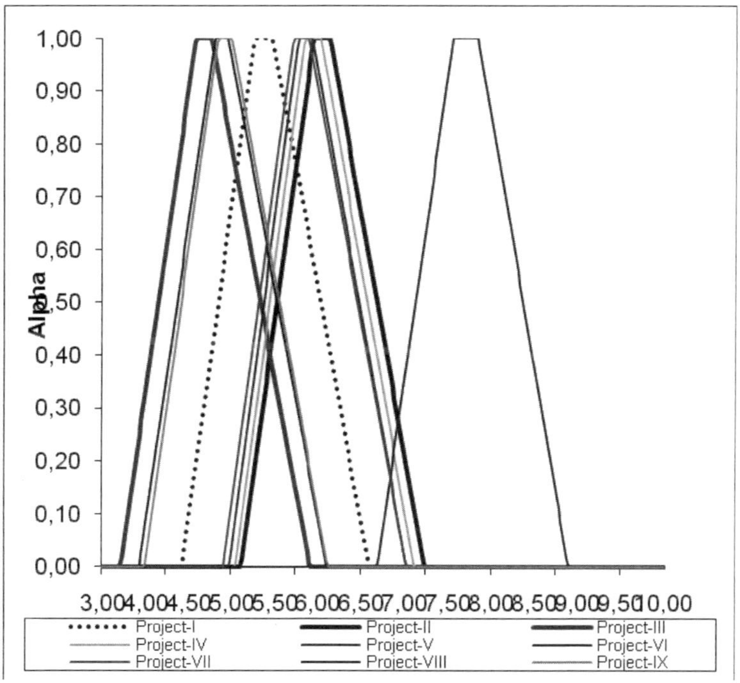

Figure 10.7 The Membership Functions of Fuzzy Scores for Alternative Projects

10.5 Conclusions

Traffic congestion occurs when a volume of traffic generates demand for space greater than the available road capacity. There are a number of specific circumstances which cause or aggravate congestion; most of them reduce the capacity of a road at a given point or over a

Table 10.10 The comparisons results for alternative projects

Alternatives	a_1	a_2	a_3	a_4	D_{max}	D_{min}	Ranking
Project-I	4.43	5.26	5.47	6.59	4.580	5.449	6
Project-II	5.11	5.94	6.13	7.22	3.916	6.113	2
Project-III	3.71	4.58	4.76	5.91	5.275	4.754	9
Project-IV	5.05	5.84	6.03	7.10	4.013	6.014	3
Project-V	4.98	5.77	5.93	7.02	4.093	5.933	4
Project-VI	6.68	7.55	7.83	8.89	2.296	7.749	1
Project-VII	4.91	5.71	5.89	7.01	4.136	5.892	5
Project-VIII	3.93	4.80	4.95	6.10	5.068	4.960	8
Project-IX	3.99	4.83	5.00	6.11	5.030	4.997	7

certain length, or increase the number of vehicles required for a given throughput of people or goods. Traffic congestion in Istanbul is unavoidable event since around 2 million vehicles are in Istanbul traffic every day. Recently, İstanbul Metropolitan Municipality and Republic of Turkey Ministry of Transportation and Communication are working on not only extending sea, highway, and railway transportations and but also improving mass transportation. After the Marmaray and Third Bosphorus Projects are finished, traffic congestion is expected to decrease. They also discuss about precautions to avoid traffic congestion. The best policy to decrease the effects of traffic congestion in Istanbul is determined as investment for railway transportation projects. The alternative projects are evaluated by a multi criteria decision making technique which includes the fuzzy set theory that is one of the most important techniques of computational intelligence. The fuzzy set theory is a powerful tool to treat the uncertainty in case of incomplete or vague information. The proposed fuzzy multiple criteria decision making methodology allows experts to be flexible and use a large evaluation pool including linguistic terms, fuzzy numbers, precise numerical values, and ranges of numerical values. Hence, the proposed methodology has the ability of taking care of all kinds of evaluations from experts. It has been successfully applied to determine the best project alternative to decrease traffic congestion in Istanbul.

In this study three out of the nine projects are related to subway, four of them are related to light rail system, one of them is related to ferry boat line and the last one is related to tramcar line, which are evaluated as a result of the municipality's policy that more investment should be made in railway systems. These projects have been evaluated to determine the most suitable. As a result the project, "tramcar line from Kabataş to Beşiktaş", is determined as the best alternative while the two next are "subway Line from Beşiktaş to Otogar" and "light rail system from Üsküdar to Tepeüstü". The authorities of IMM should give the first priority of project for the "tramcar line from Kabataş to Beşiktaş". If it is not possible to perform the project, the other projects should be considered by taking into account the proposed order.

In the future research, the proposed fuzzy multiple criteria decision making approach can be used to evaluate alternative projects for sea and highway projects in Istanbul.

Bibliography

[1] Almeida, A.T., 2007, Multicriteria decision model for outsourcing contracts selection based on utility function and ELECTRE method, Computers & Operations Research, 34, 3569–3574.

[2] Bezdek, J. C., 1994, What is computational intelligence?, In: Zurada, J.M., Marks, R.J., Robinson, C.J., (Eds.), Computational Intelligence, Imitating Life, IEEE Computer Society Press, 1–12.

[3] Boer, L.D., Wegen, L.V., Telgen, J., 1998, Outranking methods in support of supplier selection, European Journal of Purchasing & Supply Management, 4(2-3), 109–118.

[4] Bozdoğan, R., 2005, Transportation Systems Of Istanbul, 8th World Congress Metropolis, Commission 4: Urban Mobility Management, http://www.stadtentwicklung.berlin.de/archiv/metropolis2005/en/dokumentation/c4.html

[5] Brans, J.P., Vincke, P., Mareschal, B., 1986, How to select and how to rank projects: The PROMETHEE method, European Journal of Operational Research, 24, 228–38.

[6] Buckley, J.J., 1985, Fuzzy hierarchical analysis, Fuzzy Sets and Systems, 17, 233–247.

[7] Chang, D. Y., 1996, Applications of the extent analysis method on fuzzy AHP, European Journal of Operational Research, 95, 649–655.

[8] Eberhart, R., Simpson, P., Dobbins, R., 1996, Computational Intelligence PC Tools, Academic Press, Boston.

[9] Gercek, H., Karpak, B., Kılınçarslan, T., 2004, A multiple criteria approach for the evaluation of the rail transit networks in Istanbul, Transportation, 31, 203–228.

[10] Gharehgozli, A.H., Rabbani, M., Zaerpour, N., Razmi, J., 2008, A comprehensive decision-making structure for acceptance/rejection of incoming orders in make-to-order environments, International Journal of Advanced Manufacturing Technology, 39, 1016–1032.

[11] Hwang, C.L., and Yoon, K., 1981, Multiple attribute decision making methods and applications, New York: Springer-Verlag.

[12] Jahanshahloo, G.R., Hosseinzadeh, L.F, Izadikhah, M., 2006, Extension of the TOPSIS method for decision-making problems with fuzzy data, Applied Mathematics and Computation, 181, 1544–1555.

[13] Kahraman, C., Cebeci, U., Ruan, D., 2004, Multi-attribute comparison of catering service companies using fuzzy AHP: The case of Turkey, International Journal of Production Economics, 87, 171–184.

[14] Kaya, İ., Kahraman, C., 2009, Fuzzy robust process capability indices for risk assessment of air pollution, Stochastic Environmental Research and Risk Assessment, 23(4), 529-541.

[15] Keeney, R.L., Raiffa, H., 1976, Decision with multiple objectives: preferences and value tradeoffs, NewYork: Wiley.

[16] Laarhoven, P.J.M., Pedrycz W., 1983, A fuzzy extension of Saaty's priority theory, Fuzzy Set Systems, 11, 229–241.

[17] Lee G.K.L., Chan, E. H. W., 2008, The analytic hierarchy process (AHP) approach for asses-

ment of urban renewal proposals, Social Indicators Research, 89(1), 155–168.
[18] Marks, R., 1993, Computational versus artificial, IEEE Transactions on Neural Networks, 4, 737–739.
[19] Marmaray Project, 2009, http://www.ubak.gov.tr/eubak/projects/marmaray
[20] Opricovic, S., Tzeng, G.H., 2004, Compromise solution by MCDM methods: A comparative analysis of VIKOR and TOPSIS, European Journal of Operational Research, 156, 445–455.
[21] Roy, B., 1974. Critères multiples et modélisation des préférences: l'apport des relations de surclassement, Revue d'Economie Politique, 1, 1–44.
[22] Rudas, I. J., Fodor, J., 2008, Intelligent Systems, International Journal of Computers, Communications & Control, 3, 132–138.
[23] Saaty, T.L., 1980, The analytic hierarchy process, New York: McGraw-Hill.
[24] Sakaeda, H., 2009, Marmaray project: Tunnels and stations in BC contract, Tunnelling and Underground Space Technology, Article in press.
[25] Smith, J., 2007, Quake fears, ancient finds have europe-asia tunnel on nonstop delay, Wired Magazine, Issue 15.09,
http://www.wired.com/science/planetearth/magazine/15-09/ff_quake.
[26] Tran, L, Duckstein, L, 2002, Comparison of fuzzy numbers using a fuzzy distance measure, Fuzzy Sets and Systems, 130, 331–341.
[27] TurkStat-Turkish Statistical Institute, 2009, www.tuik.gov.tr
[28] Ülengin, F., Topçu, İ., 1997, Cognitive map: KBDSS integration in transportation planning, Journal of the Operational Research Society, 48, 1065–1075.
[29] Wang, J.J. and Yang, D.L., 2007, Using a hybrid multi-criteria decision aid method for information systems outsourcing, Computers & Operations Research, 34, 3691–3700.
[30] Zadeh, L., 1965, Fuzzy sets, Information Control, 8, 338–353.
[31] Zeng, J., An, M., Smith, N.J., 2007, Application of a fuzzy based decision making methodology to construction project risk assessment, International Journal of Project Management, 25, 589–600.
http://www.ofmdfmni.gov.uk/practical-guide-policy-making.pdf
[32] Çalışkan, 2006, A decision support approach for the evaluation of transport investment alternatives, European Journal of Operational Research, 175, 1696–1704..

Chapter 11

Evolutionary Computation Methods for Fuzzy Decision Making on Load Dispatch Problems

Guoli Zhang[1], Guangquan Zhang[2], Ya Gao[2], and Jie Lu[2]

[1] *School of Mathematics and Physics, North China Electric Power University, Baoding 071003, China*

E-mail: zhangguoli@ncepu.edu.cn

[2] *Faculty of Engineering and Information Technology, University of Technology, Sydney, PO Box 123, Broadway NSW 2007, Australia*

{zhangg, yagao,jielu}@it.uts.edu.au

This chapter introduces basic concepts relating to a day-ahead market in a power system. A load dispatch model considers a ramp rate and valve-point-loading effects. An environment/economic load dispatch model is presented to handle uncertainty factors. The model provides theoretical foundations for the research on operations and decision making in the electric power market. To solve load dispatch problems from day-ahead markets in power systems, a hybrid evolutionary computation method with a quasi-simplex technique, a weight point method for multi-objective programming, and a fuzzy-number-ranking-based optimization method for fuzzy multi-objective non-linear programming are developed.

11.1 Models for Day-ahead Markets

The load dispatch in a spot market is one of the kernel problems in an electric power market. It not only relates to the benefits of every participant in the market, but is also a key issue to assure safety, reliability of the power system and order operation of the electric power market. Although a lot of achievements have been obtained, there are still many problems to be solved for the power market operation. This section introduces the basic concepts of electric power markets and builds up two load dispatch models for a day-ahead market.

11.1.1 *Introduction*

In a traditional generation electricity plan, the electricity price is determined by the generated electricity cost. In general, one price corresponds to one unit, and the price is fixed for a long time. Under an electric power market environment, since the previous pricing mechanism is unreasonable to represent fair trading and reflect the market status of supply and demand, many new price methods have been proposed. There are two typical electricity prices widely used in electric power markets. One is the so-called uniform market clearing price (MCP) or system marginal price (SMP) which can be obtained by the highest bidding of the unit committed. The other is pay-as-bid price (PAB). SMP represents the fairness of merchandise price, i.e., the same quality electric energy should have the same electricity price in the same power grid. It represents the fairness of market competition by using PAB to compute the fee of purchasing electricity and dispatching load, which is consistent with the purpose of an opening electric generation market. Both SMP and PAB are reasonable, but they still have insufficiencies. A reasonable price should consider the fairness of both the merchandise pricing and the market competition. Therefore we propose the principle of the market clearing price determined by SMP and load dispatch calculated by PAB. This mechanism combines the merits of SMP and PAB, solves simultaneous fairness of the price of merchant and market competition, and is feasible and simple. This mechanism encourages generation enterprise to uncover the inner potential, decrease generation cost, increase competition capability, realize lower bid, and finally benefit consumers.

The basic structure of a power market [1, 19, 21] consists of power exchange (PX) and independent system operator (ISO). In this market structure, PX takes charge of the spot trading in the day-ahead market, with the main task to solve the dynamic economic load dispatch problem. In the practical process of electric energy exchange, ISO takes responsibility for both network security and the auxiliary service. In other words, the congestion management and spinning reserve are controlled by ISO. In this study, we use this market structure and build two load dispatch models.

11.1.2 *A Load Dispatch Model for a Day-ahead Market*

Economic dispatch (ED) is very important in power systems, with the basic objective of scheduling the committed generating unit outputs to meet the load demand at minimum operating cost, while satisfying all units and system constraints. Different models and techniques have been proposed in the literature [3, 5, 6].

A conventional economic dispatch (CED) considers only the output power limits and the balance between the supply and the demand. If ramp rate constraints are included, the model becomes the dynamic economic dispatch (DED). Great efforts have been devoted to economic dispatch problems and various models have been proposed [1, 4, 6, 8, 15, 13, 14, 17, 19, 22, 23, 24]. In general, since the CED model does not take into account the ramp rate constraints, its solution may not be real optimal. In order to assure the optimization of solutions, the load dispatch model must consider the ramp rate limit. Therefore, the DED model is needed. Due to the inclusiveness of ramp rate constraints, the number of decision variables involved in the problem will increase dramatically compared with the corresponding CED problem. The sharp increase of the number of variables implies the increase of searching dimensions, which furthermore results in the difficulty of solving the problems of DED. On the other hand, CED problems usually formulate the objective function as smooth, which are solved by using equal λ rules [22], which, however, are not always adequate for real ED or DED problems. A non-smooth function sometimes has to be used to account for special factors, such as the voltage rippling [23, 24]. A more accurate ED model that can account for special cost factors leading to a non-smooth objective, and also including the ramp rate constraints would be highly desired. In addition, there are different constructions and operation modes in power markets, such as the England and Wales power market, California power market, Norway power market, Chile power market, and the Australia and New Zealand power markets [1, 3, 6, 7, 19, 21]. Among some of these power markets, a power exchange-independent system operator model (PX-ISO model) has been adopted in the Chilean power market [19], and the California power market [1, 21]. In this model, PX administrates the day-ahead market and the ED is the major task for PX. ISO will verify the dispatch schedule against a set of criteria, including network security, transmission congestion and spinning reserve. Hence, constraints on the spinning reservation can be ignored in the DED model. Based on the analysis above, a dynamic economic load dispatch (DELD) model for a PX-ISO power market can be described as follows:

$$\text{(M1)} \qquad \begin{cases} \min f(P_j(t)) = \sum\limits_{t=1}^{T} \sum\limits_{j=1}^{N} F(P_j(t)) \\ \sum\limits_{j=1}^{N} P_j(t) = P_D(t) + P_L(t) \\ P_{j\,\min} \leqslant P_j(t) \leqslant P_{j\,\max} \\ -D_j \leqslant P_j(t) - P_j(t-1) \leqslant R_j \end{cases} \qquad (1)$$

where $P_j(t)$ is the output power of the j-th unit during the t-th time interval, T is the number of time intervals per dispatch cycle, N represents the number of committed units, and $F(P_j(t))$ is the generation cost function and can be formulated as

$$F(P_j(t)) = a_{0j} + a_{1j}P_j(t) + a_{2j}P_j^2(t) + \left|d_j \sin[e_j(P_{j\min} - P_j(t))]\right| \quad (2)$$

where a_{0j}, a_{1j}, a_{2j} are constants, $\left|d_j \sin[e_j(P_{j\min} - P_j(t))]\right|$ represents the rippling effects caused by the steam admission valve openings, d_j and e_j are coefficients of the j-th unit, $P_D(t)$ and $P_L(t)$ are the load demand and network loss in the t-th time interval respectively, $P_{j\min}$ and $P_{j\max}$ are the minimum and maximum output power of the j-th unit respectively, D_j and R_j are the maximum downwards and the maximum upwards ramp rate of the j-th unit respectively.

The objective function in the above model (M1) can also be the expense of purchasing electricity.

The model (M1) describes a non-linear programming problem with multiple local optimal points. The prospective algorithms for solving this model must have a stronger global searching capability. The new algorithm to solve this problem will be given later in this chapter.

11.1.3 *An Uncertain Environment/Economic Load Dispatch Model*

A conventional economic dispatch problem is mainly concerned with the minimization of operating costs or purchasing electricity fee, subject to the diverse constraints in terms of units and systems. However, an environmental pollution problem caused by generation has been presented in recent years. A variety of feasible strategies [1, 17, 19] have been proposed to reduce atmospheric emissions. These include installation of pollutant cleaning equipment, switching to low emission fuels, replacing the aged fuel-burners and generator units, and emission dispatching. Petrowski referred the first three options as the long-term ones, and the emission dispatching option as an attractive short-term alternative [17]. In fact, the first three options should be determined by the generation companies, not by the regulatory authorities, especially in the circumstances of the electric power market. The desired long-term target is to reduce the emission of harmful gases. In other words, the emission of harmful gases required to generate electricity should be curtailed in accordance with laws and regulations. Therefore, the environmental/ economic load dispatch problem considering emission of harmful gases is a kernel issue in electric power markets.

Some researchers pointed out that the environmental/economic load dispatch problem is to simultaneously minimize two conflicting objective functions, i.e., minimization of fuel cost and emission, while satisfying load demand and system constraints. The emission of thermal units mainly includes SO_2, NO_x and CO_2, which are not distinguished in this chapter for reasons of simplicity. In general, these harmful gases mentioned above are all functions of output power P_j, and their emission (*ton/h*), written as $E(P_j)$, can be described as

$$E(P_j) = \alpha_j + \beta_j P_j + \gamma_j P_j^2 \tag{3}$$

where α_j, β_j and γ_j are coefficients of the j-th generator emission characteristics.

In a typical environmental/economic load dispatch model, the coefficients of both cost function and emission function are constants, and generally can be obtained by experiments. However, there exist many factors which affect these coefficients, such as: experiment errors, different operation situations, the quality of coal and the aging of facilities. Therefore, it is not precise to describe these coefficients as fixed values. Aimed at characterizing the cost and emission more precisely, we present these coefficients described by fuzzy numbers. A new load dispatch model with uncertainty, called the fuzzy dynamic environmental/economic load dispatch model (FDEELD), is built as follows:

$$\text{(M2)} \quad \begin{cases} \min f = \sum\limits_{t=1}^{T}\sum\limits_{j=1}^{N} F(P_j(t)) = \sum\limits_{t=1}^{T}\sum\limits_{j=1}^{N} (\widetilde{a}_j + \widetilde{b}_j P_j(t) + \widetilde{c}_j P_j^2(t)) \\ \min e = \sum\limits_{t=1}^{T}\sum\limits_{j=1}^{N} (\widetilde{\alpha}_j + \widetilde{\beta}_j P_j(t) + \widetilde{\gamma}_j P_j^2(t)) \\ \sum\limits_{j=1}^{N} \mathrm{P}_j(t) = P_D(t) + P_L(\mathrm{t}) \\ \mathrm{P}_{j\,\min} \leqslant \mathrm{P}_j(t) \leqslant \mathrm{P}_{j\,\max} \\ -\mathrm{D}_j \leqslant \mathrm{P}_j(t) - P_j(t-1) \leqslant R_j \end{cases} \tag{4}$$

where $\widetilde{a}_j$, $\widetilde{b}_j$, $\widetilde{c}_j$ are fuzzy cost coefficients of the j-th unit, e is an emission function, $\widetilde{\alpha}_j$, $\widetilde{\beta}_j$, $\widetilde{\gamma}_j$ are fuzzy emission coefficients of the j-th unit. The meanings of the other symbols are the same as the symbols in the model (M1).

The model (M2) describes a fuzzy multi-objective non-linear programming problem, from which it is very hard to obtain an optimal solution. In Section11.2, we will propose a weighted ideal point method, a hybrid evolutionary method and a fuzzy number ranking method to solve FDEELD.

11.2 Evolutionary Computation Methods and Fuzzy Decision Making

The model (M1) built in the above section is a non-linear programming problem with multiple local optimal points, and (M2) is a fuzzy multi-objective non-linear programming problem. These optimization problems are hard to solve; we will develop some new algorithms to solve these problems.

11.2.1 *Evolutionary Computation*

Conventional optimization methods suffer from local optimality problems and some of them require a function with good characteristics, such as differentiability, continuity, which, to a certain extent, limit their application. In recent years, stochastic optimization techniques, such as simulated annealing (SA), genetic algorithms (GA), and evolutionary algorithms (EA), have drawn many researchers' attention because the stochastic optimization techniques are capable of finding the near global optimal solutions without putting restrictions on the characteristics of the objective functions, although they require significant computing burdens and generally take a fairly long time to reach a solution. A great amount of effort has been devoted to improving these methods and some of them have been successfully used in a variety of real world problems [17, 26].

GA was initially introduced by John Holland in the seventies as a special technique for function optimization [9]. Hereafter, we refer to it as the classical GA (CGA). A typical CGA has three phases, i.e., initialization, evaluation and genetic operation, which consist of reproduction, crossover and mutation. The performance of CGA precedes the traditional optimization methods in aspects of global search and robustness on handling an arbitrary non-linear function. However, it suffers from premature convergence problems and usually consumes enormous computing time.

In the CGA, the ability of local search mainly relies on the reproduction and crossover operations, which can be referred to as exploitation operations, while the capability of global search is assured by the mutation operation, which can be regarded as the exploration operation. Generally speaking, the velocity of local search increases when the probability of crossover increases. Similarly, the level of capability of global search will increase when the probability of mutation increases. Since the sum of probabilities of all the generic operations must be the unity, the mutation probability has to be reduced to increase the crossover probability for a reasonable level of capability of local search. This contributes to the fact that the probability of mutation in CGA is very low, with a range of 0.1-5%. On the other hand, to achieve a satisfactory level of capability of global search, the probabilities of reproduction and crossover have to be decreased to increase the mutation probability. This will weaken the capability of local search dramatically, slow down the convergence rate and make the global search ability unachievable eventually. In the process of balancing exploration and exploitation based on reproduction/crossover and mutation operations for a fixed population, it is hardly possible to achieve a win-win situation for both sides simultaneously. Therefore, how to create a balance between exploration and exploitation in

GA-type algorithms has long been a challenge and retained its attractiveness to many researchers [10, 17].

We present a new method to enhance the capability of global search by increasing the probability of mutation operation while assuring a satisfactory level of capability of local search by employing the idea of simplex method, the so called quasi-simplex technique: a new hybrid real-coded genetic algorithm with quasi-simplex technique (HRGAQT) is used. HRGAQT has the following aims: (1) we assure the capability of global search by increasing the probability of mutation; (2) mutation is implemented by using an effective real-value mutation operator instead of traditional binary mutation; and (3) we enhance the capability of local search by introducing the so-called quasi-simplex techniques into the CGA since the capability of local search will be significantly weakened by the probability of reproduction/crossover decrease as a result of increasing the probability of mutation. In each iteration, HRGAQT first divides the population into a number of sub-populations and each sub-population is treated as a classical simplex. Then for every simplex, HRGAQT applies four operations in parallel to produce offspring. The first operation is the quasi-simplex evolution in which two prospective individuals will be chosen as the offspring. The other three operations are reproduction, crossover and mutation respectively, which are very similar to the traditional genetic operation, except that the probability of mutation is fairly high. All four operations together will produce a new sub-population with the same size as the corresponding parent sub-group. The new generation is the collection of all the newly produced sub-groups. In short, HRGAQT maintains the diversity of a population to enhance global search capability eventually because a higher diversity of population leads to a higher level of capability to explore the search space, while the local search is mainly implemented by the quasi-simplex technique and reproduction including the elitist strategy and crossover operations.

11.2.1.1 *Function optimization and quasi-simplex technique*

We consider the global minimization problem described by Yao and Liu [25] for the purpose of development of new search algorithms. According to Yao and Liu, the problem can be formalized as a pair of real valued vectors (s, f), where $S \subseteq \mathbb{R}^n$ is a bounded set on $\mathbb{R}^n$ and $f : S \to R$ is an n-dimensional real-valued function. f needs not be continuous but must be bounded. The problem is to find a point where $f(x_{\min})$ is a global minimum on S. More specially, it is required to find an $x_{\min} \in S$ such that

$$\forall x \in S, \quad f(x_{\min}) \leqslant f(x) \tag{5}$$

On solving the above optimization problem by genetic algorithms, an effective method, which can speed up the local convergence rate, is to combine the CGA with conventional optimization methods. Since it has been highly recognized that GA has no special request on the characteristics of the objective functions, the conventional optimization methods that go with GA should not require that the objective functions have special characteristics. In this light, Simplex method is promising because it demands less function characteristics. Therefore, we choose to combine the conventional GA with simplex technique to form a hybrid generic algorithm in which a real-value scheme and a dynamic sub-grouping are used. To understand the HRGAQT algorithm, we briefly introduce basic ideas of the simplex technique. Simplex is a type of direct search method, which is a widely accepted search technique. A simplex in an n-dimensional space is defined by a convex polyhedron consisting of $n+1$ vertices, which are not in the same hyper-plane. Assuming there are $n+1$ individuals, denoted by x^i, with function values denoted as f_i, $i = 1,2,\ldots,n+1$, the worst and the best points in terms of function values are denoted by x^H and x^B, respectively, and can be determined by

$$f(x^H) = f_H = \max_i f_i, \quad i = 1,2,\ldots,n+1 \tag{6}$$

$$f(x^B) = f_B = \min_i f_i, \quad i = 1,2,\ldots,n+1 \tag{7}$$

where f_H and f_B denote the worst and the best function values, respectively.

To determine a better new point than the worst point x^H, the centroid x^C of the polyhedron are all the points but the worst one needs to be calculated by

$$x^C = \frac{((\sum_{i=1}^{n+1} x^i) - x^H)}{n} \tag{8}$$

A better point predicted by simplex techniques lies on the line starting from the worst point, towards the centroid, which can be referred to as the worst-opposite direction. The actual location can be determined by the following formula:

$$x = x^C + \alpha(x^C - x^H) \tag{9}$$

where α is a constant and can be a different value for different points lying on the worst-opposite direction, such as the reflection point, expansion points, and the compression points. The actual value ranges of α for different points are shown in Table 11.1.

Conventional simplex techniques mainly consist of four operations, i.e., reflection, expansion, compression, and contraction. The simplex algorithm produces a new simplex by either replacing the worst point by a better point produced using the simplex technique or contracting current simplex towards the best point in each iteration step. The process will

Table 11.1 Points obtained using the simplex techniques with different α

$x = x^C + \alpha(x^C - x^H)$	$\alpha = 1$	reflection point	Reflection point of x^H respect to x^C
	$\alpha > 1$	Expansion point	A point farther than the reflection point from x^C
	$0 < \alpha < 1$	Compression point	Points between x^C and reflection point
	$-1 < \alpha < 0$	Compression point	Points between x^H and x^C

be continuous until the termination criterion is satisfied. The crucial idea of the classical simplex techniques is to track the local optimal following the worst-opposite direction of each simplex, which can be regarded as guidance in the search landscape. Therefore, the simplex algorithm has a higher level of ability of local search.

11.2.1.2 *Hybrid real-coded GA with Quasi-Simplex techniques*

HRGAQT is established by combining a technique evolved from the traditional simplex technique, which is referred to as a quasi-simplex technique with the CGA. In doing so, HRGAQT can achieve a substantially high level of global exploration by increasing the probability of mutation, while its capability of local exploitation can also be reasonably high by using both reproduction/crossover and quasi-simplex techniques.

The process of HRGAQT can be described as follows: First, HRGAQT initializes a random-generated population with μ individuals (real-coded chromosomes) and each individual has n components. The population starts to evolve. At the beginning of each iteration, the generation is divided into a number of sub-populations (or sub-groups) with each sub-group having n+1 individuals. Each sub-group will then evolve into a new sub-population of the same size by four operations in parallel, which are quasi-simplex operation, reproduction, crossover and mutation. The quasi-simplex operation (QS) will generate two new individuals, and the reproduction will retain the best individual by applying the elitist strategy and also produce some individuals based on the probability of reproduction (R). The crossover operation will also generate a number of pairs of individuals according to the probability of crossover (C) and the left-over individuals will be produced by mutation (M). At the end of each evolution iteration, all the new individuals from the sub-populations will merge together and evolution enters new generation. If the termination criterion is not met, evolution starts a new iteration. This process continues until the termination criterion is satisfied. The best individuals of population in the final generation will be taken as the optimal solutions.

HRGAQT has a number of outstanding features which enable both local exploitation and global exploration. HRGAQT adopts the dynamic sub-grouping idea to ensure each simplex consists of reasonably correlated individuals in the entire evolution process to enhance the convergence rate. HRGAQT implements population partition different to the strategies proposed in the literature by two methods. One is to take into account the dimension of individuals on deciding the number of sub-groups. HRGAQT divides a population into a number of sub-groups with each sub-group consisting of $n+1$ individuals to ensure the search validity and efficiency in terms of computing times. The detailed discussion about the size of a sub-population and the number of sub-populations to be used will be presented in another paper. The other method is to make a partition for each iteration. Although the computation time for each iteration may increase due to the partition process, the enhancement in the convergence rate could decrease the number of iterations needed.

Secondly, HRGAQT employs the quasi-simplex technique with ancillary reproduction and crossover operation to assure the local exploitation. The quasi-simplex technique absorbs the idea of classical simplex techniques to perform a guided search. It produces four prospective individuals using the reflection, expansion and compression operations along with the worst-opposite direction. The quasi-simplex technique also expands the conventional simplex technique by looking at the prospective individuals lying on a line starting from the centroid towards the best point of the simplex. We refer to this direction as the best-forward direction, in contrast with the worst-opposite direction. Three prospective individuals x^e, x^m and x^n will be produced along the best-forward direction by the expansion and compression operations using the following formula:

$$x = x^B + \beta(x^B - x^D) \tag{10}$$

where x^D denotes the centroid of the remaining points except for the best point x^B and can be calculated by

$$x^D = \left(\left(\sum_{i=1}^{n+1} x^i \right) - x^B \right) \Big/ n \tag{11}$$

The points x^e, x^m and x^n can be determined by the value of β in (10) and the range of β is shown in Table 11.2.

To avoid a situation in which too many individuals are similar so that the diversity of the population decreases dramatically, HRGAQT selects the best one from the two prospective individual groups along the worst-opposite and the best-forward directions to produce two new individuals as a part of offspring.

11.2.1.3 *A new mutation operator*

To guarantee the local search effect, GA usually uses a very small mutation probability. A typical mutation probability ranges from 0.001 to 0.05. The mutation operators have two

Table 11.2 Range of β in (10) for x^e, x^m and x^n

Formula	Range of β	Calculated point
$x = x^B + \beta(x^B - x^D)$	$\beta > 1$	x^e
	$\beta = 1$	x^m
	$0 < \beta < 1$	x^n

kinds in real-coded GA: one is to generate a new random real number within the domain and the other is to add a new random real number to the original one. Both of these two operators lack support from the principles of biological natural mutation processes. In a process of biological evolution, a gene often changes dramatically after it is mutated. In real-coded GA, decimal digits are used to represent genes. According to the principles of a natural biological mutation, these digits should also change significantly after a mutation operation. In other words, they should become bigger when they are small enough (< 5), or become smaller when they are big enough ($\geqslant 5$). Based on this idea, we propose a new real-coded mutation operator, which is described as follows. Suppose x_{ij}, $i = 1, 2, \ldots, \mu$, $j = 1, 2, \ldots, n$, represents the j-th component in the i-th individual, where μ is the size of a population and n is the dimension of each individual. In a real-coded scheme, x_{ij} can be expressed as a sequence of decimal numbers including the decimal point:

$$x_{ij} = d_{ij}^{w_1} d_{ij}^{w_2} \cdots d_{ij}^{w_p} \bullet d_{ij}^{f_1} d_{ij}^{f_2} \cdots d_{ij}^{f_q} \tag{12}$$

where superscript w and f denote the integer part and the fractional part respectively, and p and q are constants representing the number of digits in the integer part and the fractional part for a given x_{ij}, respectively. In application, p is determined by the maximum value that this sequence can represent, q is determined by the precision required by the problems and its maximum value will be determined by the hardware used in computing. If the digits in the sequence are randomly selected to undertake a mutation, the new sequence after the mutation can be represented as:

$$\overline{x_{ij}} = \overline{d_{ij}^{w_1}}\, \overline{d_{ij}^{w_2}} \cdots \overline{d_{ij}^{w_p}} \bullet \overline{d_{ij}^{f_1}}\, \overline{d_{ij}^{f_2}} \cdots \overline{d_{ij}^{f_q}} \tag{13}$$

where each decimal digit is determined by:

$$\overline{d_{ij}^{r}} = 9 - d_{ij}^{r} \text{ if } d_{ij} \text{ is selected} \tag{14}$$

or

$$\overline{d_{ij}^{r}} = d_{ij}^{r} \text{ if } d_{ij} \text{ is not selected} \tag{15}$$

where $r = w_1, w_2, \ldots, w_p,\ f_1, f_2, \ldots, f_q$.

11.2.1.4 *HRGAQT algorithm procedure*

The HRGAQT algorithm can be outlined in the following steps:

Step 1 Initialize a random population X with size $\mu = K(n+1)$.

Step 2 Divide the population X into K sub-populations with each sub-group consisting of $n+1$ individuals.

- Step 2.1 Select the best individual x from the population X.
- Step 2.2 Select n individuals which are most close to x in terms of their Euclid distances.
- Step 2.3 Combine the individuals obtained from steps 2.1 and 2.2 to form a sub-population S.
- Step 2.4 Remove S from the original population.
- Step 2.5 Repeat Steps 2.1 – 2.4 for the sub-population until no individuals are left.

Step 3 Each sub-population evolves into a new group.

- Step 3.1 Produce two new individuals using quasi-simplex techniques.
- Step 3.2 Implement elitist strategy, i.e., reserve the best one in the sub-population to be a part of offspring.
- Step 3.3 Produce new individuals by reproducing by linear ranking. The reproduction probability of the i-th individual x^i, in the target sub-group (sorted by descending the fitness) calculated by the following formula

$$P_i = \frac{1}{n+1}\left(\eta - 2(\eta-1)\cdot\frac{\text{rank}(x_i)-1}{n}\right) \tag{16}$$

  where $\eta > 1$, which can be determined by the desired probability of the best individual.
- Step 3.4 Crossover operation is processed as follows:

  Select $[{}^{(n-2)Pc}/_{2}]$ pairs of parents randomly, where $[]$ is an operator producing the maximum integer which is less than or equal to the operand. For every pair of the selected parent,

$$x^i = (x_1^i, x_2^i, \ldots, x_{m1}^i, \ldots, x_{m2}^i, \ldots, x_n^i) \tag{17}$$

$$x^j = (x_1^j, x_2^j, \ldots, x_{m1}^j, \ldots, x_{m2}^j, \ldots, x_n^j) \tag{18}$$

  where the superscripts i and j denote the i-th and the j-th individual in the population respectively. The subscript $m1$ and $m2$ are two random numbers between

1 and n. The two new individuals will be:

$$x_{\text{new}}^{i} = \left(x_1^i, x_2^i, \ldots, x_{m1}^j, \ldots, x_{m2}^j, \ldots, x_n^i\right) \tag{19}$$

$$x_{\text{new}}^{j} = \left(x_1^j, x_2^j, \ldots, x_{m1}^i, \ldots, x_{m2}^i, \ldots, x_n^j\right) \tag{20}$$

Step 3.5 The remaining individuals will participate in the mutation operation. For each individual, a new individual will be produced by (12)–(15).

11.2.2 *A Fuzzy Multi-object Non-linear Optimization Method*

11.2.2.1 *A weight idea point method of multi-objective optimization problems*

Both weighting and reference point methods are all powerful methods to achieve Pareto optimal solutions for multi-objective non-linear programming problems. Strictly speaking, the weight method only represents the relative importance of goal values from an objective rather than from different objectives. It is hard to know the magnitude of effect of the set of weights to each objective function value. The reference point method is a relatively practical interactive approach to multi-objective optimization problems. It introduces the concept of a reference point suggested by decision makers and presents some desired values of the objective functions. It is very hard to determine weightings and reference points in applications, and the interactive approach increases computing burden heavily. This section proposes a new weighting ideal point method (WIPM), which doesn't require any interaction, and can predict the magnitude of effect of the set of any weights to each objective function value.

To describe the proposed WIPM method, we write a general multi-objective non-linear programming problem as:

$$\min_{x \in S} f(x) = (f_1(x), f_2(x), \ldots, f_k(x)) \tag{21}$$

where $f_1(x), \ldots, f_k(x)$ are k distinct objective functions and S is the constrained set defined by

$$S = \{x \in \mathbb{R}^n \mid g_j(x) \leqslant 0,\ j = 1, \ldots, m\} \tag{22}$$

In this section, we propose a weighted ideal method (WIPM) as follows: let

$$g(x) = w_1 \left(\frac{f_1 - f_1^{\min}}{f_1^{\min}}\right)^2 + \cdots + w_k \left(\frac{f_k - f_k^{\min}}{f_k^{\min}}\right)^2 \tag{23}$$

where

$$f_i^{\min} = \min_{x \in S} f_i(x),\ \ f_i^{\min} \neq 0,\ \ i = 1, 2, \ldots, k.$$

$f^{\min} = (f_1^{\min}, \ldots, f_k^{\min})$ is a so-called ideal or utopia point, $w = (w_1, \ldots, w_k) > 0$, $\sum_{i=1}^{k} w_i = 1$ is a weight vector.

To get the Pareto optimal solution of the problem (21), it can be transferred to solve the single objective optimization problem below

$$\min_{x \in S} g(x) \tag{24}$$

Since the values of different objective functions in (21) can be very different, it is hard to know the magnitude of the effect of the set of weights to each objective function value. In the model (24), all objectives are converted into the same magnitude by the formula

$$\frac{f_i - f_i^{\min}}{f_i^{\min}}.$$

We can therefore predict the effect quantity of the set of weights to each objective function value. For example, if $w_1 = 2w_2$, then

$$\frac{f_2^* - f_2^{\min}}{f_2^{\min}} \approx 2\frac{f_1^* - f_1^{\min}}{f_1^{\min}},$$

where $f_i^* = f_i(x^*)$, $i = 1, 2$, x^* is the optimal solution of (23). In other words, the weights given in WIPM can reflect the trade-off rate information among the objective functions.

11.2.2.2 *A weight idea point method of fuzzy multi-objective optimization problems*

A problem becomes a fuzzy multi-objective non-linear programming problem if the objective function f_i includes uncertainty represented by fuzzy numbers in the multi-objective non-linear programming problem (21). We will give a solution based on the weight idea point method and the fuzzy number ranking.

When the non-linear objective functions are fuzzy functions, we also use (23) to convert (21) into a corresponding single objective fuzzy optimization problem. Now we need to solve a single objective fuzzy programming problem (SOFPP). One of the methods to solve fuzzy optimization problems is the maximum satisfaction factor method [11]. Another one is to convert a fuzzy optimization problem into several classical optimization problems. In this section we do not use the above methods, but directly apply HRGAQT to search for optimum solutions. We then compare the function values of different solutions by the method of ranking fuzzy numbers.

Different methods for ranking fuzzy numbers have been proposed [5, 10, 15, 19]. The definition below comes from Lee and Li [15].

Definition 11.1. Let $\widetilde{a}$, $\widetilde{b} \in F(R)$ be two fuzzy numbers. The definition of ranking two fuzzy numbers is as follows:

$$\widetilde{a} \leqslant \widetilde{b} \text{ if } m(\widetilde{a}) < m(\widetilde{b}) \tag{25}$$

or

$$m(\widetilde{a}) = m(\widetilde{b}) \text{ and } \sigma(\widetilde{a}) \geqslant \sigma(\widetilde{b}) \tag{26}$$

where mean $m(\widetilde{a})$ and standard deviation $\sigma(\widetilde{a})$ are defined as

$$m(\widetilde{a}) = \frac{\int_{s(\widetilde{a})} x\widetilde{a}(x)dx}{\int_{s(\widetilde{a})} \widetilde{a}(x)dx} \tag{27}$$

$$\sigma(\widetilde{a}) = \left(\frac{\int_{s(\widetilde{a})} x^2\widetilde{a}(x)dx}{\int_{s(\widetilde{a})} \widetilde{a}(x)dx} - \left(m(\widetilde{a})\right)^2 \right)^{\frac{1}{2}} \tag{28}$$

where $s(\widetilde{a}) = \{x \mid \widetilde{a}(x) > 0\}$ is the support of fuzzy number $\widetilde{a}$.
For a triangular fuzzy number $\widetilde{a} = (l,m,n)$,

$$m(\widetilde{a}) = \frac{1}{3}(l+m+n) \tag{29}$$

$$\sigma(\widetilde{a}) = \frac{1}{18}\left(l^2+m^2+n^2-lm-ln-mn\right) \tag{30}$$

The main steps of the weight idea point method for fuzzy multi-objective optimization problems are as follows:
Step1 Convert problem (21) into a single objective optimization by using (23) and (24);
Step2 Solve the single objective optimization (24) by HRGAQT.
Note:

(1) $f^i_{\min}$ can be given by a desired value or determined by solving the corresponding single objective optimization problem by HRGAQT.
(2) In solving the single objective optimization by using HRGAQT, for each individual we compute fuzzy function values according to the fuzzy number operation principle, then directly compare the function values of different solutions by the fuzzy ranking method given above.

Table 11.3 Technical data of units

Unit No.	P_{min}(MW)	P_{max}(MW)	a	b	c	d	e	D	R
1	00	680	550	8.10	0.00028	300	0.035	60	50
2	00	360	309	8.10	0.00056	200	0.042	50	35
3	00	360	307	8.10	0.00056	200	0.042	50	35
4	60	180	240	7.74	0.00324	150	0.063	40	30
5	60	180	240	7.74	0.00324	150	0.063	40	30
6	60	180	240	7.74	0.00324	150	0.063	40	30
7	60	180	240	7.74	0.00324	150	0.063	40	30
8	60	180	240	7.74	0.00324	150	0.063	40	30
9	60	180	240	7.74	0.00324	150	0.063	40	30
10	40	120	126	8.6	0.00284	100	0.084	30	25
11	40	120	126	8.6	0.00284	100	0.084	30	25
12	55	120	126	8.6	0.00284	100	0.084	30	25
13	55	120	126	8.6	0.00284	100	0.084	30	25

11.3 Illustrations on Load Dispatch for Day-ahead Market

11.3.1 *An example of load dispatch in a day-ahead market*

To test the effectiveness of the proposed HRGAQT in solving a DED problem (M1), a typical dynamic dispatch case consisting of 13 committed units and 24 time intervals is chosen. The data of the unit techniques and predicted load demands in each dispatch period are listed in Tables 11.3 and 11.4. Experimental results are as follows.

Because the objective function is a high-dimensional function with multi extremum points, it is unknown where the real optimal solution is. In order to demonstrate the effectiveness of the proposed algorithms, the mean value and standard deviation of total cost corresponding with optimal outputs would be significant and convincing. Table11.3.1 lists the optimal total cost, the mean value and standard deviation of 10 results obtained by the proposed algorithm running independently 10 times. Table 11.6 gives optimal power output of units and total cost corresponding to the best results.

The best result occurred in the 7-th time, and the optimal power output of units and total cost corresponding to the best result is listed in Table 11.3.1. It is obvious that the standard deviation is small and the results are believable.

The experiments show that the proposed method with hybrid real-coded generic algorithms and the quasi-simplex techniques is very effective and the results are convincing.

In Table 11.4, T is time interval, $P_D(t)$ is the load demand.

Table 11.4 Load demands in different time intervals

T	1	2	3	4	5	6	7	8	9	10	11	12
$P_D(t)$	1550	1500	1520	1540	1600	1680	1780	1880	1950	2010	1970	1970
T	13	14	15	16	17	18	19	20	21	22	23	24
$P_D(t)$	1910	1830	1850	1880	1920	2150	2370	2280	2130	1950	1790	1670

Table 11.5 The total cost, the mean value and standard deviation

i-th time	1	2	3	4	5
i-th result	461839	461138	460893	461382	460562
Mean Value	46113.47				
Std Dev	582.5868				
i-th time	6	7	8	9	10
i-th result	461540	459898	461779	461134	461182
Mean Value					
Std Dev					

11.3.2 *An Example of Uncertain Environment/Economic Load Dispatch*

In this section, we solve an uncertain environment/economic load dispatch problem (M2) by using the WIPM, HRGAQT and fuzzy number ranking methods. We convert (M2) into a single objective optimization problem by using WIPM. We then use the Lagrange relaxation method to form a Lagrange function. Finally, we use the HRGAQT to optimize the Lagrange function. In the process of the iteration, the fuzzy number ranking method is used to compare fuzzy function values of different points for the single objective function.

Tables 11.7–11.10 show the test data of the units output, cost function, emission function, and load demand, respectively.

Penalty function h is a high-dimension non-linear function, and therefore it is hard to know where the global minimum point is. In order to demonstrate the effectiveness of the proposed algorithm, the mean and standard deviation of fuzzy fuel cost, fuzzy emission and fuzzy total cost corresponding with the optimal outputs are tested. In addition, in order to compare the magnitude of effect of the set of weights to fuzzy fuel cost and fuzzy emission, we calculate three group weights. Table 11.11 lists the means and standard deviations of fuzzy fuel cost, fuzzy emission and fuzzy total cost. Table 11.12 shows results obtained by the proposed algorithm through 10 independent runs.

Table 11.6 Optimal power output of units and total cost

Time	Unit number												
Interval	1	2	3	4	5	6	7	8	9	10	11	12	13
1	359.04	188.05	185.14	94.88	91.76	96.90	94.75	94.62	93.25	42.41	61.47	55.32	92.40
2	355.22	174.74	150.39	98.53	89.47	99.36	60.03	89.58	99.78	67.83	40.02	55.00	120.04
3	358.60	194.27	171.71	95.95	98.97	95.05	95.05	60.00	96.98	40.44	40.25	55.00	117.72
4	355.86	191.76	170.36	94.75	94.41	93.27	93.41	93.67	92.31	64.67	40.01	63.12	92.40
5	359.07	195.37	209.22	95.14	97.82	98.79	96.65	109.10	99.99	51.47	40.00	55.00	92.40
6	359.92	220.06	219.94	108.86	109.86	108.75	107.60	106.96	109.34	42.50	48.31	55.00	82.91
7	429.37	214.85	224.40	104.71	109.48	108.45	109.67	108.96	111.03	72.50	76.61	55.00	54.99
8	447.57	224.22	224.40	114.39	114.28	117.04	113.02	112.42	120.43	75.81	77.40	55.00	84.02
9	448.80	236.88	236.66	112.20	112.45	121.77	123.68	118.19	113.14	78.15	77.72	77.78	92.60
10	451.33	244.58	239.12	116.05	121.79	126.59	114.95	136.89	120.75	81.82	79.05	84.67	92.41
11	450.08	247.24	234.06	122.68	125.44	111.44	126.06	126.88	120.07	77.66	80.75	55.07	92.58
12	452.43	247.49	227.11	155.96	111.87	111.35	153.38	120.04	114.74	78.89	77.43	55.00	64.31
13	448.18	244.02	233.11	116.56	117.81	111.47	114.24	110.29	113.09	77.39	76.49	55.00	92.34
14	448.77	224.37	224.35	113.11	108.14	114.43	110.06	109.66	115.02	69.20	46.70	55.00	91.20
15	448.80	224.36	224.37	110.91	112.02	113.43	110.03	109.86	110.14	75.72	76.72	55.00	78.65
16	448.80	230.23	234.55	114.92	114.41	114.51	113.52	113.41	124.86	47.12	76.09	55.02	92.56
17	449.96	234.55	238.24	111.35	115.71	110.27	114.63	129.68	115.84	76.26	75.85	55.00	92.65
18	470.15	245.53	251.87	114.17	120.11	113.43	112.95	115.91	118.19	75.88	78.42	75.85	67.55
19	539.01	285.47	288.81	147.11	152.92	147.66	147.38	150.76	152.97	103.90	98.27	93.78	91.98
20	538.64	298.90	287.01	143.60	150.57	159.74	158.98	147.86	159.84	77.40	77.45	92.48	57.54
21	519.91	251.07	244.73	131.80	154.34	152.89	120.22	122.64	158.77	77.40	78.20	57.67	60.35
22	448.23	240.95	234.14	116.17	114.36	113.01	111.22	120.62	132.66	80.32	77.28	71.37	89.68
23	440.31	218.10	224.41	109.87	109.86	109.87	112.50	110.42	109.87	77.43	55.55	55.01	56.80
24	360.31	224.52	224.46	109.87	109.68	109.86	108.57	109.82	109.90	52.85	40.00	55.00	55.15
Total cost		459898											

Table 11.7 Limits of unit output and ramp rate

Unit No.	1	2	3	4	5	6	7
$P_{\min}(MW)$	20	20	35	35	130	120	125
$P_{\max}(MW)$	125	150	150	210	325	310	315
D_j	40	40	40	50	60	60	60
R_j	30	30	30	40	50	50	50

Table 11.8 Fuzzy coefficients of the cost function

Unit No	a_0	a_1	a_2	b_0	b_1	b_2	c_0	c_1	c_2
1	800.95401	825.72578	846.36892	37.46062	38.53973	39.46468	0.15813	0.16218	0.16559
2	625.96538	645.32513	661.45826	41.32673	42.51721	43.53762	0.12050	0.12359	0.12619
3	1107.49967	1135.89710	1158.61504	38.83637	39.83217	40.62881	0.02651	0.02705	0.02754
4	1168.89357	1198.86520	1222.84250	36.90654	37.85286	38.60992	0.03403	0.03472	0.03534
5	1555.00481	1586.73960	1610.54069	36.58126	37.32782	37.92507	0.02478	0.02521	0.02559
6	1269.74602	1295.65920	1315.09409	38.29901	39.08062	39.70591	0.01653	0.01682	0.01707
7	1466.71867	1496.65170	1519.10148	36.52011	37.26542	37.86167	0.01979	0.02013	0.02043

Table 11.9 Fuzzy coefficients of the emission function

Unit No.	α_0	α_1	α_2	β_0	β_1	β_2	γ_0	γ_1	γ_2
1	15.18178	15.65132	16.04260	0.28456	0.29276	0.29979	0.003822	0.00392	0.00400
2	15.18178	15.65132	16.04260	0.28456	0.29276	0.29979	0.00382	0.00392	0.00400
3	34.69310	35.58267	36.29432	−0.54136	−0.52816	−0.51760	0.00698	0.00712	0.00725
4	34.69310	35.58267	36.29432	−0.54136	−0.52816	−0.51760	0.00698	0.00712	0.00725
5	42.03762	42.89553	43.53896	−0.52138	−0.51116	−0.50298	0.00453	0.00461	0.00468
6	40.92147	41.75660	42.38295	−0.53245	−0.52201	−0.51366	0.00464	0.00472	0.00479
7	40.92147	41.75660	42.38295	−0.53245	−0.52201	−0.51366	0.00464	0.00472	0.00479

In Table 11.10, T represents a time segment, $\mathrm{P_D}(t)$ represents the load demand of the correspondence to the time segment.

In Table 11.11, MFC, MEC, and MTC present the means of the fuel cost, the emission, and the total cost respectively, STDEV-FC, STDEV-EC and STDEV-TC present corresponding standard deviations. As the standard deviations of every result are all significantly small, the results are believable. It can be seen that the fuel cost decreases and the emission increases when the weight of the fuel cost increases.

The model (M2) is a new environmental economic load dispatch model which considers

Table 11.10 Load demands in different time intervals

T	1	2	3	4	5	6	7	8	9	10	11	12
$P_D(t)$	690	670	670	680	730	800	870	840	890	920	950	910
T	13	14	15	16	17	18	19	20	21	22	23	24
$P_D(t)$	890	890	930	970	930	950	1070	1040	950	850	760	730

the uncertainty in coefficients of the fuel cost and emission functions. The weighting ideal point method, hybrid genetic algorithms with quasi-simplex techniques and fuzzy number ranking method are developed and used to solve the optimization problem described in model (M2). Compared with other fuzzy multi-objective programming methods, the proposed method has three main advantages:

(1) To describe the coefficients of the fuel cost and emission functions by fuzzy numbers can more precisely characterize the fuel cost and emission, and can get a more accurate FDEELD model(M2).

(2) The results described by using fuzzy numbers can provide more information than real numbers. The fuzzy minimum tells not only the approximate fuel cost and emission, but also the dispersivity of the minimal fuel cost and emission.

Table 11.11 The comparison of the results obtained for different weights

(w_1, w_2)	(0.3, 0.7)	(0.5, 0.5)	(0.7, 0.3)
	1067359	1061711	1053936
MFC	1092154	1086218	1078110
	1112300	1106213	1097695
	291.4	472.8	57
STDEV-FC	303.8	377.1	58.3
	312.4	615.9	60
	11423.23	11466.7	11600.89
MEC	11993.81	12041.25	12184.12
	12539.55	12596.67	12744.69
	2.2	4.2	1.3
STDEV-EC	2.5	5.3	1.4
	2.7	9.4	1.5
	1078780	1073181	1065537
MTC	1104148	1098320	1090295
	1124838	1118805	1110440
	290.7	468.5	55
STDEV-TC	300.7	540.6	58.2
	310.4	607.9	60.9

(3) The optimum solution obtained is steady and trustworthy, because the solution of minimum dispersivity has been chosen when candidate solutions have approximately the same total cost.

Table 11.12 Optimal power output of units for weights (0.3, 0.7)

Time segment	Unit number 1	2	3	4	5	6	7
1	51.46	53.05	91.02	88.99	136.41	134.07	134.99
2	49.21	49.30	89.04	88.18	131.88	130.08	132.34
3	49.52	49.59	88.67	87.94	132.89	129.43	131.96
4	50.27	50.22	89.99	89.38	133.92	133.12	133.10
5	56.06	61.42	95.36	93.57	141.20	140.42	141.96
6	68.33	71.53	100.77	99.66	153.84	152.07	153.80
7	76.66	82.65	110.36	107.55	165.83	164.45	162.50
8	69.73	78.13	106.59	105.29	160.19	160.29	159.79
9	80.40	86.77	111.39	110.45	168.51	165.29	167.20
10	86.43	90.07	114.66	112.83	174.17	170.07	171.78
11	90.33	92.03	119.42	116.21	181.36	174.44	176.22
12	86.41	87.87	113.15	112.45	171.72	168.67	169.74
13	80.76	85.96	111.19	110.33	169.91	165.58	166.26
14	75.09	88.24	111.12	110.66	169.85	165.97	169.07
15	87.70	89.80	116.03	112.73	176.57	172.51	174.67
16	94.07	98.21	119.83	116.49	183.22	177.82	180.37
17	86.22	90.68	118.52	114.26	175.70	172.11	172.51
18	87.79	93.94	120.20	116.19	181.15	176.30	174.42
19	103.47	111.97	132.23	130.48	200.75	195.36	195.75
20	106.17	104.57	128.55	126.04	194.27	190.44	189.96
21	89.82	92.90	119.69	115.03	181.85	174.92	175.78
22	68.41	81.11	109.17	105.86	163.49	161.03	160.93
23	57.34	66.97	98.25	97.35	147.49	145.48	147.11
24	55.12	62.23	94.79	94.43	141.83	140.30	141.30
Fuel cost		Emission			Total cost		
1066800		11427.6			1078220		
1091570		11998.6			1103570		
1111700		12544.8			1124240		

11.4 Conclusions and Further Research

Aiming at power markets characterized by the PX and ISO structure, and based on the analysis of market competition mode, this chapter proposes a competition mode of "SMP plus PAB", and establishes a load dispatch mode which considers both ramp rate and valve-point-loading effects. As the pollution caused by power generation becomes an increasingly urgent issue, we analyze the uncertainty of power generation cost function and harmful gas emissions function, and develop a fuzzy environment/economic load dispatch mode by fuzzy set theory to minimize power generation costs and harmful gas emissions.

To solve load dispatch problems, we develop an evolutionary method, which combines an evolutionary method and the quasi-simplex technique to improve the convergence rate and global search capability. This method imposes no special requirement on objective functions, and has very wide applications.

To solve fuzzy dynamic environment/economic load dispatch problems, we propose a weight point method, which converts the FDEELD problem into a single objective fuzzy optimization problem. We also present a fuzzy-number-ranking-based optimization method, which can make the most of available information and give more powerful assistance to decision makers. Experiments reveal the effectiveness of this method.

Based on the research in this chapter, we will focus our future research as follows:

Considering the profit for both generating companies and power corporations at the same time, we will use bilevel programming technique, together with Game theory, to develop bidding models.

We will apply multiple objective techniques and fuzzy non-linear programming technique on our current methods.

Multiple leaders multiple followers bilevel game models will be studied for more practical methods.

Bibliography

[1] Abido, M. A. (2003). Environmental/economic power dispatch using multiobjective evolutionary algorithms, IEEE Transactions on Power Systems, 18, pp. 1529–1537.

[2] Albuyeh, F. and Alaywan, Z. (1999). California ISO formation and implementation, IEEE Computer Applications in Power, 12, pp. 30–34.

[3] Alvey, T, Goodwin, D, Ma, X. (1998). Security-constrained Bid-clearing System for the New Zealand Wholesale Electricity Market, IEEE Transactions Power Systems, 13, pp. 340–346.

[4] Attaviriyanupap, P., Kita, H., Tanaka, E. and Hasegawa, J. (2002). A hybrid EP and SQP for dynamic economic dispatch with nonsmooth fuel cost function, IEEE Transactions on Power Systems, 17, pp. 411–416.

[5] Cheng, C. H. (1998). A new approach for ranking fuzzy numbers by distance method, Fuzzy Sets and Systems, 95, pp. 307–317.

[6] Cheung, K. W., Payman, S. and Asteriadis, S. (1999). Functional Requirements of Energy and Ancillary Service Dispatch for the Interim ISO New England Electricity Market, IEEE Engineering Society Winter Meeting, pp. 269–273.

[7] Danai, B., Kim, J. and Cohen, A. I. (2001). Scheduling Energy and Ancillary Service in the New Ontario Electricity Market, IEEE Power Industry Computer Applications Conference. Sydney, pp. 161–165.

[8] Gao F. and Sheble G. B., Stochastic Optimization Techniques for Economic Dispatch with Combined Cycle Units, Probabilistic Methods Applied to Power Systems, 2006. PMAPS

2006. International Conference on, pp.1–8.

[9] Holland, J. H. (1975). Adaptation in Natural and Artificial Systems, Ann Arbor, MI: Univ.

[10] Herrera, F. and Lozano, M. (2000). Gradual distributed real-coded genetic algorithms, IEEE Trans. Evol. Comput., 4, pp. 43–63.

[11] Huang, C. M., Yang, H. T. and Huang, C. L. (1997). Bi-objective power dispatch using fuzzy satisfaction-maximizing decision approach, IEEE Transactions on Power Systems, 12, pp. 1715–1721.

[12] Irisarri, G., Kimball, L. M., Clements. K. A., Bagchi, A. and Davis, P. W. (1998). Economic dispatch with network and ramping constraints via interior point methods, IEEE Transactions on Power Systems, 13, pp. 236–242.

[13] Li Y., McCalley, J.D. and Ryan S. (2007), Risk-based Unit Commitment, Power Engineering Society General Meeting, IEEE, pp. 1–7.

[14] Li D. P., Pahwa A., Das S., and Rodrigo D. (2007), A New Optimal Dispatch Method for the Day-Ahead Electricity Market Using a Multi-objective Evolutionary Approach, Power Symposium, 2007. NAPS '07. 39th North American, pp. 433–439.

[15] Lee, E. S. and Li, R. L. (1988). Comparison of fuzzy numbers based on the probability measure of fuzzy events, Comput. Math. Appl., 15, pp. 887–896.

[16] Morgan, L. F. and Williams, R. D. (1997). Towards more cost saving under stricter ramping rate constraints of dynamic economic dispatch problems-a genetic based approach, Genetic Algorithms In Engineering Systems: Innovations And Applications, pp. 221–225.

[17] Petrowski, A. (1996). A clearing procedure as a niching method for genetic algorithms, in Proc. IEEE Evolutionary Computation, pp. 798–803.

[18] Rughooputh, H. C. S. and King, R. T. F. (2003). Environmental/economic dispatch of thermal units using an elitist multiobjective evolutionary algorithm, Industrial Technology, 2003 IEEE International Conference on, 1, pp. 48–53.

[19] Venkatesh, P., Gnanadass, R. and Padhy, N. P. (2003). Comparison and application of evolutionary programming techniques to combined economic emission dispatch with line flow constraints, IEEE Transactions on Power Systems, 18, pp. 688–697.

[20] Watts, D., Atienza, P. and Rudnick, h. (2002). Application of the Power Exchange-Independent System Operator Model in Chile, Power Engineering Society Summer Meeting, 2002 IEEE, 3, pp. 1392–1396.

[21] Wen, F. and David, A.K. (2002). Coordination of bidding strategies in day-ahead energy and spinning reserve markets, International Journal of Electrical Power & Energy Systems, 24, pp. 251–261.

[22] Wood, A. J. and Wollenberg, B. F. (1996). Power Generation, Operation and Control.

[23] Walters, D.C. and Sheble, G. B. (1993). Genetic algorithm solution of economic dispatch with valve point loading, IEEE Transactions on Power Systems, 8, pp. 1325–1332.

[24] Yang, H. T., Yang, P. C. and Huang, C. L. (1996). Evolutionary programming based economic dispatch for units with non-smooth fuel cost functions, IEEE Transactions on Power Systems, 11, pp. 112–118.

[25] Yao, X. and Liu, Y. (1999). Evolutionary Programming Made Fast, IEEE Trans. Evol. Comput., Vol. 3, pp. 82–102.

[26] Zhang, G. Wu, Y, Remias, M. and Lu, J. (2003). Formulation of fuzzy linear programming problems as four-objective constrained optimization problems, Applied Mathematics and Computation, 139, pp. 383–399.

Chapter 12

Intelligent Decision-Making for a Smart Home Environment with Multiple Occupants

Andres Muñoz [1], Juan A. Botía [1], and Juan Carlos Augusto [2]

[1] *Dpto. de Información para la Ingeniería y las Comunicaciones, University of Murcia, 30100 Murcia, Spain*

Email: {amunoz, juanbot}@um.es

[2] *School of Computing and Mathematics, University of Ulster, BT37 0QB Newtownabbey, United Kingdom*

jc.augusto@ulster.ac.uk

Ambient Intelligence (AmI) systems rely on the use of environmental information to seamlessly assist users in their daily lives. As the development of AmI architectures is involving a larger amount of users and devices information, the potential occurrence of conflicts derived from the use of this information becomes higher. These conflicts are usually represented as inconsistencies between different pieces of information. As a result, the AmI systems need a mechanism to decide upon these conflicting situations in order to still give an appropriate response. In this chapter we propose the use of Argumentation as a methodology for automatically detecting and solving these conflicting situations. More specifically, we describe a smart TV service which combines different information about viewers' presence and preferences and TV programs data to elaborate a list of recommending programs. Several arguments for and against recommending a same program are presented to the AmI system. Then, by means of argumentative techniques and several meta-decision criteria, the system is able to assist through mediation in the context of conflicting preferences or needs.

12.1 Introduction

Technological advances allow now the realization of a dream which decades ago was confined to the science fiction genre. A revolution is taking place in Computer Science driven by the availability of affordable sensing and actuating devices that can help a computing system to diagnose specific situations of interest and act consequently, all autonomously and unobtrusively [1]. These computing systems are grouped generically under the term

Intelligent Environments because at the core of each of these artificial systems a software module is providing both an intelligent analysis of the information gathered through the sensors and intelligent-decision making that will drive the actuation of the system upon the environment. The intelligent component is often termed *Ambient Intelligence* (AmI) [2, 3, 4, 5, 6, 7, 8] and the physical infrastructure (that also has some degree of intelligence embedded) is often referred as *Smart Environment* [9]. Intelligent Environments understood in the sense described above can be succinctly defined as: *a digital environment that proactively, but sensibly, supports people in their daily lives* [10]. This new paradigm can be exercised in many ways and examples of systems being explored at the moment by the scientific community and some leading companies are: Smart Homes, Smart Cars, Smart Offices, Smart Classrooms to name those that so far have attracted more attention.

Let us consider Smart Homes [11] as this is one of the areas more intensively explored and the one (together with Smart Cars) that is succeeding to reach a significant number of people. The development of this area has been so far largely dominated by a progression of pre-existing communities that were developing technology for telecare/telehealth. Researchers in those areas were mainly focused on building isolated systems that will help people to measure vital signs or to provide some level of speedy response to a problem. For example, people will have a device connected to Internet such that they can take their blood pressure and transmit that to a doctor's computer who will monitor the progress of that parameter. Pendants with an emergency call button where offered as a necklace or a pull down cord will be placed in the bathroom allowing people who felt unwell or unsafe to transmit an alarm via a phone line to a response center which will call by phone and/or send a qualified person to visit the location where the alarm was issued. Researchers in this area progressively came into contact with different types of sensors that opened up the range of problems they were taking care of. For example a bed occupancy sensor allows to estimate how often a person was getting up from bed during the night and a combination of these occupancy sensors coupled with PIR (Passive InfraRed) and RFID (Radio Frequency IDentification) sensors allowed to gather substantial information of the whereabouts and habits of people in a house. Governmental organizations at political and health-care level realized of the potential to restructure health-care provision and decentralize the service shifting the care from the hospital to the home.

There is a substantial body of literature reporting interesting progress in this area [12]. Most of these solutions however are still at a seminal level and relies on important infrastructure constraints. One such common hypothesis is that there is only one person in the house or at least only one to care of (e.g., being actively tracked by the system). However, the reality is that houses are inhabited often by more than one person and when caring for an elderly who is living alone at home is very important so it is that these systems are able to take care of an elderly couple, a family with children, etc. It is this latest scenario that will be the focus of this chapter. If Smart Homes are going to be massively adopted by society then they have to take into account that homes are inhabited by several individuals and each one will require a personalized service from the artificial system. As each individual has different preferences (some prefer TV news whilst others will mainly watch sports programs) and needs (some want the system to entertain them with music whilst others need a quite environment to study or to relax) then conflict seems unavoidable and the responsibility to harmonize will be on the artificial system to balance these preferences and needs. This presents a challenge to the research community focused on decision-making and this is the problem that we want to consider in detail here.

Digital TV (DTV) has brought a revolution in the growth of the number of channels and programs broadcast. Although it represents a wide offer for viewers, they must now cope with hundreds of different channels and programs. Consequently, viewers spend more time searching for a suitable option than watching a specific program, and they eventually get bored and stop looking for other proposals that could have fulfilled their preferences better. In order to avoid viewers wasting time in unsuccessful searches, we propose here an intelligent system which is able to display a small list of recommended programs. Options in this list will be based on the viewers' preferences, program information such as the importance of the event (e.g., breaking news, live event, etc.), external reviews (e.g., magazines), or similarities with other recommended programs. Moreover, this system could be extended with ambient information to perform more intelligent decisions when recommending programs. For example, if the system detects an under-18 viewer, programs which have an advisory "+18" parental guidance (PG) could be discarded from the list.

Our proposal is focused on an Ambient Intelligence system which identifies the current viewers in front of the TV in a particular moment. This identification may be performed in different manners. For example, it could take place when the user initiates the recommending service. In that moment, the service displays a list of the members living in the house, and the user selects the current viewers through the TV remote control. Another more advanced type of identification could be achieved by using RFID tags. In this case, the viewers wear these tags and they are automatically detected by the recommending service when they stay in proximity of the TV. Once the viewers are identified, the AmI system combines the viewers' preference and personal information with the TV programs data retrieved by e.g., Internet Web Services. Based on this combination of information, the AmI system builds a set of *justifications* for and against recommending a program. In this context, a program could be recommended and discarded at the same time by means of different justifications. Consequently, the AmI system must evaluate all the related justifications to take a final decision.

Taking this description as a starting point, the main goal of the AmI system is to display a list of recommended programs according to the evaluation process. To this end, we have devised two approaches to integrate the evaluation process into the AmI system. Firstly, the AmI system acts as a central entity which builds favourable/unfavourable justifications for recommending a program and then it applies a set of *domain criteria* to rule out those justifications that do not fulfill some conditions. On the other hand, the second approach enables the AmI system to build justifications in a distributed manner, having an agent as responsible for finding reasons to recommend a program, while another agent performs the opposite action, i.e., to find reasons against recommending that program.

Both these approaches fit well in a methodology explored by an area of Computer Science in the latest three decades: Argumentation Systems [13, 14, 15, 16, 17]. They naturally model the existence of conflicting views and the need of preference criteria to select, when possible, a most preferable option within those being examined. This has provided a useful framework for the multi-agent systems and robotics communities [18]. For example, a team of agents cooperating to solve a task (e.g., a team of robots in a soccer team trying to score a goal) may have conflicting views on what to do and how to do it. This inconsistent pieces of knowledge within a system would have rendered useless a system based in classical logic but it is tolerated and managed through a meta-decision criteria within an argumentation system.

An argumentation process takes place between two agents, by starting a persuasion dialog [19, 20] where they exchange their justifications (or *arguments*) about their different views (e.g., recommended programs). The goal of this dialog is to persuade each other about the validity of the exchanged arguments. The domain criteria is again used here to evaluate the strength of the arguments.

Therefore, while the domain criteria employed to evaluate justifications or arguments could be the same in our two approaches, its implementation differs depending on the approach selected. Both of them are introduced here in order to evaluate their advantages and drawbacks. In the first approach, the AmI system defines a hierarchical scale of criteria, assigning one level to each specific criterion. Then, the justifications for recommending/discarding a program are evaluated according to the scale in a bottom-to-top manner. Finally, those justifications that fulfill all levels in the scale are classified as acceptable. In the second approach, the implementation of the criteria is integrated in the argumentation process itself. Hence, during the persuasion dialog, an agent A could put forward an argument U_1 defending a program as recommended according to a specific criteria C_1. An agent B could show a disagreement with U_1 by giving another argument U_2 discarding the same program with a criteria C_2, where C_2 is preferred to C_1. However, A could then put forward an argument U_3 against U_2 by using a new criteria C_3 (and C_3 is preferred to C_2). The disagreement between arguments is known as "*attack*". Hence, the argumentation process follows until one of the agents runs out of new arguments for attacking the ones received previously. An argument is then accepted when it has not been attacked or its attackers have been defeated by other accepted arguments in the dialog.

The rest of this chapter is structured as follows. In Section 12.2 the abstract architecture of this AmI system is depicted. Then, Section 12.3 shows the argument structure and how they are built in the AmI system, and Section 12.4 reviews the different domain criteria that are applied to the scenario of recommending TV programs. Section 12.5 explains the two approaches for resolving conflicts when several inconsistent justifications are found, giving some examples in practice. A comparison between these two approaches is offered in Section 12.6. Finally, Section 12.7 points out the conclusions and it gives some future research directions.

12.2 SmartTV System Architecture

The AmI system introduced in Section 12.1 is devoted to obtain an intelligent and context-aware system which recommends a set of TV programs according to different types of information (viewer's presence and preference, program information, etc.). This system will be referred as *SmartTV* system henceforth.

An abstract architecture of the SmartTV system is depicted in Figure 12.1. This design shows two components, the *Information* and *Decision* modules, which form the core of the SmartTV system. In this level, the system is conceived as a black box which collects viewers and programs data and returns a list of recommended programs. The next subsections describe in detail each module.

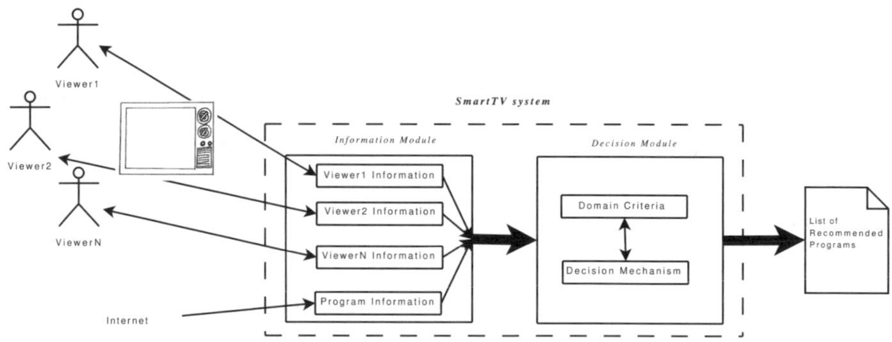

Figure 12.1 An abstract representation of the SmartTV system architecture

12.2.1 *Information Module*

The Information module acts as the input source of data in the system. This module has three specific tasks:

(1) To describe a knowledge model for representing the viewers and programs information.
(2) To collect the viewers and programs data through different kinds of interfaces and properly transform these data to the format established in the knowledge model.
(3) To deliver the knowledge model about current viewers and programs to the Decision Module.

Some characteristics must be taken into account when selecting the knowledge model representation. Firstly, the model should be easily *shareable*, as it will be used by different entities in the system (elements in the Information and Decision modules). Secondly, it should be expressive enough for modeling the targeted situations in the domain. And last but not least, a *formal representation* is needed for the entities in the SmartTV system in order to process and infer the knowledge given. Thus, the inference process will allow the system to find justifications for recommending/discarding a specific program. Moreover, a *semantically annotated* model will enable the definition of domain criteria to be used when evaluating arguments for a program (see Section 12.2.2).

A compelling knowledge model representation which fulfills the previous requirements is OWL (Web Ontology Language) [21], the standard Semantic Web [22] language. In particular, we adopt here the OWL-DL version[1] of this language. This decision is based on

[1]http://www.w3.org/TR/owl-ref/

the next characteristics of OWL and the specific OWL-DL version:

(i) OWL's syntax is written in XML (Extensible Markup Language), which enables an easy and standard manner of interchanging the knowledge model.
(ii) OWL enables the conceptualization of both viewer's personal and preference information and program data by means of ontologies. Different kinds of relationships among these concepts are also possible when modeling ontologies (e.g., a viewer *likes* a program, a program *is similar to* another program).
(iii) OWL-DL is based on Description Logic (DL) [23], a subset of First-Order Logic. DL empowers several types of automatic knowledge manipulation and reasoning processes (see Section 12.3).
(iv) OWL-DL ontologies can be explicitly augmented with semantic axioms (e.g., subsumption, union and intersection of concepts, disjointness, etc.). Thus, other concepts or relationships may automatically be derived from them.

Therefore, the knowledge model in the SmartTV system is represented by means of OWL-DL ontologies. Some examples of concepts and relationships in the SmartTV ontologies will be given throughout this chapter. The interested reader is referred to [21, 23] for more details about OWL and Description Logic.

The collection of input data in the SmartTV system involves two types of actors: Viewers and programs. Graphic user interfaces (GUI) are the common means to obtain viewers' personal (name, age) and preference (preferred programs, genres, actors, etc.) data. Other techniques such as preference learning [24] could also be studied. The collected data is stored in the SmartTV system according to the knowledge model representation selected (OWL-DL ontologies in our approach). Then, when the SmartTV system is requested to offer a list of recommended programs, it first detects the current viewers to only obtain and use the information about those particular viewers.

The information related to TV programs could be obtained from the Internet, by using Web Services retrieving specific and detailed data [25] (program's genre, cast and reviews, similar programs, etc.). These Web Services could even use OWL as the language to represent the information [26]. Therefore, it could easily be integrated into the knowledge model used in the system. GUIs and Internet files could still be part of the input sources.

Finally, all the information about viewers and programs must be separately maintained and timely delivered when the Decision module is to process it. As a result, the Information module may be composed of two software agents, the *Personal* and *Program* agents, which are responsible for the viewers and programs information, respectively. Hence, the Personal agent will keep different viewer's information, delivering it to the Decision module when that particular viewer is detected in front of the TV. On the other hand, the Program agent will maintain an up-to-date information about programs by subscribing to the correspondent Web Services, for example.

12.2.2 *Decision Module*

The Decision module is provided with viewers and programs knowledge from the Information module. Using this knowledge, the module builds arguments for recommending or discarding a program. In this context, some *conflicts* may arise between arguments (e.g., an argument recommends a program because it is one viewer's preference, while another argument discards the same program because it is classified as +18 and a teenager viewer has been detected). To solve this situation, a *decision mechanism* is needed. This mechanism uses some *domain criteria* (e.g., information about parental guidance of a program is more relevant than information about preferences on that program) to evaluate and select which argument must prevail in case of conflict. Therefore, the Decision module has three specific tasks:

(1) To allocate the domain criteria in the knowledge representation model.
(2) To build arguments for recommending and discarding a program according to the knowledge provided by the Information module.
(3) To solve conflicts between inconsistent arguments by employing a specific decision mechanism.

The addition of domain criteria to the knowledge model could be achieved by including *semantic annotations* in the model. Thus, a relation $moreRelevant(x,y)$ between two types of information x and y (e.g., x and y could be concepts and relationships in the OWL ontology) expresses that any element belonging to the type of information x is more important than any element belonging to y when they are compared in different arguments. Let us see an example of a simple domain criteria.

Example 12.1. Suppose an OWL ontology where the concept $ExplicitProg$ represents the type of all programs that are classified as explicit content, since they contain violence, sex, etc. Moreover, suppose that the concept $FavouriteProg$ represents the type of all programs that are classified as preferred, since some viewers like them. Finally, suppose an argument U_d discarding a program p because it is classified as $ExplicitProg$, whereas an argument

U_r recommends the same program p because it is classified as *FavouriteProg*. U_d and U_r are conflicting arguments, but introducing the domain criteria *moreRelevant*(*Explicit-Prog*, *FavouriteProg*) in the OWL ontology as a semantic annotation between concepts, argument U_d prevails over U_r since it contains more relevant information.

Several domain criteria and their integration into the knowledge model will be developed in Section 12.4.

Another question that must be resolved when managing domain criteria is related to *who* is the responsible for defining them. If the domain is well defined and easy to understand, the users themselves may use GUIs for this task. However, a more practical solution will involve system administrators defining domain criteria according to users' requirements. Once the criteria have been established, then users will select which kinds of criteria must be employed as default option or/and on-demand.

The Decision module performs a deductive inference process for building arguments for and against recommending programs. This inference process takes the viewers and programs knowledge from the Information module together with some *domain rules* introduced in the Decision module (see Section 12.3). Domain rules are of the form of

$$IF\ \{\text{conditions on domain element } e\}\ THEN\ \{\text{new information on } e\},$$

meaning that whenever a set of conditions about a particular element *e* in the domain (e.g., a program) are true, then new information about *e* can be inferred according to the THEN part (the conditions part of the rule are called *antecedents*, while the new information part is called *consequent*).

Then, by using a reasoning engine (e.g., Jena [27] or Pellet [28]) and these domain rules, new conclusions are obtained from the viewer and program knowledge. In turn, the inferred conclusions could again be used as knowledge to fulfill the conditions of other rules, and therefore obtain new conclusions by means of a sequential deductive inference process. As a result, this process could be seen as the construction of arguments for supporting different conclusions, which in turn could be supported by other arguments. Section 12.3 shows the argument structure and inference process in detail.

As it has been commented along this chapter, when different arguments about the same domain element coexist, some inconsistency among these arguments could arise. In these cases, the SmartTV system needs a decision mechanism in order to select which argument is more acceptable (if possible). Two approaches are presented here. The first proposal (see Figure 12.2(a)) shows the decision mechanism as a central entity. After receiving the viewers and programs knowledge from the Information module (steps 1 and 2), the central entity builds all the arguments possibles (step 3). A hierarchical scale of domain criteria is allocated in it (step 4), and the arguments generated by this module are then filtered according to the scale (from Criterion 1 to Criterion n). Those arguments that fulfill all the criteria are evaluated as acceptable.

The second proposal (see Figure 12.2(b)) is centered on a distributed construction of arguments, where agent *RecommenderAg* uses the inference process to build arguments recommending programs, while *DiscarderAg* finds arguments for discarding them (step 3). Then, an argumentation process is commenced as a dialog between the agents, where they exchange claims and their justifications to persuade each other about the validity of the claims (step 4). One of the agents is the *proponent* of the dialog by claiming an initial proposal (e.g., that a program p should be recommended), whereas the other agent acts as the *opponent*, trying to invalidate that claim with its own justifications. The result of this argumentation indicates whether the initial claim is accepted by the opponent, or otherwise the proponent must retract it. Both decision mechanisms present advantages and drawbacks, and they will be developed in Section 12.5.

12.3 Arguments in the SmartTV System

As previously stated in Section 12.2.1, the domain model in the SmartTV system is represented by means of OWL-DL ontologies. These ontologies establish the domain concepts and relationships. Furthermore, ontologies also contain *assertions* about these elements, representing the current state of affairs in the domain. In OWL-DL ontologies, two types of assertions are found. Hence, suppose that C and R are a concept and a relationship in the ontology, respectively. Suppose that a and b are two domain elements (e.g., two specific TV programs), known as *individuals*. Then, a *concept assertion* $C(a)$ states that individual a belongs to the concept C (i.e., *a is-a C*), while a *role assertion* $R(a,b)$ satisfies that individual a is related to b by the relationship R. Let us see a simple example of each assertion.

Example 12.2. Suppose an OWL-DL ontology containing the concepts *Viewer* and *Program*, and the relationship *likesProgram(Viewer, Program)*. This relationship relates a viewer with a program which she likes. Then, the concept assertion $Viewer(Peter)$ indicates that $Peter$ is an individual that belongs to the concept *Viewer*. Likewise, the role assertion *likesProgram(Peter, Friday the 13th)* states that $Peter$ likes *Friday the 13th*, which is a program according to the relationship $likesProgram$.

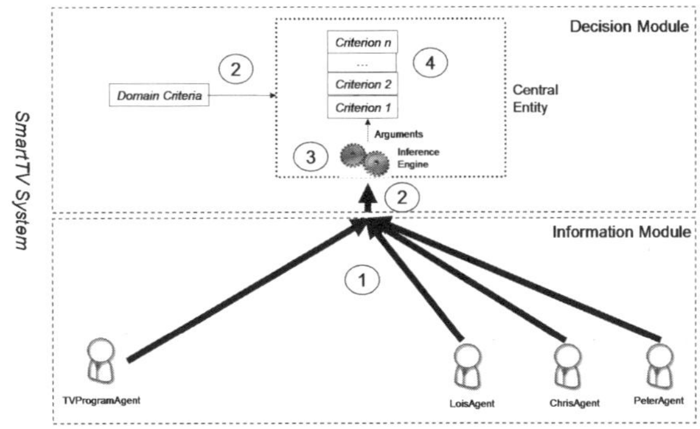

(a) Centralized approach

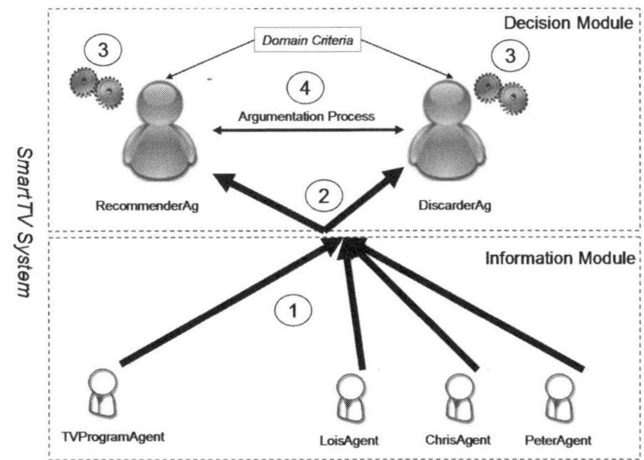

(b) Distributed approach

Figure 12.2 The decision mechanism as a central unity which builds arguments and then filters them using a hierarchical scale (a), and as an argumentation process between recommender and discarder agents (b)

In this context, an argument is defined as the justification for an assertion (e.g., $RecommendedProg(p)$, where p is a TV program) through a deductive inference process [29]. The entailed assertion in the argument is known as *conclusion*, while the justification is called *support set*. This support set is formed by *premises*, which are a group of assertions in the model and exactly one domain rule. Thus, the assertions in the support set match the rule's antecedents, and according to the deductive inference process, the rule's consequent is entailed as the conclusion. The assertions forming part of the premises could be *categorical* (or grounded) facts obtained from the input sources (e.g., the viewers' preferences or the programs' genre), or *derived* assertions from other arguments (e.g., the assertion p *is an explicit program* could be derived by an argument). Then, an argument U supporting a conclusion could in turn be supported by other arguments $V_1,\ldots,V_n$ if some of the U's premises are conclusions supported by $V_1, \ldots, V_n$. Let us put this argument definition by means of a symbolic definition.

Definition 12.1 (Argument). Let $\mathcal{O}$ be an OWL ontology representing a domain model. Let $\rho_1, \ldots, \rho_n$ be assertions about the domain model, $\rho_i \in \mathcal{O}$, $1 \leqslant i \leqslant n$. Then, we define U as an ***argument*** supporting an assertion φ by means of a support set Σ_U, represented as

$$U = (\varphi, \Sigma_U),$$

where:

- φ is the conclusion in U
- Σ_U is a premise list $\{\rho_1, \ldots, \rho_n, DomainRule\}$, where
  - The assertion ρ_i represents a grounded fact stated in the model by an input source or the conclusion of another argument, $V = (\rho_i, \Sigma_V)$,
  - *DomainRule* is an IF-THEN rule whose antecedents are matched by assertions $\{\rho_1, \ldots, \rho_n\}$ and whose consequent is instantiated to φ
- $\Sigma_U \vdash \varphi$, where $\vdash$ is the **modus ponens** operator (performing the deductive inference process).

According to Section 12.2.1, the grounded facts involved in arguments are delivered by the Information module. Regarding domain rules, they could be part of the knowledge model (designed by the domain expert) when the decision mechanism is a central entity, or they could be partially held by the argumentative agents when the argumentation process is used to solve conflicts. This distinction between the type of the rule distribution will be explained at the end of this section. Domain rules are expressed by means of SWRL [30] (Semantic Web Rule Language). This rule language adds a new kind of axiom to OWL-DL, namely Horn clause rules, which extends OWL's syntax and semantics in order to express IF-THEN rules such as the one in Section 12.2.2. SWRL rules are of the form of an implication between a conjunction of antecedents (*body*) and a consequent (*head*). Both parts of the rule consist of *atoms*: unary ($C(x)$) or binary ($R(x,y)$) assertions from the OWL-DL language—where x, y are variables or OWL-DL individuals—and *Built-ins*. These built-ins are functions that offer different operations on variables (comparison, math,...).

Let us see some domain rules for the SmartTV system. To this end, an OWL-DL ontology must be previously defined to conceptualize the concepts *RecommendedProg* and *DiscardedProg* as recommended and discarder TV programs, respectively. Moreover,

$DiscardedProg \equiv \neg RecommendedProg$ according to this ontology, i.e., they are contradictory concepts. Other concepts, such as *Viewer* or *Review* have been also defined in the ontology. Likewise, relationships such as *likesProgram(Viewer, Program)*, *dislikesGenre(Viewer, Program)* and *hasSimilar(Program, Program)* are available in the ontology, among others. The rest of concepts and relationships are referred in the domain rules, therefore it is not necessary to explain them here.

Once the SmartTV ontology has been defined, it can be used as a knowledge model for creating rules. The design of the domain rules has been divided into two groups. Rules in group A are designed to classify a program as recommended, whereas rules in group B are directed to discard a program. This a convenient manner of grouping rules, in order to clearly differentiate the proposal of each rule and easily add future rules to their corresponding group. Note that the following set of rules is not exhaustive, but a small model of the logical rules employed to classify a TV program as recommended or discarded[2]:

(A) These three rules classify a program as recommended whenever it is classified as favourite, interesting or important:

$$\begin{array}{ll} \textbf{RuleFav}: & FavouriteProg(?p) \Rightarrow RecommendedProg(?p) \\ \textbf{RuleInt}: & InterestingProg(?p) \Rightarrow RecommendedProg(?p) \\ \textbf{RuleImp}: & ImportantProg(?p) \Rightarrow RecommendedProg(?p) \end{array}$$

Now, the following rules are necessary for classifying a program as favourite, interesting or important:

(A.1) This set of rules classify a program as favourite according to the viewer's preferences on the program, its genre or the program's cast, respectively:

$$\begin{array}{ll} \textbf{RuleLikeP}: & Viewer(?x) \wedge Program(?p) \wedge \mathrm{likesProg}(?x,\ ?p) \Rightarrow FavouriteProg(?p) \\ \textbf{RuleLikeG}: & Viewer(?x) \wedge Genre(?g) \wedge Program(?p) \wedge \\ & \wedge\ \mathrm{likesGenre}(?x,\ ?g) \wedge hasGenre(?p,?g) \Rightarrow FavouriteProg(?p) \\ \textbf{RuleLikeA}: & Viewer(?x) \wedge Actor(?a) \wedge Program(?p) \wedge \\ & \wedge\ \mathrm{likesActor}(?x,\ ?a) \wedge cast(?p,?a) \Rightarrow FavouriteProg(?p) \end{array}$$

(A.2) These two rules classify a program as interesting according to some magazine reviews about that program or due to its similarity with some other favourite pro-

[2]In this chapter, *IF* ($\mathrm{cond}_1, \mathrm{cond}_2, \ldots, \mathrm{cond}_n$) *THEN conclusion* rules are represented by the following syntax: $cond_1 \wedge cond_2 \wedge \ldots \wedge cond_n \Rightarrow conclusion$, where *IF* is omitted, *THEN* is substituted by $\Rightarrow$, and '$\wedge$' is a conjunction operator read as "and". Variables in rules are represented by preceding their name with the symbol '?', whereas OWL-DL individuals start with a capital letter.

grams:

$$\textbf{RuleRev}: \quad Review(?r) \wedge Program(?p) \wedge hasReview(?p, ?r) \wedge \\ \wedge\ rating(?r, ?v) \wedge greaterThan(?v, 5) \Rightarrow InterestingProg(?p)$$

$$\textbf{RuleSimilar}: \quad FavouriteProg(?s) \wedge Program(?p) \wedge \\ \wedge\ hasSimilar(?p, ?s) \Rightarrow InterestingProg(?p)$$

Observe the use of the built-in *greaterThan* in the rule *RuleRev*. This built-in is matched if the rating value in $?v$ is greater than 5. Notice that when $?v$ is lower than 5, the built-in is not matched and the rule will not be fired.

(A.3) This rule classifies a program as important when it has some relevant tags associated, as for example an "urgent" tag:

$$\textbf{RuleUrg}: Tag(?t) \wedge Program(?p) \wedge tagValue(?t, Urgent) \wedge \\ \wedge\ hasTag(?p, ?t) \Rightarrow ImportantProg(?p)$$

(B) These three rules classify a program as discarded whenever it is classified as non-favourite, non-interesting or containing explicit content:

$$\textbf{RuleNonFav}: \neg FavouriteProg(?p) \Rightarrow DiscardedProg(?p)$$
$$\textbf{RuleNonInt}: \neg InterestingProg(?p) \Rightarrow DiscardedProg(?p)$$
$$\textbf{RuleExp}: ExplicitProg(?p) \Rightarrow DiscardedProg(?p)$$

Now, the following rules are necessary for classifying a program as non-favourite, non-interesting or explicit:

(B.1) This set of rules classify a program as non-favourite according to the viewer's dislikes on the program, its genre or the program's cast, respectively:

$$\textbf{RuleDislikeP}: \quad Viewer(?x) \wedge Program(?p) \wedge dislikesProg(?x, ?p) \Rightarrow \neg FavouriteProg(?p)$$

$$\textbf{RuleDislikeG}: \quad Viewer(?x) \wedge Genre(?g) \wedge Program(?p) \wedge \\ \wedge\ dislikesGenre(?x, ?g) \wedge hasGenre(?p, ?g) \Rightarrow \neg FavouriteProg(?p)$$

$$\textbf{RuleDislikeA}: \quad Viewer(?x) \wedge Actor(?a) \wedge Program(?p) \wedge \\ \wedge\ dislikesActor(?x, ?a) \wedge cast(?p, ?a) \Rightarrow \neg FavouriteProg(?p)$$

(B.2) These two rules classify a program as non-interesting according to some magazine reviews about that program or due to its similarity with some other non-favourite programs:

$$\begin{aligned}
\textbf{RuleNegRev}: \quad & Review(?r) \wedge Program(?p) \wedge hasReview(?p,\ ?r) \wedge \\
& \wedge\ rating(?r, ?v) \wedge lessEqThan(?v, 5) \Rightarrow \neg InterestingProg(?p) \\
\textbf{RuleNegSimilar}: \quad & \neg FavouriteProg(?s) \wedge Program(?p) \wedge \\
& \wedge\ hasSimilar(?p,\ ?s) \Rightarrow \neg InterestingProg(?p)
\end{aligned}$$

Observe the use of the built-in *lessEqThan* in the rule *RuleNegRev*. This built-in is matched if the rating value in ?*v* is lower or equal than 5. Notice that when ?*v* is greater than 5, the built-in is not matched and the rule will not be fired.

(B.3) This rule classifies a program as explicit when it has a parental guidance (PG) and there is a viewer younger than the recommended age in the PG:

$$\begin{aligned}
\textbf{RuleAge}: \quad & Viewer(?x) \wedge Program(?p) \wedge hasAge(?x, ?a) \wedge \\
& \wedge\ PG(?p, ?g) \wedge lessEqThan(?a, ?g) \Rightarrow ExplicitProg(?p)
\end{aligned}$$

After defining the domain rules, some examples of arguments can be given.

Example 12.3. Suppose that *Peter* is a viewer using the SmartTV system, whose preferences are represented by the agent *PeterAg*. Peter likes the TV series *Lost*, and a *ProgramAg* in the Information module stores information about that program. Then, all this knowledge is passed to the Decision Module. This module builds the following arguments:

$$\begin{aligned}
U_1 &= (RecommendedProg(Lost), \{FavouriteProg(Lost), RuleFav\}), \\
U_2 &= (FavouriteProg(Lost), \{Viewer(Peter), Program(Lost), likes(Peter, Lost), RuleLikesP\})
\end{aligned}$$

Note that argument U_1 concludes *Lost* as a recommended program, based on the knowledge that the program has been classified as favourite. This classification is justified by the Peter's liking to *Lost* and the use of the rule *RuleLikeP* in argument U_2. A graphical representation of both arguments is shown in Figure 12.3. Each argument is contained in a box with a solid black line. Conclusions are represented with a rectangular box, while premises are drawn in an oval shape. Premises being grounded facts have a solid line, whereas derived assertions have a dashed line. Domain rules are represented by means of arrows next to the rule's name.

After defining the argument structure and how they are built, we can now explore the type of conflicts between arguments [31]. This notion of conflict is also known as *attack*. Thus, when an argument U supports a conclusion which is conflict with another argument V, it is said that U *attacks* V. As mentioned in Example 12.1, different arguments can support inconsistent conclusions. In this case, the conclusion in argument U attacks the conclusion in V, and vice versa. This attack is known as *rebut*. Moreover, the conclusion in U may

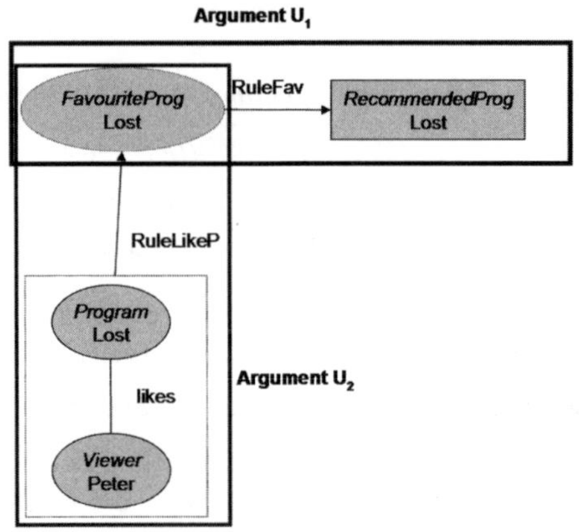

Figure 12.3 Argument U_1 supports *Lost* as recommended program, while U_1's premise is supported by U_2

attack the premises in the support set of the argument V. This attack is known as *undercut*. Let us see a formal definition for both attacks.

Definition 12.2 (Rebut). Let $\mathscr{O}$ be an OWL ontology representing a domain model. Let $U = (\varphi, \Sigma_U)$, $V = (\gamma, \Sigma_V)$ be two arguments in $\mathscr{O}$. Then, U **rebuts** V iff

- $\varphi \cup \mathscr{O} \nvdash \bot$,
- $\gamma \cup \mathscr{O} \nvdash \bot$, and
- $\varphi \cup \gamma \cup \mathscr{O} \vdash \bot$

Note that a rebut between U and V is detected in the SmartTV system when the addition of the conclusions of both arguments entails an inconsistence in the knowledge model, and besides this inconsistence is not generated when adding each conclusion separately. Next, the definition of the other type of attack between arguments is given.

Definition 12.3 (Undercut). Let $\mathscr{O}$ be an OWL ontology representing a domain model. Let $U = (\varphi, \Sigma_U)$, $V = (\gamma, \Sigma_V)$ be two arguments in $\mathscr{O}$. Then, U **undercuts** V iff $\exists \rho_i \in \Sigma_V$ such as

- $\varphi \cup \mathscr{O} \nvdash \bot$,
- $\rho_i \cup \mathscr{O} \nvdash \bot$, and
- $\varphi \cup \rho_i \cup \mathscr{O} \vdash \bot$

The concept of undercut may also be applied to the domain rules employed in the support set, although this attack is beyond the scope of this chapter and it will not be explored here.

Once attacks between arguments are detected, now it is necessary to evaluate them in order to decide which argument is more *preferable*. Thus, when the argument U is evaluated as more preferable than argument V, it is said that U *defeats* V. In the SmartTV system, we consider that U defeats V if the two following conditions hold: Firstly, U rebuts V and the premises in U are more relevant than the premises in V according to a particular domain criteria. And secondly, U is not undercut by any other argument. A formal definition of the concept of defeat is given as follows.

Definition 12.4 (Defeat). Let $\mathcal{O}$ be an OWL ontology representing a domain model. Let Ω be the set of all arguments built in $\mathcal{O}$. Let $U = (\varphi, \Sigma_U)$, $V = (\gamma, \Sigma_V)$ be two arguments in Ω. Then, U **defeats** V, represented as $U \gg V$, iff

- U rebuts V and U is preferable to V according to a domain criteria in $\mathcal{O}$,and
- $\nexists V' \in \Omega$ such as V' undercuts U, and besides V' is not defeated.

The domain criteria used to determine the preferable relationship between arguments will be introduced in the next section. Observe that Definition 12.4 only states a defeat relationship between two arguments. However, as the second condition of the definition states, an argument can be attacked by other arguments. Therefore, it is not sufficient to compare pairs of arguments. The status of an argument (i.e., acceptable, defeated or undecided) must be defined based on the interactions among an argument and the rest of arguments in the domain. In order to establish such a status, a decision mechanism is employed. As previously commented in Section 12.2.2, we propose here two different types of implementations of this decision mechanism. They will be explored in Section 12.5.

Finally, it is important to notice how domain rules are distributed depending on the decision mechanism selected. If a central entity (Figure 12.2(a)) is in charge of building the arguments, it will contain all rules in the domain (A and B rule groups in the SmartTV system). Contrarily, when the construction of arguments is distributed as in the approach of Figure 12.2(b), domain rules will be distributed as well. For example, in the SmartTV system, *RecommenderAg* will control all rules in group A, whereas rules in group B are separately maintained by *DiscarderAg*. Observe that this distribution means that *RecommenderAg* is not aware of the rules in group B, and vice versa, *DiscarderAg* is not aware of group A rules.

The type of the rule distribution has several inherit implications. One of these implications is related to the placement of the domain criteria used to evaluate conflicting arguments. Thus, the domain criteria could be defined on the rules when a central entity keeps

the whole set of domain rules. For example, the relationships[3] (*RuleExp* > *RuleFav*) and (*RuleExp* > *RuleInt*) could be stated in the central entity, meaning that an argument discarding a program p because it based on the rule *RuleExp* prevails over arguments recommending p when they are based on the rules *RuleFav* or *RuleInt* (see Example 12.4). However, this type of rule relationship cannot be held when rules are distributed. If an agent does not know the rules maintained by other agents, it is impossible for it to set a prevailing relation between its own rules and those ones. For instance, *DiscarderAg* cannot set its own rule *RuleExp* as more relevant than *RuleFav* or *RuleInt* (both rules belong to group A), since the agent does not even know the existence of such rules.
The solution proposed here is to shift the placement of the domain criteria from the rules to the assertions in the premises, or more specifically, to the "type of information" of the assertions in the premises. This means that the concept or relationship in the knowledge model to which the assertions belong will be used to evaluate the prevalence of any argument. That is to say, the domain criteria takes the information in the assertions used as premises to evaluate conflicting arguments. Let us see an example.

Example 12.4. As shown in the groups A and B of domain rules, the concepts *ExplicitProg*, *FavouriteProg* and *InterestingProg* represent the set of programs that have been inferred as explicit content, favourite and interesting, respectively. Now, suppose that the relationships (*ExplicitProg* > *FavouriteProg*) and (*ExplicitProg* > *InterestingProg*) are defined on the SmartTV ontology, meaning that the type of information about the explicit content of a program is more relevant that its preference or interest. Moreover, the following arguments about the program *Lost* have been built:

$$\begin{aligned} U_F &= (RecommendedProg(Lost), \{FavouriteProg(Lost), RuleFav\}), \\ U_I &= (RecommendedProg(Lost), \{InterestingProg(Lost), RuleInt\}), \\ U_E &= (DiscardedProg(Lost), \{ExplicitProg(Lost), RuleExp\}) \end{aligned}$$

According to the SmartTV ontology, argument U_E is inconsistent with arguments U_F and U_I since their conclusions are in conflict. However, the U_E premise set contains an assertion belonging to *ExplicitProg* (*ExplicitProg*(*Lost*)), which is more relevant than the type of information of the premises *FavouriteProg*(*Lost*) and *InterestingProg*(*Lost*) in arguments U_F and U_I, respectively. As a result, $U_E \gg U_F$ and $U_E \gg U_I$.

The feasibility of this solution is based on two features of the knowledge model representation. Firstly, this representation is shared by all the entities involved in the AmI system, as commented in Section 12.2.1. Therefore, the argumentative agents are totally aware of the

[3] The operator > represents the relationship "moreRelevant"

knowledge model used in the system, and the domain criteria is included in it. Secondly, the modeling language OWL-DL allows for semantic annotations on the different concepts and relationships that constitute the domain. Due to these annotations, the domain criteria are easily added to the model. Examples of these criteria and how they are introduced in the model will be given in Section 12.4.

12.4 Domain Criteria in the SmartTV System

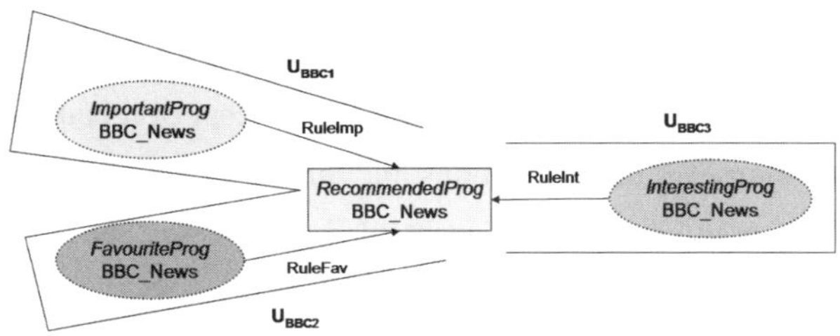

(a) Several arguments (based on different type of information) supporting the same conclusion

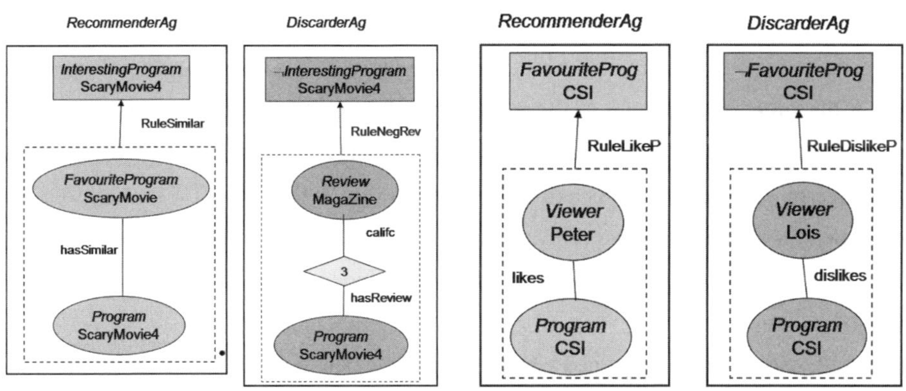

(b) Two argument supporting conflicting conclusions, based on different type of information

(c) Two argument supporting conflicting conclusions, based on the same type of information

Figure 12.4 Three different situations when building arguments in the SmartTV system

According to the domain rules listed in Section 12.3, three different situations could happen when building arguments:

(1) The same conclusion may be justified by **different** types of information. For example, the conclusion *RecommendedProg*(*BBCNews*) could be inferred due to *BBCNews* is classified as an important, favourite and interesting program (see Figure 12.4(a)).

(2) Inconsistent conclusions may be justified by **different** types of information. For example, the conclusion *InterestingProg*(*ScaryMovie*4) could be inferred due to its similarity with another preferred program (e.g., *ScaryMovie*). Contrarily, ¬*InterestingProg*(*ScaryMovie*4) could be inferred because there is a review about the program assigning it a low rating (see Figure 12.4(b)).

(3) Inconsistent conclusions may be justified by the **same** type of information. For example, the conclusion *FavouriteProg*(*CSI*) could be inferred due to one viewer's liking. Contrarily, ¬*FavouriteProg*(*CSI*) could be inferred because there is another viewer who dislikes the program (see Figure 12.4(c)).

Note that the situations 2 and 3 are equivalent to the concept of rebutting given in Definition 12.2. When dealing with these situations, the SmartTV system needs some criteria in order to decide which argument is more acceptable in each case. The next subsections give some ideas about how to define a criteria in each situation.

12.4.1 *Same Conclusion Supported by Different Type of Information*

This subsection deals with criteria for deciding the "best option" between arguments supporting the same conclusion. This best option is understood as the argument whose assertions in the support set belong to the most relevant type of information according to the knowledge model. Thus, we include here a new association between the elements of the knowledge model (i.e., concepts and their relationships in the SmartTV ontology) to express when an element is more relevant than others. This association will be referred as *preferred* in the examples of this section, and it is included in the SmartTV ontology as an OWL-DL relationship.
As a result, two criteria are defined which include this new association: A criterion C_+ for the arguments' premises supporting the conclusion φ is proposed, and another criterion C_- is given for arguments' premises supporting the conclusion $\neg\varphi$. Let us see several examples of these criteria in the SmartTV system.

Case 1: Recommended Criteria

Three types of arguments can be built for the conclusion *RecommendedProg*(p):

- Based on the importance of p, e.g., because it is tagged as urgent (*ImportantProg*(p)).
- Based on the viewers' preferences on p , e.g., because someone likes the genre of the program (*FavouriteProg*(p)).

- Based on some interesting features about p, e.g., due to a similarity found with another favorite program p' ($InterestingProg(p)$).

Then, the following criteria $RecCriteria_{+}$ may be established (see Figure 12.5):

(i) An argument recommending p because $ImportantProg(p)$ contains a more relevant type of information than those based on $FavouriteProg(p)$ or $InterestingProg(p)$. An important program could represent breaking news or a live event.

(ii) An argument recommending p because $FavouriteProg(p)$ contains a more relevant type of information than those based on $InterestingProg(p)$. The viewer's personal preferences on a program are superior to reviews or similar features to other programs.

Likewise, three types of arguments can be built for the conclusion $DiscardedProg(p)$:

- Based on the PG of p, e.g., because it is not suitable for some viewers according to their ages ($ExplicitProg(p)$).
- Based on the viewers' preferences on p , e.g., because someone dislikes the actors playing in it ($\neg FavouriteProg(p)$).
- Based on some interesting features about p, e.g., due to a bad review in a magazine ($\neg InterestingProg(p)$).

Then, the following criteria $RecCriteria_{-}$ may be established (see Figure 12.5):

(i) An argument discarding p because $ExplicitProg(p)$ contains a more relevant type of information than those based on $\neg FavouriteProg(p)$ or $\neg InterestingProg(p)$. An explicit program could contain violence or sex, therefore it is a powerful reason to discard it more than not being favourite or interesting.

(ii) An argument discarding p because $\neg FavouriteProg(p)$ contains a more relevant type of information than those based on $\neg InterestingProg(p)$.

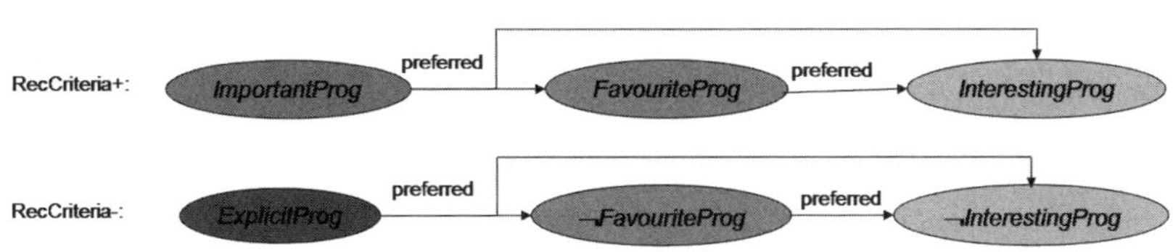

Figure 12.5 Diagram representation of $RecCriteria_{+}$ and $RecCriteria_{-}$.

Case 2: Favourite Criteria

Three types of arguments can be built for $FavouriteProg(p)$ / $\neg FavouriteProg(p)$:

- Based on the direct viewer's like/dislike of program p ($likesProg(x,p)$/$dislikesProg(x,p)$).
- Based on the viewer's like/dislike of p's genre ($likesGenre(x,g)$/$dislikesGenre(x,g)$).
- Based on the viewer's like/dislike of p's cast ($likesActor(x,a)$/$dislikesActor(x,a)$).

Then, the following criteria $FavCriteria_{+}$/$FavCriteria_{-}$ may be established (see Figure 12.6):

(i) An argument classifying p as $FavouriteProg(p)$/$\neg FavouriteProg(p)$ by means of direct information ($likesProg(x,p)$/$dislikeProg(x,p)$) contains a more relevant type of information than those based on the program's genre or cast.

(ii) An argument classifying p as $FavouriteProg(p)$/$\neg FavouriteProg(p)$ by means of p's genre information ($likesGenre(x,g)$/$dislikesGenre(x,g)$) contains a more relevant type of information than those based on the program's cast.

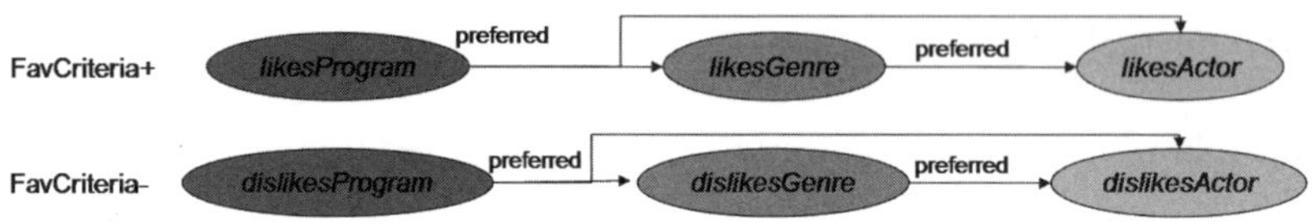

Figure 12.6 Diagram representation of $FavCriteria_{+}$ and $FavCriteria_{-}$.

Case 3: Interesting Criteria

Two types of arguments can be built for $InterestingProg(p)$ / $\neg InterestingProg(p)$:

- Based on the review of a program p ($hasReview(p,r)$).
- Based on the similarity between p and other programs ($hasSimilar(p,s)$).

Then, the following criteria $IntCriteria_{+}$/$IntCriteria_{-}$ may be established (see Figure 12.7): An argument classifying p as $InterestingProg(p)$/$\neg InterestingProg(p)$ by means of similar information ($hasSimilar(p,s)$) contains a more relevant type of information than those based on the program's review.

12.4.2 *Inconsistent Conclusions Supported by Different Type of Information*

This subsection deals with criteria for evaluating arguments supporting inconsistent conclusions. In this case, the arguments are based on different types of information. By combining the criteria C_+ and C_- defined in Section 12.4.1, it is possible to define an evaluation mechanism for this type of inconsistency.

Looking deeply in the examples of criteria C_+ and C_- given in the three cases of Section 12.4.1, there are similarities between the associations *preferred* defined over the types of information in each case (see Figures 12.5, 12.6 and 12.7). For example, in $RecCriteria_+$ and $RecCriteria_-$, the assertions based on the type of information $FavouriteProg$ are more relevant than those based on $InterestingProg$, careless of the type of information being positive or negative.

As a result, it is possible to find *groups* of types of information composed of positive and negative assertions about the same information. These assertions belonging to the same group have an equal strength. However, we can now define prevailing relationships between groups of types of information. Let us see an example of a comparison between two groups.

Example 12.5. Suppose that $FavouriteInfoGroup$ is the group of type of information about the favorite status of a program (positive or negative), and $InterestingInfoGroup$ is the type of information about its degree of interest (again, positive or negative). Then, the relationship between these two groups could be ($FavouriteInfoGroup > Interesting$-$InfoGroup$). Now, suppose the two following conflicting arguments:

$$U_F = (RecommendedProg(Lost), \{FavouriteProg(Lost), RuleFav\}),$$
$$U_D = (DiscardedProg(Lost), \{\neg InterestingProg(Lost), RuleNonInt\})$$

Since U_F is based on the $FavouriteInfoGroup$ type of information, and U_D is based on the $InterestingInfoGroup$ one, $U_F \gg U_D$ according to the type of relevant information of each group.

Note that the decision reached in Example 12.5 does not mean that U_F will finally be ac-

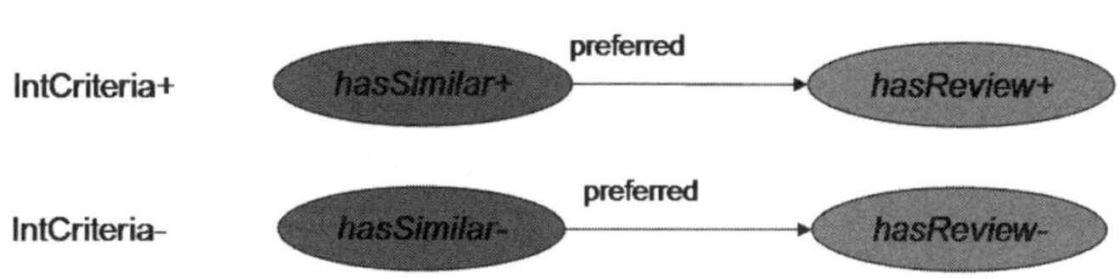

Figure 12.7 Diagram representation of $IntCriteria_+$ and $IntCriteria_-$.

cepted in the AmI system, since new attacks on the argument employed to infer *Favourite-Prog*$(Lost)$ are still possible.

The groups of type of information are modeled as OWL-DL concepts in the SmartTV ontology, whereas the association *preferred* defined in Section 12.4.1 is used again to represent the prevailing relationships between these groups. The following examples show how a criterion $C_{+/-}$ could be defined by creating a new $XXXInfoGroup$ concept and merging the criteria C_+ and C_- previously given. Obviously, there will be cases where groups of type of information cannot be found. In these situations, new relations of preference between types of information must be defined in $C_{+/-}$.

Case 1: $RecCriteria_{+/-}$

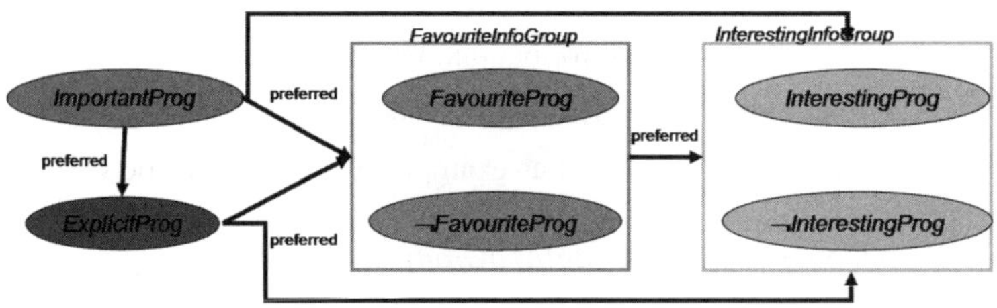

Figure 12.8 $RecCriteria_{+/-}$ as a result of combining $RecCriteria_+$ and $RecCriteria_-$.

$RecCriteria_+$ and $RecCriteria_-$ can be merged by grouping the same type of information as depicted in Figure 12.8. Thus, an argument based on $ImportantProg(p)$ is preferred to those based on $FavouriteInfoGroup$ or $InterestingInfoGroup$ type, careless of this information being positive or negative. For instance, suppose the following arguments are built in the SmartTV system:

$$\begin{aligned}
U_{Imp} &= (RecommendedProg(BBCNews), \{ImportantProg(BBCNews), RuleImp\}),\\
U_{\neg F} &= (DiscardedProg(BBCNews), \{\neg FavouriteProg(Lost), RuleNonFav\}),\\
U_{\neg Int} &= (DiscardedProg(BBCNews), \{\neg InterestingProg(Lost), RuleNonInt\})
\end{aligned}$$

Then, $U_{Imp} \gg U_{\neg F}$ and $U_{Imp} \gg U_{\neg Int}$. Here it is important to remember that U_{Imp} can still be attacked by other arguments whose conclusions oppose to the premise *Important-Prog*$(BBCNews)$ in U_{Imp}.

Note that there is a question that must be resolved in this criteria: What happens among $ImportantProg$ and $ExplicitProg$?. They cannot be grouped since they represent different types of information. As a result, a new relation of prevalence between them is needed. For example, we can agree that an argument recommending p because it is classified as important is preferred to an argument discarding p because it includes explicit content (e.g., p could be breaking news or a live event containing high relevant information which must be broadcast although it contains violence, deaths, etc.). Thus, a new preference relation from $ImportantProg$ to $ExplicitProg$ is depicted in Figure 12.8.

Case 2: $FavCriteria_{+/-}$

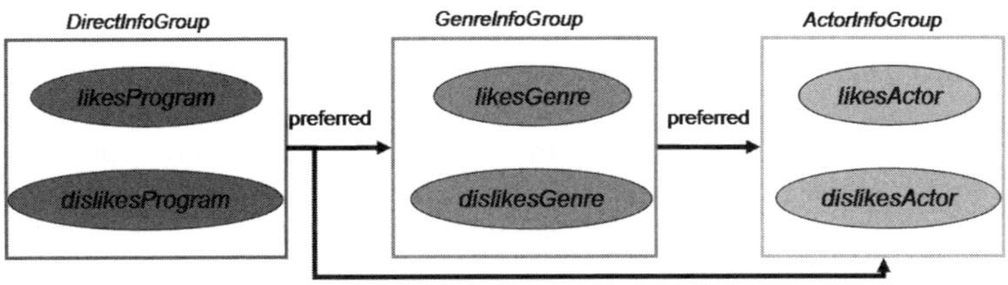

Figure 12.9 $FavCriteria_{+/-}$ as a result of combining $FavCriteria_{+}$ and $FavCriteria_{-}$.

$FavCriteria_{+}$ and $FavCriteria_{-}$ can be merged by grouping the same type of information as depicted in Figure 12.9. Observe the three groups of type of info in the figure, which have been modeled as OWL concepts. Now, suppose the following arguments in the SmartTV system:

$$
\begin{aligned}
U_P &= (FavouriteProg(XFiles), && \{Viewer(Peter), Program(XFiles), likesProg(Peter, XFiles),\\
&&& RuleLikeP\}),\\
U_{\neg G} &= (\neg FavouriteProg(XFiles), && \{Viewer(Lois), Genre(Sci-Fi), Program(XFiles),\\
&&& dislikesGenre(Lois, Sci-Fi), hasGenre(XFiles, Sci-Fi),\\
&&& RuleDislikeG\}),\\
U_{\neg A} &= (\neg FavouriteProg(XFiles), && \{Viewer(Chris), Actor(D.Duchovny), Program(XFiles),\\
&&& dislikesActor(Chris, D.Duchovny), cast(XFiles, D.Duchovny),\\
&&& RuleDislikeA\})
\end{aligned}
$$

Then, the prevailing relationships among these arguments is inferred as $U_P \gg U_{\neg G}$ and $U_P \gg U_{\neg A}$.

Case 3: $IntCriteria_{+/-}$

$IntCriteria_{+}$ and $IntCriteria_{-}$ can be merged by grouping the same type of information as depicted in Figure 12.10. As an example of this criteria, suppose the following arguments in the SmartTV system, where $U_{Sim} \gg U_{\neg Rev}$:

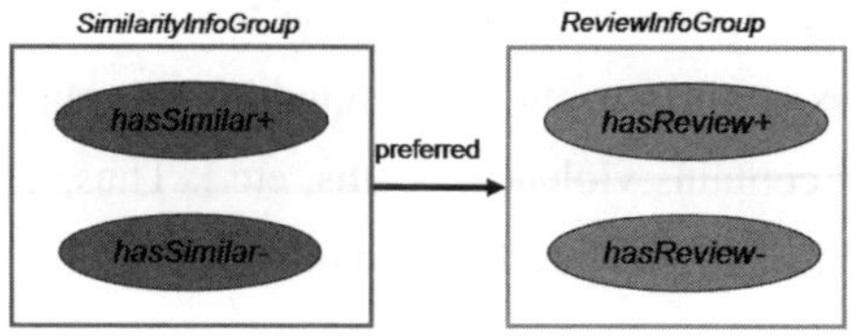

Figure 12.10 $IntCriteria_{+/-}$ as a result of combining $IntCriteria_{+}$ and $IntCriteria_{-}$.

$$
\begin{aligned}
U_{\neg Rev} &= (\neg InterestingProg(ScaryMovie4),\ \{Review(MagaZine\_001), Program(ScaryMovie4),\\
&\qquad hasReview(ScaryMovie4, MagaZine\_001),\\
&\qquad rating(MagaZine\_001, 3), RuleNegRev\}),\\
U_{Sim} &= (\neg InterestingProg(ScaryMovie4),\ \{FavouriteProg(ScaryMovie), Program(ScaryMovie4),\\
&\qquad hasSimilar(ScaryMovie4, ScaryMovie), RuleSimilar\})
\end{aligned}
$$

12.4.3 *Inconsistent Conclusions Supported by the Same Type of Information*

This subsection deals with criteria for evaluating arguments supporting inconsistent conclusions. In this case, the arguments are based on the same type of information. The question here is how to decide which argument is preferable when their premises have the same type of information value. An example of these type of inconsistency is given in Figure 12.11. In this figure, the argument U_{RA1} concludes *Lost* as a recommended program based on the *FavouriteProg* type of information, whereas U_{DA1} discards the same program based on $\neg FavouriteProg$. As we have seen in Section 12.4.2, both types of information are equally strong according to $RecCriteria_{+/-}$ (see Figure 12.8). Two situations can be developed in this scenario.

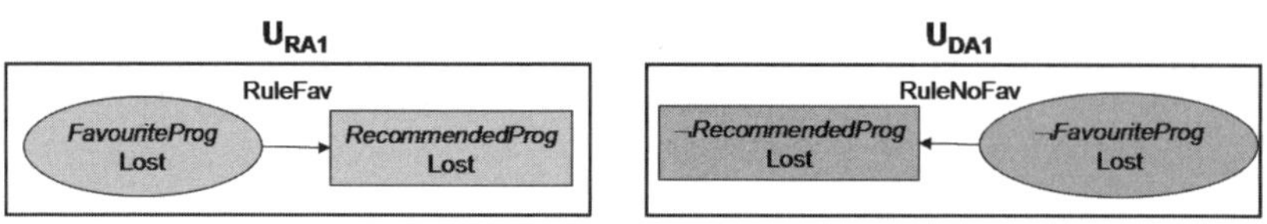

Figure 12.11 Two conflicting arguments based on the same type of information.

Firstly, if the premises with the same type of information are derived assertions from other arguments (let us call them *subarguments*), then it is possible to compare these subarguments using the criteria described in Section 12.4.2. In this case, an attack to the support set (the *undecutting* concept given in Definition 12.3) may exist with respect to the two conflicting arguments if the subarguments can be evaluated according to that criteria. An example of this situation is given in Figure 12.12. In this example, the premise $FavouriteProg(Lost)$ in U_{RA1} is supported by the argument U_{RA2}, which is based on the direct viewer's preference on a program. Contrarily, $\neg FavouriteProg(Lost)$ in U_{DA1} is supported by the argument U_{DA2}, which is based on the viewer's genre preference. When comparing these two subarguments, U_{RA2} is preferred to U_{DA2} according to the criteria $FavCriteria_{+/-}$. Then, U_{RA2} *undercuts* argument U_{DA1}, as its support has been defeated. As a result, U_{DA1} is not a valid argument now, and eventually U_{RA1} defeats U_{DA1} according to Definition 12.4. Observe that comparing subarguments could be a recursive process, since these subarguments may be supported by other subarguments.

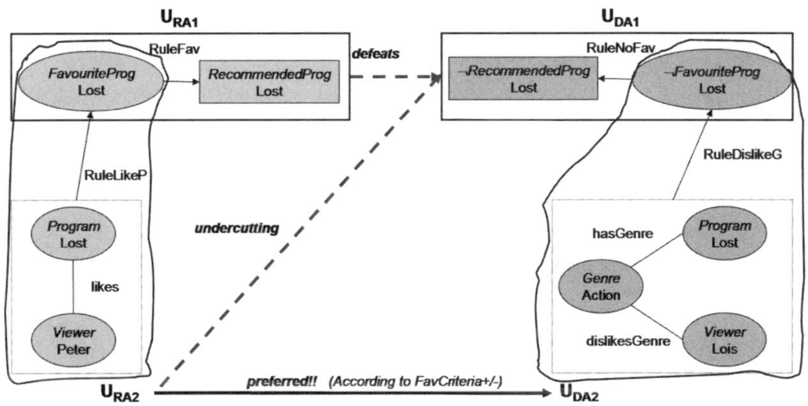

Figure 12.12 Subarguments for the derived assertions $FavouriteProg(Lost)$ and $\neg FavouritePorg(Lost)$ based on different type of information.

Secondly, when all premises are grounded facts (i.e., they do not come from a subargument), the previous solution is not possible. Then, the inconsistent situation between arguments could be left as unresolved, as shown in Figure 12.13. In this case, both subarguments U_{RA2} and U_{DA2} are equally strong too, according to criteria $FavCriteria_{+/-}$, and both are composed of grounded facts.

A possibility to solve this unresolved situation could be to use *implicit* semantic information in the premises. This "implicit" sense means that some other information about the assertions in the premises, which is not explicitly present therein, could be use to evaluate the conflicting arguments. For instance, implicit information about the premises $Viewer(Peter)$ and $Viewer(Lois)$ in arguments U_{RA2} and U_{DA2}, respectively, could be the key to set a prevalence between the two arguments. Thus, a relationship $superiorViewer(Lois, Peter)$ could be included in the knowledge model. Then, the criteria that an argument with a viewer who is superior is preferred may be established in the knowledge model (i.e., $U_{DA2} \gg U_{RA2}$). This new information is not explicitly included in the premises of the arguments. However, a the argumentation process may be extended to take into account implicit information. This solution is beyond the scope of this chapter and it is being studied as a future line of work.

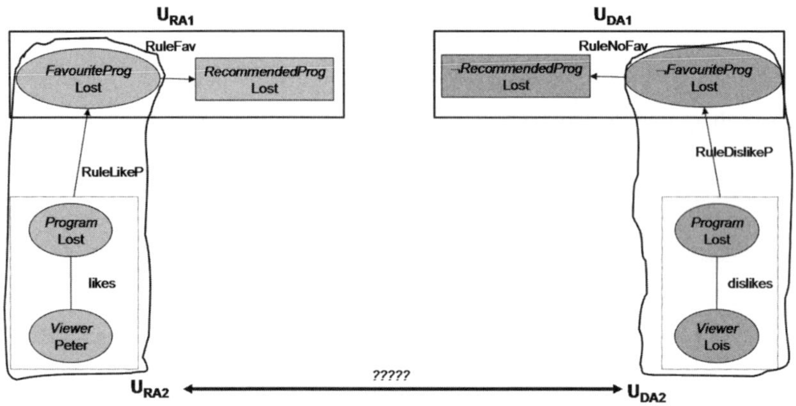

Figure 12.13 Subarguments for the derived assertions $FavouriteProg(Lost)$ and $\neg FavouritePorg(Lost)$ based on the same type of information.

12.5 Decision Mechanism: Two Approaches

Sections 12.3 and 12.4 have shown that different arguments may support inconsistent information about the same domain element (e.g., a TV program). Moreover, premises in these arguments could be supported by other arguments, which in turn may be involved in sequent conflicts. As a result, the evaluation process of inconsistent arguments must also consider all the subarguments related to them, and the subarguments related to these, and so on. This evaluation process is implemented here as a *decision mechanism.*

Two main approaches have been devised to implement the decision mechanism in the SmartTV system. The next two subsections explain these alternatives. To illustrate both alternatives, some SmartTV scenarios are then evaluated.

12.5.1 *A Centralized Approach*

The first idea is based on a centralized design. Hence, a central entity builds all the possible arguments for and against recommending a program. To this end, the entity receives all the domain knowledge from the Information module, along with the whole set of domain rules integrated in it.

The domain criteria for comparing arguments (including their subarguments) are captured in a hierarchical scale. Each level in the scale contains a criterion $C_{+/-}$. In each level, conflictive arguments which are defeated by a prevailing argument according to the specific criteria are not considered in the next level. For example, let us take the arguments U_F and U_D in Example 12.5. Now, suppose that the first level in the hierarchical scale is $RecCriteria_{+/-}$. Then, argument U_F will pass to the second level, while U_D is eliminated from the evaluation process since it is defeated by U_F. The arguments that fulfill all the levels in the hierarchical scale are then considered as acceptable. Note that inconsistent arguments could reach the status of acceptable after covering all levels in the scale, when their premises are equally strong according to the criteria. In that cases, the decision to take could be left to the viewers.

The specific domain criteria scale in the SmartTV system is composed of three levels. The bottom (or first) level contains the criteria $IntCriteria_{+/-}$. The middle (second) level incorporates the criteria $FavCriteria_{+/-}$, and finally the top level is controlled by $RecCriteria_{+/-}$. Examples of the employment of this scale are given in Section 12.5.3.

12.5.2 *A Distributed Approach*

The second idea is based on a distributed construction of arguments. Here, an agent builds arguments trying to support a particular claim (e.g., a TV program should be recommended), whereas another agent finds justifications which are inconsistent to that claim. The domain knowledge is delivered to both agents, thus sharing the same information. However, each agent has now an independent set of domain rules. Moreover, the intersection set of rules of both agents is disjoint (i.e., they do not share rules).

Centering on the SmartTV system, a *RecommenderAg* agent is in charge of building arguments for recommending programs. Contrarily, a *DiscarderAg* agent builds arguments for discarding programs. Hence, *RecommenderAg* owns the rule set A given in Section 12.3, whereas rule set B is maintained by *DiscarderAg*. Once they have built their respective arguments, the agents begin an argumentation process.

The argumentation process starts with an agent claiming a specific proposal, denoted by α. In this case, we have chosen *RecommenderAg* claiming a specific program p as recommended (i.e., $\alpha \equiv$ "p is recommended")[4]. After the initial claim, *DiscardedAg* asks the

[4]Note that a start with *DiscarderAg* claiming p as not recommended is also possible. As this decision does not affect the final result of the argumentation process, it seems to be more natural to begin with a claim recommending

justification for α. Suppose that *RecommenderAg* has the finite set of arguments

$$\Omega_{ic} = \{U_{RA_1}, U'_{RA_1}, U''_{RA_1}, \ldots\}$$

supporting α. Then, *RecommenderAg* selects the best argument in Ω_{ic} according to the correspondent C_+ criteria (see Section 12.4.1). Let us denote this argument by U_{RA_1}, which is then communicated to *DiscarderAg*.

Now, *DiscarderAg* evaluates U_{RA_1} to find a better or at least equally-strong argument against it. To compare its own arguments against U_{RA_1}, *DiscarderAg* employs the criteria defined in Section 12.4.2. Therefore, three situations can occur when *DiscarderAg* receives U_{RA_1}:

(S1) *DiscarderAg* has no stronger arguments than U_{RA_1}. Two sub-cases are detected:

- (a) If any premise in U_{RA_1} is a derived assertion, *DiscarderAg* must then ask for the justifications of it, in order to try to undercut U_{RA_1}.
- (b) If all the premises in U_{RA_1} are categorical facts, *DiscarderAg* must accept the argument.

(S2) *DiscarderAg* has some arguments just as stronger as U_{RA_1}, denoted by the finite set $\Omega_{eq} = \{U_{DA_1}, U'_{DA_1}, U''_{DA_1}, \ldots\}$. Let U_{DA_1} be the best argument in Ω_{eq} according to the correspondent C_- criteria defined in Section 12.4.1. Two sub-cases are detected:

- (a) If any premise in U_{RA_1} is a derived assertion, *DiscarderAg* must then ask for the justifications of it, in order to try to undercut U_{RA_1}.
- (b) If all the premises in U_{RA_1} are categorical facts, *DiscarderAg* utters the argument U_{DA_1} to attack U_{RA_1}..

(S3) *DiscarderAg* has some arguments stronger than U_{RA_1}, denoted by the finite set $\Omega_{st} = \{V_{DA_1}, V'_{DA_1}, V''_{DA_1}, \ldots\}$. Let V_{DA_1} be the best argument in Ω_{st} according to the correspondent C_- criteria defined in Section 12.4.1. Then, *DiscarderAg* utters the argument V_{DA_1} to attack U_{RA_1}.

Next, if U_{RA_1} has been challenged by asking the justification of any derived assertion in its premises (S1.a and S2.a cases), *RecommenderAg* must give the best argument for it. Let U_{RA_2} denote this argument. Then, *DiscarderAg* compares U_{RA_2} with its own arguments as shown above. On the other hand, if U_{RA_1} has been attacked by a counterargument (S2.b and S3 cases), then it is *RecommenderAg* who compares U_{DA_1} or V_{DA_1} with its own arguments as

a program and then exchange arguments supporting/defeating that claim.

above. In this manner, a dialog is developed where arguments of both agents are exchanged. The argumentation process ends when an agent has run out of new arguments for attacking the ones received previously. For a more detailed explanation on the argument process, the interested reader is referred to [32]. Likewise, the formalization of the argumentative dialog is given elsewhere [33].

Two special situations must be noticed in this process. Firstly, the case S1.b is possible due to the agents totally share the domain knowledge. Therefore, the categorical/grounded assertions found in the premises (viewers' preferences, programs' features) are also accepted by both agents and cannot be attacked. However, if the agents could have their own *local* categorical facts (i.e., non-shared facts only asserted by one agent), the situation would be different. Let us see an example.

Example 12.6. Suppose that *DiscardedAg* receives an argument W_{RA} containing a *RecommendedAg*'s local categorical premise (e.g., the assertion *"Peter likes musicals"*, which is not asserted in the shared knowledge model). Then, *DiscardedAg* could have another local grounded fact[5] asserting *"Peter does not like musicals"*, which is in conflict with W_{RA} local assertion. As a result, the argument W_{RA} could not be accepted by *DiscardedAg* as stated in S1.b, and a new evaluation method will be needed here.

Secondly, the case S2.b could lead to the second situation of inconsistency detected in Section 12.4.3, where two arguments based on the same type of information support conflicting conclusions. Hence, if argument U_{RA_1} and its counterargument U_{DA_1} uttered in S2.b are both based on premises which are all grounded assertions, the result of the evaluation is unresolved. Since *RecommendedAg* cannot send a new attack to U_{DA_1}, a new argumentation path must be explored, if possible. To this end, *RecommendedAg* has to utter a new argument V_{RA_1} for supporting the proposal whose previous supporting argument U_{RA_1} led to the blocked path. If a new path can not be started, the argumentation process is left unresolved, and the final decision about the program is again left to the viewers. An example of this situation is given in Scenario 3 of Section 12.5.3.

Observe that during the argumentation process, $V \gg U$ when argument V attacks argument U according to the situation S3, since V contains prevailing information. However, V could be defeated later if any of its subarguments is defeated. As a result, the main goal of the argumentation process is to determine whether the initial claim α is accepted or not by taking into account all the related arguments. Thus, if any argument in the dialog supporting α is accepted because it has not been attacked (case S1.b) or all its attackers have been

[5] This fact could even be the conclusion of a *DiscarderAg*'s argument.

defeated by other accepted arguments, α is accepted by the system. Contrarily, if all the arguments for α have been defeated, it is rejected. Let us see some examples in the next subsection.

12.5.3 *SmartTV Scenarios*

The following scenarios evaluate the use of the two decision mechanisms previously introduced. In each of them, several arguments are given in favor and against the inclusion of a program in the final list of recommendations. Notice that the state of affairs in each scenario is represented by means of OWL-DL assertions, which are contained in the SmartTV ontology.

Scenario 1: BBC News

In this scenario, the SmartTV system discovers the viewer Peter in front of the TV. The following information is collected by the Information module:

- Program(BBCNews)
- Viewer(Peter), dislikesProg(Peter, BBCNews)
- Review(TheTimes_001), hasReview(BBCNews,TheTimes_001), rating(TheTimes_001,8)
- Tag(TagBBC1), tagValue(TagBBC1, Urgent), hasTag(BBCNews, TagBBC1)

The above OWL-DL assertions represent the ongoing situation in the domain. This information is then delivered to the Decision module to set *BBC News* as recommended or not. According to the decision mechanism employed, two situations are developed:

12.5.3.1 *Case 1. Centralized entity:*

From the information listed above and the domain rules given in Section 12.3, the following arguments are built:

$$\begin{aligned}
U_{Rec_1} &= (RecommendedProg(BBCNews), \{ImportantProg(BBCNews), RuleImp\}),\\
U_{Rec_2} &= (RecommendedProg(BBCNews), \{InterestingProg(BBCNews), RuleInt\}),\\
U_{Dsc} &= (DiscardedProg(BBCNews), \{\neg FavouriteProg(BBCNews), RuleNoFav\}),
\end{aligned}$$

$$\begin{aligned}
U_{Rev} &= (InterestingProg(BBCNews), && \{Review(TheTimes_001), Program(BBCNews),\\
& && hasReview(BBCNews, TheTimes_001),\\
& && rating(TheTimes_001, 8), RuleRev\}),\\
U_{Imp} &= (ImportantProg(BBCNews), && \{Prog(BBCNews), Tag(TagBBC1),\\
& && tagValue(TagBBC1, Urgent),\\
& && hasTag(BBCNews, TagBBC1), RuleUrg\}),\\
U_{\neg Fav} &= (\neg FavoriteProg(BBCNews), && \{Viewer(Peter), Program(BBCNews),\\
& && dislikesProg(Peter, BBCNews), RuleDislikeP\})
\end{aligned}$$

Observe that there are two arguments supporting *BBC News* as recommended program, based on an urgency annotation (e.g., breaking news, U_{Imp}) and a positive review of a newspaper (U_{Rev}), respectively. Contrarily, an argument for discarding the program is found, supported by the Peter's dislike for it ($U_{\neg Fav}$).

This set of arguments is now evaluated according to the domain criteria scale defined in Section 12.5.1. The first level of the scale contains the criteria $IntCriteria_{+/-}$. Argument U_{Rev} is the only one affected by this criteria. As it is not defeated by another argument according to the criteria, the arguments passes to the next level with the rest of arguments which can not be evaluated yet.

Likewise, argument $U_{\neg Fav}$ is the only one affected by the criteria $FavCriteria_{+/-}$ in the second level of the scale. Therefore, the entire set of arguments reaches the top level, where the criteria $RecCriteria_{+/-}$ is applied. Three arguments are evaluated with this criteria: U_{Rec_1}, U_{Rec_2} and U_{Dsc}. The type of information related to $FavouriteInfoGroup$ is more relevant than the $InterestingInfoGroup$ one. Thus, $U_{Dsc} \gg U_{Rec_2}$. However, U_{Rec_1} is based on the type of information $ImportantProg$, so $U_{Rec_1} \gg U_{Dsc}$. Finally, *BBC News* is accepted as recommended program because U_{Rec_1} is an accepted argument after applying the scale, and moreover there are no other acceptable arguments which are inconsistent with it.

12.5.3.2 *Case 2. Argumentation process:*

RecommenderAg (*Rag* henceforth) creates the arguments U_{Rec_1}, U_{Rec_2}, U_{Rev} and U_{Imp} shown in the Case 1 from the knowledge received from the Information module and the rule set A. On the other hand, *DiscarderAg* (*Dag*) builds the above arguments U_{Dsc} and $U_{\neg Fav}$ from the knowledge received from the Information module and the rule set B.

The argumentation process starts with *Rag* claiming *BBC News* as a recommended program. The persuasion dialog developed from this claim is depicted in Figure 12.14. When *Rag* is asked for justifications of this claim, it must select between arguments U_{Rec_1} and U_{Rec_2}. Since U_{Rec_1} is based on more relevant information according to $RecCriteria_{+}$ (i.e., $ImportantProg(BBCNews)$ is preferred to $InterestingProg(BBCNews)$), it is given as justification. Namely, to recommend a program because has an urgent annotation is more convincing than to use newspaper information.

Now, *Dag* tries an attack to U_{Rec_1}. *Dag*'s argument U_{Dsc} is inconsistent with U_{Rec_1}. However, it is based on a type of information less prevailing than U_{Rec_1} is, according to $RecCriteria_{+/-}$ (i.e., $ImportantProg(BBCNews)$ is preferred to $\neg Favourite\text{-}Prog(BBCNews)$). Therefore, U_{Dsc} can not be used as counterargument, since the viewers' preferences should not block important news ($U_{Rec_1} \gg U_{Dsc}$). The only possibility for *Dag* to attack U_{Rec_1} is to ask for its justification of $ImportantProg(BBCNews)$, as it is a derived assertion.

Rag responds the argument U_{Imp} as justification for $ImportantProg(BBCNews)$. Since this argument is totally composed of categorical facts, *Dag* must accept it. Moreover, *Dag* also accepts U_{Rec_1} since the agent does not have stronger counterarguments nor U_{Rec_1} has any other derived assertions. Finally, *Dag* concedes the *Rag*'s claim about recommending *BBC News*, and the program is added to the list of recommendations.

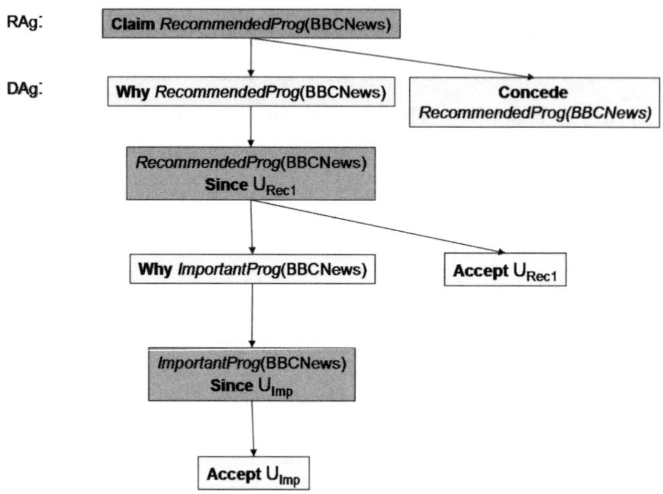

Figure 12.14 Argumentation dialog to decide on recommending *BBC News*

Scenario 2: Friday the 13th

In this scenario, the SmartTV system discovers viewers Peter and Chris in front of the TV. The following information is collected by the Information module:

- Genre(Terror)
- Program(Friday_the_13^{th}), hasGenre(Friday_the_13^{th}, Terror), PG(Friday_the_13^{th}, 18)
- Viewer(Peter), likesGenre(Peter, Terror)
- Viewer(Chris), hasAge(Chris, 13)

This information is delivered to the Decision module to set *Friday_the_*13th as recommended or not. According to the decision mechanism employed, two situations are developed.

12.5.3.3 *Case 1. Centralized entity:*

From the information listed above and the domain rules given in Section 12.3, the following arguments are built:

$$V_{Rec} = (RecommendedProg(Friday\_the\_13^{\text{th}}), \{FavouritetProg(Friday\_the\_13^{\text{th}}), RuleFav\}),$$
$$V_{Dsc} = (DiscardedProg(Friday\_the\_13^{\text{th}}), \{ExplicitProg(Friday\_the\_13^{\text{th}}), RuleExp\}),$$

$$V_{Fav} = (FavoriteProg(Friday\_the\_13^{\text{th}}),\ \{Viewer(Peter), Genre(Terror), Program(Friday\_the\_13^{\text{th}}), likesGenre(Peter, Terror), hasGenre(Friday\_the\_13^{\text{th}}, Terror), RuleLikeG\}),$$
$$V_{Exp} = (ExplicitProg(Friday\_the\_13^{\text{th}}),\ \{Viewer(Chris), Program(Friday\_the\_13^{\text{th}}), hasAge(Chris, 13), PG(Friday\_the\_13^{\text{th}}, 18), RuleAge\})$$

Observe that argument V_{Rec} supports $Friday\_the\_13^{th}$ as recommended since Peter likes terror movies (V_{Fav}). Contrarily, argument V_{Dsc} discards the program due to the information about the Chris's age and the parental guidance of the movie (V_{Exp}).

According to the scale criteria, none of the arguments are affected by the first level ($IntCriteria_{+/-}$), and only the argument V_{Fav} is evaluated (as accepted) by the second level ($FavCriteria_{+/-}$). As a result, the whole set of arguments reaches the top level. Here, arguments V_{Rec} and V_{Dsc} are detected as rebutting each other. By employing $RecCriteria_{+/-}$, $V_{Dsc} \gg V_{Rec}$ since the type of information $ExplicitProg$ is more relevant than $FavouriteInfoGroup$. Finally, $Friday\_the\_13^{th}$ is accepted as discarded program because V_{Dsc} is an accepted argument after applying the scale, and moreover there are no other acceptable arguments which are inconsistent with it.

12.5.3.4 *Case 2. Argumentation process:*

Rag creates the arguments V_{Rec} and V_{Fav} shown above from the knowledge received from the Information module and the rule set A. On the other hand, *Dag* builds the above arguments V_{Dsc} and V_{Exp} from the knowledge received from the Information module and the rule set B.

The argumentation process starts with *Rag* claiming $Friday\_the\_13^{th}$ as recommended program. The persuasion dialog developed from this claim is depicted in Figure 12.15. As the only argument supporting this claim is V_{Rec}, *Rag* answers it when the claim is challenged. Then, *Dag* searches an attack to that argument: the counterargument V_{Dsc} rebuts V_{Rec}, and moreover, V_{Dsc} is based on more relevant information according to $RecCriteria_{+/-}$ (i.e., $ExplicitProg(Friday\_the\_13^{th})$ is more relevant than $FavouriteProg(Friday\_the\_13^{th})$). Therefore, $V_{Dsc} \gg V_{Rec}$ and *Dag* can attack V_{Rec} directly with its argument V_{Dsc}. Namely, an argument saying that the program has explicit content must be considered as more important than those recommending the program due to viewers' preferences.

Now, *Rag* detects that its best argument for supporting the initial claim has been attacked. Its only possibility is to challenge the derived assertion $ExplicitProg(Friday\_the\_13^{th})$ in V_{Dsc}, trying to undercut this argument. Afterward, *Dag* utters V_{Exp} as the justification for the derived premise. Since all the premises in this new argument are categorical facts, *Rag* has to accept V_{Exp}, and therefore V_{Dsc} must also be accepted by this agent. As the only argument supporting the initial claim has now been defeated, Rag must retract the recommendation for *Friday_the_*13th, and eventually the program is not included in the list of recommendations.

Notice that the acceptance of the argument V_{Exp} by *Rag* is possible due to all the premises in it are categorical facts shared by both agents. However, suppose that the premise $PG(Friday\_the\_13^{th}, 18)$ in V_{Exp} is a local categorical fact only maintained by *Dag*. Suppose also that *Rag* holds the local categorical fact $PG(Friday\_the\_13^{th}, 12)$. Moreover, the relationship *PG* is defined as *functional* in the SmartTV ontology, meaning that for the same program, only an age rating is allowed. In this new situation, *Rag* can not accept the argument V_{Exp}, since the premise $PG(Friday\_the\_13^{th}, 18)$ is in conflict with its own local fact $PG(Friday\_the\_13^{th}, 12)$. As commented in Section 12.5.2, a new method to resolve this "local-local" conflict is needed, but it is out of the scope of this chapter.

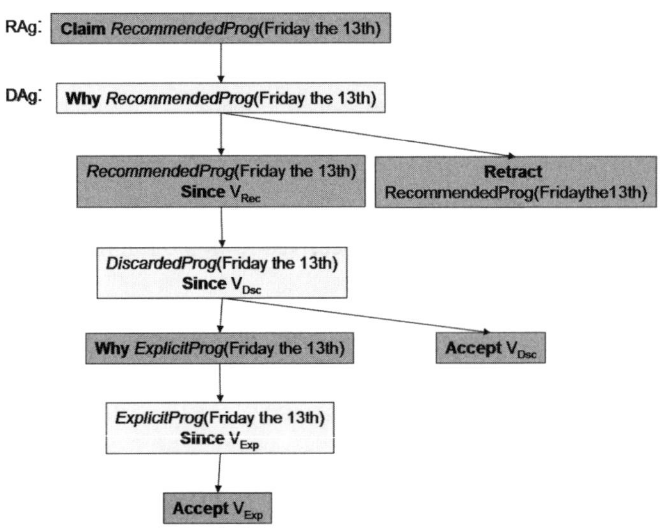

Figure 12.15 Argumentation dialog to decide on recommending *Friday_the_*13^{textth}

Scenario 3: Lost

In this scenario, the SmartTV system discovers viewers Peter and Lois in front of the TV. The following information is collected by the Information module:

- Genre(Action)
- Program(Lost), hasReview(Lost, MZine_1), rating(MZine_1, 8), hasSimilar(Lost, Fringe)
- Program(Fringe), hasGenre(Fringe, Action)
- Viewer(Peter), likesProgram(Peter, Lost), likesProg(Peter, Fringe)
- Viewer(Lois), dislikesProg(Lois, Lost), dislikesGenre(Lois, Action)

This information is delivered to the Decision module to set *Lost* as recommended or not. According to the decision mechanism employed, two situations are developed.

12.5.3.5 *Case 1. Centralized entity:*

From the information listed above and the domain rules given in Section 12.3, the following arguments are built:

$$\begin{aligned}
T_{Rec_1} &= (RecommendedProg(Lost), \{FavouriteProg(Lost), RuleFav\}),\\
T_{Rec_2} &= (RecommendedProg(Lost), \{InterestingProg(Lost), RuleInt\}),\\
T_{Dsc_1} &= (DiscardedProg(Lost), \{\neg FavouriteProg(Lost), RuleNonFav\}),\\
T_{Dsc_2} &= (DiscardedProg(Lost), \{\neg InterestingProg(Lost), RuleNonInt\}),
\end{aligned}$$

$$\begin{aligned}
T_{Fav_1} &= (FavoriteProg(Lost), & &\{Viewer(Peter), Program(Lost), likesProg(Peter, Lost),\\
& & &RuleLikeP\}),\\
T_{\neg Fav_1} &= (\neg FavoriteProg(Lost), & &\{Viewer(Lois), Program(Lost), dislikesProg(Lois, Lost),\\
& & &RuleDislikeP\}),\\
T_{Fav_2} &= (FavoriteProg(Fringe), & &\{Viewer(Peter), Program(Fringe), likesProg(Peter, Fringe),\\
& & &RuleLikeP\}),\\
T_{\neg Fav_2} &= (\neg FavoriteProg(Fringe), & &\{Viewer(Lois), Genre(Action), Program(Fringe),\\
& & &dislikesGenre(Lois, Action), hasGenre(Fringe, Action),\\
& & &RuleDislikeG\}),
\end{aligned}$$

$$\begin{aligned}
T_{Int} &= (InterestingProg(Lost), & &\{Review(MZine_1), Program(Lost), hasReview(Lost, MZine_1),\\
& & &rating(MZine_1, 8), RuleRev)\}),\\
T_{\neg Int} &= (\neg InterestingProg(Lost), & &\{\neg FavouriteProg(Fringe), Program(Lost),\\
& & &hasSimilar(Lost, Fringe), RuleNegSimilar\})
\end{aligned}$$

In this scenario, arguments T_{Rec_1} and T_{Rec_2} support the recommendation of *Lost*, based on the Peter's preference (subargument T_{Fav_1}) and the positive review of a magazine (subargument T_{Int}), respectively. On the other hand, T_{Dsc_1} and T_{Dsc_2} discard *Lost*, according to the Lois's preference (subargument $T_{\neg Fav_1}$) and the similarity of the program with another one classified as non-favourite (program *Fringe* in subargument $T_{\neg Int}$). Moreover, the latter subargument is in turn supported by the Lois's dislike for the genre of the similar program *Fringe* (subargument $T_{\neg Fav_2}$).

Let us apply the scale of domain criteria to this set of arguments. Firstly, arguments T_{Int} and $T_{\neg Int}$ rebut each other about the degree of interest on *Lost* and both can be evaluated according the criteria in Level 1, $IntCriteria_{+/-}$. Hence, $T_{\neg Int} \gg T_{Int}$ as the former is based on the type of information $SimilarGroupInfo$, which is more relevant than the type *Review-GroupInfo* used in T_{Int}. Therefore, T_{Int} does not pass to the next level, and besides the argument T_{Rec_2} is also removed from the set. The reason for this elimination is founded on the dependence of T_{Rec_2} upon T_{Int}. As a result, if its supporting subargument is defeated, T_{Rec_2} is then defeated too.

Next, the second level of the scale evaluates inconsistent arguments based on the criteria $FavCriteria_{+/-}$. Here we find the pairs of inconsistent arguments (T_{Fav_1} , $T_{\neg Fav_1}$) and (T_{Fav_2}, $T_{\neg Fav_2}$). A relationship of defeat between the arguments in the first pair can not be established, since T_{Fav_1} and $T_{\neg Fav_1}$ are both based on the same type of information, $DirectInfoGroup$. Consequently, both arguments are held in the set, with an unresolved relationship between them (i.e., *Lost* cannot be set as favorite neither as non-favorite).

On the other hand, a prevailing relationship between arguments in the second pair exists, such as $T_{Fav_2} \gg T_{\neg Fav_2}$ since the former is based on a direct preference on the program *Fringe*, and $T_{\neg Fav_2}$ only relies on the Lois's dislike for the genre of that program. As a result, $T_{\neg Fav_2}$ is removed from the set of arguments, together with $T_{\neg Int}$ and T_{Dsc_2}, since $T_{\neg Int}$ is supported by $T_{\neg Fav2}$, and in turn, T_{Dsc_2} is supported by $T_{\neg Int}$.

Thus, $\{T_{Rec_1}, T_{Dsc_1}, T_{Fav_1}, T_{\neg Fav_1}, T_{Fav_2}, T_{\neg Int}\}$ are the remaining arguments in the set when the top level of the scale is reached. Now, arguments T_{Rec_1} and T_{Dsc_1} rebut each other in the conclusion of recommending/discarding *Lost*, and they are evaluated according $RecCriteria_{+/-}$. Again, the two arguments are based on the same type of information, $FavouriteInfoGroup$. Consequently, there is not a defeat relationship between T_{Rec_1} and T_{Dsc_1}. It means that both arguments are equally acceptable, and the final decision about recommending/discarding *Lost* can not be set by the SmartTV system. Eventually, the system asks the viewers to decide about that program.

12.5.3.6 *Case 2. Argumentation process:*

Rag creates the arguments T_{Rec_1}, T_{Rec_2}, T_{Fav_1}, T_{Fav_2} and T_{Int} shown above from the knowledge received from the Information module and the rule set A. On the other hand, *Dag* builds the above arguments T_{Dsc_1}, T_{Dsc_2}, $T_{\neg Fav_1}$, $T_{\neg Fav_2}$ and $T_{\neg Int}$ from the knowledge received from the Information module and the rule set B.

The argumentation process starts with *Rag* claiming *Lost* as recommended program. In this case, the agents build two argumentation paths in the dialog. The first branch of the dialog is depicted in Figure 12.16. It starts with *Rag* giving a justification for the initial claim after the challenge posed by *Dag* to that claim. In that moment, both arguments T_{Rec_1} and T_{Rec_2} can be used by *Rag*. According to $RecCriteria_{+}$, T_{Rec_1} is preferable to T_{Rec_2} since the type of information in the premise $FavouriteProg(Lost)$ is more relevant to the information in $InterestingProg(Lost)$. Namely, the viewer's preference is a better type information than that based on reviews. Therefore, T_{Rec_1} is used as justification for the initial claim in this branch.

Now, *Dag* detects that its arguments T_{Dsc_1} and T_{Dsc_2} are in conflict with T_{Rec_1}, as they support *Lost* as discarded program. According to $RecCriteria_{+/-}$, $T_{Rec_1} \gg T_{Dsc_2}$, so *Dag* can not use it here. However, T_{Dsc_1} is as stronger as T_{Rec_1}, since they are based on the same type of information, namely $FavouriteGroupInfo$. Moreover, the premise $Favourite$-$Prog(Lost)$ in T_{Rec_1} is a derived assertion. As a result, instead of uttering argument T_{Dsc_1} to attack T_{Rec_1}, *Dag* challenges first this derived assertion (see Figure 12.16).

The *Rag*'s response for this new challenge is the argument T_{Fav_1}, which is its only justification for $FavouriteProg(Lost)$. Then, *Dag* detects its argument $T_{\neg Fav_1}$ supporting $\neg FavouriteProg(Lost)$ as a possible attack to T_{Fav_1}. Since argument T_{Fav_1} does not have any derived premise, *Dag* can only utter $T_{\neg Fav_1}$ to attack it. However, as argument $T_{\neg Fav_1}$ is also composed of categorical premises uniquely, and both are based on the same type of information ($DirectInfoGroup$ according to $FavCriteria_{+/-}$), the agents have now arrived to a blocking situation, i.e., the case S2.b commented in Section 12.5.2. Neither can *Rag* find an new attack to $T_{\neg Fav_1}$, nor does *Dag* have a better argument to attack T_{Fav_1}. Thus, *Rag* utters the message *"Undecided($FavouriteProg(Lost)$)"* to notify to *Dag* that the classification of that program as favorite/non-favorite can not be established.

Now, *Rag* finds a new argumentation path after going back in the dialog and evaluating the question *"Why($RecommendedProg(Lost)$)"* again. The previous argument T_{Rec_2} can be employed as a new justification for the initial claim, as shown in Figure 12.17. After receiving this argument, *Dag* detects its argument T_{Dsc_2} to be in conflict with T_{Rec_2}, and equally strong to this according to $RecCriteria_{+/-}$. Moreover, the premise $Interesting$-$Prog(Lost)$ in T_{Rec_2} is a derived assertion. As a result, instead of uttering argument T_{Dsc_2} to attack T_{Rec_2}, *Dag* challenges first this derived assertion.

The *Rag*'s response for this new challenge is the argument T_{Int}, which is its only justification for $InterestingProg(Lost)$. Then, *Dag* detects its argument $T_{\neg Int}$ supporting $\neg InterestingProg(Lost)$ as a possible attack to T_{Int}. Furthermore, $T_{\neg Int}$ is supported by

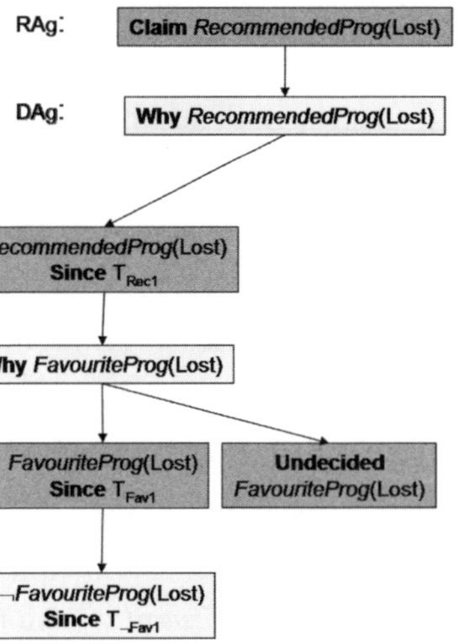

Figure 12.16 Argumentation dialog to decide on recommending *Lost*. The first argumentation path is left unresolved

a premise in the *SimilarGroupInfo* group ($hasSimilar(Lost, Fringe)$), whereas T_{Int} is supported by a premise in the *ReviewGroupInfo* ($hasReview(Lost, MZine\_1)$). According to $IntCriteria_{+/-}$, $T_{\neg Int} \gg T_{Int}$. Namely, the information based on programs similarities is more important than that based on reviews. Consequently, *Dag* utters $T_{\neg Int}$ to attack T_{Int} directly.

After receiving the counterargument $T_{\neg Int}$, *Rag* needs to attack it to reinstate its argument T_{Int}. The premise $\neg FavouriteProg(Fringe)$ is detected as a derived assertion in $T_{\neg Int}$, so *Rag* challenges it. *Dag* answers the argument $T_{\neg Fav_2}$ as a justification, which relies on Lois's dislike for the genre "Action" to classify *Fringe* as non-favourite. Afterward, *Rag* finds the argument T_{Fav_2}, which classifies *Fringe* as favourite based on the Peter's direct preferences, as an attack to $T_{\neg Fav_2}$. Due to T_{Fav_2} uses the premise $likesProg(Peter, Fringe)$ and T_{Fav_2} employs $dislikesGenre(Lois, Action)$, $T_{Fav_2} \gg T_{\neg Fav_2}$, and therefore *Rag* utters it directly (see Figure 12.17).

Now it is the turn for *Dag* to find an attack to T_{Fav2}. However, this agent does not have more counterarguments. Moreover, all the premises in T_{Fav_2} are categorical facts, so *Dag* must accept this argument. By accepting it, *Dag* must then retract its claim $\neg FavouriteProg(Fringe)$). Subsequently, since *Dag* does not have new counterarguments for T_{Int}, neither can the agent challenge it again, T_{Int} is also accepted. Following the same steps, *Dag* also accepts the argument T_{Rec_2}. Eventually, *Dag* concedes the program *Lost* as recommended.

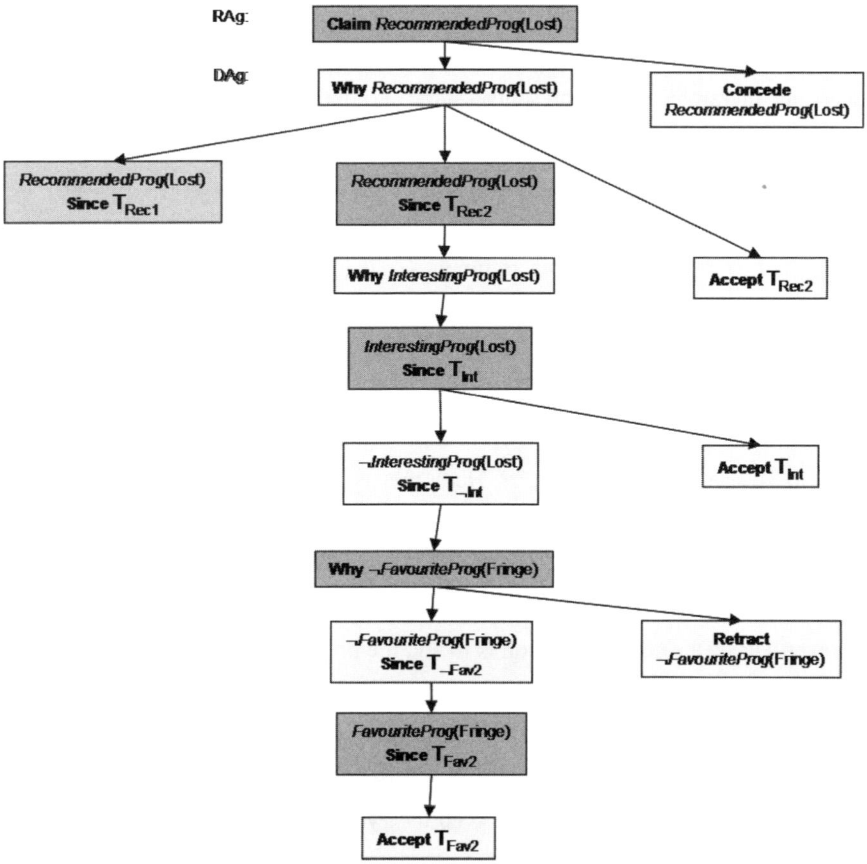

Figure 12.17 Argumentation dialog to decide on recommending *Lost*. The second argumentation path ends conceding the program as recommended

12.6 Comparing Decision Mechanisms in the SmartTV System

The scenarios in Section 12.5.3 have revealed several differences when using a centralized entity or an argumentation process as the decision mechanism in the SmartTV system.

The first and most important contrast among the two approaches resides in the application of the domain criteria. The hierarchical scale in the centralized entity avoids the exchange of arguments and thus the necessity of defining a dialog as in the argumentation process, but two main problems are detected when using the scale. Firstly, all the domain criteria must be pre-arranged before employing the scale. It could be easy to put in order a low number of criteria, but this task is not scalable. Moreover, to find the optimal order among all the criteria could be a rather handmade and fallible task. Contrarily, the argumentation process does not enforce a pre-defined order in the use of domain criteria, and the agents select the most suitable one depending on the argument that is currently being processed. Secondly, the hierarchical scale presents a static and fixed evaluation of arguments. Therefore, an argument ruled out in the level n can not be reinstated even though the argument(s) defeating it is(are) ruled out in subsequent upper levels $n+i$, $i \geqslant 1$. In fact, this situation is shown in Scenario 3-Case 1 of Section 12.5.3. Hence, argument T_{Int} is ruled out by argument $T_{\neg Int}$ in Level 1. However, this argument T_{Int} is later defeated in Level 2. As a result, T_{Int} (and the arguments that are supported by it) should be reinstated in the set of argument. However, this is not possible in the hierarchical scale, as previously evaluated arguments are not taken into consideration again. Instead of this, the argumentation process does allow for the reinstatement of arguments, since they are re-evaluated in the dialog as shown in Scenario 3-Case 2 of Section 12.5.3. Here, the argument T_{Int} is first ruled out by $T_{\neg Int}$, and then T_{Int} is restored again when T_{Fav_2} undercuts $T_{\neg Int}$.

Indeed, the outcome in Scenario 3-Case 1 is an unresolved decision due to the pre-arranged order of domain criteria and the failure of reinstating arguments during the evaluation process. Nevertheless, the correct solution is to add the program as recommended, as demonstrated in Scenario 3-Case 2.

A second difference between both approaches is the possibility of including *local* grounded facts. This option is feasible when employing a distributed architecture as in the argumentation process, where each agent could keep its own separate facts about elements in the domain. Contrarily, the centralized entity can not represent this kind of facts, since all the information managed by this entity comes as if provided by a sole source. Therefore, in scenarios where asserting different local grounded facts is enabled, the argumentation process is the only suitable approach.

Finally, the use of a dialog for exchanging arguments is more intuitive and easy to show in case an explanation about the decision of recommending or not a program is requested by the viewers. A step-by-step process showing the creation of the dialog tree in the argumentation process could be implemented as a graphical tool, thus providing the minimal information to understand the interaction between arguments and the final outcome. Contrarily, the viewer has to cope with more information when asking a explanation to the central entity, where all the arguments are shown at the same time from the beginning of the decision process, and then they are eliminated according to each level in the hierarchical scale.

In conclusion, the argumentation process approach is preferable when a distributed architecture can be employed in the decision mechanism, since it offers a flexible and dynamic implementation of the domain criteria, the possibility of using different local facts, and a more compelling explanation.

12.7 Conclusions and Further Research Directions

The problem we addressed in this chapter offers plenty of challenges for the scientific community. Decision-making is hard for any artificial system. We humans find it hard too. There are plenty of disasters reported in human history due to errors in human judgment. Still the scenario we have considered offers a good starting point to explore the improvement of artificial systems for taking decisions, as it is focused on a well-defined and restricted set of choices, and the consequences, in case of misjudgment on behalf of the artificial system, may not be that disastrous after all. This type of applications will become more common as the area of Intelligent Environments advances and transitions from a one-user focus to a many-users focus. Whenever there is a group of humans there will be a difference between their needs and preferences, and therefore a need for mediation. We believe argumentation systems offer a valuable tool in these cases as a way to naturally encode different views and preference mechanisms.

In order to illustrate this problem, we have introduced here an Ambient Intelligence (AmI) system controlling a smart TV recommending service. This system is integrated with argumentation techniques as a means of detecting and solving the conflicts derived from different viewers' preferences and TV programs data. In this manner, the new information inferred in the AmI system is presented as *arguments*. They consist of a *conclusion*, representing the new inferred piece of information, and a *justification* for that conclusion, which comprises a set of premises and a domain rule entailing the conclusion by means of a deductive reasoning process. Now, when conflictive conclusions are detected, the AmI system uses the information given by their supporting arguments to take a decision on which conclusion is preferable. In order to measure the information contained in the arguments, several *domain criteria* are defined. These criteria establish relationships of relevance among the type of information employed in the arguments' premises. Hence, an argument based on a more relevant type of information has a more preferable conclusion that another argument with a conflictive conclusion using less relevant information. In turn, the same conclusion could be supported by different arguments, and moreover, arguments could be supported by other sub-arguments. Consequently, it is not sufficient to just evaluate conflictive arguments, but also all arguments related to them. To this end, we propose two decision mechanisms. The first approach consists in a centralized entity gathering all the arguments built in the system and evaluating them through a hierarchical scale of domain criteria. The second approach uses a distributed architecture to implement an argumentation process. This process is developed by means of a persuasion dialog between two agents which exchange arguments to defend their claims about conflictive conclusions.

As a result, the final goal of the AmI system presented here is to recommend/discard a set of TV programs depending on the current viewers detected in front of the TV. Different type of information about the viewers' preference, along with TV program information (parental guidance, genre, cast, reviews, etc.) collected from the Internet constitutes the domain model in this scenario. Moreover, information about the viewers' age is also considered in order to take more intelligent decisions (e.g., if an under-18 viewer is detected, TV programs containing sex or violence may be discarded by the system).

A set of domain rules is defined to reason about this information and entail program recommendations/discards, together with several domain criteria to evaluate the arguments built from the reasoning process. Then, the two decision mechanism approaches are instantiated in the smart TV service by means of specific use cases. Finally, a comparison between both approaches is given.

Still there is a long way to go until these systems become trustworthy and accepted. There are at least two bottlenecks the community should address. One is the connection between the argumentation system and the environment. Thus, it is necessary to provide ways for the argumentation system to: (a) gather ID information of the different users the system should be aware of (i.e., knowing Andrés, aged 26, is a user), (b) gather the different views of the users (who likes what), (c) update the information easily as there are new users or they change their preferences with time, (d) detect an implicit demand for the system to act (do not miss an opportunity to mediate positively), (e) know when it is pertinent and adequate for the system to act (do not interrupt too much). The other major challenge for these systems is to acquire good preference mechanisms in a natural way. Two questions are relevant here: How can this preferences be fed to the system or learn by it in a natural way (minimizing work for the users)? What mechanisms to chose the best options are adequate in each case (each group of people in each house)?

All these questions remain challenging, although solutions for them have been explored before and they seem viable. We are now in the historical position to put these systems to work and help humans in daily life matters, and offer the opportunity to bring science to our living rooms. The importance and relevance of this step should not be underestimated. Moreover, it could be seen as a reference toward the application of argumentation techniques to other AmI scenarios, as for example Assistance Living [34, 35, 36] or Smart Cars [37]. In the first scenario, the argumentation techniques could help to select an action when a possible alarming event (e.g., a person falls) is detected. This action will be reached as a consensus between the agent on behalf of the person living in a house (e.g., a patient or an elderly person) and the agent on behalf of the nurse caring for that person. In the Smart Car scenario, the argument process may advise the driver about which route is preferable according to her profile and preferences. Several arguments will be built for and against different routes, supported by weather information, real-traffic conditions, number of times that a route has been selected, etc.

This chapter represents a natural first answer to one of the challenges highlighted recently in [38]. It may not represent a final and conclusive solution to the challenge but it is a first step in that direction the overall complexity involved in the challenge is huge and will take probably many years for a community as a team to be able to deliver systems which are aware of a group of users and capable to optimize the way they are satisfied as a group. Still this is a necessary step for AmI in its road to widespread acceptance and sooner or later the scientific community will have to make that committed and focused investment in this problem. We hope this chapter will inspire other colleagues to develop AmI in that direction.

Acknowledgements

The authors would like to thank the Spanish Ministerio de Ciencia e Innovación for sponsoring this work under the FPU grant AP2006-4154, and also thank the Fundación Séneca for the grant "Programa de Ayuda a los grupos de excelencia 04552/GERM/06".

Bibliography

[1] M. Weiser, The computer for the 21st century, *Scientific American*, **265**(3), 94–104, (1991).
[2] E. Aarts and L. Appelo, Ambient Intelligence, *IT Monitor*, **9**, 7–11, (1999).
[3] E. Aarts, R. Harwig, and M. Schuurmans. Ambient Intelligence. In *The invisible future: the seamless integration of technology into everyday life*, pp. 235–250. McGraw-Hill, (2002).
[4] E. Aarts and S. Marzano, Eds., *The New Everyday: Visions of Ambient Intelligence*, (010 Publishing, Rotterdam, The Netherlands, 2003).
[5] E. Aarts, Ambient Intelligence: a multimedia perspective, *IEEE Multimedia*, **11**(1), 12–19, (2004).
[6] W. Weber, J. M. Rabaey, and E. Aarts, *Ambient Intelligence*, (Springer-Verlag New York, Inc., Secaucus, NJ, USA, 2005).

[7] C. Ramos, J. C. Augusto, and D. Shapiro, Ambient Intelligence: The Next Step for Artificial Intelligence, *IEEE Intelligent Systems*, **23**(2), 15–18, (2008). ISSN 1541-1672.

[8] D. J. Cook, J. C. Augusto, and V. R. Jakkula, Ambient Intelligence: applications in society and opportunities for Artificial Intelligence, *Pervasive and Mobile Computing*, (2009). (to appear).

[9] D. J. Cook and S. K. Das, *Smart Environments: Technology, Protocols and Applications*, (Wiley-Interscience, 2005). ISBN 978-0-471-54448-7.

[10] J. C. Augusto, *Ambient Intelligence: The Confluence of Ubiquitous/Pervasive Computing and Artificial Intelligence*, pp. 213–234. Intelligent Computing Everywhere. Springer London, (2007).

[11] J. C. Augusto and C. D. Nugent, *Designing Smart Homes. The Role of Artificial Intelligence*, (Springer-Verlag, 2006). ISBN 3 540 35994 X.

[12] (to appear), Ed. *3rd International Conference on Pervasive Computing Technologies for Healthcare 2009, London, UK*, IEEE Explore, London, UK, (2009). IEEE Computer Society.

[13] H. Prakken. *Logical tools for modelling legal argument*, PhD thesis, Vrije Universiteit Amsterdam, (1993).

[14] D. V. Carbogim, D. Robertson, and J. Lee, Argument-based applications to knowledge engineering, *Knowledge Engineering Review*, **15**(2), 119–149, (2000).

[15] J. C. Augusto and G. R. Simari, Temporal defeasible reasoning, *Knowledge Information Systems*, **3**(3), 287–318, (2001).

[16] S. Parsons and P. McBurney. Argumentation-based communication between agents. In *Communication in Multiagent Systems*, pp. 164–178, (2003).

[17] P. Besnard and A. Hunter, *Elements of Argumentation*, (MIT Press, 2008).

[18] I. Rahwan and P. Moraitis, Eds. *Fifth International Workshop on Argumentation in Multi-Agent Systems (ArgMAS'08)*, vol. 5384, *Lecture Notes in Artificial Intelligence*, Estoril, Portugal, (2009). Springer.

[19] D. N. Walton and E. C. W. Krabbe, *Commitment in Dialogue: Basic Concepts of Interpersonal Reasoning*, (State University of New York Press, Albany, NY, 1995).

[20] L. Amgoud and S. Parsons. Agent dialogues with conflicting preferences. In *ATAL '01: Revised Papers from the 8th International Workshop on Intelligent Agents VIII*, pp. 190–205, London, UK, (2002). Springer-Verlag.

[21] M. Dean, D. Connoll, F. van Harmelen, J. Hendler, I. Horrocks, D. L. McGuinness, P. F. Patel-Schneider, and L. A. Stein. Web Ontology Language (OWL), Technical report, W3C, (2004).

[22] T. Berners-Lee, J. Hendler, and O. Lassila, The Semantic Web, *Scientific American*, **284**(5), 34–43, (2001).

[23] F. Baader, D. Calvanese, D. L. McGuinness, D. Nardi, and P. F. Patel-Schneider, Eds., *The Description Logic handbook: theory, implementation, and applications*, (Cambridge University Press, 2003).

[24] X. Shi and J. Hua. An adaptive preference learning method for future personalized TV, In eds. C. Thompson and H. Hexmoor, *Integration of Knowledge Intensive Multi-Agent Systems*, pp. 260– 264. IEEE Computer Society, (2005).

[25] J. Xu, L.-J. Zhang, H. Lu, and Y. Li. The development and prospect of personalized TV program recommendation systems. In *MSE '02: Proceedings of the Fourth IEEE International Symposium on Multimedia Software Engineering*, pp. 82–95. IEEE Computer Society, (2002).

[26] D. Martin, M. Paolucci, S. Mcilraith, M. Burstein, D. Mcdermott, D. Mcguinness, B. Parsia, T. Payne, M. Sabou, M. Solanki, N. Srinivasan, and K. Sycara. Bringing Semantics to Web Services: The OWL-S Approach. In eds. J. Cardoso and A. Sheth, *SWSWPC 2004*, vol. 3387, *LNCS*, pp. 26–42. Springer, (2004).

[27] J. J. Carroll, I. Dickinson, C. Dollin, D. Reynolds, A. Seaborne, and K. Wilkinson. Jena: implementing the Semantic Web recommendations. In *Proceedings of the 13th international World Wide Web conference*, pp. 74–83. ACM Press, (2004).
[28] E. Sirin, B. Parsia, B. C. Grau, A. Kalyanpur, and Y. Katz, Pellet: A practical OWL-DL reasoner, *Journal of Web Semantics*, **5**(2), 51–53, (2007).
[29] J. Fox, P. Krause, and S. Ambler. Arguments, contradictions and practical reasoning. In *ECAI '92: Proceedings of the 10th European conference on Artificial intelligence*, pp. 623–627, New York, NY, USA, (1992). John Wiley & Sons, Inc.
[30] I. Horrocks, P. F. Patel-Schneider, H. Boley, S. Tabet, B. Grosof, and M. Dean. SWRL: A semantic web rule language combining OWL and RULEML, Technical report, W3C (May, 2004).
[31] J. L. Pollock, *Cognitive Carpentry: A Blueprint for how to Build a Person*, (MIT Press, Cambridge, MA, USA, 1995).
[32] A. Muñoz and J. A. Botía. ASBO: Argumentation System Based on Ontologies. In eds. M. Klusch, M. Pechoucek, and A. Polleres, *Cooperative Information Agents XII*, vol. 5180, *Lecture Notes in Artificial Intelligence*, pp. 191–205. Springer, (2008).
[33] A. Muñoz, A. Sánchez, and J. A. Botía. A Software Architecture for an Argumentation-Oriented Multi-Agent System. In eds. Y. Demazeau, J. Pavón, J. Corchado, and J. Bajo, *7th International Conference on Practical Applications of Agents and Multi-Agent Systems (PAAMS'09)*, vol. 55, *Advances in Intelligent and Soft Computing*, pp. 197–207. Springer, (2009).
[34] M. E. Pollack, Intelligent Technology for an Aging Population: The Use of AI to Assist Elders with Cognitive Impairment, *AI Magazine*, **26**(2), 9–24, (2005).
[35] F. Natale, O. Mayora-Ibarra, and L. Prisciandaro. Interactive home assitant for supporting elderly citizens in emergency situations. In eds. J. Plomp and P. Tealdi, *Proceedings of Workshop on AmI Technologies for WellBeing at Home*, EUASI2004, Eindhoven, Netherlands, (2004).
[36] H. K. Aghajan, J. C. Augusto, C. Wu, P. J. McCullagh, and J.-A. Walkden. Distributed Vision-Based Accident Management for Assisted Living. In eds. T. Okadome, T. Yamazaki, and M. Makhtari, *ICOST*, vol. 4541, *Lecture Notes in Computer Science*, pp. 196–205. Springer, (2007).
[37] K. Ducatel, M. Bogdanovicz, F. Scapolo, J. Leijten, and J.-C. Burgelman. Scenarios for Ambient Intelligence in 2010. Technical report, IST Advisory Group, (2001).
[38] J. C. Augusto. Past, Present and Future of Ambient Intelligence and Smart Environments. In *Selected Papers from the 1st International Conference on Agents and Artificial Intelligence (ICAART)*, Springer Verlag, (2009). (to appear).

Chapter 13

Applying a Choquet Integral Based Decision Making Approach to Evaluate Agile Supply Chain Strategies

Gülçin Büyüközkan

Galatasaray University, Industrial Engineering Department, 34357 Ortaköy, İstanbul, Turkey

E-mail: gulcin.buyukozkan@gmail.com

This chapter proposes a multi-criteria decision-making approach based on the Choquet integral for assessing and selecting a suitable agile supply chain strategy. In the real world, most evaluation criteria have inter-dependent or interactive characteristics; hence, they cannot be evaluated by conventional additive measures. Thus, to approximate the human subjective evaluation process, it would be more suitable to apply a fuzzy integral model, where it is not necessary to assume additivity and independence. For this reason, in this chapter the conventional multi-criteria approach based on weighted mean has been replaced by the 2-additive Choquet integral. A case study is given to demonstrate the potential of the methodology.

13.1 Introduction

For a variety of reasons product and technology lifecycles are shortening, competitive pressures force more frequent product changes and consumers demand greater variety than ever before. To meet this challenge, an organization needs to focus its efforts on achieving greater agility such that it can respond in shorter time-frames, both in terms of volume change and variety change [9]. In other words, it needs to be able quickly to adjust its outputs to match market demand and to switch rapidly from one variant to another.

The agile supply chain paradigm relates to the interface between companies and markets, an external perspective on flexibility. Successful implementation involves responding to rapidly changing and continually fragmenting global markets by being dynamic, context-specific, growth-oriented, flexible across the organization, and driven by customer [2, 22, 10]. An agile supply chain focuses on responding to unpredictable market changes and capitalizing on them through fast delivery and lead-time flexibility. It deploys new technologies, methods, tools, and techniques to solve unexpected problems. It utilizes information systems and technologies as well as electronic data interchange capabilities to move information faster and make better decisions. It places more emphasis on organizational issues and people (knowledge systems and empowered employees), that decision-making can be pushed down the organization. It is a systemic approach that integrates the business, enhances innovations across the company, and forms virtual organizations and production entities based on customer needs.

In recent years, there has been a growing interest in the design and implementation of agile supply chain strategies [2, 25]. The idea of agility in the context of supply chain management focuses on 'responsiveness' [10]. Conventional supply chains have been lengthy with long lead-times and hence, of necessity, have been forecast-driven. By contrast, agile supply chains are shorter and seek to be demand-driven. A further distinction is that since conventional supply chains are forecast-driven, they are inventory-based. Agile supply chains are more likely to be information-based [12]. It has been suggested that an agile supply chain has a number of strategies [11, 3]. Specifically the agile supply chain is market (customer) sensitive, virtual, network-based and process aligned.

The purpose of this chapter is to increase the understanding of agile supply chain management and its strategies in supply chain networks. To attain the expected benefits of the agile supply chain, companies have to identify the suitable strategies for them. For this reason, this chapter proposes to use an analytical model in order to support the effective evaluation of agile supply chain strategies.

Due to its multi criteria nature, the agile supply chain strategies evaluation process requires an appropriate multi criteria analysis and solution approach. Selecting a proper method requires an insight analysis among available multi-criteria decision making (MCDM) techniques [16]. Among numerous methods of MCDM, this study presents a decision framework based on the Choquet integral aggregation for evaluating and selecting agile supply chain strategies. The main feature of such aggregation is that it can take into account interaction among decision criteria, which is generally ignored in other MCDM methods [7, 6, 8]. More precisely, we use 2-additive Choquet integral described next, which is relatively simple with only quadratic complexity and enables the modeling of interaction only between criteria pairs. Recently, Tsai and Lu [20] have applied this approach to evaluate the service quality of e-stores while Saad *et al.* [17] used Choquet integral to aggregate several attributes in the objective function of a flexible job-shop scheduling problem. Similarly, Feyzioğlu and Büyüközkan [5] used this method in a benchmarking procedure to rate competing systems and find which customer requirements should need improvement for effective product development.

The proposed evaluation process is composed of four main steps:

(1) Identify the evaluation main and sub factors of agile supply chain strategies and describe the relationships between them;
(2) Quantify the importance degrees of each evaluation factor by the Choquet based aggregation technique;
(3) Evaluate each agile supply chain strategy based on the identified criteria;
(4) Elucidatïon and make a decision with proposed approach and its verification.

The remainder of this chapter is organized as follows. The next section presents the details of Choquet integral method and the related elucidation procedure to identify strong and weak dimensions of alternatives. In the section that follows, evaluation of agile supply chain strategies as a case study and the results of analysis are discussed. Finally, some concluding remarks are given in last section.

13.2 Multi Criteria Decision Making with Choquet Integral

Until recently, the most common tool which is used in multi criteria decision making is the weighted arithmetic mean. But, this aggregation function is too poor to model the three main attitudes of a decision maker: conjunction (tnorm, like the min), compromise (like the weighted mean) or disjunction (t-co-norm, like the max); all the intermediate attitudes can also be imagined [19]. Moreover, it is important that an aggregation operator can satisfy other behavioral properties: possibility of expressing weights of importance on criteria, and interactions among them. All operators are not able to model all these properties. However, this problem has been partially solved since the introduction of fuzzy integrals [7]. Indeed, aggregation operations based on the family of fuzzy integrals include many operators (weighted mean, min, max, median, ordered weighted average) and can thus express a variety of decision maker's behaviors (severity, compromise, tolerance) and various effects of importance and interaction among criteria [6]. In the next paragraph, we briefly present the Choquet fuzzy integral and its principal properties as an operator of multi-criteria aggregation.

13.2.1 *Background and Notation*

Simultaneous satisfaction or dissatisfaction of some criteria can be significant. For example, if the key can be easily inserted to a lock and if it can also be easily turned, this will further affect the product presentation positively. Being sufficient in only one criterion can have much less meaning for the decision maker. Until recently, the most common aggregation tool, which is used in MCDM, was the weighted arithmetic mean, as it is general the case in the supply chain evaluations. Fuzzy integral based operators have been introduced notably in order to consider interactions between criteria to be aggregated [19, 7]. Especially, the 2-additive Choquet integral which takes only a pair of criteria interactions into account [7, 6, 13]. In the next paragraphs, we recall briefly the notations of the Choquet fuzzy integral and its principal properties as an operator of multi-criteria aggregation

In the remaining of the chapter, we will work in a finite universe $C = \{c_1, c_2, \ldots, c_n\}$ of n criteria, $P(C)$ is the power set of C, $x = \{x_1, x_2, \ldots, x_n\}$ represents the numerical satisfaction values of the criteria, such that x_i is the satisfaction degree of criterion c_i. Let us still consider a set of solutions (candidates) $S = \{s^1, s^2, \ldots, s^p\}$. Each solution $s^k \in S$ is associated with a profile $s^k = (x_1^k, x_2^k, \ldots, x_n^k)$, where x_i^k represents the partial evaluation (score) of s^k related to the criterion c_i. For the sake of simplicity, it is assumed that we deal with scores on criteria, expressed on a $[0, 100]$ scale, 100 corresponds to the complete satisfaction of a criterion, and 0 implies no satisfaction under a criterion. The problem of aggregation is the construction of a function $C_\mu : [0, 100]^n \rightarrow [0, 100]$, so that, for each solution $s^k : C_\mu(s^k) = C_\mu(x_1^k, x_2^k, \ldots, x_n^k)$, where $C_\mu(s^k)$ represents the overall evaluation of the solution s^k according to the all n criteria.

Let μ be a fuzzy measure on C. The (discrete) Choquet integral of $x = (x_1^k, x_2^k, \ldots, x_n^k)$ w.r.t. μ is defined by:

$$C_\mu(x_1, x_2, \ldots, x_n) = \sum_{i=1}^{n} \left(x_{(i)} - x_{(i-1)}\right) \mu(a_{(i)}) \tag{1}$$

where $(\cdot)$ in the subscript indicates a permutation such that: $x_{(0)} = 0$, $0 \leqslant x_{(1)} \leqslant x_{(2)} \leqslant \cdots \leqslant x_{(n)} \leqslant 1$, and $a_{(i)} = \{c_{(i)}, \ldots, c_{(n)}\}$.

According to the application context, we will consider only a particular case of Choquet fuzzy integrals known as the 2-additive measure [6]. This type of Choquet integral can be expressed in the interpretable form as follows [6]:

$$C_\mu(x) = \sum_{I_{ij}>0} \min(x_i, x_j) I_{ij} + \sum_{I_{ij}<0} \max(x_i, x_j) \left|I_{ij}\right| + \sum_{i=1}^{n} x_i \left(v_i - \frac{1}{2} \sum_{j \neq i} \left|I_{ij}\right| \right) \tag{2}$$

with the fact that $v_i - (1/2)\sum_{j \neq i} |I_{ij}| \geqslant 0$ and where v_i are the Shapley indices, representing the importance of each criterion relative to all the others. Also, $v_1 + v_2 + \cdots + v_n = 1$; and

I_{ij} represents the interactions between pairs of the criteria (c_i, c_j) with values contained in the interval $[-1;1]$. A value 1 means a complementarity between the two criteria, a value of -1 indicates redundancy, and a null value means the criteria are not interacting or are independent. We may thus decompose the Choquet integral into three parts: one conjunctive, another disjunctive and the third additive:

- a positive I_{ij} implies that the simultaneous satisfaction of criteria c_i and c_j will have a significant effect on the aggregated performance, and that satisfying only one criterion will have no effect;
- a negative I_{ij} implies that the satisfaction on c_i and c_j is sufficient to obtain a significant effect on the aggregated performance;
- zero I_{ij} implies that there is no interaction between the two considered criteria: the v_i indices correspond to classic weighted means.

The coefficients of importance v_i and I_{ij} are more natural to decision maker and can be determined by surveying the decision maker. Note that, it must be verified that the monotonicity conditions are satisfied [6] in order to use the transformation relation with the conventional fuzzy measure representation. Other methods based on the identification of these coefficients from experimental data exists, but are not discussed here.

13.2.2 *Elucidation of the Aggregation Result*

The need for elucidation aims at providing better quality information to decision maker during phases of process decision. This elucidation is explained in the "how" (and the "why") such a decision is taken. This understanding of the "why" (and how) of the decisions derived by the fusion system, can be expressed qualitatively or/and quantitatively at several levels [4]. The why can be quantitatively expressed in terms of the relative influence or dominance of particular criterion satisfactions on the ultimate decision? Indeed, we are interested in the partial contribution of a specific criterion for a considered fused result.
Let us consider that the solution that has been elected is s^k: it has been adopted following an aggregation strategy (relative importance weights and interactions between criteria) identified with the aggregation operator C_μ. Thus for all $l = 1,\dots,p$ (where p is the candidates-solutions number), we have $C_\mu(s^k) \geqslant C_\mu(s^l)$. Our approach to determine the contribution of partial evaluations is to decompose the aggregated value as a sum of terms where partial evaluations are involved [1, 15]. Two kinds of elucidations are considered as summarized in the following.

First, it may be pertinent to identify the elements related to the value of s^k: it is an absolute elucidation. The latter consists of decomposing the aggregated score in a ranked sum of criteria score contribution. It should then be possible to parameterize the level of detail required for the explanation. We might wish to include several levels of detail in the argumentation: a "one-word" justification, the main reason for this preference, detailed reasons, or an exhaustive report.

For this, by Eq. (1) we have:

$$C_\mu(s^k) = \sum_{i=1}^{n}(x^k_{(i)} - x^k_{(i-1)})\mu(A^k_{(i)}), \text{ let us note: } \mu^k_{(i)} = \mu(A^k_{(i)}), \text{ then:}$$

$$C_\mu(s^k) = (\mu^k_{(1)} - \mu^k_{(2)})x^k_{(1)} + \cdots + (\mu^k_{(i)} - \mu^k_{(i+1)})x^k_{(i)} + \cdots + \mu^k_{(n)}x^k_{(n)}$$

$$C_\mu(s^k) = \sum_{i=1}^{n} \Delta\mu^k_{(i)}x^k_{(i)} \tag{3}$$

where $\mu^k_{(n+1)} = 0$, and $\Delta\mu^k_{(i)} = \mu^k_{(i)} - \mu^k_{(i+1)}$. We can initially simply re-rank the terms of the sum Eq. (3) so that

$$\Delta\mu^k_{(j)}x^k_{(j)} \geqslant \Delta\mu^k_{(j+1)}x^k_{(j+1)}, \quad \forall j = 1,\ldots,n-1.$$

We can then partition the absolute contributions of the scores related to the criterion $c_{(j)}$, $\Delta\mu^k_{(j)}x^k_{(j)}$ (this term is defined as the absolute potential of criterion $c_{(j)}$) into classes relative to the orders of magnitude of the $\Delta\mu^k_{(j)}x^k_{(j)}/\Delta\mu^k_{(1)}x^k_{(1)}$ ratio. The closer is this ratio to 1, the greater is the contribution of the score of the criterion $c_{(j)}$, and the more $c_{(j)}$ represents an essential dimension in the decision (local interpretation of elucidation). In the case of 2-additive fuzzy measure, the expression $\Delta\mu^k_{(i)}$ in Eq. (3) becomes [15]:

$$\Delta\mu^k_{(i)} = v_{(i)} + \frac{1}{2}\sum_{j>i} I_{(i)(j)} - \frac{1}{2}\sum_{j<i} I_{(j)(i)} \tag{4}$$

where, $v_{(i)}$ is the relative importance of criterion $c_{(i)}$ and $I_{(i)(j)}$ are the interaction between criteria $c_{(i)}$ and $c_{(j)}$.

Another aspect of elucidation consists in providing evidence concerning the dimensions according to which a_k is preferred over a_l, i.e., the axes along which a_k makes the difference over a_l. We use the following analysis criterion:

$$\Delta C_{\mu R}(x^{a_k}, x^{a_i}) = C_\mu(x^{a_k}) - C_\mu(x^{a_l}) = \sum_{i=1}^{n} R^{k,l}_i, \quad \forall a_k, a_l \in A, \ \ k \neq l, \tag{5}$$

where $R^{k,l}_i = \Delta\mu^{a_k}_{(i)}x^{a_k}_{(i)} - \Delta\mu^{a_l}_{(i)}x^{a_l}_{(i)}$. This is a relative argument in which the quantities analyzed are the sums of the individual relative potentials $R^{k,l}_i$.

13.3 Evaluation of Agile Supply Chain Strategies

Evaluation criteria: A set of evaluation criteria has to be defined prior to evaluate the identified four main agile supply chain strategies. Based on our literature survey [see for instance [9, 2, 18, 23, 12, 22, 25, 10]] and on our expertise in the domain, we identify the agile supply chain evaluation criteria as given in Fig. 13.1.

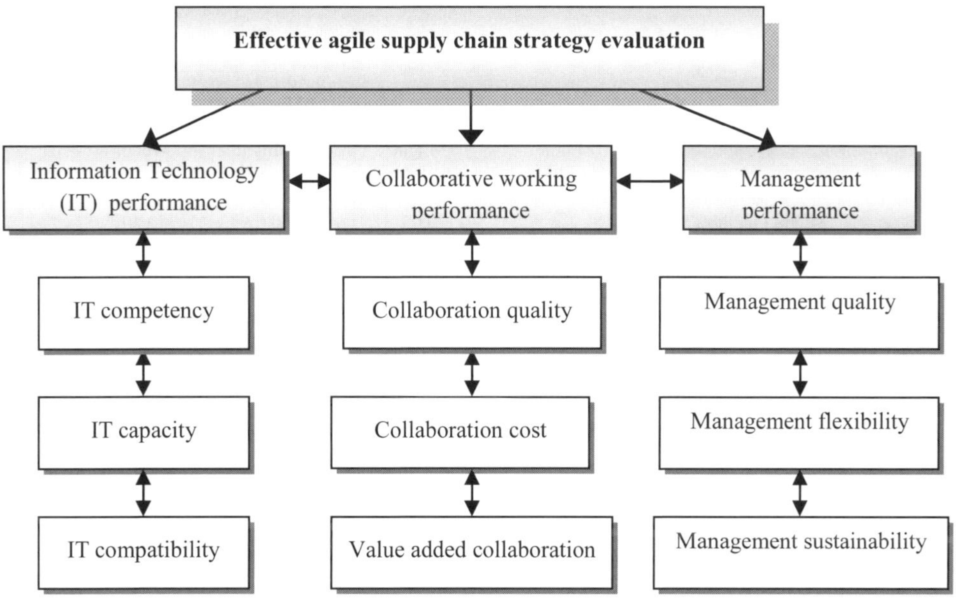

Figure 13.1 Decision criteria hierarchy for supply chain strategy selection in agile environment

Criteria interaction: The interactions among criteria have been identified as shown in Tables 13.1-13.4. We assume that in the criteria hierarchy of Fig. 13.1, only level two criteria belonging to the same first level criterion and all first level criteria are interacting with each others. Hence possible interactions among all second level criteria are considered in the first level.

Table 13.1 Interactions among and weights of criteria belonging to IT performance.

	IT Compet.	IT Capacity	IT Compat.	Weight
IT Competency	-	0.05	0.05	0.30
IT Capacity	0.05	-		0.30
IT Compatibility	0.05		-	0.40

Table 13.2 Interactions among and weights of criteria belonging to collaborative working performance.

	Collab. Quality	Collab. Cost	Val. Add. Collab.	Weight
Collaboration Quality	-	0.05	0.05	0.50
Collaboration Cost	0.05	-	0.01	0.20
Value Added Collaboration	0.05	0.01	-	0.30

Table 13.3 Interactions among and weights of criteria belonging to management performance.

	Mngnt Quality	Mngnt Flexibility	Mngnt Sustain.	Weight
Mngnt Quality	-	0.05	0.02	0.40
Mngnt Flexibility	0.05	-	0.02	0.40
Mngnt Sustainability	0.02	0.02	-	0.20

Table 13.4 Interactions among and weights of criteria belonging to agile supply chain strategy selection.

	IT Perfor.	Collab. Perfor.	Mngnt Perfor.	Weight
IT Performance	-	0.05	0.10	0.30
Collaborative Performance	0.05	-	0.01	0.50
Mngnt Performance	0.10	0.01	-	0.20

Evaluation of alternatives: An agile supply chain possesses different strategies [11, 3, 10]. Firstly, the agile supply chain may be ***customer (market) sensitive*** **(CS)**. By customer sensitive it is meant that the supply chain is capable of observing the real demand responding to it. Most organizations are forecast-driven rather than demand-driven. In other words, since they have little direct feed-forward from the marketplace by way of data on actual customer requirements, they are forced to make forecasts based upon past sales or shipments and convert these forecasts into inventory. The breakthroughs of the last decade in the form of Efficient Consumer Response and the use of information technology to capture data on demand direct from the point-of-sale or point-of-use are now transforming the organization's ability to hear the voice of the market and to respond directly to it. The use of information technology to share data between buyers and suppliers is, in effect, creating a ***virtual*** **(V)** supply chain. Virtual supply chains are information based rather than inventory based. Conventional logistics systems are based upon a paradigm that seeks to identify the optimal quantities of inventory ands its spatial location. Complex formulae and algorithms exist to support this inventory-based business model. Paradoxically, what we are now learning is that once we have visibility of demand through shared information, the premise upon which these formulae are based no longer holds. Electronic Data Interchange and now the Internet have enabled partners in the supply chain to act upon the same data i.e. real demand, rather than be dependent upon the distorted and noisy picture that emerges when orders are transmitted from one step to another in an extended chain. Shared information between supply chain partners can only be fully leveraged through ***process integration*** **(PI)**. By process integration is meant collaborative working between buyers and suppliers, joint product development, common systems and shared information. This form of co-operation in the supply chain is becoming ever more prevalent as companies focus on managing their core competencies and outsource all other activities. In this new world a greater reliance on suppliers and alliance partners becomes inevitable and hence, a new style of relationship is essential. In the extended enterprise, as it is often called, there can be no boundaries and an ethos of trust and commitment must prevail. Along with process integration comes joint strategy determination, buyer-supplier teams, transparency of information and even open-book accounting. This idea of the supply chain as a confederation of partners linked together as a ***network based*** **(NB)** structure provides the fourth ingredient of agility. There is a growing recognition that individual businesses no longer compete as stand-alone entities but rather as supply chains. We are now entering the era of network competition where the prizes will go to those organizations who can better structure, co-ordinate and manage the relationships with their partners in a network committed to better, closer and more agile relationships with their final customers. It can be argued that in today's challenging global markets, the route to sustainable advantage lies in being able to leverage the respective strengths and competencies of network partners to achieve greater responsiveness to market needs.

These four agile supply chain strategies are accepted as alternatives in this study. Based on our expertise in the domain, we have evaluated each strategy under the identified criteria. The results are given in Table 13.5.

If Eq. (2) is used to compute the aggregate score of each strategy considering only second level criteria, results given in Table 13.6 are obtained.

Finally, if we look into overall aggregate scores, we have 72.88 for the first strategy, 77.88 for the second, 81.99 for the third and finally 76.81 for the fourth strategy. This implies

Table 13.5 Evaluation of supply chain strategies.

Criteria	Alternatives CS	V	NB	PI
IT Competency	70	90	80	70
IT Capacity	70	80	80	80
IT Compatibility	80	90	80	90
Collaboration Quality	80	80	90	90
Collaboration Cost	60	60	80	70
Value Added Collaboration	80	80	90	70
Mngnt Quality	80	90	80	80
Mngnt Flexibility	60	70	70	60
Mngnt Sustainability	60	60	70	70

Table 13.6 Evaluation of supply chain strategies.

	2-additive Choquet		*Integral*	
	CS	*V*	*NB*	*PI*
IT Performance	73.75	86.75	80.00	80.25
Collaborative working performance	75.40	75.40	87.70	79.00
Mngnt Performance	67.30	75.10	73.65	69.30

that the network based strategy should be selected as the best agile supply chain strategy since it has the highest score. We could also rank strategies based on their desirability as NB > V > PI > CS.

Elucidation of the aggregation: According to the proposed elucidation procedure, the quantities are computed from Eq. (4) and are given below in Tables 13.7-13.10. For each agile supply chain strategy alternative, the criterion ranking is modified according to the partial score ranking. The real criterion is indicated in superscript before the detail of the computation for the first column. For others columns, only the results are given with the criterion rank in the superscript on the left of the value.

Table 13.7 Absolute potentials and aggregation results for IT performance.

$\Delta\mu^k_{(i)}x^k_{(i)}$	*CS*	*V*	*NB*	*PI*
IT Competency	$^{(1)}24.50$	$^{(2)}26.00$	$^{(1)}28.00$	$^{(1)}24.50$
IT Capacity	$^{(2)}19.25$	$^{(1)}27.00$	$^{(2)}22.00$	$^{(2)}22.00$
IT Compatibility	$^{(3)}30.00$	$^{(3)}33.75$	$^{(3)}30.00$	$^{(3)}33.75$
Aggregation	73.75	86.75	80.00	80.25
Rank	4	1	3	2

Table 13.8 Absolute potentials and aggregation results for collaborative working performance.

$\Delta\mu^k_{(i)}x^k_{(i)}$	*CS*	*V*	*NB*	*PI*
Collaboration Quality	$^{(2)}13.80$	$^{(2)}13.80$	$^{(2)}18.40$	$^{(2)}16.10$
Collaboration Cost	$^{(1)}40.00$	$^{(1)}40.00$	$^{(1)}45.00$	$^{(3)}22.40$
Value Added Collaboration	$^{(3)}21.60$	$^{(3)}21.60$	$^{(3)}24.30$	$^{(1)}40.50$
Aggregation	75.40	75.40	87.70	79.00
Rank	3	4	1	2

Table 13.9 Absolute potentials and aggregation results for management performance.

$\Delta\mu^k_{(i)}x^k_{(i)}$	*CS*	*V*	*NB*	*PI*
Mngnt Quality	$^{(2)}26.10$	$^{(3)}13.20$	$^{(2)}30.45$	$^{(2)}26.10$
Mngnt Flexibility	$^{(3)}12.00$	$^{(2)}29.05$	$^{(3)}14.00$	$^{(3)}14.00$
Mngnt Sustainability	$^{(1)}29.20$	$^{(1)}32.85$	$^{(1)}29.20$	$^{(1)}29.20$
Aggregation	67.30	75.10	73.65	69.30
Rank	4	1	2	3

Table 13.10 Overall absolute potentials and aggregation results.

$\Delta\mu^k_{(i)}x^k_{(i)}$	*CS*	*V*	*NB*	*PI*
IT Performance	$^{(3)}17.16$	$^{(3)}19.15$	$^{(3)}18.78$	$^{(3)}17.67$
Collaborative Performance	$^{(1)}20.28$	$^{(2)}39.21$	$^{(1)}22.00$	$^{(2)}41.08$
Mngnt Performance	$^{(2)}35.44$	$^{(1)}19.52$	$^{(2)}41.22$	$^{(1)}18.06$
Aggregation	72.88	77.88	81.99	76.81
Rank	4	2	1	3

As previously, the overall aggregated results indicate that the Network Based strategy has to be selected as the most appropriate strategy, and the Virtual strategy takes the second place. There is a need to clarify now the rationale of such a ranking, i.e., to give more explications about "why" these results are obtained. By absolute elucidation, we observe that for all strategies, the more significant scores come first from collaborative performance, then from IT performance and finally from management performance. For almost all strategies, scores for IT and management performances are approximately equal to the 25 % of the overall score, and thus collaborative performance accounts to 50 % of the overall scores.

More valuable information is the relative elucidation between the four strategies. Table 13.11 presents the corresponding individual relative potentials according to Eq. (5).

The NB strategy outperforms the CS and PI strategies on all performance criteria. When comparing NB – CS we observe that collaborative performance is most important and when comparing NB – PI, it is the IT performance that makes the most difference. Meanwhile, NB does not surpass V on all criteria. While NB has better scores for IT and collaborative performance, it has a slightly lower score on management performance.

Table 13.11 Individual relative potentials.

	IT Perfor.	Collab. Perfor.	Mngnt Perfor.
$R^{3,2}_{(i)}$	2.48	2.01	-0.37
$R^{3,4}_{(i)}$	3.94	0.14	1.11
$R^{3,1}_{(i)}$	1.72	5.78	1.62

13.4 Concluding Remarks

To attain the expected benefits of the agile supply chain approach, companies have to identify the suitable strategy. In this chapter, we have proposed a multi criteria decision making framework to identify the most suitable agile supply chain strategy among some discussed in the literature. In traditional multi-criteria evaluation approaches, each criterion is assumed to be independent of the others. Therefore, the characteristics that have interactions and mutual influence among criteria in a real system cannot be handled by the concept of traditional additive measures alone. For this reason, in this study, the conventional multi-criteria approach based on the weighted mean has been replaced by the 2-additive Choquet integral. An important aspect of the proposed model is its ability to consider decision criteria dependently. To our knowledge, no previous work investigated such a problem and we believe that this research will lead to a greater body of literature on the topic.

In the near future, we aim to develop a user interface that will facilitate assessments and automate calculations of the proposed methodology. As a second perspective, we want to concentrate on the case where evaluation could be made with verbal terms [24, 14]. This will clearly enrich the assessment capability of decision-makers.

Bibliography

[1] Büyüközkan, G., Mauris, G., Berrah, L., and Feyzioğlu, O., 2003, "Providing Elucidations of Web Site Evaluation based on a Multi-Criteria Aggregation", Proceedings of the Interna-

tional Fuzzy Systems Association World Congress (IFSA), İstanbul, Turkey, 131–134.

[2] Christopher, M., 2000, "The Agile Supply Chain: Competing in Volatile Markets", Industrial Marketing Management, 29, 1, 37–44.

[3] Christopher, M., 2007, Presentation of 9th. Logistics Management Summit, 28-29 March, Istanbul.

[4] Dasarathy, B.V., 2000, "Elucidative fusion systems – an exposition", Information Fusion, 1 (1), 5–15.

[5] Feyzioğlu, O. and Büyüközkan, G., 2008, "An integrated group decision-making approach for new product development", International Journal of Computer Integrated Manufacturing, 21, 366–375.

[6] Grabisch, M., 1997, "K-order additive discrete fuzzy measures and their representation", Fuzzy Sets & Systems, 92, 167–189.

[7] Grabisch, M., and Roubens, M., 1996, "The application of fuzzy integrals in multi criteria decision making", European Journal of Operational Research, 89, 445–456.

[8] Grabisch, M., and Roubens, M., 2000, "Application of the Choquet integral in multicriteria decision making", In: M. Grabisch, T. Murofushi and M. Sugeno, Editors, Fuzzy Measures and Integrals: Theory and Applications, Physica-Verlag, Wurzburg, 415–434.

[9] Gunasekaran, A., 1999, "Agile manufacturing A framework for research and development", International Journal of Production Economics, 62, 1/2, 87–106.

[10] Gunasekaran, A., Lai, K. and Cheng, T.C.E., 2008, "Responsive supply chain: A competitive strategy in a networked economy", Omega, 36 (4), 549–564.

[11] Harrison, A., Christopher, M. and van Hoek, R., 1999, "Creating the Agile Supply Chain", Chartered Institute of Logistics and Transport, 1999.

[12] Lin, C.-T., Chiu, H. and Chu, P.-Y., 2006, "Agility index in the supply chain", International Journal of Production Economics, 100, 2, 285–299.

[13] Marichal, J.-L., and Roubens, M., 2000, "Determination of weights of interacting criteria from a reference set", European Journal of Operational Research, 124, 641–650.

[14] Meyer, P., and Roubens M., 2006, "On the use of the Choquet integral with fuzzy numbers in multiple criteria decision support", Fuzzy Sets and Systems, 157, 7, 927–938.

[15] Montmain, J., Mauris, G. and Akharraz, A., 2005, "Elucidation and decisional risk in a multicriteria decision based on a Choquet integral aggregation - a cybernetic framework", International Journal of Multi-Criteria Decision Analysis, 13 (5-6), 239–258.

[16] Pomerol, J.-C., and Barba Romero, S., 2000, "Multicriterion Decision in Management: Principles and Practice", Norwell: Kluwer Academic Publishers.

[17] Saad, I., Hammadi, S., Benrejeb, M. and Borne, P., 2008, "Choquet integral for criteria aggregation in the flexible job-shop scheduling problems", Intenational Journal, Mathematics and Computers in Simulation, 76, 447–462.

[18] Stratton, R., and Warburton, R.D.H., 2003, "The strategic integration of agile and lean supply", International Journal of Production Economics, 85, 2, 183–198.

[19] Sugeno, M., 1977, "Fuzzy measures and fuzzy integrals: a survey", In M.M. Gupta, G.N. Saridis and B.R. Gaines (Eds.), Fuzzy Automata and Decision Processes, North-Holland, Amsterdam, 89–102.

[20] Tsai, H.-H. and Lu, I.-Y., 2006, "The evaluation of service quality using generalized Choquet integral", Information Sciences, 176, 640–663.

[21] Tzeng G.-H., Ou Yang Y.-P., Lin C.-T. and Chen C.-B., 2005, "Hierarchical MADM with fuzzy integral for evaluating enterprise intranet web sites", Information Sciences, 169, 3-4, 409–426.

[22] Vonderembse, M.A., Uppal, M., Huang, S.H. and Dismukes, J.P., 2006, "Designing supply chains: Towards theory development", International Journal of Production Economics, 100, 2, 223–238.

[23] White, A., Daniel, E.M. and Mohdzain, M., 2005, "The role of emergent information technologies and systems in enabling supply chain agility", International Journal of Information Management, 25, 5, 396–410.

[24] Yang, R., Wang, Z., Heng, P.-A. and Leung K.-S., (2005), "Fuzzy numbers and fuzzification of the Choquet integral", Fuzzy Sets and Systems, 153 (1), 95–113.

[25] Yusuf, Y.Y., Gunasekaran, A., Adeleye, E.O. and Sivayoganathan, K., 2004, "Agile supply chain capabilities: Determinants of competitive objectives", European Journal of Operational Research, 159, 2, 1, 379–392.

Subject Index